A TROUBLEMAKER'S HANDBOOK 2

HOW TO FIGHT BACK WHERE YOU WORK— AND WIN!

by

Judy Ancel, Peter Ian Asen, Steven Ashby, Rob Baril, Dave Bleakney, Ellis Boal, David Borer, Paul Bouchard, John Braxton, Aaron Brenner, Gene Bruskin, Joe Burns, Sheila Cohen, Ellen David Friedman, Tim Dean, Joanna Dubinsky, Steve Early, Kay Eisenhower, Betsy Esch, Miriam Frank, Pam Galpern, C.J. Hawking, Robert Hickey, Steve Hinds, Sonya Huber, Justin Jackson, William Johnson, Tom Juravich, Mike Konopacki, Paul Krehbiel, Chris Kutalik, Dan La Botz, Nancy Lessin, David Levin, Ricardo Levins Morales, Stephanie Luce, Trudy Manderfeld, Paul McCafferty, Julie McCall, Sheila McClear, Paul McLennan, Sara Mersha, Hanna Metzger, Kim Moody, Ruth Needleman, Roni Neff, Marsha Niemeijer, Matt Noyes, Julie O'Donoghue, Amy Offner, Mike Parker, Tony Perlstein, David Pratt, Peter Rachleff, Teófilo Reyes, Charley Richardson, Nick Robinson, Sarah Ryan, Simone Sagovac, Leah Samuel, Robert Schwartz, Linda Shipley, Gregg Shotwell, Jane Slaughter, Patricia Smith, N. Renuka Uthappa, Dorothy Wigmore, Rand Wilson, Jason Winston, Matt Witt, David Yao, Andy Zipser

Edited by Jane Slaughter

A Labor Notes Book
Detroit 2005

A Labor Notes Book
Copyright © 2005 by Labor Education and Research Project

About the publisher:
Labor Notes is a monthly magazine of labor news and analysis intended to help activists put the movement back in the labor movement. It is published by the Labor Education and Research Project, which holds a biennial conference for all labor activists, acts as a resource center, and puts on schools and workshops on a variety of topics.

Reprints:
Permission is granted to workplace activists, unions, rank-and-file union groups, and labor studies programs to reprint sections of this book for free distribution. Please let Labor Notes know of such use, at labornotes@labornotes.org, 313-842-6262, or 7435 Michigan Ave., Detroit, MI 48210. Requests for permission to reprint for other purposes should be directed to Labor Notes.

Cover Design: Barbara Barefield

Inside Design: Jim West and David McCullough

Cover photos:
Top: Rally in support of Detroit newspaper strikers. Jim West.
Top left: Striking teachers arrested in Middletown, New Jersey. New Jersey Education Association.
Middle left: Immigrant Workers Freedom Ride, Detroit. Jim West.
Bottom left: Striking nurses, members of OPEIU. Jim West.
Top right: Organizing meatpacking workers in Omaha. David Bacon.
Bottom right: Demonstration in Seattle against the World Trade Organization, 1999. David Bacon.
Bottom: UAW strike against General Motors. Jim West.
Back cover: UNITE members picket the Gap to protest sweatshops. Jim West.

Library of Congress Control Number: 2004116172
ISBN # 0-914093-12-6

Contents

How To Use This Book vii

List of Abbreviations viii

Thank You ix

Donors x

Foreword by Baldemar Velásquez xi

1 Power on the Job 1
by Jane Slaughter

Why work matters. What power on the job looks like. How employers try to undermine it. How we can win it back.

2 Basics of Organizing 5
by Ellen David Friedman

The organizing attitude. How to get started. Respect is the foundation. Your legal rights. Apathy isn't real.

3 Shop Floor Tactics 9
by Dan La Botz

Why grievances are not enough. Speaking truth to power. Using ridicule. Visit the boss, collectively. Mapping the workplace. Member-to-member networks. Recruiting stewards. Stewards councils. Rotating stewards. Work-to-rule. Fighting harassment with solidarity. Using quality programs. Locking out the boss. Politician on the shop floor. Workplace newsletters.

4 Creative Tactics 31
by Julie McCall

Why have fun? When leaders are reluctant. Mass t-shirt wearing. Using cartoons. Songs on the job. Street action. Picket sign parties. Props, costumes, puppets. Writing songs. Writing skits. Energizing meetings. Putting on a show.

5 Fighting Discrimination/Building Unity 43
by N. Renuka Uthappa

Contraceptive equity. Fighting disability discrimination. Dealing with snitches. Dealing with harassment. Anti-harassment training. Defeating management's divide-and-conquer racism. Building gay/straight solidarity. Getting the local to take discrimination seriously. Fighting two-tier contracts. Defending affirmative action. Building a demonstration. Building a coalition. Uniting black and white tradeswomen. Informal caucuses. Formal black caucuses. Leadership training for women.

6 Saving Good Jobs: Fighting Lean Production and Outsourcing . . . 61
by Jane Slaughter

The "continuous bargaining" approach to workplace changes. How to survive in joint labor-management programs. Code of conduct for joint programs. Fighting "team concept." Fighting de-skilling. Working within management's program. Submitting information requests. Fighting privatization. Fighting consultants. Use the enemy's mistakes. Fighting disinvestment. Making the case for insourcing.

7 Organizing for Health and Safety 79
by Marsha Niemeijer and Roni Neff

Mapping hazards in the workplace and on body maps. A continuous bargaining approach. Fighting "blame the worker" programs. Action toolbox. How to use (and not use) OSHA. How a health and safety fight can revitalize the union. Enforcing contract language with on-the-job action. Substituting safer materials. Working with a COSH group in a non-union workplace. Health and safety in an organizing drive.

8 Contract Campaigns 92
by Chris Kutalik

Fifteen-minute strikes and 15-second strikes. Mini-corporate campaign. Bringing members to the table. Mobilization and pressure tactics on the job. Community support. Turning away potential scabs. Mobilization network. Rank-and-file websites. A "vote no" campaign. Keeping members informed.

At the bargaining table: Keeping management off balance. Tips for bargainers.

After the campaign: Matching evaluation to goals. Drawing the right lessons. How to get an informed vote.

9 Strikes 108
by Dan La Botz

Why strikes win or lose. A "demonstration strike" (limited duration). Rolling strikes. A better burn barrel. Fun on the picket line. Road warriors. Running the strike from the rank and file. Community support. The 1997 UPS strike: picking a clear message, building public support, gradual build-up in contract campaign. Countering permanent replacements—your legal rights and strategy. Winning a wildcat. Heat walkout. Sit-down strike. Strike guidelines.

10 Inside Strategies 127
by Aaron Brenner

When to choose an inside strategy. How to get members on board. How to work to rule. Working safely. Creative tactics. Legal rights.

11 Corporate Campaigns 140
by Steven Ashby

How to pick the right target. Pressuring customers. Reaching out locally and nationally. Road warriors. Solidarity committees. Running a boycott. Getting student support. Caravan and tour. Hunger strike. Corporate campaign combined with shop floor organizing in an organizing drive. When to end it.

12 Allying with the Community: Single-Issue Campaigns 157
by Sonya Huber

Getting members on board. Living wage campaigns. Building coalitions. Educating the public. Effective lobbying (the council-o-meter). Holding politicians accountable. Winning community support for a contract campaign. Uniting workers and consumers. Fighting privatization, organizing province-wide. Finding and using members' community connections. Creating a job training program. Getting labor into the public schools.

Building student-labor alliances: what students can do, how to find student groups, building long-term relationships, doing Union Summer right, advice to students from students.

13 Allying with the Community: Multi-Issue Coalitions 178
by Steve Hinds

Jobs with Justice: building a solid chapter, contract campaign support, organizing drives, workers' rights boards, winning ordinances.

Labor-environment alliances: using each other's strengths, dealing with the culture clash, the Alliance for Sustainable Jobs and the Environment, free trade as an issue that unites, fighting for clean water during a lockout, tips and challenges.

Labor-religious coalitions: collaborating on contract campaigns and organizing drives, finding members' church connections, bargaining in church.

A "Social Contract": making joint community/union demands on the city's largest employer, power analysis, developing leaders.

14 Union Solidarity 195
by Aaron Brenner

Plant gate fundraising. Flying squads. Supporting strikers at your company but in a different union. Secondary boycott, legally. Citywide electronic solidarity newsletter. Cross-union solidarity school. Local cross-union solidarity committee. Uniting locals for an area-wide contract. How to make contacts at other workplaces.

15 Organizing New Members 208
by Aaron Brenner

Which tactics work? Strategic targeting. The relationship between staff organizers, member-organizers, and workers at the target workplace. Building on previous defeats. Building a workplace committee. Organizer training. Building on the job to create member-organizers. Mass action for quick recognition. Striking for recognition. Salting. Choosing a union. Building with small steps. Using management's mistakes. One-on-one meetings. Going public. Community outreach; peeling off management's support. Rallies, buttons, puppets, petitions, surveys, collecting cards, short strikes, fighting fear.

Wining card check and neutrality: Pressuring management through mobilization, political leverage, and using the NLRB. Organizing once you've won card check. Is card check too easy?

Winning the first contract: large bargaining team, open negotiations, contract surveys, defeating decertification, corporate campaign, strike, boycott, civil disobedience, bargaining with future organizing in mind.

Nonmajority unions: training stewards, small actions, contact with union members at other locations, patience.

16 Bringing Immigrants into the Movement 244
by Teófilo Reyes

Unions: Welcoming and involving immigrant members, training new leaders. Coping with documentation issues. Dealing with "no-match" letters. Building an immigrants' rights coalition. Demonstrating at the airport. Training new organizers. Organizing a union for immigrants from different countries, together. A union drive run jointly with a community organization.

Immigrant workers centers: Organizing workers from different countries together. Building an independent union. Winning community support. Monitoring an industry. Training peer mentors. Pressuring the garment industry to adopt standards for contractors.

17 Workers Centers 260
by Dan La Botz

What is a workers center? Workers' rights education. Getting government agencies to cooperate. Fighting for unpaid wages. Hooking workers up with unions. Helping to democratize a local. Forming a workers' cooperative. Organizing day laborers.

18 Reform Caucuses and Running for Office 272
by Aaron Brenner

Why does union democracy matter? Starting a rank-and-file caucus. Intervening in a union meeting. Consolidating a base. A caucus runs a contract campaign. Connecting on-the-job action to changing the union. Running for office. A caucus fights undemocratic restructuring and wins an election. Defeating a trustee. Building a caucus over years. Doing the union's job from the grassroots. Association for Union Democracy. Teamsters for a Democratic Union. Your legal rights inside the union.

19 Running Your Local/Strategic Planning 290
by Robert Hickey

Strategic planning: analyzing strengths and weaknesses, setting goals. Budgeting by program (rather than line-items). A communication director. Why is an "open door" not the best policy? Setting up a member-to-member network. Part-time officers. Stewards committees for accountability. Using lost time. Leading and managing staff. Dealing with union politics. Junior executive board. Candidates' debate. Dealing with language differences. Building long-term goals into your daily functioning as an officer.

20 Troublemaking on the Home Page 306
by Matt Noyes and David Yao

For rank-and-file reformers: Designing your site to build your group and encourage action and discussion. Your legal rights online.
For local unions: Designing your site. Using email to mobilize. Using online campaigns. Holding online discussions. Promoting international solidarity. Locals that rely on the Internet.

21 Developing Leaders 322
by Tony Perlstein

What is a leader? Making space for leadership development in the local's plan. Leadership Institute, Apprenticeship for Member Organizers, Stewards College, learning through developing projects. Using popular education methods. Training leaders through workplace traditions.

22 Dealing with the Media 329
by Andy Zipser

Inventory the media in your area. Care and feeding of the media. A multi-union communications campaign. How to talk to reporters. What's "off the record"? When the crisis hits. Get the members talking. The jobs of a communication director.

23 International Solidarity 339
by William Johnson

How to get started. How to approach unions abroad. List of international labor organizations. Solidarity within a multinational company. Ongoing international networks. A corporate campaign to support Mexican workers. Outreach to U.S. unions. Organizing a solidarity tour. Hosting an international visitor. A model of international cooperation: the UE-FAT alliance. Worker-to-worker exchanges. Help in an organizing drive. Working with the global justice movement. Educating about globalization.

24 Troublemaking for the Long Haul 353
by Jane Slaughter and Dan La Botz

If you think it's bad now... How movements are built. Learning from history. Where should we be organizing? How can activists sustain themselves? Do's and don'ts for a strong labor movement.

25 Resources 359
by Peter Ian Asen

Organizations, periodicals, handbooks, videos, web sources, labor history and analysis.

Appendix: How To Research Employers 364
by Stephanie Luce and Tom Juravich

How to dig out the dirt.

Index 367

How To Use This Book

"WHY DO YOU CALL IT a *troublemaker's* handbook?" a few readers wanted to know. "It's management that makes trouble—workers are just trying to do their jobs. When we stand up for ourselves, *they* call us troublemakers (and a lot of other things, too)."

We've found that most activists get a kick out of taking management's put-down and wearing the moniker with pride. Both our 1991 *Troublemaker's Handbook* and our "Troublemakers Union" t-shirts are our bestsellers.

But if you'd like a disclaimer, here it is: By "troublemaker" we mean an activist who dares to defend her or his rights and those of fellow workers. That often means making waves and causing some discomfort among managerial types. In our view, it's management that causes trouble in the workplace and employers who cause trouble in society, when they speed us up, treat us disrespectfully, and squeeze us for every last drop of profit.

So this book is an organizing manual for workers who want justice from their employers and control over their lives at work and beyond.

Our Method

Instead of presenting a book full of checklists—"this is how you do it"—we're letting the experts tell their own stories: "This is how *we* did it. See what you can learn from our story." We've found that people generally remember a story about "how we locked out the boss" better than a checklist on "how to lock out the boss."

Action Questions

However, at the end of each chapter, we do list "Action Questions." These are to get you started thinking about how you could implement similar tactics at your job, and are best tackled in a small group.

If You Don't Have a Union

Most of the actions and tactics described in this book were carried out by union members—but not all of them. Although it's less risky to stand up at work when you belong to a union, a good many of the ideas we present here could be carried out by workers who don't have a union.

One worker who's worked non-union all her life says, "We successfully ganged up on management from time to time. We wage slaves got together to challenge management on practical issues either in a subversive or a pragmatic way. More hints on how to go about that would be useful." You'll find such advice in Chapters 2, 3, 4, 5, 7, 10, 11, 15, 16, 17, 20, and 22.

Resources

Right before the Action Questions in each chapter, you'll find "Resources"—pamphlets, books, videos, and organizations for further advice. The Internet has quadrupled the number of easily available resources, so we urge you to search further than our relatively short lists.

Credit Where Credit Is Due

The authors of each chapter usually got plenty of help, so you'll see many different bylines in the book ("by so-and-so"). If a particular story has no byline, you can thank the overall chapter author for it.

Abbreviations

Ever notice how unions tend to have really long names? Rather than spell them out each time, we've included a list of abbreviations on page viii.

Troublemaker's Handbook on the Web

Our new Troublemaker's page at www.labornotes.org includes some extra information and some longer stories that didn't fit into this already-long handbook (for example, you can read about how to plan a sit-in, a statewide organizing project, or a citywide general strike). See the paragraph at the end of each chapter for related stories on the Troublemaker's page. The page will be frequently updated, so come back to it for more advice.

Tell Us Your Stories, Subscribe

This book does not include all the many, many examples of good work that go on every day in workplaces across the country. Our aim was not to mention every union or every struggle, nor to create a history of the last decade, but to choose examples that would be easiest for readers to learn from and to try on their own.

If you know of a great story that doesn't appear here, call us at Labor Notes. Perhaps we can run that story in our Steward's Corner column in the monthly *Labor Notes* magazine, or add it to the Troublemaker's page on our website. We urge you to subscribe to *Labor Notes* so that you can continue to get troublemaking advice delivered to your door. See the ad at the end of this book.

Old but Still Reliable

Finally, if you like this book, you'll like the Troublemaker's first edition too, from 1991. Almost all the ideas presented there are just as usable today as they were then, and we know plenty of folks who are still carrying around "the bible." See ordering information, and a discounted price, in the back.

List of Abbreviations

ACLU	American Civil Liberties Union
ACORN	Association of Community Organizations for Reform Now
AFGE	American Federation of Government Employees
AFSCME	American Federation of State, County and Municipal Employees
AFT	American Federation of Teachers
AFTRA	American Federation of Television and Radio Artists
APWU	American Postal Workers Union
ATU	Amalgamated Transit Union
AUD	Association for Union Democracy
BA	Business agent
CAW	Canadian Auto Workers
CBTU	Coalition of Black Trade Unionists
COPE	Committee on Political Education
CUE	Coalition of University Employees
CWA	Communications Workers of America
DARE	Direct Action for Rights and Equality
EEOC	Equal Employment Opportunity Commission
EPA	Environmental Protection Agency
FMLA	Family and Medical Leave Act
FOPE	Federation of Public Employees
FTAA	Free Trade Area of the Americas
HERE	Hotel Employees and Restaurant Employees (now UNITE HERE)
IAM	International Association of Machinists
IBEW	International Brotherhood of Electrical Workers
IBT	International Brotherhood of Teamsters
IFPTE	International Federation of Professional and Technical Engineers
ILA	International Longshoremen's Association
ILWU	International Longshore and Warehouse Union
INS	Immigration and Naturalization Service (now Immigration and Customs Enforcement)
IUE	International Union of Electronic Workers (now part of CWA)
Labor Board	National Labor Relations Board
LCLAA	Labor Council for Latin American Advancement
NAACP	National Association for the Advancement of Colored People
NAFTA	North American Free Trade Agreement
NLRA	National Labor Relations Act
NLRB	National Labor Relations Board
NOW	National Organization for Women
OSHA	Occupational Safety and Health Administration
OPEIU	Office and Professional Employees International Union
PACE	Paper, Allied-Industrial, Chemical and Energy Workers International Union
PATCO	Professional Air Traffic Controllers Organization
PSC	Professional Staff Congress
SEIU	Service Employees International Union
TDU	Teamsters for a Democratic Union
TWU	Transport Workers Union
UA	United Association of Plumbers and Pipefitters
UAW	United Auto Workers
UE	United Electrical Workers
UFCW	United Food and Commercial Workers
ULP	unfair labor practice
UNAP	United Nurses and Allied Professionals
UNITE	Union of Needletrades, Industrial and Textile Employees (now UNITE HERE)
UNITE HERE	The merged union of UNITE and HERE, completed summer 2004
USWA	United Steelworkers of America
WTO	World Trade Organization

For a complete list of the unions that appear in this book, see the index.

Thank You!

THANKS ARE DUE MOST OF ALL to workplace troublemakers everywhere, who stick their necks out and show others that it can be done. You are leaders, teachers, and inspiration for all troublemakers yet to come.

This book represents the collective effort, over two years, of 72 authors and more than 250 activists who have told us their stories in order to share their successes with others. This handbook could not have been written if these grassroots activists had not donated their time to share their experiences.

The authors, all of whom are activists themselves, listened, asked questions, and wrote the stories down. Together, back and forth, activists, authors, and editor distilled their experiences into stories that we hope will both teach and inspire. Many authors are experts themselves in the topics they covered; others would be the first to admit that they're not—but they dove in and went straight to the sources who knew the answers.

You will learn about the activists as they tell their stories. To learn more about the authors, you can read a little about them at the end of each chapter. We are proud that this book is the product of so many interactions. It indicates that the labor movement is best served when it encourages the participation of as many as possible.

You'll notice that Dan La Botz, author of the first edition of *A Troublemaker's Handbook* in 1991, contributed a lot to this all-new edition as well. You'll find Dan's stories, along with the work of labor historian and writer Aaron Brenner, throughout the book. Besides the sheer volume of material they contributed, Aaron and Dan, in very different ways, were a pleasure to work with, and their insights improved the book greatly. Dan and Marsha Niemeijer of the Labor Notes staff did many of the initial interviews that got the book under way—back in 2002. Dan also conducted many interviews in Spanish to help other authors with their stories.

Many people read at least one chapter of the book, gave us their comments, and helped us to understand what our audience would need. They are Judy Ancel, Jan Austin, Sherry Baron, Elaine Bernard, Carl Biers, Ellis Boal, Aaron Brenner, Kate Bronfenbrenner, Alex Brown, Sheila Cohen, Jeff Crosby, Mark Dilley, Steve Downs, Steve Early, Barry Eidlin, Kay Eisenhower, William Erffmeyer, Joe Fahey, Lynn Feekin, Janice Fine, Pam Galpern, Katie Griffiths, Martha Gruelle, William Johnson, Jelger Kalmijn, Brian Kearney, Chris Kutalik, Dan La Botz, Michael Laslett, Ken Leap, Elly Leary, Eric Lee, Nancy Lessin, David Levin, Paul Alan Levy, Gary Lipsius, Jon Liss, Dave Livingston, Stephanie Luce, Sheila McClear, Paul McLennan, Yanira Merino, Craig Merrilees, Hanna Metzger, Ruth Milkman, Kim Moody, Frank Natalie, Marsha Niemeijer, Bruce Nissen, Matt Noyes, Tom O'Connor, José Oliva, Ken Paff, Mike Parker, David Pratt, Teófilo Reyes, Charley Richardson, Robert Rodriguez, Hetty Rosenstein, Sarah Ryan, Simone Sagovac, Tim Schermerhorn, Bob Schwartz, Gregg Shotwell, Kelsey Sigurdur, Sam Smucker, Rachel Szekely, Wendy Thompson, Roberta Till-Retz, Jerry Tucker, N. Renuka Uthappa, Suzanne Wall, Jim West, Rand Wilson, Ilene Winkler, Michael Woo, David Yao, Andy Zipser. Thank you for your generous and incisive comments.

Volunteer editors helped polish the stories. We thank especially Hanna Metzger and Ilene Winkler. Ilene contributed not only her editing skills but her long experience in the labor movement ("that's not how it would have gone down in my local"). Hanna was my right-hand woman throughout the project, always available to take on editing chores of any magnitude, quickly and thoroughly. Other skilled chapter editors were Donna Cartwright, David McCullough, Robert Newell, Rosalyn Kawahira, Jim West, and Andy Zipser.

Andy also painstakingly proofread almost the entire book, aided by Hanna Metzger and Marilyn Penttinen. Jim West and David McCullough designed it, and Barbara Barefield created the cover.

Ellis Boal contributed his expertise as a labor lawyer. Jim West, former editor of *Labor Notes*, donated many of the best photographs you'll see in these pages, and he laid out the whole book. As always, Jim is a model of forbearance. We thank the many photographers and cartoonists who contributed their work, and the many activists who donated snapshots of the events they participated in.

Labor Notes interns helped with a variety of tasks large and small, but all crucial: thank you to Nick Robinson, Victoria Snowden, Randy Voss, Abe Walker.

Special thanks are owed to those who heeded my last-minute plea to help fill gaps. They jumped in, did interviews, and wrote them up under pressure: Aaron Brenner, Jeff Crosby, William Johnson, Dan La Botz, Simone Sagovac, N. Renuka Uthappa, Andy Zipser. You won't see their names on those last-minute contributions, but they are no less appreciated.

Of course, not all those who helped will agree with all of our advice and conclusions. Only Labor Notes is responsible for the ideas here—and we hope that the Troublemaker's page at www.labornotes.org will encourage more discussion of them.

—*Jane Slaughter*

Thank You, Labor Notes Donors

WE'D LIKE TO THANK AND RECOGNIZE HERE the activists and unions who have given us financial support to get *A Troublemaker's Handbook 2* printed and distributed to as many new troublemakers as possible. Their donations came at an important time. Thank you also to those who asked to remain anonymous.

Special recognition must be given to Kay Eisenhower and to others who gave very generously in memory of John D. Bowers, Kay's late husband and a longtime representative for SEIU Local 535 in California.

AFSCME Local 1723
Anonymous Industrial Hygienist
Royce Adams
Jan Arnold
Steven Ashby & C.J. Hawking
Stephen Barton
Erwin & Estar Baur
Joe Berry
Paul Bigman
Paul Bouchard
John Braxton
Aaron Brenner
Mark Brenner
Karl Edwin Bretz
Amy Bromsen
Steve Brown
Tom Brown
Gene Bruskin
Joe Burns
Margaret Butler
CAW-Canada
CAW Local 88
CAW Windsor Environment Council
CSEA/SEIU Local 1000
CWA Local 1037
CWA Local 1168
CWA Local 1180
CWA Local 1298
Art Carpenter
Neil Chacker
Dan Clawson
Bruce Cohen
Lance Coles
Jeff Crosby
Paul D'Ambrosio
Ellen David Friedman
Enrique Delacruz
Mark Dickman
Eric Dirnbach
Steve Downs
Joanna Dubinsky
Steve Early
Barry Eidlin
Kay Eisenhower
Madelyn Elder
Frank Emspak
Todd Erickson
Sean Farley
Lynn Feekin
Jean A. & Wesley J. Felton
Randy & Gillian Furst
Marisela Garcia
Rick Garrett
Greg Gigg
Gary Goff
Norbert Goldfield
Marie Gottschalk
Don Grinde
Martha Gruelle
IBT Local 206
IFPTE Local 21
Al Hart
Barbara Harvey
Robert Hatfield
Steve Hinds
Margaret Jordan
David Kandel
Ron Kaminkow
Michael Kaufman
Kathy Kleckner
Betsy Krieger
Paul Kriehbiel
Labor Power
Gary Lawrence
Dan Leahy
Elly Leary
Vance & Kimberlie Lelli
Dennis Levendowski
Traven Leyshon
Larry Lipschultz
Stephanie Luce
Sarah Luthens
Frank Maio
Chris Mark
John Martinez
Gary McHugh
Terry Meadows
David Melnychuk
Pat Cason Merenda & Doug Merenda
Paula Murray
Bruce Nissen
Shirley Noles
Steve Ongerth
Paul Ortiz
PSC-CUNY
Ken Paff
Bill Parker
Mike Parker
Robert & Laverne Parker
Guillermo Perez
Greg Poferl
David Poklinkoski
Charles Post
Labor Power
Paul Price
Peter Rachleff
Diane Radischat
Virginia & Rebekah Ravenscroft-Scott
Jeremy Read
Terrence Ryan
Margaret & Frank Roemhild
Michael Rubin
Rick Sather
Robert Schwartz
Joseph Serba
Fatih Shakir
Gregg Shotwell
Sharyn Sigurdur
Mike Slott
Dawn Stanger
Doug Swanson
Renee Toback
Merry Tucker
Voices at Work/ KPFT
Terry Weber
Carol Weidel
Thurman B. Wenzl
Justin West
Chris White
David Williams
Mary Winzig
David Wolfe
Matt Yamamoto
Barbara Zeluck
Andy Zipser

We are also grateful to the foundations that are helping us to get this book distributed, especially into the hands of low-income workers: the Solidago Foundation and the Unitarian Universalist Veatch Program at Shelter Rock. Thanks also to the Boehm Foundation, Funding Exchange, North Star Fund, and New World Foundation for general support during the time the book was in progress. And we also want to acknowledge the support of major donors and foundations that remain anonymous.

Our readers' support enables us to put out our monthly magazine, publish books like this one, provide trainings and tailored support, such as the upcoming Troublemakers Schools, and hold large international conferences every two years. Ask for a free sample copy of the magazine by calling 313-842-6262 or by visiting our website at www.labornotes.org. Check for the dates of upcoming schools and conferences and for local Labor Notes events in your city or for your union.

Foreword

by Baldemar Velásquez

THE HEART OF WHAT I'VE ALWAYS APPRECIATED about the Labor Notes community is embodied in this book: honest discussion and investigation. A willingness to question conventional wisdom on how best to represent and organize workers and challenge entire industries is found in very few quarters.

This book walks you through countless tactics, strategies, and stunningly creative approaches to the new realities faced by our rapidly changing workforce—black, Latino, Asian, and white, women and men, young and old. Having done grassroots organizing for 37 years and having been a preacher for 11 years, I continue to be astounded at how much I still have to learn from the experience of others and the miraculous creativity that flows from the hearts and souls of those organizers who care enough to take risks for the sake of others.

Perhaps this is what profoundly moves me more than anything: that while self-interest may be a motivator, collective action requires risking self-accommodation and therefore learning that solidarity requires some sacrifice. This is the common thread that has created and sustained not only the labor movement but also struggles for change and progressive revolutions throughout history.

While history has shown that revolutionaries and reformers have sometimes been outflanked, out-organized, and even quashed, it is perhaps out of the most distressful situations that new leaders have emerged from the ranks of the previously unseen and unheard. As a well-known hillbilly gospel song goes, "the darkest hour is just before dawn."

Understanding Others

All the many everyday heroes of the civil rights and labor movements emerged when oppressive powers were confronted by those who decided to risk self-preservation and self-interest for the benefit of the whole. The quiet actions of a seamstress named Rosa Parks, as part of a committed group of organizers, sparked a boycott that would be the envy of any labor organizer. The following pages chronicle the experiences and lessons of labor's Rosa Parkses—and perhaps tomorrow's Martin Luther King Jr.'s and Malcolm X's.

What stands out and underlies the stories are the efforts to truly understand what others' life experiences are and what they think. We are reminded that top leadership cannot become disconnected from the realities of the shop floor and the field. It is difficult enough to practice democracy in a large union and maintain the required high level of communication, but to do it across language and cultural barriers requires commitment to understand others. Many references throughout these pages show us how that has been accomplished, and they can teach us much to advance our organizing agendas.

Cultures, languages can be an impediment to organizing, but when those barriers are broken and communication begins to take place, we realize that human beings don't differ too much in their aspirations to feed, educate, and clothe their families. It takes time, effort, and money to overcome the natural obstacles to organizing, but translating and understanding cultural nuances takes an additional investment—thinking beyond the workplace and helping workers in their lives beyond the shop floor!

I've always believed in community organizing as a base to organizing workers in a workplace but now, in an age of globalization, our challenge is more daunting. Our worker communities are no longer defined by a metropolitan area or a neighborhood. International solidarity can no longer be a mere slogan; we need honest debate over how to program it. I have been to many Labor Notes conferences, with their workshops on cross-border organizing and their participation from labor leaders from across the globe. They make us realize that globalizing the union movement is a must, like water is to a human being. These pages and the discussions at Labor Notes conferences are the opening volleys on this serious issue.

As a pacifist, preacher, and labor organizer, I often relate how I first met Cesar Chavez and Martin Luther King, Jr. within an eight-month period in 1967-68. They had one thing in common, one thing that stood out without a doubt: they had both given themselves to the cause, regardless of the cost to themselves. It made me want to join them and be one of them. I knew that they would never give up their struggles for others. They personified John 15:13, where Jesus said; "Greater love has no one than this, that he lay down his life for his friends."

I see that same spirit in many of the organizers whose stories breathe life into the pages of this book. In their own ways, they are our new Walter Reuthers and Joe Hills, our Mother Joneses, our Cesar Chavezes.

[Baldemar Velásquez is president of the Farm Labor Organizing Committee.]

In memory of Victor Reuther

1. Power on the Job
by Jane Slaughter

EVER SINCE THE FIRST BOSS hired the first worker, workers and owners have struggled over how hard we would labor, for how long, with which tools, and with how much skill.

We care about what goes on during the work-day not just because we spend half our waking lives on the job. The way we spend our working hours determines so many other facets of our lives, not just individually, but as a society. Do we work so long that our employers can lay off other workers? Do we work for so little that we can't afford decent housing or to buy the products we make? Do we work with such dangerous chemicals that our neighborhoods are polluted? Do we work so intensely that our families and community life suffer?

The struggle for power at the workplace is about more than money and more than working conditions. It is about who wields power over some of society's most important decisions: What are we going to make? How are we going to make it? And who benefits from our labor? We struggle at the workplace so we can have a say in those decisions. The workplace is where we learn either that we have power over our lives, or that we don't.

Tug of War in the Workplace

EMPLOYERS "GET IT" ABOUT THE WORKPLACE—it's where their profits come from. So they're always trying to increase their power vs. ours. Today they are:

- Speeding up work, through new technologies that set our pace and then monitor us.
- De-skilling our jobs by putting our brains in the machines or giving our skilled work to people outside the bargaining unit.
- Demanding longer hours (without overtime pay) and irregular schedules, in the name of "flexibility."
- Controlling the way we work more tightly, with "lean production" schemes. Telling us not just what to do but how to do it, every little step.
- Changing jobs from lifetime to short-term, from full-time to part-time.
- Outsourcing jobs, both inside this country and overseas, to places where working conditions are worse.
- Sowing division in the workforce with "two-tier" contracts—hiring new workers at much lower wages and benefits.

With these attacks, management undermines two sources of workers' power:

- The first is our job knowledge—*we're* the ones who do the work, who are the experts about our jobs, who know what the patient needs or where to kick the machine to make it go. If work is standardized, computerized, robotized, it's easier to outsource it—say to a call center across the country or across the world. When management harvests our knowledge and embeds it in software, we lose the skills that give us leverage. It's harder to dissent, to make trouble.
- The second source of power that's undermined is

Is This Where 'Apathy' Comes From?

The best unions not only run an efficient operation and get out the vote; they have a presence members can feel inside the workplace. But in too many unions, elected leaders are far removed from the shop floor and the hogwash that workers put up with every day. They tend to be concerned with gains that they can count—new members, wage increases, votes for a candidate—rather than working conditions, which are harder to put a figure on. Staffers who've never worked in the industry may not understand just how important working conditions are.

But when unions neglect the workplace, they teach defeatism. If we don't fight back collectively against harassment, monitoring, layoffs, we learn through experience that there is little we can do to control our lives at work.

What's the result? Union leaders are inclined to call it "apathy." "Why don't the members come to union meetings?" they say. But workers who haven't been helped to fight over the day-to-day basics aren't likely to heed the union's call to come out for the "bigger" issues. One local president said, "I have seen it often in my own local, where I think we are doing great stuff in the outside world (where I am focused) and so many members think the union sucks because of things in the shop (where they are focused)."

If we don't know how to fight as a group, instead we look for individual solutions—a different job, a promotion, going back to school, scratching the supervisor's back, alcohol. We decline the union's invitation to volunteer on an organizing drive—why should we think we can win? And second-tier workers wonder why they should have a union at all.

Apathy is something you're trained in, not something you're born with.

What Does Power on the Job Look Like?

by William Johnson

Like hospital nurses everywhere, nurses at Los Angeles County hospitals were understaffed and overworked. Managers would assign them to care for eight, 12, 20, or more patients.

Joel Solis, a registered nurse and shop steward in Service Employees Local 660, says that such workloads are unsafe for both nurses and patients. "We were so understaffed and tired," remembers Solis. "We decided we had to do something."

So Solis and another Local 660 steward, Fred Huicochea, began meeting with their co-workers to develop "a strategy of resistance." The two stewards focused first on meeting with nurses on wards that were chronically understaffed, and where there were nurses who were already involved in union activity.

To avoid management, they had their first meetings on the night shift. "Managers leave at five o'clock," Solis explains, "so we'd have really good meetings around nine p.m., after the patients had their dinners and went to bed. We wore our county badges and our scrubs, so management wouldn't notice we were there. In our initial conversations, we just listened to the other nurses voice their frustrations."

After weeks of meetings on different wards, a strategy began to emerge. The nurses began discussing how to confront management and refuse to accept unsafe assignments.

"We did a lot of role-playing—manager versus nurse," says Solis. "We knew that when we refused the unsafe assignments, managers would be threatening, claiming we were insubordinate. We told the nurses, 'If they threaten to discipline you, there'll be union reps outside. Demand to have a union rep present.'"

One tool the nurses had was a new California law (AB 394) that nurses' unions had fought for. AB 394 mandated a maximum ratio of six patients to each nurse in most areas. Though the hospital had been ignoring it, the law also gave nurses the right to determine what is and isn't safe in caring for patients.

Showdown

On September 7, 2004, the nurses on a medical-surgical ward at Harbor/UCLA Medical Center told management they would care for no more than six patients at a time. To do so, they explained, would violate AB 394 and jeopardize patient safety. When management threatened to discipline them, the nurses told management they couldn't be forced to break the law. They called in their union reps, who were waiting outside the hospital.

The reps backed the rank and filers up—even when management called the police to throw them out. During a four-hour confrontation, nurses refused to accept unsafe assignments, union reps stood their ground, management fumed, and the police scratched their heads. Finally, management was forced to hire temp nurses to care for all the patients.

"We caught them completely off guard," says Solis. "All of a sudden, they were not in control. The nurses were in control, and that drove management up the wall."

Meanwhile, SEIU 660 members were leafleting nurses on other shifts at other hospitals, letting them know about the campaign at Harbor/UCLA. Soon, more wards there and at Los Angeles County/USC Medical Center were refusing unsafe assignments, and as this book was being completed, management had been forced to staff within the ratios or close to them—but only on the floors where nurses had demanded their rights.

What's more, Solis says that the nurses' success led them to question other safety hazards. "Nurses are looking into what needles are being used on a ward, asking, 'are they safe?' Nurses are checking out ergonomics, looking into things they never had the courage to question management about before."

More Involved in the Union

And the shop floor organizing has gotten nurses more involved in the union. "We've got a bunch of new stewards, and more people are showing up for meetings," says Solis. "Nurses are engaging with management, saying, 'We want meetings, we want to come up with solutions to these problems,' when it used to be management saying, 'We'll meet once a month, and here's what we're going to do.' Nurses want a greater say in how things are decided."

Though AB 394 was a useful tool for the nurses in this campaign, it was their ability to talk with each other, decide on a joint course of action, and stick to it in the face of threats that gave the law some teeth. Solis notes that once the nurses began organizing around staffing ratios, they discovered that, under hospital policy, they already had the right to determine what is and isn't safe. "All along," he says, "nurses had those rights, without knowing it."

What laws or clauses in *your* contract aren't being enforced? What do you need in order to work safely and without going home exhausted? How would your job be different if you and your co-workers got organized to demand your rights?

[Read more about the members of SEIU Local 660 organizing on the job and in the community in Chapters 3 and 12.]

POWER ON THE JOB 3

where the daily conflict lies that makes it impossible to snuff the union movement out."

Workers' power at work has ebbed and flowed over the years, but resistance never disappears. The stories in this book prove that. While management was busy working to remake the workplace and disorganize these sisters and brothers, they were working to preserve their relationships and push back. The troublemakers you'll meet in this book:

• Created informal friendship groups at work to keep themselves informed and to lay the basis for action.

The struggle for power at the workplace is about more than money and more than working conditions. It is about who wields power over some of society's most important decisions: What are we going to make? How are we going to make it? And who benefits from our labor? We struggle at the workplace so we can have a say in those decisions. The workplace is where we learn either that we have power over our lives, or that we don't.

---

our solidarity. Workers who are sped-up and monitored can't socialize with each other; we can't organize. We become electronically tethered to the work process but not to each other. And when we accept a two-tier contract, we're voting for daily tension and resentment on the floor. If we tell younger workers that we're not concerned about their future, why should they fight for decent pensions for us?

So employers want to set new ground rules for the next round of struggle. Two-tier, in particular, sets some very bad terms—if newer, younger union members are angry enough, the next battle could be over whether it's worth having a union at all.

Troublemakers at Work

AS LONG AS THERE ARE WORKERS AND BOSSES, there will be resistance to the daily grind-up. Even before there were unions, workers organized on the job to protect themselves.

Labor historian David Montgomery says, "Unions had their origins in the attempt to get some sort of collective control over the conditions of work.... The workplace is both where the union movement had its birth and

• Organized small workplace actions to resist supervisors' bullying and challenge management authority.

• Constructed formal organizations such as union organizing committees or stewards committees or workers centers.

• Took direct action in the form of job actions and strikes.

• Formed rank-and-file alliances to act together when their union would not.

• Worked to build economic power by organizing new members strategically.

• Spread their movement from the workplace and the union hall to the community and to society at large.

On page 2, hospital nurses in Los Angeles provide a terrific example of how to take power on the job, protect workers' health and sanity—and make common cause with the public (their patients).

If it's strong enough, shop floor organization like the nurses' can be maintained even after defeats and in the worst of times. It can provide a lifeline. In Chapter 8, on

Contract Campaigns, you'll read about the flight attendants at Northwest Airlines, whose "shop floor" is all over the world. They learned how to connect through a Contract Action Team and to mobilize themselves for a decent contract.

Then when September 11, 2001 hit the airline industry, the flight attendants had a system in place to talk to each other by phone, for instant crisis counseling. Facing huge layoffs, they mobilized to convince management to make the rules flexible so as many flight attendants as possible could keep their jobs. They could do these things because after their contract campaign, they had kept their rank-and-file network in place.

We Have Power

THE NURSES AND THE FLIGHT ATTENDANTS had power because they had built daily relationships of mutual trust, cooperation, and common courage. These relationships lay the basis for bigger actions—getting a union, contract campaigns, strikes. When workers have this sort of power in our workplaces, we can affect production, profits, services, public relations, and political power, as well as our own working conditions. The fight starts in the workplace, the only place in our segregated society where we are brought together with people of other races, generations, genders, and religions. It's where we learn from our sisters' and brothers' experiences and pass on our own.

When we're organized on the job, we can establish relationships with community groups and social movements that multiply our collective power inside and outside the workplace. Such coalitions aren't built on the basis of weakness, but on our ability to take our strength from the workplace into the community.

Teamsters Local 174 in Seattle provides one example. Reformers won office and set about building up the union on the job. They started new-member orientation, set up member-to-member workplace structures, taught members how to fight management's "team concept," and recruited a volunteer organizing committee. Before too long, they began alliances with environmentalists and with global justice protesters battling the World Trade Organization (see Chapters 12 and 23). Would 600 members of Local 174 have come out to march against the WTO if they hadn't had confidence in their union on the job?

In the last chapter we will look at how the labor movement needs to change if it is to build on grassroots organizing like the truck drivers' and the nurses' and the flight attendants'. Between here and there, you'll meet a host of troublemakers who fought to recruit new union members, stop discrimination, keep their jobs from killing them, end two-tier wages, slow down the pace of work, win a solid contract, set an example for the next generation, build ties overseas, welcome immigrants to this country, connect with each other in cyberspace, build equal relationships with community allies, throw out rotten union leaders, do smart research, run their locals without burning out, and poke corporate power in the eye.

If we've done our job right, their examples will inspire you and educate you. You'll be an educated troublemaker—an organizer.

Authors

WILLIAM JOHNSON joined the Labor Notes staff in 2003 and covers SEIU, teachers, and the public sector. His writing has appeared in *Z, The Nation,* and *Counterpunch.*

JANE SLAUGHTER is the editor of this book and has worked with Labor Notes since 1979.

On the Troublemaker's Website

"Surrendering the Shop Floor Means Surrendering the Future," by Charley Richardson. Go to www.labornotes.org.

Organize, Not Just Unionize

It's not enough just to make your own workplace strong, of course. One gutsy local union in a sea of non-union competitors can't hold out alone. As everyone knows by now, we need to bring our non-union sisters and brothers into the fold.

But although organizing drives for new members are crucial, they don't always answer the question of power in the workplace. Organizing needs to be more than just unionizing.

It works both ways. Unions that are strong in the workplace are likely to be more successful in organizing: they can point to their gains as reasons to join, and they have enthusiastic members who can look prospective members in the eye and spread the word.

And when we get a bigger chunk of our industry into the union, we need to remember that the job's not over. We shouldn't tell new members that they can sit back now and leave it to the negotiators. They'll need to be organized at work, if the now-larger union is to make good on its promises.

2. The Basics of Organizing

by Ellen David Friedman

YOU HAVE PICKED UP THIS BOOK. That means you are at least interested in the idea of troublemaking at work. That's where many of us start. It's not that we want to cause trouble for its own sake, but that we want to fix problems we see around us at our workplaces. It may be that something unfair has happened to you, or to someone you work with. This chapter is about doing something about it. For us…that's organizing. For the boss…that's trouble.

The Organizing Attitude

Organizing is an attitude. It's the attitude that you and your co-workers together can do something to make things better. It's the attitude that action is better than complaining. It's the attitude that all problems are just situations waiting for a solution. It's the refusal to be discouraged—at least not for long. It's the willingness to listen to others with respect, so that the plan you come up with reflects the good ideas of many people. If you have the attitude, you feel it is necessary to respond to unfairness. You are committed to building power with your co-workers, not just talking about it. You believe in collective action, even if you're just starting to understand it.

Don't Be Afraid

You are not alone. There are always more workers than bosses in any workplace. The workers will always have a lot to gain by banding together and organizing. Whether you work in an office, factory, hospital, coal mine, restaurant, or school, just do the math: there are lots of people in the same boat as you. Of course it looks like the boss has more power, and we can't kid ourselves—the power to fire, the power to harass, the power to discipline or make your life miserable are considerable powers. But we can limit the boss's power by reaching out to one another, by organizing, and by challenging unfair and exploitative treatment.

If you want to do something, but are afraid, try these steps to get going:

• Think clearly about the problem you're facing. Maybe you have a supervisor who humiliates and belittles someone in front of co-workers. You've tried reasoning with him, but nothing changes. Try to get past the emotion—the anger, resentment, shame, or whatever you're feeling about it. Write down the simple facts.

• Resist the urge to act only on emotion, or to do something all by yourself. That's often when you're most vulnerable, and might make more trouble for yourself than you've made for the boss. Instead… take a deep breath and reach out to co-workers.

• Find someone at work you trust. Show them what you've written. Ask them for their honest opinion. If they agree that this is a serious problem to address, see if you can come up with the names of other co-workers who are affected by it too.

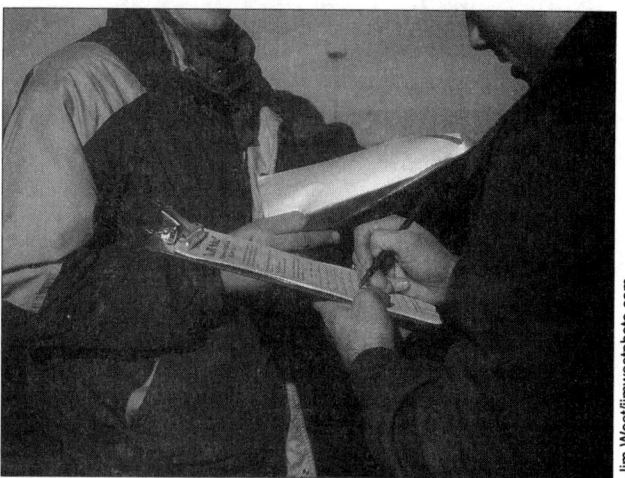

Organizing is an attitude. It's the attitude that you and your co-workers together can do something to make things better.

• Talk one to one with these other people. So far, you're just checking to see if others agree with you, not deciding what you're going to do about it.

• Some people will be more concerned than others. Don't be discouraged. Keep talking—without pestering people—until you find even one person who shares your desire to do something.

• If you find even a small handful of co-workers who share this problem, then this is your "core group." Get them together, perhaps just sharing a cup of coffee. First share your fears about what could happen if you did something. Then, talk about what will happen if you do nothing. This will usually help make up your mind to do something! Then start talking about steps you could take.

• Figure out together who in management is the decision-maker on the problem or issue. Does this boss know about the problem? How could you approach the boss, collectively, about the problem? What are the risks and advantages of different approaches?

• Use the information in this chapter to make a plan. Take small steps to build your trust as a group. This is the best way to overcome fear.

Your Legal Rights to Organize

THE FOLLOWING RIGHTS OF PRIVATE SECTOR WORKERS are protected under the federal National Labor Relations Act, also known as the Wagner Act.

General

The most important "legal" advice is to be well organized. Legal strategies aid day-to-day work. They don't take the place of it. Any position, legal or otherwise, is going to be enhanced if the people behind it act as a group, have plans that are thought out, and follow through on the plan. If the matter comes to a hearing or to court, any judge is going to be impressed by a well-attended and well-organized presentation.

Don't set yourself up. Be a model worker, come on time, and be above reproach.

Keep a notebook of all suspicious things. Record the Five W's: What happened, where it happened, when it happened, who saw it (names, addresses, phones), and why each party claimed to act as they did.

Your Right To Talk Union

If workers are routinely allowed to carry on conversations on personal or non-work topics, then you can discuss union topics or collective concerns too, as long as it doesn't interfere with getting your work done. Even if there is a rule against talking about non-work issues, you may do so anywhere on non-working time.

Your Right To Distribute Literature

You have a legal right to distribute literature to your co-workers. If you're allowed to pass around other kinds of written information in the workplace (flyers for bands, announcements about community events), union literature (or employee-to-employee materials) cannot be treated differently. Even if there's a rule against non-work-related written materials, if you are getting signatures on petitions but not distributing literature, you may do so in working areas on non-working time.

If you have just started a union drive (and you can prove that supervisors know there's a union drive going on), management cannot suddenly put no-literature rules into place or suddenly start enforcing a rule no one has ever known about. The same thing is true about wearing t-shirts or buttons with slogans—if you've always been allowed to wear them, the "content" can't be censored by the boss just because it's union-related. But stay away from obscenity!

The law says you can always distribute literature to co-workers on non-working time in non-working areas. This includes the parking lot, the time clock, the cafeteria, or any place where people go on break out of the work area.

Using email, phones, or voice mail at work to communicate with co-workers about issues is an area of the law that is being tested continually. If you have a work manual that says you are allowed "reasonable" use of email to communicate personal information, you're probably technically safe. Remember that email and voice mail are easy for the employer to monitor.

Small warning note: The National Labor Relations Board (NLRB) may allow employers to prohibit the distribution of literature which tends to disparage the employer, if the primary target of that literature is the customer base or general public, and there is no strike occurring at the time.

You have an absolute right to distribute literature at or in common areas of the union hall, including at union meetings.

'Concerted' Activities—Work Actions

Work actions are only protected under federal labor law if done by two or more individuals together—that's what "concerted" means. Striking, picketing, petitioning, grieving, and group complaints to the Department of Labor are the classic examples of work actions. Work actions are of course most effective when done by a huge majority of workers.

While most union contracts prohibit strikes while the contract is in effect (because it's assumed you can use the grievance procedure to resolve problems), you still have the right to engage in most other forms of collective action. This right is protected by the NLRB, which must receive and serve your charge within six months. However, the NLRB has a policy of deferring legal prosecution on such cases if there is a grievance procedure in effect that theoretically could resolve the issue.

Legal Rights of Public Employees

Note that public employees—state, municipal, school—are not covered by the National Labor Relations Act. Labor relation laws for public employees are a state matter, and you will need to check your own state's statutes. The majority of states do have laws on the books that guarantee rights similar to those in the NLRA.

Respect Is the Foundation of Organizing

In most workplaces, workers aren't respected. Most of us don't get paid well enough, or get a real voice on the job. Additionally, the American value system is very distorted at this moment in history—celebrity seems to be valued over integrity, wealth is more important than talent, and power is its own justification. All of this means that regular working people and our occupations are given little respect by the media or politicians, and certainly not by the corporate class.

What we as workers can do—whether we have a union or not—is to show respect for one another and ourselves. This is the foundation for powerful organizing. When you have self-respect, it means you won't put up with bullying, intimidation, or exploitation. When you respect your co-workers, it means you value their experience and know they have something important to add to the plan for solving problems at work.

This is not always easy to do. We get frustrated, impatient, or agitated about differences over religion, morality, political views, or personal habits. But you, as an organizer, can work hard to get past those feelings and find a basis of shared respect simply as workers. It is important to encourage open and honest talk about issues, without personal judgment or criticism. This will make people want to organize at your side.

Make Personal Relationships

Kris Rondeau, the lead organizer for the successful union drive among Harvard's clerical and technical workers, is a strong proponent of relationship-building as the basis for organizing. "The key is organizing one-to-one, or one person at a time," says Rondeau. "It's a type of organizing based on building deep personal relationship by connecting workers to each other in important ways."

There is a reason we have to approach organizing this way. What we "troublemakers" do is scary for most people, at times even ourselves. Whether we are trying to organize a union, revitalize a union, democratize a union, win a contract, or just solve problems at a workplace that has no union, we will find that our co-workers are nervous. No one wants to get in trouble for rocking the boat.

So, we have to address that fear. And the most effective way to do it is by linking people together in a personal way. When the relationships are real, close, and strong, it is easier for everyone to feel safer to take risks.

Rondeau suggests, "You build a strong organization by connecting people to each other. The union grows out of this network of relationships. Without this, all you ever have are superficial connections which will never withstand the hot breath of management's anti-unionism."[1]

Good organizing involves more listening than talking. Your job is to find out what your co-workers care about and then work together to make a plan to solve a problem. Don't feel that you need to sell something.

Apathy Isn't Real

For many new to organizing, the biggest obstacle may be the apparent apathy of your co-workers. You wonder whether anyone else cares. If there is a union at your workplace, you might resent the fact that very few people show up for meetings. If you are one of the people who are active in the union, you might be angry that "it's always the same few of us doing all the work."

But this leads you nowhere, except to feeling powerless, overwhelmed, and mad at your co-workers. Instead, try to step back from your anger and frustration and look at things from an organizing perspective. Your goal is to help make change, so you'll need to get in the habit of seeing things in new ways, without despair.

Think for a minute about what you're really seeing. Here are some other ways to understand what looks like apathy, and to respond to it.

- **No one seems to care.** Everyone cares about something. Pick out a few people at work who you'd like to know better. Make a point of talking with them, and find out what's going on for them. Maybe workplace problems aren't at the top of the list because things are hard at home. Show them respect and understanding. When they feel that from you, they're more likely to show respect for the things you care about.

- **It's hard to see how things could change.** Just as it's true that everyone cares about something, it's also true that hopelessness can be a strong habit. It's easier to break a habit with group support. So bringing people together who really want a change can help individuals get past their discouragement.

- **No one's willing to do anything.** Most of us aren't natural-born organizers. Many of your co-workers won't initiate activity, but they will respond if asked directly. Figure out some very small, specific request and personally approach a co-worker. This might be as simple as answering a few survey questions, coming to lunch with other workers to discuss a problem, or signing a group letter. Be respectful of time constraints in their lives, and show lots of appreciation for anything they're willing to do. This attitude of respect will make them comfortable in doing more in the future.

- **No one comes to meetings.** Think about how people are notified about meetings. A notice on the bulletin board, or newsletter dropped in their mailbox, isn't a good method. Personal, face-to-face invitations are the very best. Divide your workplace up and find several other people to share the work of inviting people individually. Make sure there is a clear agenda, a time-frame for the meeting, and a reason to attend—such as a hot issue. People are incredibly busy these days, and you will convey respect for their participation by planning a meeting ahead of time.

- **They think everything is fine.** Maybe things are fine for the majority of your co-workers. Maybe they're completely secure about their jobs, love their supervisors, make excellent money with terrific benefits, have no worries about downsizing or layoffs, face no health or safety hazards on the job, and are confident about their

Basic Principles of Organizing

1. Talk One on One. Listen to what your co-workers are saying. Share your own ideas. Don't just gossip or gripe, but help create a focus about problems that can be solved.

2. Encourage People To Feel Confident. Challenging authority is always hard. You and your co-workers may feel scared or hopeless. A calm and confident attitude can be helpful.

3. Be Willing To Challenge Authority. Organizers don't need to demonize the boss. We do need to encourage people to question and challenge authority.

4. Identify Common Problems (or Hopes). We organize to bring people together. Talk and listen until you've found a problem that matters to lots of your co-workers. Share what you've heard.

5. Set Concrete Goals. Goals should not be general, but very specific. State clearly what a victory would be. Make sure the majority of people share this goal.

6. Make Realistic Action Plans. Invite everyone's ideas. Develop plans that involve small steps. Each step should slowly increase the visibility and strength of the group.

7. Get People Active. Even simple collective activity is better than just talking. Circulate a petition. Wear buttons. Put up posters. Action breeds commitment.

8. Build a Group Identity. Design activity that brings people together. Send a group to talk to the boss. Write a letter that everyone signs. Organize social get-togethers.

9. Go from Modest to Ambitious. Start with small actions that can succeed. With new confidence, people will be able to take bigger and riskier steps to achieve their goal.

10. Confront Power. Don't just talk among yourselves. Figure out how to directly confront the people in authority. As long as the action is collective, you won't leave individuals vulnerable.

11. Evaluate as You Go. Keep talking one on one and in groups. Assess whether the goals are still correct and clear. Evaluate whether new plans are needed.

12. Organize Democratically. Include everyone who is, or might be, affected. Reach out beyond your friends. Don't let class, ethnic, gender, or age differences get in the way. Solicit opinions and involve as many people as possible in decisions.

13. Encourage Good Leaders. Take note of who is naturally respected and encourage them to take on leadership. Look for each person's talents and find ways to use them. Don't encourage the whiners.

14. Organization Is Everything. Your organization doesn't need to be too formal, but it does need to do the job. Even if you just have a phone tree, or a set of mail labels, you are on your way.

retirement. If so… put down this book and get another hobby! But it's more likely that people are scared, or feel powerless and directionless. They say everything is fine because they don't believe it can change. Organizing is the antidote to this attitude.

Action Questions

1. What is a problem you're facing at work? Have you talked about it with any of your co-workers? If not, who is someone you trust to talk with? Can you find time, either on the job or after work, to get together with them? Have you found other people who share the same problem, or who agree with you that something should be done about it?

2. What are the obstacles to workers getting together to solve problems at your workplace? Do people seem scared, apathetic, or too busy? What can you say to someone to break through these barriers? When did someone reach out to you? What do you know about how to make strong personal contact with someone?

3. Organizing is often a question of judging different individuals' strengths and helping to draw out their talents. Make a list of the closest ten people with whom you work. Which two or three would you begin by talking to? Why? What are their strengths?

4. If you wanted to meet discreetly, where would you meet? Could you talk at work, in the cafeteria, in the parking lot? Would it be best to meet in a coffee shop or a bar? Would it be good to meet at someone's home?

5. What problems are on people's minds? Can you identify a problem or two that many people share? Can you describe the problem in one or two sentences? Can you think of a solution that most people would support?

6. Once you have identified a common problem, can you list three or four steps you could take as a group? How will you involve co-workers? What preparation needs to take place? How many people can contribute to the preparation? Who will coordinate the plan? How will you communicate among members of the group?

7. Have you considered how you'll respond if you run into difficulties with the plan? How will you get people together to adjust the plan? What kind of attitude will be most helpful as you follow through the steps to solve the problem?

Author

ELLEN DAVID FRIEDMAN has been an organizer in Vermont for over 20 years, and on the staff of Vermont-NEA since 1986. She also organizes with the Vermont Livable Wage Campaign and the Vermont Workers Center, and is as vice-chair of the Vermont Progressive Party.

Note

1. "Finding Their Voice: Kris Rondeau Discusses Organizing with Richard Balzer," *Boston Review*, Sept./Oct. 1993.

3. Shop Floor Tactics

by Dan La Botz

THE TROUBLEMAKER'S TURF is the workplace. We spend most of our waking hours there. Work is where the boss makes his money. It's where we feel the stress. It's where the union is born and lives if we want it to be real and powerful. Yet workplace organization is often neglected by union officials whose attention is on negotiating contracts, national union business, or elections.

What do we do when we have a problem in the workplace? The usual answer, if we have a union, is to file a grievance, set paper in motion. But most problems aren't even grievances—they are simply the result of someone else having power over you. And the grievance procedure can be invisible, slow, and fruitless.

If we act on the job, we may not need to file a grievance. Hetty Rosenstein, president of a public employees union in New Jersey, CWA Local 1037, says, "When workers confront management at the worksite, and as a result they correct something that is wrong, or they improve their conditions, or they get a fired worker reinstated, a power shift occurs right before their eyes. It happens in real time and workers witness it.

"Not only does worksite mobilization work, it shifts the power for the next fight. Management holds the power over the situation and workers take it away. Mobilization is something that occurs outside of management's experience. And that alone gives the union leverage."

Of course, we may also want to pursue the paper process and win a precedent. But grievances will be won more quickly and more often if we also fight them on the shop floor, by making them:

• **Visible and public**, so that members are aware of what is taking place, the result, and who is accountable

• **Collective, using group grievances** to involve as many members as possible

• **Active**, involving members in actions to resolve them

• **Confrontational**, mobilizing members to face the company officials who have the power to resolve the problem, and upping the ante if necessary.

So we can organize to enforce the contract, or we may simply need to deal with the felt needs of our co-workers. The contract language may not be specific, but members can decide that 100 pieces an hour is too many, or that over 85 degrees is too hot, or that calling us "Hey, you!" is unacceptable. We can use our own power to weaken the boss's confidence and resolve such matters.

Direct Action

Organizing on the shop floor to exert power and solve problems is often called "direct action," that is, taking action ourselves, rather than waiting for others to solve the problem. Direct action means we:

• **Disrupt** the normal flow of work, the usual chain of command, and the employer's system of control. When we disrupt the system, we get attention and results.

• **Alter and improve**. We want to change the employer's way of doing things to one that treats us right and functions better. Sometimes we can change a practice simply by working differently: slow down production, take a longer break, change the way work is organized. Once something becomes an established practice, it is harder for the employer to change it back.

• **Take control.** When the boss gives an order, he sets a chain of events in motion. When we act collectively, we start a train of events in a different direction.

No shortcuts: shop floor organization takes thought, discussion, and planning. But we can think and talk on the job, and discuss in the break room. Everyone having lunch together in the cafeteria or meeting after work for a beer may be the beginning of a more formal organization, or may be all the organization we need. The key is to build a level of organization that works for the matters we're dealing with. We may just need to speak with three or four people in the department to get together a group to talk to the foreman. Or we may need to build a council of stewards who can organize throughout the worksite.

Whatever the size, the elements of a successful shop floor organization are:

• **Communication.** Lays the basis for mutual understanding. It can be informal—a conversation at work or over coffee—or more formal—through a member-to-member network, a newsletter, a leaflet, or a phone call or email.

WARNING!

1. Troublemakers can't be slackers; do your job consistently and do it well. Don't make yourself an easy target for management. Fellow workers will respect you more too.

2. If you don't have a union or you're a new worker on probation, be careful. Management can make up a bogus reason, any reason, or no reason to get rid of you.

Why Grievances Are Not Enough

The contract is a historical record of the achievements of the union, a sediment left behind by past organizing drives and strikes. It institutionalizes the victories of the past and establishes the minimum that a worker should be able to expect from the employer.

It is a mistake, however, to view the contract as a sacred document. It's only a deal. It was the result of a struggle between the employer and the union, which eventually resulted in a compromise. The employer wanted more, and we wanted more. We were at war and a truce was reached—until the conflict breaks out again.

In the meantime, every time management gets a chance, it will attempt to encroach into the territory that we have won, taking away things we thought the contract protected. The contract is never interpreted literally; it is combed by both management and the union in a search for possible interpretations. In the hands of a good steward it is interpreted creatively in the interests of the members.

Being a steward, however, is not a matter of mastering the art of interpretation. Winning your point often depends not so much on the contract language as on the power of the union.

Since the contract is the sediment of *past* struggles, it can tell you only what the balance of forces between management and labor was, say, in April three years ago, not what it is today. Winning a grievance or any other shop floor struggle depends on the balance of forces today.

Simply filing a grievance does nothing to alter that balance of forces in the members' favor. It is usually not a collective activity. It takes the issue off the shop floor and out of the members' hands. While the grievance goes its way from step to step, the members have nothing to do but wait.

How Can Just Grievances Be Lost?

Besides these problems, there is no way that simply filing grievances could begin to redress the injustices that go on in every workplace every month. Let us imagine that there are 1,000 violations of the contract or of the law by management in a particular workplace of 1,000 workers over the course of a month—probably a low estimate.

Then think about the workers who have these legitimate grievances:
- Some are probationary employees who are wise not to file a grievance yet.
- Some are not knowledgeable about the contract and do not know that they have the right to grieve.
- Some hope to go into management.
- Some are too shy or timid to speak up.
- Some who already face discrimination, such as members of racial minorities, women, or gays, may fear that filing a grievance will only add to their problems.
- Some fear they will be marked as troublemakers and singled out for transfer or discipline.
- Some are immigrants who do not know English or are not familiar with the workings of unions.

Now think about the steward:
- Even a good steward has limited time and will not be able to constantly comb the shop getting all the shy or fearful workers to submit their grievances. Even the pretty good steward is likely to work with the grievances that are submitted and not worry about those that are not.
- In any case, the steward has to pick her fights, to exercise judgment about which of the many possible grievances to pursue.
- If a grievance is not settled at the first or second step and goes into the machinery, it may no longer be settled on its merits. In a strong workplace, every grievance may get its due. But the norm may be to see half to nine-tenths of grievances traded away.

So, in the end, of the thousand just grievances which might have been filed, only perhaps a dozen are actually filed. Finally a few are won months later, but perhaps only the workers directly involved ever know about them.

If one could read the thoughts of the thousand workers in this shop, some would be satisfied. But there would be hundreds who were resentful because they had suffered an injustice at management's hands.

Strengthening the Grievance System

What can a union do to partially counteract these weaknesses of the grievance system? Besides the many tactics spelled out in this chapter:
- The union can periodically hold department or shop meetings in the plant, perhaps in the lunch area, to explain the members' rights and ask if they have problems.
- The stewards can create assistant stewards so that in the course of a week or two the steward or the assistants have talked to all the workers in the area, just to see how things are going. In this way shy workers are encouraged to come forward.
- If part of the workforce does not speak English or speaks it as a second language, the union can translate the contract and all leaflets and make sure that stewards or assistant stewards can talk to workers in their own language.

- **Solidarity.** Built every day in the workplace by being considerate and helpful to each other, by rejecting favoritism, and by building friendship and, at best, a sense of family among co-workers.
- **Joint action.** Action grows out of communication and solidarity. You do something together, if only to show yourselves you can. You may begin with something as small as showing up for work at the same time and meeting in the parking lot. If you can do that together, you can take action to disrupt and improve together.

Shop Floor Power

In any mobilization or organizing campaign, the basic, underlying issue is power: who has it, who wants it, and how it's used. Power is "the whole ball of wax," says Rosenstein. Yet many people are uncomfortable with power, find it hard to talk about, and are reluctant to avidly seek it. Part of that difficulty comes simply from non-use. "We don't recognize what it is because we don't have it," she explains.

Power is up for grabs: you can't gain power without someone else losing it, and many people shy away from the conflict and unpleasantness that implies. "People want to believe that if we're fair and we're brilliant, then we'll get what's right," Rosenstein observes. "And it's true that this helps, but it isn't enough. You can't just empower yourself. You have to take it from management."

A third reason people avoid seeking power at work is that they recognize, if only subconsciously, that it is only the first step in a never-ending struggle. Power, once taken, must be guarded against inevitable management attempts to retake it. "It's a huge amount of work," Rosenstein concedes, "and yes, it never ends." Even when workers and management reach a balance of power, no workplace is a closed system: there are always external factors, such as competition, new technology, or legislative changes, to upset the balance.

Troublemakers need to understand what makes it hard for people to act for power. Then you can help them take the first step. Troublemaking is like cooking—know the ingredients. See Chapter 2.

We look in this chapter at how union activists have built their power on the shop floor through clever tactics and strong organization. We first take up the use of "speaking truth" and ridicule as ways of challenging management's authority. Then we turn to collective action, groups of workers taking their complaints to the boss together. But how to keep that group together? This leads us to building shop floor organization—mapping the workplace, building a member-to-member network, recruiting stewards, and building a stewards council. We then look at how workers have used shop floor power to organize work-to-rule campaigns, to protect co-workers, and even to throw the boss out of the workplace. Finally, we look at workplace newsletters.

Trumpet the Truth

MOHANDAS K. GANDHI, called the Mahatma, the leader of the Indian movement for independence in the first half of the twentieth century, developed a theory of struggle that he called *satyagraha*. The essence of the idea is that by simply asserting the truth, and standing up for that truth in the face of greater power, a movement can win a moral victory that undermines the authority of its opponents.

Martin Luther King, Jr. took up satyagraha as a method of struggle for the civil rights movement. And workers have discovered the power of the method without necessarily studying Gandhi or King.

Justin West, who works at the Mitsubishi factory in Normal, Illinois, tells how he and his co-workers "spoke truth to power."[1] "An area of the plant where I work went through a week of various blatant contract violations by managers, and we workers talked about strategies.

"One night, on second shift, a majority of the workers in the area taped 8½ x 11 signs to their backs, stating things such as 'Pride,' 'Respect,' 'Dignity,' 'Stop Walking on the Contract,' 'I have rights.'

"Within minutes, upper management got wind of the battle and demanded that the signs be removed. The workers and I protested and held our ground. Labor Relations was called down.

"After 20 minutes of battling, management threatened disciplinary action against everyone, and demanded the signs be removed. The workers did remove their signs, under protest, and management was notified that NLRB charges would follow.

"The next day, the union received a settle-

How To Strategize

How do we know which workplace strategies are likely to work?

Hetty Rosenstein, president of CWA Local 1037, says, "In our local we sit down and think about using many different tactics at once to move the target—the boss. We use the word 'POLEMICs' as our checklist—Political, Opportunity to Organize, Legal, External Education, Membership Mobilization, Internal Education, Community Support—and we look at which of these tactics to use. A particular campaign may require some or all of these things.

"We train our stewards to think through the steps:

"1) What exactly do you want? (It's amazing how far along folks can be in a campaign, without having identified what their goal is and whether or not it's winnable.)

"2) Who the target of their action is—who has the power to fix the problem?

"3) Why the tactics selected have the potential to work.

"When a group of stewards figures this out and can articulate it to members, they are more likely to get members on board, and their tactic is more likely to work."

ment in our favor on one of the major grievances we were protesting, short-notice mandatory overtime."

Asserting the truth, by itself, may work only when the employer retains some shred of human feeling, however small. Assert the truth, shame the boss, and if you cannot appeal to management's sense of humanity, because they have none, at least appeal to the sense of humanity of your fellow workers and draw them into the struggle. It's a good place to start.

Using Ridicule

Union contracts often include the right to a bulletin board in the workplace. Some are pretty drab, a glassed-in board with a faded union meeting notice from last year and a candy wrapper someone stuck through the crack in the glass. But one union uses its bulletin boards to deflate management's credibility. When CWA Local 1037 is involved in a fight, says Hetty Rosenstein, "we strip the bulletin board and turn it into a billboard"—perhaps just a short slogan in huge letters. "It's amazing the impact this has," she says. "Management can't take it." Local 1037 represents some 6,000 New Jersey state workers.

"The New Jersey Department of Personnel was trying to eliminate seniority," Rosenstein recalls. "So the union put up a picture of the department commissioner, but we made his head into a garbage can and showed job security being tossed into his head. It caused a huge furor. Management sent out notices to managers all over the state to take down pictures where the commissioner was a garbage can. They'd take down the pictures, we'd put up another one, equally inflammatory.

"We grieved it and eventually won—the arbitrator said we had broad latitude to use our bulletin boards. And we forced them to back down on the seniority issue by raising so much hell at the worksite. They tried to take our seniority rights three times, and never succeeded.

"They were also mad because we were calling the Department of Personnel the 'DOPE'. They said they were going to take down anything with the word DOPE because it was inflammatory. The response revealed how weak, petty, and ridiculous the employer was.

"I'm a great believer in ridicule. It debunks them and makes them seem less strong. It's easier to stand up to somebody who's ludicrous."

Paul Krehbiel, who now works for SEIU Local 660 in Los Angeles, agrees: "Whenever you can point out the hypocrisy of management and make people laugh at it, you've weakened management and strengthened the union.

"This cartoon was produced by the stewards in a campaign to discredit a new company policy on alcohol and drug testing at Boise Cascade in Orange County, when I worked for the UE. We knew some of the managers were pretty heavy drinkers, so our leaflet, with the cartoon, pointed out the hypocrisy of the policy.

"The leaflet was a big hit; workers plastered it on the walls of the plant, and the drug and alcohol testing program fell onto the back burner."

Acting Collectively

THE FIRST TIME A GROUP OF WORKERS went together to face the boss and say "we want things to be different here," a union was born. Each time that primal confrontation takes place for the first time in a workplace, the union is born or reborn. The union in law and in fact is a group of workers acting together, confronting their employer for their common concerns.

Most of us fear being seen as a troublemaker, facing a write-up, discipline. And most of us are nice people, who find nothing harder than being rude, contrary, or disobedient. Few really enjoy these dust-ups. We are all vulnerable, and most vulnerable as individuals. So we find strength by going as a group to confront the employer. Often the slogan is, we have no leaders here, we are all spokespersons, everyone is in this together.

When we confront the employer, we show that we can act together as a group, and we gain power vis-à-vis the employer. And the union is reborn.

Confronting the Boss

by Michael Ames Connor

In the history books of labor militancy, professors claim a short chapter. Academic laborers carry a heavy weight of socialization against direct action. Discussion, compromise, and the ever-present option of another meeting make taking on the boss unlikely.

Nowadays about half of university teaching jobs are contingent: temporary, part-time, seasonal, unsteady. For these adjunct faculty, the barriers to confrontation multiply. Short contracts and tenuous relationships undermine solidarity. Fear of sticking out encourages conformity; keeping your head down becomes an art form.

In fall 2002, some adjunct faculty members at Portland State University in Oregon bucked the odds, rallied students, and confronted the boss, a college dean. Victory meant three faculty members got their jobs back, three canceled courses were reinstated, and little seeds of solidarity were planted. Here's what happened.

The PSU administration reserves the right to cancel classes due to "low enrollment." When Pedro Ferbel-Azcarate found out two weeks into the term that his class in Black Studies was to be canceled, he was not pleased. "I was hired to teach a spe-

Let's go back to the plant and start the drug and alcohol testing program.

Yea, they all look impaired to me.

cialized seminar class. I had nine students ready to learn. We had bought books and course-packs and were well into the topic. Without any guidelines in my contract about class sizes, I had no reason to believe my work was in jeopardy."

Ferbel-Azcarate called me, the organizer for the PSU Faculty Association (AFT Local 3571), and a plan came together. He would speak up at an upcoming faculty meeting, trying to get other faculty members to object. And he would notify student activists, including members of the Association for African Students and the Black Cultural Affairs Board.

Meanwhile, I circulated a letter among AFT members. The letter, addressed to the dean, objected to the late date the classes were canceled. It reminded the administration that small classes should be seen as assets and that it would be better for students and faculty members if so-called low enrollment was treated as a signal to the university rather than as a failure requiring layoffs. Within two days, 18 faculty members signed on.

Ferbel-Azcarate scheduled a meeting with the dean. Four faculty members attended, and our union president. Five students joined in. Another student, an activist with his own show on college radio, sat in with us.

The dean came in, saw 11 people around his beautiful conference table. He was not pleased. He read the letter, and still was not pleased.

The dean spent the first 15 minutes explaining how this wasn't his fault. He spent the next 15 listening. It took him another 15 minutes to agree to reinstate Pedro's canceled class and two others. When we heard that, we left. He was still talking as we exited his conference room.

The small victory had lasting effects on participants. "I learned that Frederick Douglass was right," Ferbel-Azcarate reflects, "that 'power concedes nothing without a demand.' As university teachers, we must remember that we are also workers and continue to demand fair labor practices. And we must teach what we have learned to our students as well."

Heard This Story Before?

From San Diego up to Maine, in every mine and mill
Where working folk defend their rights
It's there you'll find Joe Hill
It's there you'll find Joe Hill
—Alfred Hayes, "I Dreamed I Saw Joe Hill Last Night," 1925

Wherever little children are hungry and cry
Wherever people ain't free.
Wherever men are fightin' for their rights
That's where I'm gonna be, Ma.
That's where I'm a gonna be.
—Woody Guthrie, "Tom Joad," 1940

Harry Bridges Prowls the Stacks at Powell's

by Michael Ames Connor

Harry Bridges works at Powell's Books. He keeps an eye out for fellow workers. At least, that's what they say.

The story, repeated by many members of International Longshore and Warehouse Union Local 5, goes something like this: Every once in a while, over the store intercom, comes a page for Harry Bridges. "Harry Bridges to manager Block's office." "Harry Bridges to the loading dock." It's a pretty good intercom system, so everyone can hear it.

These union folks who work at Powell's—clerks, booksellers, loaders, techno-cats, and book buyers—they know, together, a little about everything: cooking, fly fishing, Japanese poetry, and labor history. They know about Harry Bridges. People know Bridges has been dead for years. But they know his reputation—fierce ILWU fighter who led the 1934 longshore strike that established the union. Part of joining ILWU means learning a little about their union and learning what Harry Bridges stands for: members know that if he's going to check out the loading dock, they should too.

When they get there (and it's usually 30 or 40 people who show up), they find one of their co-workers in a little difficulty with the boss. A disagreement, an argument, a confrontation. Before they show up, maybe that co-worker is in a little trouble. Maybe the boss is taking a hard line, getting ready to make an example, thinking about tossing a troublemaker out the door. That's why Harry Bridges gets the call.

So 30 or 40 people show up, and the manager backs down. Happens every time. With one or two people there, the boss can do what he likes. But with 30 or 40 people, as Arlo Guthrie once pointed out, you got yourself a movement.

Nobody's ever seen Harry Bridges at Powell's. They just know he's there, watching to make sure nobody gets picked on, or picked off.

(For the story of how the Powell's workers organized themselves to join the ILWU and its militant traditions, see Chapter 15.)

Build Everyday Connections

Don't forget that there are many everyday ways of creating a group feeling in the workplace. That group feeling can help make more confrontational actions possible, when needed. Setting up a coffee club, potlucks, sports teams, drinks after work, collecting for significant events like having babies and getting married, all build social networks that are useful when more militant action is required.

Kay Eisenhower was a "founding mother" of Service Employees Local 616 in Alameda County, California. She recalls, "One of my favorite examples from my days as a billing department employee at the hospital was when the clerks got together to create a break space out of a deserted nurses station. We cleaned out the refuse, brought plants and kitchen stuff from home—we carved out our own little space.

"Many of the tactics we employed in the County were 'softer' techniques, but they still built workplace strength and developed skills. These might be less threatening to new activists just starting out. For example, we did lots of petitions or group letters to the department head protesting one thing or another.

"Postcard campaigns and phone-ins to local politicians are useful too. We did delegations to the elected County Board of Supervisors to enlist their intervention with the department head, since they are the ultimate boss. We felt empowered when we could get the attention of elected officials.

"And we did informational picket lines to alert the public to our issues. At the county library we did this on a Sunday, which is the busiest day, and we felt supported by patrons, who know the workers much better than they know management.

"It's true that some workers are hesitant to confront management, and some might assume that being a steward or an activist tends to get one into trouble. But in general we had just the opposite experience. My co-workers believed that I was protected by my union role, that my aggressive, usually successful, representation of members ensured that I would not be personally targeted, and that if I were, the union would come in like a ton of bricks to defend me. I was able to point to myself as an example of how being outspoken didn't necessarily lead to trouble with management, as long as you did your job."

★ ★ ★

Whether your tactics are "soft" or hard, most workplaces need some level of ongoing organization. The next set of stories deals with these issues. How do we get a picture of the workplace and know who is where? How do we create a member-to-member network? How do we support the steward? How do we build a stewards council?

Mapping for Organizing

by Dorothy Wigmore

LOCATION, LOCATION, LOCATION! It matters in shop floor organizing as much as it does in real estate.

Maps bring new perspectives to organizing. These visual tools help you and others see who's where, who hangs out with whom, and common problems. They can help you set up a member-to-member network (see the next section) or identify where more stewards are needed. Maps are useful in workplaces where not everyone speaks the same language or where literacy is low. They also make power relationships more visible.

Making a map should be a group effort. First, use a flipchart or large sheet of paper and black marker to outline the area or building, showing entrances, exits, and windows. Label the offices, production lines, storage areas, shipping and receiving docks, lunchrooms, bathrooms, and so on. Add details such as machines, desks, and water coolers. If the building is large, make maps of different areas. Be sure the map is large enough to show the information clearly.

Then draw, in color, the flow of work or production, or the paths (movements) that different people take through the space regularly. It's easier to see this information if you use colored string or wool, rather than a marker.

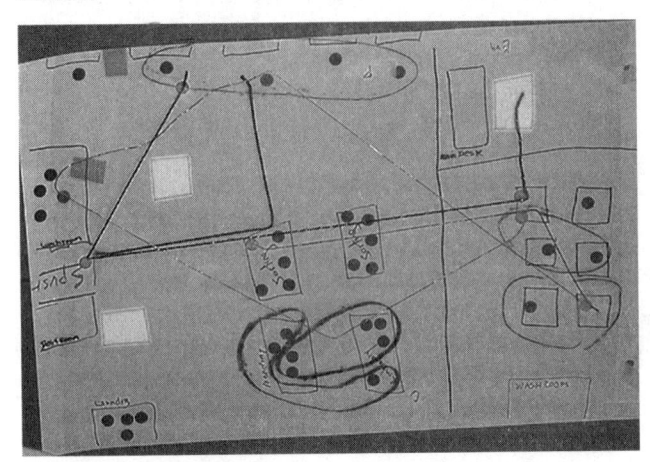

A workplace map might look something like this.

Then add the workers. Colored sticky dots work well for this. Use different colors to indicate supervisors and union activists. You might also use color to indicate workers who have the same kind of job. You can mark the dots with initials for names.

Mark groups by drawing a circle around those in them. These might be work groups—people connected by the work they share—or social groups (just be clear about which is which). Who are their primary and secondary leaders? Mark them in some way—knowing who influences whom is key information any time you are trying to move people to action. Who talks to whom (or doesn't)?

You now have a great deal of information about interactions in your workplace. This is a good place to stop and ask yourselves, "What do you see?" Even when people know their workplace well, the map will let them see it with new eyes. Ask open-ended questions such as, "What's going on here?"

The stories that come out will be about issues that are bothering people. Keep track of participants' information using other marks. Workers whom management is harassing could be indicated one way and those subject to layoff another. If the map's too crowded, start keeping track of the information another way (you could use post-its to record, sort, and prioritize issues).

As your organizing progresses, add to the map, or make new ones, to analyze where you're at in your campaign.

Fancier Maps

If you want to bring out even more information, think about other aspects of work. Check out an arts and crafts or office supply store for items that add color and texture to your map. (Different textures make the maps easier to understand and use.)

Different-colored strings can show the lines of communication for the union, management, and the "grapevine" (purple looks good). You can show where people hang out and are comfortable talking to one another (green's a good color for these "free zones") and where they don't feel safe (red gets the point across about these "danger" or "hot zones"). Use colored see-through paper to show the zones, or outline them with markers. Indicate spots where problems occur, such as harassment, health and safety hazards, or bottlenecks that cause strife.

Crowded maps are hard to read. One way to avoid them is to put different categories of information on plastic or acetate layers, and use the layers as needed. Keep the basic layout on the flipchart paper, and put the people and groups and your other information on separate layers.

Making workplace dynamics visible puts valuable information on the organizing table. But there still is work to do: identify key issues, set targets, make a timeline, give assignments. "See this group over here, the one we've never had contact with? Who can talk to someone in that group?" "We need to know more about what's behind that hot zone. Who can talk to folks about that?"

A final point. It's important to remember that some people may not want to map everything on your list. Respect privacy and acknowledge fears. Encourage people to build maps over time. They will become more comfortable with making and using these kinds of maps as they see what you and others do with them.

★ ★ ★

Most organizing manuals advocate member-to-member networks, where each shop floor leader is responsible for communicating with five or ten fellow workers—and organizing them to take action when necessary. Such a structure is easiest to set up when the local union can devote the resources, call the meetings, and do the training to get the network started. For an example of such a network, see "AFSCME Local 3299: From Internal to External Organizing," in Chapter 15, and see Chapter 19 for more advice.

In our example here, rank-and-filers created their own shop floor network from the ground up. They found that the network worked not only for confronting management day to day but also for organizing to elect their own leaders to union office.

Building a Member-to-Member Network

by David Levin and Marsha Niemeijer

FOR YEARS MANAGEMENT HAD ITS WAY with Local 556. María Martínez explains, "Before workers started organizing ourselves in 1997, no one had stood up to the company in a long time. Management was used to doing whatever they wanted. They've had a hard time adjusting to the new Local 556."

Teamsters Local 556 represents meatpackers at Tyson Foods, one of the huge multinational corporations that dominate the industry. About 80 percent of the local's members at plants in southern Washington and Oregon are immigrants, primarily from Mexico and Central America. Tyson's Pasco, Washington plant also employs workers from Bosnia, Laos, Vietnam, and the Sudan.

The transformation of Local 556 began when the workers at Tyson (then IBP, before a merger) became fed up with injuries, unfair discipline, and a do-nothing union. Martinez and others gathered petition signatures from half the workers in the plant, calling for the ouster of their full-time chief steward, Martha Pérez. The local's top officer, John Carter, refused. Pérez reportedly said, "These people don't even speak English; how are they going to get me out of here?"

The workers sent their petition to the Teamsters International, where it found its way into the hands of Joe Fahey, then an international rep. Fahey was also co-chair of Teamsters for a Democratic Union, the union's national reform movement. A new vision of the union was about to be introduced in Pasco.

No Savior from On High

Fahey agreed to meet workers in a local park, and meatpackers turned out in droves. For two hours, Fahey encouraged members to take three minutes each to talk about what they were going through at the plant. "Flaco" Pereyra describes the scene: "This was the biggest meeting we had ever seen from the plant—maybe 200 people. Two hours passed with people telling their stories: about the injuries, not being allowed to go the bathroom, never seeing our officials."

The workers saw Fahey as the person who was going to change everything overnight. But to their disappointment, all Fahey said was, "What you need is education." His prescription didn't get a welcome response. "We were pissed," Martínez remembers.

"I knew what my job was," says Fahey. "It was to tell them that only *they* could solve the problems. I was

Mapping Supplies

Basic
- flipchart paper
- black marker
- colored markers
- colored sticky dots

Advanced
Try arts and crafts, office supply, or hardware stores.
- colored string or wool
- see-through colored paper (try the mac-tac variety used to cover books or binders)
- clear tape
- clear plastic, such as rolls for covering tablecloths (at hardware stores) or the acetates used in overhead projectors

very clear: I could come back for a training session and not for anything else. Flaco told me later, 'That was the day we got our voice back.'"

Building Worker to Worker

The Local 556 bylaws gave the principal officer the power to appoint all stewards. In January 1998, members held their first TDU meeting, to learn the process for amending the bylaws so they could elect their own stewards. Activists needed a way to teach union civics to more than 1,500 uninvolved members, and to organize them to travel to a union meeting an hour away, on a work night, to vote for change.

María Chávez was at that first workshop. "We drew a map of the plant and made a list of all the production lines," she says. "We sat down by lines to choose 'volunteers.' The job of the volunteers was to inform people on their line, to distribute flyers, invite them to meetings, and answer their questions."

"Our goal was to have three 'volunteers' on each line," says Martínez. (A line can have from 20 to 40 workers.) "We looked for people who didn't let management push them around. And for people who had a good way of expressing themselves and speaking out. That didn't mean we were looking for the loudest or pushiest people. Some of the best leaders had a really quiet way about them. We looked for people that management respected and that workers respected."

Martínez also looked for people who were responsible and who weren't disciplined often. People—including management—were more likely to listen to these workers. "When you see a person like that speaking up," she says, "you think there must be a real problem going on here. Also, it was harder for management to retaliate against members who were known as hard workers with good records."

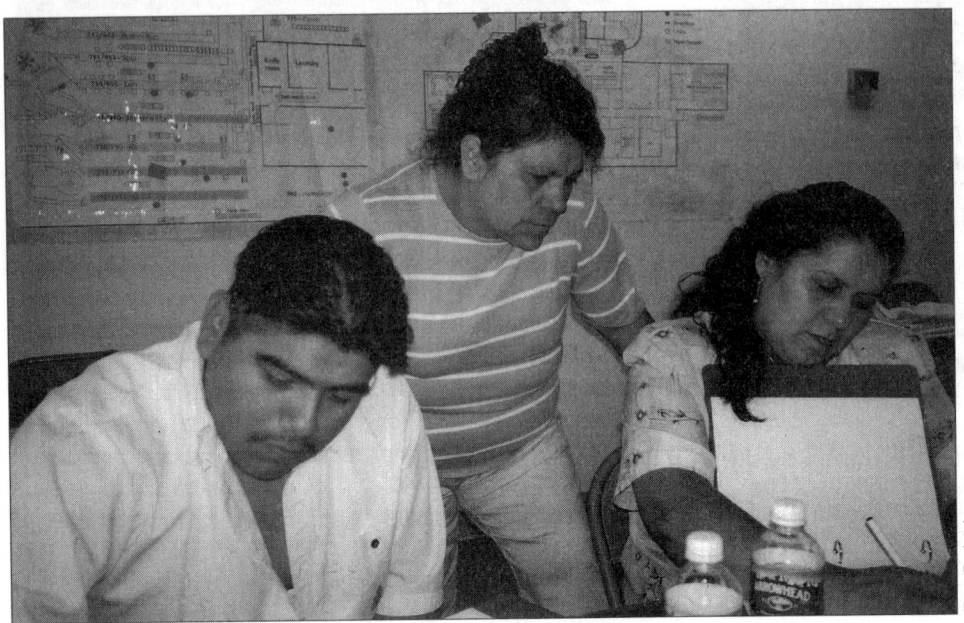

"You have to listen," says Maria Martínez (center). "It's really important to let people see that someone cares about what they have to say. Then you can ask, 'What do you think we should do about it?' You can say, 'I think we should do this.' But it's more effective when the ideas come out of them."

Volunteers Meet

When Martínez and the other planners had their list of potential recruits from each line, they sat down with each one in the cafeteria and asked how they felt about work, giving them a chance to express their frustrations. "That's when I'd explain what we were doing," Martínez says. "That we were building a network to get people together to try to make changes. I'd invite the person to a meeting so they could learn what rights we had to speak up for ourselves and for others."

"The meetings for the volunteers were key," says Chávez. "That's when we started to lose our fear. We saw that we weren't alone. And we had a plan for working together to achieve something."

At those meetings, workers would talk about how to recruit other volunteers, how to talk and how to listen to get other people involved. "You have to listen," says Martínez. "It's really important to let people let out their feelings and for them to see that someone cares about what they have to say. Then you can ask them, 'What do you think we should do about it?' You can say, 'I think we should do this.' But I've learned it's more effective when the ideas come out of them."

The new activists submitted a bylaws amendment to the local for elected shop stewards. In the plant, the volunteers distributed flyers explaining the vote and stickers that read "Vote *yes* for democracy." They had members sign a pledge that they would attend the meeting and organized a carpool to the union hall, an hour away.

On election day, the hall was packed far beyond capacity. The workers demanded that John Carter go out to the parking lot to personally count the votes of members who didn't fit into the hall. Hundreds of IBP workers voted unanimously to give members the right to elect stewards. Soon Martínez was elected chief steward, defeating the incumbent 547 to 84. In the following months the members elected another ten new shop stewards.

Taking on Supervisors' Harassment

Workers used their network to organize line meetings in the cafeteria to teach members about their rights and to make plans for dealing with shop floor problems. "The company wasn't happy about the meetings," Martínez says. "First they started sending supervisors to listen to us. But we confronted management about that. They said we weren't allowed to hold union meetings in their cafeteria. I told them that the National Labor Relations Act gives us the right to organize and to hold meetings in non-work areas at non-work times. Management told me to put it in writing. So I did; I wrote a grievance and had 100 people sign it. That was the last I heard from management about that. And we kept on meeting in the cafeteria."

A common topic at the line meetings was harassment. The volunteers would organize their lines to document it and stand up together. "If a supervisor said something, we'd say real loud to other people on the line, 'Did you hear what he just said?'" When incidents piled up, members would go as a group to higher-level managers to expose the problem. Members prepared in advance to tell their stories so that one person wouldn't be stuck doing all the talking.

For example, workers had to ask a supervisor's permission to go to the bathroom, and often the supervisor would say there was no replacement available. Workers began "calling supervisors out on this," Martínez remembers, "and demanding that workers be allowed to go when they had to. If that didn't work, we would go to the office and complain together.

"Finally, we got to the point where we would just leave and go to the bathroom. Workers on the line wouldn't stress out about the line going down. They would just stack the meat, or let it pile up at the end of the line. The supervisors wouldn't shout at us, they would just bring big gondolas to the end of the line and re-feed the meat or give it to someone else. And now, people have the right to go to the bathroom."

"Now the supervisors act very differently," says Arturo Aguilar, who became a steward. "There are still incidents. If you are alone and there are no witnesses, a supervisor might say something nasty. But in areas where we are strong they know they can't do this openly, because we stand up for each other."

Supervisors never stopped harassment altogether, of course. One tactic the volunteers use is grievance forms modeled after disciplinary tickets, on which workers can "write up" their supervisors by checking off violations. One copy goes to the offending supervisor, one to the union, and one to management. The forms are mainly used to have all the people from one line sit down and document harassment together.

Building a Committee To Work with the Steward

by Paul Krehbiel

A group of workers who have power on the job usually has these characteristics:

1. One or more leaders who speak up, provide leadership, and take action.

2. A normally small group of co-workers who work with and assist the leaders.

3. The support of most or all of the work group.

In this model, the leader becomes a steward, those who assist the steward become "union contacts" (this is the term we use in SEIU Local 660), and together this core leadership group becomes the "union committee" for a particular work area.

Flexibility and need should determine how many stewards and contacts a work area has. It could be one or more stewards, and two, three, or more union contacts. Those who function as a union committee should be elected or confirmed in a democratic way. We use a Steward Support Petition—anyone who wants to be a steward must get a majority of the workers in his or her work area to sign. Since in most of our bargaining units we don't have limits on the number of stewards in a work area, we want as many stewards as we can get. If a work area has 25-30 workers and two or three stewards, we are much stronger there than in a similar area with just one steward.

In a couple of bargaining units, management has forced the union to agree to limits on the number of stewards. There, elections are used when more people want to become a steward than we have slots for. But that doesn't stop us from electing alternate stewards and union contacts.

This model gives protection to the steward. Too often in the past, management would retaliate against the stewards, giving them the worst assignments, targeting them for discipline, and banishing them to undesirable shifts or locations. The message this sends to all the workers is: don't get involved in the union or you will be punished too. Now there are too many leaders for management to single out.

Another advantage is that the work becomes easier to handle. Many people who would like to become a steward don't do so because they are afraid that the burden of all the problems will fall onto their shoulders alone, and that they won't be up to the task.

Finally, of course, when a *group* of people assumes a leadership role, the group generally comes up with better and bolder ideas, and members feel they have the strength and support to carry them out. And it's a lot more fun!

The union committee doesn't have to be highly structured. It should have regular meetings, and sometimes it will have to meet on the fly when a crisis comes up, or meet informally for a few minutes every day while members are working.

We have sometimes used a leaflet to hand to someone we are trying to recruit as a union contact or steward, as an adjunct to the one-on-one conversation. The leaflet says at the top, "Want a Stronger Voice at Work? Become a Union Contact or Steward." It explains what the duties are and asks for their work location and phone number. A number of us carry copies of our recruiting leaflet with us wherever we go. When we meet someone who seems like a good candidate, we show them the leaflet and explain how the union is being built and strengthened.

A Stewards Council

In some unionized workplaces, the union is nonexistent on the shop floor. If workers have a problem they have to call the hall. In others workplaces, there may be a

The Harbor Stewards Council helped organize a large SEIU Local 660 rally demanding a "Fair Share" contract from Los Angeles County in 2000.

steward someplace—but who knows where? In yet other plants or offices, a few stewards carry out a heroic effort to handle grievances, always over-stretched, never quite on top of things, forever falling further behind.

A scarcity of stewards encourages the idea that the union is a kind of emergency service like a fire department, to be called when things have gotten out of hand. How can workers rebuild a union that's a force in everyday life on the floor?

Starting with very little, workers at the Harbor UCLA Medical Center in Los Angeles County created a stewards council based on one steward for every 20 to 25 members. Thus every member now has a steward close at hand, and the union is no longer something "out there" but an organized daily presence in the hospital.

The workers belong to SEIU 660, a diverse local of African Americans, Latinos, whites, and other groups from Asia, the Middle East, and "all over the world." Local 660 represents some 1,500 workers at the hospital—nurses, technicians, clerical workers, and many others.

Field rep and organizer Paul Krehbiel remembers the situation when he was first assigned to the hospital. "Every hour of every day management was violating some provision of the contract or labor law. We didn't have the internal structure to identify those violations, much less an organization equipped to resolve them. Out of five stewards for 1,500 workers, one or two were trying to do something, a couple others were pretty demoralized, and they were not organized amongst themselves. I would get 20 phone calls a day from members with complaints, and the next day there were 20 more."

Developing an Organizing Plan

To begin, Krehbiel called a meeting of the five current stewards at a restaurant across from the hospital. "I tried to do a lot of listening," he recalls. "I let them talk as much as possible: 'I feel I'm all alone.' 'There are too many problems.' 'Nobody's helping. Everybody else is demoralized.' I asked them for ideas to fix the situation. I wanted to instill the idea right from the beginning that the union is not the union office, or me—the union is the workers on the job. Before, they always had the idea, 'I called someone at the union, and they didn't come and help us.' I told them the union is all of you here, and our goal is to organize the people in the hospital so they actually become the union."

So Krehbiel and the five stewards began meeting every week. "In each of these meetings we took notes, and then put them together into an Organizing Plan, and this was before we made any organizing forays into work areas.

"Management was real clear: if you get involved with the union, you're going to be punished. So we knew that we needed to organize in a way that we could defend people when they stepped forward.

"The key was to pick something manageable. If you try to handle all the problems at once, anyone would be overwhelmed, so you have to break it down into small parts.

"Everybody pitched in some ideas, and we boiled it down to two main criteria. First, let's pick a small work area of 10 to 30 workers where there's a problem people feel strongly about. And second, let's choose a department where there's already somebody who is a leader or who has the potential to become a leader, and if more than one, that's better yet. Those were our criteria for developing a worksite campaign."

Carrying Out an Action and Creating Stewards

An opportunity came on Ward 4-West, a medical-surgery ward with 27 workers. It was getting close to December, and management put out a memo saying that workers who were sick for even one day in December would have to bring a doctor's note. It had been long-standing policy that a doctor's note was required only for a three-day absence.

The stewards and workers on 4-West decided to write a petition asking for a meeting with management and to try to get everyone to sign it within three days. When they succeeded, they asked management to meet with 12 to 15 people. Krehbiel remembers, "Management said, 'You've got to be kidding, we're short-staffed. There's no way we can release that many people. We'll release two.' Our response was 'no, at least 10' and they said two, then we said eight, then six, and finally we got four."

The union people suggested a 10:00 am meeting because, Krehbiel explains, "that's when workers get their breaks. We brought in two people on their breaks every 15 minutes to join the meeting. When the first two came in, management said, 'Why are you here?' They said they were on break. We then asked all the workers, the original four and those who had come on their break, to explain why the new policy was causing them problems. We now had six workers at the table." Managers kept looking nervously at their watches, Krehbiel remembers, and after 15 minutes said that the workers on break had to return to the ward.

"I told management that they were going to return, but first they needed to tell their story. As they were telling their stories, two more workers began their breaks and came into the meeting, so now we had ten workers at the table. Management was clearly upset. 'Those first two workers have to go back now,' they said emphatically. 'Their break is over. We can't have so many people off the ward at once.' 'We know,' we responded, 'he's just finishing up now.' Then the worker talked another two or three minutes. We did this for about two hours, and a majority of the people from the department came down for this meeting. We pushed the envelope as much as possible to have people stay in the meeting as long as they could.

"The result was that management lightened up on implementing the new policy, and we got one new steward in that department and three people to work with her."

With similar actions in other departments, new union activists were recruited to be stewards, and the number of stewards gradually expanded. Each new steward was invited to attend the weekly meetings at the restaurant, the embryo of the future Stewards Council.

How many stewards do you need in a workplace? "We say we will have as many stewards as we want," says Krehbiel. "Management may only recognize one, but the stewards are part of *our* organization, and we make the decision about how many stewards we want. Our goal for Harbor-UCLA was 60-70."

Training the Stewards

As the union recruited, it organized stewards training, with six classes: stewards' rights and responsibilities; communication and informal problem-solving; getting to know the contract, especially the grievance procedure, non-discrimination, and just-cause language; investigating and writing a grievance; presenting a case to management, with role-playing of both formal grievances and other meetings; organizing around worksite issues.

In the last class, the new stewards talked about the actions that had already happened at Harbor. "We talked about why it's important to find issues that affect a number of people and organize issue campaigns rather than file individual grievances," says Krehbiel. "Filing individual grievances alone would not have helped us build the Stewards Council and build power in the workplace."

Stewards Council in Operation

After eleven months the group had recruited 17 stewards—enough to start the Stewards Council—and six months later it had doubled its size. Now it became possible to take up bigger issues in bolder ways. "A couple of the nurses said they were really having problems getting nursing administration to meet with them over anything," says Krehbiel.

"The entire Stewards Council took up this problem and it was decided that the Council would send a delegation to nursing management and go up to their office and raise hell. When the date came we had 10 or 11 people—nurses, clerical workers, lab workers, warehouse workers, and myself—and we all marched up to the nursing administration office. The office is not very big, so with 11 people in there, it got crowded really quick.

"We lambasted the nursing administrator for about 15 minutes about managers not meeting, managers running roughshod over nurses. Once the floodgates were open, everything came out. The workers told her, 'Managers are browbeating people, shouting at them, discriminating against them.' Management had not seen this before. We definitely got their attention.

"Then the 11 stewards walked down to the office of the Chief Operating Officer. The secretary said, 'Do you have an appointment?' But we were so loud that he came out to see what the noise was. People started saying loud-

Steps in Building the Stewards Council

- Call a meeting of the existing stewards in the workplace to assess the situation.
- Hold a frank discussion of the situation, where everyone describes the problem and how each feels about it.
- Begin holding regular meetings of a committee of the current stewards to develop a plan.
- Look over the existing problems, find what looks like a winnable issue, and take it on.
- Mobilize members to win the fight in that area.
- Recruit those who become involved through the action to become stewards.
- Repeat in other areas.
- Hold stewards training classes to bring everyone up to speed.
- The stewards council now has the strength and training to take on bigger issues and mobilize more people. It can begin to put management in its place.

ly why we were there, that nursing management wouldn't meet with the nurses. After 15 minutes he could see we were not ready to leave, so he told his secretary to cancel his meetings and hold his calls. We were in there for an hour.

"Again, everything came out. Clerical workers, medical records workers, nurses, everybody who was there told about their problems. We had told everybody before we went in to try to say something. It might be hard, and you don't have to be first to speak, but say something. Some of their managers were looking for the workers because they were gone so long, but when they called the COO, he said, 'They're in a meeting with me.'

"After that day nursing administration started meeting with nurses and taking up problems. I am not saying that this was now a perfect place to work. It's not. But we had turned a corner."

Direct action like this helped to build the Stewards Council. "During this period, of the 35 stewards that we recruited," says Krehbiel, "probably half came in as a direct result of an organizing action in their work area. The other half came in when these stewards talked about their actions to their friends in other work areas.

"We had discussions at Steward Council meetings about the composition of the Council. We agreed that we wanted the Council to be representative of the medical center workforce, with all races and nationalities represented, all departments and job classifications, men and women and workers of all ages. We had discussions of setting quotas, but the group wanted to try other methods. Instead, the Council organized special activities and campaigns among groups that were underrepresented."

Now SEIU's Stewards Council is an established institution in the hospital. It meets monthly, with reports from each work area as the first item on the agenda. There are regular elections of Council officers, who usually talk every day on the phone or meet in the hospital. Workers get a roster of all the stewards, with their work location, shift, job classification, and phone number. And the Council sends representatives to monthly meetings of the countywide SEIU Local 660 Stewards Council.

Rotating Stewards Share the Work—and the Burnout

by Paul McCafferty

THOSE OF US in the Heat and Ventilation Department at Massachusetts Institute of Technology had a problem. Our SEIU shop steward, an experienced worker of 20 years, was resigning.

No one was immediately interested in the job. A steward had a lot of stress, had neither super-seniority nor dues reduction, and could make enemies with both management and co-workers. In addition, though we were only about 35 workers, we were spread out on all three shifts over seven days and had six supervisors. Many of us saw the union as an insurance plan against management and our stewards as insurance agents. We paid our dues (premiums) and wanted service, but otherwise, leave us alone.

A group of us came up with the idea of a shared, rotating stewardship. The idea was that four of us would share the steward position. We would each stand a three-month watch, and after a year we'd see how the whole thing had worked.

We wrote up this idea, along with the names of the volunteers, posted it over the time clock, and asked our co-workers to sign the sheet as an endorsement. The majority signed, and we got the support of our business agent. Soon the four of us were armed with grievance forms, a new system, and no experience.

Over the next three years we had eight stewards, all for three-month terms. Some of us volunteered more than once, others only once, but we always filled the four yearly slots. Usually, people who hadn't put in their time got some friendly pressure from those who had stepped up. Our annual sign-up sheet said in capital letters: "A union can't work unless we all participate!"

The most important change we saw was that the union was viewed less as an insurance plan, and more as something that we all had to make work. Because eight of us had processed grievances, there was a more widespread understanding of the strengths and weaknesses of the grievance procedure.

The biggest drawback to rotation is that a new steward, by definition, has little experience, and in three months has little opportunity to accumulate much. So mistakes can be made. Fortunately, there are benefits that can help rotation work. Beyond the first step in a grievance, the business agent is present. This is a big help to new stewards. And because there is a growing pool of present or former stewards, it's easy to get advice informally day to day. Each year, as more workers get involved, fewer grievances go to the second step. More are settled with the immediate supervisor.

The biggest advantage of rotation is that it offers a manageable way for workers to get involved in the union. A commitment is required, but it's limited. The worker can—or can choose not to—sign up again. You can take a year off if you need to.

In short, more hands, less work. More involvement, less burnout.

Working to Rule

SOMETIMES WE NEED TO UP THE ANTE, beyond group grievances and group visits to the boss. To get management's attention, we need to affect production itself. Short of a strike, nothing focuses management's mind like a work-to-rule or a slowdown. In the private sector the employer loses productivity and profit. In the public sector the agency hears the complaints of the public, creating a political problem. When organized with care, and that may mean clandestinely, we can squeeze the boss until he yields. We look now at how some workers in very different workplaces have organized work-to-rule campaigns. See Chapter 10 for much more detail on working to rule, including your legal rights.

Work to the Safety Rule

Companies look foolish if on Monday they insist on safety and on Tuesday they complain that workers follow the safety rules. Union contracts or various laws may give workers the right to strictly follow safety rules or to refuse unsafe equipment or unsafe work. For these reasons, work-to-rule campaigns can use the slogan "safety first."

Brian Chapman, a trucker who hauls cars out of a terminal near London, Ontario, is a chief steward for Teamsters Local 938. When we interviewed him, he was in the midst of a safety-first work-to-rule campaign, undertaken because the company had begun violating the contract by unfairly suspending drivers.

"The guys got really upset," Chapman explains, "so 30 or 40 of us got together to discuss what we could do. Legally we can't strike. The only thing we really have is to work by the contract. That sounds like something you should be doing all the time, but people let things go and cut corners, either to give the company a break or because it's to your own advantage. But now we decided to work to rule." The campaign had two aspects: taking unsafe trucks out of service, and drivers taking their rest time according to the law, not at the company's convenience.

In organizing the work to rule, Chapman gave this advice to his fellow drivers: "Make sure when you take a truck out of service that it's a legitimate safety issue. The company won't mess around with safety. Under the law that is the one thing they can't do. If you feel it's not safe, the driver has the last call. They cannot force you out, and they know it.

"Same with hours-of-duty. Guys shouldn't be lying or cheating on their log books. All you have to do is exactly what the company tells you to do, *everything* they tell you to do."

Chapman explains that in the carhauling business, a conscientious inspection can be very time-consuming: "If you do the inspection the way they tell you to do, it will take you at least half an hour per car.

"The trucks are all '89, '90, '91 trucks. A lot of guys have been working with junk. So they reported worn ratchets, cracked decks, worn-out chains, broken safety pins or missing safety pins. It takes a long time to replace these ratchets. The shop was swamped, and they fired the guy that was running the Canadian shops because the numbers were so out of whack."

When the company did release their trucks, drivers used the driving and working time they were allowed by law—and then rested, no matter how it affected the company's schedules.

"People started going to bed, taking their rest time whenever their hours of service indicated," Chapman explains. "They showed all their actual on-service and went to bed.

"That was our action, working to rule, doing exactly what they told us to do. We're paid by the unit, and it's cutting into people's pay. That's why it's hard to carry it on, after a month. I think we had 30 or 40 guys who went along with doing this for a month. I get frustrated with my members. If I could get all 300 of them to do this, we could fix our problem."

Still, with only ten percent of the workers participating, "the action had an effect," says Chapman. "The company has backed off somewhat. They know that we're willing to do something about it. It's still ongoing."

Lunch to Rule

In many jobs workers and employers come to an understanding about work practices without ever codifying these arrangements in contract language. Many workers will happily work with their boss to help him get the job done, provided that he will be flexible with them. So it was on a military base where a group of aircraft maintenance workers happily interrupted their lunch in order to deal with urgent problems, with the understanding that, once the problem was solved, they would go back to their sandwiches even though the lunch period had ended. The situation was mutually acceptable for several years—until a new supervisor came along. We all know how that is. Had to prove himself. Show who's boss. Take no guff. Etc.

Steve Eames, an international rep for the Boilermakers union, explains that about 30 of his members worked on a facility at a U.S. naval air base. These aircraft maintenance workers work closely with the pilots and travel with them all over the world. So when a pilot came back with a plane that had a problem, they interrupted their lunch. "If something needed to be done they did it." But the new supervisor insisted that the maintenance workers take their lunch between 12:00 and 12:30, period. "I'm tired of coming in and you're still here eating lunch at 1:00 in the afternoon," he said. The steward tried to explain the arrangement that had worked so well in the past, but the boss would hear none of it.

"So the steward said, 'Okay, we'll play by the rules,'" Eames remembers. The maintenance workers had previously eaten at a lunch table in the work area. But now, when 12 o'clock came, they left and went to a fast food restaurant on the base. For three or four days they all went as a group, leaving the shop unattended.

Soon a plane came in during the half-hour lunch period. No one was there to help bring in the plane, or to check it out. The supervisor himself had to park the plane. "It really stopped productivity," says Eames. "The boss went and talked to the steward, and the steward said, that's our time, we're at lunch. You got what you wanted."

The steward and the other workers went out for lunch for a couple more days, and then they ended what we might call "lunch-to-rule." "They didn't want to file a grievance," says Eames, "because the company would have won on the basis of contract language.

"Without anything in writing, it went back to the way it had been before. It empowered the guys. It told the supervisor, we'll be a little flexible if you'll be flexible.

"My guys never made a big deal out of it, they just said, 'you want to play by the rules, we'll play by the rules.'" Lunch to rule.

★ ★ ★

Most of us spend the greater part of our waking life at work. We have democratic rights in society, supposedly: freedom of assembly, of the press, of speech. But when we get to work, we lose our rights. The boss takes over, a little dictator in the banana republic that is our home-away-from-home.

We don't have to accept the notion that the boss has all the rights, as our next examples show.

Solidarity Defends a Fellow Worker

WHAT DO WE DO when management attacks one of our members? Management often goes after those who appear to be weak or disadvantaged. Gregg Shotwell, who works at a Delphi auto parts plant in Coopersville, Michigan, tells how members protected one of their own.

"There was a woman in our department who had attention deficit disorder," says Shotwell. "It made it difficult for her to learn new tasks. She was often late—both arriving at work and leaving work. She was a thorn in management's side."

A supervisor wanted this worker—we'll call her Rosie—to learn a new machine that made part of a fuel injector. When Rosie had trouble, the supervisor lost patience, disqualified her from the job, and switched her to another job, which only made matters worse. The supervisor monitored Rosie excessively, with constant questioning and criticism, which heightened her learning disability.

"The supervisor wouldn't have bothered me or many of the other workers," says Shotwell, "but she picked on Rosie because she was less able to defend herself. It was cruel." Rosie wasn't the most popular worker. Shotwell admits that she often got on other workers' nerves as well, but, he says, "we could clearly see that she was being mistreated by this supervisor, whom we had nicknamed 'the Terminator.' Rosie would be in tears after the Terminator talked with her."

Shotwell was working the third shift when he heard how Rosie was being harassed. It occurred to him that one way to defend her would be to simply use his seniority to bump her off the first shift. "I thought if we traded places, she would be safe, as my supervisor was more understanding." So Shotwell transferred to the first shift, but the lead supervisor would not move Rosie off the shift, even though as a result there were too many workers on the first and not enough workers on the third. "It was obvious that she wanted to fire Rosie," says Shotwell.

And fire her she did. A few weeks before Christmas, the boss accused Rosie of running scrap and walked her out of the plant.

The supervisor then told Shotwell to run Rosie's machine. "I immediately shut it off and refused to run it," Shotwell says. "The Terminator told me that I had to run it. I told her, 'This machine is running scrap. I'm not going to get fired too.' She insisted that I run it. I said, 'I want an AVO'—that stands for 'avoid verbal orders.' In other words, I wanted her to put it in writing. She said, 'I don't give AVOs, I give direct orders.'

"That put the ball in my court. 'Fine,' I said. 'I will run scrap under direct order, but get my committeeman [steward], because I have to get it documented that you ordered me to run a machine that is producing scrap.'"

Then Shotwell proceeded to run the machine as ordered. Sure enough, the machine produced scrap. "I made sure of that." When the committeeman came, Shotwell showed him examples of the scrap and got it documented that he had been ordered by the supervisor to continue operating.

Do Quality Work

"All companies have quality programs," Shotwell advises, "and we have to use their own programs against them. In our Quality Network, we have something called Document 40, in which an employee can document what they feel is a quality problem. First, the document goes to the committeeman and the quality rep, who then consult with the supervisor. If it is not resolved, it then goes to the general supervisor, then Quality Council (a union-management committee which includes the plant manager and the bargaining chair). If it's still not resolved, it eventually goes all the way up the corporate ladder.

"This process creates a paper trail, and management is afraid of documentation. Since the quality problem couldn't be resolved without the involvement of production workers, job setters, and the trades, we had control. It rapidly became evident that this Doc 40 was going all the way to the top."

The quality problem became contagious. Soon other workers experienced problems with their machines as well. Job setters who were usually quite skilled at making appropriate adjustments and small repairs appeared stumped. So they called out skilled trades. "We explained to tradespeople what was happening. Nothing got fixed," says Shotwell. "Production slowed to a trickle."

Rosie's co-workers weren't satisfied, though.

"The second thing we did," says Shotwell, "was take up a collection for Rosie. We wanted management to know that she's not fired, she's on vacation. She's going to be paid one way or another."

Then they demanded a meeting with the general foreman, who said he would meet with one or two members of the department. Management, Shotwell notes, doesn't like to be outnumbered. "We decided, we're all going in." They packed the conference room with workers from the shop floor. "We outnumbered and overwhelmed the four managers," Shotwell says. And management was well aware that as long as the workers were in the conference room, there was no production in the department.

"Management views me as an instigator, so I held

back. I think they were surprised by the general animosity," Shotwell says. Management had not expected such a strong reaction, thinking that Rosie was an easy target. Workers took turns relating the incidents of harassment they had witnessed and the chronic problems with quality that management ignored: "Firing Rosie doesn't change a thing." "It doesn't solve the poor quality problems." "She's a scapegoat, not a solution."

"We let them know we would pursue the Doc 40 all the way to the top of the corporation,' says Shotwell.

Civil Rights Investigation

Then people from the department went to the union meeting, including a lot of folks who didn't usually attend meetings. The union reps were reluctant to defend Rosie because, in their eyes, she was a chronic problem. But her co-workers demanded a civil rights investigation for harassment. The bargaining chairman did not favor this type of complaint—he found them too messy—but there were too many vocal members, so he felt pressured to respond.

The civil rights chairman, Rick Majors, was a good advocate, and he understood. Majors could be very intimidating. "Rick is a big teddy bear," Shotwell says. "But if you don't know him as a friend, all you see is a big bear." Majors took every person in the department off the floor into a private room and interviewed them—every worker, engineer, supervisor, anybody who had anything to do with the department. "We workers talked, and talked, and talked. We ate up time like popcorn," Shotwell says. Production suffered. "We were getting a lot of attention, the whole plant was buzzing." Management was showing a great deal of anxiety.

Along with the slowdown, union members also refused overtime. The Christmas shutdown was approaching, the company needed the parts, and union members were saying, "No, if you can afford to fire somebody, then you must not need the parts very bad." Many people who usually liked overtime before Christmas made a sacrifice.

Then the workers took up a collection to buy red and black t-shirts that said, "Stop Harassment" on the front, and on the back, "An injury to one is an injury to all."

Shotwell says, "One of the reasons this solidarity action was so successful was that a woman who is well-liked and respected, Kathy Tellier, was so incensed by the way Rosie was treated that she got involved. She had credibility. Women, I often find, are brave in these situations. They really understand harassment. Kathy helped to rally the troops, both men and women.

"Because there was so much pressure from the floor and loss of production, management couldn't do their usual routine and drag out the settlement for months. They settled the grievance quickly and brought Rosie back to work. The supervisor had to go to 'charm school,' which wasn't such a severe discipline, but it acknowledged the problem and embarrassed the Terminator.

"The day Rosie returned to work, she was the only one, on all three shifts, who wasn't wearing a 'Stop Harassment' t-shirt. She didn't feel intimidated; she felt loved and protected. Management saw a demonstration of our solidarity and solid proof that we would not tolerate harassment and discrimination.

"I felt really proud to be part of this action. It brought us together and made us feel our power as a union. Many people who are not usually outspoken or active or confrontational stepped forward. As an instigator my part was easy. I only had to appeal to the goodness in people's hearts.

"Rosie wasn't, if truth be told, a very good worker. And often times she irritated us too. But she was family.

"Given time and a patient instructor, Rosie did learn the job she was originally disqualified from. She proved capable. And management learned a valuable lesson: workers rule when they work to rule."

Locking Out the Boss

by David Bleakney

AT TORONTO'S POSTAL STATION E, the harassment was unbearable. Union leaders and supporters were constantly being disciplined. The employer routinely violated the contract. Several stewards had been fired in quick succession and it looked as if more firings were coming. And members complained the union was powerless.

One steward, Mike Skinner, noted, "We faced Neanderthal supervisors who acted as if the station was their personal kingdom. The workplace was full of fear and anger as we struggled to be good stewards, defending the contract but trying not to get fired."

In the past, workers had gone out on wildcat strikes, but such strikes are not protected by the collective agreement and pay was docked. Some workers were afraid that the employer would be more than happy to make an example of them all.

A new approach was needed. Union leaders thought, if people aren't going to wildcat but they are really angry, why not fire the bosses so people can go to work in peace?

The trigger for action occurred when Dennis Dorey, a temporary worker still waiting for permanent employment after four years, was fired. Dorey had driven his kids a few blocks home in his mail van. Admittedly, he violated the rules. The question was whether he deserved to be fired, since in other parts of the country Canada Post routinely allowed people to take mail vans home and occasionally use them for personal reasons. Skinner says that in management's eyes Dorey's worst crime was to be an outspoken union supporter.

Skinner says, "The mainstream assumption is that if someone is fired they must have done something to deserve it. The local media didn't care at all about the harassment of shop stewards, which they saw as purely an industrial relations matter. But a human-interest story is different. The Dennis Dorey firing helped us learn the importance of focusing your story for your audience."

Locking out the boss for a day improved productivity and reduced harassment at Toronto's Postal Station E.

Planning the Action

The action to lock out the bosses was led by postal workers who were full-time officers. Skinner says, "We used full-time union people, such as activists in other unions like the Steelworkers and the Auto Workers. We also contacted members of the labor council, activists from the neighborhood, support groups, supportive customers, and OCAP (Ontario Coalition Against Poverty). We had supported OCAP in the past and they reciprocated on many occasions. That is what grassroots solidarity is about. And all of these were folks who had nothing to fear from our employer. They couldn't lose their jobs because they didn't work there.

"We didn't feel we were getting adequate support from the local executive. We knew we had to act, but we were not sure whether the local would support us. We decided that it was up to us to build a credible event and the local would follow. After we got the support of a large coalition of activists from the community, the local had no choice but to add their support as well.

"Organizing was kept very quiet. We didn't want to risk reprisals. Many people were not told about the event, and there was a deliberate misinformation campaign, including floating false dates, to cover up some of the obvious planning activities. At the same time, we had to make sure we had enough people to pull it off."

How It Worked

Locking out your bosses isn't as hard as you might think. Skinner smiles and says, "The activists arrived at the station early in the morning, locked arms, and prevented the employer from entering the building. The supervisors were given a disciplinary notice of interview like the ones they give postal workers. It stated they were temporarily suspended pending further notice. Meanwhile, letter carriers were welcomed with smiles, coffee, and applause as the line opened to allow their entry." No letter carrier was engaged in the job action, which eliminated the possibility of discipline. It's hard to discipline workers for showing up on time to do their jobs.

Inside the station, a big banner over the work floor said "Harassment-Free Zone." A banner outside said "Postal workers fighting for good jobs and service for the community." A meeting was called on the floor to discuss the situation. A resolution firing the bosses for the day was put forward. It passed unanimously. The message was delivered to the supervisors.

For the first time in months letter carriers were able to work in peace. They helped each other sort up their walks. The carriers proudly marched out of the building together as a unified force, while their bosses cowered on the street.

The local media reported that the mail was on the street an hour earlier than normal. "We were learning the art of messaging," says Skinner. "It helped that the action started at 5 in the morning, which allowed it to get on morning local news shows hungry for something beyond the traffic report."

The story gained national prominence and postal workers were presented as reasonable, hard-working, and dedicated. Management was portrayed as thugs. On talk-show radio, phone lines lit up with callers who couldn't understand why an employer would use someone like Dorey for four years without giving him a job. Many said that his "probation" had passed a long time ago and the punishment was way out of line. According to the national vice-president of the Canadian Union of Postal Workers, "It was the greatest national coverage we had had since the last national postal strike, and this coverage was generally positive."

The local executive had come out in full support, never failing to include the other incidents of workplace harassment along with that of Dorey when speaking with the media.

Gains and Losses

In the end there were some gains and some losses. Dorey never got his job back. But the station manager was given a new non-supervisory position instead of merely shuffling her off to another station to do it all over again, as often happens. "Bosses like to move a problem, not resolve it," says Skinner, "and with her gone, the others were less bold."

A Station E worker notes, "For a few days Canada Post had security everywhere. The ratio was one supervisor to every three to four workers. Their covert security and investigation people were inside. Some did nothing but stand behind us. This only made us feel stronger. I think it was very disempowering for them to have all these goons standing around being mocked by workers."

Skinner says, "People really enjoyed the day. It was fun. I was concerned that people would knuckle under to the pressure that followed. Just the opposite happened—they were emboldened by the action. When the security goons appeared, we laughed it off, made fun of them, asked them what they were getting paid and whether they didn't have anything better to do. They stopped firing stewards for a while.

"We were nothing special, and this could happen on any work floor with some organization. We had a message for management, one for the community, and most importantly, one for the members. We were a typical work floor with a mix of people, not only in culture and ethnicity, but also in levels of union support. For one day we all came together. This was a no-loss situation for people on the floor. We worked outside the box and all of us shared in the victory."

A Politician on the Shop Floor

LIKE THE TORONTO POSTAL WORKERS, AFSCME Local 3299 has found some levers outside the workplace that help workers gain power on the shop floor. Local 3299 has found it useful to have politicians visit the workplace and take a stand for the workers—even on issues that are normally way under any outsider's radar.

Craig Merrilees is director of the local, representing 17,000 blue-collar, health care, and service employees on ten campuses of the University of California. "We try to bring the politician in unannounced to management," Merrilees explains. "This would be in the midst of a struggle or a mini-campaign, for example over an issue like unfair scheduling or denial of regular breaks.

"The politician can walk in, say hello, meet the workers, shake hands, and invite the workers into the break room to talk for a few minutes. This typically creates a lot of buzz and excitement among the workers and freaks out management in a big way. The line supervisor gets on the phone calling his boss—'there's a state senator on the floor, what can I do?' [If outsiders are forbidden entry, the politician can be invited to the gate, the parking lot, or the managers' entrance with media in tow.]

"Meanwhile the state senator is convening a meeting of workers and pledging his support to their cause. It's a can't-lose situation.

"If the University blunders and kicks the politician out, it causes lots of problems, nasty letters, and a frosty relationship. In most cases the managers head for the hills, while the workers often walk off the job, join the politician, get affirmation of their struggle. They walk out of the meeting feeling they're pretty hot stuff, after the state senator told them to keep fighting.

"We've done this over many different issues, from firing for union activity to whatever you can imagine. It doesn't have to be a big issue."

Following Up

After the visit, the union follows up with a flyer, a letter from the legislator, and more agitation on the shop floor. "We usually put out a flyer the same day," says Merrilees, "or at most the next day, with a photo of the state senator meeting with the workers. The headline says something like 'We're winning support in our struggle for fair schedules.' The leaflet goes on to say that Senator Z pledged her support and said that her office will be watching this closely.

"We then ask the legislator to write to the University chancellor or the boss, saying, 'I had the pleasure of visiting workers in Unit X, and I was shocked by what they told me about the scheduling problem. I hope you're going to take this seriously, because you know I do.'

"They may also say, 'I sit on the budget committee, and we'll be taking this into consideration when we talk about the budget this year.' (We often help write the letter that the politician sends.)

A staffer for State Assemblyman John Laird listens to Abel Salas and Maria Ventura at the University of California Berkeley campus.

"Typically, after the visit, the flyer, the letter, and activity on the shop floor, most bosses are brought to heel pretty quickly and have an attitude change."

Making Politics Personal

Merrilees says that the shop floor invitation tactic is beneficial to members but it can also change the politician: "When we invite politicians later to speak to our leadership meetings, they inevitably cite the experience they had at our workplace. It definitely changes their attitude.

"We want them to get their hands dirty, to have an experience on the shop floor being with people they don't usually see, in an environment they don't usually work in. We want them to take a position on the class struggle: where do you stand on the struggle between this boss and these workers? It seems small, but it separates the wheat from the chaff.

"The other benefit is to break down the alienation our folks feel towards politics and politicians. Because we depend on the budget process, we're incredibly dependent on politicians. We desperately need workers to be involved. But people are so alienated from politics that it's hard to get them to volunteer to walk the precincts. The politician's visit to the workplace is personal and concrete and it shows the reciprocity that should be inherent in the political process.

"We've had a huge increase in the number of workers who respond to our requests to get involved in campaign work. It seems the most natural thing to help Senator Chris Kehoe, since she's the one who helped us out when we had the fight over breaks."

Endorsements also come into the picture. Should the union endorse candidate X? Should it give money to candidate Y? The workplace visit becomes one criterion for deciding. Merrilees says, "If a politician doesn't answer our call, then we make it clear we can't support him or her, because he or she didn't respond when our members needed help."

Shop Floor Newsletters

A SHOP FLOOR NEWSLETTER is born when people wants to get something off their chests. The content can include lambasting of management, information about what's happening in other departments, criticisms and proposals for the union, and news and opinions from the outside world. It can be a one-person show—widely read and appreciated, but with little participation from others—or it can be the voice of a caucus that's contending for power in the local, or something in between.

At the very least, a newsletter lets people know that *someone* is doing *something*. It can serve several functions:

- Information.
- Communication. A way to reach beyond the immediate work area.
- Opinion maker.
- Organizer of campaigns. Around shop floor issues like toxics, around union hall issues like bylaws, around contract issues such as health insurance.
- Voice of a caucus. When a group publishes a newsletter that does all of the above, in effect it's developing a new leadership for the local. Those who work together to put out such a newsletter become a team that is well-informed, has clear ideas, and develops a reputation as fighters for the members.

In a local that is very badly run, a rank-and-file newsletter can be one of the only ways that members find out what's going on and have a sense of unionism at all.

Why a newsletter in the computer age? Why not just a website? Aside from the fact that not everyone likes to or knows how to spend time at a computer, it's important to have a visible presence in the workplace. When people can see each other reading the newsletter, it's evidence that dissent from management's authority exists. You want your co-workers to be able to read the newsletter at work and discuss it with each other. When one worker turns to another and says, "Hey, get a load of this!" you're having an impact.

Producing a Newsletter

A newsletter creates jobs for people with all sorts of different skills: news gathering, writing, editing, cartooning, taking photos, designing, laying out, dealing with the printer, distributing, and fundraising. The more people involved, the stronger your credibility and base of support.

Email and desktop publishing make production much easier today than it was even ten years ago. If no one in your group knows how to lay out a page, someone's kid can surely be enlisted.

It's best for a newsletter to have a regular publishing schedule, and it's better to put out a one-pager once a month than something more elaborate less often.

What makes a newsletter readable and credible? It's:

- Nice to look at, with cartoons and articles of reasonable length.
- Accurate. Most workplaces are awash in rumors. Earn a good reputation by printing the facts, not speculation.
- In good taste. Different workplaces have different standards of appropriate language. People who don't mind bad language won't notice if it's not used, but those who do mind will definitely notice it if it is there, and hold it against you. Use your creativity; there are plenty of synonyms for "bullshit." It's okay to name names, but avoid name-calling. Don't attack people, attack the issues.
- About the workplace itself. People can read about the company and union in other forums. What has an electric appeal is reading about something you actually experienced in your department, so include shop floor issues in every issue. Write about the industry, the big picture, and union politics if appropriate, but keep it grounded.
- Open. Encourage readers to question authority, to develop their own opinions. Promote debate and let the other side have a say.

A Newsletter for Warehouse Workers and Truckers

John Zartman of Teamsters Local 355 in Baltimore is a yard jockey, the driver who moves trailers in the yard and to the warehouse. A member of Teamsters for a Democratic Union, he helps put out a newsletter for workers at Sysco Corp. called the *355 Informer*. "That way it has some association with the local, but it's not the local's," Zartman explains. "The guys pitch in to get it printed at a local print shop, 125 copies."

The four-page *355 Informer* has regular columns with news from the different departments—"The Warehouse Watch," "Driver Doings"—and a Stewards' Corner with information on union rights. A column called "What do you say?" is a witty saying, and, says Zartman, "we try to include a cartoon, something that pertains to our warehouse."

Anonymous or Not?

Although conditions vary from workplace to workplace, anonymous articles may not be a good idea. If you don't sign your articles, readers may feel that the authors are afraid to stand up for their opinions, and you may lose credibility. If readers think you have reason to be afraid, you may reinforce their own fears. In addition, workers who sign articles may have more protection under the law (see "Your Right To Publish and Distribute").

Some newsletters, rather than putting bylines on particular articles, print a list of names of everyone who contributes to the work—writers, editors, layout person, distributors. This indicates that the newsletter is a collective product.

The Local 355 leadership did not react well to the new information source. "When the newsletter first came out there was a problem," Zartman says. "We had information that a business agent gave away seniority rights in the warehouse. We chastised him in the newsletter, and said you should never give away seniority rights in the union. The editorial got the people at the executive board upset, because they said we were attacking the union. Our view was that this was constructive criticism. You do something right, we'll pat you on the back, and if you do something wrong we'll criticize your actions.

"Well, the president made several threats against the people doing this newsletter. We replied saying we were within our legal rights under the national Teamsters Constitution, plus the Landrum-Griffin Act, which specifically state you have free speech, and also under the First Amendment of the U.S. Constitution.

"We sent a letter saying we were not going to stop doing this. I personally asked everyone involved in the newsletter, in writing, distributing, or whatever, if they wanted to sign the letter. Thirteen people put their names down.

"We began to publish in January 2002, and in less than a year we increased our TDU membership by 30 people in our warehouse alone. It's because they're tired of nobody helping them, and the newsletter people are willing to help.

"We've had results. We had ineffective business agents who've been moved away from our company, and we got a new business agent. When we were getting ready to go into contract negotiations, all our stewards went to meet with the business agents to develop a proposal, instead of just sitting down with the old contract. The business agents wanted to know if they could submit an article to our newsletter."

The Barking Dog

Caroline Lund, an executive-board member in UAW Local 2244, works at the NUMMI auto assembly plant in Fremont, California, the famous flagship team-concept plant that is a joint venture of General Motors and Toyota. Since 1997, Lund has published *The Barking Dog*, which initially grew out of her work as a "union coordinator," a position like a steward representing about 30 people.

"Our union was in such a crisis," Lund says, "that

Your Right To Publish and Distribute

Freedom of the press is a great American tradition, specifically defended in Article I of the Bill of Rights. In addition, free expression in the workplace is guaranteed by the National Labor Relations Act of 1935 through the "protected concerted activities" clause, which says that workers can join together to improve their situation. Speaking and writing about the workplace is part of such joint action.

In fact, the law has established that speech and writing in the workplace have rather more latitude than exists in the general public. Under the NLRA, you have the right to distribute newsletters and other materials in non-work areas during non-working hours (including breaks) in your workplace (see Chapter 2). The Labor Management Reporting and Disclosure Act of 1959 ("Landrum-Griffin") specifically guarantees workers' right to freedom of expression within the union. You have the right to distribute materials at the union hall or during union meetings and other union events.

Employers and even union officials have sometimes threatened rank-and-file newsletters with libel suits. Usually such threats come to nothing. To prove a case against you, it must be shown that when you wrote the statement you knew it was false or probably false. Even a losing lawsuit is a major hassle, however, so verify your facts and concentrate on issues rather than persons.

we hadn't had our regular union newspaper for over a year due to infighting between the caucuses. So I figured that the members would appreciate some information about union matters, and I started putting out just a leaflet every month reporting on what happened at the monthly membership meetings. People seemed to enjoy getting that information, so I decided to put out a regular newsletter and pass it out more broadly than just my two groups that I represented." Today Lund also distributes *The Barking Dog* to auto workers around the country via email, and it can be found at www.geocities.com/abarkingdog/.

Lund stays organized by keeping a folder. "As I read newspapers and magazines, I tear out articles or cartoons and put them in the folder. Or I get a little story from someone in the plant, and I put it in the folder for the next issue. I have a feature called 'quote of the month,' and I collect relevant quotations; for example, I've used quotations from Martin Luther King, Thomas Paine, and Abraham Lincoln.

"Having the newsletter is important for my thinking, because it motivates me to read about what's happening in the plant and in the world. I'm always thinking about what's important to put in *The Barking Dog*, and how to help us all think about how to change the workplace and the world for the better. It helps me be more political, I think, more alert to what's happening."

One of the biggest problems the editors of rank-and-file newsletters face is the fact that most people think they can't write. The answer is to interview them or take dictation. Lund says, "I get those people to tell me their stories, and I write them up, and then I take what I've written back to them to get their approval." She also prints articles—sometimes as short as a paragraph—from people who do write up their own pieces. She usually prints their name and department, unless they ask to be anonymous.

The *Barking Dog* focuses on management's workplace abuses and workers' experiences. It always leads off with "what everyone is most interested in and reads first—an article about the plant. I have a lot of stories about speed-up by rank-and-file members. That's the one biggest issue, together with favoritism." One recurring theme the newsletter has stressed is the need for adequate time to study the contract before members vote on it.

If Lund includes an article about a broader topic—in 2003, for example, the war in Iraq—that comes later. "I have thought sometimes I should have a sports column," Lund says, "but I can't find anyone to do it."

The tone is rather serious and always respectful of the members, even of officers whom it criticizes. In this way, it attempts to rise above the mutual backbiting of rival factions, who often seem motivated primarily by a desire to make a career in the union.

"I try to make *The Barking Dog* always constructive and respectful," Lund says. "In the UAW it's a tradition to have union members writing flyers here and there, everywhere, especially around election time. And I would say the majority of them are harsh and factional, and they turn off the average member to union politics. I try to make my *Barking Dog* the total opposite. Very calm and cool and respectful and non-factional. I try to give recognition when anyone has done something good, whatever faction they are in.

"The members like that. In fact, I was passing out my latest issue, and one guy, with his table all covered with factional leaflets, said, 'Ah, *The Barking Dog*, a breath of fresh air.'"

When Lund's paper criticized local union officials, they threatened to sue her for defamation. "The chairman and president got a lawyer to send me a letter, saying that *The Barking Dog* was calling into question their qualifications to hold office. So I was forced to get a lawyer as well, and I put out a special issue with their lawyer's letter threatening me, and my lawyer's answer. I passed out 1,000 copies of that issue, which were very well received by my co-workers.

"My lawyer noted that Supreme Court rulings have said that in union settings free debate must be encouraged, even if this means 'bitter and extreme charges, countercharges, unfounded rumors,' etc. It is not enough to prove a statement is false to prove libel; you must prove 'actual malice,' i.e., you have to prove that the person 'realized that his statement was false or that he subjectively entertained serious doubts as to the truth of his statement.'"

The union leaders' attack on the shop floor free press failed, said Lund. "In the election two months later I was elected trustee and a member of the executive board."

Resources

• *Grievances: Using the Grievance Procedure to Defend Our Rights and Build Power on the Job,* from Teamsters for a Democratic Union. The mechanics of the grievance procedure and organizing tips to involve members. $8. In Spanish: *Los Agravios: Usando Agravios para Defender Nuestros Derechos en el Trabajo.* 92 pages, $10. Box 10128, Detroit, MI 48210. 313-842-2600. www.tdu.org.

• *The Legal Rights of Union Stewards,* by Robert M. Schwartz. Available in Spanish. $12.95 plus $3 shipping. Work Rights Press, P.O. Box 391066, Cambridge, MA 02139. 800-576-4552. workrights@igc.org. Information from the pamphlet is available in lesson form on the SEIU website at www.seiu.org/olc/.

• *How to Win Past Practice Grievances,* by Robert M. Schwartz. $12.95. Work Rights Press (see above).

• *The Union Steward's Complete Guide.* Basic how-to and survival skills for new stewards, and new tactics for old hands. 226 pages. $19.95 plus $3 shipping.

Inquire about Spanish version. Union Communication Services, 165 Conduit St., Annapolis, MD 21401. 800-321-2545. www.unionist.com.

• Also from UCS: Online or CD-ROM training course for stewards, with interactive scenarios. $69.95. *Steward Update*, bimonthly newsletter. 20 subscriptions (minimum): $227/year; additional subscriptions $5/steward/year. English or Spanish. Free samples available.

• Videos: *Power at Work: Building a Member-to-Member Action Network* and *Turn It Around: Teamster Stewards Solving Problems on the Job*. By the Teamsters International. *Power at Work* (1997, 15 minutes) explains how to build an internal communications structure in a local, and *Turn it Around* (1994, 17 minutes) provides basic steward training and tips for how stewards can solve problems by mobilizing members, without having to file grievances. The union does not have copies for distribution, but they can be borrowed from John Braxton, 4712 Windsor Ave., Philadelphia, PA 19143. 215-724-1571. morbraxton@aol.com.

• "A Worker's Guide to Direct Action," by the International Workers of the World (IWW). Ideas on slowdowns, work to rule, sitdowns, selective strikes, sick-ins, and more. www.iww.org.au/lit/sackboss.html.

Action Questions

When there's a problem:

1. What happens when you file a grievance where you work? Does the union take up all the grievances workers bring to its attention? How long does the process take? What percentage of grievances does the union win? Does the union organize any action to support grievances?

2. What is a common problem or grievance in your workplace? How many workers does it affect?

3. Who is the supervisor with the power to do something about that issue? How could the issue be brought to his or her attention?

4. How would you word a petition about this grievance? Where would you go to get the first bunch of signatures? To whom would you present the petition? The union? The company? Both?

5. What group would sign a group grievance? Would that group also take it to the boss? Would you do it on your break or during worktime (affecting production)?

Direct action:

6. Would it be appropriate to use a work-to-rule campaign to deal with the issue? What rules would you use? The company manual? The union contract? Health and safety regulations? Other government regulations? What would be the key rule to enforce?

7. In some work-to-rule campaigns, one group of workers, or even one worker, can be key. Make a drawing of the work process showing how your product or service moves through your workplace. Where is the key place to create a bottleneck? Who would be the key workers?

8. Who should give the signal to begin a work-to-rule campaign, and who to end it? How can that be done discreetly, if necessary?

9. Would it be appropriate to use a slowdown, where you go beyond the rules to make sure production is cut? Where is the key place to create a bottleneck? Should you set an (informal) numerical goal for how much you want to slow production? (See "The Legal Limits of Working to Rule" in Chapter 10; slowdowns are often considered a violation of the union contract.)

10. Who would be the key workers in a slowdown? Are there weak links among the membership? Who should talk to them? Who should give the signal to begin the slowdown, and who to end it? How can that be done discreetly?

11. Would an overtime ban be an appropriate tactic? What does your contract say about such actions? Do workers feel strongly enough about the issue to give up overtime? (See Chapter 6 for two examples of overtime bans.)

Building solidarity:

12. Do some people donate time by beginning early, working through breaks or lunch, or working late? Does it create expectations for other workers to do the same? What action could be taken to stop the practice?

13. Are your members often disciplined when they try to protest speed-up or unfairness? Does the fear of losing money keep people from standing up for themselves? Would it help to create a fund to aid those who have been disciplined for defending job standards?

14. Is there a boss whose behavior is outrageous and who should be shown up for the fool that he is? How does that person act, how does he treat others? Does that give you any ideas about how to make fun of him?

15. If you were all going to do something to show management that you are united and want a change, what would you do? Would you all wear a button? All wear the same color on the same day? All march into the office together? Would you all march out of the shop at break time and have a solidarity break? Would you all stand on your chairs and sing "Solidarity Forever"? Would you march down the aisles with picket signs? Hold an informational picket visible to the public? What is the appropriate level of action for where your people are right now?

Formalizing on-the-job organization:

16. Is your workplace large enough to need a stewards council? Would such a council help make your union more visible, more pro-active, and stronger? Who could begin to take leadership to organize such a council? That is, who are the most active stewards now? Would you have to recruit more stewards? How would you involve members in identifying and developing stewards?

17. Would it be helpful to have a newsletter in your department, workplace, or union? Do you need one to organize people to deal with shop floor conditions? A coming contract? Issues of union democracy? Who could you get involved in producing such a newsletter?

The politician gimmick:

18. Would an invitation to a local politician put pressure on your employer? Who should make the contact? What do you want out of the politician in terms of follow-through on the issue, and in terms of long-term commitment?

Authors

DAVID BLEAKNEY is National Union Representative for Education in the Canadian Union of Postal Workers.

MICHAEL AMES CONNOR was member/organizer of the Portland State University Faculty Association (AFT 3571) and is an editor of *LeftField*, the baseball and politics 'zine.

PAUL KREHBIEL is a Lead Field Representative/ Organizer for SEIU Local 660 in Los Angeles. He first belonged to the United Glass and Ceramic Workers Union in Buffalo in 1968, where he helped organize shop floor campaigns including a slowdown. Later, in two other unions, he was elected a steward and local union president.

DAN LA BOTZ wrote the first edition of *A Troublemaker's Handbook* in 1991. He is an activist, teacher, and labor historian based in Cincinnati, where he writes frequently for *Labor Notes*. He was a founding member of Teamsters for a Democratic Union in the 1970s and wrote a book about that movement, as well as books on unions in Mexico and Indonesia. He is editor of the monthly web publication *Mexican Labor News and Analysis*.

DAVID LEVIN is an organizer for Teamsters for a Democratic Union.

PAUL MCCAFFERTY is a heating, ventilation, and air conditioning mechanic who was a member of SEIU Local 254 for 14 years. He served as a steward and bargaining committee member.

MARSHA NIEMEIJER staffs Labor Notes' New York office, where she covers longshore workers, telecom workers, and Canadian and European labor, as well as international economic issues. She has worked with the Transnationals Information Exchange since 1995 and helps coordinate international and cross-border programs for TIE and Labor Notes.

DOROTHY WIGMORE is a longtime health and safety specialist who has worked with and for unions in Canada, the United States, and Mozambique. You can find her at dorothyw@web.ca. www.wigmorising.ca.

Note

1. "A Small Victory at Mitsubishi," *The Barking Dog*, January 18, 2000, Issue #21, page 1.

On the Troublemaker's Website

"The Quota," by Paul Krehbiel. Workers in a mirror factory organize a slowdown to protest higher production quotas.

4. Creative Tactics

by Julie McCall

Why Have Fun?

by Ricardo Levins Morales

THE GREAT UNION ORGANIZER and troubadour Joe Hill once observed that nobody walks around reciting a leaflet to themselves. Put your message into a song, however, and they'll be humming it for days. This chapter describes many examples of art, song, theater, and humor that give your message the wings it needs to take off. Like the proverbial spoonful of sugar, they help to make organizing tasty, fun, and—well—habit-forming.

Tapping into the creative genius of your members works its magic in a number of ways:

- It helps to dissolves the atmosphere of intimidation that dominates the workplace. A cartoon or song that parodies management and gets the workers laughing undermines the boss's sacred authority.
- It builds the sense of community among workers that they need to confront the power of management.
- It encourages member involvement. When excited members return from caroling at the CEO's home or dramatizing their demands on the street, their co-workers will want to know how they can get involved.
- It can bring your story to a broader public, either directly or through the media, and win support for your position.

Put all that together and you can transform the power dynamics of a workplace, winning victories with the help of a creative spark. These tactics can electrify an organizing drive or contract campaign, galvanize public opinion for a boycott, or stimulate interest within a dormant local whose members are barely aware that they belong to a union.

Sometimes the simplest ideas can have the greatest impact. Veterans of the coffee workers union in Puerto Rico still remember marching to the city with their pockets turned inside out to dramatize the need for higher wages. Sometimes the wildest ideas can work. Indiana University workers hired an Elvis impersonator to write union rock-and-roll songs; he helped turn the tide in an uphill unionization battle. Sometimes jujitsu does the trick. Workers in a Minnesota machine shop responded to a rash of arbitrary suspensions by forming the "Suspension Club." Everyone who got suspended was awarded a pin. Those who were suspended multiple times got bigger prizes. That took the wind out of management's intimidation campaign.

All you need to get started is a willingness to have some fun. No previous experience is required. If one of your members is always doodling on her napkin at break, get her together with the one who's always telling jokes and—presto!—you have a cartoonist. Using popular ads,

When Leaders Are Reluctant

ONE OF THE MOST CONSISTENT OBSTACLES that creative organizers encounter is leaders' fear that we might do something that looks frivolous or that the members will think is silly. Most of us who have tried introducing new ideas have met with everything from censorship to an outright ban on our proposed activities. Our challenge, then, is to create a situation where leaders will actually witness the excitement and support that these tactics generate. This usually requires some chutzpah at first, but that's a requirement for a good organizer anyway!

You can just show up at the picket line with drums and whistles to hand out. Or a good song parody about the issues at hand is one way to get your foot in the door. Recruit a couple of other members for moral support, and at your next union meeting raise your hand whenever questions are taken from the floor. Instead of asking a question or debating a point, stand up and sing your position. When members start clapping, stomping, and singing along, your chairperson will get the idea and may even jump on the bandwagon. This was actually done at the 2001 AFL-CIO convention.

Volunteer to open your next stewards meeting or conference. Start reading a really boring speech and have an audience "plant" start harassing you and complain that they are tired of boring union events. A good lead-in to your guerrilla skit or song is "Are you telling me that it's legal to have fun at a union meeting?"

You may be able to eventually develop a tradition of beginning your events with creative actions—when the members line up to participate, your leadership will have a hard time arguing against it. And once you get going, creative organizing takes on a life of its own.

The bottom line is: JUST DO IT!

songs, and films as your starting point, anyone can get into the act. If you need a professional touch for a particular idea, you can contact the people listed in this chapter. Most often, though, there is plenty of talent hiding out in your own rank and file.

One of the rewards of creative organizing is watching the creative blossoming of your members and co-workers. As you hoot and holler over the boss's reaction to your last outrage and your ideas for the next one, a transformation is taking place. Members are analyzing what's going on, thinking strategically, gaining confidence, building rapport—in short, learning to be leaders. And they're having so much fun they don't even notice.

BOSSES BEWARE!

When we're screwed we multiply!

Shop Floor Actions

T-Shirt Messages— Bunnies on the Move

by Julie O'Donoghue

NOTHING HAD WORKED for the American Postal Workers in Danbury, Connecticut. Postal authorities continued to refuse to honor their contract, which required that workers whose jobs were eliminated be offered new work within 50 miles.

So on the day that the Postmaster General visited from Washington, D.C., every worker at the General Mail Facility came to work wearing the same t-shirt. "Bosses Beware: When We're Screwed We Multiply" read the backs of 300 bright red shirts, with an image of militant bunnies marching arm in arm; the local's logo was emblazoned on the front. Mortified, management began to pay attention.

The attention wasn't the welcome kind. Fuming with embarrassment, management sent a letter to all employees prohibiting the shirts because they violated the Postal Service's "zero tolerance for violence" policy. The workers, amused but not deterred, knew they had disoriented the boss. They contacted the Northland Poster Collective, the group that had designed the t-shirt, and ordered 300 more shirts, this time without the offending text. They requested other bunny paraphernalia and threatened to picket national postal officials who were scheduled to come to town.

Management knew they would look ridiculous whether they accepted the right of workers to wear the shirts or not. Fearing more embarrassment, managers reached a settlement with the local, discovering that they could find local jobs for their workers after all. They also backed down on their t-shirt ban, and the replacement shirts stayed in their boxes.

Bosses at the *Minneapolis Star Tribune* also faced the power of the bunny tees when shop steward Rick Sather began to distribute them to Teamster drivers on the loading dock. Workers began to wear the bunny t-shirts some days and other days to wear plain red t-shirts under their jackets. Supervisors got sore necks trying to figure out whether the shirts had bunnies or not.

Management said that the wording was threatening, but the supervisor was not satisfied when Sather covered the letters with masking tape. When management tried to discipline one worker for wearing the shirt, others decided that was unfair and started sporting them as well. In the end management agreed to drop disciplinary action in an unrelated case if only the workers would stop wearing those pesky wabbits!

Coordinated Cartoons

by Julie O'Donoghue

Members of UFCW Local 789 in St. Paul didn't even have to put their cartoons on t-shirts, the summer that Rainbow Foods went too far. In 1999 Rainbow management installed a new "anti-shrinkage" policy and set up a toll-free anonymous hotline where employees could rat each other out for shoplifting. If management busted a person called in by a worker, the worker was given a substantial cash reward. Lunch bag searches and other intrusive policies were instituted. Morale plummeted. Management ignored the union's requests to meet, refusing to even return phone calls.

Local 789 chose a creative first strike: it enlisted Ricardo Levins Morales of the Northland Poster Collective in Minneapolis to design a series of cartoons expressing the workers' frustration. A brainstorming session with the artist, Rainbow workers, and union staff resulted in cartoons that renamed the company "Blameyou Foods" and lampooned company policy (see page 34). At a membership meeting, representatives from every store decided to distribute the cartoons among workers in all 11 stores at 8 a.m. the next morning.

Some cartoons also ended up under managers' doors. By 8:30 management had left a message on Local 789's answering machine, asking to meet with President Bill Pearson. Workers had started making badges out of the cartoons for their uniforms and were passing the cartoons on to truck drivers, who carried them to other parts of the country.

Rainbow Foods' speedy and unprecedented response was to agree to five informal meetings with workers rep-

CREATIVE TACTICS   33

Barbecue the Boss

MIKE KONOPACKI AND GARY HUCK *are the labor movement's two best-known cartoonists. They publish* Huck/Konopacki Labor Cartoons *monthly, and their distinctive styles have appeared in union newspapers throughout the country. Here Konopacki tells us how labor cartoons can spark discussion and spur folks to action:*[1]

by Mike Konopacki

WHILE LABOR CARTOONS aren't the fuel of the labor movement, they certainly can be (and have been) the match.

Bosses hate being caricatured. They're not like politicians, who, from time immemorial, have weathered the jabs of political cartoons. Bosses are used to being cloistered in their executive privileges. So when they become objects of derision, it drives them nuts. And workers love it.

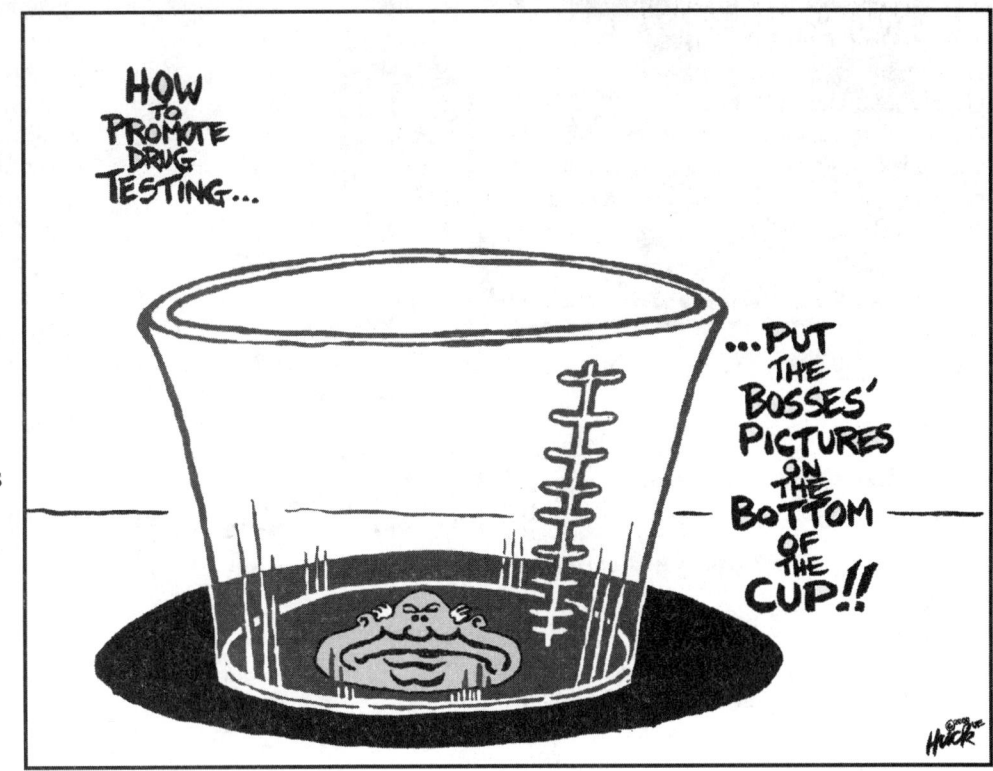

Consequently, "barbecuing the boss" has become our favorite pastime. Bosses derive their power from fear. When you ridicule the dictator, you diminish his power. In doing so, you—the worker—take on at least a little of the power he's lost. In the end, poking fun at the boss might not make or break a campaign, but workers come away knowing they got to him in a psychological sense. And that helps compensate, at least a little, for the treatment they've endured on the job.

• In 2002 I did a cartoon for *Labor Notes* on the Bush Administration's plans to intimidate the West Coast dockers union, ILWU. It showed an arm, labeled "Bush," holding a gun to the head of a longshoreman, with the caption "Work or else." Shortly after it ran, management for the Pacific Maritime Association showed up for an ILWU bargaining session with two armed bodyguards. Some inventive longshoreman took my cartoon and changed the name on the arm from "Bush" to "Miniaci," the head of the PMA. The revised cartoon circulated up and down the coast, not just in the ports but in unions supporting the dockworkers.

• When General Electric wanted to institute drug testing, UE responded with a workplace campaign. Part of it was Gary Huck's cartoon captioned "How to promote drug testing...put the bosses' picture in the bottom of the cup."

• During the Detroit newspaper strike in 1995, the Teamsters made a billboard out of a cartoon: the Statue of Liberty wore a gag labeled *"Detroit Free Press"* and a blindfold labeled *"Detroit News."* Who needed a caption?

• In Connecticut, our billboard lampooned Miller's Red Dog beer. We created a very ugly, very stupid-looking red dog, flies buzzing around it, with the message "Red Dog bites. Connecticut drivers canned. Don't buy Miller products." The cartoon ended up on posters all over town, especially at local watering holes.

• In Providence, Rhode Island, the Teamsters were boycotting a Budweiser distributor, and we used the Budweiser frogs to get our message across. We showed a worker's feet sticking out of a swamp and a frog croaking, "No Bud." The caption: "Budweiser croaks Rhode Island jobs." The billboard companies balked, so the Teamsters painted our ad on the side of a semi and drove it all over town. It became a mobile billboard that reached even more people.

★ ★ ★

For more information, contact H/K, PO Box 1917, Madison, WI 53701; huckkono@solidarity.com; www.solidarity.com/hkcartoons. Huck/Konopacki Labor Cartoons provides a monthly package of eight cartoons plus a column on Women Workers' History and a humor column by Will Durst. They also provide cartoons and art for corporate campaigns (flyers, t-shirt designs, logos, posters, banners, and web and video animation).

"It's all part of our new morale shrinkage program."

representing different stores and to listen to their complaints. These meetings rapidly brought about noticeable changes, including improved lighting in the parking lot. New cartoons showed thermometers rising and falling, according to the workers' happiness or dissatisfaction with Rainbow Foods' behavior.

A well-coordinated action and the accompanying surge in worker morale convinced management that a more humble approach to worker relations might be a wiser course.

Songs and Whistles

Joe Uehlein, director of the AFL-CIO's Center for Strategic Campaigns, tells this story about the power of song in an organizing campaign in an Alma, Georgia meatpacking plant. Organizers were encountering a great deal of fear. One of management's most effective scare tactics was sending in their slick-looking Atlanta-based union buster, who walked up and down the killing floor without saying a word. "This guy would show up in his three-piece suit and just exude power," says Uehlein. "So I began thinking about how to fight this, and I remembered a song I had heard called 'The Union Buster.' It's a parody written by Paul McKenna to the tune of 'Oh Susannah,' and the chorus goes:

He's a union buster, the boss's trusty aide

He helps keep our employees overworked and underpaid.

"I always carry my guitar in my car, so I brought it in, taught the song to the organizing committee, and we recorded it on a cassette."

At that time the company had a policy allowing employees to select the music that was played over the loudspeaker while they were working. The next time the union buster appeared on the shop floor, "The Union Buster" cassette suddenly began playing throughout the plant. "The guy just went nuts," recalls Uehlein. "The committee saw immediately how a single song could bust through that veneer of invincibility."

Predictably, by the following day, the company had rescinded its policy of allowing employees to select the music. So the next time the consultant appeared, the workers began singing "The Union Buster" song. That, of course, resulted in a rule against singing. On the union buster's next visit, the workforce was whistling the now-familiar tune. When whistling was banned, workers hummed.

Uehlein says: "In the course of one week we built strength and solidarity among that workforce. Workers learned that they could become a force by taking action on just that one small thing. Not only were we able to poke through the boss's shield of power, but we were able to anticipate management's response and plan our next moves. We illustrated the organizing principle that 'Properly goaded, the adversary will trip and make mistakes.' And by the way, that plant is a union plant today."

Street Action [2]

THROUGHOUT HISTORY AND IN MANY CULTURES, the medium of "the street," or common public space, has served as a venue for voicing concerns creatively. It is both immediate and affordable. Some common forms of street theater include:

- Sidewalk skits.
- Processions, pageants, or parades, often with music and costumes, sometimes festive, sometimes somber.
- Ritual performances. These can also be punchy adaptations of standard ritual formats, such as alternative shrines or mock exorcisms, funerals, or incantations.
- Inspired leafleting. In the 1980s, activists opposed to U.S. military intervention in Central America dressed up as waiters and carried maps of the war in Central America on serving trays. They went up to people in the street and said, "Excuse me, did you order this war?" and then followed up with an itemized bill and the line, "Well, you paid for it."
- Anti-advertisements that mock and parody a real ad. These can take any form a real ad takes: TV spot, magazine ad, poster, direct mail piece. The idea is to mimic the texture and components of the real ad but twist the message into a new and opposing meaning.
- Media stunts: a creative event with a strong symbol designed to hook the media. Understanding what the media wants is important in getting coverage. Editors are looking for a short punchy event in which people like

their own audience do something visually interesting. This doesn't have to be a funny gimmick—it can also be a dramatic way of showing the seriousness of the problem. For example:

Dramatize a phrase. One candidate held a press conference outside a waffle house to dramatize how his opponent was "waffling" on the issues.

Hand out symbols, not just leaflets. Passing out flyers rarely attracts the media. AIDS activists have handed out condoms and environmental activists, gas masks.

Create a symbol or replica of the problem. In the 1980s, students protesting apartheid erected South African shantytowns on campuses all across the U.S. In Paris, with each person adding one pair, citizens assembled a tragically huge pile of shoes to commemorate all the victims of land mines.

When creating your action, remember:

- Less is more. Figure out the *one* thing you need to say, then say it well and repeat it over and over. You can say the next one thing next time.
- Keep text to a minimum. Nothing is more deadly than lots of text without interruption.
- Maintain a consistent look and feel. The design of any slogans, flyer graphics, banners, props, and press releases should all be coordinated to develop a single message and visual identity.
- Use powerful metaphors. Portray the economy as a game with unfair rules. Use a fashion show to expose sweatshops. Use metaphors and motifs that are common in the culture and rework them to carry your message.
- Offer vision, not complaints alone. Convey hope and offer do-able alternatives. Show people it can be done and how.
- Don't preach. Try to embed the important information right in the performance. Avoid lecturing. Try to *show* more and *tell* less.
- Use the power of ritual. Imagine a corporate executive and a politician tossing huge bags of money to each other across a wide expanse, slowly and with exaggerated effect. Nearby, a support person hands out a fact sheet that tells the rest of the story. Often this kind of nonverbal performance that repeats a simple but visually arresting motion is more powerful than a full-length skit.
- Involve your audience. Choral chants, mass sound effects such as roars or murmurs, or simple physical movements are all ways to get an audience participating.
- Use humor to undermine authority. Imagine a labor action where the corporate target has to arrest Barney or escort Santa off the property. Authority requires respect and an aura of formality and seriousness. Humor can disrupt this aura and undermine a target's authority.

Picket Sign Parties

Planning street action and designing your props can be a powerful organizing opportunity in itself. Anything that brings people together to make something, whether it's a puppet show, a skit, or a picket sign, creates enthusiasm and solidarity. Assemble materials and turn your group loose with their creative ideas.

Hand-made picket signs are better than pre-printed ones, especially when they're made by union members and their families. Peter Rachleff, chair of the cross-union "Meeting the Challenge" committee in the Twin Cities (see Chapter 14), describes the successful sign-making workshops conducted during the United Transportation Union's strike against the Canadian Pacific/Soo Line railroad.

"The activists knew that their issues would not get much media attention," Rachleff says, "and they were worried about family pressures as the strike went on, especially on members of the other rail unions that were honoring the UTU's picket lines. So they decided to picket Soo Line headquarters smack in the middle of downtown Minneapolis, in order to reach thousands of passersby.

"The union coalition ran sign-making workshops for members, spouses, children, and other supporters and provided all the materials. Before participants started making the signs they discussed how to convey the strike issues to the public. These discussions resulted in dozens of ideas and hundreds of signs, in many colors, as well as a UTU leaflet for picketers to pass out.

"The enthusiasm carried over onto the picket lines, and that got the media interested. When the strike ended, public understanding of rail labor issues was much improved."

The American Postal Workers Union in the Twin Cities also used a sign-making workshop, as part of a barbecue for six different postal locals held at the APWU hall. Stewards circulated flyers in the workplaces urging members to bring their families. Over a hundred turned out, with children playing a big role in making the signs. At the barbecue, rank and filers from the three postal unions spent time getting to know each other, another benefit of the workshop.

"The sign-makers, of course, showed up

Monkey Business

WHEN 6,000 OUT OF 10,000 WORKERS at the state-owned aircraft manufacturer PTDI in Indonesia were laid off in late 2003, they took their case first to legislators, government officials, and the courts. They got the cold shoulder.

So hundreds of workers traveled by motorcycle from West Java to Jakarta to rally and spend the night near the Ragunan Zoo.

"It is useless to meet and negotiate with people who do not possess a conscience or logic," rally coordinator Toto Siswantoro told the press. "It is much better for us to meet with monkeys and apes.

"It is clear that these monkeys and apes will not be able to provide us a solution," Toto said, "but at least they can make us happy and will listen to our aspirations."

the next day to picket," says Rachleff, "looking for 'their' signs in the union van. Over 400 people showed up at two locations, including families."

Props and Costumes

Creative visual symbols and props can make your members, the public, and the media sit up and take notice.

When members of the Washington-Baltimore Newspaper Guild/CWA Local 32035 began gearing up for a contract campaign at the *Washington Post*, they already had their slogan: "We make the *Post*—The *Post* Makes Money—We Make Peanuts." They passed out peanuts in the cafeteria and on picket lines and built a repertoire of "peanut songs" such as "The *Post* Is Playing a Shell Game" (sung to the tune of "Take Me Out to the Ballgame").

But the peanut campaign really took off when an enterprising Guild member came across a Mr. Peanut costume (complete with top hat and cane) on E-Bay, and bought it for $65. To the delight of Guild members and the chagrin of management, Mr. Peanut began appearing at union meetings and events, joined informational picket lines in front of the *Post*, and even attended a bargaining session. Member volunteers took turns wearing the molded plastic outfit, which during the summer months necessitated frequent volunteer switches and a constant drinking water supply. "Not only did our members love to see Mr. Peanut on our picket line," says Guild Organizer Calvin Zon, "but passersby stopped to pose for pictures with him. Mr. Peanut really opened the door for the public to take a look at our literature." Ultimately the *Post* backed off its "final" offer on pay and union security, and a contract was signed.

Joan Papert Preiss, in her work to support the Farm Labor Organizing Committee (FLOC) in Durham, North Carolina, attracted plenty of attention when she handed out leaflets urging shoppers to honor the Mt. Olive pickle boycott: she wore a giant cardboard pickle. Preiss doesn't let her limited budget curb her creative ideas. She has designed a number of props that can be made from common materials. She was known for doing her grocery shopping while wearing a posterboard "tiara"; on the front was the image of a large pickle jar bearing the slogan "Boycott Mt. Olive Pickles." Preiss also distributed paper plates with the message: "No Mt. Olive pickles on my plate till after you negotiate." The plates were folded so that they fit into an envelope pre-addressed to the CEO of Mt. Olive, and the public was asked to sign the plates and mail them in. In 2004 the CEO signed a historic agreement with FLOC, and the boycott was ended.

Here are some other low-cost props and symbols that union members have used to dramatize their messages at work or on the picket line:

• Cardboard coffins or gravestones symbolizing "the death of workplace justice"

• A giant Union Busting License or subpoena delivered to the boss

• A huge greeting card containing an appropriate message for management and signed by employees

• Oversized Band-aids with a message such as "your contract offer makes us sick" (crutches, ace bandages, slings, and other medical items can be used too)

• A skeleton symbolizing a "bare bones" benefits package

• A "Justice-Mobile" (also known as the "Wheels of Justice") made from a huge cardboard box cut into the shape of a car

• A block of ice to protest a wage freeze

• Bags of dirt left outside the office of a CEO who treated his employees "like dirt"

• An inflatable plastic dinosaur denoting prehistoric management policies

• Kites instructing the boss to "Go fly a kite"

• Leaflets designed to resemble parking tickets and placed on cars

• Police crime scene tape wrapped around an area where an outrageous offense against workers has taken place

• Red capes and devil horns worn by employees as they welcome co-workers to "the gates of Hell"

• Large cardboard picture frames held so that they frame the face of organizers whose slogan is "put yourself in the picture by signing a union card."

You can easily supply your "special effects" box with a few visits to your local dollar store or party supply store, especially right after Halloween when everything is on sale. And there are countless novelty websites that feature everything from noisemakers to gummy worms (for use in a "survivor" skit).

Crashing the Party

The California Faculty Association used street theater to give its contract issues high visibility on the San Francisco State University campus. On the day of a planned rally, Association members organized a procession to the rally site. They borrowed costumes from the drama department and asked everyone to bring caps and gowns as well as drums and noisemakers.

"Everyone took a look at the materials and supplies we had available and came up with their own creative images," says CFA Regional Representative Nina Fendel. "Rags were stitched onto the caps and gowns to represent 'the tatters of academia,' someone pushed a trash barrel representing the 'faculty suggestion box,' and we even had a 'vampire' complete with mask and cape. It was fun to see how people's personalities changed when they put on a costume. Normally reticent members were calling out to the crowd to join in the parade. And because the spectacle generated interest, it swelled the ranks of our rally."

Later, when the CFA members found out that the university chancellor was scheduled to give a speech at a conference at a non-union hotel, they decided to rally outside the hotel. But they realized that they needed some inside action as well.

To dramatize the lack of health benefits for some part-time faculty members, they organized an event they called "The Inside Game." They made a banner that read "Families need benefits too," designed so that it could be folded up and carried inside a briefcase. CFA members, dressed as though they were conference participants, entered the hotel and placed their union flyers on all the literature tables and also posted them in hotel restrooms.

They then got into the room where the chancellor was speaking and unfurled their banner at the back of the room. Some members brought their children, who completed the tableau by holding up their own signs.

"We even managed to hijack the press coverage of the event," says Fendel. "Reporters from the major trade paper ended up writing more about our issues than about the chancellor's speech."

Puppets on the March

The Steelworkers union took to the streets of Europe to win support and publicity for 1,700 aluminum workers in Ravenswood, West Virginia. In 1990, these USWA members were locked out of the plant where they had worked for years. Union organizers traced control of the company back to Marc Rich, a multibillionaire commodities trader wanted by the U.S. government for tax evasion, who was hiding out in Switzerland. Because Rich did business in at least 22 countries on five continents, the union wanted to create a multinational campaign.

"Our challenge," says Joe Uehlein, "was how to communicate a lockout in West Virginia to trade union-

Hand Puppets on the Street

EVEN HAND PUPPETS can be called into service for street theater. Moshe Bialac, an internal organizer for IATSE (Theatrical Stage Employees) Local 720 in Las Vegas, helped organize a puppet show to support HERE members on strike. Appropriately enough, the show was a lampoon of a Vegas production, including "corporate sharks"—shark puppets with neckties—and a rap song at the end.

Although IATSE members are professional theater people, they did this show without any elaborate paraphernalia. Bialac says, "We did this right on the picket line so we could demonstrate the issues to both the rank and file and the public. Let me tell you about my 'fancy equipment.' The portable sound system for the show was an old car stereo, and the recording was made on a home cassette unit. Most of the sound effects were made with a toy synthesizer inside a garbage can, to get the echo.

"Most of my materials were donated. I put an ad in my local union newsletter asking for old jeans and shirts. And our hairdressers came in with swatches of real hair for the wigs. We didn't actually need real hair—but it brought those members into the union hall.

"You can use anything in a puppet show. There are no rules. Think about when you were a kid. You took a refrigerator box and cut a hole in it. All of a sudden you've got Solidarity Theater. Look at Shari Lewis's Lambchop—it's made out of a sock. You can go to Toys 'R Us for plastic dolls and use them as puppets.

"We needed three people to perform the show, plus five volunteers from whatever local we were performing for. The sound track was on tape, so all they had to do was learn to move the props to the cues, and we had cue sheets and the director there to help them.

"We had already learned to make our own t-shirts, so we could also silkscreen materials for the show. I got a third-grade silk-screening kit from a company that puts out instructional materials for schools, and I picked up a book on how to make t-shirts, and we found eight members who wanted to learn.

"It costs us a little more because we make mistakes, but that's eight more members who are involved."

ists around the world." Uehlein remembered that a giant puppet portraying legendary mineworker organizer Mother Jones had been used during the Pittston coal strike some years earlier. He took Mother Jones to a meeting of locked-out workers and their families to see how she would be received.

"It was an unbelievable hit," recalls Uehlein. "The union commissioned the building of two huge puppets by the Antioch College Department of Art (where the original puppet was created), and taking the puppets, puppeteers, and a group of locked-out workers to various locations around the world." Transporting the puppets turned out to be a major challenge that was eventually solved when the aluminum workers created collapsible frames for the puppets and traveling cases that could be taken on airplanes.

As the group flew to Switzerland, the Netherlands, Britain, Venezuela, Romania, and Czechoslovakia, it put on street theater in any available public place. While the two puppets representing Marc Rich and Mother Jones engaged in a dialogue about the issues, workers handed out leaflets. One side told the story of Mother Jones and the other side explained the story of Marc Rich and Ravenswood.

"The puppets attracted the attention of the media," says Uehlein. "We were on the front page of all the Eastern European papers and even had seven minutes on national TV in Switzerland. Marc Rich, who had been trying to keep a low profile because of his status as a fugitive, was in the news everywhere we went."

When the union found out about a hotel in Romania that had been purchased by Marc Rich, they approached the hotel workers' union there. "At first they were hesitant to engage with us," says Uehlein, "because they were trying to attract Western capital to beef up their economy. The locked-out workers and the puppets totally changed their mind, and they ultimately held their own press conference at which they blasted Rich."

The workers got their jobs back and a contract, thanks in big part to the "art attacks" they had launched against Marc Rich.

Union Songs and Parodies

SONGS ARE SOME OF THE BEST SPIRIT-BUILDERS in the creative toolbox. You can, of course, print a song-with-a-message in the union paper, but to inspire members to "Roll the Union On," you can't beat group singing. This is where to enlist the aid of members who play or sing in church or community choirs.

Holiday events are a good place to introduce the idea of "singing for the union." A federal worker who attended holiday festivities for two different locals in his building tells this story: "The first party consisted of a buffet luncheon followed by introductions and speeches. At the second party there were raffles, auctions, and a chorus of union members who handed out song sheets and led everyone in singing union parodies of holiday songs. I looked at photos of both events later on. The photo of the first party showed members interacting only with the one or two other people near them while eating lunch. In the photo of the second party, the entire group was on their feet and enthusiastically engaged in singing. It was a graphic illustration of how the music brought everyone together. And that second party got rave reviews from the members."

Writing Your Song

You can write a song quickly and simply by changing a word or two in a line of a well-known song. These are commonly called "zipper songs" because you "zip in" a line about your issue. Zipper songs are easy to teach on a picket line, and they let picketers create an infinite number of verses.

For example, "This Little Light of Mine" can be changed to

All over (insert the name of your workplace), I'm gonna let it shine

or

Go tell (your boss) that we're gonna let it shine. . .

Children's songs are good sources: "She'll Be Comin' Round the Mountain" can become "We'll be fighting for our health care when we come." In one campaign, the song "That's the Way I Like It" became

Organize, uh-huh, uh-huh, you'll like it, uh-huh, uh-huh.

At an indoor event or in a situation where you have an audience, you can try out something that's even more impressive: a complete song parody. Tap into the popular culture of your members to come up with a song they will relate to. Many current songs are hard to sing, but lots of oldies are familiar to just about everybody, such as show tunes, Motown-era tunes, country tunes, and movie or TV themes. Here's an example:

My Union (Tune: "My Guy")
Nothing you can say could take me away from my union
Nothing you can do, 'cause my point of view is union

One AFT organizer who is also a church choir director, pianist, and gospel singer says that it changed her life to discover how her union work and her musical life could be connected. She has since created many union songs based on gospel tunes that bring down the house at every event, such as "I'm a Soldier in the Army of the Union."

Although writing completely new words to an existing song is not as easy, the process and the result are worth the effort. Members' enthusiasm is boundless when they're working together on a song that's about them. For this you'll need a flipchart and a rhyming dictionary, available at most bookstores. These handy books give you a list of all the words that rhyme with a particular sound. Pocket-sized editions are available too, so that you can be prepared to add new verses while you're on the march.

First make a list of the terms that will personalize

the song for your group: the names of the "good guys" and "bad guys," your issues, the names of your union and workplace, the tools of your trade, any references to the culture of your workplace that will be understood by everyone.

Then pull out the rhyming dictionary and make a second column of words that rhyme with the words on the first list. Before long your song will be writing itself.

Participants at an AFL-CIO Working Women's Conference tried this technique to write a song about pay equity:

Close the Wage Gap (Tune: "Hit the Road, Jack")
Close the wage gap! Cause women deserve much more, much more, much more, much more
Close the wage gap! Cause women deserve much more!

Energized Meetings

MAKING MEETINGS LIVELY is a major challenge. Skits, songs, and game show parodies can help keep people awake and interested in the message.

Say It in a Skit

If your union president will probably drone on for hours at an important meeting about contract issues, or if few members show up in the first place because of your local's history of holding meetings that turn into snoozefests, you've got a problem.

A group of hospital workers anticipated this scenario, wrote a series of satirical skits and songs about their issues, and volunteered to perform at their contract gathering. Since they also anticipated that their president wouldn't voluntarily turn over the microphone to anyone else, they wrote a part for him in several of the scenes. Much to everyone's surprise, their normally uninspired leader turned out to be a big hit as a comic actor. And members came away with a much better understanding of contract language after seeing scenes such as the one in which hospital administrators were portrayed concocting a wicked plot to steal workers' sick leave benefits. The scene ended with an uproarious parody of "Rock of Ages" entitled "Dock Their Wages."

To get members to attend this event, the organizers handed out flyers in the workplace. The flyers, designed to look like theater playbills, announced "The World Premiere Performance of the Not-Ready-for-Prime-Time Players." They created such a buzz around the hospital that by the night of the meeting, there was standing room only.

Skits and satire are not only a great way to get information out: they are also excellent techniques for combating fear. It can be empowering for workers to play the part of supervisors who have been on their backs for years. Boss characters such as Contractula the Vampire (who sucks the blood out of union contracts), Bosszilla, Boss Hogg, Bozo Boss, and Ramboss (a Rambo-type evil-doer who rams concessions down our throats) can demonstrate the ridiculous nature of many of management's policies and actions. You can also create union super-heroes such as Captain Solidarity and Super-Rep, who arrive on the scene and help workers organize against injustice. And getting together with a group of co-workers to brainstorm ideas for the script can be one of the best parts of the whole experience.

As you put your skit together:

• Exaggerate! Take an issue or situation that's outrageous to begin with and carry it to the extreme. One group of poultry workers wanted to satirize a "bathroom study" that management was conducting to determine how much time each employee spent there.

This seemed so outrageous that at first they couldn't see how to exaggerate it. They finally came up with a "home bathroom study" for their skit, in which management came to workers' homes to monitor bathroom use.

• Evaluate your space before you write your material. If you'll have the use of a large space or stage, you can write in more movement of characters and more props. If you're doing a picket line performance on a public sidewalk, you'll have to adapt to a fairly small area. For a street theater production in front of a building that had little public sidewalk space, the United Electrical Workers once rented a flatbed truck to use as a stage.

If you won't have room for elaborate props, have cast members hold signs to denote the setting, such as "Company Board Room," or the passage of time, such as "Two Hours Later." Holding a sign is one way that a stage-shy member can easily participate.

• Evaluate the conditions you will be working under. If you will have to contend with street noise, limit the amount of dialogue. If you have a bullhorn, consider

The "Bird of Flight" hijacks jobs in a skit at the Conference on Creative Organizing.

Liven Up a Union Convention

WHEN SOMEONE SAYS "UNION CONVENTION," you might picture hundreds of glassy-eyed delegates passively sitting and listening to endless rounds of speeches. That would mean you hadn't participated in Solidarity Education Day at the international convention of the Brotherhood of Maintenance of Way Employees.

The BMWE, which represents 45,000 railroad maintenance workers, was facing contract negotiations with more than a dozen carriers. The leadership was determined to avoid a repeat of the 1991 negotiations, when Congress imposed a contract with big setbacks in wages and working conditions.

This time the BMWE dedicated an entire day of its convention to membership education and mobilization. "Solidarity Education Day was staged as a step in preparing the membership for negotiations that would be different from past rounds," explained Paul Swanson, BMWE's Membership Mobilization Coordinator.

Each of the more than 500 delegates chose to attend one of 15 work groups designed to generate ideas and develop their skills. Work-group topics ranged from discussions of railroad tactics, a workers' bill of rights, and cross-union coalitions to the specific skills of designing t-shirts, cartooning, songwriting, planning picket line chants, and making campaign buttons.

One group came up with a song addressed to Congress called "Leave Us Alone" (to the tune of "Bring It on Home to Me").

Except for the songwriting and chants work groups, all the groups met in the main convention hall, with chairs set up in different parts of the room. It was extraordinary to see a convention hall literally abuzz with discussion groups, overhead projectors, flipcharts, and so on. Groups seemed to feed on the energy of the other groups, and in an hour and a half, everyone had completed their tasks. Yes, there was a high level of noise and chaos, but that was part of what made the whole event exciting.

After lunch, each work group had five minutes on stage to give a report. For some groups, this was an oral presentation. But for others, the report was an actual picket line circling the stage and chanting, a t-shirt design or cartoon projected on the screen, or the group singing a song they had written.

Members and officials alike considered the day a huge success. As Swanson summed it up, "We got a feeling of optimism and pride that I've never seen come out of a convention before. This was my fifth convention, and I've never before seen delegates come away feeling like they had a plan of action."

---

having one narrator who reads the script while the rest of the cast acts it out. This is a good way to involve people who may be too nervous to take on a speaking role. If you are doing an indoor production in a large space, think about how to use microphones. It can be helpful to assign one cast member to be responsible for holding the microphone up to whoever is speaking, as most people have limited experience with sound systems.

• Consider the culture of your audience. A punch line has no punch if the audience can't identify with the situation and the characters. You can base your skit on a well-known television show, comic strip, children's book, or movie. For example, the "Survivor" TV series was the basis for many clever skits depicting employees figuring out how to survive their working conditions.

And don't forget commercials. The annual AFT Solidarity Night production features the Energizer Bunny walking across the stage while pounding on a drum and announcing that "the union keeps growing, and growing, and growing." Each time the bunny comes through, more audience members get up and follow.

• If you are short on preparation time, try using one main prop that the action can revolve around. In a skit called "Prime Time Lies," CWA Local 1180 board members made use of a "Lie-o-meter" to help evaluate the boss's latest pronouncements. This was a large wheel on which an arrow spun and landed on sections marked "whopper," "white lie," or "Lyin' King."

• Make it as easy as possible for people to participate. If some members don't feel comfortable memorizing lines, write out the script and let them read their parts. Give each person a cue sheet or designate a prompter. Don't give your group anything to feel nervous about, and everyone will have a great time. And once they experience the enthusiastic response from the audience, they will be hooked.

Game Shows

A game show parody is a way to get information out and a way to involve members without their having to rehearse beforehand. You can include everyone in the room, unlike the traditional talking-head format used at most union events.

Perhaps you're holding classes on contract issues, or training new shop stewards about the grievance procedure. Maybe you're training members to go out and organize. Any information can be put into a game show format—and best of all, because players have to discuss and choose between several possible answers, the information has time to sink in.

Questions can be general, such as "On average, how much more do union members earn in a week than non-union workers?" or they can be based on your specific situation, such as a question about the company's profit margin or the CEO's salary.

Here are ideas to help create a union game:

• To find labor statistics for your questions, use the AFL-CIO website, www.aflcio.org. Better yet, come up with questions about your own workplace. Buy a game show theme-song CD to play while contestants are deliberating (available at most record stores), and a hotel desk clerk bell to ring when their time is up.

- The "Million-Member Organizer" game uses qualifying rounds to select contestants, just like "Who Wants To Be a Millionaire?" You can put a single contestant in the hot seat, or have a group play as a team. Let them use their "lifeline" when they're not sure of an answer and want to poll the audience.
- A "Union Jeopardy" game can be used to review material covered in training classes. The game can be projected on a screen with Power Point slides or even with an overhead projector, and players compete in different categories. Remember that as in the Jeopardy game, contestants are given the answers and need to figure out what the questions are.
- A "Price Is Wrong" game can dramatize money issues. For example, workers who make furniture for an upscale store in Las Vegas staged an elaborate version of "The Price is Wrong" on the sidewalk in front of the store. The grand prize question was "How many weeks of grocery bills for your family of four would it take to purchase this lovely armoire that you've helped create?"
- The "Family Feud" game requires polling the audience ahead of time. The contestants try to guess the answers that the majority of the audience has selected. At a Union Women's Summer School, the questions included "Name something you'd like to see in a first union contract" and "Name something that makes the union strong." Be sure to throw in comical questions such as "Name something you'd like to give your boss."
- For the "Organizing" game, paint a huge game board on a tarp and lay it out on the floor. Contestants answer questions about making house calls, and a panel of judges decides whether or not their answer entitles them to move ahead on the board.
- In a "Which Side Are You On?" game, you display questions and hold up two different answers on opposite sides of the room. Audience members get up and walk to the side of the room with the answer that they think is correct. This gets the audience out of their usual passive mode and literally gets them moving.

A Musical Revue

Sometimes it's not just the content of the fun that makes members enthusiastic, it's who they get to see up on stage. CWA Local 1180 used a musical revue to enliven its annual stewards' conference. After dinner on the first evening, the entire local executive board provided entertainment for the stewards.

Most Local 1180 members are New York City government workers, so the e-board presented satirical skits and songs like "The Titanic City Ship," in which the mayor tossed workers' benefits and security overboard to keep the City Ship afloat, and "They've Been Working on the Railroad," which depicted the railroading of city workers and their rights. "The stewards were surprised and delighted to see their officers on stage spoofing the mayor," says one executive board member.

Saturday Night Live with AFT

Imagine a 90-minute show that includes the music of James Brown and Tina Turner (with choreography), a gospel choir, a talent show, and much more. The American Federation of Teachers doesn't have to spend much money to provide this kind of entertainment because the entire production is put on by members of AFT's paraprofessional division. It's all part of the annual Solidarity Night that has been a tradition since 1987.

The AFT is not unusual in having so many talented members, say the organizers. It's mostly a matter of providing the opportunity for them to show their stuff. Organizer Tom Moran first suggested that the paraprofessionals' conference offer workshops on song- and skit-writing. He had to do some serious recruiting ahead of time to get people psyched up to try something new. But when word got around that the morning workshop had written several Motown parodies and some satire about the bosses, by the afternoon session there was standing room only. The workshop participants put together the entertainment for that Saturday night, and the rest is AFT history. The shows are bigger and better each year, and in addition to whatever comes out of the workshops, many locals come with acts already prepared.

One year, the opening act was a parody of James Brown's "I Feel Good" (Since I Stood With the Union), using a karaoke back-up tape while members played instruments that were items from the members' workplaces. A custodian's broom became an air guitar. Two of the favorites performed by a choir were "You Really Need a Union" (tune: "You Really Got a Hold on Me") and "Rollin' With the Union" (tune: "Proud Mary"), the chorus of which goes:

> *AFT set us burnin'*
> *We set the tables turnin'*
> *Rollin' (rollin'), rollin' (rollin')*
> *Rollin' with the union*

The acts are usually tied together with a skit that continues throughout the evening. This involves creating a nasty boss character, such as "Ramboss," who appeared complete with a Rambo outfit. Ramboss announced that all the school systems were going "on-line" and would have no further use for union workers. He explained that he had hired a privatization expert to help him use the Internet to find ways to steal union jobs. The expert, who had recently starred in a movie called "Privatization Parts," was none other than Howard Stern. Howard proceeded to try to surf the Internet with a surfboard, visited chat rooms, and replaced the computer discs with "computer disco."

Union members sabotaged Howard at every turn, and after doing him in they broke out in a rousing version of the "Union Macarena":

> *Come on everybody now, it's time to join the Union*
> *When we get together all the workers will be*
> *groovin'*

*Brothers and the sisters going to get us all a-movin'
Hey—join the Union!*

Songbooks were distributed to the audience, and throughout the show the crowd was on its feet clapping, dancing, and singing along. One keyed-up participant went from row to row after the performance collecting extra songbooks to take back to his local. "I've been looking for a way to put some life into our meetings," he said. "My members won't believe this."

Resources

- For help in getting your members involved in creative activities, contact Julie McCall at the Labor Heritage Foundation, 888 16th St. NW, Washington, DC 20006, 202-974-8041, jmccall@aflcio.org. The Foundation conducts workshops on using cultural tools and maintains a regional directory of labor artists.
- Every June the Foundation holds the Great Labor Arts Exchange, a gathering of labor artists and activists from throughout the country, and the Conference on Creative Organizing, a training program for union staff, organizers, and members. Both conferences are held concurrently at the George Meany Center for Labor Studies in Silver Spring, Maryland. For more information visit www.laborheritage.org.
- Northland Poster Collective designs for the labor movement: posters, cartoons, t-shirts, buttons, and more. P.O. Box 7096, Minneapolis, MN 55407. 800-627-3082. info@northlandposter.com. www.northlandposter.com.

Action Questions

1. Is your executive board open to new ways of doing things? If not, how can you convince board members that creative strategies are good organizing tools?

2. Which of your union events and programs could benefit from a dose of creative thinking?

3. How will you recruit to creative organizing? When you sing a song at your meeting, who in the audience is singing along? Who is known as an artist? Who sews? Who plays piano in their church choir? Who leaves clever cartoons about the boss around your workplace? Who tells the best jokes? Do you have a plan for involving them?

4. Are you prepared to put on an event, say on a picket line, on short notice? Does your local have a collection of costumes, song sheets, props, and chant books that you can draw upon quickly?

5. For event planning: Who are you trying to reach? Your own members, the public, the media, unorganized workers, a combination?

6. What result are you trying to achieve? Are you informing an audience that is not familiar with your issues, or are you "preaching to the choir" but trying to inspire them and build solidarity?

7. Do you want your audience to take action after your event? Is your action message crystal clear?

8. What conditions are you working under? Will you be outdoors or indoors, and will you have a bullhorn or sound system at your disposal? Will you have a stage? If not, can you create your own "stage" by clearing an area of the sidewalk or the room? (You do need to create a situation where your audience can see and hear what you're doing.)

9. Do you want the audience to participate? If so, will a song or chant sheet help (they can take it home and use it again)? Can you ask them to make sound effects, such as booing the villains and cheering for the union?

10. Have you designed your action to involve as many people as possible? Have you created an atmosphere in which other people will feel free to participate?

11. What are your priorities—having a professional-looking performance, or involving as many people as possible? (The two aren't always mutually exclusive, but the union member who "can't carry a tune in a bucket" may be your most enthusiastic performer—and best organizer.)

12. When all is said and done, *did you have fun?*

Authors

MIKE KONOPACKI is a former Teamster bus driver. He began labor cartooning in 1977 for the Madison, Wisconsin *Press Connection,* a daily created by striking newspaper workers. In 1983 he and Gary Huck created their own cartoon syndication service and have published five books of labor cartoons.

RICARDO LEVINS MORALES is an artist/activist who works for the Northland Poster Collective in Minneapolis, which provides art and organizing materials to the labor movement and other grassroots movements. He is part of the Meeting the Challenge Labor Education Committee.

JULIE MCCALL is Project Director for the Labor Heritage Foundation. She teaches workshops on creative organizing for unions across the country and has written hundreds of song parodies for union and political campaigns.

JULIE O'DONOGHUE interned with the *Union Advocate* newspaper, Workday Minnesota (a web-based union news service), and the Twin Cities Religion and Labor Network.

Notes

1. Excerpted from the RESIST Newsletter (Vol. 11 Number 9), www.resistinc.org.

2. This section is adapted by permission from *The Activist Cookbook, Creative Actions for a Fair Economy,* by Andrew Boyd. Published by United for a Fair Economy.

5. Fighting Discrimination, Building Unity

by N. Renuka Uthappa

UNCHALLENGED, discrimination is management's dream. What happens in a workplace where no one believes that "an injury to one is an injury to all"? A workforce that is divided can't muster the unity it needs to thwart harmful management actions. This is true whether a particular attack is directed at just "your group" or at the workforce as a whole.

For management, discrimination is an entrenched mechanism and attitude that ultimately serves the bottom line. We live in a society where people's race, gender, nationality, or sexuality help determine their power, their access to jobs, and their quality of life. When management denies promotions to African Americans, pays women less, refuses the union's demand for domestic partner benefits, fails to translate safety information into workers' language, or sets up a two-tier wage system, the employer benefits from discrimination.

When discriminated against, the troublemakers in this chapter chose to fight back to survive and thrive. They fought for equal benefits, against harassment, and for their group's right to advance on the job and in the union. Their tactics ranged from petitions and departmental meetings to a strike and a statewide march. They negotiated anti-harassment programs with management, prodded their union leaders, and built independent caucuses and support groups.

The workers in the first set of stories organized campaigns to fight specific instances of discrimination. As part of these efforts, they looked for allies among their union brothers and sisters who weren't directly affected but wanted to help. As transgendered grocery worker Lincoln Rose advises, "Don't discount anyone. Some of my strongest allies were straight, older, married women, people who had been in the union all their lives."

The workers described in the rest of the chapter were up against daily, deeply entrenched, and often institutionalized discrimination in their workplaces, trades, and unions. They built formal and informal caucuses to support each other and fight for changes. African American labor leader Curtis Strong explains, "Independent self-organization within the union—not only for African Americans but for any group fighting for a voice—was the only strategy."

The activists in both groups made trouble over weeks, months, and sometimes years. They all got results. In some of the cases, as you can imagine, the discrimination did not end for good. People found they had to keep on fighting. But they also found that their organizing had created connections that made continuing actions possible.

Discrimination attacks both the personal power and the collective power of its targets. Unions exist to fight for members' power over our working conditions. That's why, whether we experience it directly or see our union brothers and sisters hurt, fighting discrimination at every turn has to be a core issue for all union members. Ending discrimination is also a necessary component of the fight for member-run unions.

Like the union activists you'll read about who fought to save affirmative action in Florida, the labor movement must also take the fight against discrimination beyond the shop floor. Besides being the right thing to do, such actions can make labor more powerful by making it more relevant to non-union workers in our communities. The more they see the labor movement support their daily struggles, the more likely they will support labor's campaigns. The more the community sees labor as a powerful force, the more likely community members will start or join the fight to unionize their own workplaces. The Florida chapter of Jobs with Justice was born out of that affirmative action fight, and continues to link labor and community activists in common struggle.

Our communities are often segregated, but on the shop floor and in union halls, workers who may not associate closely with each other otherwise are forced together. In both spaces, bigotry and what it costs those who suffer it, or tolerate it, comes with a human face. Like the workers in this chapter, we can use that proximity, our creativity, and our identity as workers and union members to unify us when other forces seek to divide us. It can, as you will see in the stories of struggle in this chapter, help to develop a stronger union, one that will truly "have our backs."

Adventures of the Viagra Lady

by Sheila McClear

KATHY BLACK DIDN'T THINK IT WAS FAIR that while 80 percent of employers in Pennsylvania covered Viagra, men's "little helper," only 29 percent fully covered all five forms of women's contraception. As president of the Philadelphia chapter of the Coalition of Labor Union Women (CLUW), she began to voice her frustration at area union halls. Some of the unions, many of them a majority men, grew so accustomed to her speech that they began to call her the "Viagra lady."

The nickname was something of a misnomer, however. It wasn't Viagra but "contraceptive equity" that Black was fired up about. CLUW, working with a coalition that included local chapters of the National Organization for Women, Pro-Choice America, Planned Parenthood, and others, simply wanted a vital type of health coverage for women workers: if a health plan covered other prescription drugs and devices, it should cover contraception, too. While most health plans in Pennsylvania covered Viagra, only 43 percent offered partial coverage for contraceptives (usually just the Pill), while 21 percent didn't cover any.

As it stands, women already pay 68 percent more than men for out-of-pocket health-care costs, largely because they pay for contraceptives and related doctor visits. But Black says that "there's no financial argument [against adding contraceptive coverage]. This is a very cost-effective benefit, very inexpensive." That is, coverage for contraceptives ends up costing much less than maternity benefits and less than the cost of abortions or of providing coverage for children that result from unplanned pregnancies. In fact, many plans cover the cost of an abortion, but not the Pill.

Black was backed up by a ruling from the Equal Opportunity Employment Commission: if employers are already providing benefits for drugs and devices for other medical uses, they may not discriminate against women in their health insurance plans by denying them benefits for contraceptives.

Philadelphia CLUW "seeks out workplaces where coverage is not provided and works up an internal campaign to get coverage there," says Black. "You don't have to wait until your next contract to have contraceptives put in. Usually, benefits can be added anytime." For example, when the group brought the issue to the attention of Laborers Local 332, they added coverage to their plan immediately.

The coalition's biggest victory was at Philadelphia's Temple University in June 2002, where 4,000 union and non-union campus workers and their families—including graduate employees, security guards, food service workers, and faculty—won full contraceptive coverage.

"We started a petition to the university to ask that it be added. That didn't work, so we threatened to sue, and then all of a sudden they decided that it would be a good idea after all," Black explains.

The Campaign

Gary Kapanowski of AFSCME Local 1723, which represents many Temple workers, says that he talked to labor relations people and to the faculty union, an American Federation of Teachers affiliate. "What we did was a campaign of sorts," says Kapanowski. We sent letters to the university, and meanwhile members were calling them up and asking for coverage. With the [Philadelphia-based] Women's Law Project representing us, acting as our surrogate, we threatened to file a lawsuit if they didn't give us coverage.

"We worked with the other unions to find people to be complainants in the lawsuit. The Women's Law Project spearheaded, funded, and coordinated the campaign. Temple studied the issue for a couple months and finally agreed to it. After a four- or five-month struggle, we won coverage effective June 1, 2002."

Although the coverage was originally requested by the faculty union and AFSCME, which together represented about 2,000 members, it ended up reaching 4,000 campus workers. "As always, the non-union workers also benefited from the struggle," says Kapanowski.

David S. Cohen, a staff attorney at the Law Project, says, "Writing that first letter, either from an individual or an organization like us, usually is enough to change policy. Often they don't even realize that they didn't offer a type of coverage." He suggests that readers get in touch with the Project to be referred to similar organizations in their town, or look for women's groups in their own areas.

A happy result of this coalition has been better relationships among the women's groups. "Originally, CLUW was the only labor participant in the coalition," Black says. However, the cross-pollination was "also a way to organize

---

Fighting Disability Discrimination— Beyond the Physical

by Sheila Cohen

When we think "disability," we tend to think about physical problems like deafness or paralysis. But unions can also fight discrimination against those with learning or cognitive disabilities. Rich Feldman, former shop chair of UAW Local 900 at Ford's Michigan Truck plant, recalls a member who was trying to get his son hired. The son had a learning disability that affected his ability to take the recruitment test; he had the skills required, but could not deal with the question-and-answer process.

The UAW took up the case and tried to get the test adapted, but initially failed. Feldman worked with the Michigan Civil Rights Commission and the Equal Employment Opportunity Commission to file charges against Ford under the Americans with Disabilities Act (ADA).

Although the company was never technically found to be in violation of the ADA, as time passed and more such cases came forward, Ford changed its policy. The union eventually got individuals' tests adapted to conform to their special needs. At first, management simply allowed the instructions to be read out loud. When problems continued, they read aloud all the questions as well. By 2002 a number of workers had taken the adapted tests and were hired.

with other women's groups in town. Now, we come to each other's events, and we've helped each other out, made sure their literature was printed in union shops. Good relationships were built out of this struggle."

Contraceptive equity affects men workers too, since coverage includes their wives. Black says that although men are supportive, some find it embarrassing to talk about. Also, Black says, "it's tough to get women to speak up about it in mostly male unions." But, she adds, "the men come over to our side pretty quickly. It's always a huge surprise to them. They've never thought of this before."

Women of Steel: Anti-Harassment Training

by Patricia Smith

THE UNITED STEELWORKERS' harassment counselors have reached more than 35,000 workers and managers in Canada in the fight against sexual and racial harassment. The USWA Canadian district's Anti-Harassment Workplace Training grew out of its "Women of Steel" program, says Sue Milling, a staff rep. "Harassment is tough to talk about, and we needed the space and time to talk about the issues."

With assistance from the Ontario government, the union got funding to train union members both to facilitate workplace sessions about preventing harassment and to deal with complaints. Counselors get three to five days of training using the Steelworkers' own materials, which are based on resources used by Canadian Labour Community Services. They also rely on community services mediation tools formulated by a local church.

Milling says, "We are very careful about setting parameters for our counselors. A counselor is trained to be a good listener and to help support our members in getting the professional services that they may need, whether that is through their own doctor, a community health and social services center, their union staff representative, or a crisis center." She adds that the counselors are not trained to be therapists or experts in the grievance procedure or human rights law. The counselors are other workers "who can help guide and support the member in making informed decisions" in a particular harassment situation.

What Counselors Do

To request the help of a counselor, says Milling, a union member contacts the area USWA office or the national office. "We call the victim, listen, and outline what we have heard and the options for moving forward. We then contact the alleged harasser, the union steward, or employer, depending on the agreed-to course of action. Our process is informal and depends on a lot of cooperation and goodwill at this point.

"If an informal resolution is not possible, we advise the victim to file a grievance, or a complaint, again depending on the circumstances and the wishes of the victim." Once the complaint is formal, it is usually handled by the union officers or by whoever else has responsibility, such as a Human Rights Commission investigator.

"In the majority of the cases," Milling explains, "the victims simply want the offensive behavior to stop. They don't want to see anyone fired but rather want assurances that there will not be any repetition of the offensive, unwanted, and inappropriate behaviors." She is pleased that in most cases the counselors can get an apology and a resolution. For example, one request for intervention involved inappropriate touching. "With the cooperation of the employer, we met with the victims and the alleged harasser. He took responsibility for his actions and apologized."

If this sort of informal mediation process does not work, "we guide the parties through the grievance process and other processes that may be available through the union."

The Steelworkers have not found much conflict with the grievance procedure. Company and union are both usually cooperative in providing space and time to work out a resolution. If a union grievance has been filed, it is often put on hold pending the outcome of the counselors' efforts. Together with the union, the harassment counselors may see whether they can deliver an anti-harassment message across the whole workplace.

"If trainings are necessary for the entire workplace," says Milling, "the national office works with the counselors, the staff, and the local union leadership and they will approach the employers. Sessions are generally two hours long in groups of 20-25, on work time and in the workplace. We try to assign two people per training, one man and one woman, who reflect the diversity of the workplace."

Milling says the Steelworkers' model has been so successful that other unions, including the Canadian Auto Workers and the Machinists, have adopted anti-harassment policies and have trained advocates and counselors to assist with complaints.

Dodging the Red Herring: When the Boss Uses Race To Divide and Conquer

The practice of "snitching"—complaining about a co-worker to management, instead of first addressing problems through union channels—can sow disunity in any local. Management can then take advantage of that disunity to divide and conquer. Members of UAW Local 235 in Detroit fought back against such a double threat: the unjust accusations of a "snitch" and management's attempt to further divide the members by using race as a red herring.

At the Detroit auto parts supplier American Axle, a little over half the workers are African American, and the rest are white. At an "Employee Participation Circle" meeting between management and workers in 2003, the union members asked management to leave, which they do regularly when union members want to discuss issues privately.

"We were talking about how to stop management from doing certain things," explains Dana Edwards, the Plant Two district committeeperson (equivalent to a full-time steward), the meeting's chair and an African

Local 235 members showed their unity in a one-day strike against a contract with two-tier wages.

American. "A white female co-worker joked, 'Kill 'em!' I responded with, 'That's a good idea.' The consensus of the group was that this was a joke."

The next day, the Labor Relations department suspended Edwards for three days for "making a threat against management." A union member had told management that Edwards himself had made the "Kill 'em" remark. Edwards explains that most members believed the "snitch" was a person known to be a management favorite, one who has, according to Edwards, openly identified herself as "not a union sister."

During the investigation period, Edwards noticed, "only white folks got questioned. In my opinion, they chose certain individuals they thought they could influence." Management's decision to question only white workers about the incident "created an angry feeling," says Wendy Thompson, president of Local 235. She calls the selective questioning a blatant attempt to create racial division. At the same time, members who had attended the EPC meeting were going to management to let them know Edwards had not said what he was accused of saying.

Meeting after Work

The next time members gathered, at a previously scheduled "Communications Meeting," they expressed their feeling that the person who had snitched to management was wrong and wondered how to approach management about her actions. Edwards suggested that they go to the union hall and set up a meeting for the approximately 280 workers in Plant Two. They scheduled an after-work meeting at the hall on the day Edwards was scheduled for his disciplinary interview.

"Having meetings at the local hall after work is fundamental," says Thompson. "Timing is key. We normally give seven days' notice about a meeting, but in this case, we waived that to put additional pressure on management."

Both Thompson and Edwards describe the importance of word-of-mouth in getting people to the meeting. To encourage one-on-one conversation, notices should be handed out to people, not just posted, Thompson says. Management definitely heard the buzz. "The frontline supervisors would have gotten a lot of feedback," Thompson remembers. "There was a feeling that they knew there would be a lot of people at the meeting and a lot of anger."

Before the meeting even took place, management informed Edwards that there would be no discipline and that he would get back pay for the three days spent on suspension. Thompson concludes that just knowing that organizing was happening made management back down.

Even after this victory, 70 people attended the after-work meeting. People were drawn, says Edwards, because they began to see how snitching could affect them. "They see the committeeperson as someone who can't be touched. If management was able to put someone in that position out, it hits close to home."

Although there is definite unity between black and white workers at the plant, Thompson notes, it was unusual for that unity to be expressed as vocally as it was at the meeting. "You got the sense that white workers wanted to make it clear that they were every bit as much against snitching as the black workers were. White workers were very vocal about not being with management."

A large number of workers filed "conduct unbecoming a union member" charges against the snitch. These would have gone to a local trial board, but on appeal the UAW International dropped them on a technicality.

"Our local is from the 1930s," Thompson explains, "and we have quite a few democratic traditions we haven't done in many years. But now we are starting to implement them gradually."

Dealing with Real Harassment

But what if real harassment had been going on among members? Although management is legally responsible for maintaining a non-hostile work environment, Thompson says that "if possible, you want to resolve things internally, in the union."

Thompson says that if a particular joke made her uncomfortable, the person who snitched should have gone to the union instead of the company. "It can be intimidating to go directly to the person you're criticizing," she acknowledges, "but the snitch could have said she wanted to see the union rep at the next highest level or could have pulled aside the alternate committeeperson."

Ideally, in a harassment situation the union rep would speak with the workers involved. If necessary, the rep would take harassment victims' concerns, clearly and fairly, to management. Without disclosing the name of the person who committed the offense, the rep could demand that management present workers with a written statement that the behavior in question is not acceptable.

If going to the union officials doesn't work, or there are some good reasons not to do so, Thompson suggests that members organize themselves to take the issue to management, again without disclosing the name of the person who committed the offense. If management does indeed issue a statement against the harassing behavior, that could be a step towards fulfilling its responsibility to maintain a non-hostile environment. If such local action is ineffective, workers could go as a group to the regional union office or to the union's civil rights or women's department.

Some months after the snitching incident, workers found two hangman's nooses—symbols of the lynching of African Americans—in a work area. Local leaders reacted swiftly. They asked any members with information to step forward, warned that such activity could lead to discharge, and called on all members to sign a group grievance demanding that management maintain a non-hostile work environment.

In a leaflet, the union leaders said, "Our future depends on our ability to be unified and treat each other with respect." The leaflet also put pressure on management to prioritize an existing diversity training program; at first, only African Americans were being sent!

Management-sponsored diversity training is often pablum and sidesteps real issues, but it's possible for union members to use the time and space to have honest discussions and promote their own unity. In Local 235's case, the diversity program was run by a community college without much management interference, and the content was good. In the aftermath of the noose incident, the local pressured supervisors to give all members time to attend and to continue scheduling trainings until everyone had gone.

Gay and Straight: Building Solidarity

by Miriam Frank

THE LABOR MOVEMENT MADE A DIFFERENCE in the lives of many lesbian, gay, bisexual, and transgendered (LGBT) workers during the 1980s and 1990s. This didn't happen at every workplace or in every community. But in organizing for fair treatment, benefit equity, and new community coalitions, we have come a long way and achieved small and large changes, from simply being able to come out at our jobs to organizing LGBT caucuses within our local or international unions. Along the way, we have found reliable allies among our union brothers and sisters, from co-workers and stewards to officials on our international executive boards.

Our understanding of ourselves as union members—queer and straight together—is changing, and that is good for our survival. Unions have realized that they can thrive only by allying with other movements outside the workplace, and we queer people know even more deeply that our only protection, in a society still ambivalent about our rights to love and live safely, is to secure strong backing in our quest for dignity and pride wherever we may work.

Unions and the movement for lesbian and gay rights need each other. The entire LGBT movement for civil rights has been based on the courageous decisions of individuals to come out and fight for their rights. People with that kind of courage should be welcomed in the unionized workplaces and union halls of America.

Still, coming out on the job when you think you're the only one can be a dangerous step to take. Many gay workers who have made their identities known have been punished by management and harassed and ostracized by co-workers. More often than not, there has been little recourse against violent attacks, sabotage, threats, and firings.

In 2004, 13 states, the District of Columbia, and over 100 cities and counties prohibited job discrimination on the basis of sexual orientation. In all other workplaces, discrimination based on sexual orientation was perfectly legal. For that reason, gay workers and their allies have fought for anti-discrimination contract language that makes coming out less risky.

Fighting Homophobia: It's Good for the Union!

When union members, straight or gay, take steps to make the workplace safe for queer co-workers, welcome us into union activities, and stand up to bigotry, they set a tone of decency that widens everyone's sense of what the union is. They are recommitting to the principle that an injury to one is an injury to all, and that the union is, above all, an organization that stands for fair and equal treatment of all workers. Here are a few things queer and straight unionists can do:

- Come out on the job. It's hard to push a gay rights agenda when your life is closeted. If you are straight, be forthright about your support when LGBT issues, such as gay marriage, are in the news. Closeted co-workers, sensing that the mood is non-hostile, may be more willing to come out.

- Encourage your local to publicly recognize the life-cycle events of LGBT members just as it does for straight members. If your local puts notices on the bulletin board for weddings, do the same for partnership ceremonies. Likewise on congratulations for births and adoptions, as well as condolences, flowers, or cards upon the death of a member's life partner.

Straight allies can educate fellow members about how deeply the union family can matter to their LGBT co-workers, some of whom may be estranged from their original families. When gay workers' partners are integrated into the union community, it's easier to persuade members to support a demand for domestic partner benefits in the contract. These include bereavement leave, which is simple and inexpensive, and, eventually, more complex domestic partner issues such as medical benefits.

- LGBT members need to be visibly active not only on civil rights committees but in all aspects of the union, such as community work, negotiating teams, and stewards councils. Local officials can encourage and appoint queer union people to union-building functions. If informal gay networks exist at the workplace, this kind of conscious inclusion may bring more gay workers on board.

• AIDS support work has often been a common cause for LGBT and labor activists. ACTWU Local 340 in New York City (retail clothiers, fine haberdashers—now affiliated with UNITE HERE) adopted the Gay Men's Health Crisis center as part of their local's charity work. In Boston, the Gay and Lesbian Labor Activists Network (GALLAN) held an ambitious fundraiser as its first major public event, in 1989. It benefited both the United Farm Workers and the gay community's Fenway Health Center. Cesar Chavez was the keynote speaker, and musical entertainment was provided by the gay a cappella group "The Flirtations."

In the 1980s the actors' union, Actors Equity, created "Equity Fights AIDS," which used theater benefits and "pass-the-hat" intermissions at Broadway shows to help members suffering with the disease.

• The local can join the fight against "hate legislation," electoral referenda designed to mandate employment discrimination against queer public employees and their advocates in education and human services. For examples of the dramatic campaigns fought by labor/LGBT coalitions in Oregon and Washington in the 1990s, see "Lesbian and Gay Caucuses in the U.S. Labor Movement," by Miriam Frank, in *Laboring for Rights: Unions and Sexual Diversity Across Nations*, edited by Gerald Hunt.

• When gay marriage emerged as a national political controversy, some labor organizations quickly affirmed their support for this crucial civil right. For example, when the Massachusetts Supreme Judicial Court said in November 2003 that it was unconstitutional to deny gay couples the right to civil marriage, opponents put forth a state constitutional amendment to ban gay marriage. Several large Massachusetts unions—including the Massachusetts Teachers Association, the Massachusetts Nurses Association, the National Association of Government Employees, and SEIU Locals 509 and 2020—pressured their state legislators to vote the amendment down, and Massachusetts legalized gay marriage in May 2004.

In April 2004, the King County Labor Council (Seattle) passed a resolution supporting the right to civil marriage for same-sex couples. The KCLC has joined several unions, including AFT, AFSCME, AFGE, CWA, and SEIU, in taking a stand against banning gay marriage in the U.S. Constitution. The Michigan AFL-CIO opposed a 2004 state constitutional amendment to ban gay marriage in that state. The federation argued that the "cynical and divisive" measure would outlaw benefits already negotiated in union contracts for both gay and straight domestic partners.

• Extend same-sex domestic partner benefits to all, and correct inequities. For example, the UAW-Big Three auto contracts cover current workers but have neglected retirees, even though straight married retirees do have coverage for their spouses.

• Bargain and lobby for pensions for queer widows and widowers. Our domestic partners are not eligible for Social Security benefits when we die and as a result are more likely to be poor when we're gone. While gay partners can name each other as beneficiaries, this usually pays out only a one-time lump sum, rather than the monthly benefits that married partners receive.

In 1990 OPEIU Local 3 in San Francisco won assurance that queer widows and widowers will receive equal financial protection when their unionized partners die. Local 3's pensions are administered through its Taft-Hartley Fund. Nancy Wohlforth, national secretary-treasurer of OPEIU, was the chair of Local 3's Trust Fund when this reform was adopted. She says the key to Local 3's victory was the decision to negotiate partner benefits for both same-sex and heterosexual couples. "I still believe this is the correct way to go," Wohlforth explains, "since then the demand becomes a unifying one, not a divider."

• Mobilize to reform the Family and Medical Leave Act of 1993, because this important law does not include domestic partners among kin entitled to care for family members in critical medical situations. A gay worker who wants to be home with a new baby adopted or borne by a partner, or who is nursing his/her ailing lover, can only rely on vacation days or on the employer's sympathy when requesting an unpaid leave. Even without a full-fledged reform of the federal law, union negotiators can propose contract language matching the FMLA provisions to cover domestic partners.

• Stop throwing around "faggot" as a curse word. Encouraging workmates to stop using such a hateful expression can be a powerful consciousness raiser. It's not against labor law to yell "faggot" at a supervisor while on a picket line, but that doesn't make it okay, even if the boss is homosexual, because it is also a clear signal to gay people marching with us to stay locked in the closet.

During a building service workers' action in the 1990s, a lesbian organizer was fed up with the "faggot" yells on the strike line. On the ride back to headquarters, she told the picket captains, "I don't care what you call the boss. If the boss is no good, there's a million things you can call him, like lousy rat, S.O.B., whatever you want. Just don't call him a faggot, all right?" Out of respect for their gay union sister, the picket captains changed their style. And it didn't make the picket lines any less rowdy.

Transgendered Grocery Worker Educates Management and Union Leadership

WHAT DO YOU DO WHEN YOU FIND your employer's support for diversity in the workplace has its limits, and those limits don't include you? And what do you do when your union rep does nothing to help? As Lincoln Rose, a Seattle grocery worker and UFCW Local 1105 member, transitioned from female to male, he met discrimination from management. With the help of an ally in Pride at Work, the LGBT worker rights group, he and his co-workers made the kind of noise that got the union leadership to listen.

The Bathroom Issue

Rose began his transition, known as "gender identity reassignment," confident in his employer's diversity policy. "A lot of gay people work at my company," Rose explains. "There were no problems when I came out as a lesbian. When I decided to transition from female to male, the people from administration were neutral, and my co-workers were very supportive. They said, 'Good for you!'"

At first, things went smoothly. The Human Resources Department explained the company's standard procedure: the person in transition agrees to use only one specified bathroom, of his or her choosing, in this case a men's room, to allow co-workers, if they are uncomfortable, to seek another bathroom.

Soon, a male co-worker filed a grievance, not wanting to use the bathroom at the same time as Rose, who was in the first stage of gender transition. Management called Rose into a meeting and told him he now had to change bathrooms and post a sign on the door each time he went inside.

Rose stopped the meeting and told management, "I feel like I'm being punished for being transsexual." He called a Local 1105 representative and also Pride at Work, where he made contact with LGBT labor activist Sarah Luthens.

That's the Best You're Gonna Get, Buddy

Luthens accompanied Rose to the next meeting with Human Resources. She and Rose waited outside the meeting room for 15 minutes while the union rep spoke privately with management. After this confab, only Rose was allowed into the meeting. Luthens waited outside.

Rose came prepared with copies of a court case, *Cruzan v. Davis, Minnesota School District*, in which the school district told a Minnesota worker who complained about sharing a bathroom with a transgenderd co-worker, essentially, "We understand your discomfort, but this is the only bathroom your co-worker can use. Please use another one." The judge in the case ruled that the school district was protecting *all* interests through its actions.

The company refused to follow this example, saying that they weren't going to inconvenience anyone. Told that hanging a sign on the door each time he used the bathroom was his only option, Rose turned to his union rep for help. "I think you're going to have to take it," the rep said. "What if a customer complains? We don't have contract language or a law. You're lucky you didn't get fired."

Concerned about the language in their contract, Rose and a gay co-worker called the union hall. A representative there told them, yes, discrimination on the basis of sex is prohibited. Luthens points with frustration to this evident lack of understanding that the word "sex" in a contract refers only to physical gender, not to sexual orientation or gender identity.

Humiliation and Frustration Lead to Action

Rose was told he had to carry the bathroom sign until he had chest surgery, which could take three years and is not covered by health insurance. Until the sign was created, a member of management walked Rose to the bathroom, checked to see that it was empty, stood outside while Rose was inside, and then walked him back to his work area. After three humiliating days of this, Rose received his sign: in giant red letters, it said "This bathroom is OCCUPIED."

Rose says that this was a stressful time and his performance suffered. Many of his co-workers were also angry, but felt powerless. When Rose's driver's license arrived, specifying his male gender, his co-workers encouraged him to send a copy of it to management, who was not moved. Then his co-workers reminded him how they had used a petition to get the company to stop requiring heavy work shirts on hot summer days. They suggested a petition to get rid of the humiliating bathroom sign. But Rose says he wanted to do something that would have a larger effect and help other people, too.

With Luthens' help, Rose drew up a petition demanding that in its upcoming contract bargaining and in the union bylaws, Local 1105 include language prohibiting discrimination on the basis of sexual orientation or gender identity. Rose started collecting signatures. People took copies for their friends to sign, and one co-worker drove Rose around to other markets, where he got more signatures.

"Once we started the petition drive," Rose explains, "people had something they could get behind, a way to make a difference. Union pride started going up. People were saying, 'We don't have to wait for the company. *We* can do something about this!'"

Rose and his fellow union members quickly collected 96 signatures. Fifteen minutes after he called Local 1105 President Sharon McCann, Rose got a call to set up a meeting about the petition with the head of the local's grievance department. After this meeting, Luthens got word from Secretary-Treasurer Jim Glibb that the local would be negotiating for new contract language prohibiting discrimination based on gender identity and sexual orientation.

Rose says his experience taught him many things, including, "if you're not getting anywhere with your local, take your ass down to the office. Make noise. Say you're not moving until you talk to someone. This is not just a technical discrimination thing. This is your job, your sanity, your sense of self-worth on the line."

An Injury to One is an Injury to All...Always

"I'm really proud of the people I work with," says Rose. "Even when they didn't know what to do, they knew what I was going through was wrong. When we found what we could do, they were on it."

Rose encourages others in similar situations not to be afraid to put a human face on any issue. "Some of my co-workers may have been on the fence about gender reassignment. But at work, they couldn't stay on the fence. At work, they saw my distress. They saw me walked to the bathroom in tears."

Rose believes his honesty about the transition helped encourage his co-workers' empathy. "Never be afraid to answer questions from your co-workers as long as they are honest questions," he notes. "If you always answer the honest questions, they'll know they can come to you." Some sources on the Internet advise transgender workers to respond to questions with, "I don't discuss that on the job." Rose disagrees, adding, "That makes you sound like you are ashamed."

His strongest advice for fellow transgender workers and others facing discrimination? "Don't discount anyone. Some of my strongest allies were straight, older, married women, people who had been in the union all their lives. One of them told me, 'When they treat you like this, they make the union look weak to all of us.'"

★ ★ ★

Contracts that specify two tiers of wages, benefits, and work rules discriminate against new workers, who are usually younger—and sometimes our own sons and daughters. If this is not literally true, newer workers are still part of the union "family." The following story gives an example of the two-tier discrimination problem and one local's solution—a strike that pulled out all the stops.

Telephone Workers Fight a Two-Tier Contract

by Patricia Smith

IN 1998 WORKERS at Southern New England Telephone were working under a two-tier wage system that had been negotiated by their previous union, the Connecticut Union of Telephone Workers. "Competitive operators" earned an average of $8 per hour while "regulated operators" took home almost twice as much.

All the more recently hired bargaining unit employees at SNET (now owned by SBC)—operators, techs, and service reps—had to pay for part of their health insurance, while those hired before 1995 had fully paid coverage. In addition, newer installation and repair technicians were paid less and subject to different work rules than the older technicians.

Many operators in the lower tier were single mothers

Workers at Southern New England Telephone defeated a two-tier system that paid new operators barely half of what veteran operators made.

in a welfare-to-work program. An SNET spokesperson announced that these women were "lucky" to be making $8 because they "just came off welfare." Meanwhile, SNET was enjoying lucrative tax breaks for participating in the program.

Angered over these inequities and many others, 6,300 workers went on strike.

Patricia Telesco, then a business agent for Communications Workers Local 1298, says that all the workers were angry about their working conditions and pay inequities: "Many people had been laid off and never replaced, and the new workers were being paid less on top of it." To build solidarity before the strike, the repair workers and technicians would wait in the parking lot and walk in together. Service reps and operators would pick a time of day and in every office across the state would stand up at their stations for five to ten minutes, or tap their pencils on their desks for five minutes.

Second-Tier Workers at the Table

To highlight the inequities of two-tier, Local 1298 brought rank-and-file members to the bargaining table. Telesco explains, "We chose members from different job titles and each of them spoke about how the two-tier system had hurt them and how working conditions hurt customer service, and each worker gave personal examples of why they needed to have what was being proposed by the union."

The SNET workers' strike succeeded in wiping out two-tier because of the union's in-your-face tactics and because of its solidarity-building in the face of management's divide-and-conquer. What did Local 1298 do?

• Called on SNET board member and feminist Connecticut College President Claire Gaudiani to take an active role in bringing justice to the second-tier workers, most of whom were women. The second-tier workers joined with others to leaflet the campus to challenge Gaudiani publicly.

• Ran ads about the unfairness of the two-tier system to the mostly female, mostly minority "competitive operators." According to Telesco, "the national union paid for radio ads and full-page newspaper ads highlighting the competitive operator position, which was the lowest-paid job in the company and had the worst working conditions." This ad, says Telesco, "drove the media and the community wild."

• Passed out red bandannas and red t-shirts to symbolize solidarity. "It got so that even months after the strike had ended, motorists were conditioned to honking their horns when they saw red shirts," says Telesco.

• Created the "Flying Circus," union members who filled two buses and drove to the home of SNET's CEO for a mass picket.

• Engaged in "electronic picketing," using an autodialer system to conduct daily "fax attacks" on company fax machines. Members also did electronic picketing via email and would jam the company's phone lines. Telesco says, "We had members dialing their supervisors' pagers all day and putting in '1298.'"

• Picketed at an SNET-sponsored tennis tournament.

• Engaged in "mobile picketing"—following supervisors in SNET trucks and picketing wherever the work was.

• Created an SBC Solidarity Coalition. Rallies or marches were held every week. At each one, a representative of SBC locals elsewhere in the country—Midwest, Southwest, and West—came to Connecticut to pledge support.

• Brought in leaders of the Independent Brotherhood of Telephone Workers, who had recently won strikes in Puerto Rico, for rallies and outreach to the Puerto Rican community.

• Paid strike pay of $200 per week and set up hardship committees. This was made possible by $3.6 million in CWA strike benefits and tens of thousands of dollars more in Defense Fund assistance from the national union.

• Worked with food banks to feed needy members.

• Demonstrated in front of City Hall to convince the police to rescind restrictions on the number of picketers allowed at worksites.

• Marched in the Newtown Labor Day parade and confronted elected officials, demanding to know which side they were on.

• Invited the press to their events, which made the local newspaper willing to publish strikers' letters to the editor. The local community responded "tremendously," says Telesco.

• Marched to the state capital.

• Held mass rallies and mass demonstrations, including one with then-Vice President Al Gore.

• Operated mass picket lines until the day the strike ended.

Less than a month after the strike began, the CWA won a new contract. It eliminated the two-tier pay, benefits, and work rules, achieved parity with other telephone workers in the Northeast, and won base-wage increases.

When it was over, the union printed a detailed 24-page, picture-packed report on the strike, "We Won It Together," so that members could remember all they'd done to achieve their victory.

Florida Coalition Forms To Save Affirmative Action

TO PROTEST GOVERNOR JEB BUSH'S PLAN to eliminate affirmative action in state government and state colleges, 10,000 people marched on Tallahassee, Florida in 2000. Looking back on the march, an outside observer might say that Bush announced his "One Florida Initiative" and the opposition just snowballed. But the small group of people who worked to get their unions and communities moving know just how much work it took, and what specific tasks. The Florida chapter of Jobs with Justice, a coalition of labor, religious, and community groups, was born from their organizing.

A Sit-In as Catalyst

Dorothy Townsend was a hospital worker and political coordinator of AFSCME Local 1363 in south Florida in 1999 when Bush announced his plans to end affirmative action in the state. As soon as they heard what was afoot, a group of union and community leaders got together, Townsend recalls, to discuss ways to stop the governor. "Affirmative action is a labor issue," Townsend notes, "because it is a workers' issue. It's about diversity, inclusion, and people having a voice at every level."

When two African American state legislators, Kendrick Meek and Tony Hill, took over the Florida Lt. Governor's office in Tallahassee on January 18, 2000, their 25-hour sit-in to protest the One Florida Initiative energized Townsend's union and fired up the African American community. "Tony is an ILA longshoreman and a close friend of ours," explains Townsend. "We had a family member locked in the governor's office, and we heard that the governor said, 'Kick their black asses out!' For us, it was a matter of disrespect. In Florida, we are tough about anyone dissin' our members of the labor family. Plus, we had worked hard to get Tony Hill elected so we would have a spokesperson in the statehouse."

Monica Russo, president of SEIU Local 1199, called Townsend, then Townsend called Sherman Henry, president of AFSCME 1184. Together they called a local radio station to say, "Look what's going on in Tallahassee!" The station put the word out, and people started calling in. "At eight in the morning," Townsend remembers, "Monica and Sherman said, 'Let's shut down the governor's office in South Dade by noon!' Everyone called everyone they knew. I called everyone I've ever spoken to." Within two hours, protesters shut down the governor's south Florida office at Florida International University.

Meanwhile, the governor called for affirmative action hearings across the state. Townsend and her fellow activists wanted Miami's hearing to be the biggest one. Their group got the word out by radio, by leafleting worksites, and by calling what Townsend describes as "all the pro-active and progressive unions." These unions and several community groups signed their members up to attend the hearings and speak. "People stood in line two hours to attend," Townsend recalls, "even though the governor changed the site twice. By the time the hearing came to Miami, we knew we had to march on Tallahassee."

The core group of five activists met every day for the three weeks they had to organize the march. They went to the Miami hearing early, armed with sign-up forms that asked for addresses and contact numbers. By the end of the event, Townsend says, "We had thousands of people committed to going on an eight-hour bus ride to Tallahassee. They figured, 'I've been here for two hours. I'm willing to do something else.' People were pissed off, saying things like, 'We are gonna be getting out of the Bushes.'"

Building for Tallahassee

Townsend's group of five grew to 150 meeting attendees just before the march. The organizers made good use of their energy. "A lot of those people we knew, and we knew their talents," Townsend explains. "So we put them in charge of certain things. We didn't wait for them to volunteer. And instead of saying to union presidents, 'Can you bring some people to the march?' we said, 'How many are you bringing?' No one wanted to be embarrassed by bringing less than they said, so they brought more!"

The group quickly organized 23 full buses of marchers, 50 people per bus. But they had no money to pay for the buses. At first, they figured they'd charge $30 per rider, but quickly realized that students and people with low incomes would not be able to afford the ride. To raise money, Townsend says, "everyone put the press on their international unions. We got 10 buses from AFSCME, five from SEIU, one from AFT, and one from IBT. Other unions who sent marchers included the Laborers, CWA, FOPE, TWU, and the Painters." AFSCME fed all 23 busloads of marchers breakfast, lunch, and dinner on the way home. Of the union members on the march, approximately 90 percent were African American, with a mixture of other races making up the remaining 10 percent.

A Coalition in Search of a Name

The group that brought together the march on Tallahassee did not stop there. Many groups had taken part in the organizing effort, including the NAACP, Haitian Women of Miami, New Shiloh Baptist Church, students from the University of Miami, and kids from the Coalition of Black Trade Unionists' Youth Labor Movement.

"After the march," Townsend recalls, "everybody was ready for something. We had just pulled off a very successful campaign. We were already together. We just needed a name to cover the unions, clergy, community, and students together." They chose to become Florida's first chapter of Jobs with Justice.

"People we would not have worked with," Townsend says, "we worked with because of that march. That's what makes the JwJ chapter here far-reaching. There is something for everybody. This chapter is the most diverse in the country. Our members are white, Hispanic, non-white Hispanics, Haitians, Jamaicans, Chinese, students, clergy, NAACP, CBTU, and LCLAA." Even though their battle ended with the enactment of the One Florida Initiative, the JwJ chapter in south Florida is going strong today.

Setting the Right Table

Townsend has specific advice for unionists looking to form such a working coalition. Her operating principle is that building a coalition means having "a table that welcomes everyone." Her advice:

• Have a theme broad enough to include everyone who needs to be included.

• Don't apologize for your theme. Not everyone will agree with you and want to join, but others will come.

• Make sure everyone at the table feels they have a voice. No voice should ring louder than the others. They should blend. Everyone wants their personal, union, and special interest at the table, but make sure no one thing takes over the coalition.

• Always remember, you may have to work with people today that you do not intend to work with tomorrow. All coalitions do not have to be ten-year coalitions. Otherwise, you are spending a lot of time trying to appease people.

• Never underestimate anybody. When you are doing all this work, you need the big dogs to sit at the head of the table, but the people who really do the work are the rank and file. It's important to acknowledge them and give them leadership opportunities. A lot of times, they aren't going to get these opportunities in their unions.

• Whenever you can give leadership opportunities to students or women, do it. And help them with their resumés when they leave. (The guys are taken care of, but not the sisters.)

• Most important of all, recognize that everyone brings their own talents, gifts, and resources to the coalition. Appreciate them!

After the march, Russo created and distributed certificates which acknowledged that the recipient "contributed to the march on Tallahassee." "People still have them," Townsend says with pride. "They had them framed."

★ ★ ★

In the rest of this chapter, you'll meet workers who met the challenge of discrimination by building their own organizations.

Tradeswomen Unite Against Racism

by Sheila McClear

WOMEN MAKE UP TWO PERCENT of skilled trades workers, and of that percentage, only five percent are women of color. To help with this isolation and with other issues around racism, the Boston Tradeswomen's Network obtained foundation funding to set up Tradeswomen United Against Racism (TUAR).

The group brought together about ten African American and ten white tradeswomen once a month, with an African American and a white facilitator. "Lots of great stuff happened in those meetings," reports Elizabeth Skidmore, an organizer for the Carpenters union. The women met together as well as breaking into two groups, with white women and women of color meeting separately. For the women of color, the benefits were mostly building relationships and unity, since many of them had never met before; for the white women, the purpose was working on their own "learned" racism. All the women involved shared the experience of often being the only woman on the job. Many wanted to be seen as a carpenter, say, rather than as a "woman carpenter."

Felicia Battley, an African American activist in the Ironworkers union, says of this experience: "Race is an issue that can be quite volatile—but I think the connections that women made through that organization are life-lasting. What's going on in your life at different times will affect your participation—at this moment, the formal network is inactive—but you can still call TUAR. The relationships we built are lifelong."

For Skidmore, who is white, "Taking on racism with this group of tradeswomen, fighting to build community with each other, and developing ways to tackle racism on the job—this was the most hopeful project I've ever been involved with. It was hard work, but boy, was it worth it!"

Starting Your Group

What about women who would like to start their own group similar to TUAR? The many steps needed to get a project off the ground can be daunting, but as Skidmore says, "anything is possible if you want to do it enough, even without funding."

Nevertheless, a good first step is getting a small grant. In Boston, the tradeswomen used Associated Grant Makers, a regional resource, to help them find a likely funder. TUAR was funded by the Boston Women's Fund.

The next step is getting the word out about the group and building a membership. TUAR started by building up its database: making lists of everyone that members knew who might be interested, having events that would attract new people, and occasionally even getting a list of members of a local. "Mainly, it was word of mouth," Skidmore says. "It was a very painstaking process."

For a meeting place, get all the space you think you might need. TUAR used three rooms in a church so that participants could break up into white and black groups, plus childcare.

Speaking of childcare, don't forget the amenities that can make a huge difference in the busy lives of working women, especially those with children. "We had a good hot meal and childcare at our meetings, and that made a big difference," says Skidmore. "The paid childcare provider showed up for every meeting. If no kids showed up, we still paid her just to be there. That was important

Women Carpenters Meet for Dinner, Build Network

by Sheila McClear

In Carpenters Local 218 in Boston, about 200 members—two percent—are women. In the late 1980s, the local formed a Women's Committee that has been meeting regularly ever since in a "low-key" way. In other words, all the women who attend a union meeting meet for dinner afterwards. Elizabeth Skidmore, an activist among women in skilled trades for 15 years and a full-time organizer in the local since 1999, argues that this gives much-needed informal support to women working in the traditionally male trades.

The format of these dinner meetings is simple: whoever has something to say gets a chance to say it. "That's the entire structure," says Skidmore. "I just try to make sure that everyone gets a chance to talk." Topics vary wildly— union- and work-related issues and beyond.

"The most important things that have come out of these meetings is that the women now have very long-standing relationships with each other," says Skidmore. "If they get in trouble—harassment on the job, unemployment, personal issues—they are calling friends."

And what about the men? "This comes up all the time," laughs Skidmore. "I always invite them, but they back down every time. Some are antagonistic and just want to come and start a fight—but a fair amount of that is good-natured hassling."

Skidmore says that these informal, women-only meetings can be useful to women in any union, regardless of the gender balance, as long as the group has a mission and leadership. However, she says, "women in places with fairer numbers usually don't feel the need as much to get together.

"The number one obstacle for women in the trades is isolation, being the only woman on a site, at a union meeting, on a picket line. These meetings have helped improve retention of women in the trades."

because parents' lives are hard enough—they shouldn't have to decide ahead of time whether they need childcare or not. If they know it will always be there, they are much more likely to come."

TUAR hired two trained facilitators to guide the women in talking about the sensitive and potentially divisive issue of race. The nonprofit world is a good place to start looking for candidates, as well as any connections your members might have. TUAR, looking for a candidate with a working-class background, asked the Boston Women's Group for recommendations.

However, if your group lacks financial resources, there are other solutions. Skidmore suggests passing a hat at meetings for food and childcare and says, "You don't even 100 percent need a professional facilitator. There's a lot that has been written on this issue. Take some books out of the library and create a curriculum yourself."

In TUAR, women from many different unions were involved—the Carpenters, Pile Drivers, Plumbers, Bricklayers, Electrical, Laborers, and Ironworkers unions. Skidmore says that the meetings led women to more activism both within their unions and on job sites. "One of our favorite activities was role-plays with situations that happened on the job. We would act out different ways of responding. For instance, if a guy said a boneheaded thing to you, what's the best way to respond? Confrontational and angry? Humorous? It was very useful."

Skidmore says that organizing tradeswomen can be like "herding cats—not because they lack unity, but because they are very independent women. After all, you have to be pretty independent to be a woman and go into the trades. But organizing is possible because the women also share a mindset that 'we're all in this together' and will help each other out whenever help is needed. Perhaps it's about solidarity even more than unity."

The Breakfast Club: Pipefitters Fight Racism and Sexism on the Job and in the Union

by Sarah Ryan

PAULA LUKASZEK AND TODD HAWKINS found out in different ways how helpful informal caucuses can be in dealing with discrimination on the job and in the union.

Plumber Paula Lukaszek was surprised when a man, a pipefitter on her worksite, asked her to a breakfast meeting in 1989. She'd had a series of jobs where "the guys had been really bad," hostile to women on the job, making her day even harder to get through. The invitation was to a meeting of the Breakfast Club, a group in her United Association of Plumbers and Pipefitters (UA) local, made up of workers who had faced and fought racism on the job.

"I didn't want to spend my free time with guys, eating breakfast," she remembers, but she couldn't resist the idea that somebody was doing something about discrimination besides complain. After her first Breakfast Club meeting, she remembers thinking, "This was the group I'd been looking for for a long time. Where have these guys *been*?"

"Those guys" had been through almost 20 years of struggle by then, and had learned a few things about organizing. To get their construction jobs, African American workers had had to close down construction sites with sit-ins, rallies, and marches. They had sued Seattle's construction industry and its unions to get them to comply with Title VII of the Civil Rights Act of 1964, which forbids discrimination in employment. Their legal victories in the early 1970s, through their group, the United Construction Workers, required the construction unions and industry to take affirmative action to finally give black workers some small part of a fair share of the skilled trades jobs.

But winning a court order was one thing; getting through apprenticeships, getting sent out on jobs, and staying in the trade was another. They'd formed a caucus for mutual support. Then, after the group made connections with other workers' affirmative action cases through the Labor Employment Law Office (LELO), a community-based action and legal organization, the caucus gradually evolved to welcome other workers of color and, eventually, women. The group changed its name to the Breakfast Club. The meetings offered friendship, support, strategy for a more progressive union, and a place to talk about issues on the job and in the wider world. The club combined the strength of women and workers of color to push for a fairer and more democratic and effective union.

When Todd Hawkins went onto the job as an apprentice in the UA, white workers tried to provoke him into doing the one thing that could get him tossed out of the apprenticeship—physically attack a co-worker. Hawkins kept his cool. But he and other black workers bumped up

"Fire your family. I'm gonna need you nights and weekends."

against a wall of resistance to their presence on the job and in the union.

Many job sites were marked by harassment, threats, and lack of cooperation. The dispatch system wasn't fairly administered, and with the complex maze of certifications in this particular trade, almost anything could be rationalized. The union seemed like a club of white families. "You'd see the same names over and over again on the membership lists," Hawkins remembers. "The way these prima donnas—no, prima-dinosaurs—saw it, black workers were taking their kids' jobs away. We had to keep a copy of the court order in our back pockets," and had to form the United Black Plumbers and Pipefitters caucus to make sure the order was complied with.

A funny thing happened, though. Although the black workers were a small minority in the membership, they were organized. They attended meetings, spoke, and voted as a group. Union officials started to take notice and to court this voting bloc. The caucus decided to support those union officials who would deal fairly and openly with the members. After a while, they decided to run for office themselves and won some key positions.

Look to History!

by Ruth Needleman

In the 1940s, black shop floor leaders in the steel mills of northwest Indiana began the organizing that would lead to the formation of a nationwide black power organization in the United Steelworkers of America (USWA) in the 1960s. A central leader, Curtis Strong, had always argued that African American workers needed—and had a right to—their own independent group, that the first step in any fight was self-organization.

"You got to coalesce," insisted Strong, founder of the first black caucus at U.S. Steel's Gary Works. "Blacks couldn't go it alone, then or now. 'We will coalesce with you,' I said, 'as long as we can coalesce with strength. We refuse to coalesce with you when you got all the horses!'" He informed his white brothers and sisters in the union that "when we are equal politically, then we will coalesce."

For Strong, independent self-organization within the union—not only for African Americans but for any group fighting for a voice—was the only strategy. First, develop a power base. "Get your horses," he advised, and then you can leverage power in a coalition. The union itself, he understood, was a coalition, but the leadership discouraged any internal organization but its own.

In 1943, Strong and four others founded the Sentinel League, a "club" for card-playing and socializing for African Americans in the coke plant. Strong believed you had to build personal relationships over time, foster trust before you could launch a political effort. With the League's backing, Curtis Strong became griever (steward) in the coke plant. From that base he built the Eureka Club, a mill-wide black caucus strong enough to place its candidates on election slates in the local.

Accused of dividing workers, destroying the union from within, being a black nationalist and an opportunist, Strong did not retreat. He expanded black power district-wide and then in 1964 helped found a national black power caucus called the Ad Hoc Committee. Ad Hoc had a three-point program: more African Americans in leadership and on staff and a civil rights department headed by an African American.

Ad Hoc's strategy was to use the international executive board elections—in which each Steelworker member had one vote—to demonstrate its ability to swing the vote from one candidate to another. Ad Hoc provided the margin that put I.W. Abel into the USWA presidency. When Abel skimped on his promises to the Ad Hoc, African Americans threw a picket line around the national convention in 1968.

"We fought the company by day and the union by night," Strong explained. They picketed three conventions in a row, getting a civil rights department established, African Americans to head it up, and more African Americans appointed to international staff.

"Some people thought that was the end of the struggle," Strong observed, "and disbanded the Ad Hoc. Without independent organization, you have no power."

Two Hats

African American steelworkers always wore two hats—a civil rights one along with the union hat. In civil rights organizations, they fought for working class leadership. In the union, they fought for equality. They established coalitions with progressive forces and used that power in short-term alliances to win an issue or a position. The co-founder of the District 31 (Northwest Indiana) Women's Caucus, Ola Kennedy, for example, came out of Ad Hoc. Kennedy brought other African American women into a coalition with white women activists to fight discrimination and harassment and to get bathrooms and decent locker facilities.

Ad Hoc and the District 31 Women's Caucus became part of the backbone of the Fight Back movement, a rank-and-file movement in the 1970s that fought in the USWA for the right to strike and the right to ratify contracts. African Americans and women participated in large numbers because they had self-organized before coalescing. Self-organization means the group develops its own leaders and recruits its own active members, thereby increasing the union's reach and power.

How It Works

The Breakfast Club is a simple but powerful idea. The club meets on Saturdays at a local restaurant, before the monthly union meeting. Sometimes the group is small, but Lukaszek remembers up to 30 people attending. In addition to supporting democratic union practices, they have encouraged others to enter the apprenticeship, spoken in the community, provided friendship and support, and worked on wider political issues.

When one of the members wants to bring up an issue in the local union meeting, they talk about it at the club and get others' ideas and assistance, "so you're not just standing up there by yourself," as Lukaszek says. They have taken part in broader labor movement and community projects, too.

In 1998, when a local right-wing group staged a statewide initiative against affirmative action, the Breakfast Club helped raise money and campaigned, unsuccessfully, to preserve fairness. The group organized union members to march against the World Trade Organization during the 1999 Seattle demonstrations.

Hawkins and Lukaszek say that workers who face race and sex discrimination on the job shouldn't rely solely on courts or outside groups but also on their own abilities to think and organize. Forming a group like this doesn't take a lot of money, just the willingness to reach out to others. Though the original members were brought together by the black caucus, the demonstrations, and the legal battle, the group continues to reach out by approaching people at job sites or in union meetings, even putting flyers in women's bathrooms on construction sites. The group is now usually about one-third women, which is far beyond their representation in the industry.

Women and people of color are still a tiny minority of skilled construction trades workers. "Two percent? Five percent? Is it that *high*?" Hawkins asks. But he and Lukaszek have both had long careers as plumbers and as union activists, and they say that having support has made all the difference.

Black Telephone Workers for Justice

by Kim Moody

THE BLACK TELEPHONE WORKERS FOR JUSTICE are a caucus of about 50 dues-paying members within International Brotherhood of Electrical Workers Local 827 at Verizon in New Jersey. They meet regularly, have their own office, put out a regular newsletter, and hold educational forums. The BTWFJ also runs twice-monthly jazz nights and is part of a coalition to fight police brutality in Newark. They take on Verizon management day in and day out, and confront a sluggish union leadership when necessary. Their major campaign since their founding in 2000 has been to make Martin Luther King Day a paid holiday at Verizon.

Born in a Strike

BTWFJ didn't start out big with an office, a newsletter, and a presence in the union. It was born out of the strike at Verizon in August 2000. Some of the company's units negotiate separately, and as a result, the New York-New England unit went back to work three days earlier than the New Jersey unit. This led to some confusion. Some of the New Jersey workers went back to work early—and even crossed picket lines.

Along with a few others, Ron Washington, founder and president of BTWFJ, tried to educate their misinformed brothers and sisters. "We were just a small informal group," says Washington. After the strike they created "Finally Got the 411," the BTWFJ newsletter. They argued the importance of solidarity and called for an organization of black telephone workers. They began to meet at Washington's house. "First meeting we had four, second meeting 12, the next meeting we had 20," says Washington. "Then we had 30, then my house became too small. We moved the meetings to a bar we all frequent."

The second edition of "Finally Got the 411" stated the case for making Martin Luther King Day a paid holiday. "We did a David Letterman," Washington says. "We wrote up the Top Ten Reasons Why We Need a Black Telephone Workers For Justice Organization." "Only as an organized force," the group argued, "can we finally force our unions to make Martin Luther King's birthday an official holiday…deal more effectively with company or union abuse or discrimination…play a more effective role in our union."

Soon the BTWFJ began to do just these things. "Before we had the organization, a lot of black workers thought the union was just a white thing," says Washington. "We began showing up at union meetings and we changed the whole character of those meetings. There used to be maybe four or five black workers at a meeting and now there were 40 or 50. As a result, there was debate and, for the first time, resolutions, putting down on paper what the members decided." One of those resolutions put Unit 4 of Local 827 on record demanding MLK Day as a paid holiday.

IBEW Local 827 is a statewide local divided into six units. BTWFJ is based in Unit 4 in Essex County, including Newark. The workforce in that part of the state is about 50-50 black and white. The idea and reality of an all-black workers' organization inside the union faced serious hostility among white workers. BTWFJ made clear in a leaflet, "We are open to debate and we want debate from all on why we need a Black Telephone Workers Organization." At the same time, they emphasized, "we are not asking anyone's permission."

BTWFJ also emphasized unity between black and white workers. Their Mission Statement stated they would "stand 'shoulder to shoulder' with workers of all nationalities…at home and abroad…against those forces that exploit and seek to divide us." They soon put their words into action.

Taking the Day

BTWFJ targeted MLK Day in January 2001. Traditionally, Verizon had allowed black workers to take the day as one of their personal days. But company policy was that no more than 18 percent of employees in an area could be off on the same day.

BTWFJ began organizing black workers to take the day off. Management said "no way." Urged on by BTWFJ, the black workers insisted on taking the day off—discipline or not. Close to 80 percent of the black workers—almost half the workforce—took the day off, according to Washington. Management did nothing! It was like a one-day strike—clearly a victory, and a boost for BTWFJ. The following year, the black workers were joined by many whites. The difference was, however, that the white workers didn't attend the rallies the BTWFJ held on that day. That's the next task, says Washington.

Soon, the group decided it needed a regular meeting place. Washington says, "You meet one week in this church, next time somewhere else, and no one is sure where the meeting is. You need a regular place." Members found their regular place by luck. One BTWFJ member installed phones at a black Masonic lodge in Newark, which agreed to rent them an office for $500 a month. BTWFJ also got meeting space upstairs and room for the Jazz Club, an addition to their activities, in the lodge's basement bar. The rent is paid by the $10 monthly dues BTWFJ members pay. The weekly telephone workers' card game that meets at the BTWFJ office one night a week also provides regular contributions.

"Finally Got the 411" is distributed regularly by members—and management doesn't like it, although the right to distribute literature in non-work areas on non-work time is well established. Washington and other members who pass out the newsletter still get harassed— and sometimes suspended. Washington knows his rights. "They give me five days off, ten days off, 30 days off. It goes into the grievance procedure and eventually I'll win back pay. If not through the grievance procedure, through the Labor Board."

In any case, he's used his suspensions to leaflet for BTWFJ's main campaign, getting MLK Day as an official holiday. Although Local 827 didn't win MLK Day in the 2003 Verizon contract, BTWFJ is determined to continue pressing the issue.

Although BTWFJ's influence in Local 827 has expanded as more of its members have become stewards, Washington sees room to grow. The group is limited mainly to technicians. It has little presence among Verizon's service reps, who are mostly women, and who are in a different union, the CWA. Washington says, however, that they have started leafleting the service reps and have gotten a good response. Surely, as BTWFJ grows, more workers at Verizon will get the 411.

Where the WILD Women Are

SOMETHING HAPPENS TO WOMEN who attend the Women's Institute for Leadership Development in Boston. They go WILD! The goal of WILD is to train and support women to gain leadership positions in their unions and, in the long run, to change the labor movement so it will address social justice issues as well as pocketbook issues.

Started by a group of women labor activists and educators in 1987, WILD runs an annual three-day, skill-building Summer Institute. WILD-trained volunteers teach the leadership development workshops, and many previous participants come back as teachers, with each workshop taught by one veteran and one new teacher. To make the program accessible to all, it is held at a different Massachusetts college campus each year and scholarships are offered.

"WILD women," as participants call themselves, have helped create women's committees in their unions, a women's network across the state of Massachusetts, and women's networks in various community organizations. Graduates of WILD helped establish a women's committee within the Massachusetts AFL-CIO and have become the heads of central labor councils in the state. A WILD woman went on to become secretary of the state AFL-CIO; another became the first female president of SEIU Local 509.

Custom-Designed Tools

Some women who attend WILD have never been active in their unions, some come as stewards, and others hold leadership positions but want to move higher in order to make more of a difference.

At the beginning of the Summer Institute, participants fill out a questionnaire to assess their current level of involvement and leadership. They answer questions about how often they attend meetings, what role they play in the union, and where they would like to be. They list the skills they think they need to achieve the level of participation they want, such as public speaking, running a successful meeting, or basic labor law. The trainers use the results of these self-assessments to tailor the sessions to match participants' needs.

Participants also fill out a "Women's Leadership Checklist" to evaluate their union's or central labor council's accessibility and inclusion of all workers. The checklist includes questions about where union meetings are held, at what time of day, whether they offer childcare, whether education programs are open to all, whether they are bilingual, and whether the union informs all members about opportunities to attend conferences. The responses help teachers and participants discuss what can be done to remove barriers to women's leadership and participation.

Workshops are run at three levels: for new leaders, for those more experienced, and for current union leadership and staff. At the 2001 summer institute, for instance, level A participants discussed what it means to lead, listed personal leadership goals, and identified tools to help meet those goals. Women at level B chose from one of three discussions: developing contract campaigns, political issue campaigns, or issues affecting tradeswomen. Women at level C ("So You're a Leader, Now What?") discussed with WILD teachers how to organize to change policy in their unions and in the nation. In addition, participants also chose skills workshops, such as Building Effective Committees, Contract Negotiations, and Stewards Training/Effective Grievance Committees.

The Anti-Racism Workshop, which all participants are asked to attend, is an essential part of the education plan. "Part of leadership development," explains former WILD Director Alison Bowens, "is anti-oppression training where we can discuss the 'isms' that can get in the way of working together as women." APWU member Mary Flanagan says that after a momentary feeling of "I'm stuck in a room with hundreds of complete strangers!" the discussions that followed helped her realize how much the women present had in common, despite differences in race, sexuality, union, and experience. "We bring together a diversity of women," Bowens says proudly, "to educate them on how to become sisters and truly support each other."

Sisterhood Brings Sense of Possibility

Of course, conferences around the country feature skills-building workshops and are open to women unionists. What makes the WILD experience so powerful is the way this program, run for and by women, gives its participants a sense of their own leadership potential through the experience of sisterhood.

"When you say 'labor leader' or 'union president,'" Bowens argues, "you often picture someone else, usually a white man. You don't assume it's something you can do." WILD seeks to help participants move away from the idea that leadership is for someone else and shows that it is attainable even to people who initially think "I can't do it."

Mary Flanagan had been a steward in the Boston Metro Area Local of the American Postal Workers Union for 12 years when she first came across WILD. She attended WILD's summer institute in 2000, ran for office the next year, and became the local's director of human relations. "Running for office?" she muses. "Before WILD, I wouldn't have contemplated doing anything like that."

"One of the specific benefits of the WILD program," says Flanagan, "was being exposed to strong union women and realizing just how effective women are, how much we have to offer the labor movement." She describes sitting in a circle of women, some already union leaders, who talked about the difference they were able to make. "As I learned more," she says, "my insecurities seemed to melt away. I had been insecure about public speaking, about volunteering to do things, about taking responsibility. But I realized that the only obstacles I had were put there by myself."

For example, the workshop "Run Sister Run: Exploring Many Roads to Women's Power in the Labor Movement" took Flanagan step by step through the process of running for office. While the workshop was "terrific," Flanagan says that "talking about the process wasn't the most important thing. I could have read a book about the process, but that wouldn't have had the same effect. It was being in that place with those people. By myself, I'm just one person, but when you gather together, you gather strength, just like in the union. When I was in a room filled with women, I felt stronger and more confident.

"After being pushed down day after day at my workplace," she observes, "what a welcome change to be lifted up by my WILD sisters!"

Getting WILD in Your Town

For union women who want to start a group like WILD in their own areas: Bowens recommends that you be aggressive about introducing yourself to other participants at women's meetings or conferences. Ask them in what areas they might like to receive training, and make a list of their responses. Talk to different unions in your area and let them know you are starting a women's education and leadership program. Ask them if you can come to their union meetings. As you begin to make contacts, form an advisory committee of women you've met. Get together and talk: "How can we raise money? Which unions will be supportive? What networks are we connected to already?"

Mary Flanagan has put the lessons she learned at WILD to good use in her local. She says she tries to reach out to new people at every membership meeting, to show that it's not elected officers against members. "I used to feel like nothing," she explains. "The officers were up there. When all the leaders were men, no one reached out to ask members for their input.

"I didn't acquire just skills through WILD," says Flanagan, "I acquired attitude, and that attitude became stronger than the things that kept me from doing what I should have done. It was in me to fight for what's right. I took that to a new level after WILD. WILD changed my personality a little bit!"

Resources

See also Chapter 16 for resources for immigrant workers.
Organizations in this chapter
• Black Telephone Workers for Justice. 883 Sanford Ave., Irvington, NJ 07111, 201-435-3362. Blacktel4justice@aol.com.
• Women's Institute for Leadership Development (WILD). 33 Harrison Ave., 4th floor, Boston, MA 02111. 617-426-0520.
• Women's Law Project. 125 S. 9th St., Suite 300, Philadelphia, PA 19107. 215-928-9801. womenslawproject.org; info@womenslawproject.org.
AFL-CIO Constituency Groups
• A. Philip Randolph Institute. 1444 I St. NW, Suite

300, Washington, DC. 20005. 202-289-2774. www.apri.org.
- Asian Pacific American Labor Alliance. 815 16th St. NW, Washington, DC 20006. 202-974-8051. www.apalanet.org; apala@apalanet.org.
- Coalition of Black Trade Unionists. PO Box 66268, Washington, DC 20035. 202-429-1203. www.cbtu.org. A list of state and local chapters is at www.cbtu.org/2003website/chapters/national.html.
- Coalition of Labor Union Women. 1925 K St. NW, Suite 402, Washington, DC 20006. 202-223-8360. www.cluw.org; info@cluw.org.
- Labor Council for Latin American Advancement. 888 16th St. NW, Suite 640, Washington, DC 20006. 202-347-4223. www.lclaa.org; headquarters@lclaa.org. For a list of local chapters, see www.lclaa.org/Chapters.htm.
- Pride at Work. Seeks equality for lesbian, gay, bisexual, and transgender workers in their workplaces and unions. PAW's newsletter and website offer news, policy statements, and model contract language. 815 16th St. NW, Washington, DC 20006. 202-637-5085. www.prideatwork.org.

Other Organizations
- Black Workers for Justice. One of the first workers centers, organizing in North Carolina and the South. 216 E. Atlantic Ave., PO Box 1863, Rocky Mount, NC 27801. 919-977-8162.
- Center for Third World Organizing. Trains grassroots community and labor organizers of color through the Movement Activist Apprenticeship Program. 1218 E. 21st St., Oakland, CA 94606. 510-533-7583. www.ctwo.org. ctwo@ctwo.org.
- Hard Hatted Women. Support for women in and seeking nontraditional jobs. 3043 Superior Ave., Cleveland, OH 44114. 216-861-6500. www.hardhattedwomen.org. info@hardhattedwomen.org.
- Tradeswomen, Inc., PO Box 882103, San Francisco, CA 94188. www.tradeswomen.org.
- Tradeswomen Now and Tomorrow. Promotes women in the trades and technical fields. Has an online forum and links to local tradeswomen groups at www.TradeswomenNow.org.
- Young Workers United. Improving youth working conditions in the San Francisco Bay Area and beyond. P.O. Box 15866, San Francisco, CA, 94115-5866. 415-621-4155. www.youngworkersunited.org.

Publications
- *ColorLines*. Quarterly magazine of race, culture, and organizing. Applied Research Center, 4096 Piedmont Ave., PMB 319, Oakland, CA 94611. 510-653-3415. Subscriptions: 888-458-8588.
- "Labor Comes Out," edited by Miriam Frank and Desma Holcomb. Issue #8 of *New Labor Forum*, Spring/Summer 2001. To order full print edition call 212-827-0200 or email newlaborforum@qc.edu. $10. Selected articles available online at Qcpages.qc.edu/newlaborforum.
- *The Manual for Survival for Women in Nontraditional Employment,* by the Association for Union Democracy Women's Project and the NOW Legal Defense and Education Fund. 718-564-1114. www.uniondemocracy.org; aud@igc.org. $10.
- *Organize To Improve the Quality of Jobs in the Black Community*, by Steven C. Pitts. A 2004 report on jobs and activism in the African American community. UC Berkeley Center for Labor Research and Education, 2521 Channing Way, #5555, Berkeley, CA 94720. 510-642-0323. Download PDF file from laborcenter.berkeley.edu/blackworkers/index.shtml.
- *Out at Work: Building a Gay-Labor Alliance*, edited by Kitty Krupat and Patrick McCreery. University of Minnesota Press, 2000. 773-702-7000. emp@umn.edu. $19.95.
- *Stopping Sexual Harassment—A Handbook for Union and Workplace Activists*, by Camille Colatosti and Elissa Karg. A Labor Notes book. 313-842-6262. www.labornotes.org. $9.
- "We are Everywhere: How (and Why) to Organize Lesbian and Gay Union Committees," by Miriam Frank. In *America's Working Women: A Documentary History 1600 to the Present*, edited by Rosalyn Baxandall and Linda Gordon. Norton, 1995. 800-233-4830. www.wwnorton.com.

Videos
- *Eyes on the Fries,* by Casey Peek and Jeremy Blasi, 2004. Looks at working conditions for young workers in the American service economy. Comes with an accompanying curriculum guide for educational uses. To order, call Young Workers United at 415-661-4155. 21 minutes.
- *Out at Work*, by Tami Gold and Kelly Anderson. AndersonGold Films, 1997. To order, 718-789-2168 or info@andersongoldfilms.com.
- *Struggles in Steel,* by Ray Henderson and Tony Buba, 1996. 58 minutes. Chronicles the history of discrimination against African Americans in the steel industry, and one campaign where they finally won equality on the job. California Newsreel, Order Dept., PO Box 2284, South Burlington, VT 05407. 877-811-7495. contact@newsreel.org. $195 list price; $49.95 selected organizations; $29.95 home video.

Action Questions

See also Chapter 16, Bringing Immigrants into the Movement.

1. Think about your experience in the workplace. Have you or any of your co-workers experienced or witnessed discriminatory actions or policies on the shop floor? Do certain groups get preferential treatment from management when it comes to raises, promotions, or transfers? Do certain groups get singled out for discipline? Are you or your co-workers the targets of violence or verbal harassment based on your race, gender, sexuality, age, or disability?

2. What mechanism does the employer have to deal with discrimination in the workplace? Does it work? If not, why not?

3. What have you and your co-workers done to bring the discrimination to the attention of the union? Have you spoken with your steward? Spoken at a union meeting? Are there particular stewards or executive board members you should be talking to, because you know they might be sympathetic?

4. What mechanisms does your union have to address discrimination in the workplace? Is there a civil rights committee? Does it function well? Does the international union have a civil-rights department? Can the discrimination be written up as grievances? Would they be more effective as group grievances or if supported by a petition?

5. What are the government agencies with jurisdiction over discrimination complaints for your workplace? Is there a city or state civil rights commission? Do you have recourse to the federal Equal Employment Opportunity Commission? (These agencies should be listed in the phone book and have websites.)

6. If the union cannot end the discrimination, either because its best efforts still do not force management to take action or because the union leadership fails to put its full weight into the attempt, what steps will you need to take, as workers and union members, to develop a voice loud enough to move management and/or your union leaders to take your concerns seriously?

7. If you don't already know, how can you find out whether some of your co-workers are dealing with discrimination? By talking one-on-one during breaks? Calling a lunch meeting or a meeting after work? Putting a letter in the union newsletter? Speaking at the next union meeting to ask people about their experiences? As you gather information, how can you also identify co-workers who are not directly affected by the discrimination but would be sympathetic?

8. Once you've identified affected and sympathetic co-workers, how can you discuss what actions to take? Can you meet at work, at the union hall, or at someone's house or a local restaurant? How would you publicize these meetings? Flyers in the break room? Word of mouth? Speaking at union meetings? Who are some of the natural leaders in your workplace that you should invite to the meetings?

9. What kinds of actions can your group take to get management's attention?

10. If you need to take your campaign beyond the workplace, what community allies should you invite to your planning meetings? Who is already out there doing anti-racist, anti-sexist, anti-homophobic, and other forms of social justice organizing? How can you find out? Is there a local university that lists activist groups? Does your city publish a listing of such groups? What are some national organizations that could have local chapters in your area? (See "Resources" above.)

11. Think about your experience as a union member. Are people of color, women, LGBT people and other groups that often face discrimination well represented among the stewards? On the executive board? On the union staff? On the district or international staff? What groups are underrepresented and why?

12. Have you experienced or witnessed discriminatory actions, practices, or policies within your union? Have you taken these issues to the union leadership? What kind of response did you get? Did the discrimination end?

13. If you are part of a group facing ongoing discrimination in your workplace and/or union, what type of organization would best help you fight back over the long term? A formal caucus to push the union leadership to recognize and act on the concerns of your group? An informal support group? A formal organization to help members of your group get the training necessary to obtain positions of union leadership or fight harassment? Do your union bylaws include a procedure for recognizing a caucus?

14. How are union members and leaders likely to react as you start organizing a caucus? Who will oppose you? Who might be won over? Who will support you from the first? What can you do to neutralize your opponents?

Authors

SHEILA COHEN is a British labor educator and activist, now living in New York, who was founder and editor of an activist newsletter, *Trade Union News*, between 1990 and 1995. Her book on trade unionism in the U.S. and the U.K. will be published in 2005.

MIRIAM FRANK teaches humanities at New York University and women's labor history for Cornell's NYC labor extension. She writes frequently about how unions connect with the movement for lesbian, gay, bisexual, and transgendered rights.

SHEILA MCCLEAR joined the Labor Notes staff in 2004. She covers UNITE HERE, farmworkers, and nurses.

KIM MOODY was a founder and former director of Labor Notes. He is the author of *An Injury to All* and *Workers in a Lean World* and writes frequently on labor issues. He now teaches labor studies and politics in New York City.

RUTH NEEDLEMAN teaches labor studies at Indiana University and is the author of *Black Freedom Fighters in Steel: The Struggle for Democratic Unionism* (Cornell University Press, 2003). Read more about the black Steelworkers in that book.

SARAH RYAN is a former steward and local officer of the Seattle American Postal Workers Union. She teaches labor studies at Evergreen State College in Olympia, Washington and never misses a Labor Notes conference.

PATRICIA SMITH is an attorney and activist from Ann Arbor, Michigan.

N. RENUKA UTHAPPA worked on the Labor Notes staff in 2003-2004, where she covered the UFCW and immigrant workers. She organized Labor Notes' first national conference of workers' centers, in 2003.

6. Saving Good Jobs: Fighting Lean Production and Outsourcing

by Jane Slaughter

REMEMBER the "high-performance workplace of the future"? That buzz-phrase of the 1980s and 1990s promised that technology and employee involvement—along with enlightened management—would lead to better jobs. Lean production, we were told, would let us "work smarter, not harder." We'd be efficient (lean, not "bloated"), and we'd enjoy our jobs more. It would be a "win-win" situation for management and workers.

It was a crock. Workers are working harder now than ever, with longer and odder hours, under the watchful eye of computerized monitoring. For many of us, lean production turned out to mean outsourcing.

These days, management has largely dropped the rhetoric of employee involvement. Employers simply implement their lean production programs top down, with names like Six Sigma or Common Sense Manufacturing. Workers are still sometimes asked to serve on joint union-management committees, however. These committees may be designed to grease the skids for new technology or to restructure job descriptions.

This chapter will deal with both types of situations: where management is unilaterally changing the way work is done (lean production), and where workers, or the union, are being asked to help (joint committees or employee involvement). The unions featured here dealt with most aspects of lean production—job cuts, de-skilling, tight attendance controls, just-in-time schedules, surveillance, and outsourcing (privatization)—as well as with disinvestment. They used joint committees on their own terms, and they used more traditional union tactics ranging from petitions, picket lines, and one-day strikes to overtime bans and messing with surveillance technology.

If these stories have one thing in common, it's that union officials weren't acting on their own; members acted together in the workplace. And often the public was brought into the fray.

To read about a sit-down strike to stop outsourcing, see the story of CAW Local 222 in Chapter 9. For a fight against two-tier wages, see the telephone workers' story in Chapter 5. For a fight against privatization in Canada, read about CUPE Local 1 in Chapter 12.

We'll start here with three sections on dealing with joint programs.

Continuous Bargaining: How To Survive in Joint Labor-Management Programs

by Aaron Brenner

CHARLEY RICHARDSON, from the Labor Extension Program at the University of Massachusetts at Lowell, suggests that unions treat joint programs as an opportunity for "continuous bargaining."

"Joint committees are often a disaster for unions," Richardson says. "Either management has used them to get what they want and put a union rubber-stamp on it, or they have simply been ineffective, making the union look bad. We need to take a very different approach: recognize that any joint committee is in fact a bargaining process. You need to be just as prepared for these as you would be for a contract bargaining session. We cannot sit back during the period of the contract and let changes in technology and work organization wash over us.

"In 1950, you could negotiate a new contract and be relatively assured that there would not be major changes in the work process during the period of the contract. Today, you can be assured that something new will come up: a new computer, a new work process.

"These create huge issues: health and safety, skills monitoring, new systems of control. They're issues of power on the shop floor. All these need to be bargained over. But when it comes up mid-contract, the system doesn't envision full discussion. The system says 'you got a problem, grieve it.' If it's something new, where you don't have contract language, you're screwed. We have the mechanisms to grieve, but not to bargain.

"So a way of having an ongoing discussion with management is critical for unions. This can happen in a joint committee."

Richardson is well aware of the pitfalls of joint committees, of course. Too often, management deals directly with members and ignores the union's sole bargaining rights, inviting workers as individuals to serve on the committees. Since different members respond differently to the appeals of joint programs, this in itself accomplishes part of management's agenda to divide the workforce. Some members want to be involved and make a contribution; others just want to take home a paycheck. Some are optimistic and want to believe the program can benefit workers; others are cynical or have been burned before. Management does not have to win over the whole workforce—if a minority buys in and begins making suggestions for cutting jobs, the union as a whole is undermined (and discord on the shop floor can become intense).

Sometimes union leaders put up with such situations, thereby abdicating their responsibility to represent workers with management. Instead, they need to win members, through education, to a unified way of dealing with the program.

The model Richardson advocates is to "treat every discussion between labor and management as bargaining, no matter whether it is called a team meeting, a problem-solving session, a steering committee meeting, or a kaizen event. The union should insist on being notified about every kind of change in the way work is done, in advance, and insist on discussing the specifics. We call this 'continuous bargaining.'

"I can't emphasize enough that the mindset of bargaining is the critical thing with joint programs. You are sitting on opposite sides of the table as far as the union's interests and management's interests go. You never want to say, 'Here is the cooperating side, in the joint committee, and we'll save our fighting side for contract time.'

"The continuous bargaining framework is built on things we already know how to do at contract time. It's just a question of learning to use them during the contract.

"Ask yourself the question, *'If I were in contract bargaining, would I act this way?* Would I disagree with my fellow committee member in front of management, or would I caucus? Would I walk into a meeting without an agenda, with no demands? Would I work off of company proposals? Would I meet without asking members what they want? Would I start meeting without first mobilizing workers to support me?'"

Educating Members for Continuous Bargaining

To gear members up for continuous bargaining in joint programs, prepare as you would for a contract campaign—but ongoing:

1. Educate members about the joint program and management's goals for it. Inoculate them against the propaganda they will be hearing, taking into account the different initial takes they are likely to have. Reinforce the need to defend their interests collectively.

2. Analyze the union's and management's strengths and weaknesses in the current bargaining environment.

3. Select the union's bargaining representatives—although they may be called something that sounds more "joint," such as "team members"—and train them in union-only sessions.

4. Learn members' concerns using surveys, planning meetings, and one-on-one information gathering.

5. Organize members to be the bargaining reps' eyes and ears on the shop floor, with a continuous flow of information about management's changes to the workplace, including rumors.

6. Organize members to back up the union's position at the table with whatever collective action is necessary.

7. Submit information requests to the company and research its financial status, corporate structure, business plan, and plans for new technology or work restructuring.

8. Prepare positions as a committee and approach management united.

9. Caucus regularly to maintain unity, to develop a common strategy, and to formulate responses to management proposals.

10. Demand that any agreements be written, clear, and enforceable.

Code of Conduct

Once continuous bargaining starts, adopt a code of conduct for participants. Here are Richardson's ten points to start a code of conduct:

No Magic Contract Language

Almost all unions faced with joint programs have negotiated language that they hope will protect members' interests. The language says that joint committees may not discuss contractual issues. But this line in the sand is a mistake. Unavoidably, joint committees will always discuss areas that are or could be covered in the contract. Work flow, new job descriptions, new software that tracks productivity—changes like these affect members' lives on the job.

Rather than trying to draw an unenforceable line, unions should admit that joint committees discuss contract issues—and therefore jump in and take control of those discussions. This is not only smart functioning but the union's duty. Under the National Labor Relations Act, the union is workers' sole collective bargaining agent and any changes in working conditions must be bargained with the union.

Unions have relied on other sorts of language, too, to protect them in joint programs: that the union can appoint 50 percent of any committee, or that the program cannot result in any layoffs. This language does not work either. See the Resources at the end of this chapter for the reasons why.

One piece of language is important, however: management should agree to fund training for committee members in a union-only setting. Ideally, they would get five days of paid training time. Make sure that the union trainer does not have a partnership mind-set (ask for references). In Muscatine, Iowa, for example, IBEW Local 109 negotiated that any members going into the joint process had to go through a union-only class, to build solidarity and become aware of the dangers.

In addition, negotiate time for the union's committee members to meet without management present. If you can't get paid time, meet on your own time, with union leaders or the affected rank-and-filers, as necessary.

1. Never go into any discussion alone. Collective participation builds the presence of the union, demonstrates unity, and provides more union brainpower to come up with ideas and evaluate actions.

2. When in joint meetings, stick to the union agenda and act together. If you are not sure what the union agenda is or how to respond to something that management says, call a caucus or wait until the next break. Caucus early and caucus often.

3. When in caucus, talk about all your concerns, no matter whether you think you have a minority view. Never ignore your gut feelings—if something makes you nervous, figure out why. While it is important to work together in meetings with management, it is equally important that any disagreements be aired in caucus. This is the only way to build unity of action.

4. Evaluate all proposals and ideas for their short- and long-term impact on the members and on the union. This takes more time than simply looking at "how it affects workers today," but it is critical to avoiding a long-term disaster. A single person can rarely do a good evaluation; it needs many different points of view to be thorough.

5. Report to the appropriate union structures on all discussions, meetings, and teams. Union leaders and members cannot act in unity if they don't know what is happening.

6. Don't keep secrets with management. Reject management attempts to keep discussions within the committee. Full and open discussion with other members is the only way to keep things on a union track.

7. No involvement, direct or indirect, in disciplining other members. The same goes for peer pressure on issues such as attendance that are essentially the company's concern. Such actions will only create divisions within the union without solving the seeming problem.

8. Always think unity with other union members, within and outside the committees. Always think about how to build the union's independence within the program.

9. Take good notes. This allows the union to coordinate across committees, to keep track of management's activities, and to have a paper trail in case the union needs to use its legal rights.

10. Do not give away information that could be used to undermine skills or eliminate jobs.

Your version of this code should be posted around the workplace and the union hall so that everyone knows what is expected.

UPS Workers Not on Big Brown's Team

by Mike Parker

THE TEAMSTERS' REMARKABLE VICTORY AT UPS in the summer of 1997 lifted the spirits of every union activist. (See Chapter 9, Strikes.) That victory was the result of long-term efforts to build rank-and-file unity and to fight management's overwhelming thought-control campaign.

One key was a union campaign against the "team concept" in 1995 and 1996.

Rand Wilson, who worked in the Teamsters' Communications Department at the time, says, "The team concept campaign foreshadowed the contract campaign. UPS geared up its team concept activity as its preparation for the contract, and by necessity we had to take them on as part of our preparation."

Ever notice what a hurry your UPS driver always seems to be in? UPS has a long history of understanding that speeding up the work requires a battle for hearts and minds. UPS pioneered in training its supervisors to "chart" the workplace, identifying the natural leaders, and working to co-opt or eliminate them. The company had maintained long-running involvement programs designed to keep its finger on the pulse of the workforce and encourage management-wannabes to demonstrate their pro-company attitudes.

The Teamsters distributed these stickers to UPS members to show management that they didn't buy the company's talk about "teamwork" while it was violating the contract.

When UPS stepped up its team concept push, the union had an advantage: the existence of a rank-and-file network within UPS. The reform movement Teamsters for a Democratic Union (TDU) had been particularly strong at UPS since the 1970s. Throughout the campaign, these rank and filers and local officers worked together with the International.

The International's Education Department developed materials, including a 15-minute video, on the UPS team programs and did a series of regional workshops for business agents, stewards, and rank and filers. The International encouraged every steward to share the video with members. "Our campaign focused on trust," says John Braxton, a former UPS worker then on the department staff. "Management kept saying that we would work better with 'trust.' And we kept pointing out that 'actions speak louder than words' (the video's title).

"How can you trust management that unilaterally increases weight limits from 70 to 150 pounds? How can you trust management that campaigns in Washington against our health and safety? How can you trust management that claims to respect workers, but refuses to negotiate the 'team' programs with the worker's organization—the union? Had we not pressed this believability and trust issue, more workers might have believed management's claim of 'last, best, and final offer' just before the strike."

Local Initiatives

The ground battle took different shapes at different worksites.

• When the company set up a trailer for team meetings at a UPS center near Modesto, California, activists responded quickly by ordering *Labor Notes* and TDU materials (via UPS overnight). The activists had sufficient numbers to counter management in each team. In one team, a union member got up and declared himself "team-leader-for-life," and all the other members bowed down before him. In six weeks management threw in the towel and declared the programs over.

• At the Madison Heights, Michigan center, activists used the meetings to shift the agenda. "When the company would try to get us to talk about costs, we talked about the cost of living and wages for part-timers. When they would talk about productivity, we would discuss health and safety," explains TDUer Dave Staiger.

The company also appointed team leaders for the various work lines at Madison Heights. Under union pressure the team leader job was changed to a seniority bid. A few people saw these jobs as a steppingstone to management, but others took them because they believed it was better that they be held by a pro-union person.

"Management hoped these team leaders would be the scab leaders for the upcoming contract," Staiger says. "But our agitation in the teams had helped sensitize them to the union issues. During the pre-strike contract campaign we asked many team leaders to be the union contract campaign coordinators—which made sense since they were often the natural leaders of the work groups."

When these team leaders actively promoted the union campaign and were solid during the strike, "I'm sure the company was disappointed," Staiger notes. After the strike the company abolished the team leader positions.

• At the Redmond, Washington, center, says steward John Misich, UPS avoided the team language, referring instead to "business reassessment," "one-step-at-a-time," and "clean sheet"—subtly suggesting that the contract could be ignored. But the topics brought up were clearly bargaining issues: incentive pay, workers screening new hires, and Teamsters auditing fellow Teamsters for mistakes.

"The company blitzed us with meetings—weekly and sometimes twice weekly—and they tried to manipulate us," says Misich. The company would appoint the note-takers, to control the interpretation of meetings. If management raised an issue that workers strongly opposed, the agenda for the next meeting would include it as "old business" for further action.

Misich filed a grievance when the company refused to pay him as a steward to attend every meeting, since contractual issues were always discussed. Members circulated a petition to back the grievance, saying they wanted union representation.

Of course, management itself taught some people a lot about the company. One member worked hard to design a new delivery route, believing it would remove some of the work overload. Then the company used the route without posting it for bidding. After six months, attendance at the voluntary meetings dropped to a trickle, and that mainly for the easy overtime pay.

• In San Antonio, meetings started out pleasantly: an hour of overtime and free breakfast. The local put out a newsletter called the *Brown Dog News,* poking fun and hitting hard at every company action that contradicted its claims of teamwork. Workers stopped attending the meetings.

• In Cleveland, clerks collectively decided to ignore a bid posting for a team-leader position with a wage increase.

• In Iowa, some activists took up a petition to cancel the programs.

• In Milwaukee, workers wore t-shirts that said, "I am already on a team—the Teamsters."

When it came time for national contract talks, International bargainers totally rejected a contract proposal that endorsed management's right to set up quality teams. In early 1998 UPS agreed in writing to terminate the program altogether.

Misich sums up the union's two campaigns: "'Empowerment' is their buzzword. What we learned from their team concept and our strike is that our union is our empowerment."

Nurses Fight De-skilling

by Nick Robinson

AT RHODE ISLAND HOSPITAL, one of the largest in the Northeast, de-skilling was the primary issue in a nurses' organizing drive. The hospital had hired a consulting firm called Advanced Practice Management to redesign nurses' jobs. "They were notorious in health care circles," recalls Rick Brooks, staff representative for the 1,900 members of an independent union called United Nurses and Allied Professionals (UNAP) at the hospital.

"We banged away at the fact that they had hired this expensive consultant to redesign the nursing model who had never spoken to staff," Brooks recalls. "We said, 'If you want the redesign to work, you need to involve us. We do the work and we know what works and right and wrong ways to improve it.' So we shamed the hospital into setting up this joint committee." UNAP won the organizing drive, and the joint committees were incorporated into the first union contract.

"We pushed our way onto committees," says Linda McDonald, an intensive care nurse and president of UNAP Local 5096. "On some committees, there were one or two union members in a sea of management. Having a single member on a committee can be more dangerous than having none at all. We did trainings on how to take down whatever information you see, to put forward your own agenda, to not become one with management."

UNAP leaders saw that they could use the hospital's rhetoric about patient welfare for their own purposes. "The health care industry is much more sensitive to rhetoric," Brooks explains. "It's not just 'We need to cut costs.' They have to package their initiatives in terms of patient care, and naturally we also care about quality and good patient care. So everyone gets in the same room to talk about quality. We used that process to get information and smoke out what they were doing.

"The big threat was to create a new unlicensed 'patient-care technician' position, who would be minimally skilled and trained with some duties of RNs while paid less. First they do an analysis of every little task nurses perform. Then they divide those tasks into those you 'truly need to be an RN' vs. 'menial' tasks, and they try to appeal to the nurses' professionalism. They ignore that 'menial' tasks like washing and feeding patients are crucial to holistic care. Feeding is also an opportunity to assess, which is critical to prevention. Nurses need to be at the bedside. In any case, their goal is fewer nurses, and more workers with less skills, who are paid less."

Using proposed job descriptions obtained through the committees, UNAP organized nurses around issues of professionalism and patient care, both inside and outside the hospital.

"Every piece of paper we could get our hands on, we viewed it—information on spending timelines, staff ratio planning," says McDonald. "Then we communicated this to members. Most of these requests were informal—we kept our ears to the ground to figure out what was being discussed at the top levels."

UNAP distributed information internally using flyers, newsletters, and open forums with nationally recognized nursing experts. A membership survey found that the vast majority of nurses viewed the patient-care technician plan as a threat, detrimental to patient care, and unnecessary.

The union made its internal leafleting very visible, and members wore stickers and buttons that said, "I am *licensed* to practice." "The leaflets are seen by everybody, not just members but other workers, patients, and their families," says Brooks. "They're half-sheets, brightly colored, big graphics. Nurses got support from patients—they're very concerned when they see a leaflet that tells them the administration's policies could endanger their safety. It really put the hospital on the defensive." Worried patients even wrote letters to hospital administration about the work redesign. "They had a major credibility problem with our members and the public," says McDonald.

Pressure increased as UNAP held a coalition-building meeting with representatives from throughout the nursing community, including Rhode Island's four schools of nursing, the state nursing association, other nurses locals, and even some RN legislators. "We said it was a threat to patient care, a threat to professional standards," says McDonald. "We held a follow-up meeting and invited the hospital's chief nursing officer to come and account to the group of nurse leaders. She actually showed up, and we told her she was undermining the profession of nursing."

"We got the Department of Health to back the hospital off on some of their plans," says Brooks. "We gave them information on what the hospital was up to, met with representatives, and explained why it was unsafe and a violation of state regulations. They ultimately agreed with us, and sent a letter to the hospital saying they viewed the plan to be potentially in violation."

"We made it clear that the hospital wanted the redesign to save money at the expense of patient care," McDonald concludes.

Eventually, the hospital dropped the plan and introduced a licensed Certified Nursing Assistant position instead.

Committees a 'Mixed Bag'

UNAP sees members' work in the joint committees as an extension of its essentially adversarial role toward management. "Committees are a mixed bag," says Brooks. "Sometimes they can be an exercise in frustration, or a vehicle for change. From our perspective, despite some pitfalls we'd rather be in the mix, as long as it means making progress. When it ceases to be that, we're very comfortable renewing our battles and resuming our previous role."

"There is good collaboration now because we have a healthy respect from management: they know how far we will go to maintain jobs," says McDonald. "We make a constant effort to participate in all the issues, not just the traditional union issues of wages and benefits. But you need constant coordination with the rank and file to know what issues to discuss in committee."

"Our goal is to have influence over every aspect over business," says Brooks, "including those things traditionally viewed as management's rights. If we don't, we cede the territory. These committees bring up questions of how work is organized, how technology is introduced—we have to get involved in that stuff."

★ ★ ★

Up till now, we've dealt with joint programs. The rest of this chapter will deal with situations where management is acting unilaterally, introducing lean production practices without bothering to talk to the union. The final story will return to the use of joint committees to save jobs.

Asking the Right Questions: How to Submit Information Requests

by Charley Richardson

YOU SIGN A NEW CONTRACT and breathe a sigh of relief. Maybe the big issues are settled for a couple of years. But before you know it, management is bringing in new technologies, starting a "work restructuring" program, and handing down new absenteeism, discipline, and drug testing policies. Health and safety, skills, advancement, and seniority are all affected. Unity, number of members, and control over critical skills—all sources of union strength—are at risk.

You know the grievance procedure won't be much help, and management is quoting the management rights clause. What can you do?

According to the NLRB, the union has the right to bargain over any change in *wages, hours, and conditions of employment* unless there is a "clear and unmistakable" waiver of that right in the contract. General management rights clauses do not meet that test. Even where management has the right to make a change (such as implementing a new technology), the union has the right to bargain over the impact of that change. But these rights exist only if the union takes action and demands bargaining.

A key piece of the right to bargain is the right to information. Submitting a formal information request to management can:

• Start the bargaining process and create a paper trail for later use
• Get more information about management's plans
• Make it clear to management that the union is not going to sit idly by
• Help to educate the membership

Most important, an information request can slow down implementation and give the union a chance to develop a strategy. Several locals have been able to stop random drug testing by asking a series of questions that management didn't want to, or wasn't able to, answer.

Preparing an Information Request

Make it a group process. Map out what you already know and then brainstorm a list of all the things you would like to know. Once you have a good list, decide which questions you want to ask now and which ones you might hold off for a second round. This approach will make sure the questions speak to your members' concerns and will create a group that can develop and carry out a bargaining strategy.

"We believe you represent the *future* of this company. That's why we're eliminating your job."

Some things to remember:

• **Ask, always ask!** Information requests should become a regular part of what we do, every time management makes a change.

• **Push the envelope.** While the NLRB requires that requested information be relevant to the bargaining process, the burden is on the company to prove otherwise. Asking one question that "goes too far" doesn't undercut the validity of your other questions.

• **Ask for specifics.** General questions can be answered generally–and you may be left without the information you need.

• **Ask questions even if you already know the answers.** It can be important to get the information directly from management, and to check on the information they are giving you.

• **Ask questions that are reasonable.** If the company doesn't give you answers, you can pass out copies of your request to members with the heading "What is management hiding?"

• **Be ready to ask follow-up questions.** Each piece of information should trigger more questions about what their plans are.

• **Ask for supporting documentation, reports, or studies.** Do this when management cites data or refers to reports that have been done.

What To Ask

Any relevant question is a good one. Say management is introducing a new time-keeping system where you place your hand on a sensor for identification. You could ask about hygiene and privacy: How will the company guard against the spread of disease? How will it ensure the security of the biometric data? What studies have been done to test the effectiveness of those plans?

If management is installing a computer system that can be used to monitor members, ask: What data does the system collect at this point and what could be collected in the future? What data is stored, where, and for how long? Who will have access to it? Are there protections against data being altered after the fact?

If management is planning a work-restructuring program, ask about any consultants they have hired. Ask for a description of the firm, any reports they have written, and a list of other facilities where they have worked.

And always ask about anticipated impact. Ask for a list of all jobs (both inside and outside the bargaining unit) that have been or will be created by this system. What changes in assignments, work processes, or job descriptions are anticipated? How will pace of work be affected? What plans are there to increase wages to match any increases in productivity and/or the intensity of work? How will the program affect stress-related illness, ergonomic injuries, or chemical exposures?

Fighting Surveillance

In the mid-nineteenth century the great American essayist Ralph Waldo Emerson wrote, "Things are in the saddle and ride mankind." Ever since Frederick W. Taylor invented time-study in the 1880s and called it Scientific Management, employers have been cooking up surveillance methods to make people work harder.

One example is global positioning systems that tell truck drivers' locations at any moment. Another is a device that measures the up-time of a worker's machine. Workers have found that such measuring devices can be fixed, fooled, or fouled up. Here Bil Musgrave of United Mine Workers Local 1189 tells how miners defeated a time-study at a Peabody Coal surface mine in southern Indiana. Musgrave worked on a land reclamation operation that used big earth-moving machines, called "pans," to move topsoil.

"The company had a five-year plan to break the union," Musgrave says. Part of that plan was to bolt a motion sensor to the pans. "We came to work one day," he says, "and found these round clocks with a paper graph inside, ticking on our machines. We asked the foreman what they were, and he said, 'Those are time-and-motion machines,' like he was Mister Wizard. 'Damn, hope they don't blow up, or we might wake up in the 1800s,' was our reaction.

"The way they worked was if the pan would sit still for more than three minutes, it would show up on the graph. They would have a print-out for each operator, and there was a spread in the print-outs of 15-20 percent. The foreman would say, 'Joe, you've got 74 percent out of this 100 percent run. That's not right. You don't have the machine performing up to its capabilities.'

"Once I started thinking about it, no wonder the percentages were low. We worked 7¼ hours with a half-hour paid lunch. So a half-hour for lunch is almost 5 percent right there. And you have 15 minutes at the beginning of the shift where you check your machine, and at the end of the shift you fuel up and clean the windows. So you're already losing an hour's run time no matter what.

Meeting To Plot

"We had a meeting of all the operators, and after that there were several things we started doing. All you had to do was move the steering wheel and it would show as machine movement on the graph. So we would make sure the steering wheel moved every three minutes. If you got out to get a drink of water, you'd shake the wheel before you got out. This increased the run times automatically.

"Now, the steering wheel is about eight foot off the ground. I hung a rag on mine, and when I was stopped for any reason I'd be sure to yank on the wheel every three minutes. And everybody else started doing that too. Next thing you know our times started getting real close together.

"We had a lunch facility that would hold six people. The first pan would come in and park. Then when the second one would come in, he'd bump the bumper on the first pan, and that would show as movement. Then the third guy would bump the next two, and so on. The graphs didn't even show we were stopping to eat lunch.

"The foreman didn't know what we were doing, but he was happy because the higher-ups were off his butt.

"One day we decided that for a week we would all be out at the machines a minute before starting time. We'd get in, shake the wheel, check the oil, shake the wheel, do the inspection, shake the wheel.

"At the end of the day, you'd wash your windows, shake the wheel, fill up, and shake the wheel. So the graph showed over 100 percent.

"Management said that was impossible, and decided the hell with it."

Management is getting sneakier, and by now, a few years further along, some surveillance technology can defeat these relatively simple tactics. The bottom line, though, is the same: you need information about how the technology works, particularly its weak spots. Where will you get it? You need to find the people in your workplace who know, and you need to make sure that they are part of your bargaining unit. The growth of surveillance technology and speed-up technologies points up the importance of organizing highly skilled workers.

★ ★ ★

A fundamental component of lean production is contracting out, which, in the public sector, means privatization—turning over public work to private contractors. In the next two sections, public employees' unions used the gamut of tactics to stop officials from privatizing their work—and to save essential public services. In the third, factory workers campaigned against both contracting out and absentee control—another key aspect of lean production—along with disinvestment. In each case, key was maximum rank-and-file involvement in planning the campaigns. In all three locals, public and private, workers appealed successfully to the public. Still another anti-privatization story is in Chapter 12 ("Sparks Fly").

New Jersey State Workers Fight Privatization

by Dan La Botz and Jane Slaughter

"WE FOUGHT A SEVEN-MONTH STRUGGLE to stop the privatization of the Department of Motor Vehicles (DMV) in 1995," says Hetty Rosenstein, president of CWA Local 1037. "We had a war here in New Jersey. We were not successful at first, but we totally discredited and obliterated [Governor Christy] Whitman on the issue."

Local 1037 represents 7,500 state workers in 13 northern New Jersey counties. "There wasn't anything we didn't do," says Rosenstein. "We stalked this woman, for lack of a better term, for many months. Workers followed Christy Whitman everywhere she went to try to expose what she was doing to 350 low-paid women workers.

"For example, she went on a trade mission to Canada. So we sent up five workers in a van, with 200 of our union hats. We met with Ontario public sector workers who were facing privatization, and they came out for us. We handed out our hats and surrounded her.

"Then when she went to Toronto, we got members of Nurses United, CWA Local 1168 from Buffalo, to send up a van. Every time she got interviewed in Canada, instead of asking about her trade plans, the reporters would ask her about the DMV—because we were following her everywhere she went.

"Then she went down to Vermont for the annual governors conference, and we sent another van full of people up to Vermont and followed her. She hid from us, she didn't come out, she stayed in her hotel.

"There was a governors' dinner at a restaurant on an island in Lake Champlain, totally away from any people. So we rented a plane and had it pull a banner that said 'Christy Whitman Equals Patronage and Privatization.' The plane flew around the dinner for an hour."

Stewards Meet Weekly

The daily anti-Whitman activity was planned by meetings of the 40 DMV stewards, held every two weeks and then weekly. But it was supported by all the locals' stewards, who knew each other because of the local's regular regional stewards meetings and annual stewards conference.

"Everybody was in on it," says Rosenstein. "The other 200 shop stewards were all completely obsessed and involved too. State workers hated Christy Whitman so much that we would get phone calls all the time. A steward at Stokes State Forest calls up: 'Whitman's going to be here tomorrow looking at the hawks, gotta get 'er.' So she's on Sunrise Mountain looking at the hawks, getting a photo op, and this plane goes by with the banner: 'Christy Whitman Equals Patronage and Privatization.' And it comes out in the Suffolk County boonies newspaper.

"There was not a day that passed that we wouldn't get her."

DMV workers regularly picketed outside their offices during lunchtime and breaks, sometimes weekly and sometimes daily. They leafleted the public and asked for their support, and they got it. The workers argued that privatization would save money only by cutting services, and ended up convincing everyone but Whitman. "Some newspapers editorialized three times," says Rosenstein. "Everybody knew it was pure patronage. Even the Republicans didn't want to do it."

One-Day Strikes

Three times, workers pulled illegal one-day strikes planned by the stewards. The first strike took place the day the legislature was holding hearings on the budget—which would or would not include the DMV. Workers gathered outside the DMV offices and took vans and buses to the hearings, where they picketed outside. For the second walkout, workers went to the state capitol. "We planned to hold a strike vote," says Rosenstein, "and the Whitman administration was trying to enjoin us—they said that even holding the vote was illegal. So the DMV workers went to the Statehouse in Trenton and held the vote right in front. We had a big picture of a pig feasting at the public trough, which represented the privatized patronage system.

"Workers were scared of what might happen to them, but they knew that if we didn't stop privatization they would be laid off. Most of what the stewards had to do was convince people that we could win and it was worth the fight.

"The one repercussion was that they got an injunction against us: any worker who walked out again would get a $300 fine and I would get a $10,000 fine. But they walked out one more time anyway—in defiance of the injunction. That time they did it in the middle of the day, with hundreds of customers on line. We just shut them down in the middle of the day. The state brought us to court, but we didn't get fined."

Later, hundreds of workers held a candlelight vigil outside the Statehouse and police, fearing they would rush the building, locked the doors. "Whitman thought we were crazy," says Rosenstein. "They couldn't believe what we would do."

Still later, two DMV workers held a hunger strike for two weeks in front of the Statehouse. "We rented a camper," says Rosenstein, "and had a banner: 'The Vigil of Conscience.' They lived right in front of the Statehouse for two weeks.

"The public was with us. We worked hard at educating people about the issue. We had met with editorial boards. We had radio spots out. We had dozens of letters to the editor that workers wrote. By the time we were done, the public knew that Whitman was a wealthy woman who was putting working women out on the street to give away patronage jobs."

In the end, the campaign won the battle of public opinion and convinced the legislators: they voted to keep the DMV. But Whitman used a line-item veto to get rid of it.

Although they had lost for the time being, the DMV workers did not end their campaign against the evils of privatization. When officials began interviewing for private parties to take over the DMV agencies, workers took down the interviewees' license plate numbers in the parking lots. "While the interview was still going on," says Rosenstein, "someone would run over to the county and find out their voter registration. Instantly, we were putting out to the press, 'here's who they're interviewing, and they're all Republicans.'

"Then later when [Democrat James] McGreevey ran for governor and asked for our support, we said, well, we want our DMVs back. He won in 2001, and he *un*privatized the DMV agencies and brought 350 DMV workers back into state service and back into the union."

The local then negotiated for a re-employment list of all workers who had been laid off from the DMV. As vacancies came up, those workers were offered jobs and received their full seniority.

Two Hospital Unions Join To Stop Privatization

PRIVATIZATION CAN MEAN selling publicly-owned assets to private entities or contracting out public services to profit-making corporations. As in the private sector, the process is often pushed along by high-priced consultants, hired guns who specialize in telling management how to slash and burn.

Using an impressive array of strategies, nurses and service workers at the University of Illinois Medical Center at Chicago (UIMCC) stopped administrators from merging with a non-union for-profit hospital, stopped them from privatizing an outpatient clinic, and kept them from contracting out housekeeping work to a low-wage non-union firm. They also sent packing some hated job-cutting consultants and forced the resignation of a whole bargaining team of anti-union administrators. Their campaign resulted in top university officials bringing in a CEO who was known for his ability to work with unions. Since that time, nurses' jobs at the hospital have increased in both quality and quantity, and more housekeepers have been hired.

UIMCC exists both to provide medical care to Illinois residents and to train the medical workers of the future; it is a "teaching hospital." In 1999 administrators floated the idea of merging with two other public hospitals in the area, plus privately owned Rush Presbyterian.

Rodney Telomen, a critical-care nurse at UIMCC, says, "If the administrators had gotten their way, the in-patient part of our hospital would have closed altogether. All departments that seemed profitable would have gone to Rush, and all the rest to Cook County Hospital. A few hundred nurses would have lost their jobs. Rush is non-union, so the nurses' ability to advocate for patients and themselves would have been lost."

Telomen is co-chair of the 900-member Illinois Nurses Association local at UIMCC. He sees himself, though, not just as an advocate for nurses but "as a citizen of this state. The county doesn't have the three-pronged mission that the University has," he explains, "to educate multiple levels of health care providers—physicians, nurses, dieticians, physical therapists, occupational therapists. Teaching and research is what would have been lost. The level of health care we can provide is never adequate, research needs to continue.

"It was clear to me that a small group of people were trying to gain private profit at the public's expense by harming or destroying the Medical Center, and that they were pursuing their plan in secret. I could not watch quasi-legal modern robber barons steal this invaluable asset without the informed consent of its owners, the people of Illinois."

At the same time they were pursuing the merger, UIMCC officials were also trying a piecemeal approach to privatization. They planned to contract out housekeepers' jobs and to privatize a new outpatient clinic that had been built with state funds. SEIU Local 73 housekeepers working under the state civil service would have been replaced by a private cleaning service paying $7-$10 an hour.

Putting Unity on the Table

The INA nurses and the SEIU stewards council at the hospital joined forces to stop the merger and the privatizations. SEIU represents the housekeepers, LPNs, clerks, and med techs, and relations had not always been friendly. "There had developed a culture of snobbishness on the part of some," says Telomen. "Some nurses were downright rude to housekeepers and clerks, and the leadership of INA hadn't done anything about it. As I got into leadership, I thought rude behavior was unjustified, and from a selfish point of view, I realized we all had to work together if we were going to save the Medical Center."

Joe Iosbaker, chief steward for the clerical workers, says, "There is a natural pecking order in hospitals, and we had to get that on the table. We held a meeting between stewards council leadership and our business rep and the officers and business rep of the INA. What came out of that meeting was two things: one, nurses expressed their desire to fight against the privatization schemes and to support Local 73. And two, when the housekeepers complained about nurses that were particularly hard on them, it turned out that every nurse that the housekeepers complained about was either not in the bargaining unit or were people that the leaders of INA themselves said, 'they give us a hard time too.' It lanced the boil."

"To begin with there were hurt feelings and anger," Telomen says. "Some nurses who hadn't realized their behavior was hurting other people were facing recognition of that, and apologizing. Certain standards needed to be maintained in the way patient rooms were kept up, but nurses could ask for that in a way that was not hurtful to the housekeeper. And nurses sometimes had legitimate

The Illinois Nurses Association and the SEIU were able to stop the University of Illinois Medical Center at Chicago from merging with a non-union, for-profit hospital, from privatizing an outpatient clinic, and from contracting out housekeeping work.

grievances. I think the clerks and housekeepers realized that sometimes if a nurse is asking for something in a rude way it's because she has no time; she's taking care of a patient and something has to be done right now.

"Anyway, there was an increase in understanding of each other's positions and a commitment to do better."

Educating Themselves and the Public

The campaign began in the usual way: education. Starting with their own members, the unions went on to educate the citizens of Illinois, the media, and the legislature—not to mention hospital administrators. "We started putting out information both verbally and in union newsletters and flyers, and we held many membership meetings, and often," says Telomen. "Instead of trying to get huge turnouts at a few meetings, we would hold frequent meetings in various locations at different times of day and night.

"We gave the members information on the plan to merge/close/privatize, and we began to learn to articulate what was wrong with this plan. We brought in the moral angle—why is it wrong? Some people don't think it's wrong to allocate health care resources based on ability to pay. But most nurses believe people who need health care should be able to get it.

"In the membership meetings, our plans developed on how to get the word out. We were writing news releases, doing interviews. Joe got some of us on radio talk shows." Says Iosbaker, "The media wanted to cover us because we were engaged in a fight."

"One of our strongest motivators, later in the struggle," says Telomen, "was what management did to cancer patients. They told patients who had begun chemotherapy that nobody could continue who couldn't pay for it. Patients would show up and would be told 'you can't have your chemo.' At that point we got more empathetic treatment from people in the news media. We got patients' relatives to come to our rallies outside the Medical Center."

The unions held multiple picket lines and rallies. They also filed unfair labor practice charges with the Illinois Education Labor Relations Board and sought to talk to hospital administrators, the board of trustees, the Civil Service Merit Board, and other decision-makers. They were rebuffed.

The unions rented vans to drive to board meetings in Urbana, 135 miles away, where they picketed and chanted outside the meetings. To build these events, they would hold sign-making parties, with families invited. "Children were good at sign-making," Telomen remembers. And the trips themselves helped to build unity. "SEIU would go with us. We talked the whole way."

The unions kept up a steady stream of meetings, picket lines, leaflets, and rallies. "One thing we did as a way of keeping ourselves in front of management," Iosbaker remembers, "is lunch-hour meetings in the hospital cafeteria. It's filled with nurses, doctors, administration, patients and students and workers, and we'd get 35-40-50 workers, pull together 10 or 12 tables, and talk openly about what was happening in the hospital and the fears people had. Everyone could hear what was going on.

"We held demos at least every four to six weeks from summer of '99 right through the coldest weather, and culminated with a demonstration in April 2000 with over 300 people."

Allies

While applying this very public pressure, Telomen was also looking for influential allies at the top. "I got sneaky," he says. "I started searching for who was on the board of trustees. The university has campuses all over the state, all under a single board. And the University Medical Center is not their major focus. There was nobody on the board of trustees that was an expert in management of this valuable state resource. We assessed each member of the board individually, and we determined that we did not have a friend.

"So I started looking around for somebody else who would be influential, and I found a head of a department at the Medical Center—a well-respected physician. He had been courted by the group of administrators trying to turn the Medical Center into a profit-driven hospital. They recognized his influence. So I showed him some memos. They showed how this group was trying to manage him, what they were saying about him in meetings.

"Yes, I did some things to get those memos. I had been given access to an office for a different purpose, and I went through some records I did not have permission for. I took them out and made photocopies, and put them back.

"I had worked with this physician before, and he had liked how I managed patients for him. Where he parted company with the others was when they said they would no longer treat patients without the ability to pay. I brought evidence, and he got on board to save the Medical Center. There was a physician on the board of trustees who wouldn't listen to anyone else until we got this physician to talk to him."

Hospital administrators finally backed down on both the merger plan and the privatization. Joe Iosbaker remembers, "The *Chicago Tribune* ran an editorial that said 'No Urge to Merge.' That editorial said that Rush looked down the street at the two heavily unionized hospitals—and lost interest. But there was nothing going on at Cook County by way of protest—it was us."

Booting the Hunter Group

Meanwhile, the unions were also dealing with the infamous Hunter Group, known for downsizing hospital staffs around the country. Management had called in these Florida-based consultants, in Telomen's words, "to show that the Medical Center was a drain and was not making money."

The activists got on the Internet and used their contacts with health care workers in other cities. "We did research into what they had done in San Francisco, where a stupid merger had to be reversed after a year or two," says Iosbaker. "Fortunately for us," says Telomen, "but unfortunately for the other people, they had already destroyed enough health care facilities—all we had to do was read. People in other areas mailed us information, people in the University of California system, in Detroit." Telomen knew nurses elsewhere from attending the American Nurses Association's annual collective bargaining conferences. "You make friends in other states," he says. "You're on the phone or writing or emailing.

"The key for us was to convince people here that the Hunter Group was evil. Every place the Hunter Group has been, they've wreaked their shortsighted 'we can improve your books for two years but afterwards you're destroyed.'

"And they are expensive—they will have a contract for $1 million or $3 million. 'I live in Florida so you have to pay for my first class airline ticket twice a week.'" The unions publicized the Hunter Group's hotel bills, expensive meals, and gifts for administrators in a barrage of leaflets and newsletters.

The Hunter Group's "study" of UIMCC was actually the same template recommendation that they made at every hospital. It said that UIMCC needed to cut jobs by ten percent and to maximize privatization and contracting out. "Bringing in the Hunter Group was the stupidest thing management ever did," says Iosbaker. "It was no longer just the nurses and service workers—everyone hated them."

The hospital administration had long held "open house" informational meetings for employees, open to anyone who wanted to come. Once the Hunter Group had been given a contract to run the hospital for a year, the unions turned out their members to these meetings and supplied them with information so they could ask hard questions. "Some of those meetings became quite contentious," Iosbaker says with satisfaction. "Sometimes they became so contentious that they would adjourn them. Again and again we used those meetings to frustrate their plans."

Use the Enemy's Mistakes

The UIMCC unions followed one of the primary rules of combat strategy: to use the enemy's own mistakes—and arrogance—against him. "The Hunter Group leadership are so cowboyish that they shot themselves in the foot," says Iosbaker. "David Hunter, when he was interviewed by the *Tribune*, was asked what message they were bringing to the hospital administrators. And his answer was: 'They have to eat what they kill.'

"Now, that was shocking to the Medical Center staff. Hunter meant, 'you can't just sit back and depend on state handouts, you have to make your own money.' But the week before, someone had died in one of our clinics, and immediately what Hunter said was spreading through the hospital. It was absurdly macho. Of course, in reality it's the workers who are eaten.

"So picture this open house meeting right after they'd just said 'you eat what you kill.' The room is packed with 150 to 200 nurses, doctors, administrators, and workers, and David Coats, the Hunter Group's acting head of the Medical Center, is at the front of the room presenting the Hunter Group philosophy. The first several questions were really meek. The docs had just no stomach to make a public fight. So I had brought along many copies of the *Tribune* article and I passed them out.

"I raised my hand at the back. I asked Coats, 'Is this statement accurate, and what did you mean?' He walked all the way down the aisle and stuck his finger in my chest. 'You, come with me'—like I was a bad kid in grade school. He said, 'Look who said this—David Hunter. My name is David Coats. That's not a quote from me.' I said, 'He's the founder of the company!' After the meeting, the head of the neonatal intensive care unit came up to me and shook my hand to thank me for standing up to Coats."

In another public forum, Coats described his vision for the future of the medical center: it would provide only care that made a profit. The INA business rep asked, "What about poor people?" Coats laughed as he replied, "We'll always need poor people. We need them for research fodder." Telomen remembers, "When several people gasped, Coats said, 'I knew someone would object to that,' and he repeated the remark and laughed again. We used this remark to show their character, also."

When the Hunter Group made a presentation to the trustees, activists went to Urbana, taking along some supporters from Jobs with Justice. They picketed outside and then went inside to hear Coats's presentation. Workers had been told not to speak, on pain of ejection. "So when Coats finished," says Iosbaker, "all 50 of us stood up silently with the signs we had prepared with 'Hunter (slash)' and held them up over our heads as we filed out of the room." (In a previous fight in the 1980s, nurses faced with a gag order went to the meeting and stood in the back with their mouths taped shut.)

The Hunter Group had thought they would run the hospital for two years, or at least a year. But after seven months, a new (highly paid) CEO, John DeNardo, sent them packing. DeNardo was clearly brought in to patch things up with employees, and he immediately announced that he wanted to work with the unions. "For the next year," says Telomen, "we had record high levels of patient and employee satisfaction in response to surveys, and record revenues exceeding expenses (profits)."

A few months after DeNardo came on, nurses negotiated a contract with good raises and some protections in the event of privatization: a guarantee of continued recognition of the INA under successor owners and limitations on RN position cuts. The contract helped to cut down on job stress, with restrictions on mandatory overtime and more opportunities to work flexible hours.

The icing on the cake was the firing or resignation of management's entire bargaining committee. And SEIU'S next contract made gains too: "After 35 years of a racially discriminatory pay differential," says Iosbaker, "we won pay equity for the mostly African American and Latino workers."

What They Did

To recap, this is how the UIMCC nurses and service workers fought merger, privatization, and a job-slashing consultant. They:

• Made the issue a moral one that would appeal to the public, hinged on patients' access to care and the need to train the medical workers of the future

• Dealt with inter-union problems first, in order to face their opponents with unity

• Educated their own members through flexible and frequent face-to-face meetings and reams of written materials, and then educated the media and the decision-makers

• Held a slew of picket lines and rallies, including outside meetings of top decision-makers

• Got spouses and children of workers and patients involved

• Held lunchtime meetings to air their grievances publicly

• Found creative ways to protest when barred from speaking

• Found creative ways to uncover useful information, and used it to persuade an influential ally to come along

• Used connections built over years in other locals around the country to get information on the consultant

• Used management's mistakes against them: the denial of chemotherapy to cancer patients, the "eat what you kill" remark

• Used management's own public forums to challenge the administration.

"Our message was always 'save the Medical Center,'" says Telomen. "When you're fighting privatization, I can state confidently that it will sometimes feel fruitless. The overall vision to keep in mind is that this medical center—or whatever your institution is—is valuable. You are finding the steps to preserve it and help it thrive."

★ ★ ★

In our final two stories, the locals addressed job loss both by using shop floor tactics that all members could be involved in and by using a bigger-picture strategy.

Fighting Disinvestment and Discipline

by Aaron Brenner and Joanna Dubinsky

OVER THE PAST 200 YEARS, the skilled machine tool workers in the "Precision Valley" around Springfield, Vermont, have been the first to build the breech-loading gun, the steam shovel, the sheep-shearing machine, the corn planter, and the spring clothespin. More recently, they have produced advanced robotics for the auto industry and machines for the plastics, textile, and chemical industries.

But management does not necessarily try to keep up with technology. After the Goldman Industrial Group took over two machine tool companies in the Precision Valley, "the new management did nothing to upgrade the equipment," says David Cohen, an organizer with the United Electrical Workers (UE). "So by the late 1990s you had this paradox. They were making ultra-modern robotics for the auto industry, the ultimate in computer-controlled equipment, on rickety old machines from the 1950s."

Management's refusal to invest in new equipment would mean eventual collapse for the shops, so the workers decided to wage a campaign to force the company to improve its machinery. "First," says Cohen, "we had all the workers do an extensive survey of what was wrong with their machines. Did they need major repairs, minor repairs? Could the workers fix it? Was a master mechanic required? There was a tendency among workers to just write, 'My machine sucks,' or 'It's a piece of crap.' So the stewards had to go back for the details. Since the workers knew their machines well, they came up with an extensive list of improvements. We got about 80 to 90 percent of the machines written up in real detail.

"We started using this information whenever the company threatened to subcontract work," says Cohen. "We would ask them why they wouldn't fix the machines. In one case, for $300 they could have bought parts that would have made the machine hold the proper tolerances when cutting metal.

"Then we held public demonstrations demanding the company reinvest and rebuild. This resonated with the public. These were some of the last machine tool shops in the Precision Valley and almost everyone in a 50-mile radius had a family member that once worked in one of the shops. Although the newspapers were not pro-union, they could not resist a story of disinvestment in their community. This publicity helped us keep the public informed.

Changing the Subject

"In part to distract the members from the issue of reinvestment, the company retaliated by instituting new disciplinary procedures, sick and tardiness programs, and because the new absentee program represented an immediate threat, the company was partially successful in changing the issue that we were fighting about. We responded to the new program with an overtime ban, which in many ways is not legal.[1] Workers at one factory refused to work overtime for nine months."

Union officials and stewards did not organize the overtime ban. "These guys had realized a long time ago that when it came to something like an overtime ban that might violate the contract, union officers and stewards did not participate," says Cohen. "This would provide the company with the legal basis to attack the union. So there was always another level of union leadership that did not hold any official position.

"The unofficial leaders included former stewards, former officers, and other natural leaders. It was not the blowhards, the workers who have never held office but want to be super-militant. Mostly, the unofficial leaders were the older workers—the mentors, if you will—who had the respect of the others. They did not hold formal meetings. They just talked amongst themselves and to the elected leadership. They did the work the elected leaders could not do. In fact, the union officials sometimes worked overtime, to make it clear that the ban was not official policy. It really was a rank-and-file effort and only succeeded for so long because the workers were behind it.

"During the overtime ban, the union committee spent months negotiating over the absentee program, making it as loose as possible," says Cohen. "Then we got workers to file grievances over every point they received for being late or absent. The only rule was that workers had to go to the grievance meeting and argue their case at the first step. This made it clear to the company that the members were opposed to this program. At one point there were hundreds of grievances pending. The union committee was spending eight hours a day meeting with the company. This in itself represented a big loss in production.

"The company kept threatening to sue us, and it eventually filed a multi-million-dollar lawsuit," says Cohen. "But we had public sympathy on our side, because we had done the publicity to explain how this company was destroying its facilities by not reinvesting. They eventually dropped the lawsuit, because, I think, they did not look like the good employer any more. We did the militant stuff—no overtime, the grievance overload—but we also projected an image of what could be done to save the two shops and revitalize them, keep them in the community."

Repairs in the Contract

Temporarily, at least, the campaign won. "We actually won language in the contract, though it wasn't perfect," says Cohen, "requiring the company to start repairing the machinery. It listed all the repairs they would have to do. We couldn't get them to rebuild everything, since we were heading into recession. But we won minor repairs that kept the machines running. There was a real victory in that sense.

"We also reversed the absentee program. Eventually, without ever admitting that the plan was a failure, they stopped enforcing the plan and installed new time clocks that could give workers a reasonable grace period."

Unfortunately, the workers could not prevent the recession. The company went bankrupt. The union developed a plan to buy the plant and invest in new machinery. Banks refused to lend money and the state government refused to help. "One lesson," says Cohen, "is that the fight for reinvestment must start before the crisis begins."

Continuous Bargaining and Confrontation Save Jobs at GE

by Aaron Brenner

"Neutron Jack" Welch, the General Electric CEO, earned his nickname by laying off tens of thousands of workers. Welch retired in 2001, but GE kept "bombing" jobs. Workers at GE's Locomotive Works in Erie, Pennsylvania found two ways to fight for theirs. They used joint committees to bring new work into the plant, and they refused to work overtime while anyone was laid off.

"I have not had a single person work overtime for the last year," says Rich Manno, a shop steward for United Electrical Workers (UE) Local 506. "Of course, there's no such thing as an overtime ban under the contract.[2] We're just exercising our right to work 40 hours. We just say, 'No, thank you' when we're offered overtime. The main issue is job preservation and the people on layoff. If they don't need those people, then they don't need us to work overtime."

The workers decided to decline overtime at a union meeting, after the company announced in March 2002 that it wanted to lay off 925 workers, 700 because of lost business and 225 because it wanted to transfer work elsewhere. After the decision, the stewards got the word out. "I went around to each person," says Manno. "I explained the vote, why we made it, and answered any questions or complaints.

"Early on, a few people in other departments worked overtime. Their co-workers and the stewards let them know there would be consequence for their actions and no one would associate with them. One worker found the cab of his truck packed with snow and another had a load of manure dumped in his driveway. 'I will not scab' stickers were placed all over their work areas and 'The Scab' cartoon by Jack London[3] appeared all over with their names on it. One worker has decided he is going to retire. They found out working overtime was not 'advisable' and they didn't do it again."

The overtime refusal is "a huge weapon for us," notes Plant Steward Dave Kitchen. "It drives the employer batty. We know they have just-in-time and continuous flow manufacturing. They must keep to a schedule, but it's hard if we're not working overtime." Plus, GE has to keep more workers on the job when no one is working extra hours.

Workers also exploited their incentive pay system to pressure management, by working to rule. "If the cable department people have been working at 150 percent efficiency to make more money, management starts to count on it," says Kitchen. "Then the workers could choose to drop down to 100 percent efficiency, which is completely within the rules, and the company cannot get its products delivered on time."

As another part of their protest against layoffs, Local 506 had a two-hour strike in November 2002. "All 2,900 people walked out," notes Manno. After that, in addition to the work-to-rule and choosing to work 40 hours, the workers showed their unity and boosted their spirits by holding rallies, wearing buttons, putting massive protest banners on plant buildings, and holding "band practice": everyone hammering away on anything that won't break for 10 minutes or more.

"We schedule 'band practice' during breaks or lunchtime," explains Kitchen. "It drives the bosses crazy," says Manno. "It rattles the windows and lets the workers blow off steam. And there's not much the bosses can do about it."

Job Preservation Committees Find New Work

The union also turned to something it had negotiated in the 2000 national contract—job preservation committees (JPCs). The contract requires the company to meet quarterly with the union and provide advance notice of layoffs and work transfer. "That gives us the opportunity for an in-plant struggle and work in the JPCs," says Kitchen.

GE had thought the JPCs would be made up of union officials, but the UE staffed them with rank-and-file volunteers. Using the company's own figures and the rank and file's craft knowledge, the JPCs demonstrated to management that the current workforce could do much of the work the company planned to outsource at a lower cost, without wage cuts.

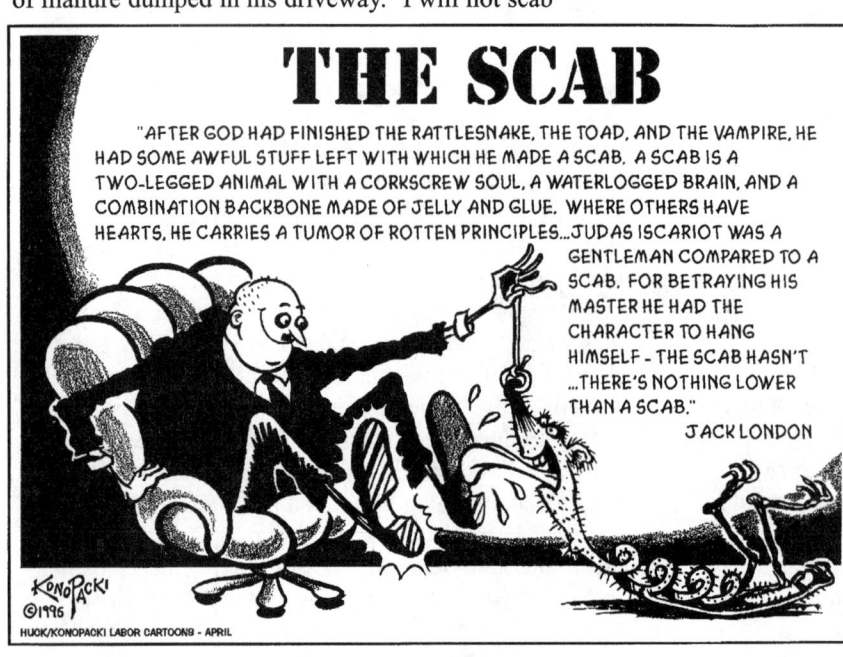

"Our JPC members were asked, and in some cases volunteered, to serve," says Kitchen. "They are qualified because they work on the shop floor and know the product and manufacturing processes better than the boss. We have one committee for each major work group: assembly, weld, indirect, maintenance, and machining. There are two persons on each committee, one with technical skills and one with organizational skills. They in turn find other volunteers to assist them, and they look for opportunities inside and outside their building."

"Basically, we are self-taught," says Manno, who leads the JPC in the assembly division. "We started by holding committee meetings to figure out which jobs we thought we could save. Then we met with the company. We asked what it would take to bring work into the plant. They said, 'Beat our price,' so that's when we knew we had to learn as much, if not more, about the business than the managers did.

"We found out that isn't too hard, because they only know what is fed to them by the source people. The source people only look at the price of the product and nothing else, such as overhead, quality, delivery time, raw material costs, etc. I developed a 'job preservation process' outline to help others in the process."

Manno gives an example from the cable department. He says when making a presentation he tries to use the company buzzwords. "The company said they could save 10 percent by outsourcing power cable production. We looked at the vendor's itemized breakdown of per-cable costs: $3.65 for materials, $1.06 for labor, and $1.46 for overhead, for a total of $6.17. We went into GE's computer and found that another vendor could provide material for $3.43. We could do the labor for $0.92, and the overhead would be only $1.27, for a total of $5.62. They didn't know their business. They used an average over four or six weeks to calculate labor costs. We pulled each worker's individual run, which is the pay they actually made, so we knew the exact labor cost. And the vendor was padding the overhead."

In another case, Manno says, "we wanted to build AC motors used in locomotives. Management was telling me it would cost $10,000 for the equipment, but they were looking at brand new coiling stands. We talked to the assemblers; they demonstrated that we could spend just $800 to adjust the equipment we already had. We got the AC motors for windmills and locomotives."

Avoiding Competition

Of course, a big danger with such committees is undercutting workers in other shops. Local 506 has a policy that if a JPC recommendation would take work away from a union shop, the union will get management to agree to replace that local's work. However, management has made no formal agreement to do this.

Manno says, "We pulled alternator rebuilds out of an IUE-CWA shop, because we could do them for less. So we got the company to invest $10 million in their shop, to rebuild wrecked locomotives." Before the JPC even made the bid for the alternator rebuilds, Manno got a verbal agreement from management to put the new work into the IUE-CWA plant.

"I had to show them a return on their investment, the time it would take on that return, how it would enhance the business, and how it would allow for future growth. That's one of the drawbacks of the JPCs; I sometimes start to feel like a manager, since I have to do their work. But if it saves or builds jobs, so be it."

JPC work takes time, and GE pays for only about two hours per JPC member per week. The union pays the rest if it is done during work hours. JPC members, Manno says, have to put in a lot of their own time.

The JPC members from all the divisions meet regularly to discuss strategy, what's working and what's not. They consult with workers in the affected areas and work out the implications of any changes they might negotiate. "I have been in assembly my whole working life, but I don't know everything," says Manno. "I do not take anything for granted. We get as many people involved as possible. That way they can help us."

Before any meeting with management, JPC members set an agenda, decide on their goals, and settle all their disagreements. "If we disagreed during a meeting with management we would call a break and work it out among ourselves," says Manno. "We don't want to get burnt. Luckily, we've never got to that point. We have disagreements, but we take care of them before the meetings."

JPC leaders report regularly to the division chief stewards and the plant steward, a full-time official. That way the officers are up to speed should they be called into a meeting with management. "We can bargain just about everything—bringing work in, the codes, the piecework price," notes Manno, "but when we start dealing with certain contractual questions, I stop the meeting and contact the plant steward. He might have a suggestion that allows us to continue, or he might join us, or he might convene his own meeting with management."

In one example, Manno was negotiating to bring in "UX" work, in which piece-rate assembly workers would rebuild broken machines. The company wanted piece-rate workers to do so-called "nonproductive" work as well, including driving jitneys and operating cranes. On the regular assembly floor, that would take work away from jitney drivers and crane operators, who do not earn piece rates.

"I knew management would only agree to the UX work if we allowed the job combination," says Manno. "I stopped the meeting and consulted with Dave, the plant steward. We decided to allow the piece-rate workers to do the nonproductive work, but only in the UX section, not on the main assembly floor." Thus no non-piece-rate jobs were lost and some piece-rate jobs were gained. The downside is that management now has a foot in the door to demand that all piece-rate workers drive jitneys.

Sometimes the plant steward and other full-time officials have to negotiate job preservation with upper management, because management reps on the JPCs are not authorized to hire new workers or recall workers from layoff. Meetings between full-time union officials and upper management occur at least once a quarter. "We brief the officers on everything we are doing, so there are no surprises," says Manno.

By wading through GE's massive purchasing material, deciphering its "Enron-like" accounting, and developing rank and filers' creativity, the JPCs saved 180 of the 225 jobs GE had announced for transfer in March 2002.

Making the Case for Insourcing

by Mike Parker

Calculating the full costs of doing a job, in-house or outsourced, takes considerable skill, time, and knowledge. Despite management's obvious advantages, unions may have some of their own.

Management rarely puts in the effort to do a serious job. The staffers assigned are usually overworked and/or lazy, and they often present crude guesstimates and mistakes (while using very precise figures). The union has access to the people who know the realities of the job. Often workers in the bargaining unit have expertise about other processes, methods, and pricing from previous jobs and/or family members. Unions do well to draw on this talent, on their union's research departments, and on local college labor studies departments.

Here we will discuss insourcing of parts in a factory, but similar considerations apply to insourcing services. To compare the costs of in-house versus outsourced work, the union will need to figure out costs for materials, labor, transportation, engineering, tooling, training, and in-house floor space or work area.

These costs are not always straightforward. Here are some factors that experienced bargainers have used to make the case for doing the work in-house:

Cost of packaging and transportation. Finished parts usually require more space, more packaging, and more care in handling than the raw materials and components.

Pipeline costs. Outsourced work usually requires a longer pipeline. Money is tied up in the extra inventory required for the pipeline, in keeping track of where things are, and in preventing damage as parts are moved.

Quality. 1) A well-paid stable workforce usually does better quality work. 2) A workforce that is in closer contact with the end result has a better understanding of and more commitment to a quality product. 3) The longer the pipeline, the harder it is to discover the source of errors and the longer it takes for a correction to have an impact. In some cases everything in the pipeline has to be scrapped.

Sequencing savings. In these days of just-in-time production, changes in customer demands drive week-by-week adjustments to quantities and to the product mix. The right parts need to arrive at the right time (sequencing). The red dashboard has to be there when the red car gets to the assembly station. In-house production and sequencing mean that parts can be more quickly ordered and matched with changes in demand.

Synergy savings. A large plant is more likely to have spare parts and knowledgeable staff available for faster repairs. Small shops with a single specialized machine are more dependent on vendors to take care of them.

When management proposes to outsource, make an official information request for the true costs. But don't expect managers to have accurate figures. Bill Parker, president of UAW Local 1700 at a Detroit-area DaimlerChrysler plant, has been very successful at bringing work back in. Parker advises unions to keep careful track whenever work is lost. Keep track of the amount of production time lost because the outsourced parts were not there in a timely fashion. Keep track of quality problems, how long it takes to get them fixed, and how much the repairs cost. These often turn out to be far more expensive than any small savings in the listed product cost.

Don't let management mix apples and oranges. Be very suspicious when they use "average" costs. For example, the stated "average" cost for labor may include a substantial amount that is covering existing pension obligations. If managers move the work out and abolish the jobs, they still have this cost. Don't let them include it in the cost for in-house labor for the specific work in question.

A similar case can be made about space. If the space is available and unused, don't let them count the cost of maintaining the building as part of the cost. In economic terms, make sure that the costs you use are the "marginal costs" (costs for the extra production), not the average costs.

Above all, remember that costing is more of an art than an exact science. There are many variables, each with a different weight. As one negotiator says, winning on these questions "requires doing a lot of homework. But it also depends on big parts of intuition, power, good notes, and b.s."

Of course, even if you have all the facts on your side, it may not matter. Management may have a different agenda—like breaking or de-skilling the union. In a number of industries the benchmark is "Harbour numbers," a measure of labor hours used per unit of production. In this case there is no mutual ground for discussions with management. Outsourcing, even if it costs more, produces better Harbour numbers and better bonuses for managers. Says UAW Local 909 President Al Benchich, "You can't beat 'em with a calculator. You have to beat 'em with a stick."

Finally, be sure to keep up front that this sort of work is dangerous terrain for unions. Avoid any situation where "putting in a low bid" leads to undermining work rules or setting bad precedents on staffing levels. It is easy to get carried away in trying to find ways to undercut the competition. But your first job is to maintain and improve good union conditions.

Of the total 925 jobs threatened, only 133 workers have been laid off permanently. "Not too bad," says Kitchen. "All the solidarity actions by our members contributed to the result."

Local 506 got good results by combining "management's work" with confrontational actions that involved the entire rank and file. Not all unions have used their "insourcing" committees this way. In some unions, contract language giving locals the right to "bid for work" has simply opened the door to concessions and a plant-against-plant mentality.

To avoid that outcome, UE 506:
• Treated all meetings with management as bargaining sessions, with unity on the union side
• Involved rank and filers and trained them on what to look out for
• Involved members with both technical and organizational skills—the shop floor leaders
• Maintained a close relationship between JPCs and the local's contract enforcement officers
• Held meetings of the different JPCs together. If one JPC was heading in the wrong direction, others could pull it up short.
• Paid attention not only to the direct effects of a change but to how it might affect workers in other departments or classifications, both immediately and down the road
• Declined to bid for work being done by other union shops unless management agreed to replace the other shop's work
• Simultaneously carried on job-saving efforts that were confrontational, not cooperative.

"Rank-and-file activities are our norm," Kitchen contends. "We take pride in not trying to drum up militancy once every decade or century or just when crisis looms. It takes ongoing education and rank-and-file involvement to walk the walk."

Resources

• *Working Smart: A Union Guide to Participation Programs and Reengineering* (with *Strategy Guide*), by Mike Parker and Jane Slaughter. Explains lean production, the appeals of "employee involvement," why "quality programs" are really speed-up or job-loss programs, the dangers of "protective involvement," the Japanese and Swedish models, and the pitfalls of training programs. Includes strategies and contract language for dealing with employee involvement and lean production, and case studies from health care, factories, the Postal Service, trucking, government, schools, and telecommunications. $15 plus $4 shipping. www.labornotes.org. Labor Notes, 7435 Michigan Ave. Detroit, MI 48210. 313-842-6262.

• See Chapter 5 of the 1991 *A Troublemaker's Handbook* for more on fighting employee involvement programs. Order from Labor Notes.

• Free fact sheets. Order from Charley Richardson, 978-934-3266 or Charles_Richardson@uml.edu.
  ✓ "Treat It as Continuous Bargaining"
  ✓ "Work Restructuring and Employee Involvement: Watching Out for the Tricks and Traps"
  ✓ "Avoiding False Security: Analyzing the Limitations of Protective Contract Language"
  ✓ "Draft Code of Conduct for Union Members Involved in Joint Programs"
  ✓ "Asking the Right Questions"

• For a list of over 200 information requests to submit when management plans to do drug testing, contact the University of Iowa Labor Center. Use a search engine to look for "Iowa Labor Center drug-testing."

• *The New Model of Bargaining: Mutual Gain or Unilateral Loss?* by Dan Holub, Roberta Till-Retz, and Laurie Clement, 1998. Order from the Labor Center, Oakdale Hall, University of Iowa, Iowa City, IA 52242. 319-335-4144. labor-center@uiowa.edu. $5.

• Video: "Stop Privatization at UIC Hospital." The fight by SEIU Local 73 and the Illinois Nurses Association described above. 10 min. $20. Labor Beat, 37 S. Ashland, Chicago, IL 60607. 312-226-3330. mail@laborbeat.org.

Action Questions

WHETHER YOU ARE DEALING with a joint program or lean production/outsourcing, you will need to research management's business plan and how its proposals fit into that plan, and to figure out where the union has leverage to resist. Most of the following questions apply to both kinds of program.

For joint programs:

1. What is management's goal for the program?

2. What level of management is pushing it? Do they want the program mainly in name (because higher management insists on it)? Which elements do they really want and which are window dressing?

3. Can the union simply refuse to accept the program? Or must the union attempt to function within it in a way that protects members? Are there elements that can be turned to the union's advantage, such as access to information?

4. Have you demanded that management bargain over the impact of the program?

5. What information requests do you need to make to aid you in bargaining? Are you prepared to back them up with more requests, or to file unfair labor practice charges if management does not comply?

6. How can you find out how the program (or the consultant) has worked elsewhere?

7. How is management trying to reach your members about or through the program? How are members reacting (interested, skeptical, apathetic)? Are you seeing divisions based on these different reactions (the "sucks" vs. the "dinosaurs")? How can you deal with each of these? How will you structure your education to promote a unified response?

8. Are joint committee members appointed (by union or management), elected, or volunteer? Can the union demand to elect or appoint its reps?

9. How can you develop a plan for approaching the meetings as continuous bargaining sessions? Can you demand union-only training for joint committee members? If not, can the union organize its own training? Whom will you ask for help?

10. If the union reps begin to act like bargainers in the joint sessions, is management likely to cancel the

program? Do you want it to?

11. What should be included in a code of conduct for joint committee members?

12. How can you organize rank and filers to channel info to the joint committee reps? How can you organize members to back up the union's position at the table with collective action?

13. If your union leaders are cooperating in the program, and you are a rank-and-filer who wants to organize against it, how can you educate co-workers? Written information, a department meeting, one on one? Can you organize in your area to boycott team meetings, for example, and then spread the word to other areas? Can you bring up the question at union meetings? See Chapter 18.

For lean production:

14. Has management already begun to introduce changes that will affect how work is done? How will these changes affect fundamental union issues such as skill levels, job security, seniority, work pace, privacy, classifications, contracting out?

15. What have been the results in other plants or offices?

16. How can you get information about the effects of new technologies on workers? What about the technology's weak spots? Can you get information from people who are not yet in the bargaining unit but should be? Can you make a plan for organizing technical workers into the union?

17. If the workforce is being organized into work teams, can you organize members to "take over" team meetings? To boycott team leader promotions? To run the most pro-union person for team leader? To try to make the team leader position a seniority bid?

18. How can your members resist the speed-up that comes with lean production? Are they willing to "work to rule" every day (refuse to cut corners, work through breaks, or let safety slide)? See Chapter 10.

19. Would the public be interested in your issues? (De-skilling cuts back good-paying jobs, disinvestment eliminates them, speed-up and privatization hurt quality of services.) What research is needed about the effects of contracting out/privatization? Who will be hurt, who will profit? How can you take your fight to the community?

20. Can you show management how your members can perform outsourced work for less money, without giving up pay or your rights on the shop floor? Are there members with the technical and organizational skills to do this work, and can the union back them up so that concessions are not made? What training would be needed?

Authors

AARON BRENNER is a labor historian, researcher, writer, and editor in New York City. He has written about international labor solidarity, union reform movements, and rank-and-file rebellions by Teamsters, telephone workers, and postal workers, and is the editor of *The Encyclopedia of Strikes in American History.*

JOANNA DUBINSKY, a former Labor Notes intern, earned a Master's Degree in Labor Studies from the University of Massachusetts, where she was an active rank-and-filer in the Graduate Employee Organization, UAW 2322. She is involved in social and economic justice projects in New Orleans.

DAN LA BOTZ wrote the first edition of *A Troublemaker's Handbook* in 1991. He is an activist, teacher, and labor historian based in Cincinnati, where he writes frequently for *Labor Notes*. He was a founding member of Teamsters for a Democratic Union in the 1970s and wrote a book about that movement, as well as books on unions in Mexico and Indonesia. He is editor of the monthly web publication *Mexican Labor News and Analysis.*

MIKE PARKER, a skilled trades member of UAW Local 1700, is the author of *Inside the Circle: A Union Guide to QWL* and co-author of *Choosing Sides: Unions and the Team Concept* and *Working Smart: A Union Guide to Participation Programs and Reengineering.*

CHARLEY RICHARDSON works at the Labor Extension Program at the University of Massachusetts Lowell. He has worked with unions across all sectors on using a continuous bargaining strategy to deal with workplace changes, including new technologies. Charley is a shipfitter by trade and was a shop steward and a safety observer in the shipyards.

NICK ROBINSON is a former student-labor activist at Miami University and *Labor Notes* intern. He is now a volunteer organizer with the Montpelier Downtown Workers Union and the Vermont Workers Center.

JANE SLAUGHTER is co-author, with Mike Parker, of *Choosing Sides* and *Working Smart*, and is the editor of this book.

Notes

1. Any legal protection for an overtime ban would depend on the particular contract language. Some contracts say or imply that concerted refusals of overtime can be disciplined.

2. See endnote 1.

3. Author Jack London's famous description of a scab was made into a cartoon by Mike Konopacki. It's in the cartoon book *Bye! American*, available at http://solidarity.com/hkcartoons/books.html.

On the Troublemaker's Website

"Preparing for a Site Visit." What to do when management invites your local on a junket to visit the "model workplace."

"Global Positioning Systems: Big Brother Is Doing More than Watching," by Charley Richardson.

Go to www.labornotes.org.

7. Organizing for Health and Safety

by Marsha Niemeijer and Roni Neff

IS YOUR WORKPLACE A SAFE PLACE TO BE? Think about it. Perhaps the odors make people dizzy, or tools are causing injuries. In some workplaces overtime hours are long. Maybe many of your co-workers have back injuries or are starting to lose their hearing. Sometimes a health and safety issue is so prominent that it can't be missed. Other times workers are not aware they have a common problem until they sit down together and start talking.

Occupational injuries and illnesses are shockingly common. Every single day in 2002, 15 U.S. workers died from on-the-job injuries, on average, and 12,877 nonfatal injuries and illnesses were reported.[1] This means that about one in 25 U.S. workers is being injured or made ill on the job every year—and many more have seen these events or dangers and want to do something about them. In Canada, workplace deaths have risen since 1998, according to the Canadian Labour Congress, where on average 2.5 people were killed on the job every day in 2002.

What's more, the damage to workers' health goes beyond what conventional statistics show. "When I talk to workers around the country, in any industry," says Nancy Lessin, Health and Safety Coordinator of the Massachusetts AFL-CIO, "and I ask them what's hurting them or what's stressing them out, most people tell me about mandatory overtime, increased workloads, and downsizing. Workers and their unions generally don't think of these issues as health and safety issues. And yet the traditional issues, such as chemicals and unguarded machines, are further down on their list of things that are hurting them."

Margaret Keith, research coordinator at the Occupational Health Clinic for Ontario Workers, says that as union power in the workplace has declined, unions have often tended to "treat health and safety purely as a technical issue, because unions don't expect to have control over the work process. Fighting for health and safety becomes an argument with the employer over how many parts per million are safe to breathe. The rank and file are disconnected from the mobilizing aspects of health and safety."

What are the "mobilizing aspects"? Because health and safety problems potentially affect almost everyone in the workplace, working on them can build unity. For example, using the mapping technique described below creates a collective analysis of the source of problems, and this in turn helps foster a collective approach to fixing them.

This chapter will not attempt to cover all the mobilizing tactics that unions use, which include member training, grievances, finding allies in the environmental movement, and fighting to change standards and laws. You can find more useful strategies, as well as technical help, in the Resources listed at the end. Instead we will start by laying out some useful approaches to health and safety organizing, and end with examples of inventive actions that workers have taken collectively. These topics are included:

• Using "mapping" techniques to pinpoint hazards
• A "continuous bargaining" approach to health and safety
• A toolbox of tips and techniques
• Strategies to counter management's "blame the worker" or "behavior-based safety" programs
• Using information requests
• How and when to use OSHA—and when not to
• Five examples of workers taking action for health and safety and building their unions in the process: building a rank-and-file grievance committee, involving the media, refusing unsafe work, demanding safe materials, demanding a fair process from OSHA, working with COSH groups and community organizations, using health and safety in an organizing drive.

Identifying Problems Collectively: Mapping

by Dorothy Wigmore

THE FIRST STEP in a health or safety campaign is to find common problems. Then comes the detective work to find the hazards behind the symptoms. Many health and safety activists use body and workplace maps to see how workers are being hurt in their workplaces now or how they are affected by what they did years ago.

Mapping is participatory and fun. It involves most senses, it can be used where workers speak different languages or don't read well, and it is a quick way to make sense of complex situations. Maps can show the different experiences of workers by age, seniority, job, or gender. Body maps can show the patterns of symptoms and the long-term effects of hazards. Workplace maps give an overview that individuals do not have. The two types of maps can be used together to see the workplace in a new light.

Body Maps

"This is the first time I've known I'm not alone in my pain," a veteran construction worker said after seeing the body map he and others made in an ergonomics workshop for operating engineers. His reaction is a classic example of a barrier to health and safety organizing—individual workers think their symptoms are just their problem.

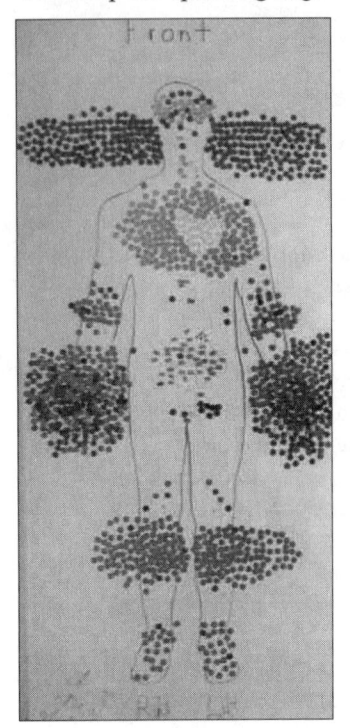

Body maps can break that barrier. The most common version is to use the front and back outlines of a body. You can get these (and much more information on different kinds of mapping) at www.hazards.org, or draw your own outlines. Make a large version for the overall group and smaller sheets for groups of workers.

Next, decide what your question is. Are you looking for aches and pains? All the symptoms workers have now? Long-term effects, such as cancer, chronic pain, stress? Do you want to be able to see the effects by gender, age, job, seniority?

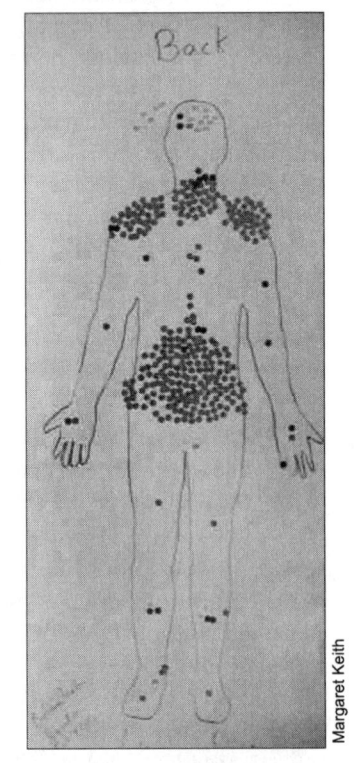

Get people into small groups. If you want information by age, for example, divide them into groups based on that category. Give each group colored markers or colored sticky dots and a code to mark their outlines. One method uses red = aches and pains, green = where does your stress show up, and blue = other symptoms that may be work-related. To get the overall picture, have them transfer their information to the large body map (see example).

When you're looking at aches and pains, one person can act out her job. The others identify which body parts are likely affected by force, repetition, awkward postures. With permission, they can mark the spots directly on the person, using "ouch" stickers.

Workplace Hazard Maps

Workplace maps usually focus on the hazards behind the symptoms that show up on the body map. If there's time before making the maps, get workers doing similar jobs to fill out a questionnaire and discuss it together. Focus on:

- How is the work *organized*? (e.g., number of workers, shifts, hours worked, and breaks)
- What is the *work process*? (How is work done? What tasks are involved? What machines and tools are used?)
- What are the *hazards*? (use the categories below)
- What *complaints or symptoms* show up in conversations?
- What *measures* are being taken to *prevent* or *reduce* the hazards? What else could or should be done?

Groups of workers then draw the layout of their workplace or work area. Be sure to include doors, windows, offices, washrooms, desks, machinery, and equipment. The larger the map, the more details you can add. Try to get the questionnaire information onto the map without making it too cluttered.

Hazards are often divided into six categories: safety (immediate kinds of injuries); physical (energy sources such as radiation, temperature, noise); chemical (dusts, liquids, gases); biological or communicable (infection, needlesticks, mold); ergonomic (force, repetition, posture, design of control panels); and work organization/psychosocial risks (things that cause stress such as long or odd work schedules, no say about the job, workload).

Draw a different colored icon or a different shape to show each category of hazard. Different sizes can show the seriousness, and the number of workers who may be exposed to the hazard can be marked inside the icon. Use sticky dots or some other format to put the people in the picture and show where they work.

It's also useful to show the flow of work and workers' usual paths (movements) in the workplace. The map is easier to read if you use string for this information. One worker made two maps using different colors of string to show her paths in a nursing home, on "normal" days and then when working short-staffed. The clear differences between the maps provided an "ah-hah" about her increased workload, a serious stressor.

Mapping the Effects of Work on the Rest of Your Life

Work takes a toll off the job—on our families, our leisure time, and our communities. "World mapping" is one way to show these effects.

Put a large sheet of paper up on a wall, with a small human figure in the center. Then draw or add words around the figure to show how your lives are affected by your work. You might draw guitars you no longer can play because of crippled tendons or broken hearts from a divorce linked to long hours and stress. See instructions and examples at www.hazards.org/diyresearch/index.htm#worldmapping.

Using the Maps

The first question to ask after you've made any of these maps is "What do you see?" Look for patterns, and the things that don't fit the patterns.

Put together maps of work areas to get the overall picture about one workplace. Over time, come back to them to record new information or check on changes. Use your imagination and creativity to make sure that everyone's story is recorded, if they want it included. If you want to add even more information, you can use see-through plastic layers for separate categories of information or to represent the experiences of different groups. See Chapter 3 on how to use workplace maps for organizing.

When setting priorities about what to tackle, use these questions and build your case accordingly:
- How serious a hazard is it—for me or others (ask about acute and chronic effects)?
- How many workers are or could be affected? How serious are the consequences?
- How often is the problem likely to occur?
- What costs does the problem cause?
- What does the law say?
- Can the problem be fixed easily?

The Continuous Bargaining Approach

by Nancy Lessin and Roni Neff

UNION BARGAINERS TRADITIONALLY NEGOTIATE a contract and then shift their focus to enforcing the rules they've established. Bargaining ceases till the next round. But in between contracts, employers may bring in new procedures, programs, and technology that can change workers' risks considerably. Scientific understanding of hazards also keeps growing. A "continuous bargaining" approach means not waiting until the contract expires to address issues but engaging in a continuous bargaining approach with management, as needed.

After an employer tells the union about a new workplace program that could affect workers, including their health and safety, the labor law regarding "unilateral changes" has been interpreted to give the union a six-month window of opportunity to request bargaining. And if the employer brings in a policy that the union wouldn't otherwise have the right to bargain over, the health and safety impact can give the union a foot in the door. The union should view health and safety broadly, to include problems caused by stress and work overload. A new work schedule, an attendance program, technology that increases the work pace, "multiskilling" or layoffs that increase the workload—all may affect workers' safety or health and thus are subject to the union's demand to bargain over the impacts of employer changes.

When applicable, the regular negotiating team should address these issues by requesting formal "midterm" bargaining. In addition, union representatives on joint labor-management health and safety committees should also adopt a continuous bargaining mindset. Too often, management tends to control the agenda of joint meetings, but this needn't be the case if the union treats the meetings like bargaining sessions. See the Canadian Auto Workers' example below, "Substituting Safer Materials."

Tips for effective continuous bargaining meetings with management:

Prepare for meetings as if they were bargaining sessions. Union representatives should be trained for their bargaining roles and should meet in advance to plan. (Ideally, seek contract language allowing planning meetings on company time.) Planning should include: understanding member concerns and identifying issues to raise; documenting the health and safety impacts; reviewing the related laws and scientific research; analyzing where management is vulnerable; deciding what solutions you want to suggest; and developing a strategy, including escalating tactics, if management is not willing to address problems.

Act like bargainers. Caucus regularly during joint labor-management meetings, to maintain a united response and to remind employers that they are dealing with the union, not a group of individuals. Agreements made, with deadlines for fixing problems, should be recorded in the minutes.

Involve members: Learn their concerns and keep them informed with one-on-one conversations, surveys, fact sheets and newsletter articles, and presentations at union meetings. Use visible strategies like t-shirts and buttons to demonstrate to management that it's not just the people sitting around the table stating these concerns, and use other pressure tactics described in this chapter.

Leverage: Besides member mobilization tactics, use information requests and consider OSHA complaints, as described later in this chapter.

For more on continuous bargaining, see Chapter 6.

Fighting 'Blame the Worker' Approaches

by Nancy Lessin and Roni Neff

EMPLOYERS' APPROACH TO HEALTH AND SAFETY is often to blame workers themselves. They claim injured workers weren't using the equipment properly, or they weren't paying attention. But what is seldom asked is—why? Why did a worker not wear safety glasses, for example? Perhaps the employer buys cheap glasses that scratch easily; or perhaps conditions make the glasses fog up. The best way to prevent injuries is to leave as little as possible to chance or human error. Personal protective equipment such as safety glasses should be a last resort. To the extent possible, longer-term solutions—such as enclosing an operation so that safety glasses aren't needed—should be used.

But more and more employers have embraced "behavioral safety programs" that focus on workers' "unsafe acts" as the primary problem leading to injuries and illnesses. In some programs, workers are made

Health and Safety Action Toolbox

Health and safety activists should have a toolbox of strategy options, from the smallest screwdriver to the largest sledgehammer. They can then fit the tool to the situation—keeping in mind that even when a sledgehammer seems needed, sometimes just threatening to use it is enough. In addition to educating members to know what to look for, filing grievances, and bargaining for contract language, you can:

• Ask the right person. If your initial request doesn't get good results, think about who else might be more able or willing to help you. Point out ways the changes you recommend will benefit the employer.

• Draw attention to problems. Does management display a sign saying, "X days with no injuries"? Unions can put up their own sign saying, "X days since we told management about the hazard in the paint shop and it's still not addressed." If you don't have rights to a bulletin board, use a daily flyer. Another tactic is to put fluorescent stickers on hazards. Or if there are frequent puddles of water or oil on the floor, float brightly colored rubber duckies in the "ponds."

• Use joint labor-management safety committees to engage in "continuous bargaining" with management (as described on the previous page).

• "Work to the safety rule": Perform jobs exactly as specified in the employer's official safety rules. The resulting decline in productivity should motivate management to talk to the union. See Chapters 3 and 10 for more on working to rule.

• Identify allies such as local environmental, community, or religious groups. Tell each other about your issues and needs, and keep them updated. Support their struggles so they'll support yours. Take advantage of their strengths. For example, are they well connected to the media or politicians? Are they able to turn out large numbers of supporters? Are they creative? Do they have legal expertise?

• Think big. Maybe your manager is suggesting a halfway solution that doesn't fully solve the problem. Maybe that's how "everybody" deals with it. But is there another, better way? For example, the workers in the "Substituting Safer Materials" story below pushed their employers to use different chemicals rather than just trying to reduce exposure.

• Go to the media to embarrass and pressure employers who fail to fix hazards. Union members can write letters to the editor or op-ed pieces, contact radio talk shows, or pitch the story to labor- or health-oriented reporters (see Chapter 22). Don't forget progressive and neighborhood media.

• Call in OSHA—or let your employer know you are considering it (see below). Despite the agency's few teeth, most employers do not want OSHA involved, and OSHA citations (or the threat of them) can lead employers to fix problems.

• Evaluate whether a different government agency can be involved, such as the Environmental Protection Agency, the National Labor Relations Board, or state or local government agencies relating directly or indirectly to health and safety and the environment. Ask a COSH group for help on this (see Resources).

• Threaten criminal prosecution. Write a letter to the district attorney about a hazardous condition, giving names and dates of conversations with management. State that if a fatality or serious injury occurs, you will seek criminal prosecution. Give management a chance to see the letter and respond before you mail it. A Steelworkers local at Simond Saw in Fitchburg, Massachusetts used this tactic, and the hazardous machine was instantly removed from operation. The union was also called in for its first real discussion with management.

Although prosecutors rarely bring such charges, managers want to avoid having to defend themselves individually in court. One progressive attorney general in Massachusetts brought two CEOs up on charges for "assault and battery with a deadly weapon" after their workers were exposed to lead and cadmium. The CEOs were convicted.

• In an emergency, call OSHA for an "imminent danger" inspection, 800-321-OSHA. Both the OSH Act and the National Labor Relations Act give the right to refuse work based on serious hazards. OSHA gives the right to workers who have told the employer of an "immediate serious risk of death or serious physical harm," but the employer did not fix the hazard, and there is not time to contact OSHA. Note that the OSH Act applies only when a "reasonable person" would concur about the danger.

The NLRA gives the right to refuse work or walk off the job when such actions are taken in good faith and are "concerted activities"—actions by two or more workers or by one worker with others' endorsement. Note that despite the law, employers may retaliate against workers who use their rights, and legal remedies for this retaliation can be slow. You may decide to exercise this right only where the danger is clear and critical.[2]

---

responsible for watching each other and noting when a co-worker performs a "safe behavior" or commits an "unsafe act." Some programs discipline workers who report injuries, or require drug tests, counseling, verbal warnings, or even firing after repeated reports of injuries. Reward programs may offer prizes or lotteries to non-injured workers, or they may use peer pressure by rewarding whole units that report no injuries.

Whether employers use the carrot, the stick, or both, the results of such programs are the same: fewer workers report symptoms, injuries, and illnesses. Employers cut their workers' compensation premiums and their chances of OSHA inspection, and they avoid the cost of dealing with the real causes of injury.

One example is the "Safety Bingo" program, in which employees compete in "Bingo" and management raises the jackpot each day. When an injury is reported, bingo cards are wiped clean and the jackpot drops nearly to nothing. At one Massachusetts worksite that used Safety Bingo as well as post-injury drug testing and a policy of disciplining for injuries, multiple minor injuries from an unguarded machine went unreported. A worker was later crushed to death in that machine.

Demand To Bargain

When management plans to start a safety incentive program or an injury discipline program, the union can say, "What an interesting proposal—we'll meet you at the bargaining table." The union should then begin to file information requests to obtain any and all information that it needs to bargain over the program, such as data on injuries and the company's evidence that this particular program will cut injuries.

Information requests are useful not only for getting data but also because the National Labor Relations Act prohibits the employer from starting the policy or program while there is an open, valid information request that the employer has not responded to in good faith. If an employer does not respond, the union can file an unfair labor practice claim for each unfilled request. Needless to say, responding to each request or dealing with each unfair labor practice claim can be a major headache that the employer will want to avoid. See Resources to get sample questions your union can ask.

Further steps to take include:

• **Tell members why you object** to the program. "Reward" programs can be popular, so be sure to explain their drawbacks. Consider offering management an alternative: instead of prizes going to workers who don't report injuries, prizes could go to workers who identify serious hazards, or who suggest ways to eliminate them. When the employer rejects this plan, it's clear how strong management's interest in safety really is.

• **Mobilize action.** Visible symbols like buttons and stickers demonstrate unity to management. At the Dunlop Tire plant in Alabama, management promised workers it would reward a low injury rate with a hot dog dinner during work hours. The union, United Steelworkers Local 915L, explained to members that the actual goal was to discourage reporting. At the end of the time period, it happened that reported injuries had gone down, and the employer organized the dinner. The union organized a boycott. On the day of the picnic, out of 1,800 members, 1,798 refused to go. The union likes to say, "Management was eating hot dogs, hamburgers, and beans for a long time."

• **Use the laws.** Section 11c of the OSH Act prohibits employers from discriminating against workers who exercise their rights under the Act. A section of OSHA's new "Recordkeeping Rule" (29 CFR 1904.36) spells out that one of the rights workers have under the Act is the right to report an injury or illness without fear of discrimination. Any employer policy or program that denies prizes or doles out discipline to workers who report injuries should be seen as a violation of the OSH Act.

Inform the employer that if a safety incentive or injury discipline policy begins, the union will encourage every member who experiences such illegal discrimination to fill out an OSHA 11c discrimination claim form, with each claim triggering an individual OSHA investigation.

A Steelworker in Oklahoma City who had been subject to discipline for clinic visits filed an 11c complaint with OSHA. Not wanting the investigations, the employer kept its "accident repeater" program but took out the disciplinary parts. A union member explains, "It was like taking the bullets out of a tank—without them, there was no more reason for the tanks to advance," and the employer has since done little with the program.

How to Use (and Not Use) OSHA

WE'VE CONCENTRATED THUS FAR on collective action rather than on using the law, for a reason. Enforcing workers' rights under the Occupational Safety and Health Act is not always easy, and using OSHA is not always the best tactic. OSHA is underfunded and often seems to lack the political will to enforce the laws. It would take 84 years for OSHA to inspect each workplace in the United States once, according to the AFL-CIO.

OSHA also lacks the authority to do its job properly. The agency has legal standards for only 500 of the 150,000 chemicals in today's workplaces[3] and has no standards addressing some of the top hazards, including musculoskeletal disorders, vehicle crashes, and workplace violence. Even where OSHA does regulate, its requirements tend to lag far behind the current science. Many of its standards were set in 1969 and have not been updated.

Jay Herzmark, a University of Washington employee trained as an industrial hygienist, and a longtime health and safety activist in AFSCME Local 1488, says that although OSHA will always follow up on a complaint, "they often don't cite the employer, and even then, sometimes OSHA has to catch the employer several times before they issue a fine." The most OSHA can fine an employer is $70,000, and the average fine in 2003 was only $871 for a "serious" violation, in which there is "a substantial probability that death or serious physical harm could result."[4] Filing a complaint can also take a long time. Herzmark explains, "OSHA has six months to do their inspection. If they issue a citation, the employer can appeal, and it doesn't have to fix anything until the final court decision.

"It's a great temptation just to file with OSHA and then let them take over. But bringing in a state or federal agency often waters down your mobilizing and organizing impact because people focus on the law and what they can get out of it." If the union has a strong health and safety committee or has experience involving rank and filers on the issue, and you have a chance to resolve the problem through direct negotiation with management, do so. In general, this will be the fastest and easiest route, and one in which you will have most control over the outcome.

At the same time, Herzmark notes that the threat of going to OSHA might get the employer to resolve the issue. "Employers don't like OSHA, even if they know that OSHA won't do anything. It is disruptive to have an inspector appear at your door, because the employer has to drop everything and walk around with her. Also, if OSHA does cite the employer, the employer will spend lots of time fighting it. However, be prepared to actually file with OSHA if the employer calls the union's bluff."

The main point is to think creatively. If the employer doesn't fix a problem after an OSHA citation, take action. "Besides going back to OSHA and trying to get citations for repeat and willful violations, there are various things you can do," says David Pratt, an organizer with Teamsters for a Democratic Union:

- Use the citation during your contract bargaining. Get the members behind it and include it in your demands.
- Use the citation as evidence for grievances.
- Approach the local media and explain to them that you have a citation from OSHA but your employer won't fix the problem.

★ ★ ★

In the rest of the chapter we tell the stories of rank and filers, stewards, a local union, a joint workplace environmental committee, COSH groups, and two groups of workers in organizing drives. All used the actions, attitudes, or techniques described above to win big improvements from management. The first story is told by a teacher whose school was making people sick.

Breaking the Mold: A Health and Safety Fight Revitalizes the Union

by Steve Hinds

WHEN I TAUGHT HIGH SCHOOL in New Haven, Connecticut, our 1,400-member union had moved away from its militant, progressive history and was functioning as a business union. Grievances were rare. Local leaders emphasized the importance of cooperating with management. There weren't any local-wide membership meetings. To explain our union's decline, local leaders complained that members were not willing to come to meetings or to organize.

At our school, instead of complaining, we began a grievance fight over unhealthy conditions that showed the city and the union what mobilized teachers can do.

How to File an OSHA Complaint

- Evaluate your chances of winning through OSHA. Call OSHA in advance to find out whether your workplace is covered, whether there is a standard covering your concern, what the procedure for processing a complaint is, how long it will take to respond, and the recommended/needed documentation (800-321-OSHA). OSHA will also tell you which area or state office to file with. If there is no standard pertaining to your problem or if it is unlikely that there is a violation of the law, don't call OSHA in for an inspection. Try another strategy.

- Build a strong foundation for your case. OSHA is responsible for doing its own investigation or inspection, but by collecting data yourself, you can assure that inspectors see what you want them to and you can check up to make sure they considered key points. Keep logs of conversations with the employer (including responses) and worker complaints and symptoms. Document your health and safety problem, including dates and times of any incidents. Try to collect technical information on the hazard: company Standard Operating Procedures, Material Safety Data Sheets (which the employer is required to make available), product labels, and scientific research on the hazard and how to reduce it.

- Involve your co-workers and keep them informed. Use leaflets, meetings, and one-on-one talks.

- File the complaint. Be as clear, organized, and comprehensive as you can when you describe the hazard. See the Resources section for guides to what to include. Note that written, signed complaints are most likely to result in in-person inspections. If you do not want the employer to know who filed the complaint, you can have it filed by the union, ask OSHA to keep your name secret, or even file anonymously (though OSHA gives anonymous reports low priority). It is illegal to discriminate against a worker who files an OSHA complaint, but it can be a long, hard process to get justice.

- Participate. The workers' representative has the right to join the OSHA inspector on the visit, and workers have the right to speak to the inspector in private. Use the chance to point out hazards and raise issues.

- Follow up persistently. Make sure you are told of all formal and informal meetings that the government and employer hold on your case. There will be many delays. Continue to keep the rank and file involved and informed about what is going on.

ORGANIZING FOR HEALTH AND SAFETY   85

Our school was old and had not been well maintained. In the late 1990s, the state stepped in to help pay for massive renovations. We were not relocated, but rather were expected to teach while whole walls were being replaced, new floors built, and new wings added. In the fall of 2001, we noticed that many teachers were suffering from sinus problems, headaches, and other respiratory illnesses. Dust, poor ventilation, and sewage leaks had been a problem for years, but the cluster of symptoms at this time was extraordinary. Several teachers were forced to leave work early for medical treatment.

A group of teachers met to decide what to do about air quality. We decided to file a grievance, and got over 90 percent of the teachers to sign the grievance form in a single day. While gathering the signatures, we also conducted a health survey, finding that 70 percent suffered from a narrow list of symptoms related to air quality. These actions helped us develop a network of activists that we used later to communicate between meetings.

There had been little grievance activity for years, so we could start fresh. We formed a school Grievance Committee that would include anyone who wanted to work on the issue. We held weekly meetings and produced our own newsletter to keep members informed. We assigned one Grievance Committee member to keep in daily contact with the president of the parents' organization at our school.

Individual teachers had asked several times to see a study of our school's air quality done six months earlier by the city. The city always said it would share the information but never did. The Committee filed an information request along with our grievance, and that forced the city to hand it over to us. Many teachers, including the newly elected stewards, were learning for the first time that we had a right to this sort of information. The report showed us that the city knew there was an infestation of molds in our building, and that the mold spores could provoke respiratory and other illnesses.

Our demands were simple. We wanted the city to do what its own report concluded it should have done six months earlier—fix the roof leaks that let moisture enter the building, remove moldy ceiling tiles, and clean the walls, floors, and other areas with a bleach solution. We gave the city a deadline to agree to these demands, including a reasonable completion date. We also demanded a walk-through by teachers and parents to inspect the completed work. The city indicated it was working on the problems, but wasn't formally agreeing to anything.

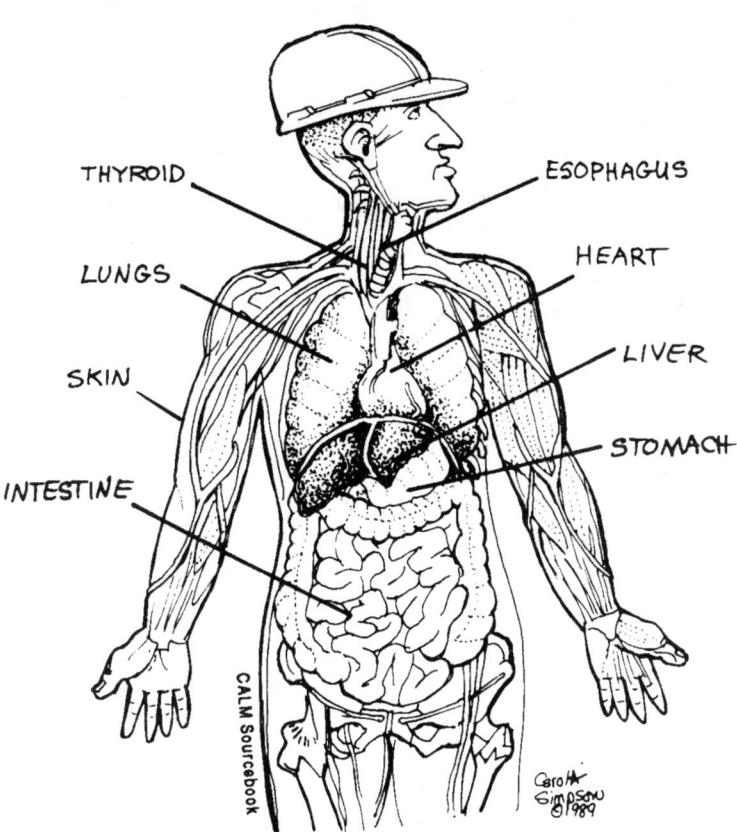

Involve the Parents

The Grievance Committee reported in its newsletters and in larger meetings of teachers at our school that the city appeared to be working on the worst roof leaks but would not agree to our specific demands nor our timetable. We needed more action. We decided to organize a meeting of all the parents the following week. In order to publicize the parent meeting and our concerns, we wore surgical masks to school the following day.

What a day it was. We didn't even need to call the newspapers and TV stations to attract attention. Word got out through student cell phones, and the cameras and reporters were at the school doors by 9 a.m. asking for interviews. Parents who heard about the masks were calling downtown with their concerns. City officials were furious, and the superintendent showed up to bully us. Most of the teachers simply walked out of this meeting. The city agreed to our timetable by the end of the day.

The following day, a crew went through the building room by room to create a master list of work to be done. This list led to some 1,000 work orders by city crews over the following weeks. More work was done to improve our school building in those few months than had been done in the previous two decades, and health complaints by teachers and students gradually eased in the ensuing months.

All of this organizing was done completely within our school, not relying at all on our timid local. We developed leadership and negotiating skills in 15 members who previously had had no experience. We built credibility with parents, who saw that the union was not interested only in salaries.

Grievance Committee activists didn't stop there—we began a petition drive and formed a group called Contract Organizing Group, calling on the local to adopt this bottom-up, aggressive kind of organizing in the upcoming contract talks. (Read more about COG in

"Labor Fights for a Community Contract," Chapter 13.) Beginning with a health and safety fight at a single school, we were able to show teachers, parents, the kids, and the city something important about collective action—it works.

'Standing By' To Enforce the Contract

LONGSHORE WORKERS in the port of Los Angeles found that their union's strong contract language gave them considerable rights, but that rank and filers needed to organize collective action to back it up. David Stock tells how he and fellow members got management to fix unsafe trucks—quickly.

Stock drives trucks on the docks. One company, Stevedoring Services of America, "had a reputation for bad equipment," he says. "The exhaust came into the cabs, the air seats didn't work, the safety gratings were missing or falling off, the wipers and heaters didn't work, and the trucks were extremely loud." The trucks were not only unsafe but a pain to operate.

One day Stock found the only trucks left "undrivable. I took them to a maintenance foreman to get them fixed. He threw a fit, screaming at me that I was just lazy and didn't want to work. I told him he should be ashamed to have these trucks in service. He said, 'Just drive the f—in' truck because there's nothing you can do.'

"I told him I was going to 'stand by' for health and safety." The International Longshore and Warehouse Union contract says that if a worker has a safety grievance he or she can "stand by" (refuse the work) until management fixes it, gives the worker something else to do, or calls the union representative to talk about whether it's a legitimate complaint. If the company doesn't agree the complaint is legitimate, an arbitrator is immediately called onto the job to decide (a notable difference from most contracts, where arbitration takes months). If the arbitrator says yes, workers are paid for the standby time. In the rare case where the arbitrator says the complaint is not legitimate, workers are docked for standing by but are not punished otherwise.

"We called the business agent and he let me handle it," Stock says. "He made me a steward on the spot [every longshore worker gets training as a steward] and gave me a printed steward's card. We agreed to go around to find out what was wrong with all the trucks and leave only one truck in service per crane, so that the job would officially keep running. We asked each driver what was wrong on his or her truck."

Stock had a stack of red tags to put on the trucks as the workers took them out of service. "We had enough legitimate safety complaints that we had 18 drivers standing by for health and safety. The job basically ground to a halt for half the shift.

"The supervisors came running and said, 'Listen, if we fix the lights on this truck, can we put it back in service?' 'We'll order the safety grates today and fix them by the end of the week.' One by one we let the trucks back in service, as they agreed to fix the stuff."

Substituting Safer Materials

THE CANADIAN AUTO WORKERS in Windsor, Ontario knew that the metalworking fluids used in their work could lead to irritation, rashes, asthma, lung conditions, and cancers. Rather than asking for better ventilation or personal protective equipment, the union took the more radical step of demanding that the hazard be eliminated altogether. Building a campaign over a period of years, they got the Big Three automakers to replace these hazardous fluids with more expensive but safer vegetable-based fluids.

Ken Bondy works at Ford (CAW Local 200), and is chair of the CAW Windsor Regional Environmental Council, a group uniting area CAW locals to speak for the environment. He describes the steps the CAW took:

• **Documented the risk.** In the late 1990s, Bud Jimmerfield, a well-known health and safety activist at the SKD automotive group in Ontario, had tried to get workers' compensation for his esophageal cancer. Jimmerfield had almost 30 years of exposure to metalworking fluids. "The company and Workers' Compensation Board did everything in their power to deny his claim," says Bondy. "Bud passed away in January 1998, but our union continued to fight for his compensation for his family, and shortly after his death we were successful. That changed everything." The union now had "a case we could refer to, that found that metalworking fluids were hazardous." The union also looked at material safety data sheets (MSDSs), gathered studies on the health effects of metalworking fluids, found professionals to look at the data, and negotiated epidemiological studies into their contracts.

• **Found safer substitutes.** CAW contacted the International Labor Organization office in Canada, which connected them with activities going on in Sweden. (The ILO is an agency of the UN.) Bondy says, "Most labor organizations are happy to share their successes."

• **Educated members**. The Regional Environmental Council educated workers through seminars and flyers. "That is really our strength," Bondy says, "the ability to say the members are behind us on this and they know all about the issue. Corporations recognize that our workforce is more apt to say, 'I will refuse to work if you can't show me it's safe.'"

• **Talked money**. "The language of corporations is money," says Bondy. "We emphasize that either they will pay now or pay later in terms of increased health care costs and, more than anything else, workers' comp claims down the road."

• **Talked to the media**. "Corporations want to be viewed in a positive light, which ultimately affects their merchandising and sales."

• **Built alliances** with grassroots organizations and other unions. "We co-sponsor information sessions in the community and participate in each others' informational pickets, protests, and rallies."

• **Bargained**. Bondy and others helped prepare proposals for contract talks. The 1996 contract required the Big Three to implement joint workplace environmental committees. "These committees gave us a venue to sit down and talk directly to the company," says Bondy. "We talked in great detail about the need to change metalworking fluids. They finally, around 1998, started to listen to us, perhaps as a result of Jimmerfield's death, the pressures we had been bringing, and a new opportunity. Ford was upgrading some of their production processes, and we said, 'While you're in the process of making those changes, why not try this vegetable-based fluid?'

"They agreed and tried it. They had to struggle to make it work, but we helped them and pushed them to find a way. They knew that we were gathering more information and we weren't going away. If they didn't deal with us through the committee, they would deal with us during the next set of negotiations."

Ford, DaimlerChrysler, General Motors, and four other Windsor-area auto plants have now substituted vegetable-based metalworking fluids in at least some systems. The safer fluids effort has become a model throughout the CAW and in other unions. Bondy says, "If we can get a corporation as large as Ford to make changes, it will give confidence to others as well."

COSH Group Helps Immigrant Workers Win Changes

During a union organizing drive at Kayem Foods, the union brought MassCOSH in because so many workers were talking about dangerous working conditions and injuries.

MassCOSH, one of the 22 state and local Committees or Coalitions on Occupational Safety and Health across the country, makes a particular effort to reach out to immigrant workers. Immigrants tend to work in the most dangerous jobs and suffer disproportionately high rates of injuries and fatalities, and immigrants without papers are often reluctant to speak up about their conditions, says MassCOSH Executive Director Marcy Goldstein-Gelb. "We reach hundreds of workers each year through English as a Second Language classes," she says. "We integrate the health and safety component right into the training. We assist unions that want to use health and safety as an organizing strategy. And we work with many immigrant community groups." MassCOSH also spearheads an "Equal Access to OSHA Coalition" that works to get OSHA to better serve the many immigrant workers in Massachusetts.

MassCOSH introduces immigrant workers to others who are fighting for health and safety. "This is an especially important resource," says Goldstein-Gelb, "because so many immigrant workers are afraid of retribution from their employers. That gives them peer support about how to go about fighting for health and safety on the job while protecting themselves. We discuss 'pressure points'—what kind of leverage do they have over the employer? Does the company get contracts through the state? Is the company sensitive to its local image in the community?"

In 1999, workers at Kayem Foods, a meat processing plant in Chelsea, Massachusetts, joined with the United Food and Commercial Workers on an organizing drive. Jean-Carmel St. Juste, MassCOSH's Immigrant Safe Work Coordinator, says that the company's fear-mongering among the 350 immigrant workers, many of whom were undocumented, worked. In the first vote, the workers voted the union down. A strong group of workers continued the effort with UFCW, hoping to win a future vote. UFCW brought in MassCOSH in 2000 because so many workers were talking about dangerous working conditions and injuries.

St. Juste explains, "The workers described to us constantly changing shifts, amputations and cuts from slicing machinery, burns from leaking chemicals, and severe injuries from falling racks. Management was ignoring basic safety measures such as allowing workers to lock the meat slicer in an off position before removing obstructions inside the machines. The workers told us that management claimed this would slow down production.

"A UFCW organizer invited us to a meeting to hear the workers' concerns. We expected about seven people, but 17 showed up. Out of this group and later meetings, the workers created a health and safety committee. This was an important way to collect all the health and safety complaints and begin functioning as they would if there were a union in place."

First Step: Hearing Tests

Goldstein-Gelb describes one of the first steps following these meetings: "Kayem Foods was required by law to test the workers' hearing on a yearly basis, due to the high levels of noise in the plant. But workers had not been given the results. When we asked what one step they felt they could do to begin to document health and safety violations, they all agreed to request copies of their hearing tests. They got them. Taking that step was an important confidence-booster. We found that while many workers had hearing loss, none was offered protection.

"The next step was to write a report documenting the health problems and safety violations and issuing recommendations to the company. We used the report to help build a strong coalition of labor, community, and religious supporters, who were appalled when they heard about conditions at the plant."

"While the organizing drives were proceeding," continues St. Juste, "the committee of workers made an attempt to become officially recognized by the company and to have their health and safety concerns recognized. First we sent a letter to the Kayem president, Ray Monkiewicz, signed by the community organizations and the workers. It was ignored.

"Towards the end of September 2001, we organized a rally at the plant. A wide range of unions, community groups, religious leaders, and elected officials turned out in support. Because we made use of the upcoming gubernatorial elections, we also got candidates to attend, including the Massachusetts Secretary of State. A delegation was chosen to take a letter with demands to Monkiewicz. The delegation even included two candidates for governor. The demands included an appeal to Monkiewicz to address the unsafe working conditions and to allow the workers to elect their own health and safety committee. Monkiewicz refused to see them. Eventually a plant supervisor met with the delegation, but all he did was blame the workers for their injuries and illnesses. He said they weren't paying enough attention to what they were doing. That's when we decided to get OSHA involved.

"MassCOSH had already been meeting with OSHA and discussing their lack of ability to serve immigrant workers. They don't have enough bilingual staff, so we knew of cases where they had asked supervisors to translate for the workers. Also, they would interview immigrant workers who fear for their status right in front of management. So we were prepared to get OSHA involved in a slightly different way."

"We helped the workers file the complaint," explains Goldstein-Gelb. "In the cover letter the workers had a few demands: that OSHA send an investigator who speaks Spanish, that they agree to meet with the workers off-site, and that OSHA meet with them during the closing conference." (Just before OSHA issues its citations and any penalty, it typically holds a closing conference with the employer and any union representatives. If there is no union at the workplace, OSHA generally does not meet with the workers.)

"On their first visit to the plant OSHA sent an investigator who couldn't speak Spanish. He walked around with management."

At MassCOSH and the workers' urging, OSHA then sent a Spanish-speaking investigator who met with workers in a confidential place at the plant and agreed to meet outside the plant to encourage workers who would normally be afraid to participate. About 13 workers went to the meeting. The OSHA staff got a much more thorough understanding of the hazards, and OSHA issued over a dozen citations and more than $16,000 in penalties. The combination of the citations and the other pressure tactics forced the company to make many improvements, including fixing leaky pipes and faulty wiring, securing the meat racks, and lowering the weight limit of meat that could go on them.

While Kayem employees have still not voted in the UFCW, their campaign will prevent future injuries and "it also was an important statement about the need for collective action in order to achieve decent working conditions," says Goldstein-Gelb.

Health and Safety in an Organizing Drive

IN THIS SECOND STORY OF IMMIGRANT WORKERS joining with a COSH, the COSH helped workers win an organizing drive at a company called Mexican Industries.

"Mexican Industries hired from the Spanish-speaking immigrant community, centered in southwest Detroit," explains Jeff Ditz, a staffer with the Southeast Michigan Coalition for Occupational Safety and Health (SEMCOSH). The company's plants made parts for the auto industry. "You could work there whether you had papers or not. The company was a paternalistic corporation—workers could borrow money to go home for a family emergency, and local churches and community groups could depend on annual contributions. There were 1,400 people working in six plants, plus management.

"In 1999 the United Auto Workers started an organizing drive. They'd learned from an earlier failure and they'd chosen Cindy Estrada, a bilingual woman of Mexican descent, as lead organizer. Cindy called the COSH because she needed research done. The office they rented for the organizing campaign was only a half-mile from our office, with three Mexican Industries plants in between.

"There are big differences in work culture between most union-side safety people and the 'model' organizer. Safety people can work for years on a policy problem. For organizers, the campaign and its fast-paced schedule are everything. The COSH folks or the safety experts from the union or the university need to adjust to fit the focused needs of the organizing campaign. So that was the challenge we were looking at—how could the COSH, with limited resources, serve this hugely important project in our neighborhood?

"The workers' biggest issues were the broken promises made by management during the earlier organizing battle. But safety issues were pretty high on people's list too. Both issues came down to dignity and quality of life."

Marisela Garcia, a Mexican Industries worker who later joined the SEMCOSH staff as a trainer, describes some of the problems: "Initially I sewed covers for tires and armrests. The leather was tough. You're constantly pulling and pushing with your fingers and wrists. There were widespread repetitive strain injuries in the plants. People were working with arm braces. Lots of people had big problems with company doctors and favoritism issues about light-duty work.

"There were also skirmishes with the company over chemical exposures. One day we stole all the labels from whatever chemicals we were working with and took them in to SEMCOSH to find out what the chemicals were. Based on what they told us, we would refuse to work with some of the chemicals."

Newspaper in the Community

Ditz explains what SEMCOSH decided to do. "What we had, that the union didn't, was a tabloid-style newspaper that is distributed by the thousands through union locals and solidarity groups, and in working class communities. A lot of the workers at Mexican Industries lived in a single zip code in southwest Detroit.

"Cindy and the organizers went through the reports they had accumulated from workers and pulled out the ones having to do with safety and health. I turned them into publishable stories. An organizer then translated them into Spanish. SEMCOSH published the first-ever bilingual issue of our newspaper and increased the print run by several thousand for distribution in the plants and throughout the Spanish-speaking neighborhoods, about ten days before the representation election. So here were the stories of the workers themselves getting into the plants and out in the streets, and getting there not through the union but through a community group."

Garcia remembers the impact. "There was a real buzz about the newsletter in the various buildings. It helped people get involved in the organizing drive. Some of the workers had believed the company's line that getting a union would be bad, especially for the undocumented workers. But when they got the newsletter a lot of people felt like 'this is the truth. We don't believe what the company is saying anymore.' And it was really important also to see that there was support from an organization which is based in our community." The workers voted the UAW in.

"The other thing we did is find volunteers to conduct health and safety trainings in Spanish," Ditz says. "So this kept safety out there as an issue through the first contract campaign.

"Our efforts paid off because we were with the campaign before it began. If organizers want to work with a COSH group, an environmental group, or some other community-based group, the union has to create that partnership early. Some organizers will call an environmental or safety group in the last couple weeks of the campaign, but that's just cosmetics. It doesn't tap the potential of the safety or environmental issue. The lead organizers need to be open to strategies beyond the 'model organizer' routine.

"The challenge to the union is that if the COSH assists the organizers in building a safety subcommittee within the workers' organizing committee, then that energy and training is going to extend beyond the election into what can be very important struggles around the first contract. For a democratic union that is trying to organize and educate its new members, that can be good."

Resources

More about strategies in this chapter:
• Mapping: See www.hazards.org/diyresearch/index.htm#mapping for blank body maps. That website and www.ilo.org/public/english/protection/ses/info/publ/barefoot.htm have great background on mapping and other tools for "do-it-yourself" research among workers.
• Behavior-based safety: See "On the Troublemaker's Website," below. Also see www.hazards.org/bs for a collection of union materials opposing behavior-based "blame-the-worker" safety programs.
• OSHA complaints: See OSHA at www.osha.gov/as/opa/worker/complain.html and the NYCOSH sheet on filing OSHA complaints: www.nycosh.org/how_to_complain.html. NYCOSH also has links to over 1,000 health and safety websites, organized by subject. www.nycosh.org/link.html.
• Substituting safer materials: Canadian Auto Workers Windsor Regional Environmental Council: http://cawwrec.org/ and Centre on Environmental Health: http://cawwrec.org/PDF/CEH_Flier_2.pdf.

Background research on health and safety problems:
• See the websites listed above under "mapping."
• National Network of Committees on Safety and Health: Website includes strategies, workers' rights under OSHA, information on hazards, and links to Material Safety Data Sheets online. www.coshnetwork.org.
• OSHA has an extensive website, including regulations, a database of OSHA inspection history by company, and statistics. www.osha.gov/as/opa/worker/index.html is the OSHA workers' page. www.osha.gov is the main OSHA page. OSHA's Hazard Advisor is a detailed survey workers can use confidentially to identify workplace hazards and find out about related laws. www.dol.gov/elaws/oshahaz.htm.
• Electronic Library of Construction Occupational Safety and Health. Search for materials by hazard, trade, and jobsite. www.cdc.gov/elcosh/index.html.
• In Canada: The Canadian Centre for Occupational Safety and Health (www.ccohs.ca/) has a great deal of online information and a free, confidential Inquiries Service. 800-263-8466, www.ccohs.ca/ccohs/inquiries/inquiries_form.html. Links to provinces' websites on regulations and procedures.
• *Disability Nightmare,* by the Labor Video Project, 2000. 21 minutes. Through interviews, tells how millions of American workers are injured as a result of bad laws and callous management. P.O. Box 425584, San Francisco, CA 94142. 415-282-1908. Email lvpsf@labornet.org. $30 plus $5 shipping.

Taking action:
• COSH groups can help you with strategy, training, and technical assistance and in other ways. To find out if there's a COSH group in your area, see www.coshnetwork.org, email the National COSH Network Coordinator at taoc99@bellsouth.net, or call 212-627-3900. Links to a variety of free resources.

- The Labor Safety and Health Project, a joint program of the George Meany Center/National Labor College and the AFL-CIO, has an extensive curriculum on a "Union Approach to Health and Safety," available in English and Spanish. The curriculum includes lots of participatory activities. The Project does training free of charge and also offers periodic train-the-trainer programs. 301-431-5414. ssimon@nationallaborcollege.edu.
- OSHA: www.osha.gov, 800-321-OSHA. See also the websites above on filing complaints.
- National Institute for Occupational Safety and Health, the government's research institute, has an extensive website, including a "Pocket Guide to Chemical Hazards." Any three private sector workers can request a "Health Hazard Evaluation," including written or verbal information about the hazard and possibly a visit to your workplace, which could help pressure your employer. Names are kept confidential. www.cdc.gov/niosh or 800-356-4674.
- Two publications from the Labor Occupational Health Program: *Tools of the Trade: A Health and Safety Handbook for Activists,* 2005. An excellent and complete guide to gathering information, organizing your co-workers, identifying hazards, using the "right to know" and OSHA, bargaining and enforcing contract language, and building community alliances. $25. *Collective Bargaining for Health and Safety—A Handbook for Unions,* 2000. $20. Order from LOHP, University of California, 2223 Fulton St., Berkeley, CA 94720. 510-642-5507. Prices include shipping. Make checks payable to "Regents of UC." For more publications, including materials in Spanish and other languages, as well as LOHP's online library catalog, information on training programs, and telephone reference service, go to www.lohp.org.
- *Labor Research Review* #16, "Organizing for Health and Safety." Available from the Center for Labor and Community Research, 3411 W. Diversey Ave., Suite 10, Chicago, IL 60647. 773-278-5418x24. www.clcr.org; email sbaer@clcr.org. $10 plus shipping and handling.
- *The Union Safety and Health Committee—Organizing for Action,* by Roberta Till-Retz, 1999. A manual for local union safety committees. Order from the Labor Center, Oakdale Hall, University of Iowa, Iowa City, IA 52242. 319-335-4144; email labor-center@uiowa.edu. $4.

Learning more:
- *Hazards Magazine* (www.hazards.org) is an international, union-friendly magazine on health and safety issues. The website has a wealth of information and resources for union members.
- Confined Space (www.spewingforth.blogspot.com) is a weblog covering health and safety news and politics from a labor perspective.

Action Questions

1. Can you gather a group of people to make a health and safety map of your workplace? Would this help to get an idea of what the outstanding issues are? First make a drawing showing the different work areas. Now using each of your sense organs (eyes, ears, nose, tongue, skin, and "under the skin"), indicate the sources of irritation, discomfort, pain, medical problems, or emotional stress. (Examples: poor light in area A, noise in area B, chemical odors that could be toxic in area C, heavy overtime in area D, awkward and repetitive work in area E, sexual harasser in area F.) Circle the area with the most dangerous problem and circle the one that affects the most people. Which problem does the group think should be tackled first? Is there one that would be easiest to get changed?

2. Make a list of the outstanding health and safety problems in your workplace. Choose one problem and list some first steps you might take in trying to change it. If you're already working on the issue, list some new ideas this book has given you about future steps. Try to be as concrete as possible. (For example, instead of writing "Contact our supporters," list who you would contact, how, and what you would say to them.)

3. Are there problems in your workplace that affect people's health or safety but that aren't considered "health and safety problems"? These could include problems with emotional stress, work hours, or how work is organized. How might you get people to change the way they see these problems? How might you use health and safety tools to win changes in these areas?

4. Would it be good to call a health and safety meeting in your department or for the whole worksite? What issue would attract people? Who would you ask to speak? An occupational health expert? Or would you simply have a discussion among co-workers?

5. To what extent does your employer's attitude "blame the injured worker"? Is health and safety considered an individual responsibility or the employer's role? What do most workers seem to think? How might you discuss this issue with fellow workers?

6. Does your employer have a "behavior-based" safety program? If so, what do you think has been the impact on workers? On safety? How supportive might your co-workers be of a challenge to the program? How might you go about mounting a challenge?

7. Most workplaces have at least some measures in place to control dangerous exposures. How good are these protections in your workplace? To what extent do they work "passively"—that is, without workers having to do anything to make them effective? (For example, are there barriers installed, or does each worker have to put on personal protective equipment? And if personal protective equipment is required, do workers have to pay for it?)

8. Could different methods or materials be substituted for the dangerous ones in your workplace? How could you find out about these alternatives?

9. Has your workplace ever been inspected by OSHA? If so, what was the outcome? How, if at all, did workers participate in the process? In hindsight, do you think OSHA was the best strategy at that time? Under what conditions do you think you would contact OSHA

to inspect your workplace? Are there creative uses you could make of an OSHA citation?

10. Do you have a health and safety committee in your workplace? Is it a joint committee, or one run by the employer or union? Who has the real power in it? Do the union members on the committee approach it with a bargaining mindset? Do they organize among the members at large to support them on the positions they take in the committee? If the committee has been management-dominated, how can you educate the union representatives to take a more aggressive bargaining outlook?

11. Do you need to get more people involved in the committee or to elect new representatives?

12. If you have no health and safety committee, should you organize one? Who are three people who would be good to get it started? Are they representative of the different areas and groups you need to involve? Do you want to make the committee a regular standing committee of the union, and/or participate in a joint committee with management?

13. In raising health and safety issues, employer discrimination can be a real concern. How can you deal with the possibility of discrimination against those who exercise their rights or take a leadership role?

14. Where can you go for outside help? Is there a COSH group in your area? What about the International's health and safety department? What about the National Institute of Occupational Safety & Health (NIOSH), OSHA, or the state OSHA? How about the Environmental Protection Agency (EPA)? A university occupational health department?

15. Is the community also affected by your workplace, such as by toxic emissions? Who would you contact to form an alliance? Can you contact a reporter who would be interested in health and safety problems? (See Chapter 22.)

16. How could you use health and safety as a tool to build your union's strength? What issues would engage the most members? How would you communicate with members about these issues to draw them in further and help motivate action? What types of strategies would be most appealing? How do health and safety issues tie in with other union concerns or campaigns?

17. How good is your employer's record-keeping about health and safety? Ask to review the OSHA 300 log of injuries and illnesses (employees have the right to see this). Can you convince the union to start keeping its own records to see how they match up? (Include logs to document workplace hazards, conversations with the employer about them, and any responses, and publicize the existence of the union's logs so you can get comprehensive information.) Beyond helping you understand problems, these logs will be very helpful in future dealings with the employer and any government agencies.

18. Does your union contract give workers rights they can use? What more is needed? Draw up a contract proposal to deal with the most pressing issues. How would you begin to organize to win it in the next contract?

Authors

STEVE HINDS teaches math in the City University of New York's adult literacy program. Previously, he was an activist in the New Haven Federation of Teachers (AFT Local 933), and before that an organizer with the United Electrical Workers (UE).

NANCY LESSIN is Health and Safety Coordinator for the Massachusetts AFL-CIO. She has worked with unions nationally and internationally for over 25 years, especially on "blame-the-worker" safety programs and on the impacts of work restructuring and downsizing/understaffing.

RONI NEFF is a doctoral student in occupational safety and health policy at the Johns Hopkins School of Public Health in Baltimore. She has worked in a variety of public health and environmental health advocacy and education positions.

MARSHA NIEMEIJER staffs Labor Notes' New York office, where she covers longshore workers, telecom workers, and Canadian and European labor, as well as international economic issues. She has worked with the Transnationals Information Exchange since 1995 and helps coordinate international and cross-border programs for TIE and Labor Notes.

DOROTHY WIGMORE is a long-time health and safety specialist and activist based in Winnipeg, Canada. She has worked with and for unions in Canada, the United States, and Mozambique and is a pioneer in mapping methods. You can find her at dorothyw@web.ca. www.wigmorising.ca.

Notes

1. U.S. Bureau of Labor Statistics, www.bls.gov. A recent study found that these numbers may miss one-third to two-thirds of actual injuries, due to underreporting and other problems. (J. Paul Leigh, James P. Marcin, Ted R. Miller, "An estimate of the U.S. government's undercount of nonfatal occupational injuries," *Journal of Occupational and Environmental Medicine*, Volume 46, Number 1, January 2004, pp. 10-18.)

2. For more details on the right to refuse unsafe work, see "Basic Health and Safety Rights," from the New York Committee for Occupational Safety and Health, www.nycosh.org/rights.html.

3. AFL-CIO, "Death on the Job: The Toll of Neglect," April 2004. www.aflcio.org/yourjobeconomy/safety/memorial/upload/death_2004_intro.pdf.

4. Ibid. The definition of "serious violation" is from the OSH Act.

On the Troublemaker's Website

TO CONFRONT a "behavior-based" safety program, see "Bargaining Over Injury Discipline Policies: Submitting Information Requests," by Nancy Lessin.

8. Contract Campaigns

by Chris Kutalik

WHEN PEOPLE THINK ABOUT COLLECTIVE BARGAINING, many picture union officials and bosses talking across a table. But today, in the face of employers' demands for mammoth givebacks, union negotiators—no matter how experienced—can't get the job done alone. When management representatives look across the bargaining table, they need to know they are dealing with the entire membership, not just a small negotiating team.

How does the union mobilize the power of the members during bargaining? The answer is a contract campaign. Negotiations are about power and proving who has it—creatively, if necessary. Since management won't sign a good contract without a threat of some kind, the union must demonstrate that members (and their allies) are ready and able to disrupt business as usual. Waging a campaign *before* the contract expires gives the union a way to build up its unity and strength if it does have to strike. And since the vast majority of contract talks don't result in strikes—because of the balance of forces, because certain strikes are illegal, and for many other reasons—the contract campaign is an essential weapon in bargaining.

When the contract expires the union has four options: settle, keep working with or without a strategy, or strike. If the contract campaign hasn't "worked" by the expiration date, the union had better be prepared for plan B.

Our case studies illustrate these key elements of a contract campaign:

Start early. A good campaign may begin even a year or two before a contract expires. Start with an honest evaluation of the union's strengths and weaknesses. Research the employer's position, especially vulnerabilities (see the Appendix). What did you lose or gain last time? What do you hope to gain this time? How will you win? If the local is part of a larger company or in an industry where locals should be bargaining together, then goals and strategies should be decided together. This is the time to plan your strategy.

Members decide. An involved membership with the power to make decisions is crucial. If a campaign is top-heavy and most members are passive, management will know it. Members must be clear what actions they are willing to take.

Prioritize. Through surveys and thorough discussion, everyone should be clear on which are the must-have goals. Knowing your goals enables everyone to agree on whether or not you've won.

Build leadership. You will need a strong contract action team of stewards and rank-and-file volunteers. Creating such a member-to-member network enables new rank-and-file leaders to step forward.

Keep information flowing. A strong communications network using one-on-ones, phone trees, shop floor meetings, videos, hotlines, flyers, websites, and email will keep members mobilized over the length of the campaign.

Escalate actions. Build momentum as you approach the expiration date, starting with actions that require less risk. Your goal at first is to get members involved in any visible way. Begin with simple actions, like putting up stickers or having members all wear the same color shirt

More on Contract Campaigns

Contract campaigns, or tactics to help win them, appear in almost every chapter in this book. See in particular "Vermont Nurses Reach In to Each Other and Out to the Community" and "Everything but the Kitchen Sink: HERE's 13-Year Campaign Beats the Marriott," in Chapter 15. The approaches these workers took in their fights for a first contract, such as open bargaining, could be used just as well by a local facing its twentieth contract. And read the story of the UPS contract campaign in Chapter 9, Strikes. Each of these three stories details a campaign from start to finish.

Most of the campaigns in this chapter were coordinated by union leaders, but rank-and-filers can take the lead and organize contract campaigns using the same principles. For three examples, see "Transit Workers Caucus Runs Contract Campaign" in Chapter 18; "Drivers Organize for Area-Wide Contract," in Chapter 14; and "Rank and Filers Take Over a Strike" in Chapter 9. In the last case, the workers did their own member survey, wrote and passed out leaflets, and challenged a two-tier contract proposal.

To read about a contract campaign that became a community-wide crusade, see "A Living Wage Contract Campaign" in Chapter 12. Chapter 10 on Inside Strategies tells how to carry on a contract campaign after the contract expires.

Finally, to win good contracts, many unions will need more than the workplace-based tactics described in this chapter. They will need to garner community support and plan long-term for a large-scale corporate campaign. See Chapter 11.

one day. Then build intensity, involving more members and putting more pressure on management. Organize petition drives, rally during lunch or break time, or leaflet customers. Later, as things really start to heat up, you can work to rule or pull a sick-out or a one-day strike. This gives bargainers more leverage over sticky issues like wages and benefits, which typically fall later in negotiations.

Mobilize community support. In some cases the union will need the help of other unions, community leaders, clergy members, and politicians to win a decent contract. Winning public support means having a message that resonates with a broader audience. For example, the union can link the company's over-reliance on part-time work or contracting out to the community's need for more good jobs, or it can explain how cutbacks in the city workforce will hurt services. Use contacts in the media to get the message out.

Some of the following stories are about specific tactics within a contract campaign. Others, such as the Barr Labs and Northwest Airlines stories, show how unions can put some or all of these pieces together in the quest for a strong contract. Most of our examples deal with contract campaigns organized by union leaders, but the Northwest Airlines and "No Scabs" sections show how rank and filers can take the lead and use the same ideas. At the end, we include three discussions with experienced negotiators on tactics at the bargaining table.

On-the-Job Actions: 15-Minute Strikes

by Hanna Metzger

YOU CAN ENERGIZE YOUR MEMBERS and get media attention by using work breaks for short demonstrations and rallies.

Workplace Actions during a Contract Campaign

- Survey days, where workers discuss their priorities together
- Signing a petition or writing letters
- Wearing buttons, stickers, t-shirts, hats, armbands
- Putting up posters
- Marching into work all together, perhaps carrying balloons or banners
- Synchronized tapping, coughing, sneezing, or whistling
- Health action days—to protest demands for givebacks, members wear bandages, canes, eye patches
- Pledge card campaigns—members pledge to take certain actions
- Stepped-up enforcement of existing language
- Lunch or break-time rallies, inside or outside the workplace
- Demonstrations to turn away potential scabs
- Family rallies
- Leafleting clients or customers
- Extra attention to safety and quality
- Working to rule or slowdowns
- Sick-outs or one-day strikes

The Pennsylvania Social Services Union, SEIU Local 668 in Philadelphia, represents workers in around 20 welfare offices. During negotiations with the state in 1996, says spokesman Ray Martinez, "we wanted to do something legal, but nonetheless an activity that would irritate the boss, educate the public, and at the same time get the members psyched up. We decided that we would all take our 15-minute breaks at the same time."

PSSU used its phone-trees to call members at home. "At the agreed date and time," Martinez explains, "all of our members would get up and walk out of the office. This meant that clients in the office, phone calls, and so on would be placed on hold. In other words, all activity ceased.

"This served a couple of purposes. First, management and clients would get a feel for what it would be like without our services if we were to go on strike. Secondly, we, the members, would be outside of the worksite having outdoor shop meetings and updating the workers on the latest on the negotiations. While this was going on, we had picket signs asking drivers to honk their horns to show us their support. The beauty of it all was that this was perfectly legal, so there was nothing management could do."

At the end of the 15-minute break, everybody went back inside and went back to work.

15-Second Strikes

Another quickie action took place while managers were in meetings to discuss strike contingency plans. Martinez explains, "With all of them in the meetings, we would have someone either blow a whistle or ring a bell. Then we would all—sometimes as many as 75 workers—start a PSSU clap and stomping of the feet. It would last 15 seconds.

"By the time management realized what was going on and came out of the meeting to see who the culprits were, we had stopped and were quietly at our desks doing our work. Since they couldn't prove who was involved, they couldn't discipline anyone. This worked to mobilize our members."

Mini-Corporate Campaign against Concessions

by Nick Robinson

IN 2001 CONTRACT TALKS WITH PACE LOCAL 1-149, drug manufacturer Barr Labs demanded over 100 concessions. Mark Dudzic, currently national organizer for the Labor Party, was president of Local 1-149, which represented two Barr plants in New York and New Jersey. Here he tells how a "quick, small campaign" beat back the concessions.

"We were initially shocked," Dudzic says, "because there were no indications that the company was really going to go after us. After the initial shock wore off, the committee turned that shock very effectively into anger.

"We were in a pretty good position because there were no real reasons for these givebacks. Barr was doing well, rolling out new products. We decided that we needed to regain the offensive." The local began by forming a 15-person contract committee and planning a multi-pronged attack, including a small-scale corporate campaign.

"Obviously, the first thing to do," explains Dudzic, "was to build solidarity in the plant. We had to break out of the secretive negotiating process and communicate with people directly. We set up email and phone trees and sent out brief updates after every bargaining session via email. We wanted a way to communicate quickly with people, and this is a multi-shift operation in two different buildings, with negotiations on the weekends."

One of Barr's demands was to contract out the jobs of 15 mostly Haitian custodial workers in the porter job classification—more than ten percent of the bargaining unit of 130. So the union leafleted with the porters' pictures. "We added up all of their salaries," says Dudzic, "and compared it to the salaries and stock options of the top five corporate officers, which was something like ten times what these folks were getting. We tried to humanize the situation. We also focused on a whole series of the givebacks in leaflets, and did a lot of internal discussion.

"People went to some of the community organizations, as there's a large Haitian community in Rockland County. A Haitian cable TV show did a brief piece on the campaign, and there was some coverage of the negotiations in the local newspaper and radio."

Dudzic emphasizes, however, that tactics should be constantly re-evaluated and based primarily on hurting the company, not simply on what has worked in the past. "We made the decision early on that community support was important, but in the context of what this company was about and where they were vulnerable, community support wasn't going to win this fight. In earlier negotiations, we had done a lot of community support, and the company was prepared for it this time."

Finding Their Vulnerability

Local 1-149 hit upon an unusual way to pressure the company. Members knew that Barr was just getting ready to release a generic version of Prozac that it expected to be a big seller, and the company's stock price was moving up in anticipation. "In the generic drug industry," explains Dudzic, "the first month, when you are the first to release a new generic drug, is the most important, because as other companies enter the field, your profitability slowly goes down."

The contract committee knew that Barr's stock price was a highly sensitive subject for the stock analysts who monitor the drug industry and send out regular notices to investors. Dudzic checked some Internet message boards. "There was a lot of activity, lots of messages recommending that people buy Barr stock, which we found through web searches. So we compiled a list of stock analysts and began to send them regular emails telling them there was no way Barr would meet their launch date, because of the likelihood of a strike.

"My name was listed on the first email we sent out, but without contact information. I came home from negotiations that night at midnight, and my answering

Where Is Our Dollar?

CWA Local 1037 in New Jersey was negotiating a first contract for workers at the Association for Retarded Citizens. "These are group-home workers," says President Hetty Rosenstein, "and they were pretty low-paid. We found out that the state of New Jersey, which funds the program, had provided the ARC with $1 an hour supposedly to go to the workers. But the workers never got it. The workers only got a bonus.

"The mobilization committee made up a great chant about the director of the program and organized a protest outside management's offices:

> *Hi ho, Diminot*
> *We've been looking high and low.*
> *Our dollar,*
> *Where is our dollar?*

"During a weekly softball game that management participated in, they organized a scavenger hunt to look for the dollar.

"Then people pinned a dollar on their shirts and wore them to work on Solidarity Fridays.

"They made up charts of things they would have done if they had gotten the dollar. They filled out the charts together and faxed them to management on one of the Solidarity Fridays.

"Those workers—people making $9 an hour—got an amazing first contract—and they got more than a dollar. In the first year we got 90 cents and in the second year 70 cents."

machine had 15 messages from stock analysts who had tracked me down on their own. It really put the company on the defensive and made them very vulnerable, because most of top management was reaping huge stock options.

"These analysts would say, 'The company says they have stockpiles, they won't be affected.' I'd say, 'Well, we make it, so we should know, and it's not going to be ready.' The company was forced to set up a conference call with their major investors just to reassure them. Instead of an anti-union lawyer advising upper management that they were controlling the situation, now upper management was telling the union-buster to end the problem."

Dudzic maintains that workers' in-plant actions were also crucial to victory. "The company uses supervisors to find weak points, so you have to keep the heat up on the shop floor, in order to maintain a credible threat to back up your words. It's things like freezing out management by walking out of the break room when they walk in, wearing buttons, whatever you can do to show some solidarity.

"People stood together until the end. The campaign changed the whole balance of negotiations. One by one they dropped the givebacks. Not only did they withdraw their demands to subcontract, they even guaranteed that all 15 porters would continue working for the length of the contract. It was an across-the-board victory. No concessions, substantial wage increases, improvement in all of our issues. We were lucky to have those kinds of circumstances."

Local 1-149 demonstrated that a union can find allies in unexpected places, including allies whose concerns are different from workers'. "Don't assume your only potential allies have the same interests you're interested in," Dudzic says. "Our 'allies' were stock analysts who were interested in shipping dates and profit margins, not the jobs of these 15 porters. You've got to look out of that box, see how the company's vulnerable.

"It took no special training. Most of this stuff was done by negotiating committee members. People only need to understand the Internet, start doing searches, find out who is interested in your company and why, and then use their interest as a pressure point. Ten years ago, we would have had to hire some kind of corporate industry analyst to access financial reports. The Internet has made all that more accessible."

Bringing Members to the Table

by Marsha Niemeijer

AT THE LAMBWESTON "PIZZA POCKETS" PLANT in Weston, Oregon, management was used to an uninvolved union membership and negotiators who did the talking for them. But in September 2000, a slate of Teamsters for a Democratic Union members, mostly Latino immigrants, swept into office. The new Local 556 officers—and the members—had to convince management that the changes in their union went beyond the executive board.

In their contract campaign against LambWeston (a division of ConAgra, a $27 billion per year agricultural giant, one of the largest in the world), members took escalating actions on the shop floor to get management's attention. According to steward Sandra Stewart, "All we had to do was make one phone call and there would be things going on in the plant."

But first, they had to get organized. Seven months before expiration, a group of workers and stewards met to talk about what it would take to win a good contract. They began by reviewing membership lists and charting each department and shift. They launched a bargaining survey and used the charts to track who had filled it out.

Besides handing out the surveys one on one, the local held a "survey day" in the cafeteria. Sitting down together enabled members to talk among themselves about what they wanted most, and by four months before expiration, nearly 90 percent of the plant had filled the surveys out. The stewards and volunteers began to meet on Sundays to analyze the surveys and review the contract line by line.

At a large meeting, members elected a rank-and-file negotiating committee. Members talked about the lack of respect from supervisors and emphasized that without respect on the job it would not be possible even to talk about the other important issues, such as low wages and health care.

Members were involved in every step of the bargaining process, but the trick was to prove that to management—to bring members, in spirit, to the bargaining table. "It is often very isolating for the bargaining team to be holed up with management behind closed doors," says Tony Perlstein, whom the new officers had hired to do internal organizing.

"What the members wanted was just one sentence in the contract that stated that there must be mutual respect and dignity in the workplace," says Stewart. "On the first day we met with the company we sat them down in a circle at our union hall. They were freaked because they'd never sat in a circle before during bargaining.

"Then we told them that we wanted them to get to know us, as workers and as the bargaining team. We told them, 'We're not just numbers, so we want respect. We want you to know what our jobs are and who we are, and you can tell us who you are.' They were nervous, because they'd never been forced to see us as people." (See more below, "Keeping Management Off Balance.")

Management dug in its heels, fearing the union would use "respect" language to grieve anything and everything. In response, the union printed up bright yellow posters in Spanish and English—"RESPETO" and "RESPECT"—and stewards asked members if they really wanted this one sentence in the contract.

Workers answered by mounting the posters on their windshields in the parking lot. "When the supervisors came to work and saw all those bright posters they weren't happy," Stewart says. "But back at the table, they still refused to put it in the contract. So the bargaining team went back to the workers and planned the next step."

Activists circulated a petition, almost the entire plant

signed, and they blew it up to poster size. Groups of workers presented photocopies of the petitions to their supervisors. "The day that workers marched into their supervisors' offices, the bargaining team hung up the big poster with all the signatures on the wall of the room where we were bargaining," Stewart recalls. "It was up there before the company walked in. They didn't want to speak to us that day. One woman took a group of ten people into her supervisor's office, who happened to be her husband—boy, was he pissed.

"Management's main line had constantly been that all those demands are just what Tony wants. But then they saw it wasn't Tony, this is what the people want, and now you have to listen."

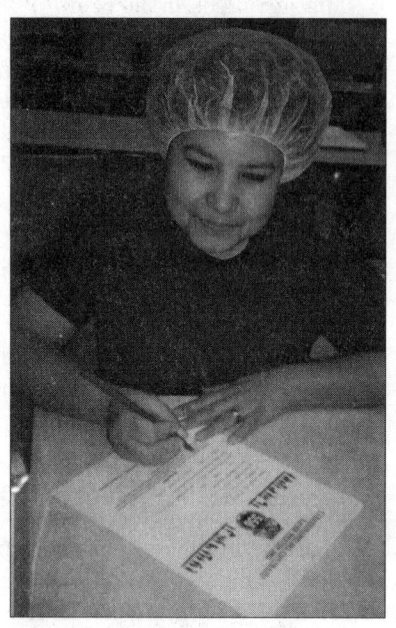

Ultimately, management agreed to print the respect-and-dignity language on the inside cover of the contract. The committee consulted with members, who agreed to the compromise.

Community Support

Meanwhile, the local was also searching out the links members had in their communities. "On the back of our contract surveys there is a question about what other groups members belong to, such as church or sports groups, or whether they know workers in other LambWeston plants," Perlstein explains. "We tell members that preparing for a good contract is also about informing the groups and community they belong to that this campaign is going on. The pay, benefits, and working conditions inside our plant have a direct impact on the place where members live, especially in a small company town like Weston."

Some workers were reluctant to answer the question because they were embarrassed or believed it had nothing to do with the campaign. "But that starts a conversation," says Perlstein. "Some people didn't want to talk about the contract campaign outside of the plant, but over the course of the campaign, and because of the conversations we started, folks became more willing.

"It's so great to see that happen, because everything in society makes us define ourselves so narrowly. It's about *my* discussion with *my* employer over *my* wages. There is so little to make us think that this contract campaign is about the standards we're going to have in our community over health and safety and a decent living."

Members were involved in every step of the bargaining process at LambWeston, from filling out a bargaining survey to lobbying management for a "respect and dignity in the workplace" clause.

The union based its public message on the "respect" theme: respect on the job, respect a day of rest (overtime was horrendous), respect the law, and respect our basic union rights. Volunteers solicited letters from church-based groups in Washington and Oregon, from the PCUN farmworkers union and other farmworker organizations, from unions, from nearby residents, from students and professors at a local college, and from the people running English as a Second Language programs. The workers even got a letter from the union representing LambWeston workers in the Netherlands.

Local politicians also wrote letters vowing to support the workers if they could not reach an agreement. Workers got press coverage for a big picnic and rally attended by 300 people, including politicians, workers from other plants in their local, and community supporters.

When management announced a layoff during negotiations, members were ready to respond. Local 556 issued a pledge card asking workers to pledge two days a week during the layoff to organize in the community, send delegations to Portland, Seattle, and possibly the Netherlands, and make signs and posters. After these efforts, management canceled most of the layoffs.

The final issue was wages. The union wanted four percent across the board each year. The negotiating committee bargained until 1:30 a.m. and when they left, made calls to mobilize members. "We told some workers that we didn't get what they wanted and that management had given us a last and final offer," Stewart says.

Fighting Words

At Smith Frozen Foods, another plant in the same local, workers were also fighting for "respect" language in their contract. Bargainers made a list of all the swear words that supervisors used against workers, translated them from Spanish into English, and made posters. Straight-faced, they went over the posters at the bargaining table: "'Pendejo,' that means pubic hair, but it is also a general term for 'idiot' or 'bastard.'"

Mormon managers turned crimson, and finally agreed to the "respect" language workers were seeking.

When she arrived at the plant at 6:30 the next morning, a group of people was organizing in the cafeteria to descend on management. On their own, they had written letters demanding the wage increase, and they posted the letters on the walls of the plant. The production manager read some of the letters and pulled them down. "The workers became really mad," Stewart says. "They were yelling at him, and he locked himself up in his office. He never did come back out."

Workers kept on posting their letters. Five would go up, get pulled down, and another ten would go up. Workers got the point across. Management agreed to a wage increase of three percent the first year and four percent in each of the other years.

No Scabs, No Strike

by Dan La Botz

WHEN UNIONS STRIKE, they need to keep replacement workers from taking union jobs. To up the ante and intimidate members, companies may begin hiring scabs even before the contract expires. How can unions stop scabs, win public sympathy, and get members united and stronger?

In 2002, rank-and-file Teamsters in Local 572 in southern California came up with a strategy that did all of those things. Frank Halstead, who belongs to Teamsters for a Democratic Union, is a steward at a perishable foods warehouse of Ralphs Grocery Co. Halstead recalls, "When negotiations took a turn for the worse and there was a possibility of a strike, and absolutely zero leadership from the elected officials, people started coming to me and asking what we could do.

"The employer placed an advertisement in the regional newspaper asking for applicants in the event of a labor dispute. This happened a couple of days after negotiations broke down, and people were worried. I said we ought not to let the company get away with running these ads and getting applicants.

Organizing a Demonstration

"In my opinion, the company made a fatal mistake. They ran the ad on Sunday but they weren't accepting applications until Wednesday, so that gave us two days to put this thing together." First, the rank and filers talked to people in the Teamsters and other unions who had been involved in turning away scabs. They talked to the national TDU office and to Tom Leedham, a leader of the union's warehouse division for many years.

"They gave us all the help we could have desired about the technical aspects of this kind of demonstration," says Halstead. "They said we needed a big presence at the beginning, before people were lined up, because it would be almost impossible to turn them away after that. Although applications would be accepted starting at 8 a.m., we knew people would start lining up at 6 a.m. So we knew we had to have a large group of people there by six or earlier."

The activists had a loose communication network throughout all shifts, with people committed to participating in the demonstration. "We showed up with 100 people at the beginning of the day, very disciplined—and management was stunned," says Halstead.

The Message: 'These Are Not Real Jobs'

When faced with people who may take their jobs, some union members will be angry. Others may understand that these are often desperate unemployed people who need work. The Local 572 members decided that their message should not be hostile.

"We wanted to talk to these workers and explain what the situation was," remembers Halstead. "We had a flyer that spelled out our message. We said that these were not real jobs, that the company has no real intention of hiring you. They just want to use your applications as a tool in bargaining to intimidate us into accepting their offer. So, number one, by filling out this application you're wasting your time.

"Number two, you're helping the employer hurt workers. And, third, you're actually helping to destroy the very good job that you came to get. We tied all of those themes into hurting the community. It was very effective."

Because they didn't want to be accused of trying to cause a work stoppage, the members didn't carry anything that resembled a picket sign. "All the signs we had were handmade poster-board signs with slogans like, 'See Me First about a Job,'" says Halstead.

Bringing video cameras was one of the most important tactics. "We told our members to bring them whether they worked or not. We wanted as many video cameras as possible. The video cameras paralyzed their security force. We had told some guys to spend the entire time pointing the cameras at the big-shot supervisors and the security goons."

Some applicants understood the situation and did not want to apply for someone else's job. For those people, the activists had prepared a list of employers that were hiring, with union employers first on the list. When a job applicant did go in, Halstead would turn on the siren noise on his bullhorn.

Although this was a serious event, it was also fun. Halstead says, "We had some warehouse comedians who would heckle the people going in. One guy came with a cast on his hand, and somebody said, 'Hey, buddy, you're not even hired and you're on worker's comp.'

The Impact

The action kept management from recruiting the pool of scabs it would need in case of a strike. "Normally when they run an ad they get over 1,100 applications," says Halstead, "but this time they got just over 300." But there were other benefits. "Even more significant, because we were disciplined and unified and effective, no one suffered a single negative repercussion. Not one person got disciplined. Not one person was even issued a traffic ticket. We showed the company that we could be effective and that we were not intimidated by them.

"After that we had two other actions, two Teamster Days with 200 people wearing shirts saying 'Ready to Strike.' On the day of the deadline we had a huge potluck in the parking lot where everybody came out for the latest report on the contract negotiations. That really freaked management out, because they didn't know if they were coming back after lunch or not. Once again, nobody was disciplined."

The rank-and-filers' actions did not force the officers to better represent the members or force the company to cave. "We ended up getting a contract, although it was not a good contract," says Halstead. He believes, though, that stopping scabs "had a tremendous empowering effect on the workers. The next day everyone's chest was stuck out as if they were saying to the supervisors, 'You don't scare me.' The culture of the warehouse has dramatically changed from that time on."

Northwest Flight Attendants: Contract Campaign Becomes a 'Vote No' Campaign

by Simone Sagovac

WHAT HAPPENS WHEN UNION OFFICIALS NEGOTIATE an agreement over the heads—or behind the backs—of the members? Even a contract campaign with maximum member involvement can be sold out if the national union does not support it. That is one of the lessons of the Northwest Airlines flight attendants' contract campaign in 1998-2000.

The flight attendants' well-organized and creative campaign did win improvements, although not what they had hoped for. We tell their story here for two reasons. It illustrates the ingredients of a potentially winning contract campaign—including, at the end, a successful "Vote No" movement. And it points out the pitfalls of incomplete democracy, when unrepresentative bargainers are in a position to make crucial decisions.

A History of Fighting Back

Long before the contract campaign began in 1998, the predominantly female flight attendants had had a history of fighting for their rights. They fought the industry's discriminatory policies that, until the 1970s, restricted age, weight, and marital status. In the early 1990s, with the election of reformer Ron Carey to head the Teamsters, they fought to consolidate all Northwest flight attendants into one nationwide local, Local 2000. With years of help from Teamsters for a Democratic Union, activists finally elected a reform-minded local leadership, who took office in January 1998.

These new leaders, the "It's Time Slate," had campaigned for more member involvement to win a good contract and immediately upon taking office began a contract campaign.

By then, negotiations had been stagnating for two years. Airline workers fall under the Railway Labor Act, which requires bargainers to exhaust the negotiations process, mediation, arbitration, and finally a 30-day cooling off period, before they can call a strike. But the Northwest negotiations were still at step one.

The 11,000 flight attendants had gone ten years without a raise. They had given the company $850 million in wage concessions alone, when the airline industry faced a severe economic threat in the early 1990s. By 1998, the company was turning out record profit increases of 325 percent, and executives were collecting million-dollar compensation packages. Executives retired with up to $600,000 per year, while 30-year flight attendants got $12,000.

"We took a 12.5 percent pay cut to save the company," explains Danny Campbell, who at the time was Local 2000's secretary-treasurer and later became president. "But mainly the concessions we made were in work rules, like 13-hour duty days. A decade later, we were way behind the industry wages and work rule language." Campbell, a TDU member, says he got his start as a union activist when he read the first *Troublemaker's Handbook*.

Contract Action Team

The new leadership created a member network called the Contract Action Team (CAT) "because there was no way we were going to be successful without a strike strategy," says Campbell. "And you can't have a strike strategy without agreement about goals and a membership that believes in them."

In contract surveys, members had identified over a hundred issues to change, but only a few could become the focus of the campaign—those that most members felt strongest about and that could best unite members and gain public support. CAT focused on pensions, stopping subcontracting, and better wages. Work rule improvements were also important: decreasing the 13-hour duty day, pay for the time passengers boarded and exited, and sensible scheduling where flight attendants could trade trips with one another.

"We faced obstacles because of the geography of our membership," says Campbell. Members lived in every state and many countries. "We would need to recruit volunteers from each of our ten bases (in nine states) and from areas where large numbers of members lived."

The local held a kick-off CAT training meeting for volunteers, base reps (business agents), and executive board members. "At that meeting," says Campbell, "we developed the infrastructure, appointed an overall coordinator for the campaign, and selected coordinators for each base. We used information from the member surveys to develop campaign messages, and we set a timeline for unity actions, starting small with a sticker day." The CAT activists discussed their common bonds as a workforce of women and many gay men, facing a management that devalued their skills and did not take them seriously.

The union then scheduled CAT trainings around the country to enlist more volunteers. At each base, members would be in charge of a CAT committee that would shape

CONTRACT CAMPAIGNS 99

The Contract Action Team used petition drives and demonstrations to put pressure on Northwest Airlines.

and build activities. Initially, the International provided field organizers for each base and paid for regular CAT bulletins, leaflets, stickers, buttons, signs, and rally props.

CAT's Out of the Bag

CAT training sessions emphasized that it was members' involvement that would create power at the bargaining table. CAT was designed for two-way communication, with information flowing up from the grassroots and back from the bargaining table. Organizers held weekly phone conferences of volunteer CAT coordinators, or "CAT calls." A 1-800 hotline gave updates on activities, sometimes daily.

"We were putting out monthly CAT bulletins," explains Campbell, "condensing contract issues and putting out talking points which had internal and external appeal. At the same time, we were simultaneously building the infrastructure at the base, with one member assigned to ten member contacts, and building a phone tree by area codes." The goal was to have 1,000 identified CAT leaders in contact with 10,000 members.

"The great thing about the CAT was an energy and light being pumped out," remembers Kristi Damis of Seattle, a rank-and-file flight attendant and CAT leader. "I would have the CAT bulletins in my arms and flight attendants were reaching, wanting whatever I had. Never was it so easy to communicate with each other. CAT was successful because we had good leaders who the members respected and could believe in. They worked hard (and weren't being paid) and they earned the members' trust."

Since members lived far and wide and worked with different co-workers every day, both the telephone and the Internet were essential for communication, but they did not replace face-to-face organizing. Even with online access to bulletins and leaflets, these were also distributed member to member to keep the network primed for response.

Rank-and-File Websites

Along with the local's website, there were three rank-and-file websites that members started up early in the campaign. They worked in tandem with CAT and supported grassroots creativity and communication. One website hosted a forum where members could converse on all aspects of the campaign and debate contract issues. Another had the full text of prior contracts as well as bargaining history. An independent email listserve managed by another member built support throughout the campaign and was critical to grassroots efforts.

"What we were saying to management was that finally we're going to release something that you are going to have to contend with, which is the membership," Campbell recalls. "Right away members were building momentum with unity actions like the first sticker day." The stickers' message warned: "CAT: It's Out of the Bag!"

The planning for the first sticker day in June 1998 started at the founding CAT training and shows how much careful effort CAT put into mobilizing members. At airport bases around the country, flight attendants volunteered in shifts to hand out stickers for members to wear on their uniforms on the upcoming sticker action day. Members got extra stickers to give to other crews along their travels. Volunteers received tip sheets that included a sample pitch about the campaign and sticker, instructions on how to respond to management, and a statement of members' legal right to talk to other members in non-work areas on non-work time.

Stickers, union pins, and ribbons on uniforms were visible proof of CAT's success in reaching members, and showed management that members were gearing up. As CAT took hold, solidarity actions spread. "We began developing unity actions with other airline work groups, like pilots and Machinists, and the community that related to our issues," explains Campbell. Early on, flight attendants organized picket support for a brief pilots' strike.

Perhaps the most successful action was the "Wake-Up Call" rally in August 1998, which was widely covered because CAT leaders had built relationships in the media. Flight attendants rallied at all ten bases simultaneously; they brought alarm clocks and set them to go off at the same time, for a wake-up call to management. Pilots, Machinists, and other airline workers came as supporters and speakers in a great spectacle for the media and show of solidarity. "We marched through the airport, up and down the escalators with picket signs and got the cops chasing us," laughs Damis.

The union also began targeting the public. Organizers dropped an early slogan, "show us the money," because they feared it would not lend itself to public sympathy, making the workers sound like the greedy party. One effective leaflet was titled "Tired of Delays at Northwest Airlines?" It linked members' concerns over long-delayed pay increases with the public's concern over flight delays and mismanagement.

In a Political Divide, the Members Led

While the members' mobilization grew, there were no signs of progress in negotiations. The flight attendants faced a difficult problem. Although members were united in support of the campaign and the new local leadership, the bargaining committee was not. Under Teamster rules, the bargaining committee had been elected separately, near the time of contract expiration in 1996, to serve for the duration of negotiations. Bargaining committee members were divided over backing the contract mobilization.

In addition, the Teamsters International held ultimate control over signing the contract. In January 1999, James P. Hoffa took office as Teamsters president. Hoffa knew that the flight attendants had overwhelmingly backed his opponent, incumbent Ron Carey. He immediately removed the international field organizers Carey had assigned to work with each of the local's bases on the campaign. Communication from the bargaining table to the members stopped, and Hoffa began a plan to divide and conquer the local leadership.

"A divide between the membership and the bargaining committee started," says Campbell, "when key issues were being settling at the bargaining table without taking them to the members." On the same day that a rally was to highlight the retirement issue, local leaders who supported CAT discovered that the bargaining committee, along with the then local president, had accepted terms that were not in line with members' demands.

The bargaining committee then agreed to an information blackout. There was no longer a strategy that worked in tandem—at the table and away from the table—between the committee and the members. So the CAT activists organized to speak for themselves.

The CAT network began a petition drive to pressure both management and the bargaining committee.

Explains Campbell, "We took ten of the issues we knew were still on the table and put maximum power behind them. In three and a half weeks we had 9,000 member signatures. No petitions were mailed to any home; they were distributed flight attendant to flight attendant. It was miraculous, coming just seven months after the birth of CAT."

"The greatest moment," remembers Damis, "was getting the thousands of signatures we gathered, calling for Raises, Routes, and Retirement. Twelve of us marched down the street and knocked on the door of the bargaining session. They opened the door a crack, then the company ran out the back." Many on the bargaining committee and some local leaders denounced the action, but at the same time it fueled the membership.

"On the heels of this petition drive," recalls Campbell, in the spring of 1999, "we took a strike vote called by the local's executive board. Ninety-eight percent of eligible members delivered a 99.31 percent authorization. It was the highest-ever turnout by flight attendants, and the highest-ever strike ratification by flight attendants. But less than 48 hours after the strike vote, the committee made a tentative agreement that didn't have seven of the ten issues that were on the petition. All hell broke loose." Members felt betrayed when their mobilizing efforts were ignored.

Organizing To Vote No

"An agonizing period of time passed between the tentative agreement and when members saw the proposed language," says Campbell. "The International put out only bullet points. There was a lot of speculation and suspicion. And internal power struggles began in the local." The executive board was sharply divided over whether to support the contract.

"Once the agreement was reached at the end of May 1999, the International stopped financing CAT bulletins. Communications started coming directly from them, bypassing the board altogether. The International began an all-out sales campaign for the contract. Their scare tactics included threatening that a rejection would delay the economic improvements for a year. The International got our local president's approval and sent six mailings and a videotape to each member's home telling them to vote yes."

The International also took a sales show on the road to every base, with its experts and the bargaining committee talking about the proposal's highlights. In turn, activists posted their contract "lowlights" on a rank-and-file website, where they could be downloaded and passed along to other members. Members prepared to speak on the proposal and leafleted at the union's "road shows." One took her copy of the agreement to the head table where bargainers were sitting and dumped a heap of kitty litter on it.

The International seized control of the voting process and put the agreement to a vote. That August, Campbell reports, "with 94 percent voting, 69 percent rejected the agreement. The International lost mostly because they asked the CAT to lay down arms and dismantle. They assumed that any opposition to the contract must be an orchestration from some small clique. They had somehow missed the point of an educated membership. Members had proposals ready with what to change for a second agreement, but the International was only interested in using scare tactics to gain control and lower members' expectations."

The bargaining committee was forced back to the table. When CAT activists demanded that bargainers be replaced, one CAT leader was given a seat at the table as a token measure. CAT was officially shut down by a divided local executive board. A program called HAVOC (Having a Voice in Our Contract) didn't get a serious start. Meanwhile, the National Mediation Board (the agency that oversees negotiations under the Railway Labor Act) claimed that the flight attendants' demands were out of line with conditions in the industry and that the union should pare down its proposals.

From August into December of 1999, stalling at the table continued. Divisions in the local leadership halted any momentum to unify against the employer. Some CAT members addressed a local board meeting to remind leaders of their campaign promises.

The CAT network then organized rallies for December 15, and there was some discussion of working to rule. Campbell recalls, "The company understaffed for the holiday season, then claimed that workers staged an illegal sick-out." The company fired members and the union did not take aggressive action to get them back. The International even allowed the company to seize members' home computers in an attempt to prove a sick-out, which made headlines because of the violation of privacy rights.

After a long period of inactivity in bargaining, the firings and seizures had the intended chilling effect. Further, the National Mediation Board declared that it would not release the union from bargaining so that it might legally strike, and instead ordered that bargaining must continue.

In May 2000, a second tentative agreement passed by 68 percent. By voting no the first time, members had gained $90 million in improvements, including domestic-partner benefits. But they didn't win enough on key issues such as retirement, and many work rules were left unchanged or made worse. Campbell notes, "A weaker voter turnout, 87 percent, showed it was a vote of no-confidence in the negotiations committee. The true power of a mobilized membership went untapped on this contract."

"We doubled our retirement, essentially, which many people were happy with," says Damis. "But we hadn't had a raise in our retirement in 17 years and to me this contract didn't make up for it." However, she feels CAT had an important impact on the members. "I have a whole new respect for offering people to get involved. All these people that I never saw have opinions on anything got involved and did the work. All the people that I assumed would get involved when we first started signing people up, didn't. It was the biggest eye-opening experience. CAT activities made workers feel a part of something, that they were going to have a voice in something. We actually got to vote a bad contract down."

Later that year, the same member network cleaned house in local elections. Members voted into office the Flight Attendant Mobilization Slate, which included the leaders and activists who had fully backed CAT. But the International's continuing efforts to quash the members and their new leadership led to lasting bitterness. In 2002, the flight attendants decertified the Teamsters in favor of an independent union, the Professional Flight Attendants Association.

★ ★ ★

Our next three sections deal with bargaining table tactics.

Keeping Management Off Balance

by John Braxton

JOE FAHEY, who is co-chair of Teamsters for a Democratic Union, was a local union president and worked with food processing workers for the Teamsters' Warehouse Division. "When I think about negotiations," Fahey says, "I never bargain the same way twice. What you are trying to do is to engage the people you are bargaining with and engage their intelligence in some way, but you are also trying to make them uncomfortable, in order to give yourself openings. It is a balance between wanting them to give in to what you are saying but you don't want to alienate them so much that you cannot get an agreement if an agreement is possible."

Fahey helped the workers in Teamsters Local 556, described above, with their negotiations. Most members of the negotiating team had never bargained before. Fahey recalls how they started their first meeting. "I wanted the workers to know that they were in control of the process, to apply the principle of equality as negotiators as described in Bob Schwartz's *The Legal Rights of Union Stewards* [see Resources, Chapter 3]. I told them, 'You have a right to be equals with management at the bargaining table. You could call them names and they are not allowed to fire you.' Not that that is a good idea, but you have a lot of choices about how to do negotiations.

"We wanted to set it up to make the company feel at least as uncomfortable at the first meeting as the workers feel. So we brainstormed ideas. The first negotiations were in the local union hall, so we had an opportunity to set the stage. The most popular idea was to arrange the chairs in a circle, with no table. We invited the management team in and pointed to the empty chairs and said, 'Have a seat.' It worked. They were polite but looked really uncomfortable. Their eyes were rolling. They had no place to open their briefcases or their laptops. They were not sure what to with their legs.

"Now that we had made them uncomfortable, we tried to put them at ease. We said, 'We want you to get to know us a bit and we want to get to know you a bit. We all have different jobs. You probably know more about our jobs than we know about your jobs. So let's go around the circle and introduce ourselves.'

"One reason for doing this is that the bosses are workers too. We look at those with more authority as a huge boss, but often they are only one or two steps above us, and they have bosses over them. We want to turn *our* problems into problems for our boss. To do that, it is good to know what our boss thinks his job is and who *his* boss is. What does he get rewarded for? What does he get punished for?

"So when it got to the plant manager, we asked him what he did and who his boss was. This company makes frozen snacks. He answered, 'My job is to make sure the lines produce 132 snacks per minute.' We asked him more questions and he went on and on, like he was enjoying the fact that someone was asking him a question. He eventually revealed some things that the human relations manager didn't like, and the human relations manager rapped him on the head with his knuckles and said, 'You shared too much! You shared too much!'"

Job actions during negotiations can also keep management off balance. "I used to bargain with Smuckers," recalls Fahey. "We decided to do things that would freak them out. Factory life is very predictable. The workers decided to take their breaks at the railroad tracks instead of at the same table and the same bench that they did every day. It was easy for the workers to do, but it was scary for management. They are more easily scared than we realize—and we need to use that to our advantage."

Stop Looking Up

Fahey explains why it's important to keep management off balance: "Sometimes I feel like the debate in the labor movement is whether workers are looking up to management with their hands folded in prayer begging for fairness or whether workers are looking up to management with their fists clenched demanding justice. In both scenarios the workers are looking up.

"I also find that management is much more constrained in its options than workers think they are. The corporate culture is not a creative culture, and we need to look at that not as a threat but as an opportunity. Also, I think union people sometimes assume that the people you are bargaining with are the same as the CEO or very close to the CEO. We want to fight the CEO and the company through the guy who is sitting across from us at the table. But we need to let it appear that they are doing what their boss wants while they are actually doing what *we* want.

"For example, I had a rocky beginning with the HR representative of a large multinational food processing company. She began the relationship by trying to con us into dropping a very expensive grievance. I started by thinking that she was the representative of all corporate evil. One day, I noticed that her clothes were very 'non-corporate.' I tried getting to know her, and by engaging her privately in conversation, it turns out she was a campus radical during the '60s and had never held the same job for more than five years. We found common points of agreement, even though they were not at the bargaining table. We both didn't like Bush, for example.

"It became clear that her job was to get this plant in line with the corporate policy, which was a 30 percent co-pay in health premiums, and we had zero co-pay. We were mobilizing and preparing the workers for war, but I also wanted to see if there was a way to get an agreement without a huge fight. What we arrived at was an agreement to create two different health insurance plans: one with a 30 percent co-pay at the end of the five-year contract, and an alternative plan with zero employee contributions for the life of the contract.

"She did her job and could tell her headquarters that the corporate goal was achieved. The zero co-pay plan had a slightly lower level of benefits, but almost everyone would benefit by electing the free plan and saving over $1,000 a year."

Keeping Members Informed

by Steve Early

BARGAINING UPDATES SERVE TWO FUNCTIONS: to keep members informed about developments at the table—and active on the job. By detailing what management bargainers are demanding (and why), your reports can alert members to the threat of givebacks. If members know that their wages, benefits, or job rights are at risk, they are far more likely to take action on the job or to join community outreach activities.

Before the talks, you will bargain guidelines for the negotiations with management. Ideally, members should be allowed to attend as observers. Such "open bargaining" is one good way to demystify the whole process. A rank-and-file presence can put much-needed pressure on management.

How does a union provide running commentary on a process that can be fast-changing, often complicated, and confusing even for direct participants?

First, someone on your bargaining committee (or the local's communications person) must review the union's notes after each session and boil them down to a one- or two-page summary. Number each bulletin in sequence to make it easier for readers to keep track of them, and post them all on your website as well as sending emails and handing them out—whatever makes sense for your workplace.

To give members a sense of the back-and-forth exchanges involved in bargaining, your summary should answer the "5 W's" of basic news reporting: who? what? where? when? and why? Who was there, for labor and management? If negotiations aren't being conducted at the worksite—where they are most visible and accessible to the rank-and-file—say when and where the meetings were held.

Most of your report will be devoted to what was discussed—and why. If bargaining has just begun, explain the union's initial proposals, listing by name the workers on the committee who may have addressed particular questions or objections raised by management in response. This information can help reassure members that their negotiators actually read the contract surveys filled out by workers and used them to set priorities. As tentative agreements are reached on particular issues, this should, of course, be noted, along with proposals amended or withdrawn and what issues remain open.

Any blow-by-blow account of a bargaining session should not neglect what management says or does. Be sure to use lots of quotes to liven up your account. Often management negotiators—particularly their lawyers—make comments at the table that don't play well for them on the shop floor.

Using the Internet

Websites and email are ideal for quick updates during contract talks. During 2003 negotiations with Verizon, for example, regular updates were sent to more than 18,000 members of CWA and IBEW. This "Unity@Verizon" electronic newsletter both reported on and promoted membership mobilization, the key factor affecting the balance of power at the bargaining table. The large email network helped Verizon workers coordinate simultaneous workplace activity at hundreds of different job sites. Some CWA locals have also provided quick, regular, and more detailed accounts of what's happening in bargaining itself.

Remember that not all members have Internet access, though. Each email update should be distributed in the workplace.

Tips for First-Time Bargainers

by Linda M. Shipley

NEGOTIATING YOUR FIRST TIME OUT can be intimidating. Here Sandy Pope, secretary-treasurer of Teamsters Local 805, offers some pointers for greenhorn bargaining committees.

These bargaining table tactics, she cautions, are no substitute for a united membership, solid research, and an aggressive contract campaign like the ones described in this book. "Negotiating committees that are not sufficiently linked to members," she says, "often make the mistake of thinking the force of their arguments alone will help them win."

Preparation

If member solidarity is the most important element in successful bargaining, preparation is the second.

Pope emphasizes that the committee should seek out training from their international or from labor educators. The training should explain the bargaining process and the basic laws that govern bargaining and prepare committee members to anticipate problems that typically occur. "For example, in almost every negotiation there is a moment when the boss gets up and yells," Pope says. "Committee members should be told to anticipate that moment, and when it actually happens, they will not be intimidated."

Many unions have begun to survey their members about contract issues. "If the stewards are doing their jobs they should already know what the major issues are," says Pope. "Membership surveys should be designed to get more deeply into those issues. For example, if members constantly complain about overtime, one question should ask whether members think overtime is distributed unfairly. The next question could ask for suggestions on how to resolve that problem.

"There should always be room on the survey forms for members to write. Don't just use a checklist. Members feel more engaged in the process when they can write about their concerns and it is an invaluable opportunity for them to express themselves."

Often existing contract language addresses the issues that members are upset about, but the contract is simply not being enforced. Do not waste your political capital, Pope warns, fighting at the bargaining table for something you already have. In such cases, this may be a signal that stewards need training in how to enforce the language. An enforcement campaign can become part of the contract campaign and help generate a spirit of combativeness on the shop floor that backs the bargainers up.

Tactics at the Table

Just as trust is important between the committee and the membership, Pope cautions, "the company must also trust the negotiating committee. They don't have to like you, but they do have to respect you. Sneakiness is not good; your word has to be good at all times. You can, however, surprise them. Small gestures like walking out of negotiations or bringing people in to testify can have a large impact.

"It is important to realize that the people who are negotiating for the company often do not have a real understanding of how the company operates on the ground. Committee members who are performing the work every day often feel frustrated talking to members of management who do not understand the realities of the shop. They need to think of creative ways to bring the reality of the shop into the bargaining room. Stewards who work in the shop can play a valuable role here.

"For example, at one company the workers were very dissatisfied about the rules for promotions. Every department was doing something different and members felt that it was all based on favoritism. The company would not budge on the issue.

"The union had done its research and knew that every department had different standards. The union really pressed for the opportunity to bring managers in to testify about the practices of their departments. When the managers came in, each said something different. This made the human resources people realize, for the first time, that the policies were inconsistent. The company agreed to standards that were fairer. Not only did the committee feel like they had accomplished a lot, but they felt empowered when they were able to question their bosses—and when their preparation paid off."

Bargaining Do's and Don'ts

• "The most common mistake greenhorn negotiators make," Pope warns, "is to bargain against themselves. For example, the negotiator will say, 'We'll take 50 cents.' When the company says no, the negotiator will then say, 'Okay, we'll take 25 cents.' A better strategy is to make an offer and leave it on the table. Wait for the company to make a counter-offer."

• "Communicating with the membership about the progress of negotiations is crucial, but the committee should not make the company's arguments for it. You may be tempted to do this to explain why you were not successful on some aspect. Report what the company says, but don't make their arguments for them."

• Pope recommends being careful about using mediators. "They may push for unnecessary compromises, or push too early in the process. On the other hand, if the company is being ridiculous, they can be helpful. Before using a mediator, try bringing in a trusted higher-ranking union officer or a company higher-up who has not been involved till this point. Sometimes company negotiators are not adhering to a bottom line handed down to them by top management but are just trying to be extra tough in order to impress their bosses."

Bringing a fresh person into the negotiations may be especially helpful when the union is threatening outside activity to push the company on an issue. For example, when the union is about to start leafleting the customers, the company vice-president may forego playing the tough act and bring the negotiations to a satisfactory close.

• Recommending the contract to the membership is a bargaining chip for the committee. Do not give it for nothing. For example, you might tell the company that the committee could recommend a yes vote if the company adds an extra 20 cents an hour and one more sick day.

• If you cannot recommend the contract, do not recommend it.

After the Campaign

by Jane Slaughter

WHAT HAPPENS when the contract campaign is over, talks are finished, and there's an offer to vote on?

Negotiators who've sweated through bargaining sessions have a natural tendency to put the best possible face on the tentative offer. For local officers thinking about re-election, the tendency is magnified.

It goes without saying that members should get a true picture of the contract, warts and all, and have plenty of time to discuss it, both at work and at union meetings.

Bargaining committee members, or stewards if they've been briefed, should lead department-level meetings at lunchtime or after work, and the union should rent a large enough hall for an informational meeting for the whole unit. The ratification vote does not necessarily have to take place at this meeting. Members will be living under the contract for the next three (hopefully not eight or ten) years, so there's no need to rush. Even in a strike situation, leaders should plan for —or rank-and-filers should demand—the maximum possible discussion period.

To avoid surprises later, negotiators should provide members the entire proposed contract, with all changes clearly indicated. This is easily done online, but make enough paper copies for those who want them too. The entire contract is difficult to wade through, however, so an honest summary should also be distributed in the workplace, with a recommendation, yes or no. Telling members "vote your conscience" is a cop-out. If you recommend rejection—and this goes for minority reports from the bargaining committee too—you'll need a clear alternative plan: keep striking (if you're on strike), go on strike, keep negotiating, inside strategy (see Chapter 10). You'll also need a clear goal for what changes would make the contract acceptable.

Be Clear on Goals

Writing an honest contract summary will be easier if negotiators have been clear from the get-go about goals and how to measure progress. Jeff Crosby, president of IUE-CWA Local 201 at a General Electric jet engine plant in Lynn, Massachusetts, says, "Part of the problem is how unions approach the contract in the first place. It's contradictory to argue throughout the contract campaign that we should negotiate on the basis of the company's ability to pay—which in the case of GE is limitless—and then at the end sum up the strengths and weaknesses on the basis of 'what everybody else is getting.'

"We should be more realistic to begin with and more honest afterwards."

Of course, being honest afterwards is only half the battle, because interpretations of the contract will differ: perhaps "the best we could do" vs. "it stinks." Bargainers and rank and file are more likely to have the same appraisal if workers have been involved in the bargaining process. They can be at the table, as the nurses of AFT Healthcare were at Fletcher Allen Hospital or as HERE members were at the San Francisco Marriott (see Chapter 15), or they can be kept informed through frequent updates, as Steve Early describes earlier in this chapter. If leaders and activists are making regular evaluations of the contract campaign as it goes along, workers should have a sense of how much leverage they have exerted, what management is feeling, and therefore what they can expect from the contract.

At General Electric in 2003, IUE-CWA Local 201 leaders felt that the new national agreement had definite pluses but fell short of being acceptable. Being crystal clear about why a contract turned out the way it did, says Crosby, will enable members "to understand the terms of the struggle for the future. If you've done your work well, then the contract represents to some degree the actual balance of power. If it's not satisfactory or what people wanted, then people need to draw conclusions that put some responsibility on themselves. The answer is not always 'shoot the latest round of union leaders,' and it's never 'hire a better lawyer.' That tends to be the conclusion that people draw.

"In our case, we didn't get sold out, but we didn't do as well as we deserved to do, given GE's profits, despite the fact that the International did a pretty good job in the mobilization. With only 20 percent of the GE workforce unionized, we just didn't have the leverage to force GE into something it really didn't want.

"People need to understand what they're up against, or they won't be willing to put time and effort into changing it. In our case that means making people understand the need to put effort into organizing the rest of GE." (See Chapter 15 for an example of Local 201's organizing efforts.)

Local 201's executive board urged members to vote down the 2003 contract—and officers were brutally frank about why. Their letter pointed to the lack of protection against outsourcing and plant closings. Business Agent Ric Casilli wrote, "All locals [will be] pretty much on their own again to fend off job loss over the next 4-year period."

At the same time, officers made sure members knew that without their efforts in the contract campaign, including several rallies and a short strike, the results would have been worse: higher medical co-pays and nothing for retirees. "We told them that what they did made a difference," says Crosby. "That's not easy to do when people are disappointed."

What They *Think* Happened

Nonetheless, the battle for hearts and minds is crucial. Crosby: "In every battle there are at least two battles: what happens and what people think happened. The second one is at least as important as the first.

"GE workers went on strike nationally for 101 days in 1969. The average member will tell you we gained nothing but a nickel. But in fact we got a number of substantial improvements, and we got better settlements for the next 30 years because of that strike—we convinced the company not to push us to a strike again.

"The same thing happened in '86. We had a local strike for four weeks which improved the discipline system and got them to stop harassing and firing stewards. The grievance procedure has worked better ever since then. But the leadership at the time didn't educate people on what they'd accomplished, so most people feel the 'respect strike' wasn't worth it.

"After every strike, or every contract, the company will spread its own version of what happened. And it's not just the company, but the dead weight of cynicism about everything in our society. People think 'the government sucks, the company sucks, politicians suck, the union sucks, of course we can't get anything, because we suck.' And there's always 'they're going to do what they want to do anyway.'

"So absent an aggressive post-contract campaign by the union, people will tend to believe the company's summation. They'll decide the struggle

---

How To Get an Informed Vote

What if union leaders won't provide a copy of the contract proposal in enough time for discussion, or won't provide the actual language? Can rank-and-filers force them to? Carl Biers of the Association for Union Democracy (AUD) says members should try to head this problem off in advance. "Try to amend the bylaws or pass a motion at a membership meeting to require that members be given the complete tentative agreement x days in advance of voting," he says. "If that fails, make the same request in writing (with a certified letter) as early in the process as possible—before expiration. If the officers won't commit to this, it may be necessary to threaten legal action beforehand. AUD is available for advice." (See Chapter 18.)

The law doesn't require unions to let members ratify contracts, but most constitutions do provide that right. "When they do," says Biers, "then the ratification vote must be fair and informed—you have to get the agreement or an accurate summary of key points, with enough time to review it. Unfortunately, this is enforceable only in federal or state court; you need an attorney. No government agency will do anything to enforce this right. You need to act yourselves.

"Even if a ratification vote is stolen, it's almost impossible, after the fact, to have a court void the contract. Pro-business courts don't like to punish the employer, who presumably bargained in good faith, for the union's violation of its own procedure. But it is possible to win a court order requiring advance notice on future contracts."

wasn't worth it, and that will make them hesitant to step up in the future.

"What we've tried to learn in our local is that you have to wage the second campaign as aggressively as the first one. That's another reason your summation has to be accurate—people can smell the b.s."

To wage the "second campaign" over "what people think happened," call post-contract stewards meetings. Explain the new contract language, but also spend a lot of time listening to what went right and wrong in the contract campaign. Brainstorm about what can be done differently next time—and think ahead about when to get started. (For example, "our leverage won't be any better unless we organize our company's competitor.")

Follow up with workplace meetings to evaluate the contract and the contract campaign. Talk about how to make the most of the contract—stressing, of course, that language is only as real as members make it on the job.

It's crucial to call lunchtime meetings by work group or department. Leaving such discussions to the union meeting means that most members will not be informed and will be that much more open to the company's version.

Resources

- *Contract Campaign Manual,* 2004. Covers research and setting goals, organizing the campaign, pressuring the employer, and conducting bargaining. SEIU Education Department, 1313 L St. NW, Washington, DC 20005. 202-898-3326. Email jtroutma@seiu.org. $15.
- *Mobilizing To Build Power*. Communications Workers of America Education and Organizing Departments, 1999. Available from Steve Early, c/o CWA District 1, 100 Tower Office Park, Suite C, Woburn, MA 01801. 781-937-9600. Lsupport@aol.com.
- *Bargaining for Power: A Teaching Manual for Staff and Local Union Bargaining Committees,* 2004 (revised edition). Handouts, guidelines, and resources for running various workshops with bargaining committee members. SEIU Education Dept., see above. $15.
- *Offensive Bargaining* by David Rosenfeld, 1995. Offensive bargaining tactics to prevent an impasse. Contains sections on the fundamentals of bargaining law, how to take on strategies used by employers to avoid a contract, ways to bargain for a first contract, and more. The Labor's Heritage Press Department, George Meany Center for Labor Studies, 10000 New Hampshire Ave., Silver Spring, MD 20903. 301-431-6400. $15 plus shipping.
- See the Union Communication Services catalog for more resources for negotiators. www.unionist.com.
- SEIU's Online Learning Center at www.seiu.org/olc includes simple lessons on figuring the cost of contract proposals.
- *The 7,000: Chicago's Hotel Contract Fight,* video by Larry Duncan/Labor Beat, 2003. 23 minutes. Documents the 2002 contract campaign victory of HERE Local 1 in Chicago. Labor Beat, 37 S. Ashland Blvd., Chicago, IL 60607. 312-226-3330. www.laborbeat.org. mail@laborbeat.org. $20.

Action Questions

1. How long in advance should you begin planning for your contract expiration? What is the overall timeline for the campaign?

2. How will you decide the union's goals for the contract? What issues were lost in the last contract that need winning back? Will there be a special union meeting? A vote?

3. What is the economic situation of your employer? Of your particular workplace? What are management's plans for negotiations?

4. Who do you need to put pressure on to win? Local management? The head of the company? The parent corporation? The state government? An outside financial or governmental institution?

5. Has your union organized contract campaigns before? What tactics worked? What would you do differently this time?

6. How will you organize this campaign? Do you have leaders in all departments, shifts, or worksites? What role will stewards play? Will there be contract action teams?

7. If your leadership is not interested in a contract campaign, can the rank and file organize? Can you pressure your leadership? Can you find help from activists in other unions?

8. How will members participate in the campaign— no matter who organizes it? What are the first simple steps to getting a member involved? Filling out a survey? Wearing a button? Signing a petition? Wearing a t-shirt?

9. What strategies will intensify the pressure on management? Rallies? Sick-outs? Quickie strikes? Media attention?

10. Who will be on the bargaining committee? Will it include rank-and-file members? Will it be representative? Do the committee members have training in negotiating?

11. What's the plan at the table? How will you coordinate the contract campaign and the bargaining? How will you keep two-way communication going during bargaining?

12. How do the campaign's issues relate to what's going on in the world? What would make others want to support your fight? What allies do you have? What organizations do your members belong to that might help you?

Authors

JOHN BRAXTON was an early leader of Teamsters for a Democratic Union at UPS and an education coordinator for the Teamsters International during the UPS strike. He is a Jobs with Justice activist and co-president of AFT Local 2026 at Community College of Philadelphia.

STEVE EARLY, a CWA representative, has worked with local bargaining committees in manufacturing, telecom, cable TV, telemarketing, higher education, and local government.

CHRIS KUTALIK is the editor of *Labor Notes*. He was formerly secretary-treasurer of ATU Local 1549 in Austin, Texas, where the local used the 1991 *Troublemaker's Handbook* to help plan a winning contract campaign.

DAN LA BOTZ wrote the first edition of *A Troublemaker's Handbook*. He is an activist, teacher, and labor historian based in Cincinnati, where he writes frequently for *Labor Notes*. He was a founding member of Teamsters for a Democratic Union in the 1970s and wrote a book about that movement, as well as books on unions in Mexico and Indonesia. He is editor of the monthly web publication *Mexican Labor News and Analysis*.

HANNA METZGER is a retired technical writer and editor living in Oregon.

MARSHA NIEMEIJER staffs Labor Notes' New York office, where she covers longshore workers, telecom workers, and Canadian and European labor, as well as international economic issues. She has worked with the Transnationals Information Exchange since 1995 and helps coordinate international and cross-border programs for TIE and Labor Notes.

NICK ROBINSON is a former student-labor activist at Miami University and Labor Notes intern. He is now a volunteer organizer with the Montpelier Downtown Workers Union and the Vermont Workers Center.

SIMONE SAGOVAC is the co-director of Labor Notes. She worked closely with the Northwest flight attendants while an organizer on the staff of Teamsters for a Democratic Union.

LINDA M. SHIPLEY is an attorney with Leonard Carder, LLP in Oakland, California, where she represents unions and works on a wide range of workers' rights issues.

JANE SLAUGHTER is the editor of this book and has worked with Labor Notes since 1979. She wrote the 1983 Labor Notes book *Concessions and How To Beat Them*.

On the Troublemaker's Website

"A Deal's a Deal," by Doug Swanson. Public employees in Wisconsin launched a statewide campaign that forced the legislature to accept their contracts. See www.labornotes.org.

9. Strikes

by Dan La Botz

STRIKES ARE AT THE HEART OF THE LABOR MOVEMENT. Strikes by unorganized workers led to the founding of unions. Strikes won the first union contracts. Strikes over the years won bigger paychecks, vacations, seniority rights, and the right to tell the foreman "that's not my job." We might say with only some exaggeration that everything we have in terms of unions and contracts and improvements in the work and life of the working class is owed to the sacrifices made by members past through their strikes.

Great national strike waves in 1877, the 1890s, 1918-19, the 1930s, 1945-46, and the late 1960s and early 1970s built the Knights of Labor, the Industrial Workers of the World, the American Federation of Labor, and the Congress of Industrial Organizations. Without the strike, we would have no labor movement, no unions, no contracts, and a far worse working and living situation for all workers.

Why do we strike? Strikes occur when workers feel they must exert power to force their employer to concede something: to recognize the union, to defend a fired member, to fight two-tier.

The key word here is "force." Strikes are not principally symbolic actions (though they usually have a symbolic component), but are intended to harm or stop production or services. In the private sector they mean to hurt the corporation's profits. In the public sector, they disrupt work and services. If you cannot have an impact on production and the provision of services, then you will find it difficult to win.

Since strikes threaten an employer's production, perhaps its public image, and above all its profits, employers will bring to bear all of their power. Employers may lock workers out. They may bring in replacement workers. They will carry out a campaign to discredit the union. They will bring charges at the National Labor Relations Board or file lawsuits against the union. They will use spies and private security forces, and they will call on the police.

Strikes Are Hard Today

Today it is more difficult to win a strike than it was in the 1950s, 1960s, and 1970s, though probably not more difficult than in the 1920s or 1930s. Why? Corporations have grown larger, with national and international operations, so that a strike at one facility represents a smaller part of production. Work can be shifted to plants in other regions or other countries. Corporations have become conglomerates; by diversifying their production, they have made themselves less vulnerable to strikes in one industry.

Looking just at relatively large strikes, those of over 1,000 workers, there were 470 such strikes in 1952, the peak; 187 in 1980; and 14 in 2003.[1]

Government has also made strikes more difficult. Federal and state laws which once gave workers the right to organize, bargain, and strike have been weakened by governors and presidents who don't enforce them and by court decisions that have effectively changed the law. Federal workers, of course, still do not enjoy the right to

Why Strikes Win or Lose

Whether workers win a strike depends partly on the strength of the enemy and partly on how they carry out the strike. Unions today have certain advantages. Employers' dependence on just-in-time production makes them more vulnerable to strategic disruption (or, we might say, just-a-little-late). New computer or information technologies may give certain groups of skilled workers the power to disrupt or paralyze production.

Many strikes are lost when a union simply hits the bricks, without taking the measure of the opponent and what it will take to win. The Detroit Newspapers strike, referred to in this chapter, and the southern California grocery strike of 2003-04 come to mind. Sometimes the union makes no serious attempt to hurt the employer. Sometimes unions undermine their own position, say when members work overtime and the company stockpiles production before a strike. Sometimes rank-and-file members get scared and cross their own lines.

Sometimes the union does nearly everything right but is still not strong enough to beat a powerful opponent with deep pockets.

Perhaps the chief reason for a defeated strike is the failure to bring all the union's muscle to bear, including that of its allies.

strike legally. Most state and local workers don't either. Private sector workers face injunctions against picketing and replacement workers are protected by the courts and the police. Unions that violate such laws face fines and sometimes threats of jail time.

The economic situation—a series of recessions or jobless recoveries accompanied by cutbacks in social welfare programs—has made workers more fearful of losing their job in a strike.

Finally, fewer workers belong to unions and only a small percentage have had the experience of striking. Workers may hesitate to plunge into the unknown.

Yet despite adverse conditions some unions have won strikes in this difficult period. This chapter is about how to beat the odds.

We will move from simpler or less risky examples to more complex and riskier strikes. We look at economic strikes, wildcat strikes, and sit-down strikes. In this chapter we will focus mostly on tactics related to the workplace, but many winning strikes these days do much more to pressure the employer. For strategies that bring in a wide array of allies and tactics, see Chapter 11 on corporate campaigns. Chapter 12 tells how students supported strikes by janitors in Boston and by university workers in Ohio. Chapter 13 deals with community and environmentalists' support for strikers and locked-out workers and with an interfaith group's work on a contract campaign. Chapter 5 includes a militant strike against two-tier wages. And you can read about a strike for union recognition in Chapter 15.

A 'Demonstration Strike': IUE & UE Strike GE over Health Care

SOMETIMES A UNION will call a short protest strike during the contract to demonstrate its anger and resolve over a specific issue. The union may inform the employer that the strike has a definite time limit—an hour, a day, two days. The union intends to stop production and make a statement but does not intend to stay off the job indefinitely.

We talked with Jeff Crosby, president of IUE Local 201, about his experience in the January 2003 two-day strike at General Electric. The International Union of Electronic Workers-Communications Workers of America and the United Electrical Workers called the strike after GE announced an increase in out-of-pocket expenses for medical care. GE had the contractual right to raise costs unilaterally, but the unions had the right to strike in mid-contract over such changes. The two-day strike, the first national strike at GE since 1969, involved close to 20,000 workers in 48 plants in 23 states, making everything from appliances to jet engines.

Local 201 in Lynn, Massachusetts was one of the larger units on strike, with 2,400 members. Crosby recalls, "We looked at the strike as the introduction to the

A two-day strike in January 2003 over health care cost increases was the first national strike at GE in 34 years.

national contract campaign which would come up about six months later. We felt that a major response to the company's implementation of cost increases would set a good tone for the contract negotiations, and that a lack of response would invite a more aggressive cost shifting."

At the same time, Crosby and the other Local 201 leaders believed they could use the demonstration strike to raise the issue of national health care: "For most people the strike was a protest against the cost increases. A smaller number understood it as part of a national campaign around the need for national health care, to relieve pressure at the negotiating table and help get health care for everybody in the United States.

"We had a public meeting of about 200 people during the strike with the Massachusetts Nurses Association and the Lynn Health Task Force. Union people, immigrants, elderly, nurses, and other providers all spoke. The meeting was a protest, but it was part of a bigger movement. We did not expect to reduce the health care costs that the company implemented on January 1. We believed that by doing this we would help ourselves in the short run and in the long run."

The union turned out hundreds of members on each shift to picket the plant. "A majority of our members picketed, around the clock," Crosby remembers, "and it was the dead of winter. It was not symbolic. We stopped traffic, we stopped production. Police got people through the picket lines here, but in some places such as Schenectady, where temperatures were at zero, they stopped the plant completely." In Louisville, Kentucky, striker Michelle Rodgers, a single mother of three, was hit and killed by a police car. The IUE-CWA immediately created a fund to help her children.

The new contract reached in June 2003 did increase workers' health care costs some. "But our belief," says Crosby, "is that it would have been considerably worse without the protest strike. We succeeded in moderating the cost shifting." Perhaps a bigger gain was the elimination of GE's right to increase health care costs during the contract. "They did it once, and they do not want to do it again," Crosby maintains, "because of the reaction, the strike, and the publicity. The strike was a loser for them."

Rolling Strikes: Teachers Strike for a Raise

by David Yao

IN 1999 TEACHERS represented by the Washington Education Association (WEA) staged a series of one-day strikes in over 30 school districts, as part of a campaign to win public support for pay increases. Their ultimate target was the state legislature, which controls funding for teachers' salaries in grades K-12.

Kevin Teeley, president of the Lake Washington Education Association, says that in early 1999, "we were in the midst of a booming economy, but the legislature didn't acknowledge that. For a number of years we had had no raise at all. There was a great deal of unrest among the members."

Teachers had begun phoning and emailing their legislators even before the start of the legislative session in January, angry at the budget proposal for two two-percent increases over two years. Teachers' strikes are illegal in Washington, and the leadership of the WEA opposed going on strike. So local officers and activists took action themselves.

"I called a bunch of other local presidents," said Teeley, "and asked, are you having the same unrest from the members? Then I came up with the idea of having rolling walkouts and a march on Olympia, the state capital. We scheduled different dates over several weeks. We had thousands marching on Olympia. It all snowballed.

"The beauty of the rolling strikes was that we could keep them up for a long time, because each strike had just one day's impact on the members. It was a lot easier to get people to buy into it if it was just one day. But the legislature was subjected to the impact for many days. They saw hundreds and thousands of us daily.

"For the most part, the strikes were planned in advance. We would notify the school district, which would schedule a make-up day, because since our target was the legislature, we wanted to step on as few toes as possible. We understood that parents needed lots of notice, and a lot of the Parent-Teacher-Student Associations arranged daycare. We notified Boys and Girls Clubs and they extended the hours of after-school programs. We notified daycare centers in the area." In one district, teachers surveyed community groups, phoned dozens of voters, and held town meetings before voting to strike. In other districts, where teachers thought striking might hurt their cause in the eyes of the public or where local school bond issues or tax levies complicated matters, the union decided not to strike.

Sick-Outs in Seattle

Although in some districts union leaders planned the walkouts, the leadership of the Seattle Education Association opposed striking. So in Seattle, activists at individual schools led the way, calling one-day "sick-outs" in two schools for March 30. Paulette Thompson, a teacher

Build a Better Burn Barrel

The open barrel burning on the picket line with a group of strikers warming their hands over it forms part of the tradition of the strike in the United States. Usually the burn barrel is just an oil drum filled with wooden pallet planks. But when engineers at Boeing went on strike in 2000, they designed a better barrel.

Tom McCarty, treasurer of the Society of Professional Engineering Employees in Aerospace, IFPTE Local 2001, explains, "The stoves did work very well, as they were more efficient than open burning, and that was satisfying to the engineers. Being engineers, they designed environmentally friendly ones."

The engineers' better burn barrels caught on. "After the strike the engineers went around and taught others—such as the [*Seattle Times* and *Seattle Post-Intelligencer*] newspaper strikers—how to build them," McCarty explains.

"The burn barrels made the picket sites a little more enjoyable, especially at night or in the rain. We also did a lot of cooking—eggs in the morning, chili at noon, and stew at night. I still meet people in the halls at Boeing I haven't seen since the strike, and they will remember something from that experience standing around the barrel."

To request instructions for making the efficient and environment-friendly burn barrel, contact SPEEA at 15205 52nd Ave S., Seattle, WA 98188 or at speea@speea.org.

and SEA building rep at Garfield High, recalls, "At a meeting in our building we passed around a clipboard and signed our names, agreeing to the sick-out and to go to Olympia. Ninety-eight to 99 percent of the staff were on board, even anti-union people. Teachers from other schools stopped by on their way to work to support us." Two hundred Garfield students marched to support their teachers, which got great press coverage. Thompson says, "Parents and students organized this. Parents even drove their kids to Olympia, where we all picketed and visited our legislators."

Two days later teachers at Seattle's Franklin High held their own strike. Joined by about 15 students, they set up information tables and organized passersby to write to their legislators on the teachers' behalf. Finally, on April 7, after two more Seattle schools scheduled strikes, the SEA held a vote on a Seattle-wide action. Thompson concludes, "Our actions pushed them to do that. The vote for a one-day strike was overwhelming."

The SEA held a large rally at the new Mariners' baseball stadium, which the legislature had helped fund with tax dollars even after voters had rejected a ballot initiative to subsidize the stadium. Teachers chanted that "money for bleachers" should mean "money for teachers."

Work-to-Contract

In the town of Bellevue, teachers at Newport High announced that they would no longer work more than eight hours in a day, grade assignments at home, or attend extracurricular activities. Kathleen Heiman, executive director of the Bellevue Education Association, says, "Some felt that more needed to be done, beyond walking out. It was 'work-to-contract.' It's hard to do that, because there's so much to do that it's easy to lose your resolve at the end of the work day. But they agreed that everyone would leave at the end of the day empty-handed." Student government leaders organized a letter-writing campaign to support their teachers. Press coverage of this three-week protest made the point that teachers routinely work longer than eight-hour days.

"Town Meeting," a Seattle-area television program, did two shows on the teacher salary issue. Local leaders made sure the audience was filled with teachers, who got up to tell their side. Kevin Teeley says, "We didn't prep people beforehand; we wanted it to be sincere. If you coach too much it sounds phony, like you're reading a line. It worked really well that way; it came from the heart and sounded genuine. We just tried to keep it focused on the pay package and not some other issue. Fortunately, teachers are articulate and used to speaking in front of an audience."

A series of one-day strikes in 30 school districts helped the Washington state legislature get the point that teachers needed a raise.

Pressuring Legislators

When teachers struck, many would picket for a while at busy intersections, then drive to Olympia to rally or lobby at the Capitol. They confronted lawmakers in other places too. Teeley recalls: "The legislators were holding their regular town meetings in their districts, which usually had only five people or so attend. We organized to inundate them with droves of teachers on our issue. We targeted every legislator in the entire state.

"We organized a rally in the Everett Civic Auditorium and called it an accountability session for legislators. Teachers' locals in seven different areas participated. We invited legislators who represented those school districts and several of them showed up. For those who didn't, we had empty chairs with their names on them. It was a pivotal event. Thirty-five hundred teachers showed up. We had people come to the mike and tell their stories, about how they had been affected by the decline in wages."

Another tactic that drew good publicity was having teachers deliver hundreds of boxes of macaroni and cheese to their legislators in Olympia. Each box had a letter attached, saying, "Dear [name], Here's dinner on me. Sorry it's not more, but I've had to cut corners since I've lost 15 percent to inflation during the past six years."

Rolling strikes led to rolling news coverage and rolling lobbying. The number of job actions, street rallies, and other publicity made the campaign one of the year's biggest stories in every media outlet in the state. The WEA supplied yard signs calling for fair pay for teachers that sprouted in many neighborhoods. News coverage frequently showed parents and students supporting the campaign. The teachers were so successful in determining the terms of the debate that the press rarely mentioned that the strikes were a violation of their contract.

Local Flexibility and Creativity

Workplace-level leadership played a key role throughout the strikes, often in the face of reluctance or opposition from WEA leaders. But the lack of central control allowed for flexibility and creativity in tactics. Local leaders or activists in individual schools were able to turn grassroots unhappiness into enthusiastic participation. As the *Seattle Times* reported, teachers realized that years of being "quiet and polite" had gotten them nowhere.

Teeley says, "At the time, it just seemed like the thing to do. There was no master plan; we got our ideas day by day. We tweaked things as we went along. I would bounce ideas off the elected building reps of the Lake Washington district, who meet once a month, and our local board, which meets twice a month."

After the rolling strikes began, lawmakers began coming up with successively more generous offers. On April 25 the legislature approved 15 percent raises for new teachers, 10 percent for senior teachers, and 8 percent for those in between, over the next two years. In return, the bill mandated three additional work days.

Immediately, local leaders began discussing a direct appeal to voters. Teachers gathered nearly 300,000 signatures to place an initiative on the ballot in November 2000. By over 60 percent, voters approved the initiative to give teachers pay increases equal to inflation, along with a WEA-supported initiative to limit class size.

It was the rolling strikes campaign that made the difference. The teachers had gotten public opinion firmly on their side, and thousands of teachers were mobilized in an unprecedented level of activity. The strike actions created an aroused and motivated membership that was ready for the successful ballot campaign the next year.

What To Do on the Picket Line? Manitoba Telephone Workers Make It a Picnic[2]

HOW DO YOU KEEP THE MEMBERS COMING TO PICKET? Women telephone workers in Manitoba created a strong, sisterly spirit of solidarity by having fun on the picket line.

During the 1990s a Conservative government privatized the Manitoba telephone service, which then became Manitoba Telecom Services. MTS management brought in union-busting consultants to impose a new contract that would gut job security. In 1999, Communications, Energy and Paperworkers Union (CEP) Locals 7 and 55, representing clerical and operator staff, voted to strike by 88.5 percent. But they thought they would win more sympathy from a public already angry about privatization and rising phone rates if they could provoke the company into locking them out.

Setting the trap to sucker management into locking the doors was a tricky business that required careful coordination and maximum secrecy. On June 2, members across Manitoba all unplugged from their computers at the same time. They proceeded to study the manuals, visit the water fountain, head for the washroom, check a few files, and discuss the weather. This caused a frantic scramble among managers, many of whom didn't know how to handle incoming calls. Ten minutes later, after a signal from the chief stewards, regular service was suddenly restored. The head office told the local managers to stay all night, just in case.

That was all right, because no action was planned until the next day, when chaos hit MTS again, this time for half an hour. Workers at a couple dozen locations suddenly stopped work. The phone rang at CEP headquarters. "This is crazy!" barked the head of MTS's Industrial Relations. "We can't run a business like this. We're locking your members out."

"Oh, no..." said CEP's Maggi Hadfield, as she smiled at the other women in the room. "That's terrible."

Strike Fun in the Summer Time

The 1,500 members of Locals 7 and 55 spent exactly a hundred days on the picket line. Whether it was a strike or a lockout didn't matter, as it turned into a fine summer of picketing, picnics, and parades.

"A lot of the women showed up for four hours on the line and spent the rest of the day with their kids," says picket captain Diane Shaver. "For an awful lot of them it was the best summer they had ever had."

While the MTS managers were cooped up inside trying to keep the system working, pickets in the town of Morden held Mexican Days, Hawaiian Days, and Western Days, with festive clothing to match. In Thompson, there was Hair Dyeing Day. The annual parade at the Selkirk Fair featured a CEP float. Picketers organized pancake breakfasts, pizza days, and barbecues. A group in Morden used their time on the line to knit an afghan, which they donated to the local women's shelter. Pickets organized a clothing swap for children returning to school.

Members also contributed recipes to the cookbook they had started to compile before the lockout, as a fundraiser for charity. When the 100-page book came out, a postscript described how a member had her bridal shower on the picket line.

Then there was the sprinkler incident, something that might have been handled differently by male strikers. In East St. Paul, one of CEP's traveling "garden parties" descended on the home of a scab manager to do some picketing. He showed his hospitality by turning his sprinkler system on the women and calling the police.

Instead of confronting the fellow and hurling abuse his way, the pickets simply moved their cars to that side of the road and began to wash them. By the time the police arrived, the scab manager was livid. The amused cops issued the man a summons for unauthorized spraying of a public area.

On a more serious note, CEP activists kept close track of the reelection campaign of Manitoba Premier Gary Filmon, who had rammed through the MTS privatization in the face of widespread public opposition. Whenever Filmon and his supporters got off their bus, there was CEP's white van, decked out in pompoms. In a scene that was often shown on suppertime newscasts, the premier made his speech with CEP picket signs bobbing in the background.

Manitoba voters swept Filmon's discredited government from office, installing the labor-backed New Democratic Party a few days after the CEP victory at MTS. Telephone workers gained a pay increase, sick leave for casual part-timers, and a new voluntary termination package. They preserved strong contracting-out language the company had wanted to dilute. Returning to work, the women all wore t-shirts bearing the CEP logo and a simple, three-word message: "Union and proud."

A few weeks later Maggi Hadfield was making small

talk with the head of Industrial Relations, trying to defuse the tensions that had built up. He said he had seen a side of the workers he had not been aware of. "You know what your problem is?" she replied. "You took on the men, but then you made us mad. And when you tick a woman off, honey, you're going to pay."

Road Warriors: Newspaper Workers Harass the Boss

WHEN A STRIKE IS PROLONGED, the union may want to take the fight on the road and to the public. If the company is national or multinational, the strikers can take their struggle to its other facilities and to corporate headquarters. Within such a corporate campaign, one element is the "road warriors," a team of mobile union activists who fan out seeking support.

The term "road warriors" first arose in UFCW Local P-9's strike at Hormel in 1985-86 and was used again at Staley and the Detroit newspapers. All three of those were unsuccessful strikes.[3] A "road warriors" squad can't win a strike by itself, but it can be an important part of a broader strategy. Road warriors can spread a strike to other workers, build a boycott, spread the word to potential supporters, harass the boss, and get media attention. See the Staley story in Chapter 10 (Corporate Campaigns) on how road warriors can build support from union members and the public. In the Detroit newspapers story here, we concentrate on the road warriors' harass-the-boss tactics.

Barb Ingalls, a member of Detroit Typographical Union Local 18, became a road warrior in February 1997. A majority of her fellow strikers were Teamsters, and Teamsters President Ron Carey had given the go-ahead for a corporate campaign against the Gannett and Knight Ridder newspaper corporations.

"Bart Nailor was the head of corporate affairs at the Teamsters," says Ingalls. "A Harvard Business School graduate who came to see the light, he was one of them and he knew their ways. With his support and advice, we launched a full-scale assault on Gannett and Knight Ridder and their corporate directors."

'Go Yell at Corporate Bastards'

The day-to-day leader of the road warriors was Mike Zielinski, a Teamster organizer. He had been pushing for a "union SWAT team" that could jump in the car, travel throughout the country, and harass the corporations. He and Nailor put together a list of corporate targets and an agenda of activities. Ingalls describes their schedule as "like boot camp: we would get up, get dressed, and go yell at corporate bastards." The road warriors faced constant confrontations with authorities, the daily possibility of arrest, and an exhausting schedule. "We got in a big red van and we drove all over the country," remembers Ingalls. "We went to their offices, their shareholder meetings, and even to their homes.

"My first day, we were in New York at the Rockefeller Foundation, where a Knight Ridder board member was the president of their board. We had picked up quite a few people from New York Jobs with Justice. We ran past the security guards and took the elevators to their floor. We were chanting and leafleting everybody, and all the workers in there were freaking out."

The point of such visits was to disrupt business as usual in corporate offices, inform headquarters employees about union members' problems with the company, and publicize the cause when the media showed up.

"One of my jobs was to calm down the female office staff," says Ingalls. "They were scared, and I am sorry about that, because we never wanted to hurt workers. We also knew that the security guard who let us in got fired, and we did feel bad about that. When we went into their office, I would go to the office manager or receptionist, and I would talk in a low voice—because a loud voice is scary—and say, 'You don't have to be afraid. We're not

The First Road Warriors

by Peter Rachleff

In 1833 Scottish immigrant carpet weavers wrote an important chapter in American labor history when they struck the Thompson Brothers' Carpet Factory in Thompsonville, Connecticut. The strikers were arrested and charged with taking part in a conspiracy to "injure" their employers' business, but they were acquitted by a jury of local farmers. According to most legal scholars, this verdict established the right to strike as a legal right of American workers.

There was, however, another dimension to the weavers' strike. One of their first actions was to write letters to Scottish carpet weavers in six other cities, asking them to resist any offers to come and work in Thompsonville.

The U.S. carpet industry was less than a decade old and all of its workers were skilled immigrants, lured from their native Scotland. Most hailed from just two counties, so they tended to know each other. The Thompsonville weavers told their counterparts about their struggle against unilaterally introduced work rules and new pay scales. Employers wanted to prohibit such traditions as the right to come and go from the workplace, drink beer or read newspapers in the workplace, and quit at will. These changes were "unjust," they wrote to their old friends, and only by standing together "like a bundle of sticks" could they prevail.

This first solicitation of solidarity established an important strategic lesson. What we now call "internal organizing"—bringing strikers together to write letters, discuss their values, choose just the right language, decide who should receive the letters—was linked to "external organizing." The same activity strengthened both the union's internal solidarity and its standing among other workers.

here to break anything, steal anything, or hurt anyone. We just want to talk to your boss. We're workers from the Detroit newspapers, and here's the leaflet about our strike that we're handing out.'

"We would do these visits for five or six days at a time. Mike Zielinski really worked us. The people that never went on the trips would say that all we did was drink beer and party. But we usually worked from 7:00 in the morning to 9:00 or 10:00 at night, going to one meeting or office after another—and then we would go out and party. Those were serious long days. We were on a little per diem, and some of the guys were so poor by then, they wouldn't eat all day so that they could send as much money home as possible."

The Detroit road warriors pursued Gannett and Knight Ridder board members from one end of the country to the other, often using humor to challenge the powers-that-be. In some cities they worked with environmentalists, and in others with Jobs with Justice. Their actions did not always affect the corporations directly, but they certainly helped morale. "On one trip," says Ingalls, "we crashed the Harvard Business School Commencement," because some Business School professors were also Knight Ridder board members.

"Boston Jobs with Justice rented us caps and gowns and made diplomas in union-busting, and we handed them out. It was hilarious. We were scared, but with the Harvard graduates no costs were spared, so it was very nice. There was beer and food everywhere. So we would go through the crowd and hand out some diplomas, and then we would drink their beer. Everybody who walked by screamed at us, 'Hey, this is my graduation, get out of here, get a job.' One of the Knight Ridder board members, James Cash, knew better than to attend. Knowing that we were there, he decided not to go.

"The visit to Harvard made us feel a little bit better. It was good to take it out on the rich. It's very cathartic."

Creating a Road Warrior Team

The union should choose the road warrior team from volunteers who are solid union members. While every team should have at least one or two experienced activists, not everyone has to be an official or an old-timer. Rank-and-file members should make up the majority, because they bring the authentic voice of the strike to other workers and the public.

While union leaders have responsibility for helping launch the road warriors, the team must use its own initiative to keep going. A good team should be largely self-financing, raising money as it moves along, and should constantly be generating its own forward motion. How does that work?

- Plan your itinerary. Start with a list of union locals or other organizations to contact and/or your list of corporate targets. When are the union meetings? When are the shareholder meetings?
- Tell your story. While traveling in the car, develop the basic speakers' points so that no matter who talks, everything gets covered: why you're on strike, what's at stake, how they can help. You need not be an experienced speaker. Often heartfelt words are the most convincing.
- Raise money. Everywhere the group visits, take up a collection to cover travel expenses and to support the strike back home. Ask locals for larger donations. No striker can afford to be shy about asking for money.
- Stay with supporters. Arrange for housing with unions or religious or student groups. You want to spend time in the homes of supporters to develop relationships with them.
- Stay in touch with your home base. Your positive experiences will encourage members back home, and you will be up-to-date on what's happening in the strike.
- Make more contacts. Ask your new supporters who they know in other unions or other cities. The road is made by walking, and in this case, the tour is made by finding out who next to see just down that road.

Rank and Filers Take Over a Strike

SOMETIMES THE RANK AND FILE has to take leadership of a strike away from do-nothing officers. Here Doug McGilp and Gillian Furst, two recently retired Teamsters, describe how the members organized to vote down a bad local contract—and then ran the strike themselves and won a better deal.

McGilp and Furst, who worked at different plants of the Honeywell corporation in Minneapolis, were activists in Teamsters Local 1145 and members of Teamsters for a Democratic Union. In the 1990s, Honeywell and Local 1145 had developed a cozy relationship, negotiating wage freezes or tiny raises, and many workers were fed up. As the 1998 contract approached, the TDU activists sensed that Honeywell workers might be willing to fight for a better agreement. The Teamsters had recently won a

Detroit Newspapers road warriors in Virginia at the headquarters of Vance Security, which provided thugs for management during the strike/lockout.

national strike against UPS, and Teamster activists had joined the picket lines and learned how to run a strike.

The TDUers began by surveying members informally. "We canvassed to see what people wanted," says McGilp. "What the members wouldn't accept was a loss of their hospitalization. We had full hospitalization and everyone wanted to keep it."

Rank and filers began their own contract campaign, saturating the main Honeywell plants with flyers pressing for improvements. TDU members from other locals helped, and here the group's history of activism stood it in good stead. "With a little dedication, two or three people could work like 50," McGilp remembers. "Because we had been active for a long time, people knew us. We knew all the break room locations and where to find the bulletin boards. We had people everywhere at different levels of involvement who could get leaflets out in the different plants.

"We did a lot of really creative leafleting on the plant bulletin boards. We used one issue of the company newsletter, 'The Circulator,' that bragged about company earnings—'Record Earnings Per Share.' I reduced the newsletter until there was a space at the bottom, and then I wrote there, 'What do you think you're going to get?' Now, you know everybody likes to mark up things on the bulletin board. So people then wrote responses on that leaflet. Whenever I did a leaflet I always left a wide margin, so that people could write their remarks on it. The members would then say all the things I wanted to say but couldn't."

Speaking Out at the Union Meeting

"At union meetings, the officials can make it hard for the members to speak out," says McGilp. "We would get up and speak, but the officials would roll their eyes and their supporters would heckle."

However, McGilp had learned a trick from observing Furst. "The officers are always sitting up high, so you have to speak up to them. But Gillian always got up, took the mike, turned her back on the officers, and spoke directly to the workers in the hall."

Just before the membership meeting to vote on the contract proposal, someone leaked information to Furst. The contract was bad, with lower wages and benefits for new-hires. The two activists worked the crowd before the meeting, letting them know what was coming. "The minute the officer presenting the contract said 'two-tier,'" recalls McGilp, "I jumped up on my seat and started shouting. And then others got up. Then it spread around the hall. Some people didn't react, but I think the fact that it got vocal was very important. Once someone gets up and makes a strong statement, then others will get up and speak." When the mikes were opened, half a dozen rank and filers spoke against the contract.

McGilp remembers, "I got up to speak, but they cut off my mike. When they do that, nobody knows what happened. People think you just stopped talking. So I started waving my arms so people would realize I'd got cut off. That forced them to put the mike back on, and I finished.

"The negotiating committee recommended the two-tier contract, but got voted down by 58 percent. And out we went on the picket lines at midnight."

The membership had forced a strike. Now they needed to force the officers to carry out a real fight and win it.

Keeping Members Informed and Active

Since they had assumed the contract would pass, the Local 1145 officers had made no serious preparations for a strike. Officers and stewards were supposed to be the strike captains, but most of them had no idea how. The union's policy was never to talk to the press, and the talks were kept secret from the members.

But because the TDU activists were well known, the media called them on the day of the strike vote. The TDUers invited reporters to come to Doug McGilp's house to interview rank-and-file Teamsters and to take pictures as they made hand-painted picket signs. "The local's printed signs just said Unfair," says Furst. "But our signs said No Two-Tier, Decent Pension for All, and A Living Wage."

"We became the media's source of information," explains McGilp. "I got interviewed on a number of radio stations and by St. Paul and Minneapolis newspapers, which really helped get our message out."

The TDU members and the other activists met every day to share information and plan strategy. Meeting daily let them stay on top of events, though it left them all utterly exhausted.

Strike logistics were a real challenge. Union leaders had set up a minimal structure, with their cronies as strike captains sitting in warm, cozy shacks. "They finally put up a shack for us two-and-a-half miles from our plant," says McGilp, "and they put me there as a strike captain to keep me off the picket lines. So I had a friend take my job, and I went out on the line to talk to people."

Meanwhile, the negotiating committee was sworn to secrecy about what happened at the table. The TDU activists developed a system to spread whatever up-to-date information they had through the membership. Furst set up a special phone line in her house with an answering machine that served as the strike hotline. Every day, or even every few hours, she recorded a new message with the latest information. She says, "We made some stickers that said 'Strike Hotline—Call This Number' and handed them out and stuck them on every sign and post. That was important because the local officers were trying to block most of the information."

Most important, the TDU activists put out a one-page strike bulletin. "The strike lasted two weeks, and we put out ten bulletins," says Furst. "We did them every day except weekends. We would come up with the information, and one of our supporters would help write and edit the articles. Then we would get the bulletins printed and hand them out at the shacks and the gates. We had done leafleting many times. This time people really wanted our bulletins because this was the only information there was."

The strike bulletin helped build solidarity. One issue quoted a union official's prediction of pressure from clients who desperately needed Honeywell parts. Another told how Teamster drivers at the Minneapolis *Star Tribune* had taken up a collection to help pay for the bulletin.

The TDUers pushed the local to hold weekly strike meetings so members could make democratic decisions. McGilp says, "At those meetings, we asked questions that we knew the answers to so they would have to tell the members what was happening." The weekly meetings kept the members together and also gave the activists a forum.

Strikers came up with ideas to make the picket lines fun and keep members involved. Taking a cue from the recent UPS strike, they organized picket line events such as barbecues. "They were bringing their kids," says McGilp. "We had a 'bring your dog to the picket line' day." All these things helped involve the workers' families and friends. The result, says Furst, was that an incredible number of people who had never been active before came to the picket lines, even when it wasn't their time of duty. "A woman I had never thought of as a union activist brought a huge truckload of wood. It was February in Minnesota, and we brought grills to the picket lines so people could warm their hands. People came with coffee, people came with wood to feed the grills. There was no organized committee either, people just did."

Building Community Support

The TDU activists brought in other groups to support the strike, though the local leadership resisted. "Because my name got in the paper that very first day," says McGilp, "I started getting calls from all over—college students, UFCW Local P-9, a church. When I brought that up at the union hall, the local leaders said they didn't want any outsiders, but the members did. The members needed to hear that the community was with them. Everybody understood the two-tier issue. That part the public could grab hold of and respond."

Furst took the lead in organizing rallies on the picket line. She turned the back of the daily strike bulletin into a rally leaflet. "We invited activists and leaders from other locals that had been on strike," says McGilp. "Northwest Airlines people, UPS people, and sometimes local politicians. We had three or four hundred people come to each one of these rallies. The union officers also felt they had to come, though they called them 'Gillian's rallies.'"

The state Attorney General and many other state and local government officials, as well as leaders from other unions, visited the picket lines to show support. The newsletter quoted County Attorney Mike Freeman: "I hope the company is listening. Two-tier wages and benefits went out with high-button shoes." The strike bulletin made sure to mention all the local supporters who addressed the strike rallies.

Because rank and filers ran such a well-organized, spirited strike, they won a better contract. Honeywell dropped a portion of the two-tier proposal, and members kept their hospitalization insurance. In the end, the workers won a partial victory, but the activists felt they could have won more if the leadership had held out longer. Many members said that one more week could have made all the difference.

At the next election for the executive board, held shortly after the strike, members elected several reform-minded candidates. It was the largest election of local opposition candidates in 25 years. When the next contract came up four years later, the union won major gains without a strike. Honeywell did not want to face off against a membership that had fought so hard in 1998.

The 1997 UPS Strike: 'Striking for Every Worker in America'

by Rand Wilson and Matt Witt

THE 1997 TEAMSTERS' UPS contract campaign and strike was one of the most successful actions by union members in the 1990s. The key to winning was a carefully planned contract campaign that began months before the contract expired, a campaign that built on-the-job unity and laid the basis for public support so that community allies would see their stake in the workers' success.

The sheer magnitude of the strike helped: nearly 200,000 UPS workers went on strike in every state in the nation. Thousands of members of other unions and many community groups joined in the picketing and other events. Polls showed that the public supported the strikers by more than 2 to 1.

Four key strategies contributed to the Teamsters' victory:
• Involve members in setting priority goals
• Build unity at the worksite before bargaining starts
• Set up a membership communications and action network
• Explain campaign goals in a way that will build public support.

TDU activists published strike bulletins daily, which provided the only strike information available to the rank and file.

The Contract Campaign Begins

UPS began preparing for contract expiration two years ahead of time—and so did the Teamsters. UPS had launched a "Team Concept" program in order to divide worker from worker, and the Teamsters mounted a national education campaign to counter it. You can read about the campaign against team concept in Chapter 6.

But the union also faced a longer-standing division, one that UPS management had routinely sought to exploit: the huge separation between full-time drivers and part-time sorters and loaders. Management assumed that full-timers wouldn't fight for better pay and more full-time opportunities for part-timers, while younger part-timers wouldn't fight for better pensions or reduced subcontracting of full-time jobs.

In addition, management used its front-line supervisors to deliver carefully scripted messages about competitiveness, productivity, and the need to avoid a strike that would drive customers to other companies. To help counteract the management message, the International's Education Department provided training on how to set up member-to-member communication networks. These networks made each steward or other volunteer responsible for staying in touch with about 20 workers, giving them information, answering their questions, and listening to their views.

Union leaders conducted a survey to find out which issues united and—just as important—divided the membership. Their major demands became more full-time jobs, improved safety, stopping subcontracting, and pension improvements. In particular, the survey showed that part-timers were ready to fight for more full-time jobs.

Union materials then emphasized common interests. Part-time workers would benefit from improved pensions for full-timers because that would lead to more early retirements, which in turn would open up more full-time promotional opportunities for part-timers. For full-time employees, higher pay for part-timers would weaken incentives for UPS to replace them with part-timers.

Implementing the contract campaign was the responsibility of each local. The International provided leaflets, petitions, videos, and other organizing tools to get members talking about the contract campaign. In many locals members of Teamsters for a Democratic Union worked hard to challenge an entrenched culture of backroom deals that discouraged member participation.

Actions Build Unity

In the months before expiration, some locals used the member-to-member networks to organize actions to build unity among full-timers and part-timers. For example:

On the day before negotiators exchanged proposals in March 1997, members held worksite rallies between shifts in UPS parking lots in seven designated cities. The next day, UPS negotiators complained that the union had never before held rallies so long before the contract expired. In response, Teamster leaders organized rallies in 14 more cities before the next bargaining session two weeks later.

The union provided members with the tools to document that UPS was one of the nation's worst job safety violators. More than 5,000 members filled out special "EZ" safety and health grievance forms. The grievances became the centerpiece of "Don't Break Our Backs" parking lot rallies where injured UPS workers spoke.

Another larger round of rallies focused on job security. Tens of thousands of members blew high-pitched whistles in unison inside and outside UPS facilities to "blow the whistle" on subcontracting.

About six weeks before contract expiration, more than 100,000 Teamsters signed petitions saying "We'll Fight for More Full-Time Jobs" and the union presented them to top management in negotiations. Part-time package sorters and full-time drivers held rallies throughout the country and marched together in public demonstrations. "In years before, we weren't as unified," said part-timer Brad Hessling in St. Louis. "Feeder drivers would sit over here and package car drivers would sit over there and part-timers over there. But this year we were talking together and I learned about other people's issues. By the end, we had enough reasons that we could all stick together."

When bargaining began, Teamster negotiators stayed on the offense. It had become common during the 1980s for union leaders to start negotiations by warning members about management demands for major concessions. "Victory" could then be measured not by gains won but by givebacks defeated. But when UPS management demanded big concessions, Teamster leaders broke off negotiations.

As more UPS workers united, they began to see their own power. At a distribution center in Jonesboro, Arkansas, members came to work wearing contract campaign stickers. Their supervisor fired the union steward and told the other workers to take their stickers off or leave. The workers left—and went straight to the news media. After the story was broadcast on television that night, management called to apologize and assure the workers that they would be fully paid for the time they missed.

While UPS spent more than a million dollars on newspaper ads featuring pronouncements from corporate headquarters, the Teamsters spent no money at all on advertising. Instead, the union concentrated on rallies and other actions to attract the media, with rank-and-file workers among the featured speakers. Bulletins, videos, and other materials featured both full-timers and part-timers explaining why they were getting involved in actions to win a better contract for all.

To help members speak for themselves, the union provided a steady stream of information through a toll-free hotline, the Teamsters website, an electronic listserve for activists, and national conference calls that members could hear in every local union hall.

Winning Public Support

From the beginning, the union designed the contract

campaign to build broad public support. For nine months, communications stressed that the campaign was not just about raises but about the very future of the good jobs that communities need. Members, in turn, emphasized the same message when talking to the media and to family, friends, and neighbors.

After the strike started on August 3, the union escalated its campaign to show that Teamsters were fighting for all workers. A few hours after picket lines went up, the Reuters newswire quoted rank-and-file driver Randy Walls from Atlanta saying, "We're striking for every worker in America. We can't have only low service-industry wages in this country." In some areas, striking UPS drivers drove their own cars along their regular routes, sometimes accompanied by a part-time package loader, to explain the significance of the strike to their

Strike Strategy: Countering Permanent Replacements

by Robert Schwartz

Unions that cannot credibly threaten to strike are not likely to do well at the bargaining table. But one reason some unions have backed off of this strategy is a heightened fear that strikers will be replaced. Researchers report that employers now hire permanent replacements in approximately 20 percent of strikes.

Hiring permanent replacements is an act of war. It is very difficult, if not impossible, to win a strike once significant numbers of permanent replacements are on board. When the strike concludes, whether by settlement or surrender, large numbers of strikers may find themselves on the street. The employer may withdraw recognition or petition the NLRB for a decertification election. If 12 months have passed, replaced workers will not be able to vote.

How can unions discourage or prevent employers from hiring permanent replacements? Vigorous internal organizing ensures that members will not cross their own picket line: employers depend on union defectors to train replacements. Community alliances mean that if the strike is supported by neighborhood, religious, and political leaders, workers in the area are less likely to apply for jobs. Militancy on the picket line makes replacement workers less likely to cross.

A union can also deter permanent replacements by making its strike an unfair labor practice strike.

Under the National Labor Relations Act, a strike is called an *economic strike* if it concerns bargaining demands over wages, hours, or working conditions. During an economic strike, the employer can hire permanent replacements to continue operations. When the strike ends, the replacements may be retained even if this means that strikers must accept placement on a preferential recall list.

Strikes in protest of employer conduct that violates the National Labor Relations Act are characterized as *unfair labor practice (ULP) strikes*. When a ULP strike ends, workers have an absolute right to their jobs—even if the employer must dismiss replacements it has promised permanent employment. Violations that can serve as a basis for a ULP strike include discharges of union leaders, unilateral implementation of new rules and policies, and refusal to supply relevant bargaining information.

A ULP strike can also have economic goals, such as an improved contract. If just one of the reasons for the strike is unlawful employer conduct, the strike will have ULP status. Moreover, a strike that begins as an economic strike can be converted to a ULP strike. This can happen if the employer commits a ULP, such as firing pickets for name-calling, that adds issues to the bargaining table and thereby prolongs the strike.

Reinstatement rules: When a union settles or calls off a ULP strike, the employer has five days to reinstate strikers. The only exceptions are workers who committed serious misconduct. When a strike has been converted, however, replacements hired before the strike acquired ULP status can be retained even if this keeps strikers on the street. This points up the importance of achieving ULP status from day one.

ULP Strike Strategy

A ULP strike strategy involves three steps. First, the union must identify—or, if necessary, provoke—an employer unfair labor practice. Second, the union must shape its strike around the ULP. Third, the union must educate the employer about the potential back-pay liability it may incur if it hires permanent replacements. The following violations can serve as the basis of a ULP strike.

Pre-strike violations:
- Surface bargaining
- Insisting on going to impasse on a permissive bargaining subject, such as a demand that the union give up positions
- Refusing to supply profit and loss data if the company has asserted an inability to pay union demands
- Implementing a final offer before reaching a bargaining impasse
- Threatening workers with termination if they should strike

Mid-strike violations:
- Refusing to meet
- Telling employees they have been permanently replaced before replacements have been hired

customers. In Seattle, thousands of Teamsters and supporters formed a human chain around a UPS hub. More than 2,000 telephone workers marched in Manhattan to show their support. Senator Paul Wellstone, Reverend Jesse Jackson, and other politicians walked picket lines.

Driver and steward Butch Traylor organized the strike at the UPS Center in Valdosta, Georgia. Borrowing a trick from management's book, Traylor made sure there were video cameras on the picket lines. "There were a couple of instances where supervisors tried to run the picket lines and could have hit somebody," Traylor says. "But when they realized they were being taped, the safety level went way up."

Traylor adds, "I had a lot of anxiety prior to the strike, but once we got going people really bonded on the strike line, people who didn't usually spend a lot of time

with an Unfair Labor Practice Strike

- Firing strikers for name-calling
- Discharging strikers for conduct that is tolerated when engaged in by supervisors, crossovers, or replacements
- Permanently reassigning work to other plants
- Violence by guards or supervisors, such as driving a vehicle into a picket line
- Videotaping peaceful picketing

One way to provoke a ULP is to submit detailed information requests for sensitive records and data. For example, if the employer contends that the members are already better paid than workers in other corporate branches, request the pay rates, benefit schedules, and union contracts in the other facilities. If a striker is discharged for picket line misconduct, request the records of non-strikers and supervisors who uttered threats or assaulted picketers, to determine if they were similarly punished.

Shaping the Strike

To shape a strike around a ULP, raise the ULP at the bargaining table, discuss it at union meetings, and cite it in union literature. Phrase the strike vote: "Does the body agree that, in view of the employer's unfair labor practices, and the employer's bargaining position, a strike should be called?" The majority of picket signs should say "On strike against bad faith bargaining" or "Unfair labor practice strike." Union spokespersons should mention the ULP when giving newspaper interviews. If the ULP occurs during the strike, hold a vote of the membership asking, "In view of the employer's unfair labor practice, does the body agree that the strike should be continued?"

File ULP charges at the NLRB soon after the illegal activity. If the strike has begun, remind the Board agent that when drawing up its complaint, the NLRB Case-Handling Manual requires the region to allege that the strike was caused or prolonged by the ULP.

Educating the Employer

With the ULP nature of the strike on the record, the union can credibly warn the employer of the consequences of hiring permanent replacements. First, such hiring will be viewed as an act of war and the union will react with fury—on the picket line, in the community, and in front of the boss's home.

Second, the employer will be responsible for unemployment insurance payments for replaced employees.

Finally, the union may respond to the hiring of permanent replacements with an unconditional offer to return to work. This will present the employer with only two lawful options:

(1) Allow the strikers to come back to work without a contract. But without a management rights clause, the employer will not be able to make new job assignments or other daily decisions without exhaustive bargaining with the union. Moreover, the union will be able to continue its contract campaign with informational picketing, boycotting, and work-to-rule activities. Since there is no no-strike clause in effect, the employer will have the constant uncertainty of another walk-out.

(2) Declare a lockout. The problem with this maneuver is that strikers will, in many states, be able to collect unemployment insurance. Moreover, under NLRB rules, permanent replacements cannot be hired.

If the employer refuses the union's offer to return, continues to operate with its replacement employees, and continues to hire permanent replacements, it will be looking at prosecution from the NLRB and an eventual reinstatement order, with back pay from the date of the union's offer to return.

Delaying a Strike

If the union cannot establish a good ULP during bargaining, it should consider allowing the contract to expire without calling a strike. In the absence of a management rights clause, the employer is likely to make unilateral changes to working conditions, which is illegal. The union can also provoke the employer by engaging in picketing, boycotting, and wearing signs and insignia. It will not be long before the employer overreacts and gives the union the opportunity to call a ULP strike.

The Teamsters made the UPS strike of 1997 "America's fight." A few hours after picket lines went up, the Reuters newswire quoted rank-and-file driver Randy Walls from Atlanta saying, "We're striking for every worker in America. We can't have only low service-industry wages in this country."

together. Being able to spend several hours together gave them a chance to talk. A lot of people didn't want to let go of that feeling of fraternity and go back to work."

On August 15—twelve days into the strike—the union announced a major escalation of community activities to show that the UPS workers' fight was "America's fight." Jobs with Justice planned actions against retail companies like Kmart and Toys-R-Us that had called on President Clinton to end the strike. Local Coalitions for Occupational Safety and Health planned news conferences and demonstrations highlighting how UPS had attacked federal job safety rights for all workers. National women's groups geared up actions focusing on the effect on women workers when good jobs with pension and health benefits are destroyed.

"If I had known that it was going to go from negotiating for UPS to negotiating for part-time America, we would've approached it differently," UPS vice chair John Alden later told *Business Week*.

Most of these planned support actions did not take place, because as the strike headed into its third week, UPS management caved in on every major issue. The company agreed to create 10,000 new full-time jobs by combining existing part-time positions—not the 1,000 they had insisted on in their July 30 "last, best, and final" offer. They raised pensions by as much as 50 percent and dropped their demand for company control of workers' pension funds. Subcontracting was eliminated except during peak season, and then only with local union approval. Wage increases were the highest in the company's history, with extra money to help close the pay gap for part-timers. The only union compromise was to accept a five-year contract instead of four years.

While some argue that unions must shun the "militant" image of the past in order to maintain support from members and the public, the UPS experience shows the broad appeal of a labor movement that is a fighter for workers' interests. The union showed its members and the public that it sought solutions to problems, not confrontation for confrontation's sake. But it also showed that it was willing to stand up to corporate greed when push came to shove.

The Teamsters' UPS campaign, like any contract fight, involved specific circumstances that wouldn't always be present in other situations. But millions of workers, both union and non-union, took away some universal lessons about the power of a revitalized labor movement to fight for a better future.

Wildcat Strikes

How Wildcats Can Work

by Aaron Brenner

ON MARCH 30, 2004, 300 workers at the Royal Mail sorting office in Oxford, England, refused to come to work. Without their union's approval, they staged a protest against bullying and harassment by managers who made their work unbearable and unsafe. Though management quickly agreed to address their concerns, it banned the strikers from receiving overtime pay for an indefinite period, as punishment for the strike.

In response, workers at other facilities joined the walkout, which continued for 16 days. They returned to work when management agreed to curtail the overtime ban. The walkout was the fifth in five months within the Royal Mail, as workers resisted work rule changes and hostile management.

The Royal Mail walkout was a typical successful wildcat strike. Rank and filers, angry at management, organized themselves and exercised their most powerful weapon. They did so without their union's approval, in the middle of a contract, against the law. They knew that others had done the same thing and succeeded. They had good reason to believe their employer could not easily replace them. In the end, they won a little and lost a little.

Wildcats like the Royal Mail walkout often appear spontaneous. But they sometimes involve significant planning—and are more likely to win if they do. Workers often have a feel for how much leverage they have, the right moment to walk off the job, and when to call the strike off. Wildcats have drawn on longstanding traditions of solidarity and shop floor organization.

But wildcats have largely disappeared from the United States in the last 25 years. They have disappeared because those traditions of solidarity and shop floor organization have been lost as management has tightened the screws and unions have paid less and less attention to conditions of workers' daily life. Fewer and fewer workers can remember a shop floor leader telling them, "At seven, we walk." High unemployment, unfavorable legal decisions, and employers' willingness to fire workers have also contributed to the decline of wildcats. Workers are often afraid of official strikes, too, so the thought of a wildcat against the employer, the contract, the law, and sometimes the union officers is particularly intimidating. As we searched for examples of recent wildcats, the stories we heard most often were of courageous non-union immigrant workers walking off the job, sometimes demanding union recognition then and there.

Still, wildcats remain a legitimate and potentially powerful tactic. Done at the right moment, a wildcat can force an employer to redress workers' grievances far more effectively than the glacial grievance procedure.

Wildcats terrify management because they demonstrate that their workforce is organized, unified, and capable of acting against management's wishes even without union leadership, with whom they may have a cozier relationship. Management cannot settle the issue while production continues, with horse-trading, but has to address workers' concerns. A successful wildcat rebuilds the traditions of solidarity and shop floor organization that give the labor movement its power.

Here, we present some tactical advice about wildcats, and our first word of advice is caution. Wildcats are risky. Failed wildcats can cost workers their jobs and demoralize the remaining workers. So evaluate your situation carefully.

Advantages and Disadvantages of Wildcats

- The element of surprise. Management is caught off guard, replacements are not on hand, there are no extra security forces, the worksite has not been locked up.
- Timing. A wildcat can happen exactly when it needs to happen. Management's peak need for the workforce—say at Christmas time or harvest time—may not coincide with contract expiration. A heat walkout happens when it's hot, not after a grievance has gone through the procedure.
- Lack of official sanction. There are no strike benefits. International or local officials may attempt to break the strike. However, rank and filers are not bound by the controls and restrictions of the international either.
- Breaking the contract. The employer may seek an injunction and a judge may order the workers back under pain of arrest. Officials and/or strikers may become liable for sizable fines.
- Rank-and-file character of a wildcat. The rank and file's willingness to fight right then and there gives the wildcat energy which many officially sanctioned strikes, called from above after a news blackout on negotiations, do not have.

Heat Walkout

When rank and filers organize a wildcat strike, they can find union support or union hostility. Some officials just want to get the members back to work. Others see the wildcat as a way to discipline management and build power on the job. Paul Krehbiel, organizer/representative in SEIU Local 660, found himself confronted with a wildcat and turned it into an opportunity to strengthen the union.

"During the summer of 1999 there was a heat wave in Los Angeles," says Krehbiel. "Workers in Medical Records at the Harbor UCLA Medical Center had complained to management for some time because the air conditioning was broken. Management claimed they were waiting for parts.

"One woman took a lead in doing something about the situation. She wasn't a steward, but she was someone who had been there for many years, and she was seen as a leader. She wasn't particularly outspoken, but she had a good idea of what justice was, and on big issues, when she knew that people felt strongly about them, she would act. So she said something like, 'We shouldn't put up with this heat any more. Let's get out of this building, and then we'll call the union,' meaning the full-time union rep. At that time their idea was that the union was the rep.

"So I got a call from a steward—the workers in Medical Records had left the building, it was too hot, they were complaining of headaches and nausea.

"When I got there the Medical Records bosses, plus the heads of Human Resources, were trying to tell the workers to go back to work. They were promising cold water and soda pop and some big fans and extra breaks. They were trying to march them back in."

Krehbiel and the department steward consulted and told management they would have to check conditions inside. They went inside and found, of course, that it was very hot. "We told the workers that in our opinion it was too hot to work in that building," says Krehbiel. "When we said that, a big cheer went up.

"Management said, 'Wait, we've got the big fans, we're putting them in now.'" So the union reps investigated again and found that the fans were just blowing the hot air around. They told the workers it was still unsafe to work in that building.

Seeking to fend off retaliation against the wildcatters, Krehbiel suggested that they go to the hospital's Employee Health department and report their headaches and nausea. "Thirty workers clogged up the waiting room, and spread halfway down the hall, and created a big ruckus—and then they went home.

"Management was really furious. 'When are they going to come back?' the manager asked. I told him, 'They'll come back when you get their air conditioning fixed.'

"Well, they not only found the parts, but they found a whole team to come to work that day and into the evening to fix the air conditioning. The workers came back the next day.

"That experience was a big boost for us. Word went around the whole Center. It really gave a boost to those workers and gave confidence to other workers. And that helped us to recruit workers and build the stewards council." See Chapter 3 for more on the building of the stewards council at Harbor UCLA Medical Center.

Think Long and Hard

Because wildcat strikes so often break out in response to some incident—a serious injury on the job, a bounced paycheck—it is difficult to plan for them. Obviously, a rank and file that is already well organized on the shop floor will be best able to deal with a wildcat strike. Following are a few additional points.

• Rank and filers should think long and hard before pulling a wildcat their union leaders will oppose. Full solidarity, excellent timing, and the ability to hurt management quickly will be necessary to pull off such a strike without firings.

• The stewards or other union activists must have a feel for the situation. Is the issue one that will unite almost all or at least a sizable majority of the workers in the affected area? Can the strike be spread quickly to everyone you want involved, whether that is the department or the whole facility?

• If the strike is going to be spread to other workplaces, get in touch with the workers at other sites before your pickets arrive, to ensure a sympathetic welcome.

• The leaders of the wildcat, especially if they are stewards or other officials, may need to conceal their role as organizers. Or stewards may want to resign at the appropriate moment, to avoid being held legally responsible. The proper line for strikers to take, at least in the initial stages, is often "we have no leaders here."

• One of the great problems of wildcat strikes is that though the rank and file leads the strike, the union leadership usually negotiates the return to work. How is it possible to insure that the wildcat is not sold out?

One answer is to get a working member into the meeting with management, perhaps the steward. That person can represent the views of the strikers and report back to them if a deal is being done.

• The all-important demand of a wildcat strike is amnesty. That means that management does not include anything in the employees' records and withdraws any police charges. Individual supervisors must also withdraw charges such as assault or battery. In the end you may have to negotiate and accept some discipline.

• Remember that the strike is likely to be short. Even while you are trying to spread the strike to the rest of the workplace, you must be figuring out how to end it in such a way as to save everyone's jobs and win your demand.

Sit-Down: Ontario Auto Workers Pull Off a Plant Takeover

THE SIT-DOWN STRIKE was American and Canadian workers' most powerful weapon when they organized industrial unions in the 1930s. Workers occupied their factories until management recognized the union and entered into negotiations. The sit-down strikes spread from factories to small shops and retail stores. Thousands of workers participated, bringing millions of workers into the union movement between 1936 and 1940.

Why the sit-down? The sit-down strike gave workers greater control over the situation and greater power over management. When workers occupied the workplace, management could not bring in scabs to replace them. While they held valuable machinery, employers were reluctant to send in the police and unleash a battle that might damage their equipment. Workers often barricaded themselves inside the buildings and could only be dislodged by force, and mayors and governors did not want to be held responsible for the slaughter that could result.

The sit-down strike also had political implications. Such takeovers challenged management's control of private property. In a sense, the sit-down strike raised the question: Don't workers and society have a stake in such powerful institutions as the corporation? Shouldn't there be government regulation of employer-worker relations and even of capital itself?

Sit-Down To Save Jobs

When the Canadian Auto Workers struck General Motors in 1996, GM made plans to remove crucial dies from its Oshawa, Ontario plant and move them to a U.S. plant to continue production. Hundreds of CAW members took over the plant, seized the dies, removed key parts, and occupied the plant until GM agreed to protect the workers' jobs. Tony Leah, today the national coordinator for the CAW's Skilled Trades Union Education Program, was one of the leaders of the plant takeover.

Leah, a welder, was the skilled trades chairperson for the GM unit of CAW Local 222. He says that the critical strike issue for the trades, and for the union as a whole, was outsourcing. It was a particular issue at Oshawa, Leah says, "because a number of former GM management people had set up a company called Mackie's, to which large chunks of the assembly operations were being outsourced. In some cases, they were just packing up the machinery and setting it up down the road where they were hiring workers at about $8 an hour, when a union assembler's rate at that time was $22 plus benefits."

The union had just negotiated a contract with Chrysler that included the concept of "work ownership." Work historically done by the bargaining unit could not be outsourced if it led to a job loss. No work could be outsourced at all for major operations, and for minor operations, work could be outsourced only if replaced by comparable work. But GM refused to accept the work ownership language, and the union was forced to strike.

Ten days into the strike, there were clashes on the picket line at the Oshawa fabrication plant. Picketers stopped GM from bringing a truck through the line to remove a die that produced metal stampings. GM then got an injunction to prevent the CAW from impeding access to the plant. The injunction gave the company the right to remove 75 dies and molds that were critical to GM's operations in the U.S. "It immediately became clear," says Leah, "that this was an attempt to break the strike by continuing production in the U.S. and starving us out."

At the CAW national bargaining committee meeting in nearby Toronto, Leah remembers, "some people suggested we should put thousands of people around that plant to keep the dies from being taken out. The bargaining committee decided that the next day we would meet in Oshawa to be closer to what was going on."

Leah doubted that a mass picket line would work. "I felt that no number of people on the picket line would really secure the situation, because sooner or later the numbers would dwindle, and the number of police would grow, and GM would get the dies out. So I approached a few people and suggested that we occupy that plant to prevent the dies from getting out. I also suggested we do it in such a way that GM got no knowledge of our plans.

"I had read all about the Flint [Michigan] occupations that built the union in GM in 1937. So I was familiar with the tactics that had been used then, and I was confident we would be able to adapt to whatever eventualities arose. We didn't give legalities much thought at all. It was more an issue of power than legality, and at that particular moment we could wield some power.

"I got a phone call at home at 12:30 that night from one of our assistants to the president, to set up a meeting at the union hall at 7:00 in the morning to make plans to occupy the plant." The next morning Leah met with a half dozen other officers. They agreed that an occupation was both necessary and practical. Each agreed to invite trusted members to the hall as soon as possible, without telling them what was afoot.

The Takeover

"In the next hour or so," says Leah, "we got together as many people as we could and explained how we were planning to occupy the plant. We would do it in such a way that nobody could accidentally or even deliberately get that information to GM. We even made sure that nobody had a cell phone. After we had discussed and arranged everything, we went to the plant as a group. We issued all the people in the room red CAW baseball caps. The national rep, Bert Rovers, who's about 6'6", would raise his cap as the signal to break through the main entrance of the plant.

"Part of the plan was to get as many skilled tradesmen as possible so we could secure the entrances by welding the doors shut. In addition, we arranged for a group of tool-and-die makers who were familiar with the dies to remove key sections and hide them. Then GM could not use the dies even if an occupation was eventually defeated. Although some of the dies are huge things, weighing tons, removing small sections that might not be readily noticeable would make the dies unusable."

When the crew arrived at the plant, Rovers waved his red cap and the workers moved. "We got to the front doors, and they were all locked and security was right inside. We had to break the door open," says Leah.

"So many people had been picked up at the hall that there were several hundred people coming in and only a couple of security guards, so they weren't in a position to prevent us. In fact, they offered no opposition at all. They contacted the other two or three guards patrolling the plant and agreed they would just gather their stuff and leave. A few management people were less cooperative, but we also rounded them up and escorted them out. Then we sealed all the doors."

Impact of the Sit-In

"Our timing was quite lucky," Leah recalls. "There had been a deadlock in negotiations, and President Buzz Hargrove had requested a meeting with GM CEO Jack Smith, who had agreed to come to Toronto. That morning Hargrove was meeting with Jack Smith and the head of Canadian GM, Dean Munger. Well, Munger's cell phone rang and he turned to the group and said, 'My God, they've occupied the fabrication plant.'"

With its plant and its dies in the hands of the CAW members, GM decided to accept the "work ownership" language from the Chrysler agreement. The company asked only for face-saving language in which the CAW recognized that GM was "different than" Chrysler and Ford. GM also agreed to withdraw its injunction. In return the CAW agreed to remove its members from the plant.

"Buzz Hargrove came to the plant. It was quite a dramatic moment," Leah says. "By that time there were a lot of people outside on the picket line, and another big group on the roof waving flags. Buzz came inside and he reported to the members of the bargaining committee the understanding with Jack Smith. So we agreed to leave the plant, taking our sleeping bags with us. But I did have to tell Buzz that we needed a couple of hours to put the dies back together before we left. GM would not object to that.

"We had been in the plant about five or six hours, but it had had a huge impact on the negotiations and on the union membership. This would not have happened as it did without the support of the union leadership. We had the support of the top leadership, the staff, and the membership." The CAW had open channels of discussion between members, middle-level leaders, staff, and national leaders. National leaders were willing to listen to local activists and trust them.

Foreseeing that the 1996 negotiations would be difficult, the CAW had authorized a special convention to consider increased dues for a long strike. That special convention was held two days after the occupation, with delegates from all sectors of the union (the CAW represents many kinds of workers besides auto workers). "Delegate after delegate rose to urge support for double dues if the strike against GM continued until November," says Leah, "and some had members who made far less than auto workers. They all understood it as a defense of the union, and that a victory in auto would raise the bar in all sectors of the union.

"That happened because those delegates had seen the determination of the GM workers in the occupation. The vote also had a very strong impact on GM when we went back to the bargaining table the next day."

Leah believes that the occupation brought all the Oshawa GM workers closer together. "We were able to rely on different strengths and abilities that people had. What the tool-and-die people could do, the trades, and the production workers, they all had a role to play.

"When we were back at the negotiating committee, GM was unwilling to meet some of the language on skilled trades. Knowing the role skilled trades had played in the occupation, the bargaining committee refused to settle until those things were taken care of. This last item, as all the other parts of the work ownership language, was a master agreement item that applied to all the GM plants in Canada. A real sense of solidarity between production and trades came out of that."

Strike Guidelines

ALL THE SUCCESSFUL STRIKES in this chapter had common themes: membership involvement, democratic decision-making, and careful planning. To summarize, we are including a checklist of the lessons of these strikes.

Deciding to strike means developing a strategy to win the strike:

• What is the economic situation of your employer? How much impact will a strike have? Who would you have to put pressure on to win your strike? Local management? The head of the company? A government agency or elected official?

• What is your leverage? Do you have a plan to prevent the work from getting done? Do you have contact with the workplaces that might be asked to scab on your strike?

• Should you strike every workplace at once, have rolling strikes, or strike selected departments or workplaces?

• Would an in-plant strategy or corporate campaign be more appropriate than a strike?

• Do members feel strongly enough about the contract issues to sustain a strike? What discussion is needed to build awareness and unity?

• Can you frame the issues, rather than letting the employer do so? (The Teamsters at UPS won public support because they framed their strike as a fight for full-time jobs. The Washington Education Association was striking for higher pay, but it held town meetings before voting to strike and got students and parents on board.)

• Will you have support from the community and other unions? Have you been supporting them on their issues?

• When did your workplace last go on strike? Do the members view it as a defeat or as a victory? What went right? What will you do differently?

• Who will run your strike? The international? Your local? An elected strike committee or the officers? Who will decide when it is over?

Running a democratic strike requires:

• An informed strike vote. In some unions, this vote is routine: everyone votes yes without really expecting a strike. You need serious debate *before* the vote is taken. What is the percentage you'll need before you'll decide to walk?

• A democratically elected, broadly representative strike committee that is larger than just the e-board and is responsible for running the strike. The strike committee and union officers should visit the picket lines regularly.

• An elected negotiating committee that overlaps with the strike committee or maintains close communication between the two.

• Constant communication with the membership. *Nothing* is worse during a strike than feeling you are in the dark. A strike website and a strike bulletin distributed to the picket lines and by email will help.

• Regular and frequent membership meetings, with childcare or a kids' meeting. Reports should include the progress of negotiations; the strike's effect on production, profits, and the employer's morale; funds raised and disbursed; other support received. Include entertainment, solidarity greetings from supporters, and, most important, open discussion of the conduct of the strike and the state of negotiations.

• A democratic vote on when and how to end the strike.

On the picket lines you will need:

• A strike headquarters near the main strike location, with phones, faxes, and Internet, to serve as a gathering point for strikers and for press conferences and community meetings.

• Picket captains, operating under the guidance of the strike committee, with the authority to organize the picket lines. They should obtain all members' phone numbers before the strike begins, establish the picket schedule, and maintain communication with their members.

• Picketing of all locations and shifts that matter, with regular turns by union members and supporters. If necessary, move picket lines to follow the work.

- Restrooms. Arrange for the all-important restroom access for picketers at friendly restaurants, churches, or other unions.
- Fun. Whistles, noisemakers, music, chants, creative signs, rallies, and parties keep up morale on the line.
- Rules to protect picketers from being fired after the strike: no drugs, drinking, or weapons. No racial or sexual harassment of scabs. No unauthorized individual violence or harassment of the police.
- A policy on bringing members' children to the lines.
- A flying squad made up of the union's most active and energetic members to follow scabs, energize the lines, and deal with difficult situations.
- A first-aid committee and medical assistance, if you expect confrontations with scabs or the police.
- Lawyers to explain picketers' legal rights and deal with injunctions, fines, or arrests.
- Cameras and video cameras to commemorate the strike and protect members' rights by recording any management outrages or disputes.

You need a strategy to deal with scabs:
- Publicity. Publicizing the strike and its goals can minimize scabbing.
- Mass picket lines. This can make it impossible for scabs to get to work, or can make them afraid to try. Supporters from other unions can help.
- Information. Have union friends sign up to work as scabs to learn how scabs are being recruited and when they are coming to work.
- Investigation. If your employer is using a day labor or temp agency to provide scabs, investigate the agency and threaten legal action or hold a protest there. Many such agencies routinely violate the law, such as by overcharging workers for transportation. Union volunteers can sign up at the agencies in order to collect information. There may be a workers' center in your city that works with day laborers and can help convince them of the disadvantages of scabbing (see Chapter 17).
- Asking them to leave. If scabs are being kept in motels or trailer parks they can be visited at night and talked to. Perhaps they can be convinced that leaving is in their best interests. If nothing else, night visits may make it difficult for the scabs to get adequate rest. Such visits are potentially dangerous and should be carefully thought out, as the courts may consider them illegal intimidation.[4]
- Speaking their language. If the scabs are not English speakers, reach them in their own language. Frequently employers take advantage of immigrants who are not familiar with the issues involved.
- Avoiding racist harassment. It is important that the pickets not engage in racist name-calling. The issue is not that the scab is of another race or ethnic group, but that he or she is a scab, period.
- Dealing with management employees crossing picket lines. Confrontations can lead to strikers being fired or harassed after the strike, so develop a policy for picket line behavior.
- Stopping deliveries. If your workplace receives deliveries from Teamster drivers, ask the Teamsters Joint Council in your area for support. Most major Teamsters contracts contain language such as: "It shall not be a violation of this agreement for employees covered hereunder to refuse to cross a primary picket line which has been approved and sanctioned by the joint council" or local union. Contact the appropriate Teamsters locals before the strike and get their support, as the joint council will pay attention to their opinion. Do the same for other union workers who might be asked to cross your lines.

Winning the strike means maximum participation, taking care of members' problems, and gaining support from their families and the community. You will need:
- An efficient strike fund committee, headed by a trusted member, to dispense strike benefits, make loans or grants, and handle bail money. In a long strike, the committee will need to expand into a welfare committee to prevent evictions or foreclosures, refer members for welfare assistance, or find temporary or part-time jobs for needy members.
- A family support committee to involve family members in the strike.
- A food committee to collect food donations and distribute them through a food bank or communal kitchen.
- An outreach/fundraising committee to seek support and money from other unions and community and religious organizations. Investigate starting an "adopt-a-striking-family" campaign.
- Media outreach. Train a group of strikers to deal with reporters, issue press releases, and hold press conferences. Don't let the company frame the issues. The union must set the tone, if possible before the strike begins.

The pressures of the strike will, if it goes on for any length of time, tend to create fissures in the leadership and the membership. Members will disagree about how to carry out the strike, about the terms of the contract offers, about when to settle. They will get through these intense struggles about strategy and principle best if they have the strongest bonds of mutual respect and solidarity.

To build up the strength to go though a strike, the union needs to be a living democratic organization. The more members have participated in and been part of the democratic decision-making of the union, they more they are likely to be committed to the union's decision to strike. And the more likely they are to rise to the occasion of the discussions and debates that take place during the course of the strike.

Resources

- *Conducting a Successful Strike.* Communications Workers of America, 2000. 30 pages. Free from Steve Early, CWA District 1, 100 Tower Office Park, Suite C, Woburn, MA 01801. 781-937-9600. Lsupport@aol.com.

- More detailed is *Holding the Line in '89: Lessons of the NYNEX Strike*, 55 pages. Free from Steve Early, see above. Info on pre-strike mobilization, mobile picketing, role of mass meetings, health care cost-shifting as a strike issue, and more.
- *Preparing for and Conducting a Strike: A UE Guide*. United Electrical Workers, One Gateway Center, Suite 1400, Pittsburgh, PA 15222. 412-471-8919. ue@ranknfile-ue.org. $4.50 includes shipping.
- *Taking on the Boss: A Union Guide to the Law of Strikes, Picketing and Lockouts,* by Robert Schwartz, 2005. Work Rights Press, P.O. Box 391066, Cambridge, MA 02139. 800-576-4552. workrights@igc.org. $25.
- *Teamster Rebellion,* by Farrell Dobbs. Monad Press, 1972. This account of the 1934 Teamsters strike in Minneapolis, by one of its organizers, is a virtual manual for a citywide strike.
- *Industrial Valley,* by Ruth McKenney. Harcourt, Brace and Co., 1939. Various reprint editions. This account of the first great rubber workers' sit-down strike in 1936 demonstrates the power of the sit-down or factory occupation within the context of a broad industrial conflict.

Authors

AARON BRENNER is a labor historian, researcher, writer, and editor in New York City. He has written about international labor solidarity, union reform movements, and rank-and-file rebellions by Teamsters, telephone workers, and postal workers, and is the editor of *The Encyclopedia of Strikes in American History.*

DAN LA BOTZ wrote the first edition of *A Troublemaker's Handbook* in 1991. He is an activist, teacher, and labor historian based in Cincinnati, where he writes frequently for *Labor Notes*. He was a founding member of Teamsters for a Democratic Union in the 1970s and wrote a book about that movement, as well as books on unions in Mexico and Indonesia. He is editor of the monthly web publication *Mexican Labor News and Analysis.*

PETER RACHLEFF teaches U.S. labor history at Macalester College in St. Paul, Minnesota. In 1985-1986 he served as chairperson of the Twin Cities Local P-9 Support Committee and since 1992 has chaired the Meeting the Challenge Labor Education Committee.

ROBERT SCHWARTZ is a union labor lawyer in Boston and the author of *Taking on the Boss: A Union Guide to the Law of Strikes, Picketing and Lockouts.*

MATT WITT served as director and RAND WILSON as coordinator of the Teamsters Communications Department before and during the UPS strike.

DAVID YAO is a chief steward for the Greater Seattle Area Local of the American Postal Workers Union, and a member of Labor Notes' Policy Committee. He writes for *Labor Notes*.

Notes

1. Bureau of Labor Statistics, "Work stoppages involving 1,000 or more workers, 1947-2003." www.bls.gov/news.release/wkstp.toc.htm.

2. Excerpted and adapted from Jamie Swift, *Walking the Union Walk—Stories from CEP's First 10 Years*, Communications, Energy and Paperworkers Union of Canada, 2003, pp. 50-53.

3. For more history of the Detroit Newspapers strike, see Jane Slaughter, "Business-as-Usual Unionism Lost the Newspaper Strike," *Labor Notes*, February 2001, pp. 8-10.

4. Legal Note: Intimidating anyone at any time is illegal under the criminal laws of every state. Violence, of course, is always punishable by the courts, whether or not there is a labor dispute. Less clear are incidents which present no specific threat, but might still be intimidating.

For instance, mass picketing which denies access to the employer has been held unprotected, even if there is no actual violence. *W T Rawleigh Co v NLRB*, 190 F2d 832, 28 LRRM 2324 (CA7, 1951). Threats may be found implicit in following nonstrikers to their homes. *Longshoremen's Local 6 (Sunset Line & Twine Co)*, 79 NLRB 1487, 23 LRRM 1001 (1948). But all cases are fact-specific, and the company has the burden of proof that any individual did anything.

The company may also have problems proving that the union is responsible. There are many court cases on the subject of whether the union is responsible for the acts of individuals and officers.

On the Troublemaker's Website:

- "How To Take Over a Building," by Amy Offner. Although a student sit-in is different from a workplace takeover, there is much union members can learn from the painstaking planning that went into the Harvard Living Wage Campaign's successful building occupation in 2001. Many of the same lessons, from scrupulous planning to media work to negotiating an end to the sit-in, apply.
- "A Citywide General Strike: Ontario Unions' 'Days of Action,'" by Dan La Botz. Between late 1995 and 1998, Ontario unions called 11 "Days of Action," a series of rolling, one-day general strikes in different towns and cites that involved not only unions but also social movements and community organizations. They were, in effect, citywide political strikes against the provincial Conservative government.

See www.labornotes.org.

10. Inside Strategies

by Aaron Brenner

WORKERS HAVE THE POWER to inflict economic damage on a company without going on strike. They can use this power to extract concessions at the bargaining table by disrupting production, undermining management control on the shop floor, and hurting the company's profits—while still on the job. Such "inside strategies" are not easy, but they can be better than walking out, especially when the company is prepared for a strike.

With an inside strategy, workers keep working, even after the contract expires. That means they can keep earning wages, keep building solidarity, and keep acting collectively against management. They will have to withstand intimidation, threats, arbitrary work orders, discipline, and dismissal. An inside strategy requires great creativity and serious collective willpower, but the rewards can be a better contract and a stronger union.

Inside strategies combine shop floor tactics with the tactics used in contract campaigns. The key difference is that the contract has expired, though the strategy begins long before. Once the contract expires everything can change. As long as bargaining continues, the old contract applies. However, the company may declare a bargaining impasse, which allows it to suspend dues check-off and impose its last contract offer. This could mean an end to the grievance procedure, radically different work hours, and inferior benefits. The company will also feel freer to discharge workers for union activity, technically still illegal but easy to get away with given government indifference. Under such circumstances, workers must rely even more on their collective power.

The most common tactic of an inside strategy is work-to-rule. Working to rule is not exactly the same as a slowdown and it is not sabotage, neither of which are legally protected union activities. Working to rule generally means restricting output, undermining quality, or cutting back on service by working strictly by the book.

Other inside tactics may include sick-outs, overtime bans, demonstrations, and button wearing. They may be accompanied by boycotts, corporate campaigns, fundraising, and just about everything else unions do in contract campaigns.

In some ways, inside strategies are harder than going on strike. Many unions ask strikers to do little more than picket a few days a week. Inside strategies require many coordinated activities among the workers throughout the workplace. Not only must workers figure out ways to hurt the company's bottom line within the bounds of the rules, they must motivate their co-workers to maintain the campaign even in the face of management hostility.

And there is more. To implement a successful inside strategy, workers must understand the economic position of the company, how best to cut into its profits. They have to know the strengths and weaknesses of their managers, how they can be frustrated. Workers must understand the ins and outs of the production process, where exactly to "throw a wrench in the works." They have to be familiar with their union contract, even if the employer has imposed a "best and final offer." They must know the basics of labor law, the limits of their workplace rights. And they must have a sense of the mood of their co-workers, how much solidarity they have built.

Work-to-Rule at Staley

by Steve Ashby and C. J. Hawking

WORKERS AT A.E. STALEY MANUFACTURING CO., a corn-processing plant in Decatur, Illinois, executed a work-to-rule campaign to near perfection for nine months in 1992-93. The members of Allied Industrial Workers (AIW) Local 837, who averaged 21 years in the plant, cut production in half. Then, upon being locked out in June 1993, they mobilized nationwide support for an aggressive corporate campaign. Despite their ultimate defeat in December 1995, the Staley workers achieved remarkable success during their work-to-rule campaign.

Preparing the Ground

When the British multinational Tate & Lyle bought Staley in 1988, nearly 80 years of peaceful labor-management relations were ended. The new owners hired union-busting experts as top managers in Decatur. During 1992 contract talks, these managers attacked seniority and the grievance procedure, and they sought to impose 12-hour shifts, with workers switching between nights and days every 30 days. The proposed to strip the existing 116-page contract down to 17 pages.

Local 837 first responded by hiring university-based labor educators for advice. The educators debunked the company's claim that the plant was "uncompetitive" by demonstrating that the value-added per worker was $467,000. They also confirmed workers' suspicions that the company wanted to provoke a strike, replace workers with scabs, and bust the union. The Staley workers had just seen UAW members in their town abandon a five-month strike when Caterpillar threatened to permanently replace them. Mike Griffin, a 27-year union activist, recalled that workers "wanted to do something, but the overwhelming majority were not comfortable with a strike."

The Staley workers' inside campaign was so successful in cutting production that after nine months, management locked them out. That ended the work-to-rule campaign, but it did not end the fight. A year later, police pepper-sprayed workers and supporters who were peacefully blocking an entrance to the plant.

One month before the contract expired, Local 837 contacted Jerry Tucker, head of the New Directions Workers Education Center in St. Louis. Tucker, a former UAW regional director, had led several locals of auto and aerospace workers in work-to-rule campaigns.

Tucker sent the AIW 837 leaders material on work-to-rule campaigns, including a chapter from the first edition of *A Troublemaker's Handbook*. At his first meeting with the executive board, bargaining committee, and stewards, Tucker explained that the goal of a work-to-rule campaign is to show that the plant cannot be run successfully without the knowledge and skills of the workers; that the union membership is a unified and determined force; and that if management refuses to bargain reasonably, production and profits will suffer.

In a work-to-rule campaign, said Tucker, workers strictly follow company rules and the contract, and do only what they are told to do. They "leave their brains at the gate" and make no extra efforts. They ask their supervisors how to solve problems rather than solving them themselves. They forget the shortcuts they have developed to speed production. They ask managers for help with every job. They perform every task meticulously. They follow all safety procedures to the letter. They do not start work a second before they must and they do not work a second longer than required. They refuse voluntary overtime and take every minute of every break. They grieve every dispute, no matter how trivial. In short, they use management's rules against the company.

Tucker then spoke to the membership, explaining that a work-to-rule campaign would require heightened rank-and-file involvement. "The word 'leadership' means something entirely different in a work-to-rule campaign," Tucker told the members. "The top officers remain the officers. But you're going to have a whole lot of people working with you now. You're going to have a whole lot of hands on the oars.

"You can't manage an effective in-plant strategy from the union hall. I like to use a phrase I heard [African American civil rights leader] Ron Daniels use: 'You are the leaders you've been looking for.'"

Tucker also explained the risks of working to rule. Workers could get fired. Under the National Labor Relations Act, workers have the right to engage in "concerted activities for the purpose of collective bargaining or other mutual aid or protection"; nevertheless, employers illegally fire thousands of workers every year. Tucker cautioned that the company could also lock them out.

The membership agreed to launch the in-plant campaign and hired Tucker to guide them.

Leave Your Brains at the Gate

In early October 1992, Local 837 members rejected the company's proposed contract by 96 percent. In response, management declared a bargaining impasse and within ten days imposed most of its demands. The company also evicted the union from its in-plant office, abolished "excused union business" for union officers to handle grievances, and eliminated dues check-off, which forced the union to collect dues by hand.

"Ending dues check-off was one of Staley's major threats that they thought would be our demise," said AIW 837 President Dave Watts. "They thought it would tear us down, but it built us up." During the nine months they worked without a contract, 97 percent of the local's members voluntarily paid their dues. Most paid at union meetings, now held weekly and including family members. The rest were collected by hand in the plant.

The in-plant campaign began as soon as the union voted to reject the contract. The first step was establishing a "Solidarity Team" that would meet with Tucker weekly. Seventy workers attended the first meeting. It was a good start, but a successful campaign could not be built with only 10 percent of the workforce. "We didn't have a critical mass," noted Tucker. "It would be mythical to say the rank and file were ready to go. They needed guidance."

The Solidarity Team started by conducting one-on-one meetings with each worker to explain the company's proposed contract, line by line. Dan Lane, an early member of the Solidarity Team, recalled, "Part of this is from my military training. You don't send green troops to fight battles. You have to create a mind-set. So I would go through the contract with people, right in the plant."

The Solidarity Team explained everything the union faced, and went over the nuts and bolts of a work-to-rule campaign. Richard Brummett, one of the strongest supporters of work-to-rule, explained that when there is a problem in your area, "you call up the boss and say, 'This piece of equipment is doing such and such,' and he says, 'What do you think we ought to do?' And you tell him, 'You come up here and you tell me what to do. That's what they pay you for.' And if he tells you to do something and you know it's wrong, you do it anyway."

For years, said Dave Watts, "we had helped to manage mismanagement. Whenever management made a decision and it was passed down through supervision and we knew it was wrong, we did the right thing on the line anyway. But with work-to-rule, that day was done. No more correcting management's mistakes."

To increase participation, in November Tucker began to hold departmental meetings on every shift, a time-consuming process that helped build a critical mass in support of working to rule. "People relate to those closest to them," says Tucker. "Tell them to come to a plant-wide meeting and they don't think it relates to them. Tell them to come to a meeting to discuss a problem in their department and everyone shows up. After a week of departmental meetings the solidarity committee grew from 60 to 350." Tucker's major purpose was to hear from the workers. "You don't get up and have big speeches or have the president harangue people. You ask people what's going on. You get them to convey the information. You get them talking, listening."

The department meetings were vital to solidifying support. After the contract was rejected, some members had been skeptical of the decision not to strike. The meetings helped convince them that an in-plant campaign was a militant alternative to a strike.

The Solidarity Team determined that there were four key departments—the refinery, dry starch, the mill, and co-generation—plus the maintenance department, whose members worked throughout the plant. The team tracked each worker's involvement. Who was participating fully, who was partially in, and who was not yet involved? Where was the union strong and where was it weak? Was the company harassing or disciplining workers? How was each department responding to intimidation? Which workers were emerging as leaders?

Daily Confrontations

In many ways the Staley plant, with 110 buildings spread over 440 acres, was ideal for a work-to-rule. It was an old plant—much of the machinery was decades old—run by experienced workers. "Everybody knows you got to kick a Model A to get it to start," said Brummett, "but it takes 20 years to know where to kick it."

It helped, too, that after the 1988 takeover, Tate & Lyle had fired about half the white-collar workforce, including the experienced supervisors. Jeanette Hawkins, one of the first African American women workers hired, explained how the new supervisors inadvertently contributed to the work-to-rule campaign: "They didn't know what was going on, and if you tried to explain to them, well, they thought they can't trust the union people. So you just did what they said and it screwed [things] up. But it was on them, because that's what they told us to do."

While the Staley workers left their brains at the gate, they did not leave their common sense. They remained extremely cautious inside the volatile chemical plant, careful not to put themselves or the Decatur community at risk.

During the weekly union meetings, workers shared stories, laughed at tales of management's ineptness, discussed successes and setbacks, and built up each other's determination to escalate the fight. At the meetings, recalled Tucker, "a worker would get up and give a report on their area to 400-500 people. They were not leaders, not used to giving speeches. Then when they sat down they would feel a little more powerful, feel a sense of satisfaction. The idea is to pull people out, get them to convey information, get them talking."

Hearing about the successful efforts of other departments, workers adapted the tactics to their own situations. The meetings always ended with the question, "What creative actions could the union take next?" Workers began to meet informally inside the plant, at lunch, on breaks, and at shift changes.

The in-plant campaign also involved actions that did not impact production but nevertheless mobilized members to confront management on a daily basis. Workers regularly wore red union shirts, union caps, and an extensive array of union buttons. They honked their car horns in the plant parking lot. They held demonstrations at the plant gate before marching together into work.

Half the workers carried company-furnished radios, and they turned them into weapons of solidarity. Recalled Emery Schrimpsher, "You started hearing 'Solidarity Forever' [being sung on the radios]. There was a [worker] preacher that came on and preached sermons [calling on the company to repent]. There were whistles being blown on the radio.... A lot of these supervisors did nothing but run around trying to find these radios."

The radios unified the membership, said Dan Lane. "There had been divisions between process workers and the [higher-paid] mechanics, between the older and younger workers, men and women, black and white. So when the radio use was broadened, people read things like Martin Luther King's 'I Have a Dream' speech. It brought people together."

Two additional methods of communication united workers: the local's monthly newsletter and *Midnight Express*. Members Jerry Dilbeck and Robert Luka, Jr. edited and mailed the two-page *Local 837 News* to every member. It publicized union rallies and related progress on the corporate campaign against Tate & Lyle that was simultaneously under way. *Midnight Express* was an underground weekly newspaper written by members. It detailed the errors and accidents of the non-union contract workers, management's harassment of union activists, and the blunders of Staley supervisors and top management.

Workers replaced Staley's grievance procedure with their own system for disputing unsafe or unfair company practices. Some carried laminated copies of "Weingarten rights" inside their hard hats, and if a supervisor reprimanded them they would read, "If the discussion I am being asked to enter could in any way lead to my discipline or termination or impact on my personal working conditions, I ask that a union steward, representative or officer be present. Unless I have this union representation I respectfully choose not to participate in this discussion."

Local 837 News reminded members, "Remember, you have the right to have as many union people present as you feel comfortable with when confronting a company or salaried person with any issue or dispute. Never go in one-on-one. You will lose!!!" Large groups of workers began to hold on-the-spot grievance hearings with lone supervisors. They used whistles to signal when such participation was needed. At one meeting with management, the group wore Groucho Marx glasses and moustaches and carried cigars.

Varying Levels of Participation

Many Staley workers speak of their nine-month work-to-rule campaign as one of the most liberating times of their lives. "It galvanized the membership," recalled Mike Griffin, "and gave them courage and faith and hope."

However, not all of the union's 762 members participated, and some were involved more deeply than others. One difficulty was that it ran counter to the workers' natural work ethic. Many were afraid they would lose their jobs, even though the union set up a Solidarity Fund to provide full pay to anyone fired because of union activity.

Art Dhermy estimated that about one-third of the plant was aggressively working to rule, while many others were supportive but not taking the lead. "My department [the boiler room] was like everybody else's. You had the ones that were going to grab the bull by the horns. You had the ones that might grab the tail and be drug along. And then you had the ones on the other side of the fence, to make sure the bull wasn't going to get them. I had no animosity to the ones not grabbing the horns. We needed some standing out in the pasture watching our backs. But the ones on the other side of the fence often came to the union meeting—at least they were in the pasture."

Added Dhermy, as time passed "that fence got expanded some," and more people stepped up their participation.

Success! Production Down

By early 1993, five months into the campaign, the number of workers participating in the work-to-rule had reached critical mass and their efforts were having a tremendous impact. Union members at Staley's customers told Staley workers that deliveries were often late, had insufficient quantity, and lacked the usual quality, resulting in a steady stream of customer complaints and returns. The workers could see the company's desperate measures to fill orders. Management scrambled to turn out product, regardless of quality. Machinery once masterfully operated by the workers now baffled the supervisors.

The company took heavy losses in December 1992 and January 1993. "Production was down from 140,000 bushels [of ground corn] a day to 80-90,000," said bargaining committee member "Dike" Ferris. By spring, the union estimated that production had fallen 50 percent. Tate & Lyle insisted that the drop was only 32 percent—still a remarkable figure.

Nine months after the workers rejected Staley's contract, management locked them out. That ended the work-to-rule campaign, but it did not end the fight. The solidarity built by nine months of working to rule together helped the Staley workers struggle for another 30 months.

Telephone Workers Pressure Verizon from Within

by Pam Galpern

VERIZON, the largest telephone company in the United States, was itching for a strike when its contracts with the Communications Workers of America (CWA) and the International Brotherhood of Electrical Workers (IBEW) expired on August 3, 2003. Management thought it could outlast the unions in a strike, impose its concession demands, raise health co-pays for workers, and eliminate strong job security language that was limiting its ability to move jobs to lower-cost states or overseas.

Workers, too, expected a strike, a long one. They cleared out their desks, emptied their lockers, and turned in their tools. They removed the batteries from their equipment and got rid of anything that might make it easier for managers and scabs to do their work.

But just hours before the deadline, the unions announced that they would work without a new contract and keep negotiating. The next day, defying their tradition of "no contract, no work," more than 78,000 union members in 13 states from Maine to Virginia returned to Verizon for their regularly scheduled shifts, working under the old, expired contract, which remained in effect as long as bargaining continued.

The Strategy

"I've got 35 years on the job," says Steve Carney, a field technician in Westchester, New York and a steward in CWA Local 1103. "At first I thought, 'hey, no contract, no work.' But different times require different strategies."

The union chose the inside strategy for several reasons.

Verizon is the largest local phone company, largest wireless company, and third-largest long distance company in the country. With deep pockets, a highly automated work process, and virulently anti-union management, it represented a more formidable foe than the regional phone companies of the past. The company had lined up 30,000 managers and scabs, many of them flown in from around the country, to work as soon as the union walked. Management had made arrangements with non-union call centers to take over customer service work. It had hired extra security to monitor strikers and had reportedly reserved eight months' worth of hotel rooms to house the scabs. These preparations cost Verizon millions each day.

Elizabeth Gurley Flynn: An Early Inside Strategist

INSIDE STRATEGIES ARE NOTHING NEW. They have been around as long as workers and bosses.

In 1916, the Industrial Workers of the World (IWW) published one of the first pamphlets about inside strategies. It was written by Elizabeth Gurley Flynn, the radical IWW organizer, free speech activist, Communist, and feminist who participated in such famous strikes as the Lawrence, Massachusetts Bread and Roses strike and the Paterson, New Jersey silk weavers' strike. Her pamphlet was called "Sabotage: The Conscious Withdrawal of the Workers' Industrial Efficiency."

As her title indicates, Flynn defined sabotage not as violence against bosses or the destruction of property, but as "an instinctive defense [that] existed long before it was ever officially recognized by any labor organization. Sabotage means primarily: the withdrawal of efficiency.

"Sabotage means either to slacken up and interfere with the quantity, or to botch in your skill and interfere with the quality of capitalist production, or to give poor service. Sabotage is not physical violence; sabotage is an internal, industrial process. It is something that is fought out within the four walls of the shop."

Flynn gives an example:

"The Scotch dockers had a strike in 1889 and their strike was lost, but when they went back to work they sent a circular to every docker in Scotland and in this circular they embodied their conclusions, their experience from the bitter defeat. It was to this effect: 'The employers like the scabs, they have always praised their work, they have said how much superior they were to us, they have paid them twice as much as they have ever paid us; now let us go back to the docks determined that since those are the kind of workers they like and that is the kind of work they endorse, we will do the same thing.

"'We will let the kegs of wine go over the docks as the scabs did. We will have great boxes of fragile articles drop in the midst of the pier as the scabs did. We will do the work just as clumsily, as slowly, as destructively, as the scabs did. And we will see how long our employers can stand that kind of work.' It was very few months until through this system of sabotage they had won everything they had fought for and not been able to win through the strike."

Sabotage brought howls of protest from corporate and government officials. The IWW withdrew the pamphlet from "official" publication, but rank-and-file activists of all kinds kept it in circulation, and its lessons remain useful nearly a hundred years later.

You can find the entire pamphlet on the web. Here's a link to the IWW's copy: http://bari.iww.org/culture/library/sabotage/index.shtml.

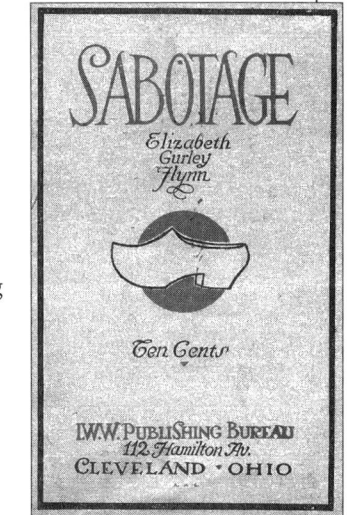

Based on its experience during a four-and-a-half month strike in 1989, the CWA estimated it would take more than two months for the company to feel the economic effects of a strike. While the unions had been mobilizing, they weren't nearly as prepared as the company was for such a long strike. The level of member mobilization was uneven; in some areas workers engaged in extensive work-to-rule activities prior to contract expiration, while other areas remained quiet. The economic hardship of a long strike would be severe in some places, since the IBEW had no strike fund and workers outside New York state would not have been eligible for unemployment benefits.

Staying inside reversed the balance of power, in a way. Without a walkout, the company's strike preparations became a big financial burden. But since the threat of a strike was still real and could happen at any moment of the union's choosing, Verizon had to keep its expensive strike contingency plan in place. Meanwhile, the unions could pressure the company from inside, mount a public pressure campaign from the outside, and extend their strike preparation efforts at the same time.

Job security, along with health care, was a key issue in negotiations, and the inside strategy preserved jobs. The existing contract had unusually strong language that prohibited Verizon from moving more than 0.7 percent of the bargaining unit work out of state or overseas and defined the circumstances under which workers could be laid off. An arbitrator had recently upheld this contract language, ordering the company to rehire 3,400 improperly laid-off workers with full back pay. A strike would void the contract and allow the company to move work at will.

"All of the jobs in my local would be at risk if we went on strike," says Don Trementozzi, president of CWA Local 1400, representing service reps in New England. "All the inside jobs period would be at risk. The company has the technology to flip a switch and move those jobs somewhere else."

Protesting on the Job

Many members weren't happy with the inside strategy. No one wanted a strike, but workers knew the company wasn't going to back down without a major fight. As the unions got information out about the strategy, the mood shifted.

"The company wanted us to strike," says Jim Zanfardino, a service rep in Massachusetts and a member of CWA Local 1400. "When we didn't, that threw a monkey wrench in their plans."

"By staying on the jobs we won customers' support," says Keith Cofresi, a field technician in Staten Island and a member of CWA Local 1102. "Every customer I saw was behind us 100 percent in fighting corporate greed."

A CWA fact sheet told workers how to work to rule, including, "Never go by memory, check your reference material" and "Never use your own judgment—ask!" The tactic was a powerful weapon for "outside" workers, the ones who install and repair telephone lines and equipment. These technicians have leeway to determine how best to complete a job. During regular times they often disregard bothersome company rules to get a job done quickly. But during the work-to-rule campaign, they followed Department of Transportation regulations, for example, to the letter.

Technicians delayed the start of their days with a 20-minute truck safety check each morning. The check involved two technicians, one to operate the truck and another to inspect such things as turn signals, brake lights, and hydraulic lifts. "Some mornings at the Watertown garage, you'd see 100 bucket trucks with their lifts spinning in the air," says Dave Reardon, business agent for IBEW Local 2222. "It drove managers crazy."

"State and federal regulations require that we put out the proper signage—signs, cones, flags—when we work in manholes and near highways," says Carney. "We refused to take trucks out that did not have the right signage.

"And the company wants us to make 'five points of contact,' with customers. We're supposed to call them before we come, introduce ourselves when we arrive, update them during the job, say goodbye, and then call the next day to make sure everything works. Sometimes, the actual problem is far from the customer's location, but we made sure to get in the truck, drive to the customer, update them, and then drive back to the job site. And we'd do it again at the end of the day. Then we'd do the paperwork in detail, which took more time away from the job."

Following company rules, technicians refused to use fire escapes, which forced management to find other ways to gain access to phone boxes. Nor would they use a customer's ladder, which, for technicians without trucks, meant waiting for a ladder to be delivered. And they refused to work in dimly lit areas, which meant extra time running a light.

Out in the streets, they spent extra time looking for legal parking places, no easy task in big cities where

Instead of striking, telephone workers at Verizon pursued an inside strategy when their contract expired in 2003. The unions held dozens of pre-work and lunchtime rallies and everyone wore red, the union color.

workers usually park in loading zones and parking tickets are an everyday occurrence.

Technicians also tried to do every job just right. When running cables up the outside of a building, the company suggests technicians install D-rings every 18 inches to keep the cable straight and close to the wall. Technicians often skip this step when the wall is brick, but during the work-to-rule they went to their trucks or back to the garage, got the special hammer, and took the extra time to pound the rings into the brick.

For slightly tricky jobs, technicians called their managers and waited for them to come out to the job to tell them what to do.

The downside of working to rule for the outside workers was that they had little contact with co-workers, making it difficult to build a sense of collective action. No one knew for certain what other workers were doing. It also allowed management to harass workers out of sight of co-workers and stewards.

To counter the isolation, rank-and-file and official mobilization coordinators brought workers together before work, at lunch, or after work to share stories and float ideas, months before the contract expired. "Each month we'd discuss a different aspect of working safely," says Reardon. "One month, we'd explain all the details of manhole safety—putting out two signs on each side of the road, testing for gas before removing the cover, setting up a blower to vent the hole, and checking for gas every few hours. The next month, we'd talk about electrical testing—in manholes, on poles, in climbing spaces."

Working to rule was harder for inside workers at Verizon, since every minute of their time is scheduled and supervised. They relied instead on tactics designed to keep management guessing. Leading up to contract expiration and then after, call center workers brought picket signs to work and leaned them against their desks, "just in case" they needed to walk out. They wore red on Thursdays as a show of unity. "We kept our picket signs on our desks," says Zanfardino. "When we went home, we took them with us. When we went to lunch we took them and practiced picketing. It drove management crazy."

Working without a contract was stressful. "The company was cracking down," says Carney. "There was a lot of fear and intimidation." Verizon put its extra managers to work following members around, looking to get people in trouble. Tensions were high as members dealt with the surveillance and the uncertainty of not knowing whether a strike would be called.

The unions maintained support for the work-to-rule and the contract campaign through a structure of "mobilization coordinators" that mirrored the steward structure. Coordinators were rank-and-file volunteers who took responsibility for getting 10 to 15 co-workers involved. They met regularly with each other and with a chief coordinator for each local. Chief coordinators also met with each other and with union officials. This structure helped disseminate ideas around a local, across locals, across regions, and throughout the unions.

Mobilizing Outside Support

Essential to the inside strategy was a campaign to build public support, pressure the company, and demonstrate workers' solidarity. The effort highlighted Verizon's greed and its threat to "hometown jobs" and quality service.

Just prior to contract expiration CWA stepped up its web-based version of the newsletter *Unity@Verizon*, with almost daily updates on bargaining and mobilization activities. The union estimated that *Unity@Verizon* reached 18,000 members. This was critical in a fight that covered 78,000 workers in 13 states. The unions also launched a campaign, with AFL-CIO help, to collect pledges of support from Verizon customers. See Chapter 20 for details on this aspect of the campaign.

In the weeks before and after contract expiration, workers held dozens of pre-work and lunchtime rallies, joined by local politicians, Jobs with Justice activists, and other supporters. "We had pre-work rallies before we went in," says Cofresi. "Everyone lined up and went in together. We wore red [the union color] every day. On Thursdays we had 100 percent of the people in red; on other days 75-80 percent."

Members from both unions leafleted company-sponsored public events.

At a sold-out Yankees-Red Sox game in Boston's Fenway Park, where it was Verizon Visor Night, they passed out stickers that said, "Yankees suck and so does Verizon." CWA members teamed up with United Students Against Sweatshops and picketed a Verizon Wireless store in New York City. IBEW and CWA members and Jobs with Justice activists held multiple protests at Verizon Vice-Chairman Larry Babbio's New Jersey mansion.

Members leafleted on city streets to tell the public about the connection between quality phone service and good union jobs. Union reps took legislators on tours to see dilapidated telephone facilities in need of repair. Members rallied outside public service regulators' meetings and protested recently relaxed regulations. Retirees held rallies protesting the company's proposal to increase their health care costs.

Several actions focused on Verizon Wireless, Verizon's non-union mobile phone subsidiary. The union set up informational pickets exposing the company's anti-union drive, which violated its pledge to remain neutral in the CWA's organizing campaign. On several occasions, the union held "store invasions," in which dozens or even hundreds of members walked into a store, leafleted customers and workers, chanted, and listened to speeches.

The unions ran newspaper ads that exposed the astronomical salaries of Verizon executives, contrasting their obscene gains with their attempt to make retirees pay for health care. The ads also countered the company's own publicity campaign, pointing out Verizon's hypocrisy in claiming it was an excellent place to work while trying to cut jobs and slash benefits. The same logic, along with the union's focus on hometown jobs and quality service, helped the union win support from many state and local politicians, who then spoke out publicly.

Reaching Agreement

The combined pressure of working to rule, informational pickets, community-supported demonstrations, the arbitrator's ruling upholding the job security language,

In the AFA's CHAOS campaign, flight attendants picketed to inform passengers of possible unannounced strikes at Midwest Express.

and the expense of the company's unused contingency plan led Verizon to abandon two of its most important concession demands: the right to eliminate jobs and that workers pay health care premiums. A month after expiration, the two sides settled. The unions did not win everything they wanted. They agreed to a five-year contract and accepted a lump sum instead of a wage increase for the first year. They let the company introduce a second tier on job security, with fewer protections against layoffs for new-hires. Still, given the balance of power, the contract represented a "defensive victory," said one CWA official.

Flight Attendants Wreak Havoc

by David Borer and Joe Burns

FLIGHT ATTENDANTS AT MIDWEST EXPRESS AIRLINES voted to join the Association of Flight Attendants (AFA) in May 1999, but by the spring of 2002 management had still refused to sign a decent first contract. Under the Railway Labor Act, which governs labor relations at the airlines, negotiations routinely drag on for two years or more. The flight attendants turned to CHAOS™.[1]

The AFA first developed CHAOS, or Create Havoc Around Our System, at Alaska Airlines in 1993. Flight attendants promised random, unannounced strikes against individual Alaska Airlines flights, cities, or aircraft. Potential passengers were told that—without warning—CHAOS might leave them stranded. CHAOS resulted in a 20 percent drop in passenger traffic at Alaska Airlines even before a single flight was struck. After striking just seven flights over a period of nine months, the union won an industry-leading contract without losing a dime of lost wages. Management settled when a federal court ruled that intermittent CHAOS strikes are legal under the Railway Labor Act.

To implement CHAOS at Midwest Express, the AFA built upon the organization created to win the representation election. Out of 465 flight attendants, all but a handful had signed union cards. The union set up phone trees and an informational representative structure, so flight attendants would have accurate and up-to-date information throughout the campaign.

To activate the membership and demonstrate unity, flight attendants wore color-coded ribbons (such as yellow for approaching CHAOS, blue for cooling off, and dark green for money), circulated petitions, and ran letter-writing campaigns. Over 100 flight attendants picketed on St. Patrick's Day at the Midwest Express Center in downtown Milwaukee, wearing Astrobright green CHAOS T-shirts. In May, a large group of flight attendants and union allies converged on the Midwest Express board of directors meeting, demanding a fair contract and threatening CHAOS.

The Milwaukee Central Labor Council actively supported the flight attendants, mobilizing other union members to AFA events, providing logistics and sound for rallies, and garnering political support. The Ironworkers donated a large billboard near the airport that warned the flying public that CHAOS strikes could occur.

Before the threat of CHAOS strikes could carry any weight, however, the union had to be released from mediation by the National Mediation Board (NMB). Under the Railway Labor Act such a release triggers the start of a 30-day cooling-off period and additional mediation. Only after the cooling-off period expires without an agreement may airline workers legally strike. By spring 2002, the union could see that a release would be coming in the summer and kicked into CHAOS mode.

Wearing CHAOS T-shirts, flight attendants picketed and leafleted airports, informing passengers of possible unannounced strikes after the cooling-off period. They encouraged passengers to fill out cards so the union could email them CHAOS updates.

In May 2002, over 95 percent of AFA members authorized their leadership to call a strike. Flight attendants switched their color-coded ribbons to CHAOS green, signaling their readiness for the coming confrontation. They wrote company reports in green ink. When management dictated that all reports be done in black ink, a rank and filer came up with the idea to seal their reports with green dots.

The union made the traditional preparations for a strike. It opened a strike headquarters staffed by international officers (who are working flight attendants) and by rank-and-file flight attendants on their days off. Rank and filers also organized a series of fundraising events, including bake sales, car washes, and parties.

The union asked flight attendants to sign a GUTS (Geared Up To Strike) list. While all flight attendants were expected to strike if called, GUTS volunteers would be called first when CHAOS strikes began, allowing the union to target flights staffed by committed GUTS volunteers.

The NMB released the parties from mediation in late July, setting the cooling-off period to expire on August 30, 2002. As the date approached, activity and media attention reached a crescendo. Solidarity and information actions were held daily, sometimes twice daily, including a constant stream of news releases and leaflets to warn passengers of potential CHAOS at the airline, mass rallies, and picketing at company headquarters.

CHAOS instilled paranoia in management. A company vice-president launched a useless investigation when a supervisor mistook a flight attendant's cigarette break for a CHAOS strike. When a union news release stated "CHAOS is coming to Los Angeles and New York" and solidarity pickets marched at those airports, management thought a strike had begun and called in reserve flight attendants. Management sent extra supervisors to watch the flight attendants and take over if a work action began. This was all wasted time, money, and effort, because the union could target individual flights wherever management's tactics provided an opening.

"CHAOS drove the company crazy," says Toni Phillips, a flight attendant and AFA Master Executive Council Chair at Midwest Express. "They spent tons of money trying to figure out our strategy. That's why it was so successful. It was actually fun to watch."

CHAOS also raised anxiety among flight attendants. Unlike a traditional strike, where everyone is in it together, the strategy called for attendants in crews as small as three to take on the company. Plus, to maximize the surprise, local and international leaders would pick strikers without notice. "In CHAOS, the flight attendants never knew if their flight would be picked that day," notes Phillips. "They were always on edge." That's why CHAOS requires more discipline and education than a regular strike.

Flight attendants debated the CHAOS strategy at membership meetings. The majority decided that, given the ability of management to permanently replace strikers, walking out in small groups allowed greater protection. The Alaska flight attendants had struck for just 20 to 30 minutes at a time, making it virtually impossible for the company to deploy its scabs.

Media coverage of potential CHAOS strikes drove away passengers. The AFA estimated a 20-25 percent drop in passengers during the CHAOS activities, even before a single strike. Still, flight attendants knew they would have to make good on their threat. While they were fine-tuning specific flight targets for maximum impact and minimum risk, management called to request a resumption of negotiations. The company then offered significant movement on the major issues and on September 20, 2002, the flight attendants won a solid first contract.

The key to CHAOS was membership mobilization. Flight attendants had to keep up constant public pressure on the airline with daily airport pickets and major rallies several times a week at company headquarters, plus all the strike preparation. And, unlike a traditional strike, they had to keep working while doing it.

Working Safe on the Docks

WHEN THE PACIFIC MARITIME ASSOCIATION (PMA) threatened to eliminate union jobs in the summer of 2002, West Coast dockworkers fought back. Knowing the Bush administration would secure a Taft-Hartley injunction against any strike, dockworkers in the International Longshore and Warehouse Union (ILWU) stayed on the job after their contract expired and cut production by "working safe."

"It wasn't a slowdown," says Vance Lelli, a member of ILWU Local 23 in Tacoma, Washington. "Five members had died on the job in the six months leading up to negotiations. With the PMA taking a hard line in negotiations and threatening to lock us out, our elected safety officers reminded us of OSHA rules and of the safety provisions in the contract. They pointed out the stop signs and the 15 mph speed limit on the docks."

The union could point to other reasons that production was slow. Leading up to the contract expiration on September 1, ports in Los Angeles, San Francisco, Portland, Tacoma, Seattle, and 24 other West Coast ports were extremely busy because shippers, worried about a strike or lockout, were trying to move as much cargo as possible for the Christmas season. The crush of ships, trains, containers, trucks, and cargo slowed operations. So did the hiring of inexperienced dockworkers to handle the rush.

"That was a safety issue," Lelli points out. "When the employers couldn't get enough people to handle the load, they would hire people from the unemployment office. They had no training. They would hurt themselves, or someone else. So we stopped that, which did put a crimp in the works."

Dockworkers' insistence on safe operations affected productivity. "When you are lashing containers to the deck of a ship, you should have a railing around you," says Lelli. "We made sure we had railings. We asked for earplugs and dust masks for some jobs. When you are in a container crane 105 feet above a truck and you are in a rush, you pick the can [container] off the truck and hoist it toward the ship before the truck moves off. That's not safe. Instead, you should lift the can from the truck, let the truck move safely away, and then begin hoisting the can toward the ship.

"Vehicles were key," notes Lelli. "If all the hustler trucks obey the stop signs and the speed limit, everything takes a little longer, the trains back up, and the just-in-time operations get out of whack. Of course, the companies put up the signs, and they put them up for a reason. In Tacoma, we have straddle carriers that take containers from the staging area to the train. They have eight wheels and straddle the containers. The cab is 45 feet off the ground. Some drivers would blow through stop signs and scream around corners. But we reminded them that several people had died when one of the carriers tipped over."

The union got the work-safe message out informally. "The ILWU is a rank-and-file union," says Lelli. "Experienced workers are the leaders on the dock. We talked to each other and to the younger workers every morning at the dispatch hall. On a bad day, there are 200 dockworkers there and usually 300 or 400 show up. We talked at the hall and then we talked on the ship. We were trying to look out for each other more."

Claiming the union was engaged in a deliberate slowdown and refusing to "pay dockworkers for being on strike," the PMA locked out the ILWU for three shifts starting the evening of September 27. When the ports reopened on September 29, productivity dropped 60 percent, according to the PMA, prompting the employers to lock out the workers indefinitely. On October 9, the Bush administration sought and received a temporary restraining order under the Taft-Hartley Act from a federal judge.

He ordered the employers and the union to stop interfering with "the orderly continuance of work in the maritime industry, at a normal rate of speed." But when the workers returned to work, a normal rate of speed was impossible under the crush of backed-up cargo.

The union continued to "work safe," noting in a press release, "safety regulations are a part of [the] contract. In compliance with the court order, the ILWU has instructed its members to obey the letter of those regulations and to follow all mandated procedures."

In the first week after the lockout, the PMA claimed the union was still slowing down. According to some PMA employers, union gangs would arrive at work missing a skilled worker or two, such as a hook checker, who tracks cargo on and off a ship, or a clerk supervisor, who oversees the movement of cargo throughout the docks.

Union members made working safely a priority when the Pacific Maritime Association threatened to eliminate longshore jobs in the summer of 2002.

Productivity dropped 34 percent in Oakland, 29 percent in Portland, 27 percent in Seattle, 19 percent in Tacoma, and 9 percent in Los Angeles/Long Beach, the PMA claimed. In Tacoma, productivity dropped only 10 percent on the first two days after the lockout, but fell sharply on the third and fourth days, which happened to follow a local union meeting. "That was a coincidence," says Lelli.

The chaos on the docks after the lockout provided cover for the dockworkers' work-safe efforts. When the PMA sought to hold the union in contempt of court for its supposed slowdown, the union was able to point to the disorder caused by the backlog of work. The Department of Justice refused to prosecute the union, blaming both sides for the drop in productivity.

The settlement, which came by the end of November, was a victory for the ILWU given the weight of government support for the employers. Although the contract was too long—six years—the union preserved no-cost health insurance and won a pay raise and better pensions. On the main issue—whether dock jobs using new technologies would be done by ILWU members—the PMA agreed that, "Technologies shall not be used to shift traditional union jurisdiction to non-bargaining unit employees or facilities."

The Legal Limits of Working to Rule

by Ellis Boal

WORKERS OFTEN FOLLOW two sets of rules: the official company or government rules and the unofficial, unwritten shop floor practices established over time. The two often conflict, but supervisors wink at rule violations in the interest of productivity by ignoring, say, paperwork or health and safety requirements. Eventually, the unwritten norms become "past practices" of an unusual sort, in that they are past practices that benefit the company.

Workers can exploit the inconsistency between official and unwritten rules by "working to rule"—collectively following a company's written rules and regulations to the letter.[2] Working to rule rests on the idea that management must make instructions clear. If there are, in effect, two sets of instructions, workers cannot be faulted for following those rules from which they benefit.[3]

Working to rule is used for four reasons:

(a) as an economic weapon to support the union's bargaining position on grievances or during contract negotiations

(b) as a means of protest

(c) to ease the burdens and risks of high-intensity work

(d) to produce a high-quality product.

Courts are skeptical of reasons (c) and (d).[4]

If working to rule were protected by law, employers could not legally discipline workers for doing it. If it were unprotected, the employer could impose discipline, possibly including dismissal. Remarkably, there is no general rule on whether or not working to rule is protected. In decisions of 1996, 1997, and 1998 the NLRB noted the "difficult issues raised by work-to-rule" and bypassed them. The Supreme Court did the same in 1960 and 1976.[5]

The law does not protect insubordination. But properly executed, working to rule for all reasons except (d) ought to be protected. Why is reason (d) different? Because the law only protects concerted activities undertaken "for [workers'] mutual aid or protection." Courts consider product quality a management prerogative outside the realm of legitimate union or worker concern.[6]

Of course, even activities protected by law can be risky due to the government's slow and uncertain enforcement. The greatest protection is still the solidarity of a well-organized union membership.[7]

Without a Contract

Working to rule occurs in two different legal contexts. The first is where there is no contract in place, and the union is negotiating for the first one or a new one.

The NLRB and the courts have reasoned that if a contract were in place, it would provide a mechanism for working out conflicts, and there would be no need for working to rule. But without a contract, working to rule can be a legitimate response to conflicting management expectations.

One frequent tactic in a work-to-rule is refusing overtime. If accepting work assignments such as overtime is voluntary, the NLRB says that workers may collectively refuse to perform them.[8] The NLRB treats such concerted refusals as legal strikes.[9]

It may seem odd, but without a contract, partial strikes, intermittent strikes, and most slowdowns are not protected.[10] On the other hand, a spontaneous full walkout in the middle of a shift to protest a particular situation is protected, even if the workers' demands are disorganized or unclear,[11] or if the strike lasts only briefly.[12]

Even though slowdowns and partial strikes are unprotected by the law, the Supreme Court has said that such actions are nonetheless part and parcel of collective bargaining.[13] This means an employer can discipline workers for the slowdown, but it cannot refuse to bargain just because they are slowing down. Thus, if workers think they can get away with it, they can use slowdowns to pressure the employer to bargain.[14]

Intermittent strikes are generally unprotected, but the company must prove a pattern of strikes if it wants the NLRB to uphold its discipline of workers for striking intermittently. That means that workers may be able to get away with random strikes, such as a short walkout at the end of the regular workday to protest overtime.[15]

With a Contract

Work-to-rule participants are at greater risk in the second context, where there is a contract with a no-strike/no-slowdown clause and a regular grievance procedure. Then the grievance procedure applies instead of the law. Not only are partial and intermittent strikes unprotected. All strikes are,[16] with the exception of some sympathy strikes.[17] As a case in point, an organized sickout is considered a strike.[18] Working to rule is still an option. Management must still make its instructions clear and members may still interpret instructions to their benefit. They just have to be sure not to violate the letter of the contract if they want to avoid discipline.

Employers may go to a judge for an injunction against any action that violates the contract. Employers try to argue, often with success, that a work-to-rule is a violation of the contract.[19] Production statistics are often part of a company's case against working to rule, although alone they are not sufficient for an injunction.[20]

Any contractual protection for working to rule would depend on the particular contract language and the particular arbitrator. The General Motors-UAW contract, for instance, specifies that certain overtime is voluntary on an individual basis, but concerted refusals of overtime can be disciplined.[21] Arbitrators at other companies have held that slowdowns to the standard production rate are protected if done individually or to make work easier (reason c), but not if done as a group or to extract a concession from management (reason a).[22]

In the 1989 Paperworkers case, New York locals instructed members under threat of fines not to help the company brainstorm quality improvements or do other non-unit work. The instruction was to remain in effect until the dispute of a locked-out sister local in Alabama was resolved. The company went to the NLRB and claimed this violated the no-strike clause, and was coercion by the locals. The NLRB disagreed. It emphasized that non-unit work was voluntary at this company, and rejected an employer claim that the union's self-help should await the outcome of grievances.[23]

Will It Work?

Unions do not always get to choose which forum—courts, NLRB, arbitrator—will hear a case about working to rule. If possible, unions unsure of their arbitrators should try to get before the NLRB. Though susceptible to political influence,[24] currently it seems to have a better overall view of working to rule than courts or arbitrators. In court, NLRB precedents can be presented, but a judge is not bound to follow them.[25]

Whether you are before a court, an arbitrator, or the NLRB, expect hostility from the decision maker:

• In one amazing case, a union of federal professional employees proposed in bargaining that members be insulated from adverse evaluations insofar as they had followed written procedures or orders. The Federal Labor Relations Authority held that management did not even have to bargain over the union's proposal: "[I]t is unreasonable to expect [from management] the total elimination of conflicts and deficiencies." The court of appeals agreed: "[T]he result could be similar to what British labor unions achieve by 'working to rule,' namely the tangle that inevitably occurs when a bureaucracy is bound and gagged with red tape—no matter that the tape is of its own making."[26]

• In a Caterpillar case, an administrative law judge (ALJ) held a member's requests for a safety rep and a steward were unprotected where the requests were just to harass management and where there was no actual contract violation to grieve.[27] This decision was not appealed to the NLRB, is non-binding, and is contrary to precedent. Grievance filing is protected even if it exceeds the actual contract language, unless the excess is extraordinary, obnoxious, unjustified, and departs from the grievance procedure.[28] But the ALJ's attitude is typical of decision makers confronted with work-to-rule.

• In a 2001 dispute between United Airlines and the Machinists, the court of appeals enjoined a union work-safe campaign. This contradicted the legal doctrine that says an employer must have "clean hands" before seeking legal relief. That is, the employer must "make every reasonable effort to settle" a dispute before filing a lawsuit against the union. The court granted the injunction against the union even though it accepted the unchallenged finding that the airline could have stopped the slowdown through individual disciplinary action.[29] In justifying its decision, the court gave credit to testimony of company officials that union calls to work safe and to work by the book are "commonly recognized signals... for a work slowdown."[30]

Despite this last case, courts, the NLRB, and arbitrators often look more favorably on working to rule for safety reasons (reason c). In one case, the union ran a work-to-rule contract campaign; simultaneously the health and safety committee posted leaflets that urged members to "work to the safety rule." The board ruled that this phrase did not encourage "unprotected activity." That is, the flier advocated that the workers engage in protected activity "in accordance with the rules of safety that have been established for their benefit." Moreover, the board refused to rule on the legality of working to rule. Instead, it found that even if working to rule were unprotected, working to safety rule is protected.[31]

Management can always deal with a work-to-rule campaign by changing ambiguous instructions to clear ones, or by giving a direct order to do something in a certain way or at a certain speed. In that case working to rule may be as unprotected as any other slowdown.[32] Though there are limited exceptions,[33] "obeying now and grieving later" would be the risk-free course.

Workers might have some protection for working to rule if the employer ever condones such activity. In one case, a UPS worker refused for safety reasons to perform his job and his immediate supervisor went along with his decision. Later the worker received a disciplinary letter for his refusal, which the NLRB ruled was illegal because the supervisor had condoned the worker's action.[34]

Even if working to rule is protected, an employer who has otherwise bargained in good faith can lock out a union that is using the tactic for reason (a). The NLRB has not addressed a lockout in response to working to rule for reasons (b), (c), or (d).[35]

Action Questions

WORKING TO RULE is nothing new. It rarely catches large companies by surprise. Therefore, those considering an inside strategy must prepare for the harshest treatment after the contract expires and the work-to-rule begins, including buyoffs, distraction, harassment, discipline, dismissal, and lockout. Preparation includes a creative understanding of the company's vulnerabilities: how to hurt production and profits within the bounds of management's rules, the contract, and the law. And it requires a keen assessment of the membership's potential for solidarity.

The questions below will help you decide whether working to rule is a viable strategy. To make that decision, they should be discussed discreetly, among a few trusted members. Once you decide that working to rule might fit your situation, you should discuss these questions with the rest of the membership, who will have many good ideas.

1. What is the economic situation of your company? Of your plant? Do you have a trusted friend in management or an office worker who can get you information about management's plans for the future? Who are its suppliers? Who are its customers? What shape are they in? Where do your company's orders stand? Who has

power in the corporation and at your location?

2. Why are you thinking of using an inside strategy? How will the members relate to the idea of an inside strategy instead of a strike? Is there a history of work-to-rules or slowdowns? How successful have strikes been?

3. Where will your core group come from? The executive board? The stewards? A committee created for this purpose? Who are the members who can be developed as leaders in a new situation? Who are the two or three key people you must talk to? Who are the next five people you must talk to? Who are the next five? Who should talk to whom?

4. How's your timing? Get out a calendar and check the vacation schedule. Will all your key people be there when you need them? Looking at management's production schedule for crunch times, when can you hurt them most?

5. What is the production process? You might want to make a map (see Chapter 3). What are the most crucial operations? What are the key departments? What are the key operations in those departments? What would it take to stop them? Who fixes them? What are the key links between departments? Where are the potential bottlenecks? Which workers have jobs that allow them to travel around from one department to another? Is there one group of workers who are particularly powerful if they impede production? Is there any group of workers who because of their skills or experience are difficult to replace? Which workers are most vulnerable and need most protection?

6. How can you use the work rules against the company? What shortcuts does the company encourage? What does the contract allow? Which rules are vague? Which managers are unclear in their instructions? Which managers are vulnerable to aggravation? Which have the power and will to discipline workers?

7. Do you have ties to unions at your company's suppliers or customers? Would they be willing to raise their quality standards or shorten their required delivery times for your company's product? Do you have ties to the unions of the truck drivers, railroad workers, or others who move your parts or finished products? Can you establish ties with those workers that can make life more difficult for your company? How does it affect production if raw materials or parts arrive late? How do your customers react if your production schedules or quality requirements are not met?

8. What will you ask people to do? What level of commitment is needed? How will you establish your solidarity committee? Where will you get your "intelligence" about what's happening at the workplace? How will you recruit people to activity?

9. What activities should you begin with? Meetings? Group grievances? Work-to-rule? Slowdown? What about lunchtime meetings or rallies? Will you have buttons? Leaflets? Newsletters? What actions will come later?

10. What kind of support can you expect from the union's district or regional office? How will the international react? What funds do you have? What can you raise?

11. Can you mobilize community support? Are your co-workers in community groups that might offer support? Do members have connections to other local unions? Religious groups? Politicians?

Authors

STEVEN ASHBY AND C.J. HAWKING organized solidarity efforts with the Staley workers. Ashby, now a professor of labor studies at Indiana University at Bloomington, was co-chair of the local's flagship support group in Chicago. Hawking, a United Methodist pastor, moved to Decatur during the lockout to assist the local in its outreach to the community. This section is based on Ashby and Hawking's book, *The Staley Workers and the Fight for a New American Labor Movement,* to be published by the University of Illinois Press in 2005.

ELLIS BOAL is a labor lawyer and the websteward for Labor Notes. He has written manuals about legal and union rights for Teamsters and UAW members.

DAVID BORER is general counsel for the Association of Flight Attendants, AFL-CIO, and JOE BURNS is former staff attorney for AFA and staff negotiator of the Midwest Express Airlines contract.

AARON BRENNER is a labor historian, researcher, writer, and editor in New York City. He has written about international labor solidarity, union reform movements, and rank-and-file rebellions by Teamsters, telephone workers, and postal workers, and is the editor of *The Encyclopedia of Strikes in American History.*

PAM GALPERN is a telephone repair and installation technician at Verizon.

Notes

1. AFA requests: "CHAOS and the CHAOS logo are trademarks of the AFA. We encourage others to use some or all of the CHAOS tactics, but please do not use the term CHAOS or the CHAOS logo without the AFA's written permission. Thanks."

2. The legal citations for this section, numbered 2-35, can be found on the Troublemaker's website, www.labornotes.org.

On the Troublemaker's Website

SEE www.labornotes.org for more on inside strategies:
- *Washington Post* Byline Strikes
- Key Elements of Inside Strategies
- Legal Notes, the case citations for "The Legal Limits of Working to Rule"

11. Corporate Campaigns

by Steven Ashby

A CORPORATE CAMPAIGN MOBILIZES LABOR and the community to tarnish the public image of a corporation and to inflict enough economic damage to get management to negotiate a fair contract or recognize the union. The first corporate campaign, although it wasn't called that at the time, was organized by the United Farm Workers in the 1960s. To convince agribusiness to recognize the union, the UFW mobilized rank-and-file members to build a national boycott against grapes and Gallo wine, involving thousands of activists across the U.S. Corporate campaigns since then have drawn from the lessons of that first crusade.

Corporate campaigns are also called "strategic," "external," or "comprehensive" campaigns. They are no magic bullet, but they can give a union more allies and more weapons to use against a company. Any union considering a strike would do well to lay the groundwork for a corporate campaign while simultaneously organizing a contract campaign to mobilize members on the job.

The downside of corporate campaigns is that they require a substantial allocation of union resources, and they rarely win quickly. When the workers involved are on strike or locked out, a corporate campaign, to be most effective, should be combined with a strategy to stop production. If a deep-pocketed corporation continues to turn out product with a scab workforce, the corporate campaign is less likely to succeed.

Our four case studies illustrate different types of corporate campaigns with different goals. UNITE's fight at "ABC Linen" targeted a small local employer, seeking union recognition. Union members at A.E. Staley were locked out, fighting a horrendous contract and a multinational employer. Non-union farmworkers are targeting Taco Bell, a customer of their direct employers, the growers, so that Taco Bell will bring the growers to the table to discuss wages. At non-union Cintas, UNITE HERE is combining shop floor organizing with a corporate campaign to win a neutrality agreement from Cintas. You can also read about three other corporate campaigns in this book. See "A Corporate Campaign To Support Mexican Workers" (Chapter 23), "Everything but the Kitchen Sink" (Chapter 15), and "Mini-Corporate Campaign against Concessions" (Chapter 8). Together, they illustrate five components of a corporate campaign:

• **A solidarity theme.** The campaign should reach out to people who may be apathetic or even hostile to unions. Standard picket signs that read "Unfair to Labor" don't resonate with most Americans.

The media, business, and politicians often portray unions as caring only for their own members. Plan your corporate campaign to counter this negative propaganda. The message should be that the fight is broader than just this group of workers—it is about morality, decency, and human rights. It is a struggle for justice for the community and should involve all good-hearted people.

For example, in the A.E. Staley campaign, placards at union rallies declared "Corporate Greed Is Tearing Decatur [their town] Apart!" At ABC Linen, a flyer asked customers, "Do you want to eat off a sweatshop tablecloth today?"

• **Mobilized members.** A successful corporate campaign cannot be run top-down by union officials, nor is it a public relations campaign run by media experts. A corporate campaign is a social movement. All of its activities—reaching out to workers, unions, and community groups locally, nationally, and internationally; organizing a national pressure campaign—require an active and organized membership.

At Staley, dozens of workers became "road warriors," traveling the country to speak for the union. In the Taco Bell campaign, farmworkers put on a 15-city "truth tour" to seek nationwide support. At Cintas, workers mobilize in small shop floor actions to build their confidence and confront management abuses.

- **Research to identify targets.** Strategic planning should start well before the union goes on strike or is locked out. The union will research the corporation to determine the breadth of its operations, which are most profitable, who its customers are, which institutions provide financial backing, which members of management sit on other corporations' boards, and what the company's safety, environmental, and tax records show. The goal is to know exactly where its operations are most susceptible to pressure. (See the Appendix on Researching Employers.)

From its research, the union selects a few aspects of the company's operations as primary targets. This step is crucial. Choosing the wrong target can lead to fruitless efforts. Often the target will be the company's customers. Once the target has been chosen, explains UNITE organizer Malcolm Emerich, "You hit them and hit them and hit them. The owner is being consistently bombarded with complaints from his clients."

At Staley, the workers first targeted the company's financial allies, but then, determining that that strategy wasn't working, switched to hitting corporate customers, Miller Beer and Pepsi. Farmworkers chose Taco Bell as the customer that would be most vulnerable to public pressure.

- **Labor-community coalition.** Naturally, the campaign begins with outreach to the labor movement. A local union needs the active support of its own international, and then the support of its local central labor council and its state federation of labor. Support from the national AFL-CIO can open the door to central labor councils and state federations in nearby cities and states. But too often official bodies may give little more than paper endorsements.

So corporate campaigns require a form of horizontal unionism—reaching out to any locals, national unions, and individuals who want to stand up to the assault on workers. A big part of this horizontal unionism is going beyond the union movement—which is just 13 percent of the workforce—for public support and for alliances with the African American and Latino communities, women's organizations, students, environmentalists, clergy and congregations, small businesses, citizen's groups, and neighborhood organizations. A website and national mailings educate the public and update supporters.

However, solidarity is not a one-way street. For many unionists a corporate campaign requires a new way of thinking: a sincere promise that just as the community comes to their aid, the union will also be there to support others' struggles. People can smell opportunism; when the union asks for solidarity, it must be prepared to reciprocate.

Corporate injury to the community can be a target. For example, the company might have been receiving tax subsidies from local or state governments. The union can appeal to homeowners and small business owners who are subsidizing the corporation's tax breaks with their own higher taxes.

If a corporation is a polluter, then neighborhood groups, civic leaders, and environmental organizations may be a natural ally. If a corporation has ties to universities—for example, the university's endowment fund owns large shares of stock or the company sells a product on the campus—then student groups can mobilize to cut those ties. If a corporation has a bad record in its treatment of women, immigrants, or people of color, the union can find natural allies in workers centers or in women's rights and civil rights organizations. The union can mobilize groups that own stock in the company to raise objections at shareholder meetings.

As AFL-CIO Secretary-Treasurer Rich Trumka put it, "Corporate campaigns swarm the target employer from every angle, great and small, with an eye toward inflicting upon the employer the death of a thousand cuts rather than a single blow."

The Cintas campaign reached out to environmentalists over the company's illegal dumping of polluted wastewater. The Taco Bell campaign got students across the country to take up farmworkers' demand for a raise.

- **Take it to the streets.** Finally, a corporate campaign requires a willingness to be creative and daring, to be courageous, to do things members might never have dreamed of doing. It requires opening up the day-to-day decision-making process to the rank and file in order to draw out the most imaginative tactics. As retired CWA leader Jan Pierce has said, "When we always throw the fast ball, management knows what's coming and they hit it out of the park. We need to throw the curve, the slider, the change-up, the screwball, the knuckleball, the spitball."

A corporate campaign means aggressively and ingeniously getting in the face of corporate leaders. It will include marches and picket lines. It may be necessary to break the law in nonviolent civil disobedience. In the thick of the 1989-90 Pittston strike, Rich Trumka said, "Labor law is formulated for labor to lose. If you play by every one of those rules, you lose every time."

At ABC Linen, members embarrassed the boss when their kids handed out flyers in his neighborhood while trick-or-treating. At Staley, workers sat down in mass nonviolent civil disobedience at the plant gates. During the Taco Bell campaign, workers launched a hunger strike.

'ABC Linen': Skirting Taft-Hartley in a Strike for Recognition

by Dan La Botz

THE TAFT-HARTLEY ACT prohibits secondary boycotts and other forms of indirect pressure on employers. But it does not prohibit a union from publicizing the causes of a labor dispute or strike. Thus it is possible for unions and workers to engage customers and suppliers as part of their struggle against an employer, if they do it carefully and skillfully. This can be particularly effective with small employers, as UNITE has demonstrated in Chicago.

Small companies can present "special challenges,"

says Pete DeMay, director of organizing for the Chicago and Central States Joint Board of UNITE, "because they take our line of attack really personally. Because it becomes less about money and more about machismo, we've learned something about how to manage these strikes. We've been victorious in all five of the strikes we've run in the last four years, but they were tough. Some of the lessons we learned would be applicable to any small industrial operation."

UNITE organizer Malcolm Emerich describes a struggle for union recognition at a laundry outside Chicago. (We have changed the name of the company at UNITE's request, because although this was a hard-fought battle, the union and company now have amicable relations.)

"ABC Linen is a specialty laundry, with about 40 production workers, that provides high-quality linens to caterers, materials with patterns and special colors. In the Chicago area there might be four other shops that do similar stuff, and three of them were unionized.

"We got involved in this shop through friends and families of unionized workers. Most of the workers come from the town of Queztalapa in Oaxaca, Mexico. A UNITE laundry up the street employed mostly immigrant undocumented workers who had family and friends at ABC.

"The workers literally organized themselves. They faxed us a petition saying that they wanted the union, and everybody in the shop had signed it. Two were young men and the rest were young women ranging in age from 18 to their mid-twenties. We had people sign cards, and then a UNITE vice-president presented the cards to the owner, and said that it would be in his best interest to recognize the union."

But the employer resisted and the union decided to pursue an unfair labor practices (ULP) strike, which provides some protection against permanent replacement workers (see the box in Chapter 9 on ULP strikes).

"Any employer, particularly with immigrant workers and folks without paper, is almost always breaking the law and they almost always violate somebody's rights," explains Emerich. "So we could walk out on a ULP strike. One of our charges was threats against union activists made in a meeting. Everybody walked out and not a single worker crossed during the strike."

The union hoped that the strike would be brief and not too hard on the employer. "These folks were making $5.15 per hour and moderate benefits, with mystery profit-sharing and pension plans. There were also many health and safety issues. But the union wasn't asking for much. The price of the first contract would have been relatively reasonable from the employer's point of view. It was intended to be a short strike, because against small employers like this we have enough angles to put the pressure on him. We have strong unions, we have folks in the community, and we thought we could do it in a nice way."

Unfortunately, the employer decided to bring in strikebreakers, escalating the confrontation. "We decided to keep his production down," says Emerich. "The workers led that. Because the community is pretty tight, many of the scabs looking for work were friends or family, or friends of friends. As a result, the picket line was so personal that a lot of temps refused to come back. We organized workers to visit the temp agency, to talk to them about the situation. We referred scabs to another agency, a community-based organization that worked as a job locator for immigrants. When scabs arrived to look for work at ABC, we would say, here's a number to see about work."

Although the union had some success turning away scabs, the employer eventually found a new workforce. "He hired newer people in the community, an Argentine, a Colombian, or Mexicans who weren't from that town, and some older people. So his production was low for months, because he had inexperienced and less capable workers," says Emerich.

Going after the Customers

UNITE now decided to attack the employer's business, going after his customers—many of whom were caterers—and even the customers' clients. The union had a pretty complete customer list. "We scheduled an organizer to go to a caterer with two or three workers from the shop," says Emerich. "The workers would tell the caterers what the conditions were like at ABC. We would ask them, 'Do you want to do business with a guy who treats his workforce like this?'

"On the surface, we were engaged in an informational campaign for ABC's customers, telling them about the situation. The implied message was: You need to stop doing business with this guy.

"You have to find their client list, find out when they are doing events, and then target the client of the client," Emerich explains. "For example, the catering industry is a relatively closed community, and we were going after wedding shows. A wedding show is a kind of bazaar for wedding services such as caterers, limousine services, florists, and so on. We would do informational leafleting there; we had a leaflet of a blushing bride, saying, 'Do you want to take any chances with your special day?' We let them know that our campaign had gone anywhere to protest and inform. So they knew it was not just the laundry or caterer that was the target; it could be their event.

"The Constitution protects free speech, so we can inform anybody of anything. Every flyer had a disclaimer—in about one-point type—saying that the flyer was produced by UNITE, that it was not in any way a direct appeal to refuse to provide service or products, or to stop doing business with anybody. There was no demand. This was just information. But in that way, you can do a lot of really nasty stuff."

In the process of going after the clients, the union also went after the related businesses of the clients. Emerich explains, "Often caterers also have a restaurant or a storefront where they serve sandwiches or salads. Those are the best. We had a banner that said, 'This business supports sweatshops.' We would explain the workers' situation at ABC, and if they said, 'this doesn't concern me,' we would show up the next day with the flyers, the megaphone, and the banner.

"Sometimes one person would even wait outside with all of this stuff while an organizer and workers talked with the owner. We demanded an answer, but we were relatively flexible. If they seemed reasonable, and said they needed time to find another linen provider, that was okay. We could not refer them to a unionized linen provider, because that would be collusion, but we could say that there are other linen providers in the area. If they were not supportive, then we would walk out and start yelling with a megaphone and rallying and passing out leaflets and having a banner. And it was embarrassing."

Going after the Corporate Clients

Sometimes a small business serves large corporate clients, so the union can target them too. ABC's clients included Abbott Laboratories, University of Chicago, and Northwestern University. "When we realized how big the client list was," says Emerich, "we hooked up with Interfaith Committee for Worker Justice, Jobs with Justice, and the regional AFL-CIO. We also had help from UFCW, UE, AFSCME, and other unions, and from community organizations, and more radical movements, such as Direct Action Network–Labor, in Chicago."

UNITE worked with these allies to develop strategies to pressure the corporate clients to drop ABC. "With JwJ and Interfaith, we planned to go after Abbott's board of directors, who are supposed to be community supporters, donating to things like the Chicago Symphony. A lot of it is psychological. The threat is scary enough to make people, especially rich people, think twice. A leading geneticist from Abbott held a symposium at the Museum of Science and Industry, and we crashed that. We also did rallies and marched on the executive offices of Abbott to present them with tablecloths stenciled with 'This tablecloth washed in a sweatshop,' to urge them to stop using ABC. We carried out these actions with the support of well-known politicians, labor officials, priests, and ministers."

UNITE's allies helped reach the right people in the universities or the churches or even in the corporations themselves. "Through USAS (United Students Against Sweatshops) and SLAP (Student Labor Action Project) we got in touch with campus organizations," Emerich remembers. "Student organizations can sit down with the president of the school and talk with them, so that was pretty easy. Interfaith could sit down with any organization with religious ties." UNITE also used its labor contacts to corporate and political figures.

UNITE's campaign was relentless, Emerich says. "It's not how big the client is that's most important, it's that the owner is being consistently bombarded with complaints from his clients. It's the psychological factor, that he's losing business every day. We had major rallies, constantly targeting more public clients in central Chicago."

UNITE's campaign to organize 40 laundry workers had become complex and time-consuming. "For a strike of 40 you have to do all the same sort of work that you have to do for a strike of 200," says Emerich. "You have to make connections with all of these people. We ended up at golf clubs, caterers, restaurants, churches, community organizations, universities."

End the Strike in Good Time

UNITE knew that the employer might let the business be destroyed before giving in. "It really does become very personal to these employers," says Emerich. "We found out that we had effectively destroyed 80 percent of his business. In the later months we were throwing our punches very warily, because we were concerned that we would be doing permanent damage to this company for years to come."

By the spring the employer realized that business was going down the drain. "Winter is generally slow, so he may not have realized how much business he was losing," says Emerich. "Then came spring season, and the business wasn't coming in because of the long-term work we had done over the winter destroying his name. But he couldn't settle because of his pride."

Because the boss refused to settle, the union made the attack even more personal. "You can say that you don't want to make it personal, but in the end it is personal," Emerich believes. "We did an action on Halloween where we brought the workers and their kids into the rich suburban neighborhood where he and his brother lived. The workers and their kids went trick-or-treating, and we gave each resident a flyer. It showed a sad-looking kid reaching into an empty pumpkin and finding nothing. We took that leaflet to all of his and his brother's neighbors, which really pissed him off.

"We arranged to have people call him constantly, political people such as state legislators, for example. We also looked for contacts in the community, so he could feel he had a way out. We sent in priests, anything. All of this was unsuccessful. We could have done a better job with that."

Finally, the union found the straw that broke the camel's back. "What turned this thing into something he couldn't handle was that he was trying to join a country club. We spoke to the club management and got that club to pull his linens." With that, the employer capitulated.

Surprisingly, after the long, bitter struggle that nearly ruined the business, once the union was recognized and a contract negotiated, the employer and the union developed reasonably harmonious relations.

Staley: Their Solidarity against Ours

by Steven K. Ashby and C.J. Hawking

IN 1988, THE FAMILY-RUN A.E. STALEY COMPANY was bought by Tate & Lyle, a British-based sugar conglomerate. In 1992, Tate & Lyle launched an assault on the 760 workers organized in Allied Industrial Workers Local 837 at Staley's flagship corn-processing plant in downstate

Staley workers reached out to members of other unions for support and solidarity (above) and also ran a corporate campaign targeting Staley's customers (right).

Decatur, Illinois.

The local responded to the company's demand to gut its contract by mobilizing in a two-phase campaign. The ten-month work-to-rule campaign is discussed in Chapter 10, Inside Strategies. The workers also launched a national corporate campaign that continued after they were locked out in June 1993. Although the workers were finally defeated in December 1995, they garnered impressive support from other workers along the way. Their struggle has important lessons for running corporate campaigns, including the importance of choosing the right targets.

In June 1992, three months before the membership voted to reject Staley's proposal, the local hired labor consultant Ray Rogers and his Corporate Campaign, Inc. (CCI). The members voted by 97 percent to increase their dues to $100 a month to pay for the corporate campaign.

Rogers told the Staley workers and their families that the only way to defeat a multinational corporation like Tate & Lyle was to launch a national and global grassroots campaign. Workers would need to donate much of their free time, he said, reaching out to other workers and community groups locally, nationally, and internationally; organizing national boycotts; engaging in visible protest actions; and putting public pressure on the corporation's banks and members of its board. Rogers emphasized that a corporate campaign has to hit the company from every possible angle.

Reaching Out Locally and Nationally

The union launched the campaign in early September 1992. Rogers and his staff researched and wrote a four-page brochure for wide public distribution. The "Crisis in Decatur" brochure declared, "Supervisors seem to believe they are running a prison camp: Employees are severely disciplined for minor infractions…and there have been ten firings. Staley is doing everything possible to instigate a strike, and if that doesn't happen, the company is ready to impose a contract or lock the workers out." The brochure described the safety violations documented in a 1991 OSHA investigation and the $1.6 million in fines levied. It detailed the enormous amount of toxic substances that the company poured into Decatur's water and air. The brochure revealed the company's huge profits, along with "sky-high executive salaries and lavish perks" and the corporate ties between Staley and its neighbor and alleged competitor, Archer-Daniels-Midland (ADM).

Over several weeks workers and family members delivered 50,000 brochures to homes and small businesses in Decatur. Distributing the brochures gave workers a real sense of accomplishment and hope. It was like "getting *my story* out," said worker Art Dhermy. Over the next year, the workers went door to door three more times to distribute literature and talk to their neighbors.

Using a CCI mailing list built up in previous campaigns, workers mailed "Crisis in Decatur" to 60,000 unions, community organizations, and individuals across the country. There were four such mailings in the nine months leading to the lockout, and dozens of national mailings during the 30-month lockout.

The first mailing got an overwhelming response. Supporters sent donations as well as the requested letters of protest to Tate & Lyle's CEO. By Christmas 1994, six months after the lockout, over $100,000 had been raised. During the three-year struggle, $3.5 million was raised through mailings, speaking engagements by union members, and the fundraising activities of local solidarity committees.

Throughout the Staley workers' fight, their literature and speeches emphasized three themes. First, the workers' fight was for dignity, respect, and safety on the job. A primary focus was the 1991 death of worker Jim Beals as a result of company negligence. Second, the fight was not just for the Staley workers but for everyone in Decatur. The slogan on rally placards was "Corporate Greed Is Tearing Decatur Apart." Third, the fight was a national and global fight for *all* working people. Corporations were united against working people, so workers, too, had to stand together. The union adopted the slogan, "It's Our Solidarity Versus Theirs! Help us Fight the Union-Busters!"

Targeting Banks and State Farm

Rogers' primary focus was Staley's financial relationships. He recommended that the union target State Farm Insurance, which indirectly owned significant shares of Tate & Lyle stock, and the banks that had Staley executives on their boards. Rogers reasoned that banks are a corporation's lifeline, supplying short-term and long-term loans. "When the bank receives pressure, it will put pressure on the targeted company. When the bank starts getting phone calls and letters, and people start asking questions and threaten to withdraw their accounts, and when unions start withdrawing their large accounts, then that captures the banks' attention. And the bank will tell the company, 'Get this thing settled, or you get off our board and we'll get off your board.' Now, that's divide and conquer!" Move the fight into the corporate boardrooms, Rogers declared. "Let them begin to beat each other up."

While working without a contract from late 1992 through spring 1993, the local sent busloads of workers and family members to picket two bank chains. The campaign against First of America Bank resulted in thousands of protest letters and many withdrawals by local unions. Two months later, the corporate campaign won its first victory when Staley Chairman Bob Powers was forced to resign from the bank's board. The union launched another bank campaign that soon resulted in Staley officer J. Pat Mohan leaving the board of Magna Bank.

The Staley workers were energized by the success of the two bank boycotts. "What the bank boycotts did was show us that we could do something," said member Barrie Williams. "It showed us that if you did organize and had a program, you could accomplish something with it. And that's what we needed, the confidence builder."

After the June 1993 lockout, Rogers' primary target became State Farm. State Farm was the largest holder of ADM stock, with 7 percent, and, through a subsidiary, ADM owned 7 percent of Staley/Tate & Lyle stock.

Union members and supporters of labor hold large numbers of State Farm policies, Rogers argued, and therefore State Farm was susceptible to a pressure campaign. The union mailed a fundraising letter and 60,000 boycott brochures to unions and progressive activists across the country. Staley workers distributed flyers when they spoke at union halls. Supporters leafleted State Farm offices in many cities.

Debating Campaign Targets

But by late 1993, the State Farm campaign began to lose momentum. The campaign wasn't working with the public, discouraged activists argued, and the Staley workers themselves weren't buying into it. The State Farm connection was too indirect. Union spokespeople had to explain that the local was targeting State Farm because the insurance giant owned part of ADM, and ADM had a British subsidiary which owned part of British-based Tate & Lyle, and Tate & Lyle owned Staley.

Union leader Dan Lane said, "People were having too hard a time connecting what the hell does State Farm have to do with this struggle in Decatur? Our own workers did not understand it and were not buying into it. Rogers went through this whole presentation, and people got hyped about it. But once people stepped away from it, they were saying, 'Wait a minute. You want me to do this to A so he'll do something to B to do something to C to do something to D? That seems like an awful long, indirect way to get something done.'"

The Staley Workers Solidarity Committees that had grown up across the Midwest also began to rebel against the campaign. Since most insurance business is done over the phone, when activists handed out flyers in front of State Farm branch offices, they found only a trickle of traffic and felt they were wasting their time.

In addition to Ray Rogers, the local had also brought

in Jerry Tucker, the country's foremost work-to-rule expert, to lead the campaign inside the plant. Tucker was increasingly critical of Rogers' focus on the banks. "If we were talking about [the old] Staley," said Tucker, "homegrown, family-run, its top executives spread out in the community—then that would have been a whole different ballgame. There was potential for embarrassment. But when [the corporation is] being run from London by a group of people who don't care if they lose the whole management [team] tomorrow, it doesn't matter."

Switching Targets

In late 1993, when Tucker began to talk with activists about switching campaign targets, he found a highly receptive audience. He listed all the company's customers, including Pepsi, Coke, Miller Beer, Smuckers, and Brach's Candy. By this time, the company had locked workers out, which was both a blow to the union and an opportunity. While workers were still on the job, it would have been impossible to organize the solidarity committees in cities across the country that were essential for a nationwide corporate campaign. The lockout raised the stakes for workers, but with the right corporate campaign targets, it also opened doors to new organizing possibilities.

Tucker and many of the local's activists began to argue aggressively that the corporate campaign should take on Miller Brewing, which accounted for 11 percent of Staley's income. Tucker believed that a grassroots campaign pressuring a purchaser of Staley's corn sweetener to switch to another company would be far more appealing to supporters, and seemed much more winnable, than the focus on Staley's financial allies.

Miller was highly vulnerable to a mass campaign, said Tucker. "Miller would be the easiest to roll, and we needed a victory. Just like in the in-plant campaign, you need something new happening every week." The beer industry is highly competitive, and the battle is fought city by city. When one beer tops the list in sales in a particular city, the brewery company highlights that fact in local advertising in an effort to solidify its dominance. Just a one percent drop in market share causes tremors in the boardrooms of the three companies that dominate the beer market: Miller, Anheuser-Busch, and Coors.

Tucker argued that to be successful the Staley workers would have to build a popular campaign and generate media coverage in only a small number of big cities where union support was strong. That would be enough to make Miller management switch from Staley to another supplier. Furthermore, Miller would be particularly vulnerable to a labor campaign because its primary customer base was blue-collar workers. Finally, there was a precedent: in 1992 Miller had succumbed to a similar corporate campaign organized by locked-out Steelworkers at Ravenswood Aluminum, which supplied Miller with material for its cans.

Although the State Farm campaign was never formally dropped, by spring 1994 the local turned its energy to Miller.

It's Miller Time!

As Staley workers traveled the country building solidarity, they found a receptive audience. "The Miller campaign went really well," recalled worker Royal Plankenhorn. "We would tell hotels, 'get this stuff out of here!' and it would be gone. When we would talk about the campaign, people said, 'I'll never drink another Miller beer again.'" Supporters were reinvigorated by having a target they could explain easily and that they believed was likely to succeed.

The union's slogan, "Miller Beer: Dump Staley!" was chosen carefully. The campaigns against Miller, and subsequently Pepsi, were never officially "boycotts." Under the 1947 Taft-Hartley Act, it is legal for a union engaged in a strike or lockout to call for a boycott only of products made by the company whose workers are on strike or locked out. "Secondary" boycotts—of a struck company's customers or suppliers—are against the law. To avoid being fined if Staley took the union to court, the local was urging supporters to "pressure" Miller, not boycott it. The goal was to convince Miller to stop purchasing Staley product.

After another 60,000-piece national mailing went out, the solidarity committees moved into high gear. Events that produced significant media coverage were immediately held in Madison, Milwaukee, and Chicago. In March 1994 in Chicago, whose large Irish-American population celebrates St. Patrick's Day by dyeing the Chicago River green, 75 unionists, community activists, and a group of Staley "road warriors" (see below) poured Miller bottles filled with red dye into the river after the parade, to signify the Staley workers' blood. The red-dyeing of the river made it onto every major local radio and television news broadcast.

In many cities, the solidarity committees organized mass leafleting at sporting and cultural events where Miller was a corporate sponsor. Flyers often had a detachable coupon at the bottom that could be mailed to Miller headquarters, and pre-addressed postcards were distributed. Local newspapers, the labor press, and student papers began to feature Local 837's campaign against Miller. At outdoor Miller-sponsored music or cultural festivals, Staley workers' literature tables were often set up next to Miller Beer tents.

The Staley fight inspired students at the University of Wisconsin-Madison to form a Student Labor Action Committee and target the campus bar—the largest beer distributor in Madison. "College students drink a lot of beer, so this is a case where students will be listened to," said SLAC leader Steve Hinds.

Road warriors also visited Miller breweries to talk to union officials and leaflet workers at plant gates. Those unions were often cool if not outright hostile. The brewery workers' leaders argued that the campaign would hurt sales and possibly cause layoffs of Miller workers. Despite many discussions with local and national union leaders, the tension with unions at Staley customers was never resolved.

Eight months after the campaign had officially

begun, Miller announced that, because of "cost considerations," it would cease doing business with Staley when its contract expired three months later, on January 1, 1995. Workers and supporters were exuberant. It had been a year since the last victory—knocking Staley officials off the boards of two banks—and this success hit A.E. Staley directly in the pocketbook.

Road Warriors

Four days after workers were locked out, 60 members had come to a training meeting, where Tucker coached them in public speaking and helped them hone their message. The Staley "road warriors" were born. Over the course of the fight, several dozen workers traversed the country, speaking at hundreds of union halls, campuses, and community centers. Initially, they called central labor councils, some of which responded enthusiastically, but most not. The best initial contacts came from lists of progressive unionists provided by Labor Notes, Jobs with Justice, and Labor Party Advocates. And as the Staley Road Warriors traveled the country giving speeches at union halls, they urged the creation of Staley Workers Solidarity Committees, which in turn provided even more contacts.

"How do you make a local fight into a bigger fight for the whole labor movement?" asks Milwaukee Central Labor Council President Bruce Colburn. "That's where the road warriors become so important. Through the road warriors, people can see [the struggle], touch it, feel it."

Joe Uehlein, director of the AFL-CIO's Center for Strategic Campaigns, says the warriors "did an unbelievable amount of good to the labor movement. When road warriors go out in any campaign, they touch people in a way that union newsletters don't, magazines don't, phone calls don't, staff to staff don't, staff speaking to members don't. We learned a lot from Staley about road warriors and we have used that approach."

Most of the Staley workers had a problem in common—stage fright. But Tucker gave them simple directions: Don't worry about being a polished speaker—just tell your story in your own words. This is a worker-to-worker program—your audiences are going to be workers who are eager to hear what you have to say. Explain why you were locked out, how you are fighting back, and what your fight means for workers everywhere.

Lorell Patterson, a road warrior known for her no-nonsense style, recalled her anxieties: "The first time I spoke, I was shaking like a leaf! I had prepared notes. I would take big breaths, calm myself down, not try to impress people, just tell people what happened to me. People were impressed that a young person was fighting for the union."

Each time they spoke, the road warriors explained that for decades their working conditions at Staley, where a typical worker had 21 years in the plant, had been fundamentally good, but that Tate & Lyle had turned their lives upside down. They spoke emotionally about Jim Beals' death and the deteriorating safety conditions. They described how the company wanted to start 12-hour rotating shifts, gut seniority, and move from a 116-page contract to a 17-page one. They explained that Tate & Lyle was trying to destroy their union.

The road warriors' message went beyond organized labor. "It's not just union talk but labor talk," said Patterson. "A lot of people aren't in unions. This is a struggle not just for union workers but for all workers." Their ideas resonated. American workers were growing skeptical of multinational corporations. Time after time, audiences remarked that it felt as if the road warriors were telling *their* story. They were grateful that someone was taking a stand.

The response repeatedly surprised the road warriors. Many people in the audiences were looking for a renewal in their own unions and the labor movement and saw the Staley workers as models. Workers made donations, registered for Local 837's mailings, and vowed to boycott corporate campaign targets.

When they made trips, the road warriors packed sandwiches; there was no money to spare on restaurants. They used their own cars and stayed in supporters' homes. If a trip required a flight, the host union paid the airfare.

For more on road warriors, see the story of the Detroit Newspapers strikers in Chapter 9.

Solidarity Committees

The road warriors wanted to create local solidarity committees to raise funds, organize speaking engagements, and publicize the corporate campaign. In some cities, such as Madison and Milwaukee, the central labor council took the lead. But when a CLC was not receptive and a Jobs with Justice chapter did not exist, they encouraged individual locals and supporters to form committees on their own.

Many unionists saw building solidarity with the Staley workers as part of the struggle to rebuild their own local labor movements. Madison CLC president James Cavanaugh recalls, "We look for a struggle where the workers are putting on a courageous and creative battle with a lot at stake. We see these kinds of things as educational opportunities.... Every time a Staley road warrior came to Madison, I would call up the local unions that were holding meetings on those days and arrange visits. I can't recall any union ever turning us down."

During the two-and-a-half years of the lockout, 30 solidarity committees were crucial to keeping the road warriors busy with speaking engagements, building the customer campaign against Miller Beer and then Pepsi, and helping raise $3.5 million. Every December, the Midwest solidarity groups gathered tons of toys and organized a huge Christmas Caravan to Decatur, where the "Solidarity Santas" were met by hundreds of delighted families.

Support work for the Staley workers had consequences down the road. The Student Labor Action Coalition that originated in Madison spread to a number of other Midwest and Northeast college campuses. Some of these activists later helped form United Students against Sweatshops. And many clergy and religious activists who supported the Staley workers came together in 1995 to form the National Interfaith Committee on Worker Justice (see Chapter 13).

Adopt-a-Family

Staley workers' picket pay was just $60 a week, so the adopt-a-family program was a key element of the corporate campaign. As road warriors traveled the country, they asked for monthly pledges. Each family adopted by a union or group of supporters received $600 a month. Without it they might well have been quickly starved into submission.

Barrie Williams, who coordinated the program, recalled, "You have to remember, everyone in that union is proud. Many them looked at it as welfare. So we had to keep each member's integrity and privacy. The way I put it to the floor [at the union meeting] was, 'You're not receiving any type of charity. These are groups out there that someday are going to be in the same fight. And if they can stop the fight here with you, and support you, then that's what they're doing.' And that made a lot of people feel better."

To ensure privacy, each Staley worker who applied for adoption filled out two forms with the same identifying number at the top. The first form asked for name, address, and phone number. On the second, workers anonymously filled out a financial statement and listed all their bills and medical and special needs. The first form went into one locked box, and the second into another.

A small committee of local unionists evaluated the statements and prioritized the families in order of need. No Local 837 member was allowed to serve on the committee. Williams received only a ranked list of numbers. Then he started at the top of the list and notified the adopted worker and the donors. The monthly contributions went directly to the locked-out worker.

As the lockout moved into its second year, it was clear that workers with special needs needed additional help. Williams asked the local's Community Service Council (CSC) to send emergency cases to an outside financial counselor, who would report back to the CSC with confirmation that the worker needed emergency assistance. Then that worker went to the top of the adopt-a-family list.

Williams asked each adopted Staley worker to write letters regularly to the adopting union or persons to tell them about progress in the union's campaign and their own role in the struggle. The personal connections did much to strengthen the national solidarity effort. When donors came to town for a union rally, there was always an Adopt-a-Family booth so that Williams could discreetly hook them up with their adopted Staley worker. Years later, says Williams, "people are still exchanging Christmas cards."

In the first year, several dozen families were adopted. By the end of 1994, more than 660 unions and groups from California to Connecticut had at one time or another adopted a Staley family. By the end of the 30-month lockout, the program had raised $1.7 million.

Initially, 240 Staley workers signed up for the program, although some got jobs and declined when adoption was offered. By the end of the lockout, 126 families had been adopted; about 85 percent were getting the full $600 monthly contribution. By that date, every worker who requested an adoption had received one. The flood of donations gave the workers and their families hope. "There were perfect strangers sending us money," recalls Mary Brummett.

A Sad Loss

After the Miller Beer victory, the union focused the corporate campaign on Pepsi. Activists were convinced that Pepsi would drop Staley when its contract ran out on December 31, 1995. Unfortunately, by then a thin majority of the local, urged on by their international, had given up hoping for victory. They voted for a concession contract.

Despite the Staley workers' defeat, their corporate campaign provides lessons for unions trying to build a national solidarity movement in support of striking or locked-out workers.

Boycotting Taco Bell: The Coalition of Immokalee Workers

by Peter Ian Asen

IMMIGRANT TOMATO PICKERS IN FLORIDA have won allies across the country in their campaign to raise their sub-poverty-level wages. The central part of their campaign is a boycott of Taco Bell, one of the largest consumers of the tomatoes they pick. The Coalition of Immokalee Workers (CIW), named after the agricultural town that is a center for tomato and orange production in southwest Florida, has used tactics that include a cross-country "Truth Tour," a hunger strike outside Taco Bell's corporate headquarters, actions at shareholders' meetings, and a campaign by students to kick Taco Bell off campuses.

The Coalition of Immokalee (rhymes with "broccoli") Workers, founded in 1995, includes workers from Mexico, Guatemala, and Haiti. It is a membership organization with a nine-member board, all of whom are workers in agriculture or other low-wage industries. Dues are minimal, but the CIW's work has attracted donations from foundations and individuals. Members meet weekly, and the group is structured to make sure that it is not dominated by staffers. Staffers are elected, receive the same pay as farmworkers, and must spend at least three months a year in the fields.

In October 1997, the CIW launched an "anti-slavery campaign" to call public attention to sub-poverty wages in the tomato fields and orange groves. The campaign won raises for 450 workers, for the first time in decades, after Governor Jeb Bush intervened and growers agreed to increase pay by 5 cents per bucket.

But these raises left the CIW with plenty of organizing to do. Tomato pickers working for major growers like Six L's Packing Co. Inc. still were paid only 40 cents for each 32-pound bucket they picked. This means that in order to make $50 in a day, they had to pick two tons of tomatoes.

Staff member Julia Perkins describes the anti-slavery campaign: "We did work stoppages, strikes, hunger strikes by six members for 30 days, a 230-mile march across the state—pretty much anything you could think of to put pressure on the growers. But the growers don't have a public face. They time and again either ignored us completely or said they wouldn't come to the table. One of the growers said to us, 'A tractor doesn't tell a farmer how to run his farm.' That was the attitude we were working with."

Follow the Tomato Trail

After years of focusing their struggle on the growers, CIW staff member and longtime farmworker Lucas Benitez says, the CIW discovered that "the power is beyond the growers. There are big corporations that are controlling the agricultural industry because they consume a majority of the products. So when we saw this new direction that the industry was going, we decided to focus on one of the major corporations that buys the products that we pick."

The Coalition chose Taco Bell as its target for a number of reasons. First, Taco Bell is part of Yum! Brands, a parent company of Kentucky Fried Chicken, Pizza Hut, Long John Silver's, and A&W Restaurants, which together make up the largest restaurant chain in the world. Benitez says that Taco Bell was also a target because "it invests a great quantity of money maintaining its public image." Finally, Taco Bell targets 16-24-year-olds as its main consumers, a group that the Coalition thought would be most sympathetic to a boycott.

The CIW wrote twice to Taco Bell, asking the company to sit down with farmworkers and bring the growers to the table to work out more humane working conditions. Receiving no response, CIW contacted the student groups on many Florida campuses, with whom it already had good relations because of its earlier work. In the early spring of 2001, the CIW and its supporters held demonstrations at Taco Bells in five cities. Local students, as well as allies from the labor and religious communities, joined 50 to 100 farmworkers at each rally. "We were giving Taco Bell one last chance to avoid the boycott," Perkins says. "But again, there was no response. So on April 1, 2001, we officially announced the boycott of Taco Bell." The Coalition could legally advocate a secondary boycott because it is not a union.

CIW had three demands. First, the farmworkers asked Taco Bell to pay its growers one penny more per pound of tomatoes, which would go directly to the workers and provide an 80 percent wage increase. Second, they demanded that the company bring the growers to the table so that three-party dialogue could occur. Third, the CIW asked Taco Bell to join with growers and farmworkers to draft a Code of Conduct for Taco Bell tomato suppliers. They wanted a code to include the right to a living wage, to overtime pay, and to organize without fear of retaliation.

CIW Director Lucas Benitez and other farmworkers from the Coalition for Immokalee Workers march on Taco Bell's world headquarters as part of the Taco Bell Truth Tour, demanding that Taco Bell increase the price it pays for tomatoes by 1¢ so that workers' wages can go up.

David Bacon/dbacon.igc.org

"What's important about the boycott," says Perkins, "is that it comes directly from the community and from the workers. The workers are spearheading it and leading it. Even though we have this national campaign, we don't want to lose our base in the community."

The Truth Tour

The first major boycott action was the Taco Bell Truth Tour. The CIW planned to send busloads of workers and allies on a 17-day, 15-city tour, from Immokalee to Taco Bell headquarters in Irvine, California, and publicize the struggle with rallies and actions nationwide. Originally planned for September 2001, the tour was postponed to the following March after the September 11 attacks.

The tour was "many months in preparation," Benitez says. The CIW worked to develop "tour committees" in each of the cities where workers planned to stop. They contacted groups throughout the country that they thought would be natural allies—global justice organizations, labor groups, religious and student activists—and they used their list of those who had contacted the CIW on their own to support the boycott.

These allies' experience in their own communities meant that they could do the crucial organizing work for the tour stops. The local committees did almost all the planning—logistics, publicity, and organizing—for stops in their cities and were in constant contact with the CIW to make sure their planning fit with the Coalition's larger vision and national planning. The one exception was in Irvine, where the CIW sent a handful of organizers to work with the local committee.

Months before the tour began, a group of ten CIW members went to the various cities to make presentations and meet with local activists. These pre-tour visits helped both to strengthen connections with local allies and to foster broader involvement in their committees. After the tour was postponed, the CIW did a second round of preparation visits, which helped the committees grow and maintain their momentum.

As awareness of the upcoming tour grew, Taco Bell suddenly took notice. Just two days before the Truth Tour was to begin, the CIW received a call, asking the group to cancel the tour in exchange for a meeting with Taco Bell executives. Perkins remembers, "It was the first time in two years or so that they'd had any kind of communication with us."

This scenario is pretty standard in the history of corporate campaigns (and of many other struggles, such as strikes). The target of a pressure campaign makes a first, relatively minor conciliatory move, and demands in return that its opponents call off their campaign. Too often, the campaigners agree, as a show of "good faith." They lay down their arms—and find themselves in the next stage of negotiations with no weapons and no leverage.

But the Coalition refused to call off the tour. Benitez says CIW leaders felt that if pressuring the company had achieved this first goal, keeping up the pressure could accomplish even more. They were determined to take advantage of the opening to press the attack. "We knew that it wasn't a sincere offer from the corporation," Benitez says. "If they'd been sincere from the get-go, they wouldn't have waited until the last moment possible to offer us a meeting. And if they'd been sincere, they wouldn't have just offered a meeting, but would have offered to meet our demands."

In addition, he says, "there had been an investment on our part, both monetary and human. People all across the country were ready and were waiting for us to get to their cities. And we knew that that was a moment that was ready for our voice and our consciousness and our commitment to get to those thousands of people who were waiting for us along the tour."

The farmworkers asked Taco Bell to pay its growers one penny more per pound of tomatoes, which would go directly to the workers and provide an 80 percent wage increase.

So the CIW said workers would be happy to meet with the company once the Truth Tour reached Irvine, and the first-ever meeting between farmworkers and executives in the fast food industry took place. The meeting was cordial but no meaningful change came of it.

Nonetheless, the Truth Tour brought the issues of farmworker wages and working conditions to a new level of attention across the country. A group of 70 workers and 30 allies traveled by bus to cities including Atlanta, Louisville (where corporate-parent Yum! has its headquarters), Denver, Salt Lake City, Oklahoma City, Little Rock, and San Francisco. "All along the way," Perkins says, "we had workers in the forefront, talking about what their situation was, and what Taco Bell could do about it." The Coalition chose cities that were on the route from Florida to California and back, but also scheduled stops in Chicago and Wisconsin because of major support in those areas.

Activities included marches and rallies outside Taco Bell restaurants. Farmworkers met with supporters at churches and union halls. CIW members talked about their working conditions and urged attendees to promote the boycott. "The best part," Benitez says, "was on the biggest day of the tour, the day that we arrived in Irvine, where we marched for around five miles to Taco Bell's headquarters with about 2,000 allies."

The tour received a great deal of media attention, which Benitez believes "came to us because of the years of struggle, of creative actions that had led us to that point." The CIW planners did outreach to media everywhere they were going to stop and gave local committees a general press release that they could customize for their cities. The local groups' connections with local media made their press outreach particularly valuable.

The Coalition also supported local organizing along the way. In Irvine, for example, the CIW co-sponsored a conference with a number of local workers centers, and bus riders went to an action to support the Garment Worker Center in its own boycott of the clothing store Forever 21 (see Chapter 16).

Hunger Strike

After the Truth Tour, the Coalition continued to up the ante. In March 2003, workers returned by bus to Irvine and did a ten-day hunger strike. Sixty-five people, including 30 farmworkers and 35 allies, camped out in front of Taco Bell headquarters and fasted for at least five days each, reiterating the CIW's three demands and engaging in possibly the largest hunger strike in U.S. labor history. The hunger strike brought more media attention.

By engaging in a hunger strike, Benitez says, "we were well aware that we were putting our health at risk." The hunger strike solidified the commitment of the people who took part in it, as well as those who supported the strikers. "It showed Taco Bell's true face," says Perkins, "because they didn't meet with us or acknowledge us in any way during the ten days that we were on their sidewalk."

"To find the workers who did the hunger strike was pretty easy," Benitez says. "We started organizing and talking about it at the beginning of the season and people came in to sign themselves up as volunteers." The Coalition recruited allies in student, labor, religious, and community groups to participate as well.

Benitez says, "We went through a process to make sure that everyone was in good health. The first day a doctor came and checked everyone out. He was there every day, keeping tabs on us and making sure that everyone was staying healthy. That also helped us to know when people had to be hospitalized." In the end, three strikers did require hospitalization.

Getting a permit to camp out in Irvine for ten days was not easy. "We had a long negotiation process with the police in Orange County and Irvine to be able to camp," Benitez says. "We also had to negotiate for the permit to be on the sidewalk 24 hours in front of Taco Bell's headquarters. Local allies, including local churches, played a strong role in helping to push for those permits. When they wanted to take our permit away in the middle of the hunger strike, the local allies were key in making sure that everyone was looked out for and taken care of."

"After the fifth day of the hunger strike," he adds, when the CIW staged a rally that drew over 1,000 supporters, "we essentially had to do a whole renegotiation process for the permit. They stopped allowing us to have tents and we had to sleep out in the elements. We kept doing that until the very last three days, when the police would only let us be there until nightfall and we had to go sleep in other places."

Students Boot the Bell

"Students have always been the key to the boycott, since they are the principal target market of Taco Bell," Benitez says. "We have gone from university to university across the country taking our message and we have found the active student groups. Through hearing about the boycott, they've decided to take it on as their first priority. We've formed strong relationships with student groups that are involved in the fight for social justice, like MEChA, the Chicano students' movement, and USAS, United Students Against Sweatshops, which we count among our closest allies."

The existence of groups on campuses that were already fighting against sweatshops and for workers' rights helped the CIW's campaign gain traction with students. Perkins says, "We were able to tap into this existing movement and give it something different, which is a worker-led boycott. And it's workers in the United States."

The "Boot the Bell" campaign was announced by a national coalition called the Student-Farmworker Alliance in early 2002. As of August 2004, 19 schools had either "booted the Bell" from campus or declared their campus a "Taco Bell-free zone."

One school where students succeeded in booting the Bell was the University of Chicago, where Taco Bell had a contract in the food court. The Anti-Sweatshop Coalition there began its campaign on April 4, 2002, to commemorate the day Dr. Martin Luther King, Jr. was killed 34 years earlier while supporting striking sanitation workers in Memphis.

Student activist Ella Hereth says the keys to success were coalition-building among student groups, a massive education program, and the use of "pretty creative tactics the entire time," such as performing street theatre on campus. The students kicked off the campaign by delivering tomatoes to the school's top administrators, along with notes that explained their concerns about having Taco Bell on campus. Chicago had a particularly strong citywide Truth Tour committee, with about 30 active members, and this committee provided a base of off-campus allies.

Hereth says that around 100 students were actively involved in the campaign, and that 300-400 regularly came to educational events and rallies. "I think they had no clue that we could do so much in that short a period of time," she says, referring to the university administration, "and that we could build that much support. They didn't know what to do when we actually did." Administrators agreed not to renew Taco Bell's contract and established a committee with student input that would choose a new vendor for the food court.

Shareholder Power

Major Christian denominations such as the United Methodist Church have supported the boycott, as has the National Council of Churches. Though few unions have officially endorsed the boycott, AFL-CIO President John Sweeney did write to a Yum! Brands board member, "I will be urging my constituents—the 13 million members of the AFL-CIO and their families—to boycott Taco Bell products until this issue is resolved."

Responsible shareholders are another ally. At the Yum! Brands annual meeting in Louisville in May 2003, about 50 CIW members and supporters chanted outside about Taco Bell's unwillingness to support farmworkers. Inside, CIW allies introduced a shareholder resolution to force the board of directors to prepare a "sustainability report" that would address the impact of corporate practices on workers' rights, human rights, and the environment. Although the resolution could not mention the boycott because of Securities and Exchange Commission (SEC) regulations, it was a statement that clearly would have helped CIW.

Part of the strategy was to take advantage of Taco Bell's recent approval of a policy to buy food from contractors that do not mistreat animals. The CIW called attention to the company's apparently greater concern for animals than for human beings.

When they introduced the resolution, which was strongly opposed by the board of directors, the CIW and its shareholder allies expected to get about three to six percent of the vote, which is typical for first-time resolutions on social justice. But between the buzz that the boycott had created and the speeches on the floor, the resolution garnered 43 percent, and the shareholder allies won a meeting with Yum! executives.

Yum! Feels the Heat

The months after the 2003 shareholders meeting were a time of increasing national recognition and support for the CIW's cause. Coalition members Lucas Benitez, Julia Gabriel, and Romeo Ramirez received the Robert F. Kennedy Human Rights Award for their leadership of the campaign. The positive attention the CIW was beginning to receive, and the many journalistic accounts of their campaign, helped add to the growing interest in the boycott.

The Coalition returned to some of the tactics that had helped it to grow early on and held another Truth Tour in spring 2004. Rallies at Yum! and Taco Bell headquarters were preceded by marches—an eight-mile march to the Yum! headquarters in Louisville and a 44-mile, four-day march from East Los Angeles to Taco Bell in Irvine.

Yum! executives agreed to meet for negotiations at the Carter Center in Atlanta, whose founder, former President Jimmy Carter, had become a supporter of the cause. Though no conclusive offers came from the talks, they represented a major step forward. "From where we were when we started this boycott," says Perkins, "when Taco Bell and Yum! said they would never, ever talk to farmworkers, to having farmworkers meet with top executives at Yum!, that definitely makes us hopeful."

The Yum! shareholder meeting in May 2004 gave the group more reason to hope. Inside the meeting, CIW allies again introduced the shareholder resolution in favor of a "sustainability report," while outside 100 CIW members and allies held a vigil and fast. Three thousand more people participated in a solidarity fast nationwide. Although the resolution received only 33 percent, CEO David Novak admitted, in a speech to the shareholders, that the wages and working conditions of farmworkers in the supply chain were a cause for concern. Novak told Benitez, "We're ready to end this boycott if you are."

But Novak's offer to encourage the growers to pay one penny per pound more to tomato pickers was contingent on the Coalition's agreeing to first end the boycott. Once again, the Coalition stood firm and rejected Novak's proposal, because Yum! was not offering to pay this surcharge themselves.

In June 2004, Taco Bell sent an unsolicited check for $110,000 to the Coalition, claiming that the amount was equivalent to a penny per pound for its tomato purchases in Florida. Apparently, the company wanted the CIW to distribute the money among tomato pickers—an impossible task—but did not want to make any permanent changes in the industry. The Coalition returned the check, demanding once more that Taco Bell establish lasting, enforceable "modern-day standards" in the tomato supply chain.

"The boycott continues, obviously," says Julia Perkins, "because we're not calling the boycott off until there is actual change for workers."

As this book was being finished, the Immokalee workers' fight with Taco Bell was not over. When workers target secondary companies they face a very high hurdle, and the farmworkers had not yet forced Taco Bell and Yum! to take responsibility for conditions at their suppliers. But in the outsourcing era, when more and more jobs are at subcontractors and temp agencies, secondary targets will be increasingly necessary.

For more information, contact the Coalition of Immokalee Workers, PO Box 603, Immokalee, FL 34143. 239-657-8311. www.ciw-online.org. workers@ciw-online.org.

Cintas: Corporate Campaign Aids an Organizing Drive

by Aaron Brenner

FROM 1998 TO 2003, the Union of Needletrades, Industrial and Textile Employees aggressively organized industrial laundry workers, growing from 10,000 to 40,000 members in the industry. Together with the Teamsters, UNITE represented about a third of all laundry workers. But to deliver real benefits, UNITE believed it had to organize the 17,000 workers at Cintas. Most of these workers are women and people of color, primarily African Americans and Latinos, many of them immigrants.

"Cintas is by far the largest company in the market," says organizer Liz Gres. "They set the standards for the industry—and they set them extremely low." Stories abound of low wages, unsafe plants, harsh management, unpaid wages, non-payment of overtime, lost vacations, and race and sex discrimination. The company is fiercely anti-union, says Gres. "Not one union has ever won an election against them. They parade that around to the workers a lot."

UNITE (which in 2004 merged to form UNITE HERE) is not organizing Cintas on its own. While UNITE HERE organizes production workers, the Teamsters organize the drivers who pick up and deliver uniforms. Although the organizers work together, each group is responsible for its own jurisdiction.

To win at Cintas, the unions calculated that an ordinary organizing drive would not be enough. They decided that they needed a corporate campaign that would get the company to agree to neutrality and a fair recognition process, namely "card check" (for more on card check, see Chapter 15).

"It is a strategy of necessity," says Gres. "We cannot organize Cintas plant by plant. They keep their plants small, about 100 to 150 workers, and many with fewer than that. They build one and then go down the road and build another, relatively close so it can perform the work of the first plant if necessary. No plants are essential. If workers in one or more plants go on strike, they have little chance and little leverage. The only way to win is with a broad movement of workers across the company and across the continent."

Pete DeMay of UNITE HERE in Chicago believes that the longer time-frame of a corporate campaign allows for a more effective organizing drive. "Organizing campaigns using the NLRB are usually much shorter," he says, "but [with a corporate campaign] we can teach people what it means to be union members. We've blitzed Cintas ten times, with no results. With the corporate campaign, we have the luxury to do some one-on-ones, try different activities. It's a stressful atmosphere, but you can't rely on a business agent. The company won't cut a deal with the union, so the workers have to fight."

The campaign against Cintas has two parts: the internal organizing of the workers and the external campaign to pressure the company. Each part employs a series of escalating tactics. The idea is that as the number of union supporters grows and their voices draw more public attention, the company will decide that the rational, prudent course is to grant neutrality and card check.

"Our demand is that the workers need a fair process to choose a union," says Gres. "We believe that the company must be neutral, no one-on-ones, no captive audience meetings, no law-breaking. We are saying that neutrality and a fair process is the only way to choose a union at Cintas, given the company's anti-union record.

"Our message to workers is that the only way to get a union is to act like a union now. It is going to be a long fight, but we have to take on the bosses right now, to show that we can do something to improve workers' conditions, whether it's getting more microwaves in the break room, filing a lawsuit against the non-payment of over-

Cintas workers and supporters picket a Starbucks Coffee shop in downtown Detroit (above) in support of the organizing campaign. UNITE said that Starbucks, which claims to be socially responsible, should stop doing business with Cintas. At right, the sign says, "Laundry Workers United for Justice and Respect."

time, or protesting against favoritism."

DeMay agrees. "We consider that there is a union at Cintas, but it's not recognized by the company and it's not recognized by the government. What's important is that workers recognize it and UNITE recognizes it."

This approach is how UNITE HERE and the Teamsters believe they can win, DeMay explains. "Cintas management will have to be made to see that they'll have to deal with the union either way. They can settle a contract and do things in a diplomatic way, or they'll have to deal with the union in the form of militant worker committees and a comprehensive corporate campaign. If folks are rallying to win raises, it's not much different than a contract—and a contract might even be easier."

Worker Organizing

As in other organizing drives, union organizers meet with Cintas workers to lay out what workers should expect. "We are firm," says Gres. "We say, 'It's great that you joined the campaign, but you are the union. You have to be willing to do things to build the union at Cintas. You have to get workers together, or do something inside the plant, or meet with community allies, or talk to other unions whose members wear Cintas uniforms.'"

Organizers encourage creative, small-scale responses to management offenses. "In Chicago," says Gres, "workers were upset that workers who rode to work with the supervisor got all the overtime. They resented the favoritism. So we helped them put together a leaflet with a picture of the 'Overtime Van,' that said other workers deserve overtime too. Right after that, they got overtime. It was a great victory."

A 12-year worker in one Chicago plant, Eleuteria Mazón, describes another way the workers acted like a union, this time to fight arbitrary supervision. "When management changed a fellow worker's shift without previously informing him and without consulting him, we had a small work stoppage," says Mazón. "We all went with the worker to the boss's office. He gave us his explanation for what had happened, but he also realized that we were capable of uniting."

The workers distribute literature about the union, often in Spanish and other languages. "On one occasion, I distributed literature in the cafeteria and they called me in and told me what I was doing was illegal," says Mazón. "I told them I had the right to do it in non-work areas at non-work times. They still threatened to fire me. But I keep doing it.

"We have now succeeded in getting workers to openly take and read our literature. They used to be afraid to take it, but now they take it and read it."

A huge source of resentment is Cintas's miserly wages. In some plants workers have pressed for a $1 an hour raise. In San Leandro, California they made copies of dollar bills and pinned them to their uniforms. In Chicago workers came up with the idea of a leaflet comparing billionaire Cintas founder Richard T. Farmer's wealth and their own paltry raises. They distributed a sticker with a piggybank and the demand for a $1 raise. In Detroit and Chicago, workers actually won 50-cent raises, larger than they had ever seen. But in San Leandro the most active workers got the worst raises, so they filed a discrimination complaint with the Labor Board.

DeMay notes that the wage campaign "puts the company in a tough spot: give a dollar or come close, or else people learn that permanent change is with a union."

The union has helped workers file dozens of OSHA complaints. In Hayward, California, OSHA found some 30 violations and Cintas was fined. Workers in Chicago also called the Fire Department for an inspection.

"We visit people who are somewhat chilly to the union," says Mazón. "They want the union, but they are afraid of losing their jobs. I talk to people who have immigrated from different countries, and I say, 'If we left our country looking for a better life, if we have gone through the trouble and danger of crossing the border, if we have gone through all this suffering and pain to get an opportunity in a country we didn't know, then why don't we now have the courage to fulfill our dreams? Why did we leave our countries—to continue being submerged in poverty? No—we have to lift up our faces here.'"

UNITE HERE holds regular conference calls with workers across the U.S. and Canada so they can share stories about their struggles. Workers also share information through a union newsletter, distributed in the shops and by mail.

In late 2003, 40 workers from eight cities and 17 plants met for two days in Las Vegas. They had done surveys in their shops to find out their co-workers' main demands. From these, they wrote a manifesto with six demands, and then took the manifesto back to work. They pass it around, post it, and get more workers to sign it. They are using the manifesto to build for another international meeting.

All of these actions help workers to see that Cintas is not almighty and that they can make gains when they act together.

Mobilizing External Support

The unions' public education—the corporate campaign part of the effort—aims to connect Cintas's treatment of workers with its treatment of customers and communities. "Workers, customers, and communities are coming together to demand the company clean up its act," says Gres.

To alert customers to the company's disreputable practices, the unions started a website, www.cintasexposed.org. It explains Cintas's uniform rental and facilities rental contracts, exposing hidden fees, escalator clauses, and other items that the company includes to extract more money from customers. The site notes that Cintas faced a class action suit from its customers for imposing an "environmental charge" that was supposedly mandated by the government. The company was forced to change this practice but still tries to impose a "service charge," even when it performs no extra service. The site includes stories from angry customers about delivery of the wrong uniforms, poorly washed or ripped uniforms, shortages, overcharges, and arbitrary price increases.

Around the country, delegations of Cintas workers have gone to union meetings to talk to workers who wear uniforms from Cintas. They ask the union workers to ask their companies to use their managerial discretion to drop Cintas as a supplier. "Unions can also negotiate contract language calling for uniforms from a 'responsible supplier,'" says Gres.

Cintas is being forced to deal with lawsuits and with government agencies. In Newburgh, New York, environmentalists intervened when Cintas applied to build a wastewater storage tank. The group publicized the fact that the state of Connecticut was already suing Cintas for illegally dumping wastewater, and when people in Newburgh found out they raised a fuss with the city, which delayed the permit.

In Louisiana, a similar mobilization led Cintas to pledge $2 million to clean up a wastewater mess outside Baton Rouge. In Union, New Jersey, the company was forced to drop plans to expand the size of a laundry it was building there. Difficulties in Newburgh and Union could slow the company's penetration of the New York market, where it has invested significant resources over the last few years.

In municipalities with living wage laws, workers have filed complaints to get Cintas to obey the law. "We filed a complaint with the City of Hayward, [California]," says worker Francisca Amaral. "We never knew that Cintas was supposed to be paying us a living wage. And they never did. We filed the complaint, but they just canceled the contract with the city."

Cintas routinely assigns jobs on the basis of sex and race, with women of color in production jobs, white women in office jobs, and white men as drivers. People of color rarely rise to management, except maybe as floor supervisors. With the union's help, a group of workers filed a class-action anti-discrimination complaint with the Equal Employment Opportunity Commission. And Cintas drivers filed a national class-action lawsuit to recoup millions of dollars in overtime pay. "The company claims that drivers are salespeople and exempt from overtime," says Gres. In 2001, the company paid $10 million to settle a similar suit in California.

The unions have signed up 91 members of the House of Representatives on a letter asking the company to agree to a fair recognition process and neutrality. "This is not just one of those soft letters that asks the company to consider the interests of its workers," says Gres. "It specifically demands card check neutrality."

Unlike in other corporate campaigns, DeMay says that in organizing Cintas, "there's a lot less emphasis on allies. It's not like strikes. We rely on a small handful of good allies, like Rainbow PUSH with discrimination, clergy, Jobs with Justice, some local politicians, people the workers trust. It is nice to have people respected in the community; workers appreciate that. We spend more time working with this small group of allies, and we do more with them, rather than casting the net real wide and not getting a lot out of them."

Summing up the relationship between the unions' internal and external campaigns, DeMay says, "A corporate campaign can never replace one-on-one organizing. You have to do the educational campaign with customers and the public, with shareholders, obviously, but you have to have some kind of militancy to back it up. Without militancy, you can't get it done. You can't get it done without worker committees."

For more information see UNITE HERE's report, "Cintas: An Industry Leader Dragging Down Standards," at www.unitehere.org/cintas/whitepaper1103.pdf. See also www.uniformjustice.com.

Lessons

THE FOUR CORPORATE CAMPAIGNS provide many lessons. Each involved extensive member activism, which is the basic requirement for success. The campaigns helped educate, build unity, and develop leadership and skills among the workers involved.

Workers are transformed in this kind of corporate campaign. Road warrior Gary Lamb expressed common sentiments at the end of the Staley fight: "The fight forever changed me. It changed my direction in life, how I treat people, how I look at people, and I think it's for the better. I will never be the person I was before—the compassion I have for others now. I'm more aware of what's going on around me.

"Now I know that there are people that will go the extra mile, for no advantage for themselves, and that there are a lot of them."

The campaigns also illustrate the weakness of a solidarity culture in the United States. The Staley workers, at a time when Caterpillar and Firestone/Bridgestone workers were also on strike in their home town, Decatur, were never able to attract more than 7,000 supporters to their national demonstrations. If the Immokalee workers were receiving the active support of even a large fraction of the labor movement's over 15 million workers, Taco Bell would long ago have granted the workers' demands. The case studies show that every major labor battle is simultaneously a fight against an intransigent employer and a struggle to awaken the spirit of solidarity.

These four stories show how a corporate campaign can be a powerful tactic. But the tactic isn't a cure-all. The ABC Linen campaign was victorious, the Staley fight ended in defeat, and at the time of this writing the Cintas and Taco Bell campaigns are continuing. This scorecard is not unusual for corporate campaigns.

The uneven results show that unions need to respond to the increasingly ruthless corporate assault on worker rights with an equally aggressive strategy that plans far in advance of a contract expiration. A principal problem with corporate campaigns is the limited support they get from other unions. Another problem is that the labor movement has not adopted a strategy to shut down production when companies hire scabs. If production is not stopped, the economic pressure from a corporate campaign alone is often not enough to win—certainly not in the short run and when the corporation has deep pockets and is intent on crippling the union.

Resources

FOR RESEARCH HELP, see the Appendix, "How To Research Your Employer."

- *Labor Research Review,* Issue #31 (1993), "No More Business as Usual: Labor's Corporate Campaigns." Published by the Center for Labor & Community Research, 3411 W. Diversey, Suite 10, Chicago, IL 60647. 773-278-5418. info@clcr.org. www.clcr.org.
- Corporate Campaign Inc. www.corporatecampaign.org.
- *The Death of a Thousand Cuts: Corporate Campaigns and the Attack on the Corporations*, by Jarol B. Manheim (Lawrence Erlbaum Associates, 2001). Written for corporations on how to stop union corporate campaigns, but useful for unionists.
- *Rules for Radicals*, by Saul Alinsky, Vintage Books, 1971. This classic work has useful ideas for organizing public support against a corporation.
- *Organizing for Social Change*, Midwest Academy, 2001 (third edition). Midwest Academy, 28 E. Jackson St., #605, Chicago, IL 60604. 312-427-2304.

Action Questions

1. What are your employer's biggest vulnerabilities that could be targeted with a corporate campaign? (The questionnaire on the Troublemaker's website can help you think this through.) If you need help with research, who can you ask? Your international? University contacts?

2. Who are your employers' biggest customers? Are they vulnerable to pressure?

3. Has your union built relationships with community groups in your town, such as students, environmentalists, civil rights and women's rights groups, farmers? Are there pro-worker groups in your town such as United Students Against Sweatshops or the National Interfaith Committee on Worker Justice? Does your local have a community outreach committee?

4. What about contacts outside your community? Do you know how to reach out regionally or nationally?

5. Does your union have a solidarity committee to support other unions' contract campaigns, strikes, and corporate campaigns?

6. Is your union educating members through classes, at-work meetings, a website, and emails about what is involved in a corporate campaign? Are they prepared to take on the large amount of work involved?

Authors

PETER IAN ASEN is a writer and labor activist based in Providence, Rhode Island. He is the former managing editor of the *College Hill Independent*, a joint publication of students at Brown University and the Rhode Island School of Design. His writing has appeared in *Labor Notes, The Progressive,* and *Against the Current*.

STEVEN ASHBY is a professor of labor studies at Indiana University at Bloomington. In the mid-1990s, he was co-chair of the flagship Staley workers support group, the Chicago-area Staley Workers Solidarity Committee. C.J. HAWKING, a United Methodist pastor and labor studies instructor, moved to Decatur during the Staley lockout, where she assisted the local in its outreach to the community. Ashby and Hawking have written *The Staley Workers and the Fight for a New American Labor Movement*, to be published in 2005 by the University of Illinois Press.

AARON BRENNER is a labor historian, researcher, writer, and editor in New York City. He has written about international labor solidarity, union reform movements, and rank-and-file rebellions by Teamsters, telephone workers, and postal workers, and is the editor of *The Encyclopedia of Strikes in American History*.

DAN LA BOTZ wrote the first edition of *A Troublemaker's Handbook* in 1991. He is an activist, teacher, and labor historian based in Cincinnati, where he writes frequently for *Labor Notes*. He was a founding member of Teamsters for a Democratic Union in the 1970s and wrote a book about that movement, as well as books on unions in Mexico and Indonesia. He is editor of the monthly web publication *Mexican Labor News and Analysis*.

On the Troublemaker's Website

Corporate Campaign Questionnaire. This questionnaire has over 300 questions to pinpoint the employer's vulnerabilities to a corporate campaign, from tax questions to quality concerns to customers and disgruntled ex-managers. Designed for use by and with rank and filers. From the 1991 *Troublemaker's*.

12. Allying with the Community: Single-Issue Campaigns *by Sonya Huber*

A FIGHT IN THE WORKPLACE can easily spill out into the community—and that's usually right where we want it. As the friends and families of workers find out about a labor struggle, they can get motivated to step in and lend a hand, and also to put moral, economic, and direct-action pressure on an employer.

By the same token, workers can put their muscle behind a community fight to benefit everyone in their neighborhood or region. The stories in this chapter illustrate that coalition work provides more options to help deliver a win. Included here are accounts of successful struggles for a living wage for low-paid workers, for better bus service, for funding public health care, to establish a job training program, against electricity privatization, to get labor taught in the schools, to keep hazardous waste out of the community, to support low-paid workers' strikes for better wages, and to build alliances with students and improve conditions for campus workers.

Thinking long-term about coalition campaigns can pay off big for workers. For example, a living wage fight can change the climate for union organizing in an area and even change local labor law—for example, if the ordinance stipulates that companies receiving city contracts must remain neutral during organizing drives. Living wage campaigns can also activate a base that will throw anti-labor politicians out of office. Ultimately, getting labor reconnected with the communities where we live will expose more non-union workers to the benefits of (and existence of!) the labor movement.

At the same time, coalition work also has immediate benefits. It provides every player with new perspectives and ideas, and may even re-energize a comatose local or organization. By working with other groups, activists see their own organization in sharper outline. They may realize that they have been stuck in a rut or running campaigns or meetings on the basis of outdated assumptions.

The way a labor group approaches its community partners for support is critical. Too often, community groups are contacted at the last minute and asked to provide bodies for a rally without getting a say in campaign strategy. Instead, smart organizers know that solidarity is a two-way street. Start your outreach well in advance. Look at your local's structure and think about how to set up an ongoing relationship with community and religious groups. Talk with your local's leadership about the best people to represent the local at meetings of community groups, and solicit names of rank-and-file members who are active in community groups or want to get involved in this outreach effort.

Rather than just donating money to community efforts or passing resolutions, consider inviting these groups in for face-to-face presentations and updates about the groups' campaigns. Can you include relevant community notices in your members' newsletter or email update, or provide a community bulletin board space in your meeting hall? What about offering resources that community groups so often need, such as use of the photocopier or meeting space, or a place to do evening phonebanking?

Then, when you have a major campaign gearing up that could use community support, set up an issue briefing for representatives from the community partners you regularly work with. Outline the fight, provide fact sheets, and answer questions about the campaign. Ask community members for their ideas and contacts, and you will inevitably be surprised at all of the avenues for outreach and action that would never have been available working alone.

Coalitions aren't always easy or neat, and as some of these stories illustrate, one major struggle may be within our own locals, convincing some members that community issues matter. But a savvy organizer knows that solidarity is better than money in the bank: sooner or later, it will be your local that needs the help.

These stories show how leaders and members made partnerships work by building them with care and respect, keeping an eye on their long-term game plan. When labor and community groups start working together around one campaign, the partnership often broadens out to take on multiple goals. Ongoing multi-issue coalitions are discussed in Chapter 13. Since in practice there's no firm dividing line, read both chapters to get a fuller picture of the possibilities.

In this chapter you will find a wide variety of tactics, from the familiar (creating a timeline) to outside-of-the box (a tent city and street theater). Look for the common threads: coalitions are about building relationships of trust and respect; education about the issues, including internal education of members, is key; alliances work best when the partners treat each other as equals.

If going it alone was ever an option for unions, it's not possible now. Our numbers are too small, and the battles facing workers and communities are too big, to win without cooperation.

Showing Members the Big Picture

by Leah Samuel

"A LOT OF MEMBERS HAVE A NARROW VIEW of what a union does," explains Bob Hasegawa, former president of Teamsters Local 174 and now a Washington State Representative. "They would say that it's just jobs and wages. The broader view sees everything as interconnected." It was this broader view that helped Hasegawa lead Local 174 into partnership with Seattle environmental groups in 2000.

"There was a ship called the Wan He carrying hazardous waste from a U.S. military installation in Japan," Hasegawa says. "Some environmental people contacted the ILWU [the dockworkers' union] about it." According to activists, the Environmental Protection Agency (EPA) had given the ship special permission to bring the waste to the U.S., although it was an illegal shipment. The company responsible for the shipment told Washington state officials that it would leave the waste there temporarily, to which the governor agreed. But activists didn't believe the waste would be "temporary." The unions and environmental groups held rallies at the docks to protest the shipment. The longshore workers refused to unload the material.

"At some point, however, they would have had to, because they would have been legally liable had they not," says Hasegawa. "So we Teamsters said, 'You can unload it but we won't haul it anywhere.' We said no to both the governor and the EPA. The Teamsters refused to haul it on the highways. The Longshoremen refused to handle it, and the stuff ended up sailing away, back to the Army in Japan."

Hasegawa says the reason for getting his union involved in the environmental fight was simple: "The environmentalists were doing the larger job and they needed our help." He adds, however, that it took him a few years to get the local to the point of being willing to take on fights around the environment or other issues.

"You can't just flip a switch, and say, 'You're all going to sacrifice your jobs, because we're not having this stuff,'" he says. "We've got a lot of members who have that narrow view. They don't unlearn it overnight."

Hasegawa says that Local 174 took specific steps to broaden members' minds. "We were always bringing in guest speakers talking about health care, poverty, and trying to break the ice on class issues," he says. "The more you talk about it, the less afraid people are to talk about it, and the less likely people are to revert to red-baiting or whatever."

The local introduces new members to social-movement unionism right away. "We've taken that on in initiates' meetings," Hasegawa says. "We take a hundred bucks off their initiation fee to attend this meeting. And it's not what they expect. They expect to hear about their benefits, and we do talk about that, but we also give them the background on the movement and labor history. We talk about democratic unionism. All of a sudden, light bulbs start coming on."

Hasegawa says that the work of turning workers into community activists is ongoing. "We do stewards' trainings on it," he says. "You've got to keep at it, talking about the big picture." For another example of Local 174's work, see Chapter 23, in which "Teamsters and Turtles" protest the WTO in Seattle.

★ ★ ★

Living wage campaigns are another tool for opening a conversation about "the big picture" and economic justice, with both organized and unorganized workers. The tactics described below—such as tracking elected officials and hitting them where it hurts—are useful for all sorts of community campaigns, and indicate one reason that living wage efforts have succeeded in so many cities.

The Fight for a Living Wage[1]

by Joanna Dubinsky

ORGANIZERS HAVE LEARNED A LOT since the first living wage fight in 1994. Soon after this initial victory in Baltimore, local coalitions composed of unions, faith groups, and community-based organizations like the Association of Community Organizations for Reform Now (ACORN) were launching and winning living wage campaigns.

Jen Kern, director of ACORN's Living Wage Resource Center, says, "Since 1994, we've won close to 100 ordinances in cities, counties, school boards, and college campuses. We've won wages ranging from $7 an hour all the way up to $14.95. The people involved in living wage campaigns believe that everyone who works should make enough to support themselves. So we start with employees whose wages can be tied to public money, and we insist on higher wages for those employees." This connection is appealing; supporters argue that our tax dollars shouldn't be used to create or subsidize poverty-wage jobs.

Three categories of jobs are linked to public money: direct public employees working for a city or county; employees of private firms that contract to provide services for the city, such as parking lot attendants or security guards; and workers whose companies have gotten a low-interest loan, a grant, or a tax abatement from the city—"what we might call 'corporate welfare,'" Kern says. "Often they have gotten these in the name of job creation."

Kern says that a campaign to make a city council pass a living wage ordinance will usually include seven elements: a broad coalition, short- and long-term goals, a timeline that drives the campaign, public education and mobilization, effective lobbying, an escalation of pressure tactics on targets, and an engagement in politics—including a willingness to make politicians pay!

Build a Broad Coalition

"The three basic legs of any good living wage coalition include the labor community, religious leaders, and community-based organizations," says Kern, and it is important to think about why different groups join. She argues, "You are only going to sustain yourselves so far by working for other people's interests," and suggests "a range of pitches to get each group invested in the coalition in a long-term, genuine way.

"Unions may join because they are fighting privatization, and they know that if private contractors have to pay a living wage, that will stop the race to the bottom. Or if a union has organized in the private sector, its employer might not be able to get the city contract because it is getting outbid by a contractor that has lower wages. Religious leaders might feel obligated to take a stand for working people and poor people. You might have a community organization that works on affordable housing, and it finds that living wage resonates with its constituents, low-wage people.

"You need to think about being as broad as you can, bringing in social service providers, bringing in civil rights groups, neighborhood commissions, but you also want to think about going deep into the coalition as well. Think about how to reach the members of that congregation, how to reach the rank-and-file members of that union, or the clients of the food bank or homeless shelter."

Create Short- and Long-Term Goals

Clear goals for a living wage campaign are critical, because these goals will drive the way the coalition is built and will shape the debate in the community. "The

A Labor Day march kicked off the 1998 campaign for a living wage in Alexandria, Virginia. Two years later, the city council passed the first living wage ordinance in the state.

short-term goal is to pass an ordinance," says Kern, "but it is also important to think about what else you, as a coalition, are doing. Do you want to organize workers? Do you want to elect a new mayor? Do you want to change the tone of debate in the town? Do you want to build a permanent economic justice organization? Do you want a turn-out machine, where every time a group of workers is in need, the living wage coalition turns out 50 people? What do you want to be? It is important to think about these things when you are starting out."

The living wage coalition in Alexandria, Virginia did just that. According to organizer Gyula Nagy, the long-term goal was to "build a permanent labor-religious-community coalition for workers' rights."[2] After winning an ordinance, the coalition went on to organize home childcare workers, and eventually it evolved into a Jobs with Justice Organizing Committee.

Once the coalition has decided its short- and long-term goals, the group should create a timeline that "has urgency and drives your work down a certain path," says Kern. Without a timeline it is too easy to "endlessly meander in the realm of the living wage.

"The average campaign is over two years long now, which is a good thing, because it speaks to people's deliberate and focused coalition-building and mobilization. We suggest at least six months of coalition-building before you even go public at all, maybe more, so that by the time you do your first public event, you are demonstrating power. So then, the first time you sit down with the city councilor, you can do that with a large list of endorsing organizations and a delegation that represents labor, community, and religious leadership in your city."

Activate Layers of Members and Supporters

Supporters should be able to work with the coalition on multiple levels, with different kinds of involvement and tasks, so that not every person has to attend every meeting. Kern warns against having "one big coalition meeting. You don't want to just have meetings where the participants learn something and walk away. People need to know what they should do next.

"Participants should have assignments: bring five new people to the next meeting, create the phone tree that the coalition can use to call the city councilors right before the vote, or research how much it costs to live in the city. The coalition should split into specific committees with specific tasks, such as mobilization, media, research, and ordinance drafting.

"The mobilization committee plans for a rally, or the action on the city councilor's home. The research committee researches what the living wage amount for that city should be, or gets information on working in poverty in that city to bring to the public." Kern warns against an over-emphasis on research, noting that each piece of research should be "campaign-driven" and that the coalition should use national resources, like the Economic Policy Institute and ACORN's Living Wage Resource Center.[3]

Nagy from the Alexandria campaign agrees: "Our research committee understood from the beginning that we weren't going to win simply because we were right. Research was focused solely on helping us build power. So we investigated city contractor information in order to talk to workers, and to wield the financial numbers offensively."

Kern argues for a paid full-time organizer to oversee the campaign, although the organizer could also be a volunteer. Many campaigns have a "donated" staff person—a person on the payroll of one of the coalition's organizations, who steps in to act as the living wage organizer for the life of the campaign. The important thing is that it should be someone's job to hold all coalition members accountable, frequently checking in to see that people are doing what they said they would do.

Get the Word Out

You can educate the public and mobilize your base in a range of ways: economic literacy training, forums, public hearings, marches and demonstrations, sit-ins at decision-makers' offices. Your message needs to be clear and compelling to counter the well-funded opposition—the Chambers of Commerce, the National Federation of Independent Business, the National Restaurant Association, and the Employment Policies Institute, an anti-living wage think tank.[4]

Activists in Pittsburgh found a way to counter the wisdom of the free market and build their base at the same time. According to Kern, "they developed an economic literacy training to present to members of the coalition's endorsing organizations—the rank-and-file union members and the congregants of churches. The trainings explored the big picture of economic justice: the decreasing value of the minimum wage over time, the growing gap between the rich and the poor, the devastating effects of union-busting. Then they tied this in with the specific proposal—the living wage law—and encouraged folks to get immediately involved in the campaign. This kind of training is designed to bring people into a coalition that has potential beyond the immediate goal of the living wage law."

Public education also comes about through creative actions and media coverage. "In Denver they wanted to cover economic development subsidies," Kern says. "They went to the place where this big Nike Town was being built, and they threw fake money into a hole in the ground, demonstrating that tax dollars were being thrown away and that these jobs would pay so little that the people who work them would qualify for public assistance. That was a fun action.

"In Dallas, ACORN had a canned food drive for the city hall janitors. They sat on the city hall steps and had people bring in canned goods for these city contract workers making just over minimum wage. In Alexandria, they had the first-ever Labor Day parade in that city, to kick off their campaign.

"In many cities, the living wage coalition has a presence at every major parade, march, and festival—Labor Day, Martin Luther King Day, Human Rights Day (December 10). Flyer the crowd, gather postcards to send to city officials, collect signatures on petitions, recruit new volunteers. Show up with your banner and clipboards, set up your table, and organize." Providing reporters with press packets, complete with pictures, will help ensure good coverage. Prepare members ahead of time to deliver the coalition's message in a pithy sound bite.

Matt Luskin, lead organizer for SEIU Local 880 and an organizer for the Chicago Jobs and Living Wage Campaign, describes how his coalition works for a good turn-out.[5] "When we are leading up to an action, flyers are out two weeks ahead of time, mailed or delivered to all of our constituents. And we usually do two weeks of phone calls, with tracking, getting a 'yes' or 'no.'

"Then there is a second round to everyone. Usually two days before, we call everyone who said 'yes,' to remind them. The night before we do confirmation calls; that morning we do wake-up calls. It's a lot of work, but mobilizing 300-400 people for these actions really makes a critical difference." Luskin also emphasizes the importance of a good database. He says, "If you can sort them by city council ward, so you can mobilize people by district, you can move on an alderman quickly." And, of course, make sure to thank the people and organizations that turn out.

Specters of Fear

"A lot of campaigns overlook the importance of effective lobbying," argues Kern. "They think: 'Oh, we've talked to the city councilors, they seem to agree, in general they think it's a good idea,' or 'She's a Democrat, or labor helped get her elected, she's fine.' We are almost always wrong on that stuff."

Kern says that council members can suddenly lose their commitment when they learn about the specific businesses (including nonprofits) that will have to raise wages. "Suddenly they have nonprofits in mind, they didn't know that you were talking about all contractors, or that you wanted such a high wage, or they didn't know contractors were paying so little in the first place and that those contractors were going to start calling them. As soon as the councilors realize they are up against the Chamber, their tune's going to change a little bit.

"You have to prove you will exact more punishment—whether it is against their political career or through public embarrassment—than their punishment from the Chamber of Commerce. This is tough, because the Chamber has the dough."

Your lobbying of council members can escalate from postcards and letters through mass phone-ins to delegations and rallies. Organizations in the coalition should write to council members on their letterheads, urging them to take leadership on the living wage and pledging to watch their actions closely. For phone calls, set a day or a week to flood their offices with calls. Delegations can even make their point through a sit-in, as living wage campaigners did at the office of the Massachusetts Speaker of the House.

"The very least you need to do is three rounds of visits with every single councilor, to coincide with different progress points in the campaign," says Kern. "Lobby visits perform two functions: they apply pressure and they assess where you are.

"The best way to do a lobby visit is in a delegation with someone from community, labor, and religious groups. These delegations should represent your broad public support—geographically and by type of organization. A city councilor may fear bad PR if his or her pastor supports the living wage and the councilor doesn't. That is a different feeling than when the labor council supports the living wage—but if labor got the politician elected, it is important to have labor there too. And if the community members are going to be protesting in the councilor's neighborhood, that presents a problem for them, too. You need to get as many specters of fear inside their offices as possible.

"In Alexandria, they thought about what moved each of their council members. They figured out who the pastor was of one of the important votes on the city council, and they had that pastor come in and do some pastoral counseling.

"The other thing the lobby visit does is to help you assess your council members' position. They may have been supportive at the start, but then you go in there a second time and they say, 'I'm with you, but I'm worried about job loss.' Well, it's a problem that this councilor thinks the living wage causes job loss. Perhaps they haven't read everything you've given them, or they haven't been listening to you, or—most likely—you haven't been doing as effective a job of pressuring them as the business community has done.

"We recommend that you create a 'council-o-meter.' You make a chart on the wall, and you write 1, 2, 3, 4, and 5. And each councilor fits under one of these numbers: '1' being someone who lives and breathes living wage, and '5' being the person who actively denounces your campaign publicly. The 2's would probably vote yes, but aren't very strong, 4's would probably vote against, and the 3's are your fence-sitters.

"You need to know where your council members are on that list—at all times. They will change positions according to where the pressure is coming from. It is your job to move people from right to left. You should know what your vote in council will be before the vote is taken."

Engage in Politics— and Make Politicians Pay!

The ultimate outcome of a living wage campaign may be to change the power dynamics in a community. "This really is about who has the power to make these decisions," argues Kern, "and aren't we sick of other people having the power to make these decisions? Don't we wish our members were city councilors? Our pitch is to get involved, run coalition members for office, do accountability forums when elections come up, make living wage a big issue—make it the litmus test of whether they stand with working people or against them. Make them pay; bring them down if they aren't with you."

The Chicago Jobs and Living Wage Campaign provides an example of holding politicians accountable. One campaign goal, according to Matt Luskin, was to "challenge the power structure of Chicago." The coalition pressured city council aldermen mostly through speakouts, public events where the coalition pushed aldermen to sign a promise to vote for the living wage. When the mayor came out against the living wage, swaying some aldermen to recant or to stall proceedings, the coalition protested at their houses and offices.

Two years into the campaign, coalition members decided to force the vote, even though they knew they weren't likely to win. Then the coalition made sure the living wage was the primary issue in the next election season. They protested publicly the aldermen's decision to give themselves a pay raise, eventually forcing them to the bargaining table. The council unanimously passed the living wage ordinance in July 1998.

Though the ordinance was much weaker than the coalition had hoped, the campaign did develop a broader coalition of progressive forces, eventually called the Grassroots Collaborative, which has gone on to fight for immigrants' rights, among other issues. In 1999 the coalition ran a member—a retired postal worker and former president of Chicago ACORN— against the mayor's machine-backed alderman candidate and won. The coalition was later able to get the council to strengthen the ordinance, using the fact that aldermen wanted another pay raise. Luskin points out, "Any time city officials want a raise, they know they have to come through us."

After winning a living wage ordinance, activists still face the challenge of making companies and cities comply. "Since our victory we've kept rolling," says Nagy. "Roving volunteers act as our 'grassroots enforcement' team. Armed with contractor information and clipboards, activists interview workers to ensure they're receiving the living wage. We're ready to launch aggressive campaigns to bring errant companies into compliance."

The living wage movement has won raises for workers around the country—and it shows no signs of letting up. Just as important as the wage gains, however, are the lessons learned about winning against government and corporations to gain power for local coalitions.

A Living Wage Contract Campaign

by Aaron Brenner

MOST LIVING WAGE MOVEMENTS focus on a legislative fight, but the Living Wage Coalition in Ithaca, New York built a campaign to help low-wage union workers win a decent contract. The LWC helped 200 low-paid teachers' aides and assistants, almost all of them women, win a raise of more than 50 percent over three years.

The LWC had 31 affiliates, including unions, community organizations, political parties, church groups, and student groups. "Back in 2000, Carl Feuer asked if we wanted to make our negotiations a living wage campaign," says Debbie Minnick, a working paraprofessional and president of the Education Support Professionals/Ithaca, a National Education Association affiliate. "He was active in the Tompkins County Labor Coalition [the local central labor council], and we had a history of working together. We presented it to the members before entering negotiations and they were very excited."

When Minnick began bargaining with the school board in January 2001, teachers' aides made about $6.70 per hour, clearly not a living wage. According to the Alternative Federal Credit Union, in Ithaca a living wage for a single person was $8.50 with employer-provided health insurance.

So the LWC built community support for a living wage contract. They used:

• A petition. "It asked people to support a living wage for the paraprofessionals and a small increase in property taxes that might be required," says Feuer. "The support was incredible. People grabbed the petition out of our hands as soon as we said 'paraprofessional.' We had between 2,000 and 2,500 signatures, which we presented to a school board meeting."

• Public hearings, at which paraprofessionals testified about their work and how their low pay affected their lives. The hearing officers were community leaders, which brought media attention. The LWC used the officers' report to educate school board members, other politicians, and media.

• A video. Using a $1,000 grant from the National Organization for Women, the LWC produced a video that told what paraprofessionals do, how they help students, and how difficult it is to get by on their pay. "We sent the video to community groups like the PTA, the school board, radio and TV stations, and religious leaders," says Minnick. "It had a huge effect as far as getting people interested in the cause."

• Candlelight vigils, rallies, and a forum with religious leaders. "The forum helped a lot," says Minnick. "The last thing board members want is a phone call from those people."

• A "parade of paras." "We had 50 different groups," says Feuer, "community organizations, PTAs, seven or eight unions, political parties (Green, Working Families, Democratic), faith-based organizations (Catholic Charities, the Unitarian Church), student groups—and they all carried banners to show the diversity of people supporting the paras."

"The parade ended at the commons downtown," adds Minnick, "and for the afternoon we had bands and speakers who talked about the living wage campaign. We had activities like face-painting for kids. We wanted it to be an event that families could enjoy while learning about the issues."

The contract campaign took 18 months, but in the end wages for teachers' aides rose to $9.36, with an increase to $10.05 in the contract's last year. Assistants went from $7.46 to $9.98, with a final rate of $10.69.

Following the success of the Ithaca paraprofessionals, the NEA put together a cadre of trainers who do workshops on living wage contract campaigns. Minnick, one of the trainers, is very willing to help anyone interested (email deppieipa@aol.com). So far, paraprofessionals in Baldwinsville and Greece, New York have won living wage contracts, and others have started campaigns.

Since the campaign, the number of LWC affiliates has grown to 38, and it has two half-time organizers, an office, and a mailing list of 375. Its religious task force hosts a monthly breakfast briefing for area religious leaders and arranges meetings with industry managers to discuss a living wage. A business task force is in the works.

"Seeing the living wage movement as going beyond legislation gives us plenty to do," notes Feuer. "So many unions need the kind of support we built for the paraprofessionals. We are trying to organize a campaign for low-wage hotel workers in the Ithaca area. We have formed a Workers' Rights Center to provide information, referrals, and advocacy, and to strengthen our movement among low-wage workers. The Center has an activist board with a majority of low-wage workers. It is hard, but over time it can achieve something."

★ ★ ★

In our next four stories, unions fought hard on issues that would benefit the community and that also impacted their own members' jobs.

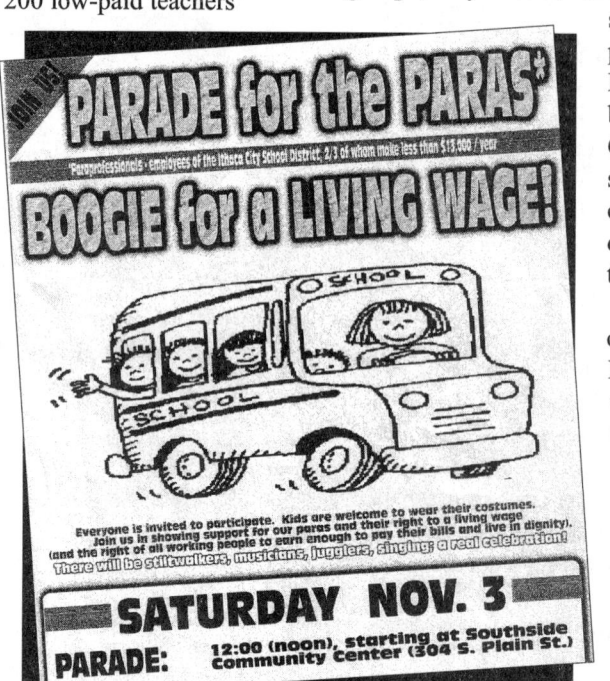

Commuters and Bus Drivers Unite

by Leah Samuel

THE TRANSIT DEREGULATION OF THE 1980s had trickled down from the airline industry to city buses. By 1989, union density among Staten Island-Manhattan express bus drivers was down to 60 percent, from a 1980 high of 90 percent. These figures, plus high bus fares, decreasing ridership, private companies threatening their jobs, and budget cuts, pushed Staten Island bus drivers to take action.

"We started in 1989 by forming a coalition with the riders," says Larry Hanley, former president of Amalgamated Transit Union Local 726 and a current vice-president at the ATU International. "But back then we didn't know that paper didn't organize people," he laughs, pointing out some of the union's early mistakes.

"We'd put out leaflets inviting people to meetings and they wouldn't come. We weren't doing the human contact, talking to people about issues, rather than just standing on a corner handing out leaflets. We opened a storefront and invited people to come to talk about transit issues. But people don't come to your door; you have to go to theirs."

Faced with budget cuts, the Metropolitan Transportation Authority (MTA) was cutting services and raising fares. In addition, private and non-union buses began picking up passengers along the city's routes. "They were just tour buses trying to pick up extra money," explains Hanley. "We had bad equipment and high fares, and the people standing on the corner just get on the first bus that comes."

One idea to fight these trends was to lobby the city and state governments to protect the bus drivers' jobs through legislation. Hanley did not think that would work. "We faced several budget cuts and decided we couldn't regulate our way out of this," he says.

The union had to figure out a way to get the support of bus riders. Hanley knew that frustrated customers often blame drivers, unaware that transit workers have little control over service or fares. "We knew that if our plan didn't benefit both riders and drivers, it wouldn't work," he says. "So we devised a plan to move buses out of Staten Island faster with express bus lanes. People would zip through Brooklyn in 10 minutes, for example, rather than be stuck in traffic for two hours."

Hanley also had to get union members on board with this plan. "Bus drivers are paid by the hour, so it was hard to tell them, 'Here's a plan where you'll be paid less,'" he says. "So, instead, we said, 'We're in a dying industry. If we don't make it more efficient, people won't get out of their cars to take the bus.'"

Hanley also had to get members to pay for a campaign. "We had meetings with sodas and pizza to explain this to members," he says. "But people voted against it twice, really close, like 51-49. So we went to the people who did want to contribute, and we got about 75 percent of those members to contribute $5 a week to the campaign. Then others contributed. We were able to get people to voluntarily contribute where we couldn't get them to vote for it."

Hanley believes the reasons are mostly psychological. "The members felt like if they voted it in, it would be something they had to do, whereas if they had the option, they could always opt out, so they felt better about contributing." The local also got funding help from the International's Committee on Political Education (COPE).

Study Shows Benefits

In 1996, the International commissioned a study of Local 726's proposal for express lanes. "The study showed the cash savings and the environmental benefits," says Hanley. "For example, if buses could carry 30 percent more people, you could charge 30 percent less." The union sent the results of the study to the local media. At the same time, members went on the buses to tell riders about it.

"We hired an organizer to organize the public," Hanley says. "We learned that you had to have one person dedicated full-time to that one piece of the campaign. We handed people flyers with a letter to the governor's and mayor's addresses and fax numbers printed on the back, and asked people to send them, and they did.

"We hired kids from Staten Island Community College, paid their fare, and sent them onto buses with a three-postcard flyer. One postcard was to the mayor, one was to the governor, and one was to the city council. The kids had people fill them out and we mailed them. But before we mailed them, we photocopied them to create a database of who was riding our buses."

By the end of 1996, the campaign was full-blown. The union was able to enlist riders to organize the buses they rode and hand out leaflets to further pressure the MTA, the mayor, and the governor to support the plan. Local 726 also mailed leaflets to people from the database they had created.

The campaign got another boost in 1997. The union did an analysis of Staten Island housing values. "The value of real estate is related to the efficiency of transit," says Hanley. "We had a public-access cable TV show where we brought riders on. We got a real estate lobby group on the show and got their endorsement for our proposal." The union took their new information to the Rotary Club, the Chamber of Commerce, parent-teacher organizations in the schools, and professional and business groups.

Local 726 also created a few unusual opportunities to win public support. "We went to the Staten Island Columbus Day Parade and handed kids balloons that supported us, so that when they stood next to the borough president, they would have these balloons," says Hanley. "And what's he going to do? Take the balloons away?"

"We rented stagecoaches to show the state of transit in Staten Island. We held a series of press conferences and invited the public. We got riders to show up and make the arguments for our plan. We were told that members of the public burned out two ribbons on the governor's fax machine, faxing him in support of us. And at one point, a bunch of riders went up to the governor's office to lobby for the proposal."

The union got media support as well. "The *Staten Island Advance* newspaper is not very friendly to unions, and I'm being kind," says Hanley. "In the end, though, they bought the plan and said that it made sense. We were in the paper so much that the MTA called the paper the Staten Island chapter of ATU."

There were small challenges along the way. "We had bus drivers who work split shifts stuffing envelopes during their breaks between shifts," says Hanley. "It drove MTA crazy. They said we couldn't do it. We said that we were communicating with riders, and that if we couldn't do that, the bosses couldn't either."

All the work paid off in 1997, when the mayor came on board and endorsed the plan. "He was up for re-election that year," says Hanley. "The governor was up for re-election the next year, so he had to come along." In March 1998, the Brooklyn express bus route to Manhattan was extended three to four miles. The express fare was lowered from $4 to less than $3 (instead of the $2 the union wanted).

Improvements such as larger buses continued after the initial campaign. Ridership on the express buses grew from 16,000 to 40,000 by 2001, which created 500 new jobs for drivers—at around $50,000 a year plus benefits—and $37 million in new revenue for the MTA.

"New demand for the improved, faster, nicer buses led to even more service. Saturday service was increased ten-fold, and for the first time Sunday service was inaugurated. Trips on routes that once ended at 8 pm now run until midnight," says Hanley. "Today, the express buses in the City of New York are about 98 percent union as a direct result of this campaign. The service is 100 percent better."

Sparks Fly: Fighting Electricity Privatization

by Jason Winston and Sonya Huber

CANADIAN UNION OF PUBLIC EMPLOYEES (CUPE) Local 1, representing 1,200 municipal electrical workers in Toronto, went head to head with the provincial government of Ontario to fight deregulation and privatization. The government had enacted legislation to deregulate the electricity system in November 1998 and planned to open the electricity market by November 2001.

"The problem we faced was a very hostile and aggressive provincial government," says Bruno Silano, president of Local 1. "They were ideologically driven to privatize and sell off everything in the province that the government owned, and that included the hydroelectric system."

In December 2000 the government sinent announced the proposed sale of Hydro One, a network which included transmission and rural distribution lines. Valued at $5 billion Canadian, it would have been the largest privatization move in Canadian history. (For stories of local unions in the U.S. fighting privatization, see Chapter 6.)

Fighting the Tide

When the plan first came to light, Local 1 spoke out against it, but the majority of Ontario residents were in favor. "They bought the government's line that it would lead to consumer choice, lower prices, and a way to deal with Ontario Hydro's debt," Silano says. Other union locals also bought the plan, including CUPE Local 1000, representing 15,000 electrical workers across Ontario. "They thought deregulation would get money in to refurbish nuclear plants," Silano says.

In February 2001, a handful of activists from Local 1 began to discuss taking action, hoping to take advantage of the publicity around brownouts and blackouts in California. California's deregulated electricity market had been used as a model for the Ontario plan. "We decided to start up a coalition, get it up and running, and let it go its merry way," Silano says. "Our first meeting was over 30 people. We brought in a facilitator who helped keep everyone on the same page.

"Our local put up $50,000. We needed to put our money where our mouth was and lead by example. We started contacting environmental groups, which generally supported deregulation because they thought it would bring green power. But with California, they saw that the promise of green power was window dressing.

"We were able get other labor groups involved. The Communications, Energy and Paperworkers union (CEP) played a large role. They saw that if electricity prices skyrocketed, the private sector, steel, mining would all be hurt. Our national union, CUPE, and the International Brotherhood of Electrical Workers came on side." Other members included retired union members, social justice groups, and the Ontario New Democratic Party. "Howard Hampton, its leader and a provincial member of parliament, was a big supporter," Silano says. "We brought academics on side that gave us a certain amount of credibility."

Organizing the Province

Most members of the Ontario Electricity Coalition (OEC), as the new coalition was named, were from Toronto, so the group decided to establish chapters throughout the province. "We put together a pamphlet and got spokespersons to go to different communities. We eventually went to over 100 communities," Silano says. "We had a simple and easy-to-understand flyer. The concept was: can you afford to pay double for electricity? The flyer also spoke to other bad things that would happen. About this time, the Enron scandal broke. The government backed off the opening date for the electricity market, saying the utilities weren't ready. We saw this as a victory.

"We seized this opportunity to fan the flames. We officially launched ourselves on December 3, 2001. We had a press conference at a statue of Sir Adam Beck, a Conservative at the turn of the century who fought to make electricity publicly owned. We had great media turnout, because they were anxious to hear opposition."

The next step was a series of public meetings to establish the chapters. "We went to Windsor, North Bay, Peterborough, Kingston, Cornwall, Niagara Falls—and all these places set up chapters. We used our website as an organizing tool (www.electricitycoalition.org). We had a 'how-to' there on what we expected a chapter to do: write an editorial for a paper, distribute the pamphlet, talk to politicians, organize a community meeting. It was a grassroots campaign."

The coalition simultaneously held successful press conferences at the legislature and organized chapters around the province. "We had a media strategy. Whenever the government said, 'This will be different than Enron,' we immediately countered. The media began calling us for a counterpoint. We entered the playing field," Silano says.

The pressure on the campaign heated up as the May 2002 deadline for the sale of Hydro One drew near. In February 2002 a lawyer reading the 1998 deregulation legislation found something that could be exploited. At that time, the government had sworn that it would not sell Hydro One, and the unions used this record in court. National CUPE and CEP filed an injunction to prevent the sale. "Most folks thought it was a long shot," says Silano. The judge ruled that the Ontario government did not have the authority to sell Hydro One.

At the same time, a new Conservative premier for Ontario, Ernie Eves, was sworn in. The ruling against the sale was his first political crisis, and it became a national story. "It really galvanized the coalition," says Silano. "They were trying to privatize health care, education, water, and this victory led to a sea change. It was a big hole in their armor. They were ignoring us, but with public pressure we beat them at their own game."

Grassroots Power Surge

In the continued campaign, grassroots support was crucial, and polls indicated that 80 percent of citizens opposed the sale. "Conservative members of Parliament were breaking ranks—there was a lot of turmoil," Silano recalls. "The Liberal Party started changing their tune to garner public support, pledging never to sell Hydro One."

The coalition helped pass municipal resolutions against deregulation, in cities including Windsor, Hamilton, and Toronto. "We used this to say that over four million Ontarians, represented by city councils, had called for this to end," Silano says.

Then the electricity markets were opened to competition, on May 1, 2002. "This took the wind out of our sails," says Silano. But that summer was the hottest on record, with temperatures over 30° Celsius (86° F) every day. Electricity consumption went through the roof—"and with a market, and demand going up, the price started to skyrocket.

"The Coalition pointed out that we had predicted this, and the government didn't listen. The people most affected were small business and consumers, who didn't have locked-in prices. Their bills were doubling and tripling. With that bill coming every month, the issue wasn't going away. A government insider said publicly they had never received so many angry calls.

"The media began to say there might be a blackout. Every day the *Toronto Star* would print the price of electricity from the previous day, and it had quadrupled. Defasco, a large steel plant in Hamilton, came out and said what the government was doing was wrong.

"We were doing tours of towns, press releases, all sorts of public events to keep the pressure on." The pressure paid off as the government decided to close the energy market and put a cap on the price of electricity. "On Remembrance Day, November 11," says Silano, "Ernie Eves went to a home in Mississauga in a staged event, and announced that he was closing the market." However, the problem was not completely solved, as the government was still allowing companies to sell electricity on the spot market, and was also subsidizing these sales to the tune of hundreds of millions of dollars.

Eves called an election for October 5, 2003, and the Coalition mobilized. A massive blackout had hit Ontario and the U.S. Northeast and Midwest that August. The Coalition used the blackout to point out the dangers of a deregulated electricity market. "The OEC said that the blackout impact was in Ontario, New York, Michigan—all deregulated. Vermont and Quebec were not deregulated, and they didn't have a problem," Silano says. "This argument stuck. A Liberal government was elected, and we pushed the Liberals to come up with a pro-public power stance. Now the OEC is holding the Liberals' feet to the fire to make sure they don't retract."

Despite its impressive record, Local 1 could have improved its work in some respects. "My only disappointment is that we could have done a better job of bringing our members along," says Silano. "They knew the OEC was Local 1, but I would have liked to do more. With limited resources, we wanted to create the coalition and hand it off. That didn't turn out to be possible—we had to continually drive the coalition. Resources, finances, meetings, website, press conferences—CUPE Local 1 was driving this. As the president I was focused on the coalition and the vice-president was focused on the day-to-day running of the local."

Overall, however, Silano is pleased with the work of the OEC. "I think working in the coalition has been a great experience for us even if we hadn't had the victories. Our local has so many friends now throughout the province and Canada. One member has been invited to talk in Mexico and Spain. I went to France to talk to unions facing similar challenges.

"I think coalitions are the way to go. Locals are facing huge sources of capital, and for a union in and of itself it's very difficult to win, but in a coalition we make links to other concerns—how this will affect hospitals, education, etc.—and that forces them to stand up and take note."

Lessons Learned

CUPE Local 1:
- Took on an issue even though it was not popular with the public at the time—and created an 80 percent majority sentiment for its position
- Was ready to commit heavily from its treasury
- Created a broad local coalition, and used a professional facilitator in case of disagreements among the different interests
- Wrote a simple, single-issue flyer that could appeal to almost everyone in the province and communicated the essential points of the campaign in clear, accessible language
- Quickly took advantage of events as they happened—the brownouts, the Enron scandal, the 2003 blackout—to help build their case
- Trained coalition members to travel to other cities and help set up chapters
- Used their website to educate and train chapters and to communicate with chapters and the media
- Used a lawsuit to challenge the sale of Hydro One
- Got city councils to pass resolutions in support of their effort
- Made ties with unions in other countries that are fighting privatization.

County Workers Get Help To Save the Hospitals

by Dan La Botz

IT'S NATURAL FOR PUBLIC EMPLOYEE UNIONS to ally with community groups. Such coalitions fight to defend the budgets that pay for both workers' wages and clients' services. Although lobbying and get-out-the-vote efforts are necessary, the best kind of coalition has members of both kinds of groups talking to each other.

SEIU Local 660 members built such direct alliances in a countywide campaign to pass a ballot initiative to save two county hospitals.[6] Local 660 represents 50,000 Los Angeles County employees and reflects the county's multicultural character, with about 25 percent African Americans, 25 percent Latinos, less than 25 percent whites, and other groups from Asia, the Middle East, and all over the world.

In the fall of 2000 Local 660 called on its members to support Measure B on the county ballot, which would generate $168 million for emergency rooms and the Trauma Network, which was on the verge of collapse. Union activists went to dozens of community meetings to talk with voters about why they should support funding for public health. Los Angeles County has one of the largest geographical areas and one of the largest populations of any county in the United States, and this effort meant mobilizing thousands of members to eventually reach hundreds of thousands of voters.

Education, Then Outreach

The campaign began when Keenan Sheedy brought his fellow executive board members a resolution to oppose health care cuts. Sheedy then led a team of union members, patients, and community residents to persuade 17 city councils in the county to pass resolutions against the cuts.

Sheedy asked workers at Bell Gardens clinic, for example, to talk to their patients about attending the Bell Gardens City Council meeting. At the meeting, he says, "one clinic worker and two patients told the council how the proposed closing of the clinic would hurt community residents, many of whom lived near the clinic and relied on it as their only medical service. After hearing this testimony, the city council voted unanimously to oppose the clinic closing.

"In Baldwin Park, we got support from the city council through the good work of José Perez, a steward at LAC+USC Hospital. The mayor invited us to set up a literature table at weekly concerts in the public park. Perez and others got thousands of signatures on petitions at the concerts."

Outreach was a multi-step campaign, starting with internal education. Joel Solis, an RN steward at LAC+USC Hospital, worked with a team at his workplace to reach out to 5,000 co-workers and their families. "The union began with a series of trainings at work about the $700 million shortfall in the budget," Solis explains. "These trainings were attended by hundreds of workers, and over 100 people signed up to be Health Care Advocates.

"These advocates got thousands of signatures on petitions and got co-workers to attend rallies and to do phonebanking and precinct-walking. And we signed up 50 new COPE [Committee on Political Education] members."

The union planned specific strategies for reaching out to churches. Lavon Luster, an ambulance medical technician, is also the Youth Pastor at the New Covenant Christian Church in Long Beach, and he was in his element talking to other congregations totaling thousands of people. He explained how as a med tech he had seen patients turned away from closed emergency services or rejected at hospitals for lack of insurance, and once had seen a patient die. Luster enlisted the help of other county workers, as well as 30 young people from the churches. "Many of the workers and patients I saw at Martin Luther King Hospital, I also saw at churches that I visited, so I could talk to them at greater length," he says.

Luster spoke before representatives of 70 churches in the Newton Area Clergy Council, representing an area that covers a large section of the county. "These congregations have a very high percentage of voters," Luster says. "They all took Measure B literature to their churches." He and his team distributed literature to some of the largest churches in Los Angeles, reaching many thousands of members.

Organizing Community Meetings and Rallies

The campaign also needed a public face. Marina Rodriguez, a clerical at Harbor-UCLA Medical Center, worked to organize community meetings and rallies. Harbor-UCLA was a particularly strong workplace within Local 660 because a stewards council had been created there over the previous few years (see Chapter 3). After hundreds of workers attended the budget training workshops held at the hospital, they organized a town hall meeting at a high school in Harbor City, and hundreds of workers, patients, and community members attended.

To help attract a crowd, the union invited Congresswoman Jane Harman and Dr. Hochberger, Chief of the Harbor ER. "We also organized three rallies outside the hospital," says Rodriguez, "and we got thousands of signatures on petitions. All of these events generated media attention, and that helped to prepare the public for our phonebanking on Measure B." The phonebank was set up in the office of the congresswoman.

Alina Mendizabal, a marketing representative, educated community members right on the job at Olive View Medical Center, one of the centers threatened by the cuts. "We began by educating the workers at Olive View," she explains. "I did a PowerPoint presentation that was attended by 350 people. Then we got sign-ups for buses to rallies, and we signed up a lot of new COPE members. We did other presentations on Measure B for staff and patients right in the ER waiting room, GYN, ENT, Pediatrics, and other clinics.

"We gave presentations to groups of seniors, parents at elementary and middle schools, and at churches. A group of us also went to Ranch Medical Center in Downey to join the campaign there to save that hospital. We helped staff and patients make 2,000 phone calls in one day to elected officials to keep Ranch open."

Lessons of the Local 660 Campaign

What did Local 660 do to build this winning campaign?

• The local used its stewards and activists as the backbone of the campaign. These more active members undertook the training of other union members on the budget and on the health needs of the community. As a result, when members went out to talk, they knew their stuff. Trainings were held in the workplace where it would be convenient for members to attend.

• Hospital workers used their own experiences as workers, patients, and community members to argue the case. In those roles they were the experts who could convince others.

• The workers undertook activities appropriate to their own experience and expertise. One worker went to the mayor in his community, an African American worker reached out to black churches, and the marketing specialist developed the PowerPoint presentation.

• While the get-out-the-vote campaign used the usual phonebanking and leafleting, the effort was made much more effective by the prior education and by the town hall meetings and rallies, including the media coverage of those events.

• All of these events made the union a visible presence in the workplace and in the community, recruited new members to the union's political action committee (COPE), and laid the basis for future labor-community alliances.

A Local Union Fills the Training Gap

by Marsha Niemeijer and Steve Hinds

SINCE THE EARLY 1990s, IUE-CWA Local 201 has been working with local businesses and community organizations in a program that trains workers for jobs as skilled machinists. Local 201 represents workers at General Electric in Lynn, Massachusetts and in other area factories.

President Jeff Crosby describes how the program was started: "We were having layoffs. Our political action committee did a survey of our membership to find out what their main concerns were, and they found that their main concern was jobs—not only maintaining their own jobs at the plant, but also getting jobs if they got laid off and getting jobs for their kids. The political and economic situation was changing, so that people who used to say that they never wanted their kids to work at GE now were saying, 'I don't know what my kids will do, because they'll never get a job at GE.'"

At the same time, the Essex County Community Organization, a local faith-based coalition, spent almost a year trying to learn about the political concerns of their parishioners. They got the same answer: jobs.

Crosby continues, "Our local formed a jobs team with ECCO. Together we did some research and found that at a time when GE had closed its apprentice program for machinists, some of the local high schools were also closing their machinist training programs. Meanwhile, the workforce was aging, and it seemed likely that there would be an ongoing demand for machinists, if not at GE then at least at smaller machine shops in the area. Machinist jobs would meet our three standards for the type of jobs we wanted to create—jobs with a living wage, with benefits, and with a career path.

"We spread the word through ECCO congregations

and within our shops that we were holding a public meeting to talk about jobs in our community. We had 600 people there, along with some elected officials and employer representatives. We called on the politicians and employers to help us set up a training program for machinists and find the funding for it."

Funding for the program, called E-Team, was secured as a line item in the Massachusetts state budget. The program was managed by union, community, and employer representatives; the employer reps came from companies that belonged to the Greater Boston Machine Tool Association and had an interest in developing trained machinists for the future. While the employers wanted to train workers narrowly in only the skills they needed to do the job, the union and community representatives fought successfully to include health and safety, organizing, and other worker rights. The union was guaranteed the chance to fill a percentage of the openings. E-Team has trained about 30 machinists a year.

Running E-Team

"We found out that it's one thing to start something up, and another thing to manage it," Crosby says. Discussions between union and employer representatives were sometimes polarized. One big issue was qualifications to get into the program, particularly the required level of math and English. Local 201 initially pushed for an eighth-grade minimum academic standard. "We wanted the program to be a place for people who hadn't had very many opportunities before," says Crosby. The employers wanted a very high standard; eventually they compromised at tenth grade. Applicants who did not meet the standard were referred to colleges or other agencies that could help them become eligible.

The program had its political costs inside the local. "At a certain point," says Crosby, "the program became very controversial. Because semi-skilled and unskilled work was tending to disappear at GE, one of our goals was to train our unskilled and semi-skilled members so that they could upgrade to machinist classification. But then low-seniority machinists felt threatened that we might train unskilled workers who had more seniority, who could then bump them out of their jobs during a layoff.

"Not only did that not happen, but GE actually hired again a couple of years ago. When they did, 18 graduates of the E-Team got into the plant. Several of them are now activists in the union. Once E-Team was seen as an avenue to employment with GE, it became really popular with members. It was a chance for their kids to get jobs."

Expanding Opportunities

After this success, the union began promoting training opportunities outside of E-Team. The local actively steered members' kids to building trades apprenticeships. The state AFL-CIO helped Local 201 win a federal Department of Labor grant to train workers at two shops. Workers took classes at the job sites and at a local community college. Starting with basic English and math, workers in the program could eventually receive an associate's degree.

"One problem we noticed," says Crosby, "was that we were not reaching the immigrant community. It was because of the entry requirements for math and especially for English. One of our original goals had been to create job opportunities for immigrants, who were arriving when decent-paying jobs, like those at GE, were disappearing. Our local labor council then created a program called PRIMO, an English-as-a-second-language program that could feed its graduates into E-Team. The state AFL-CIO helped us write the funding proposal to the Massachusetts Department of Education to create the program and hire staff. PRIMO has helped us maintain diversity in the E-Team."

The program has had to adapt to economic changes. "When the number of machinist opportunities declined, E-Team added welding to the curriculum," says Crosby. "We want to train people for jobs that exist. The program has run into budget problems because of state cutbacks, and so our local has had to search for other funding."

Crosby says that the job training effort, which started mainly with volunteers, has "created opportunities for families and expanded our members' view of what the union can do for them. It has also created long-term relationships with churches, immigrant groups, and nonprofits in the education field. The positive effects have been both practical and political.

"I think it's changed our members' views of community organizations. Originally, even among the leadership of the local, there was some doubt about working with clergy and what some referred to as 'poor people.' That's changed. Our members see faith-based and immigrant groups more as natural allies of the union. But it's still a struggle. It's never easy to get people to put time into community efforts."

Labor Goes to School

by Leah Samuel

SCHOOLCHILDREN may come closest to learning about workers' issues when their teachers go on strike. By then, the message about unions is overwhelmingly negative, as administrators portray teachers as selfish and lazy. How are kids to know that because of the labor movement, their parents are free to take them to soccer practice on the weekend, or that their allowances and movie tickets can be the direct result of union contracts?

Officers from the Calgary and District Labour Council decided that labor needed to be a part of what kids were learning. They wanted to see labor history, economics from a labor point of view, and international labor issues taught in the public schools. "It's not as radical a concept as one might think," says Gary Hansen, a teacher who is now executive director of the Aspen Foundation for Labour Education. "Kids should be familiar with these kinds of things."

First, representatives of the Labour Council sent a letter to the Calgary Board of Education outlining their concerns. This led to meetings with a social studies curriculum specialist from the board. A series of other meetings followed, during which they brainstormed issues that were currently missing from the curriculum. They researched resources, wrote and rewrote lesson plans, presented material to the council of social studies teachers for critiquing, tried out the results in classrooms, and revised the material again.

This resulted in a collection of course materials called "The Missing Perspective," which included sections on Media Literacy, Canadian Labour History, Labour Leaders, Labour/Management Relations, Anti-Union Government Policies, Harassment (racism, sexism, and homophobia), Technological Change, and International Labour Issues.

The course materials use simulations, role-playing, collaborative reading, pairs reading, research, and reporting as learning tools for different grade levels. The lessons are flexible, made to be used individually or sequentially to suit the needs of different classes. Materials are contained in a binder, to be easily removed for photocopying, and copyright permission was obtained so that teachers can reproduce materials for classroom use.

Once the materials were developed, the union activists had to get teachers to use them. They delivered copies of the binder to each high school in Calgary and worked with the Board of Education's Social Studies Council. They contacted the Alberta Teachers Association (the main labor body for teachers) and the provincial government about using the material as an educational resource and as a submission to the review that the government was then doing of the social studies curriculum.

At the same time, they recruited volunteers—teachers, unionists, and others with an interest in seeing the materials used in the schools—to their ad hoc "The Missing Perspective" movement. These volunteers distributed the binders and spoke at teachers' conventions, union conventions, and social studies conferences, from one end of the province to the other. Feedback from teachers and students was strong and positive. During presentations, teachers asked for areas in their schools' existing curricula where the material could be used and offered suggestions.

"The common feeling was that teachers do not present a pro-labor perspective because they do not know how to access resource materials or plan lessons around them," wrote Calgary and District Labour Council delegate Joan Thomson in *Labor Notes*.[7] "During in-class workshops, students consistently demonstrate their interest and a natural curiosity about unions and labor law for youth. They display strong feelings about how young people are discriminated against in society and by legislation."

The word about "The Missing Perspective" spread to the Alberta Federation of Labour (AFL). Through discussion at its Education Committee and resulting convention resolutions, the AFL endorsed the development of a non-profit organization called the Aspen Foundation for Labour Education (AFLE), which would develop further bridges with the Alberta Teachers Association and other coalition partners. In 2001 the AFL convention endorsed a resolution to support the foundation in any way possible, including strongly encouraging affiliates to make sustaining donations.

Hansen says the unions had a big incentive for supporting AFLE. "There has been a major push by business to get involved in schools," he says. "So a lot of labor activists see this as leveling the playing field."

In 2002, AFLE elected its first board, developed a curriculum committee, launched its website, and contracted with a teacher to develop two new sets of lesson plans: "Doing Work and School" and "Looking into Sweatshops."

★   ★   ★

Of all the possible partners that labor activists can reach out to, students have been some of the most responsive over the last decade. Coalition work with students has its own set of advantages and challenges. A workers' struggle that taps into the energy of students is bound to receive a jolt of energy and enthusiasm.

Here we give advice on making contact with students, and follow it up with two examples where student activists were a major support in union campaigns. The first story involves campus workers and the second, workers off campus. We end with some advice on running a Union Summer program for student interns.

Labor Lessons

Here are some low-cost ways teachers can help youngsters learn about the labor movement. Union parents can volunteer to help.

• Real-life examples: When a strike happens, teachers can assign students to study the issues as a current events project. Strikers can speak to classes and can volunteer at schools when they're not on the picket lines, which can give young people a positive view of union members.

• Field trips: Teachers can take students to a labor-related exhibit at a museum or to a union hall (one more reason to commission that mural). Locals can sponsor such trips, with members serving as tour guides.

• Career Day/Week: Along with the firefighters, doctors, and journalists who speak in schools every year, union organizers or officers can offer to tell why they do what they do. They can help kids recognize that making sure workers are treated fairly is an honorable, meaningful job.

• Visuals: Have a local activist dress up as Mother Jones or some other famous activist and come to the classroom to talk about her life and struggles. This might be good for just after Labor Day or on Halloween.

• "Bug Hunt": Have students search for and bring in items from around their homes with union "bugs" on them, and research the unions indicated.

Students and union members picket sweatshop garment manufacturers in San Francisco. Building ties between unions and students has become easier in recent years because of increased interest in social and economic justice on campuses.

Building Student-Labor Collaborations

by Joanna Dubinsky

STUDENTS CAN BE IMPORTANT ALLIES—they are creative and energetic, and they can organize campaigns, like secondary boycotts, that unions legally cannot. But unions should approach students not only for what students can bring to campaigns, but because students—and young people in general—are important to a strong labor movement. Young people are the organizers, rank and filers, and union troublemakers of tomorrow.

Building ties between unions and students has become easier in recent years because of increased interest in social and economic justice on campuses. In the late 1990s students began organizing student-labor action committees and anti-globalization groups on their campuses, and built national organizations such as United Students Against Sweatshops (USAS) and the Student Labor Action Project (SLAP). While most of these groups were originally formed to support garment workers abroad who made university apparel or to protest unfair trade agreements, these student-labor activists quickly began looking for ways to work with U.S. workers as well.

According to Lenore Palladino, a national organizer for USAS and a former student activist at the University of Chicago, there are two kinds of local campaigns student-labor activists support: "The first is the campus-worker organizing campaign or campus living-wage campaign. Right now there are over 40 of these campaigns across the country.

"The other kind of campaign is the more community-focused campaign, where there is union-busting somewhere in the community outside of the campus. In this situation, chances are that company has some sort of relationship with the university that students can use to exert pressure on the company. It might be a business relationship, or a person from the company's board is on the university's board. Our role as student activists is to form relationships with workers on and off campus and to investigate what we can do from our position to leverage power and support workers."

Locals can reach out to student groups to build on-the-ground relationships. "I love it when unions take the pro-active stance and contact me to talk about working with students, not only as a 'rent-a-rally' but to develop longstanding relationships," says Ana Rizo, a national organizer for SLAP. "A lot of times unions will scramble two days before an event to get students out. Unions often treat students or Jobs with Justice this way. They think they can always call on us because we are the radical ones. But these campaigns work best when students and workers have already been developing relationships. SLAP is really focused on long-term change, and we don't think you can do this if you haven't built long-term relationships."

"The first step in building a relationship is to collaborate together, for instance on SLAP's annual April 4 National Student Labor Day of Action event," says Andrea Calver, student liaison for the Hotel Employees and Restaurant Employees. "Events take place across the country on April 4, the anniversary of the assassination of Martin Luther King, Jr. Actions include pickets, sit-ins, teach-ins, and more.

"So for both unions and for students who want to start building a relationship when there isn't a crisis, April 4 is a fabulous opportunity to look for a local campaign and do some kind of action. These events have completely strengthened HERE's relationship with students. Through these events, our locals know who the student activists are and continue to work with them. April 4 has become an institution."

SLAP is connected nationally to Jobs with Justice, and on the local level it may bring together student organizations on various college campuses in a given city. In 2004 local SLAP coalitions put on 309 actions around April 4. In some cities the Day of Action was expanded to a week of action honoring the lives of King and Cesar Chavez.

Ella Hereth, a University of Chicago activist, confirms that actions during the Student Labor Week of Action have helped strengthen relationships in a mutually beneficial way. "In Chicago, April 4 looks a little bit different every year. In 2003 it was very much about having students support unions. In 2004 it looked more student-focused." Union members came out to support a fight at City College against budget cuts and tuition hikes. "The budget cuts were due to a lot of factors that affect working people, so there are a lot of connections there," says Hereth.

She gives another example of union support for student issues: "Two years ago students at the University of Illinois had a big campaign around faculty diversity. There was a cut in funding to certain departments, and fewer people of color were becoming tenured. The workers at University of Illinois helped students organize a campaign around that issue. They did a big march on the administration, collected signatures of workers in support of the campaign, and sent delegations to visit administrators."

When reaching out to students for the first time, ask the national USAS and SLAP offices about groups in your area. Or look on the college website; contact the campus student affairs office for a list of student groups; look for flyers on or near campus; or do a web search for student activist websites or a local Indymedia website.

If there are no labor-focused groups at the college near you, look for other social or economic justice organizations, like a progressive student union. Hereth points out that while not every college or university has a USAS chapter, "there will be an organization of black students, or an organization of Latin American students, or a students-of-color coalition. I'm willing to bet that there is some student group working on some important student issue on a campus, who will appreciate support and in turn will help with a union's struggles."

Once you have found student contacts, Hereth argues that the best way to approach them is to first find out what they are doing. "Solidarity is a two-way street. A union may have a specific campaign that it wants students to work on, but it should approach students by asking what they are doing and how the union can support them." Ask about campaigns they've done in the past, too. Simply inviting students to your rally or picket line does not build a real relationship. Figure out where your interests intersect. Creating a dialogue through sending reps to each other's meetings (when appropriate), turning union folks out for student events (like the rallies against tuition hikes at City College in Chicago), and co-organizing events helps students and workers feel comfortable working together.

Organizing activities around the Student Labor Week of Action is considerably easier if your city has a Jobs with Justice chapter and a SLAP coalition. If you don't have this infrastructure, seek out suggestions from national organizers. Don't just plan rallies or strike support. Sponsoring speakers and screening movies like "At the River I Stand" (about Dr. Martin Luther King's support of the 1968 sanitation workers' strike) help motivate workers and students. Don't forget social events; this will give students and workers a chance to get to know each other. And, of course, nothing gets students more committed than being involved in planning actions and making trouble.

University Workers Seek Students' Help

by Dan La Botz

RANDY MARCUM, president of AFSCME Local 209 at Miami University in Oxford, Ohio, developed a plan to transform his union, and part of that plan was to establish a closer relationship with students. Over a period of four years Marcum, a plumber in the maintenance depart-

The worker-student alliance on Miami University's campus was not a gimmick to win a strike but part of an ongoing campaign for worker justice. After the strike, professors, students, and AFSCME Local 209 members continued to work to help the clericals organize.

ment, led a reform movement in his union, established working relationships with students, and led his union through its first-ever strike to a modest victory. The union's relationship with students was key, as he would be the first to argue.

Local 209, representing food service, grounds, and maintenance workers, was the only union on campus at Miami University. The state university, located in a small college town set in a rural, conservative community, had never seen a strike. Professors and clerical workers had no unions. In 1990, the university had illegally decertified Local 209.

In 2003, the local had its bargaining rights back but had been reduced to a pathetic state, with only 220 members in a bargaining unit of over 900. The union had little presence in the workplace and virtually none in the broader campus community. Yet in less than a year campus workers and student activists joined together to carry out the first strike since the founding of the university in 1809.

Marcum explains how he first became active in the local. "I came up with a plan," he says. "I was going to take a speech class and then run for president. The next thing I had in mind was unionizing the clerical employees. And I was going to get a student coalition going.

"One of the first things I wanted to do was to write about wages for the union newsletter. We had lost our step raises back in 1990, which had affected our wages 25 to 40 percent." The change had cost workers hundreds of thousands of dollars.

Union officials wouldn't let Marcum publish his findings in the union newsletter, "because it stepped on too many toes in upper management," he says. So he decided to take the information to the members and to the students. "My perspective was that in order to get a decent wage here at Miami University you had to have an alliance with the customers, who were the students."

Students in Solidarity

With the support of Local 209, students:
- Did the local's research and writing, distributed union publications by email, and put out tens of thousands of leaflets on campus
- Swayed the opinion of the 16,000 mostly conservative students by engaging in conversations and raising the question of the strike in classes
- Helped draw professors into strike support activities, gaining 200 signers for an open letter in support of the living wage and the strike
- Produced a "curriculum" for professors that dealt with the living wage issue and the history of the union and its negotiating efforts, so that professors could teach about the strike in their classes
- Arranged for Local 209 members to speak in classes about the contract issues and later about the strike
- Organized marches and rallies on campus and at the president's residence that challenged the administration and forced students to take sides
- Organized large groups to "rush" dining halls and put pressure on management and scab workers
- Joined Marcum and other union activists in "Tent City" in front of the administration building
- Joined workers in blocking trucks that attempted to make deliveries to the campus
- Joined clerical workers, professors, and the staff at broader meetings of a strike council.

Students Step Up

Two students, Nick Robinson and Nicolle Schaeffer, who were working with the local chapter of United Students Against Sweatshops, had contacted Local 209, but the past president hadn't returned their phone calls. So they had started working with clerical workers on campus and had conducted a survey of clerical workers' problems and interests. Teresa Harper, a secretary who had initiated a drive to organize the clerical workers into AFSCME, passed Robinson's and Schaeffer's names along to Marcum.

Marcum remembers when he first met with Nick. "I was ecstatic when I heard about the students who wanted to work with our union," Marcum says. "I met with Nick Robinson and told him what I was looking for. He wanted to get involved. I went over the facts and figures with him. We discussed a lot of things that day."

Nick Robinson remembers, "When I met with Randy, I knew immediately this was who I was looking for. Randy had this detailed plan to organize a coalition between students, graduate students, professors, and clericals to support Local 209 when its contract expired on June 30, 2003."

With Marcum's support, the two students set up a group called the Miami University Fair Labor Coalition, made up of staff, clericals, students, and professors interested in strengthening Local 209 and in helping to organize the clerical staff.

Marcum, meanwhile, had run for president on a platform calling for union reform and a campus-wide alliance. As part of his campaign, he invited Robinson and Schaeffer to speak to the executive board about the possibilities of an alliance with students. Marcum won the election in December 2002 and set to work building the coalition. He spent every free moment going from department to department and shift to shift, talking to the workers in the bargaining unit and recruiting them to the union. In a few months, he succeeded in raising the union's membership from 220 to 470, a little more than half of those eligible.

At the same time, he worked with the new Fair Labor Coalition to reach out to students, professors, and clerical workers. Local 209 had a contract clause preventing it from publicly criticizing the Miami administration, so union members used the coalition for crucial agitation. "We set up some meetings," Marcum explains. "I made some speeches to students. I helped them recruit more student members to the coalition." Sometimes the outreach to students also brought in new workers. "One of the students, Jon DeVore, brought along his father, Bill DeVore, a campus worker, and both of them joined the Fair Labor Coalition." Bill DeVore became a leading union activist. Marcum estimates that 40 percent of new union members joined as a result of publicity created by the Fair Labor Coalition.

Living Wage Campaign

The coalition decided on a living wage campaign, and publicized a study by Professor Anne Bailey that said many campus workers could not survive on their low wages. Bailey presented the study at a coalition meeting, and its results were turned into educational leaflets and widely distributed on campus. "In essence, what we were doing was bringing out the facts and the issues, and we were hoping that a lot of students would have compassion and a drive to get involved, because it is their fees that pay for the university," says Marcum.

Robinson and Schaeffer graduated in the spring of 2003 but returned to the campus the next fall as volunteer organizers. For the next several months they slept in Marcum's cabin, in friends' apartments, or in a local professor's house while doing research, writing, and organizing in preparation for the coming strike.

"I kept up the lectures to classes and campus organizations. Nick and Nicolle had their own recruitment techniques. We had a really good personal relationship," Marcum says. "It was phenomenal how hard they worked. I went to a lot of meetings with the students and the coalition, and threw out ideas about what I wanted to see in leaflets about what would be productive for union goals."

The coalition served as an arm of the union, doing things that for legal reasons the union could not do or could not do as effectively. "I used the coalition to get out information about union demands that the union couldn't distribute yet because we hadn't yet filed to negotiate with the state public employee collective bargaining board," Marcum explains.

"The Fair Labor Coalition was very, very successful in motivating students and professors. By the time the strike came around the issues were out there pretty darned good." Marcum functioned as one of the central leaders of the Fair Labor Coalition. He treated the students and professors with whom he dealt as equals, as partners in the fight to improve labor conditions on campus.

Tent City

When negotiations began, Marcum set up a cot and slept on it in front of the administration building. When the weather turned rainy, he got a tent. For a time he even went on a hunger strike. He explained that he wanted to rally and inspire the union and its supporters, and it worked. A couple of other AFSCME members brought tents and joined him. Students also began to bring their tents, and by the time of the strike there were a couple dozen tents in front of the building, a little community that became known as "Tent City." Even a couple of professors braved the elements for a night. Tent City became the symbol of the worker-student alliance that challenged the administration.

Perhaps the high point of the strike came when about

Advice from Student Activists

Nicolle Schaeffer and Nick Robinson offer their advice to students:

Instead of approaching the campus union with your idea for a campaign, find out what their issues are and how you as a student can help engage rank-and-file workers. It's easy to survey workers or use workers' narratives as class assignments.

Also, we tried not to relegate ourselves to "unquestioning supporter" status. We brought up ideas that we thought would help and suggested tactics and strategies that had worked in similar circumstances.

Our Fair Labor Coalition maintained an identity of its own and autonomy from AFSCME (though it had AFSCME officers and members in it). Clerical workers used the space created by the Fair Labor Coalition to continue their workplace activism side by side with organizing into AFSCME. When some clericals complained that the regional AFSCME organizer wasn't taking their advice seriously, they said that they still wanted to organize for a living wage, but put more energy into the Fair Labor Coalition.

Similarly, we began a kind of corporate campaign by focusing on Miami's ties to Cintas, a corporation that makes and cleans uniforms. As a result of the AFSCME International's benign neglect, we had more freedom to plan actions, although we lacked some resources and funds. Billionaire Cintas founder and Miami alum Richard T. Farmer sits on Miami's Board of Trustees, and a Cintas director is the Trustees' chair. Through our contacts in the student-labor movement and UNITE, we twice brought fired Cintas workers to speak to Farmer at trustees meetings, and dumped a load of old bed sheets on Cintas' career fair table. Farmer and Cintas Director Roger Howe resigned as trustees in spring 2004. [See Chapter 11 for more on UNITE's corporate campaign against CINTAS.]

One question we kept in mind was, What can students do that workers can't? What privileges do we have, and what is the best way to use them? On picket lines, we tried blocking trucks when workers were reluctant to do so.

During the strike, about 40 of us "rushed" a dining hall to pressure the scabs. We ate dinner together, pointed out to management that many of the scabs weren't wearing gloves while serving food, created havoc, and left as the police arrived. Four student activists (ourselves included) were later arrested (and acquitted) on charges including "tampering with a salad bar."

Effective tactics should be molded around your administration's vulnerabilities.

100 students, strikers, clericals, and faculty crammed into a room to hear Miami President James Garland dedicate MacMillan Hall, which had cost $4 million to renovate. As Garland spoke, students held up signs that said "shame" and "millions for buildings, pennies for workers." After the speeches, Bill DeVore stood up and read a statement supporting the strike, signed by the heads of all five departments to be housed in the building. The protesters then converged around Garland and chanted, "Shame on you!" forcing him out of the room with the aid of a security escort.

"During the 13-day strike in September and October of 2003 it was kind of like an army with different battle groups," says Marcum. "The students organized the rallies and passed out leaflets. The students worked with professors; without the students I don't think we would have gotten all those resolutions of support from the different departments and from the Faculty Senate. And the professors were so supportive too, and that really helped the cause. The students did their thing, the professors did their thing, and the union did their thing, and all of that got the media involved. It was like a three-front war, which I think was highly successful."

During the strike itself, the coalition grew from 20 to 50 activists, and as many as 100 students could be mobilized within hours to join a march or to "rush" a dining hall being staffed by scabs. Workers and students picketed the culinary support center off campus and turned away some trucks. Students, workers, and professors became friends on the picket line.

In the end, the strike's monetary gains were small. "From my perspective, this isn't the end of the movement," says Marcum. "It's just the beginning of it, and I think we've had a phenomenal start. I didn't think we'd get a living wage the first campaign. That will have to be the next campaign in two and a half years."

What did Randy Marcum do to create a successful relationship between the union and the students?

• First, he had a plan to reform the union that included reaching beyond its own members to the clerical workers, professors, and students.

• Second, he took time to meet with students, educate them, and learn from them. He spoke at student meetings, in classrooms, and in public debates.

• Third, he treated the students the same way he treated the union members, as part of the movement. Students attended and even spoke at union meetings, and some workers participated in the Fair Labor Coalition. When the union held mass meetings of 300 union members, there would always be 20 or 30 students there. When the full Fair Labor Coalition met, roughly one-third of the participants were workers, including union officers, clerical workers who wanted a union, and curious, previously uninitiated workers.

• Fourth, Marcum recognized that the students could do some things better than the union and some things the union could not do for legal reasons.

• Finally, Marcum didn't see the alliance as a gimmick to win a strike. The worker-student alliance on Miami's campus is part of an ongoing campaign for worker justice. After the strike, professors, students, and AFSCME Local 209 members continued to work to help the clericals organize.

Student Solidarity in the Boston Janitors' Strike

by Amy Offner

WHEN BOSTON-AREA JANITORS in SEIU Local 254 went on strike in October 2002, students throughout the city mobilized an impressive set of support activities. Organized independently through the Boston chapter of the Student Labor Action Project (SLAP), students participated in events sponsored by SEIU and Jobs with Justice and planned their own complementary actions.

Students in Boston participated in some high-profile events in support of striking janitors, including civil disobedience.

Their efforts helped to embolden striking workers, most of whom were Latino immigrants, amplify the pressure on employers, and generate positive media coverage of the strike.

Over the course of the strike, students throughout the city helped maintain and strengthen union picket lines, especially those set up in the middle of the night to block deliveries. They independently organized a citywide student march to support the janitors, a series of rallies, and a letter of support signed by Boston-area faculty. Students at Northeastern University camped out on the university president's lawn to get him to put pressure on janitorial contractors.

"My favorite action was when we targeted the second-largest building owner in Boston," says Lara Jirmanus, who was working as a SLAP staffer during the strike. "She was refusing to negotiate, so we made 'Wanted' posters with her picture and put them up all around her house in Beacon Hill."

A key moment for student support was the first night of the strike, when workers were scheduled to walk off the job. At Northeastern, one of the struck job sites, students held a support rally by the punch clock where workers gathered to start the strike. "Even though the police forced most of the students to stay 100 feet away, having the students close by gave the workers a lot of confidence," recalls Aaron Bartley, a staff organizer for Local 254. "It was an uncertain point—the police and supervisors were trying to intimidate workers—but the students were able to counteract that intimidation."

Students also organized some high-profile events, including civil disobedience in the Prudential building, a posh downtown skyscraper that houses a shopping mall and offices. Students combined street theater and civil disobedience to support the union's demand for health benefits. Entering the mall dressed in bandages, the students feigned illness in the middle of the food court, explaining that the janitorial contractors' denial of health benefits made them sick. With TV cameras recording, students groaned, writhed on the floor, and vomited fake blood all over the mall. The police dragged them out in what became a humiliating scene for the janitorial contractors. The sensational arrests helped focus media attention on the janitors' demand.

Northeastern Law School students also staged a one-day strike in support of the janitors. Before the strike, workers convinced a few sympathetic faculty members to turn their classes over to the janitors for a day. Workers came to classes, told students their own stories, and asked them to join the walkout.

Lessons of Student-Labor Work

The student network in Boston proved a valuable resource to labor organizers. "There was an existing network of student-labor activists the union could rely on," explains Bartley. "They were able to organize pretty autonomously. They had contact people on each campus who communicated periodically with the union about the timing and nature of actions."

It was important to student activists that SLAP was a student-run organization that operated independently of both Jobs with Justice and SEIU. JwJ provided institutional support, hiring Jirmanus as a long-term SLAP staff person and three other student organizers for the duration of the strike. One of the three was hired specifically to strengthen support among students of color, who were underrepresented in SLAP.

Anna Falicov, a Harvard student active in SLAP, argues that the group needed to be autonomous in order to attract experienced student activists who did not want to be used or micro-managed. "It was important that the union communicated with us and gave us information on the status of negotiations," she says, "but we didn't want them to directly control our actions." This insistence on independence reflected the past experiences of students in Boston who felt that some unions had dealt manipulatively with student and community supporters.

"When SEIU or JwJ would say to us, 'Tomorrow we need 100 people arrested,' people really didn't like it," says Jirmanus. "We would just say no." The students periodically conferred with the union, and were careful not to take actions that would put SEIU in legal trouble or otherwise hurt the strike. They argued that maintaining independence was good for the strike, because the union could truthfully say that it could not control its supporters. The janitorial contractors were threatened by the idea of unruly students, and the union was protected from legal responsibility.

The Prudential arrests were just the kind of action that the union would not have carried out itself, but which helped the strike. "With the Prudential event, we definitely pushed the limit," explains Falicov, who was arrested in the action. "There was some concern about whether the union would want us to do it, but we thought it would generate good media, we wanted to get arrested, and it was something that the janitors could not do themselves because of their immigrant status."

Bartley agrees: "Students could leaflet on campuses that we were striking, whereas workers couldn't because the campuses were private property. It's easier for students to get arrested than workers who are not citizens. And in cases of direct action, it can be easiest for students to enter a building first. Their presence makes it easier for workers to get inside."

The union was organizing powerful actions of its own: enormous marches that shut down downtown streets every night for three weeks and direct actions inside struck buildings. The student actions strengthened the workers' campaign and helped provide public protection to workers who would otherwise have been more vulnerable.

Doing Union Summer Right

by Joanna Dubinsky and Amy Offner

SINCE 1996, thousands of college students have taken part in the AFL-CIO's Union Summer program, each spending several weeks working with a union to learn about the labor movement and develop organizing skills. Some unions have also developed their own summer internship programs.

Students' experiences in Union Summer have varied considerably: for many, the program has inspired long-term involvement in the labor movement, but others have found the program disorganized or uninspiring. Here are some steps unions can take to make internships worthwhile for both the union and the students.

DO:

• Assign students to locals, not to regional or federation offices. At locals, they'll have more opportunity to participate in organizing and work with members; federation offices give a more bureaucratic introduction to the labor movement. Among locals, the ones that benefit most from interns and which give students the best experiences are those with exciting, well-planned campaigns in progress.

• Put the students in contact with workers as much as possible. Students can help turn out workers for rallies, membership meetings, and other events. Some can help translate at multilingual meetings. Andrea Calver, Student Liaison for HERE, notes, "Contact with workers is key to students feeling like they are part of real change."

• Pair students with experienced organizers so that they can observe worksite meetings, job actions, house visits, and other day-to-day functions of the union.

• Let students attend union meetings to observe.

• Although the focus should be on organizing, other projects can be interesting to students and useful to your local. Students can provide resources you might not have thought of:

✓ Your intern likes to write? How about an article for a local newspaper, magazine, or the union's paper? Students can also help write press releases.

✓ Your intern likes research? Provide a crash course in corporate research, so she can help research a potential organizing target. Some students will already know how to do this.

✓ Your intern has video production experience? Get him equipment to interview workers and make a short film about your local.

✓ Your intern is an artist? Let her paint a mural at the local hall or draw a comic for the union paper.

✓ Your intern has graphic design skills? Let him design flyers and posters for your events.

✓ Your intern has experience working with the media? Let her call reporters to help get coverage for a rally.

✓ Students are great at livening up actions. They can help organize a drum corps for marches and rallies, come up with creative chants and signs, or pull off banner drops from buildings and bridges.

• Make sure you have enough work for the students to do. Also be flexible and elicit their feedback. For instance, if they are excited about some activity you've given them, let them keep doing it if something else is not urgently needed.

• At the beginning of the program, give the students a tour of the city and its working class areas.

• Teach the students labor history as part of the program. If possible, bring in labor historians from the area to help. A book that students usually love is *Labor's Untold Story*.

• Teach the students about racism, sexism, and homophobia in the labor movement.

• Talk with the students about current debates in the labor movement: how unions should organize and function internally, labor's relationship to other social movements and to labor movements in other countries, and questions about how labor can revitalize itself.

For many students, Union Summer has inspired long-term involvement in the labor movement.

• Stay in touch with your interns after the summer is over, via email. They will want to know what happened to the campaign they worked on. Staying in touch also provides an important benefit—students can be great allies in future campaigns.

DON'T:

• Don't take on too many interns at one time. Aim for a 2:1 intern-to-supervisor ratio. Calver says, "Many locals may be enticed by the help they could get from a large number of interns, but they do not have the supervision to make sure interns have a good experience."

• Don't make students phonebank all day. It is not the same as meeting workers.

• Don't make students spend the summer doing office work or painting the union hall. A summer filing papers won't add to anyone's enthusiasm for the labor movement.

• Don't hand students a stack of flyers and leave them standing on a street corner all summer.

• Don't assume that all students are new to the labor movement. Many will have experience in student-labor groups on their campuses and will have worked with unions before. Most will have job experience, usually low-wage. Make sure the experienced students are challenged.

• Don't hold students captive 24 hours a day. Give them some down time to explore the city and relax.

• Don't spend money printing oversized t-shirts that no one wants to wear.

Resources

• ACORN Living Wage Resource Center. Living wage ordinance summaries and comparisons, tips for drafting a local ordinance, research summaries, talking points, and links to other living wage-related sites. http://livingwagecampaign.org. Write Living Wage Resource Center, 1486 Dorchester Ave., Boston, MA 02122, or call 617-740-9500.

• *Winning Wages: A Media Kit for Successful Living Wage Strategies*. Produced by the SPIN project and the Tides Foundation. Useful for both living wage and other economic justice campaigns. 415-284-1420, lw@spinproject.org. Free for members of organizations that work for living wages or broader economic justice, $15 for others.

• Aspen Foundation for Labour Education (AFLE).

Curricula for teaching about labor in the schools. 11 Bonin Place, Leduc, Alberta, Canada T9E 6H6. 780-986-1745. afle@telusplanet.net. www.afle.ca.
- United Students Against Sweatshops (USAS), 1150 17th St., NW, Suite 300, Washington, DC 20036. 202-NO-SWEAT. www.studentsagainstsweatshops.org, organize@usasnet.org.
- Student Labor Action Project (SLAP), a joint project of Jobs with Justice and the U.S. Student Association. SLAP coordinates the National Student Labor Week of Action. See www.jwj.org or call 202-393-1044.
- Union Summer, unionsummer@aflcio.org.
- *At the River I Stand,* by David Appleby, Allison Graham, and Steven John Ross, 1993. 56-minute video. Recounts the Memphis sanitation workers' strike and the assassination of Dr. Martin Luther King while in Memphis supporting the strikers. California Newsreel, Order Department, P.O. Box 2284, South Burlington, VT 05407. 877-811-7495. contact@newsreel.org. $195 list price; $49.95 selected organizations; $29.95 home video.
- *Occupation,* by Maple Rasza and Pacho Velez 2004. A 42-minute video on the Harvard Living Wage Campaign, an alliance between students and custodial, food service, and other workers, and the campaign's culmination in a three-week student sit-in at an administration building. www.enmassefilms.org.
- *AFL-CIO Communities@Work Toolbox*. Aimed at organizers who want to enlist their communities to help workers form unions. How to gain community support for card check, employer neutrality, and local and state initiatives. 800-442-5645. First copy free; additional copies $15.
- *Coalitions Across the Class Divide: Lessons from the Labor, Peace and Environmental Movements,* by Fred Rose. How to bring together movements that have often clashed in the past. Cornell University Press, 2000. $19.95.

Action Questions

FOR ACTION QUESTIONS see the next chapter, Allying with the Community: Multi-Issue Coalitions.

Authors

AARON BRENNER is a labor historian, researcher, writer, and editor in New York City. He has written about international labor solidarity, union reform movements, and rank-and-file rebellions by Teamsters, telephone workers, and postal workers, and is the editor of *The Encyclopedia of Strikes in American History.*

JOANNA DUBINSKY, a former *Labor Notes* intern, earned a Master's Degree in Labor Studies from the University of Massachusetts, where she was an active rank and filer in the Graduate Employee Organization, UAW 2322. She is involved in social and economic justice projects in New Orleans.

STEVE HINDS teaches math in the City University of New York's adult literacy program. Previously, he was an activist in the New Haven Federation of Teachers (AFT Local 933), and before that an organizer with the United Electrical Workers (UE).

SONYA HUBER is a writer and teacher living in Columbus, Ohio. She is a founder of Columbus Jobs with Justice.

DAN LA BOTZ wrote the first edition of *A Troublemaker's Handbook* in 1991. He is an activist, teacher, and labor historian based in Cincinnati, where he writes frequently for *Labor Notes*. He was a founding member of Teamsters for a Democratic Union in the 1970s. He is a professor at Miami University and worked with the Fair Labor Coalition and Faculty for Staff during the strike described in this chapter.

MARSHA NIEMEIJER staffs *Labor Notes'* New York office, where she covers longshore workers, telecom workers, and Canadian and European labor, as well as international economic issues. She has worked with the Transnationals Information Exchange since 1995 and helps coordinate international and cross-border programs for TIE and Labor Notes.

AMY OFFNER was a member of the Harvard Living Wage Campaign when she was a student. She has also worked as an SEIU organizer and as a co-editor at *Dollars & Sense* magazine in Boston.

LEAH SAMUEL is a former *Labor Notes* staffer and now a freelance journalist who covers social justice issues. Her work has appeared in *The Chicago Reporter, In These Times,* and *The Progressive.*

JASON WINSTON is a union organizer and a former co-president of the Vermont Workers Center.

Notes

1. This section was developed from an interview with Jen Kern and a speech by Kern given at the Indianapolis Living Wage Teach-In, Butler University, November 23, 2002. Audio can be found online at www.indyaccess.org/library/living_wage.htm.
2. Interview with Gyula Nagy and "Winning a Living Wage Ordinance from the Grassroots," by Gyula Nagy, *Labor Notes*, January 2002.
3. See the Economic Policy Institute's website, www.epinet.org, and http://livingwagecampaign.org.
4. The Employment Policies Institute has a book and website dedicated to fighting living wage campaigns, www.epionline.org.
5. Developed from Matt Luskin's speech at the Indianapolis Living Wage Teach-In.
6. This account has been adapted from Paul Krehbiel's article, "Local 660 Members Push Measure B Over the Top," *660 Voice*, November-December 2002, p. 5.
7. "How We Brought Labor into the Schools," *Labor Notes*, June 2001.

13. Allying with the Community: Multi-Issue Coalitions

by Steve Hinds

TO BUILD DURABLE LONG-TERM ALLIANCES, unions and community groups have found there's a golden rule: don't take each other for granted.

For Jobs with Justice chapters, that can mean ensuring community representation in decision-making. For a still-young labor-environmental coalition, it has meant finding common ground while sidestepping and respecting differences. In labor-religious coalitions, an organized religious community has its own leadership, credibility, and expertise to offer. And in an alliance in New Haven, Connecticut, unions spent years working with community leaders on community demands, resulting in a contract fight that was far broader than traditional wage-benefit unionism.

In these and other instances, labor has moved away from the old model of asking for bodies at rallies. Instead, labor and community groups have shown not only that alliances built on shared leadership and decision-making broaden the vision and improve understanding between groups—they have also shown that they are more likely to win.

Jobs with Justice

by Steve Hinds and Dan La Botz

DURING THE LAST 15 YEARS, and especially in the last five, Jobs with Justice has become an important activist force in many regions. From 12 chapters in 1992, by 2004 JwJ had grown to more than 40 homegrown local coalitions of unions, community groups, and faith-based organizations. At their best, JwJ chapters can offer a model of creative organizing and teach activists skills they can take back to their own organizations.

After describing a workable structure for a JwJ chapter, we give examples of good chapter work. We offer some tools to start and to build an effective chapter, and conclude with some of the challenges that JwJ faces.

Structure

"From the beginning, we realized that there could not be a cookie-cutter approach to JwJ," says Fred Azcarate, executive director since 1992. "While there would be some core principles, we thought folks would know best how to organize locally. JwJ does not really match trade union structures. Our organizational form is coalitional—an organization of organizations—but chapters allow for participation by both groups and individuals."

Most JwJ chapters have a steering committee and working groups. Steve Cagan, a coordinator of Cleveland JwJ for seven years, says, "We have dues-paying member organizations which include local unions, the labor council, and several church groups. Each organization has one representative on our steering committee, which meets monthly and makes all the fundamental decisions—budgets, projects (adopting or terminating them), strategic plans, and staff hiring. Every member organization has one vote on the steering committee, no matter how big that organization is.

"Most of our actual program work is done through our working groups. Currently we have four—Living Wage, Workers' Rights, Health Care, and Globalization. This is what we do and what the public sees. Each working group is responsible for developing its plans, executing them, and developing relationships with other organizations and labor groups that aren't members of our coalition.

"The working groups operate somewhat autonomously within general strategic guidelines. To give an example, the Living Wage group has decided to emphasize three or four suburbs and make them our targets. They wouldn't carry out such a program without the steering committee's approval, but once they have such approval they can move forward. The working groups are the place where individual activists can participate, and where they can make decisions and carry out things as equal partners. Once the overall strategy has been approved, there's a lot of room for individual activists to take a leadership role in making it happen."

This openness to individual activists in JwJ is important. In some cases, a potential activist may not be a union member or may not belong to a union that has an activist vision. JwJ can be a place where individuals do this important work and later demonstrate the benefits to their co-workers.

JwJ chapters across the country have been involved in an enormous number and range of campaigns. Here, we focus on some impressive examples of chapter work in support of both labor and community issues.

Workers' Rights Boards

Workers' Rights Boards were first developed as a JwJ strategy in 1993, out of frustration with the National Labor Relations Board's weak enforcement of the right to organize. Their goal is to bring employer abuses out into the open and to advocate for fair treatment.

Typically, a WRB is made up of community leaders, religious leaders, academics, elected officials, and other prominent members of the community. WRBs have no legal authority, but they have investigated and publicized cases of worker abuse in dozens of campaigns around the country.

WRBs conduct public hearings, giving the targeted employer the chance to participate, and then seek follow-up meetings with management to report their findings and, if possible, resolve the dispute. WRBs have worked best when combined with direct action by JwJ activists. Margaret Butler, a staff organizer with JwJ in Portland, Oregon, says, "Our WRB has largely focused on new organizing and first-contract support. It gives workers a chance to get a sympathetic ear from local big shots. It makes a big difference in their morale, and they feel much less isolated in their fight."

Some WRBs have established hotlines that give out information on workers' rights and make referrals to unions or government agencies. To answer calls effectively, activists must be trained to answer common questions on unemployment, OSHA, wage and hour concerns, rights of fired workers, and more.

JwJ's experience with hotlines is mixed at best. Many activists say the hotlines are extremely time-consuming, and that many calls are frustrating for both the caller and the activist, because employers often act unfairly but not illegally. And while the JwJ activist can encourage callers to take collective action to solve problems, calls many times come too late—after the caller has been fired, for example. Before you set up a hotline, you will need to devise a system for distributing any organizing leads that arise to the appropriate unions. But activists report that few calls to their hotlines have led to organizing drives.

Supporting a Contract Campaign

When Cleveland JwJ decided to support a contract campaign for Cleveland State University food service workers employed by Aramark, a private contractor, activists saw it as a first step to other campaigns. "If Aramark workers at Cleveland State could win real advances in their contract," says Steve Cagan, "it would boost organizing efforts at other campuses and for other food service workers in the area." Most of the workers were African American women.

Aamir Deen, organizer and business agent for HERE Local 10 at Cleveland State, tells the story: "We were halfway through negotiating a new contract, and Aramark was really playing hardball. We called JwJ to witness the negotiations, because we could see there was trouble coming. Our relationship with JwJ has been successful because we get them involved early."

Local 10 President Ken Ilg adds, "JwJ helped set the strategy. They met with our staff and organizers. It was actually JwJ that laid out the pattern for that campaign, and taught us how to reach out to unions on campus, because they had had some work with professors and students. They developed the plan to reach out to students."

"On campus there was the professors' union (AAUP), the SEIU, and CWA, the clerical workers' union," says Deen. "Each had a representative come to our next negotiating session, and they witnessed the company's hard-line stance firsthand.

"At one time Aramark called out the professors and asked them if they wanted to pay more for food. It was very demeaning and got everyone really angry. Aramark refused to budge on health insurance and basically refused to make any offer. Seeing the company's behavior up close gave our new allies a lot of motivation to help us.

"Our contract was well past the deadline. We informed Aramark of our intent to strike, but we decided to first organize for a one-day boycott of the cafeteria. That was in March, and because April 4 was a national day of action for JwJ and students [see the student section in Chapter 12], it made sense to have the boycott on that day. We organized the staff, clerical workers, and professors, and another organizer and I spoke to every student group. Inside, the workers were all wearing blue buttons saying, 'We support cafeteria workers.'"

"The day of the boycott," says Ilg, "where we had to turn out 1,000 people, it was JwJ's phone calls, emails, mailings that insured they would turn out. Those were resources we couldn't have duplicated as a single local union."

A Model Workers' Rights Board

These are some of the struggles the Portland, Oregon Board has supported through hearings over the past few years:

• Workers trying to win their first contract at Powell's Books testified at a WRB hearing. Because of the owner's concern for his public image, the publicity helped to spur negotiations, and a settlement was reached just two bargaining sessions later. See the story in Chapter 15, Organizing.

• Locked-out workers at Oregon Steel testified on the company's labor and environmental violations. WRB members went on to successfully pressure the area transit authority to stop buying scab steel from the company.

• Workers from the Justice for Janitors campaign testified about their workplace issues. Since that hearing, WRB members have put effective pressure on building owners to "go union."

• Portland teachers turned to the WRB during a thorny contract negotiation. A hearing was attended by more than 1,000 people, where teachers told their emotional stories.

• As a part of the national Immigrant Workers Freedom Rides in 2003, immigrants testified on the weak legal protections for immigrant workers. WRB members promoted a resolution in support that was passed at the city level.

A cafeteria worker at Cleveland State University cheered as a boycott supported by Jobs with Justice resulted in an empty cafeteria.

"On April 4 it was a complete success," says Deen. "On that day it seemed as if Aramark had flown in management from everywhere. They were apparently expecting workers to strike, and they had spent money hiring temps, so that made our boycott more effective. We went to the area called The Cage, the student hangout, and we set up tables with free food donated by the AFL-CIO and JwJ, as an alternative to cafeteria food.

"We had free food, music, and speakers from every union on campus declaring their support. We had students from Case Western Reserve University come down and talk about how they were helping the cafeteria workers there organize. We finished up with a march to the cafeteria, and there were the workers, with spotless aprons and big smiles on their faces. We had 200 or 300 people in The Cage, and no more than four or five people ate in the cafeteria. That very day the company got in touch with us, and a week later, we had a negotiating session, and it was a completely different story. We got just about everything we wanted."

"This is a good example of what JwJ is able to do," says Cagan. "We created a focus that changes the environment, changes the context."

Supporting an Organizing Drive

An active JwJ chapter can be incredibly important for workers in an organizing drive. These workers are often just learning how to support one another, and they can be vulnerable to severe or illegal intimidation from the boss. Community leaders giving support and pressuring management to obey the law can sometimes tip the scales.

Cagan describes an example involving food service workers at Cleveland Stadium who were organizing with HERE Local 10: "Everybody else there was organized—the ushers, the clean-up crew, the groundskeepers, even the players and the umpires—but not the food service workers. There had been an unsuccessful drive before, and so they knew the company was prepared to use a full-scale anti-union assault of one-on-ones, captive audience meetings, and illegal threats. The odds against winning an NLRB election were great. The workers needed neutrality and a card check agreement. [See Chapter 15 for more on such agreements.]

"Instead of asking for a meeting with the concession company—SportService—we decided we would focus on the Cleveland Indians' corporate management. The Indians rely at least partly on their image in Cleveland, and they also had the power to force SportService's hand," Cagan says. "We had political, religious, and labor leaders sign a letter asking for a meeting. The Indians' management refused, saying they didn't think their involvement was necessary.

"Together with our leaders who had signed on to the letter, we went to the Indians' corporate offices and asked for an immediate meeting with management. They were busy. We went in anyway and occupied the lobby. That got us our meeting. The next day, the Indians' lawyer was calling, asking what it would take to get rid of us. I was active in the '60s, and compared to those times, this action was a tea party, but for them, they'd never seen anything like this before and didn't want to see it again.

"They didn't agree to card check, but they did agree to something called 'super-neutrality.' Under this agreement, every time the employer held a meeting, the union was invited to the same meeting." This gave the union access to workers so they could challenge misleading statements made by the boss, and it showed workers that solidarity was strong enough to force the boss's hand even before the union had won. "The union and the workers won the victory," says Cagan, "but we made it possible by changing the environment and showing we don't have to play by the same rules."

Because JwJ is a coalition of community and labor leaders, it can put pressure on companies or individuals that rely on maintaining a good public image. That was crucial at Cleveland Stadium. In addition, JwJ wouldn't take "no" for an answer. This combination—the right strategy and a willingness to use aggressive tactics if necessary—won the day.

Winning Ordinances and Electoral Initiatives

South Florida JwJ was created out of the labor and community upsurge against Governor Jeb Bush's "One Florida Initiative," which would have ended affirmative action in state government and colleges. (For more on this campaign, see Chapter 5.)

"In my opinion, the way for labor to start growing again is to start working with the JwJ model," says Dorothy Townsend, a former AFSCME shop steward and later director of South Florida JwJ. "We have clergy, labor, white, black, Haitians, Jamaicans, Chinese, Latinos, and it's one big family. If organized labor doesn't catch on to this model, we're going to continue to lose. The reason we have been so successful here is because of who is at the table. People take ownership of what's going on. That alliance has to exist, people have to feel it."

Perhaps because of its membership, South Florida JwJ has focused on issues not just of interest to union members but to all working people, including the poor. We focus here on the chapter's involvement in three electoral victories. South Florida's Miami is the poorest large city in the country, with a poverty rate of nearly 29 percent. JwJ came up with some innovative tactics in three related campaigns to combat poverty: living wage, better mass transit, and smaller class sizes in area schools.

The first campaign was to win a living wage ordinance in Miami-Dade County. Says Townsend, "We had to start from zero because there was a new mayor who didn't know anything about the living wage. On Christmas Eve of 2001, we held an all-night vigil, spending the night with the homeless to begin publicizing the need for a living wage. We followed this with a 2,000-person Poor People's March the following month.

"Our support and visibility grew with each event. Our first Workers' Rights Board hearing, titled 'Organizing Out of Poverty,' was a huge success partly because Danny Glover agreed to sit on the WRB. This showed us that celebrity support goes a long way to attracting media attention. After these months of educational and organizing work, the mayor became a supporter of the ordinance, and it soon passed." The chapter then helped another county to pass an ordinance and started work on a third.

South Florida JwJ also understood that mass transportation was needed to take workers to jobs. Transit, seen in this way, is a poverty issue. A proposal to increase bus and metro service by adding a half-cent to the sales tax had been defeated twice, and JwJ decided to gather support for the issue's third appearance on the ballot in November 2002.

JwJ's third front in its anti-poverty war was the Smaller Class Size Initiative to amend the state constitution. With a coalition of groups across the state, JwJ gathered thousands of signatures at worksites, community meetings, schools, graduations, hospitals, shows, and concerts. JwJ also organized phonebanking parties every Wednesday where its members made thousands of calls to encourage voters to vote for the amendment.

But Florida is not known for clean elections. Thousands of voters, especially African Americans, were systematically disenfranchised in 2000 and 2002. To protect voters this time, the community won a historic two-week early voting period. JwJ took advantage of this voting period to lead a mobilization on behalf of mass transit and class size.

The voter drive included a town hall meeting at Antioch Baptist Church to educate the community and encourage people to vote early. JwJ also turned out over 50 students for a "Democracy Enforcers" Training where the U.S. Student Association, Black Youth Vote, and People for the American Way trained students to be election monitors. The highlight of the campaign was the hugely successful Early Vote Rally on October 26, led by South Florida JwJ.

"Before election day, over 100,000 people had already voted," says Townsend. "The transit initiative passed in every one of the 720 precincts in the county. The victory immediately doubled the bus fleet and will add seven metro rail lines over the next decade. It will also create over 2,000 full-time union jobs in South Florida." With the help of South Florida's votes, Florida voters also amended the constitution to limit class sizes.

South Florida Jobs with Justice asked actor and activist Danny Glover to sit on their Workers' Rights Board and participate in a day-long mobilization.

Building a Solid JwJ Chapter

Starting a chapter: The Jobs with Justice national office provides local coalition starter kits, which include information on the history of JwJ, how to build a coalition, and descriptions of common chapter work. Fred Azcarate says, "We have a field team that works with local coalitions, especially newer coalitions, to help them with their local strategy. I wouldn't tell people how to carry out local campaigns, but we might have some good questions to help them think it through."

To be recognized as an official chapter, you must: support JwJ principles; have the support of at least 10 local member organizations, including five unions and five community groups; have 100 signed pledge cards (see below); adopt bylaws and have a clear decision-making process; and participate in the annual JwJ meeting, the national days of action, and other national activities (when possible).

JwJ regional and national campaigns—which have included health care, fair trade, welfare reform, and the right to organize—create opportunities for local chapters (especially new chapters) to quickly plug into an organizing issue. Each year there is a national student-labor week of action between Cesar Chavez's birthday and the anniversary of the assassination of Dr. Martin Luther King, Jr. Resources for these campaigns, from information to leaflets to full-blown organizing kits, are on the website, www.jwj.org.

Building individual participation: JwJ can help individuals learn the nuts and bolts of organizing and can give union members as well as non-union activists a chance to see what the labor movement can be like when it's a *movement*.

Al Cholger, an international representative with PACE in the Detroit area, says, "I have been using Jobs with Justice really as a classroom for PACE members to experience rallying on behalf of other people. I took two members down to support locked-out tunnel workers in Detroit. They really got pumped up. As it turned out, AFSCME was demonstrating the same day against the City of Detroit, right down the street. Our PACE members got to see about 300 AFSCME workers march down from where they were picketing at the city building to support the tunnel workers. It was great for them to see solidarity come from an unexpected source. Two days later, there was a settlement. Our members were able to see the connection between getting people out and actually winning a struggle."

JwJ can also help rank-and-file members build leadership and organizing skills, if such learning is planned for. When chapters encourage less experienced members to learn tasks such as creating newsletters and leaflets, speaking at meetings, or doing corporate research, they not only help JwJ but also put these member-activists in a position to win leadership positions in their own locals.

The JwJ affiliate in Vermont, for example, the Vermont Workers Center, organized support for local GCIU and IBEW contract campaigns. Leaders of those locals became JwJ activists, and then, in 2003, won positions as president and vice-president of the Vermont State Labor Council, advocating JwJ-style tactics statewide.

Portland JwJ uses the pledge cards created by national JwJ to track and organize the group's activists. Signers of these cards promise to come out at least five times a year "for someone else's fight, as well as my own. If enough of us are there, we'll all start winning."

"Anytime we do anything," says Margaret Butler, "we ask people who come to sign the pledge cards. We then put the names in our database and immediately send anyone new a JwJ welcome letter. We use the database to send out postcard announcements to everyone for any major actions (about one per month). We have also organized a system of 'phone tree stewards.' Each steward is given eight to ten pledgers, and stewards call their list to give a further reminder of any mobilizations."

Building group participation: The best way to demonstrate the benefits of JwJ to unions and other groups is to offer support to their struggles. When you first approach a group that needs help, offer your support first and your advice later. Gradually, you will find ways to provide ideas where they are needed. James Haslam of the Vermont Workers Center says, "We offered to help a group of AFSCME mental health workers with their contract campaign. The AFSCME members were a bit tentative about us at first, but we showed up regularly at their strategy meetings, and when their committee members heard our suggestions, they often took them. Now a number of their members are coming out in support of another of our campaigns in Montpelier."

Once you have demonstrated your solidarity for unions or community groups, let them know that their help is needed by others. Ask them to affiliate with the chapter and appoint JwJ delegates who will give regular reports to their membership.

You don't have to wait for groups to come to you, of course. JwJ speakers should schedule visits to community groups and union meetings to ask for support for campaigns. Rather than spending much time on the history or structure of JwJ, focus on how they can plug into current campaigns.

Make sure that individual activists in JwJ are reporting back to their groups or locals, whether or not their group or union is formally affiliated. You might want to publish monthly "JwJ talking points" to help activists remember all of the important work. These speaking opportunities are chances for your activists to further develop their skills. To help individuals win a JwJ affiliation from their organizations, help them develop a strategy for bringing a motion before the executive board, the membership, or whichever body makes sense.

Ensuring community involvement: Jacob Carton, an organizer for Washington State JwJ, describes the task of balancing labor and community issues in their chapter: "We don't want it to be a one-dimensional, labor-dominated coalition. In the end it's a workers' rights coalition, so we're going to find the greatest interest among labor organizations, but we very much want to focus on balancing it with community groups, faith-based organizations, and youth. The challenge is not just to balance them, but to tie them together."

One way to ensure shared leadership from community groups is to formally build it into the chapter's structure. Cagan of Cleveland JwJ says, "We have one more level of structure [besides the steering committee and working groups], and that's our executive committee. It meets monthly and is a more hands-on, agile group than the steering committee. One of its tasks is to prepare proposals for the steering committee. The executive committee is made up of all current officers, a representative of each working group, and a couple of at-large people elected from the steering committee.

"The purpose of the at-large members is to give us a mechanism to maintain racial, gender, and community diversity at the executive committee level. We have three co-chairs and a treasurer, for a total of four officers. Of the three co-chairs, one must be from labor, one from a religious organization, and one from a community organization. In addition, at least two of the four officers have to be people of color and at least two have to be women. With this structure, we ensure that our labor, religious, and community constituencies are represented in decision-making."

Building your reputation: In a workplace with a union that aggressively organizes around grievances, management will learn to check itself before doing something unfair. The same can be true for a JwJ chapter at the city level, once you have built your reputation as effective troublemakers. Before a mayor, factory boss, or developer does something stupid, you want them to say to themselves, "Ugh, those damn JwJ types are going to be out here yelling if I do this."

In order to maintain a reputation for consistent, fierce organizing, avoid giving empty endorsements. You want a commitment by JwJ to mean something.

Challenges and Limits of JwJ

In most places, JwJ chapters, AFL-CIO unions, and independent unions all work closely together. In other areas, union officials have been hostile to the idea of an independent activist organization, or have said JwJ is not needed because the labor council is the proper vehicle to mobilize workers and community support. But community activists and other non-union workers do not have a voice in labor councils. A true labor-community alliance is built when both groups share decision-making and responsibility. If a labor council is threatened by a JwJ chapter, it may be that JwJ is especially needed.

Sometimes JwJ chapters are approached by workers who are unhappy with their own local unions. It gets more complicated if the local in question belongs to JwJ. Chapters usually decide, rightly or wrongly, that preserving the coalition comes first. They don't criticize union officials, take sides in a union election, or blast a concession-filled contract. "Portland JwJ," says Margaret Butler, "has a policy that we do not get involved in internal union disputes, or in staffer organizing drives within our member organizations. One of the criteria we ask ourselves before participating in a campaign is 'Will this build JwJ?' Internal union disputes and disputes within our member organizations don't help us build our coalition."

Such a policy may be frustrating to rank and filers—perhaps dedicated JwJ activists themselves—who want JwJ to take up the "justice" of their cause. In practice, even if they wanted to, JwJ chapters have limited ability to impact the internal workings of locals, although JwJ may be a great place for reformers from different unions to meet each other and exchange ideas. In most cases, JwJ as an organization will best lead by example, demonstrating how militant organizing and democratic decision-making can work. And it can help educate activists so that they can go on to run for office and become leaders of their locals.

Coalition work is hard. Activists who think they "get it" can become frustrated when more conservative or newer activists have different ideas. It is important to meet your fellow coalition members where they are while still pushing against the status quo in your community. Beware of pushing for militant tactics (such as civil disobedience) without having first built a foundation among your coalition members through a history of good organizing. If you ignore this advice, you could find that your coalition shrinks rapidly.

For example, there was debate within and between JwJ chapters about whether JwJ should take a position against the wars in Afghanistan and Iraq. Some activists argued that taking a position would be divisive; there was concern that an anti-war stance would drive away some members or potential members and thus waste the opportunities for organizing in support of JwJ's other goals. Some chapters explored ways to agree to disagree but still allow for discussion. Several chapters held public forums on the subject, and others promoted meetings of union members who were military veterans to discuss the war issue.

Other activists argued that because workers are so negatively affected by a war climate, JwJ should take an explicit stance against the current war. Leaders of Washington State JwJ argued, "We must view the right to organize, global justice, budget crises, health care, and other issues affecting working people in the context of ongoing war. We [Washington State JwJ] recognized that militarization leads to attacks on civil liberties and workers' rights, and to increased hostility to immigrants."[1] Steering committee member Paul Bigman reports that their chapter's overtly anti-war stance led to increases in member and financial support. Nationally, JwJ took no position, leaving local chapters to decide what best fit their circumstances.

You can read more about actions by local JwJ chapters throughout this book. See in particular the story "Secondary Boycott, Sort Of," in Chapter 14.

Blue and Green: Labor-Environmental Alliances

OVER THE LAST DECADE labor and environmental groups have found ways to work together at the local level to battle corporations that abuse workers and the environment. While there have been victories, the movement is still young and faces many challenges. Activists continue to look for useful ways to build what the Alliance for Sustainable Jobs and the Environment (ASJE) calls a future "where nature is protected, the worker is respected, and unrestrained corporate power is rejected." In this section we share some lessons learned by the Steelworkers union and by ASJE.

Labor and environmental groups have not had a cooperative history. A decade ago and earlier, they often saw each other as enemies. Corporations had a lot to gain from this tension and used propaganda to distort the intentions of environmental activists, workers, and rural communities. Some early environmentalists argued that they needed to organize alongside workers, but as Kim Marks of Earth First! remembers, "When I was young I thought it was insane to build alliances with these people [loggers and rural community members]. Some people who lived in rural areas, because of the corporate propaganda, were so upset they seemed to want to kill us. While this was mostly people from the towns, loggers did get very upset sometimes. We have a history of not getting along."

Marks was involved in a coalition against Maxxam, Inc. and its notorious anti-worker and anti-environmental practices.

Shared Foe

In the late 1990s the Steelworkers were in difficult negotiations with Kaiser Aluminum, which is owned by Maxxam. Instead of getting provoked into a strike, which they believed the company wanted, over 3,000 Steelworkers in aluminum plants in Washington, Ohio, and Louisiana agreed to continue working under the old contract once it expired. The company had other ideas, and locked the workers out in January 1999. Once the lockout began, the Steelworkers realized they had better look for allies.

The union researched Maxxam and learned that members had something in common with Earth First! activists who were fighting the aggressive logging of redwoods by the Pacific Lumber Co. PL had also been purchased recently by Maxxam, and the company had enraged environmentalists by tripling the previous logging rate of northern California redwoods. The logging created short-term jobs, but PL eventually laid off many of its workers in favor of contract labor. PL's logging practices in old-growth forests endangered area homes with potential floods and landslides on steep, unstable slopes. Steelworkers and Earth First! had a shared foe in Maxxam and its CEO, Charlie Hurwitz.

According to Kim Marks, "We said to the Steelworkers that we can help you. We're good at shutting things down and getting media. As our first action together we blocked one of Maxxam's ore ships by taking over the cranes and a conveyor belt. We draped a huge banner across the crane to bait Hurwitz. It said 'Charlie cuts jobs like he cuts the forest.' We blocked that ship for the remainder of the day, and later went back to the USWA hall to grill hot dogs, tofu dogs, and have a party."

Environmental activists continued their support for the Steelworkers by appearing at Kaiser picket lines in Spokane and Tacoma. "We learned from the workers that you had to keep moving on a picket line. We were used to sitting down and blocking entrances," says Marks. "We often brought music to the picket line—banjos or guitars. We also made it more likely that media would show up because our support for the workers was new and different."

Steelworkers returned the solidarity in California, where environmentalists were battling Pacific Lumber. Steelworker activists went to Humboldt County and picketed PL for its unsustainable logging and to reach out to PL's non-union workers. And despite having no members anywhere near Humboldt County, the Steelworkers opened a "Road Warriors" office there to maintain a presence in the community.

Gradually, the Steelworkers and environmental activists began to coordinate their actions more explicitly. The two joined in impressive demonstrations at Maxxam shareholder meetings in Houston in 1999 and 2000. The two also filed separate lawsuits against PL in California. The environmentalists' lawsuit focused on PL's unsustainable logging, while the Steelworkers focused on the economic impacts. Because PL would cut too many trees in the short term and deplete the forest long-term, the short-term boost to jobs would be offset by long-term job losses for the region.

Alliance for Sustainable Jobs and the Environment

A bond developed between the unionists and environmentalists who came together to fight Maxxam. Guided by David Foster, director of Steelworkers District 11, and David Brower, founder of Friends of the Earth, a new group was founded, the Alliance for Sustainable Jobs and the Environment.

ASJE quickly grew beyond the original anti-Maxxam coalition. A board composed equally of environmental and labor activists was elected at the first annual meeting in 1998, and 250 members (both organizational and individual) joined in the first year. ASJE first gained national attention with its appearance at the Seattle protests against the WTO in 1999. Bill Carey, now ASJE labor co-chair and a staff rep for the Steelworkers in Illinois and Indiana, says, "The Pacific Lumber coalition rolled in to the WTO protests, and that was where I first ran into students and environmentalists who were working on labor issues. The first question I asked was, 'Are any of you in Chicago?'"

ASJE has built a loose structure of local chapters. Most activity thus far is in the West and Midwest and revolves around four areas of work:

• Restoration—Restoring nature, especially the woods, in a way that maintains long-term jobs

• Energy—Moving to an economy more based on sustainable energy, in a way that does not put the pain of that transition on workers

• Rogue corporations—Mobilizing against corporations that are beating up on the environment, on workers, or on both

• Globalization—Educating and mobilizing citizens against the threats of "free trade."

The March to Miami

ASJE activists have been part of dozens of labor/environmental campaigns, but none was larger than the November 2003 March to Miami. Protests were planned there against the Free Trade Agreement of the Americas (FTAA), a NAFTA-like free trade agreement that would encourage investment abroad to the detriment of workers and the environment. As at the Seattle WTO meeting in 1999 and the FTAA meeting in Quebec in 2001, the FTAA delegates in Miami were surrounded by protesters from a huge array of groups, including the AFL-CIO. ASJE activists wanted to be a part of these protests and to make a connection between the Seattle protests (where the "Teamsters and Turtles" slogan originated) and Miami, so they decided to organize a bus tour between the two cities.

At the St. Louis stop on the March-to-Miami tour, ASJE members rallied with members of Steelworkers Local 9014.

ASJE raised $18,000 from local unions, member organizations, and individuals, then bought an old bus and painted it blue-green. Gas money was raised by passing the hat at each event along the way. The goal was to have discussions about the impact of globalization in local communities along the route. The route was organized to pass through ASJE chapter areas, but also through areas where new alliances could be built. The entire tour lasted seven weeks and included events in 24 cities.

Dan Leahy, executive director of ASJE, was on the bus. "The basic program we gave on the FTAA included literature, a skit, and some songs," he says. [See the "FTAA No Way" song on the Troublemaker's website.] "We were almost a troupe. For those who didn't know about the FTAA itself, we could quickly explain that the FTAA was NAFTA in 30 more countries. They tended to see it as corporations messing around with everybody, and not country versus country. That's good, because racist stuff wasn't evident.

"Generally, we tried to organize an educational event and a rally at each stop along the way. We managed to link up with a huge array of struggles.

• "In Bismarck, North Dakota, we rallied with farmers against multinational corporations who dump foodstuffs in order to drive small ranchers and farmers out of business.

• "In Chicago, we rallied in front of what used to be the Brach's candy factory that employed 6,000 workers. It moved to Mexico, and Wal-Mart is coming in. We were joined by the South Austin Community Coalition, the Teamsters, the Coalition Against the Homeless, SEIU, UNITE, and others.

• "In St. Louis, we held a teach-in on trade co-sponsored by Teamsters in their hall. The next day, ASJE joined Jobs with Justice, Steelworkers, and environmentalists in a march to four sites to highlight the problems with trade agreements.

"What interested me," says Leahy, "were the intense feelings of isolation that local groups had. A bus coming through on something called the March to Miami helped to 'nationalize' their local work. We were going to take their struggles with us to Miami. That old bus helped to break workers' isolation."

Fight for Clean Water

In Ohio and Pennsylvania the Steelworkers and several environmental groups joined forces to protect worker rights and the health of local communities.

AK Steel locked out the 600 workers in its Mansfield, Ohio plant in 1999. Mike Zielinski from the Steelworkers' Office of Strategic Campaigns says, "As we were gearing up our corporate campaign, the story broke regarding AK Steel and the town of Zelienople, Pennsylvania." Zelienople was downstream from the company's Butler plant, and residents were endangered by AK's discharges in Connoquenessing Creek. AK had more than tripled its discharges since 1995, dangerously increasing the amount of nitrates in the water. According to the Environmental Protection Agency, drinking water with high concentrations of nitrates can cause serious illness and death in infants from "blue baby syndrome." Nitrate levels in Connoquenessing Creek had been measured between 10 and 17 times as large as the EPA's safe water limits.

"Clean Water Action (CWA) was already there, had been canvassing, and had built a local organization," Zielinski says. "We contacted them. They were receptive to us right away. Town officials were less certain they

When 600 steelworkers were locked out by AK Steel in Mansfield, Ohio, they joined with Clean Water Action to fight pollution the company was dumping into streams around its plants. During the campaign, "our own members learned a great deal about environmental issues," said Steelworkers rep Mike Zielinski. "Their consciousness was definitely raised."

wanted to get into the middle of a labor dispute. Part of their hesitance probably came from the company propaganda that was all over the region. The company had filmed some picket line violence from the opening days of the lockout and were using that to portray us as thugs in the media. AK even bought a commercial spot during the Super Bowl.

"We developed our relationship with Clean Water Action and with the residents of Zelienople by showing that we cared what happened in their town. One of our first actions was to raise money for a caravan of bottled water from Mansfield. Later, there was a town-wide meeting to discuss the water issue. AK Steel didn't bother to send a representative to hear the residents' concerns, or to offer an explanation for why they were refusing to abide by an EPA order to reduce their discharges and provide an alternative water source. We, on the other hand, listened to them. We also brought 15 locked-out members from our local to talk about *their* experience with AK Steel. After that meeting, town officials saw that we had a lot of knowledge and experience with the company. Trust was building.

"Along with Clean Water Action, we held a press conference and rallied at the State Capitol offices. At the University of Pittsburgh, we joined with environmental groups, student groups, and Jobs with Justice to rally outside the building where AK was receiving an award as employer of the year. We gave AK Steel our own award—Inhumane Employer of the Year."

More Filth, More Organizing

As the campaign on behalf of the residents of Zelienople continued, the Steelworkers found another outrageous blot on AK Steel's environmental record, this time in Middletown, Ohio. The company's flagship plant was located alongside a creek that passed by an elementary school where the EPA had discovered high levels of PCBs. The EPA filed suit, but the company denied any involvement or responsibility. Zielinski notes, "Ohio Citizen Action and the Cincinnati branch of the Sierra Club had publicized the case, so we met with them to coordinate some actions.

"We testified together at permit hearings, highlighting AK's environmental record. The Sierra Club came to Mansfield and trained our local's members to take and monitor our own water samples. We also did some door-knocking in the poor neighborhood around the Mansfield plant to try and identify health problems that might be linked to AK. Citizen Action launched its own AK campaign, literally knocking on 100,000 doors to generate thousands of personal letters challenging AK Steel's policies.

"We even went to Delaware to spoil their shareholder meeting by delivering emissions dust we scraped off of workers' cars and homes near the plants. At our press conference, we used a magnet to show how metallic the dust was. We also took a bottle of water from the Middletown creek, listed the potential toxins on the side, and challenged the CEO to take a sip.

"Everyone gained," says Zielinski. "The lockout ended in December 2002, though it took almost a year for all of our members to get back into the plant. In September of 2003, the CEO and president were forced out by the board of directors. There is no question that a lot of the issues raised by the union, including AK's confrontational negotiating stance and their environmental record, led to the change.

"The new CEO has done an about-face in terms of reaching out to the union and the communities. He actually sat down with Ohio Citizen Action and has communicated directly with the Sierra Club. AK agreed to build a fence around the creek in Middletown to keep any schoolchildren out of the area. They agreed to pay for a water purification system for the town of Zelienople, and to technological changes that would limit emissions into the water supply. Our own members learned a great deal about environmental issues. Their consciousness was definitely raised."

Tips and Challenges in Building Labor-Environmental Coalitions

Finding common ground: "I think organizing around trade is the easiest," says Bill Carey of the Steelworkers and ASJE. "It is not hard to find common ground. It is when you get into energy that things are more difficult—burning or not burning coal. Let's not talk about those things yet, if there are other areas we agree on." Mike Zielinski has similar advice: "Be honest about any differences you have as organizations, and be up-front about the commitment you are making. You may or may not be talking about long-term alliances. Our track record in communicating our goals isn't perfect. We can improve on that."

The most difficult issue for labor and environmental groups has been the question of jobs. Bill Carey notes, "Environmentalists sometimes think that all you have to do is talk about jobs, and unions will be happy. 'Our solar project will mean this many jobs, so don't worry about no more power plants.' That shows a real lack of understanding about organizing difficulties and union density. Environmentalists also sometimes believe that efficiency translates into better wages. It doesn't. Better wages come from more power. There is still a gap there."

Cultural and other differences: While they have been exaggerated at times, there are cultural, class, and organizational differences between the labor and environmental movements. Being sensitive to those differences helps. Barbara Dudley, formerly of Greenpeace, suggests, "Pulling off a successful meeting between union members and environmentalists can be tricky. Union members: if you are inviting environmentalists to your home, don't only serve lunchmeats and Styrofoam. Environmentalists: don't get so uptight over lunchmeats and Styrofoam. Also, don't make union members eat out of used yogurt dishes on their first visit to your house.

"Be aware of the different organizational cultures in the two movements. The labor movement tends to be very hierarchical and disciplined. A shop steward cannot go to a meeting and commit his organization to join a coalition without talking to the executive board. Environmental organizations, by contrast, can almost be anarchists in that they often believe in consensus decision-making,

"Be aware that even though unions are in conflict with a company, they do not want to put that company out of business. They want to make the best deal possible with that company. Environmentalists, on the other hand, would maybe prefer putting a company out of business if it is resource-extracting or poisonous. This is still a fundamental difference."

Thinking long term: Dan Leahy comments on the promise and challenges of the local coalitions visited by the March to Miami: "A lot of alliances I saw were broader than they would have been in the past. At most events, there was a range of speakers— a labor person, an environmental person, etc. Still, the groups need to move past supporting one another at rallies to organizing together in strategic, long-term ways."

Barbara Dudley believes it is easier to form alliances on a local level than nationally. "Trusting relationships are definitely being built between groups, because we work together in the same community and see the immediacy of the alliance." Dudley was a member of the Blue-Green Working Group, an alliance of national unions and environmentalists that was trying to address climate change in the early years of John Sweeney's leadership of the AFL-CIO. She says, "We were talking with national unions for the first time about what it would take to move the country towards renewable energy. We discussed scenarios where workers in affected industries would be protected by something similar to the GI Bill. We also worked on creative ways to reduce global emissions.

"Working against us was the incredible pressure on unions to stem the huge membership losses they were facing. Once the economic downturn after 9/11 set it, job losses mounted and unions were even more focused on the members they had. Ultimately, we must stop acting on an emergency basis, and instead do the necessary planning for our long-term futures."

Building Labor-Religious Coalitions

by Nick Robinson

KIM BOBO, executive director of the National Interfaith Committee for Worker Justice, knows the pitfalls and rewards of coalition-building. One of her pet peeves is a phenomenon she calls "Dial-a-Collar." Bobo says, "The labor folks would call the religious folks at the last moment and say, 'Will you come offer a prayer at the picket line?' They viewed that as having the religious community involved. The religious community will often go and do that, but that is not real involvement." The National Interfaith Committee is a network of over 60 local committees that organizes the religious community to form lasting coalitions with workers and their organizations.

"Religious folks want to be partners with labor," says Bobo, "but they don't want to be handmaidens of labor. We all want to work on things that reflect the values we both share. Some in the labor community don't really understand that for a lot of people in the faith community, doing this work to support workers is what their faith is all about. It is who they are to want to do this work. It is not that the religious folks are doing the labor folks a favor, or that there has to be a quid pro quo, or that the labor folks trick the religious folks into this. Justice, fighting poverty, human dignity—these are joint

Religious folks want to be partners with labor, but they don't want to be handmaidens of labor.

goals, not just labor goals."

Katherine Bissell, director of the Chicago Interfaith Committee on Worker Issues, says that when unions change their priorities toward working with the lowest-paid workers, "this brings religious groups into the mix." The Committee runs a workers center for the Latino and Polish immigrant communities and a program for minorities in the building trades, and is looking into starting a worker-owned day-laborer hiring hall. These difficult-to-organize constituencies have often been ignored by organized labor but embraced by religious groups.

"To be honest, when we started our group in 1991," says Bissell, "the unions said, 'Who are these crazy people?' Today we're helping to build connections between unorganized workers and unions interested in organizing them. The unions we work with most are the ones who are organizing low-wage workers, women, and immigrants."

Both Bissell and Bobo have experienced what Bobo describes as a "tension that unions face between representing their members and representing the broad class of workers." She says, "Take the issue of raising the minimum wage. The religious community is deeply committed to that, across all religions and denominations. It's a no-brainer for them. Some of our labor people have said, 'Why should we be working on the minimum wage? How does that affect our members?' I think the religious community often pushes the labor community to think beyond just their members."

Strong religious-labor coalitions can lead to stronger organizing campaigns because they can allow unions to reach hesitant workers in a way that puts the workers at ease. (See "To Organize a Union, Organize the Community," in Chapter 16.) As Jennifer Barger, religious outreach programs coordinator for the Chicago Interfaith Committee, puts it, "Religious groups can play a strong role in translating these struggles in communities. Also, the religious community is often uncomfortable with the level of conflict in labor struggles, so we can be predisposed to play a mediator role and encourage dialogue. Mediation gives the employer space to save face and look like they're doing the right thing."

Faith and Hotel Workers in Chicago

The relationship between the Chicago Interfaith Committee and HERE Local 1 illustrates the potential for these kinds of alliances. Both the Committee and Local 1 have evolved dramatically since 1991, when their relationship began with a drive to organize airport concessions workers.

The Chicago group was the first local labor-

Bargaining in Church[2]

The Stamford Organizing Project in Stamford, Connecticut is a joint endeavor among four unions that represent workers in low-paying service-sector jobs, mostly women and almost all African Americans. They are nursing home workers in District 1199 New England (SEIU), childcare and municipal workers in UAW Region 9A, janitors in SEIU 531, and hotel workers in HERE 217. Instituted by the AFL-CIO, the project has had notable success in community organizing to win affordable housing.

Ever since staff organizers began talking with workers, they have asked about workers' community connections—whether they belong to a church, what community organizations they belong to, if they are married, where their spouse works, whether he or she is a union member, and whether the member is registered to vote and actually does so. All that information is put into a database, making it possible to determine how many union members live in a particular housing project or neighborhood and how many attend each church. The unions can then determine which neighborhoods or churches or community groups they have a presence in. The project quickly learned that by far the most important community connections were with churches.

So the unions have brought together groups of workers by church for discussion and training. First, the group talks about workers' need for allies to increase their power in general, and then more specifically about a local labor issue. The emphasis is on parishioners' and workers' personal stories and how the issues play out in their lives. Next, the group agrees on what it will ask their own pastor to do, and prepares for the meeting with one-on-one role-playing. The workers then arrange a group meeting with their pastor and three to 15 workers.

As a result of this intensively personal yet collective organizing, clergy have become involved with the unions' campaigns, both on the job and in the community. For example, the four unions have begun holding their contract negotiations in churches. Why not? Negotiations are, after all, typically held at a "neutral" site. But neutral for whom? Most are held in a businesslike setting like a hotel conference room, where managers are at home and workers are less comfortable. A black church is a setting where these workers feel at home and the (usually white) managers can feel uncomfortable.

Frequently, the minister comes at the beginning of negotiations to offer a prayer, expressing hope that everyone involved will do the right thing. You would hate to be the public relations manager for a company that refused to negotiate in a church, but the setting almost invariably alters the "balance of comfort" and hence, power, at least marginally.

interfaith committee, formed in 1991 by a core group of activist clergy. The group, including Bobo, approached an enthusiastic Don Turner, then president of the Chicago Federation of Labor (CFL). When Bobo talked with other religious leaders, she says, "It was not hard to get them involved. They just had never been asked to help by the labor folks."

The coalition had some growing pains. After the Interfaith Committee supported the airport concessions workers with prayer vigils and rallies, the CFL invited religious groups to participate in the Labor Day parade next to HERE Local 1's float. The float promoted casino development, while the United Methodist bishop, who was standing next to HERE leaders on the platform, had led the opposition to casinos.

"Folks just have to agree to disagree on certain things," says Bobo. "HERE wasn't going to change its position. And the Methodists weren't going to change theirs. The Catholic Church is not going to change its position of supporting vouchers for private schools, and the teachers union will not support vouchers. But you find what you can agree on and work on that, and leave the other stuff behind."

By 2001, Local 1 had made a major shift—from tactical to strategic, in Bobo's words—in how it conducted its coalition work. The HERE International had ousted old local leaders, citing Mafia ties and corruption, and the local needed to prepare for master contract negotiations with over 30 downtown hotels. New President Harry Tamarin believed that starting early was the key, and Local 1 began preparing over a year in advance of the August 31, 2002 expiration. HERE organizers developed committees with the goal of one representative for every ten workers.

"It started with agitation," says Local 1 Research Director Lars Negstad, an architect of the campaign. "People knew they were getting screwed, but they didn't know how badly until we put together some materials on a map, where we pulled out wage examples from San Francisco, New York, and Los Angeles." Chicago's hotel dishwashers and room attendants earned under $9 per hour, less than half their counterparts' wages in New York. Members wore buttons that said "I ♥ New York Pay," one of the campaign's key themes.

Local 1 approached area religious leaders in January 2002 to determine how to build a community base to support a potentially massive strike. These joint brainstorming sessions led to a survey, at the Interfaith Committee's suggestion. The survey asked members for their priorities in the contract, and also what church or community organizations they belonged to. Local 1 developed a database of members' personal information, including over 250 religious institutions to which they belonged.

The Interfaith Committee then trained a hundred-person religious outreach committee, composed of union members working with the Committee, to reach out to the churches that workers attended.

"We had a few good activist clergy, but this was a good way to get new clergy involved, when their members were involved in the struggle," says Bissell. Negstad agrees. "We wanted to avoid the 'rent-a-collar' mentality and develop relationships with allies beyond the small group of usual suspects. Workers have multiple identities—we all do—as churchgoers and as residents in the community. If there is a powerful minister we want to support our cause, and if we can get a number of members of his church to ask him to sit down and talk, he's much more likely to give his support."

The coalition was also an effective way to empower church members within the union. In February, Interfaith Committee members held trainings that included member-activists whose faith was an important part of their lives. "Probably 30 people came to the meeting, and we followed up by planning outreach to get their clergy involved," says Barger. "It didn't occur to these workers that they could ask their clergy to support the campaign.

The Bitter and the Sweet[3]

After forming in 1997 during a successful living wage campaign, Clergy and Laity United for Economic Justice has grown to over 400 religious leaders in Los Angeles County.

In April 2001, CLUE's annual worker rights procession used religious symbolism to support workers organizing at the Loews Santa Monica Beach Hotel. The 300 Loews workers faced intimidation and mandatory coercive meetings during management's harsh anti-union campaign. The nearby Pacific Shore Hotel, in contrast, had become unionized through card check neutrality in 2000.

The 500-person march, including 70 clergy in religious regalia, began at City Hall, where participants were given plastic bags of traditional Passover items: unleavened bread (matzo), bitterroot, and parsley. Blocking rush hour traffic for over half an hour, the marchers stopped to recognize several sites of recent labor struggles.

At the first stop, the crowd held out their matzo and sang as SEIU members performed street theater about conditions in local nursing homes. They then marched to Loews, where the crowd held bitter herbs—the Passover symbol for slavery—towards management in their outstretched hands.

"As long as there is harassment by threat or innuendo, this hotel and places like it will be places of bitterness," said Rabbi Neil Comes-Daniels as he presented a piece of bitter herb to the hotel's head of security.

The march concluded at the Pacific Shore Hotel, where participants left parsley—a symbol of spring—and milk and honey—symbolizing the bounty of the promised land—to congratulate hotel workers for their victory.

In California's East Bay Area, Seminarians for Worker Justice supported low-paid workers at the Claremont Hotel. In Chicago in 2002, seminarians visited more than 100 congregations and collected commitments for eight tons of food to sustain the city's hotel workers in case they were forced to strike. "It made hotel management think, 'Whoa, they're serious about going on strike,'" said HERE Local 1 Research Director Lars Negstad.

A lot of them were the quiet ones at meetings, and they got excited when they could bring this important part of their life into the campaign."

Religious supporters organized marches and vigils, wore buttons that read "We love Chicago workers—they deserve more money," and obtained a letter of support from Chicago's Catholic cardinal.

HERE also received help from two seminary students who acted as full-time organizers for the campaign. The students were interns through a ten-week program, jointly sponsored by the AFL-CIO and the National Interfaith Committee, called Seminary Summer, a part of the Union Summer program.

"At the end of the summer, the seminarians came back and said, 'The unions are doing God's work, and we've got to work with them,'" says Bobo. In Chicago, where there are more seminaries than in any other city besides Rome, the Interfaith Committee created a group called Seminarians for Worker Justice. The seminarians visited over 100 congregations to obtain letters of support and to organize a "Hungry for Justice" campaign, collecting commitments for over eight tons of food and additional strike funds.

"The concept was, if there's a strike, we'd make sure they'd have enough food to eat," says Barger. "We wanted to give our congregations something concrete to do; who hasn't had a food drive in their congregation? It's something they already know how to do. It's key to find something that's within the context of the religious community and put it in the context of a labor struggle." The Interfaith Committee received reports that even the generally less supportive, wealthier congregations were bringing in carloads of food.

In mid-July, religious leaders spoke at a press conference to open the "Hungry for Justice" food warehouse donated by Teamsters Local 705. "It was symbolic," Negstad says. "It brought in member volunteers, a big organizing program, and a media component. It also made people feel invested in the fight. It made hotel management think, 'Whoa, they're serious about going on strike.' And when members look at a stack of cans of lima beans, they think, 'We're really serious about going on strike.'"

The members' readiness was demonstrated on August 12 with a 3,952-67 vote to strike. On August 23, thousands of workers and supporters, including a strong religious contingent, marched down Chicago's "Magnificent Mile" of extravagant hotels. The newly active members, many of whom had never participated in any union before, handed out leaflets to the public and demanded their rights on the job. After workers protested, an activist at one hotel got his job back with the help of a supportive priest.[4]

As it turned out, a strike became unnecessary. The 67-member negotiating committee accepted the hotels' offer, and members ratified it 892-153. The contract gave hotel attendants a $3.27 raise by the end of the four-year contract and dishwashers a $1.25 immediate raise. It also reduced health care costs from $85 to $30 a month by the end of the contract.

Local 1 and the Chicago Interfaith Committee have maintained a close relationship since the 2002 campaign. When management at the Congress Hotel refused to follow the pattern agreement and instead implemented wage cuts, workers struck in June 2003. The Interfaith Committee helped organize many vigils and marches in support, including a march based on the scripture passage about the Wall of Jericho. In the Bible, Joshua and the Israelites trusted God's instructions and marched around the city of Jericho seven times, having faith that Jericho would fall and that they would win justice. In July 2003, led by six clergy, supporters marched around the Congress Hotel seven times with trumpets resounding.

The two partners also worked together to sponsor the Chicago visit of the Immigrant Workers Freedom Ride in fall 2003. To read about the Interfaith Committee's work with immigrants and as a liaison between immigrant workers and unions, see Chapter 17.

Labor Fights for a Community Contract

by Steve Hinds and Rob Baril

HERE LOCALS 34 AND 35 represent clerical, technical, and maintenance workers at Yale University in New Haven, Connecticut. During a difficult contract campaign and strike in 1996, the unions won important support from community allies and political leaders. This labor-community alliance took a traditional form: unions asked for help and got some. After the strike, union leaders sat down to think about their future with Yale, the most anti-union campus in the country. In order to change the balance of power with Yale, they needed a better strategy.

The locals approached the New England Health Care Employees Union, District 1199 SEIU, with a proposition. If 1199 could organize workers at Yale-New Haven Hospital, the largest hospital in the state, the combined university/hospital memberships could leverage greater power against Yale. District 1199 already had a strong record of organizing nursing home workers across the state, and any serious organizing in the hospital industry meant organizing Yale-New Haven. A further incentive for 1199 was its desire to improve conditions for the members it already had at the hospital, 150 dietary workers with little power inside an enormously rich institution. District 1199 decided to join in this alliance, beginning its campaign to organize 1,800 blue-collar workers at the hospital.

The strategic alliance forged by 1199 and the HERE locals was unique because at this very early stage (years before the HERE contracts were due to expire), the group began building a broad-based community coalition to support worker rights. Instead of doing this work directly, the unions funded a new organization called the Connecticut Center for a New Economy. CCNE's mission was to provide organizing, leadership development, and research in support of issues affecting workers, people of color, and the poor in Connecticut's cities. CCNE would not be a simple union front but an independent organization that advanced demands from the grassroots of New Haven.

The unions and CCNE understood well the centrality of race in New Haven, where the majority of residents are people of color. CCNE's second hire was a prominent African American minister, and four of its seven staffers are people of color. After two years of organizing in New Haven, and especially in black and Latino churches, CCNE activists could speak of a black-brown alliance that held significant political and community power.

Community and Unions Develop Joint Demands on Yale

CCNE's early work consisted of small meetings with community and church groups across New Haven. At these meetings, District 1199 brought hospital workers to talk about what it was like to work at the hospital and support a family on $10 an hour without benefits. University workers spoke about meager pensions and low pay. The difference between these meetings and the more traditional labor-community work was that there was two-way dialogue. Community members had issues of their own: housing, education, jobs. CCNE activists found out early that community members did not want to be a part of something that only supported unions.

Community-based meetings continued for almost two years. By this time, the contract covering university employees was set to expire, and organizing at the hospital was heating up. It was time for a more public community campaign to begin. The unions had been flexible enough to incorporate social change demands raised by community leaders into their own demands. That meant that the unions' goals had grown beyond contracts and union organizing to include the community's goals. CCNE condensed the union and community demands into a unique document, a "Social Contract" with Yale. In addition to being a platform for organizing in the community, the Social Contract became HERE's central contract demands at the bargaining table.

Organizing around the Social Contract

Armed with a program for change, CCNE activists fanned out into the community once again to educate and mobilize support for the Social Contract. CCNE staff used a PowerPoint presentation to give a short history of the changing New Haven economy. New Haven had been a manufacturing city, but plant closings over the past two

HERE Locals 34 and 35, graduate student teachers, and hospital dietary workers—more than 5,000 workers—struck for five days. "Yale is too rich for the workers to be so poor," said the Rev. Jesse Jackson as he led a mile-long march.

decades had meant drastic change. Lower-paid, non-union service jobs in retail, education, and health care had replaced higher-wage factory jobs. Remarkably, one-quarter of the city's residents were now connected to Yale. CCNE's presentation also focused on how the Social Contract addressed some of the community's most pressing needs. This educational campaign was impressive—more than 100 meetings were held in church basements alone across the city.

If CCNE was going to build a community mobilization that went beyond a few rallies, community activists would need to be developed as leaders. CCNE began holding monthly strategy meetings, where they brought together impressive people they met in the smaller meetings around the city. At these events, CCNE asked for a higher level of commitment from the activists, but also looked for guidance on the direction of the campaign. As long as these meetings lasted, the Social Contract was more likely to belong to the community and not just to CCNE or the unions.

To begin to pressure Yale, massive community meetings, most in churches, were held in six New Haven neighborhoods. Clergy, workers, parents, kids, teachers, and others crowded into meetings where speeches, music, singing, and chants helped make the Social Contract feel like a movement for the first time. Each meeting culminated with everyone signing on to huge placards that displayed the Social Contract. This was an important early test for politicians and other community leaders; as the campaign gained momentum Yale had been trying to co-opt many community members.

Once the Social Contract had been endorsed by thousands at the community meetings, actions began. Large rallies and marches were held in support of the Social Contract at the hospital and in a "Community Revival" on the town green. CCNE activists appeared at city council and other hearings. The most impressive demonstration was a march and rally in Yale's backyard, where 750 were arrested for blocking traffic in an act of civil disobedience.

Ripple Effects

Organizing around the Social Contract had effects beyond its original scope. CCNE activists got to know a group of activists from the New Haven Federation of Teachers, AFT Local 933. These activists had formed a group inside their local called the Contract Organizing Group that was organizing to promote union democracy, union militancy, and good schools. COG challenged many of the ineffective, undemocratic, and corrupt practices of the local.

COG's survey of the membership in advance of contract negotiations showed that class-size reduction was one of the biggest issues for teachers. Until pressured by those results, union leaders were concerned only with wage increases. Because class size was also a focus of the Social Contract, COG was able to keep that issue alive throughout negotiations. COG brought teachers to CCNE meetings and events, where they talked with and listened to New Haven parents about problems in the schools. And CCNE lent COG legitimacy by bringing workers and parents to COG-planned contract rallies and urging Local 933 leaders to follow COG's organizing lead. The teachers' contract settlement ultimately did not reduce class size, but teachers were very positive about the changes in democracy and action that accompanied the campaign.

Meanwhile, at community events, CCNE was constantly looking for workers from the hospital or the university. CCNE activists found Yale connections were everywhere. Besides helping build an organizing committee at the hospital, another issue began to rise in these conversations: medical debt.

Yale-New Haven Hospital, like many hospitals, receives government funds to help cover the costs of caring for uninsured poor patients. Instead of telling patients about these funds, the hospital often adopted a "don't ask, don't tell" approach. Even though Yale-New Haven had $30 million in funds set aside for uninsured patients, sick patients were running up medical bills they could not hope to pay. Making things worse, Yale-New Haven charged an unusually high 10 percent interest rate on medical debts and would even place liens or foreclose on the homes of patients who were far behind in their payments. There were instances where Yale-New Haven employees themselves were in terrific debt to the hospital. For example, one nurse's aide earning $12 per hour

---

A Social Contract with Yale

- **Organizing Rights:** Yale must remain neutral in organizing campaigns by its employees, especially blue-collar workers at Yale-New Haven Hospital and graduate teachers at the university.
- **Access to Jobs:** Yale must end the historic under-representation of Latinos in its workforce and provide training opportunities so service workers can advance into higher-skill, higher-paid trades classifications.
- **Affordable Housing:** Yale must extend its program to subsidize home ownership for its employees to neglected areas of New Haven, especially Fair Haven, the most populous Latino neighborhood.
- **Education:** Yale's tax-exempt status on almost all of its property robs the city of important tax revenues. Like other universities with Yale's wealth (now over $10 billion), Yale must make voluntary yearly payments to the city to make up for this loss of revenue. These new funds would support class size reductions in public school grades K-3.
- **Good Contracts:** Yale must negotiate quality pensions, wage increases, and other benefits so that its employees are treated as if they worked at a world-class institution.

owed the hospital $40,000 in medical debt, resulting in Yale garnishing 25 percent of her wages and initiating foreclosure on her house.

Even though medical debt was not among the original Social Contract goals, the abuses deserved immediate action. Rallies, publicity, and hearings were held to question the debt practices. The organizing led to several victories. CCNE action called for and won state legislation that cut the maximum interest rate on medical debt from 10 percent to five percent. Foreclosures were banned, and regulations were set on liens. The hospital was shamed into forgiving the debts of dozens of patients and "voluntarily" altered its free-care policy.

Strike for the Social Contract

Despite the impressive organizing in New Haven churches, in council hearings, and in the streets, Yale was not budging in negotiations with Locals 34 and 35 and would not agree to neutrality for the organizing campaigns. In addition, there was no agreement on housing or hiring issues, and Yale's wage and pension proposals were far below workers' goals. Stronger tactics were needed.

During a frigid week in March 2003, the HERE locals, graduate student teachers, and the dietary workers at the hospital—more than 5,000 workers in all—held a five-day strike for the Social Contract. Pickets and rallies were held daily on contract issues, and the culminating community march of 10,000 was led by the Rev. Jesse Jackson. This was the largest rally in New Haven since the Black Panther trial of the early 1970s. At this point in the campaign, fence-sitting community leaders were forced to take a side. Yale continued its efforts to court and co-opt local leaders, including the Republican president of the New Haven NAACP, but in the end, it became politically impossible for many to take Yale's side. After sitting out years of community-based work, the NAACP president put himself at the front of the community march.

As negotiations continued through the summer, the unions built for an open-ended strike. That strike began in August, when Yale students returned for the fall semester. The Rev. Jackson played another active role in this strike, spending an entire week at CCNE events, with workers, and in a 24-hour sit-in with Yale retirees demanding pension improvements. After five weeks, progress was being made at the bargaining table for Locals 34 and 35 and for some elements of the Social Contract, but neutrality and an improved contract for dietary workers were not happening. The HERE locals made the difficult decision to settle.

The locals signed a contract with big gains in several areas. Perhaps the most significant was in pensions, scheduled to double by the contract's expiration in 2009. Wages rose an average of 30 to 40 percent over an eight-year period (six years from the settlement because of two years of retroactivity). The settlement also established a committee on Latino hiring and extended the home-buyer program to the targeted New Haven neighborhoods.

Challenges still lay ahead for CCNE and the unions. Hospital management continued to fight vigorously against a fair contract for dietary workers, not wanting to fuel 1199's organizing of the rest of the hospital, which continues. The settlement did not include neutrality for the organizing drives. One fear was that the eight-year agreement would make it difficult to maintain the energy that was built by the contract campaigns. And while the committee on Latino hiring was a step forward in access to jobs, the union did not win the training program it sought for service workers.

Lessons

The unions and CCNE learned the importance of:
- Strategic analysis—HERE's analysis of the need to build power at Yale led to creation of the alliance.
- Time to build—It took time and resources to build CCNE, precisely because CCNE carefully created a Social Contract that reflected the needs voiced by the community and not just the unions.
- Centrality of workers—The fact that workers themselves were speaking in their neighborhoods and at their churches was the reason the community linkages were so strong.
- Centrality of race—CCNE's work led to sincere dialogue between residents of different New Haven neighborhoods, and a new black-brown alliance emerged.
- Leadership development—The unions certainly provided leadership in CCNE's growth, but CCNE also spent time building the community's voice in the unfolding campaign. Once the activity level became furious, however, some of this leadership development work subsided. For a lasting labor-community coalition to emerge, leadership development cannot stop, even during busy organizing periods.
- Creating an organizing culture—The campaign for a Social Contract provided a model and support for other progressive labor organizing, particularly in the teachers' union.
- Social unionism—CCNE's collaboration with the community led to a struggle that went far beyond wage-and-benefit unionism. CCNE and the unions were leaders in building an entire community's demand for justice.

Resources

- Jobs with Justice, 1325 Massachusetts Ave. NW, Suite 200, Washington, DC 20005. 202-393-1044. info@jwj.org. www.jwj.org.
- Alliance for Sustainable Jobs and the Environment, Security Building, 203 E. 4th Ave., Rm 207, Olympia, WA 98501. 360-709-9324. www.asje.org.
- National Interfaith Committee for Worker Justice, 1020 W. Bryn Mawr Ave., 4th Fl., Chicago, IL 60660. 773-728-8400. www.nicwj.org. For a list of local committees, www.nicwj.org/pages/outreach.LG.html.
- Seminary Summer, 815 16th St., NW, Washington, DC 20006, 800-952-2550. unionsummer@aflcio.org.
- Connecticut Center for a New Economy (CCNE),

425 College St., New Haven, CT 06511. 203-785-9494. www.ctneweconomy.org.

• *The Next Upsurge: Labor and the New Social Movements*, by Dan Clawson. Clawson presents case studies of innovative union organizing strategies and styles and argues that unions don't grow slowly and incrementally, but rather in bursts. For there to be a new upsurge, labor must fuse with social movements rooted in communities of color and the global justice movement. Breaking down barriers between union and community could create new forms of organization we can barely imagine. Order from Labor Notes, $17.

Action Questions

1. How do you define your workplace's community? Is it the surrounding neighborhood, the entire city, or the region? An ethnic group within the area? Does the community include your customers or clients?

2. To what communities does your workforce have the closest ties? Can you survey your members to find out which organizations, including religious ones, they belong to?

3. Make a list of the most important organizations in your community. Include religious, social, political, civil rights, women's, immigrants', consumers', and other groups. What are your relations with those organizations? Do any of these groups have labor committees or liaisons?

4. What group in your union is responsible for maintaining contacts with the community or with your customers and clients? Is there a community relations or social action committee? Do union members regularly speak to community groups? How often have you been in contact with community groups?

5. What issues in your workplace also affect the community or your customers or clients? Economic (quality, cost)? Environmental? Health and safety? (For example, pollution affects workers' health and community health. Caseload size affects working conditions and service to clients.)

6. What do community members see as their pressing needs? Are these issues that the union might take the initiative on? Recreation programs for youth? Low-cost housing? Improving health or educational facilities?

7. How can you best approach community groups to show respect for their work and their issues? How would you present the issue so as to make common cause with your community? Who would you talk to first?

8. What are the most important media in your community (TV, web, radio, press)? What union body keeps in touch with them? What have you done lately? Is there a way to promote your union in the public eye? Does your union have a website that the community can access, and do you promote this resource?

9. What existing community programs are you involved in? Does your union simply donate money, or does the program build bonds between rank-and-file workers and grassroots community people? Is power shared equally between labor and community groups? Are women and people of color involved and represented in the leadership? Do rank-and-file members and grassroots community people set the direction for the program?

10. What concrete resources can you provide to community groups—meeting space, phones for phonebanking, computer/fax/office equipment, flyers or signs, labor networks and contacts—that might help build and solidify your relationship?

11. How can you keep in touch with your community allies and give updates about the union's activities? Is there a regular labor meeting that you can invite community allies to attend, or a community meeting that union representatives can attend?

Authors

ROB BARIL is a community-labor organizer in New Haven with District 1199 New England/SEIU.

STEVE HINDS teaches math in the City University of New York's adult literacy program. Previously, he was an activist in the New Haven Federation of Teachers (AFT Local 933), and before that an organizer with the United Electrical Workers (UE).

DAN LA BOTZ wrote the first edition of *A Troublemaker's Handbook* in 1991. He is an activist, teacher, and labor historian based in Cincinnati, where he writes frequently for *Labor Notes*. He was a founding member of Teamsters for a Democratic Union in the 1970s.

NICK ROBINSON is a former student-labor activist at Miami University and Labor Notes intern. He is now a volunteer organizer with the Montpelier Downtown Workers Union and the Vermont Workers Center.

Notes

1. Paul Bigman, Lynne Dodson, Mary Ann Schroeder, and Lonnie Nelson, "Unity Is Achieved by Confronting Differences, Not Avoiding Them," *Labor Notes*, May 2002.

2. Adapted from Dan Clawson, *The Next Upsurge: Labor and the New Social Movements*, 2003, Cornell University Press, pp. 110-111, 119-121.

3. Adapted from a July 2001 article in *Faith Works*, the National Interfaith Committee's newsletter. For more information on CLUE, visit www.cluela.org or call 213-239-6770.

4. David Moberg, "Cheap Hotels: Labor takes on Chicago's hospitality industry." *In These Times*, August 2, 2002.

On the Troublemakers' Website

ON THEIR SEATTLE-TO-MIAMI BUS TOUR, the Alliance for Sustainable Jobs and the Environment sang "FTAA No Way" to the tune of "YMCA." See www.labornotes.org.

14. Union Solidarity

by Aaron Brenner

SOLIDARITY IS A BEDROCK PRINCIPLE of the labor movement, resting on the simple fact that together we are more powerful than we are separately. But solidarity is not automatic. It has to be built through personal and institutional contacts that nurture respect, trust, and support. And to be effective, solidarity has to mobilize power in the form of people, money, and publicity.

The official labor movement has mechanisms for building solidarity: international unions, the AFL-CIO, central labor councils. These institutions have the personnel and resources to support workers in struggle.

Unfortunately, much of this potential solidarity is wasted. Many internationals simply do not build connections between their locals, or if they do the networks are intermittent (say, only at contract time) and operate only among officials.

The AFL-CIO lacks the strength, authority, and tradition to compel affiliates to act in solidarity. Its Industrial Union Department used to facilitate about 80 corporate or industry bargaining councils in which multiple unions coordinated bargaining and solidarity at a particular company (like all the unions at General Electric) or within a single industry (like meatpacking), but the IUD and all but a few of the bargaining councils are now gone. As for central labor councils, too many are inactive, conservative, and focused exclusively on local and state politics.

Thankfully, the labor movement has many creative people, some in the rank and file and some in official positions, who know how to build alliances. In this chapter, some of them tell us how they do it.

Solidarity takes an almost infinite number of forms. In other chapters, we discuss how to build support through labor-community alliances, Jobs with Justice, labor-student connections, corporate campaigns, the web, and international networks. Here we focus on local-to-local solidarity within the same union or among different unions. This can be as simple as phone contact between rank and filers in different locals at the same company, or as complicated as long-term cooperative agreements between unions within an industry. Our stories start with one-time solidarity actions and conclude with ongoing cross-union coalitions. Our emphasis is on activities for rank and filers and local union officials.

The examples in this chapter highlight several lessons. First, solidarity takes time. Do not wait for a crisis before you reach out for help. Try to establish solidarity long before you need it. How? By offering support in whatever form you can, such as sharing information or walking a picket line. Your actions will build trust and give your new friends reason to support you in the future. That points up a second lesson about solidarity: it is reciprocal. It's not enough to get it; you have to give it.

Third, solidarity is not abstract. Give people concrete ways to express their support, whether it's by joining a march, donating money, boycotting your employer, or reaching out to others. Statements of support can build morale, but to be really useful they should pledge action.

Finally, institutionalize solidarity where you can, so that it doesn't have to be rebuilt each time it's needed. We give examples in this chapter: flying squads, solidarity schools, a local cross-union education and solidarity coalition, and Teamsters for a Democratic Union. Through regular meetings, conferences, classes, or parties, you can build long-term connections that become the basis for solidarity.

Plant Gate Fundraising[1]

SIMPLE ACTS OF SOLIDARITY, such as walking a picket or collecting money, have obvious practical effects, but they also foster a culture of solidarity that encourages workers to help each other. That builds the labor movement.

When the UAW International cut off strike funds to a local of locked-out workers in Henderson, Kentucky, a group of rank and filers at a GM plant in Pontiac, Michigan organized a plant-gate collection for them. They set up a planning committee of six and got some of them to write down their thoughts about Local 2036's struggle against Accuride, a maker of truck wheels.

At their first meeting, the committee chose an editor, who used their thoughts to write educational flyers to prepare their fellow workers for the plant gate collection. Two members recruited collection volunteers for all three shifts. One member designed the donation canisters, using the large plastic jugs that pretzels and animal crackers come in, and printed a sign for each jug.

The committee kept the campaign secret as long as possible, to avoid opposition from the local leadership. Email helped speed communication. One member got coin rolls and dollar organizers ahead of time.

On the Friday prior to the actual fundraising, the volunteers handed out the first educational flyer at the nine plant gates. They followed that up with a second flyer on Monday. Then they collected for two days, so that those who had forgotten a donation on day one could have a second chance. Both days coincided with payday.

Committee members paid for the union printing and for two $50 gift certificates. The flyers included a coupon that members could clip and drop into the canisters with their donation. One coupon was drawn at the end for the gift certificates.

The thorough preparation paid off. "I'll never forget the moment when we were all assembled in the plant lobby, turning our canisters over on the counters," wrote Gene Austin, a rank and filer who was later elected chair of the Local 594 bargaining committee. "People were still filing by stuffing in money. We were all dead tired, but happy because we knew we had done quite well. The rank and file at Local 594 raised $7,155.64 for the rank and file at Local 2036. It's an accomplishment which is still talked about today."

Afterwards, the committee printed a thank-you flyer to those who assisted in handouts and collections and to all those who donated to help their union brothers and sisters.

Flying Squads Swoop In

WHEN NAVISTAR INTERNATIONAL TRUCK announced it would use scabs to break a strike by Canadian Auto Workers Local 127 in Chatham, Ontario in June 2002, the workers had a powerful weapon: flying squads from other CAW locals around the province. They mobilized hundreds of picketers from Windsor, Tilbury, St. Thomas, London, Woodstock, Ingersoll, Kitchener, Cambridge, and Waterloo to block the plant gates and keep buses of scabs from entering.

But CAW flying squads do much more than just strike support for auto workers. They sit in at immigration offices to prevent the deportation of refugees. They rally to prevent the eviction of squatters. They picket the headquarters of scab-providing employment agencies. They invade department stores that operate with scabs during strikes, and they demonstrate for anti-scab legislation. They protest against "free" trade. They organize rallies and leafleting to raise the minimum wage. And they trek hours to show support for striking nickel miners.

"These are the kinds of activities flying squads are suited for," says Steve Watson, a national representative with CAW. "They involve direct action, are easy to organize, get results, and make the point. They help build alliances with various communities. Poor immigrants, like the Somali community, see that unions can be their allies, and that has huge potential."

Loose Organization Promotes Creativity

Rank and filers organize the CAW flying squads in each local. Open to anyone, including non-CAW members, they range in size from half a dozen to over 40. They meet each month or every other month, and members decide what actions they will take. No one gets paid, and funding usually comes from donations, though some locals provide official support. Sometimes the flying squad is an extension of a local committee, like the political education committee. Other times, a squad is just a group of activists without formal standing in the local.

T-shirt designs used by CAW flying squad members.

"There are no bylaws around the flying squads, because we are grassroots and only informally recognized by the national union," says Anne MacMeekin, an auto worker at the GM-Suzuki plant in Ingersoll and co-chair of the CAW flying squads for Ontario. "I guess you could say that availability and varying levels of activism govern the participation."

The squads wear CAW flying squad bandanas and t-shirts with bilingual logos. One popular logo is a cobra with the caption, "If provoked we will strike." Some local squads have their own hats, jackets, sweatshirts, and badges. Many also have CAW Flying Squad flags.

"Our first mode of communication is email," says MacMeekin. "If something comes up on short notice, then we get on the phone. Local flying squad leaders—chairpersons or coordinators—are responsible for communicating short-notice events and talking to people without Internet access."

Across Ontario, there are about 1,000 CAW flying squad members. Every two years, they elect two co-chairs to coordinate flying squad activity for the province. They also elect a recording secretary who takes care of the email list and meeting minutes. A financial secretary helps with fundraising. A trustee is chosen to audit the squads' money, though so far that's been unnecessary.

"We are not a ruling body, just a coordinating group," points out MacMeekin. Nor is there a hierarchy to the local squads. "Officers just schedule meetings and let people know what's going on. Meetings are very informal. Sometimes, someone will say we are not following parliamentary procedure, but we don't need to vote on everything. There's a balance between consensus and voting."

The freewheeling nature of the flying squads allows for creativity. "People bring all sorts of ideas to the meetings," says MacMeekin. "We have guest speakers. Meetings can be diverse and all over the map, depending on what's piqued members' interests. A while back we had a debate about whether the squad should be only about picket lines and supporting workers or also do work with social justice issues, like free trade, minimum wage, immigration, and anti-scab legislation." The members agreed on the broader approach.

Teamsters Support Grocery Strike

THE DEFEAT OF THE 2003-2004 STRIKE of 70,000 southern California grocery workers was a tragedy, but it need not have been. Although they faced a united group of employers, the strikers might have won had United Food and Commercial Workers (UFCW) and Teamsters officials expanded the strike to more stores and warehouses and encouraged the local solidarity efforts carried out by thousands of supporters around the country. There are many lessons to be drawn from the strike.[2] Here we concentrate on the rank-and-file inter-union solidarity efforts of Los Angeles-area Teamsters warehouse workers, led by Teamsters for a Democratic Union.

Unions and workers supported the grocery workers' strike in many ways. The International Longshore and Warehouse Union, for example, shut down Los Angeles harbor for a day and held a demonstration of 5,000. They threw parking lot barbecues at stores on strike and brought hundreds of supporters.

Teamsters, however, had the potential to play a larger role. Seven thousand of them work at warehouses that supply the supermarket chains: Albertsons, Ralphs (owned by Kroger), and Vons (owned by Safeway). Because the chains own the warehouses, the UFCW could legally picket the warehouses and Teamsters could legally honor their pickets, making it virtually impossible for the stores to get the supplies they would need to keep operating during the strike.

The Teamsters had every reason to join the UFCW's fight. If the companies succeeded in introducing a two-tier wage scheme and cutting health care for store workers, they would inevitably seek the same at the warehouses. The Teamsters could help themselves by helping the UFCW.

Knowing this, TDU members in L.A. began preparing to walk off the job in support of the grocery workers.

"Prior to the strike, we did our best to educate our co-workers about the importance of the strike," says Frank Halstead, a TDU leader and warehouse worker in Local 572 at Ralphs in Compton. "We had a real problem in our local because of the widespread misconception that the clerks did not honor our last strike in 1985, when in fact the majority did honor the picket lines. So the first thing we had to do was explain the importance of the issues at stake in the clerks' contract battle and get over the excuses.

"We had so many co-workers whose wives worked in the stores that we got good information. We TDUers would be in the break room and a guy would say, 'they crossed our picket in 1985,' and we would say, 'no, they didn't, and even if they did, we need to unite now to protect our jobs and our health care.' Then another guy would come up to us after and say, 'I'm glad you said that, because my wife works at Vons, or my daughter works at Albertsons, and I want to support them.' So I'd say, 'bring us all the contract literature they get, every letter they get.' So before you know it, workers are posting UFCW literature on our boards, putting up hotline phone numbers. Of course, the [Teamsters] union was doing nothing, providing no information.

"The UFCW had buttons that said No Concessions. We got a couple hundred buttons and handed them out at the warehouse to show the employers we knew the issues and would support the clerks' struggle. We wore the same buttons as the clerks to show unity."

The strike started on October 11, but the UFCW picketed only the stores, not the warehouses. "We encouraged our members to help at the store level by walking picket lines and attending demonstrations and rallies," says Halstead.

Pressuring the Local

"We tried to get our local to create some kind of hotline or put information on the website or bulletin boards and play some kind of role in blessing the rank and file to participate in supporting the strike. Workers would ask, 'What does our leadership say?' They felt more comfortable if the leadership encouraged the strike support. The officials did approve some of the things we suggested, like going to rallies and demonstrations. But they were mostly paralyzed and overly cautious about lawsuits, so they discouraged workers from going to picket lines. They said to just go drop off water or coffee, absurd little stuff. They said we'd be sued and subject to discipline if we picketed, which was nonsense."

Workers from all over the region, union and non-union, were joining UFCW pickets, with the encouragement of the Los Angeles Central Labor Council and virtually the whole labor movement.

"We had to prove our union leadership wrong in terms of our First Amendment rights," says Halstead. "A core of us was willing to go and walk the picket lines and prove that we could do it. For those who were afraid, we said, 'Go and walk the pickets at Vons or Albertsons and don't go to Ralphs.'"

"I tried to be everywhere, but I soon realized that was a mistake," says Frank Villa, a TDU member in Local 630 who works at a Sysco warehouse in Walnut, California. "I concentrated on stores in my neighborhood, where I could get to know people. We got the idea to picket a motel where the companies were housing scabs. We got about 150 people out there and we got news coverage about how the companies were bringing in out-of-state scabs to take our jobs."

Sympathy Strike

On November 24, the UFCW extended the picket lines to the ten local warehouses owned by the chains. "A majority of workers knew what was at stake and why to support the strike," says Halstead. "That's why we saw 90 percent honor the pickets at my facility.

"The leadership said we couldn't walk the picket lines. Even though we have language to honor picket lines, they claimed that because we still had a contract in place, we risked being disciplined and sued by the company if we engaged firsthand in any strike activity. So they told us to go home. We knew they were full of it, and we talked to some lawyers to make sure. I don't know any strike that has been won from home with workers sitting on their couches.

"So we defied the leadership. And just to make it clear that it wasn't us on strike, we didn't 'picket.' We didn't walk back and forth. Instead, we 'demonstrated' and 'exercised our basic constitutional rights' and raised hell in front of the warehouse. The leadership and the company weren't happy, but they couldn't tell us to move.

"More and more people came and they were energized by being on the line. We demonstrated that the leadership was wrong legally and strategically."

Bolstering the UFCW pickets with Teamsters also sent a message to any Teamsters who had thought about crossing. "If no Teamsters are there to convince other Teamsters not to cross, who would stop them?" asks Halstead. "Scabs would have to look us in the eye and know that we would know they crossed.

"It was a learning experience for many of us who had not been on strike before. We saw how they brought in scabs and housed them at hotels, how they outsourced using vendors to make direct store deliveries that bypassed the warehouses, how they pressured vendors to send their workers to perform the work of stocking the shelves, how they advertised for scabs in local papers, how they brought in strikebreaking security companies.

"We also learned how to deal with the police. They were trying to deny us access to stand on the corner outside the warehouse. They would tell us to move and we'd move. Then they'd drive off and we'd go back. Finally, we decided to stay. When they came back, we said, 'This is a public walkway and the company lets other people walk here, so they cannot deny us.' The police called their sergeant, who said we could stay. That was a huge victory for us.

"It was a running battle out on the picket line. The company turned on sprinklers to drive us away, so we got towels and threw them over the sprinklers. They had cameras mounted to video us, so we got a bunch of spotlights and stuck them right in the camera. That made them furious. In the end, the security people came out and negotiated with us. We got most of what we wanted, which was our right to be there without hassle."

Most Teamsters around the region honored the UFCW pickets. "Riverside had only 25 out of 1,100 cross," says Halstead. "Glendale has 500 workers and maybe 10 crossed. So Ralphs was solid. Vons was 100 percent. Albertsons had over 500 people cross, which was a problem.

"We were out from November 24 to December 22. Then the Teamsters leadership shut it down. They did not want to pay the strike benefits. There was also concern that so many crossed at Albertsons. They were worried the sentiment was so anti-union that they could lose representation and see the union decertified. The leadership just wanted it over.

"Having the TDU network and the resources was important. Where we had a large TDU presence, you saw heavy participation from workers. Where there was not TDU presence, there was no one offering ideas or pressuring the leadership or saying how we could win this. Through TDU, we could talk to attorneys who told us what we could do on the picket lines, when the leadership was telling us we couldn't do anything. We brought that to the union meetings, and the leaders had to admit that we were right. That built the strike solidarity and it built our reputation."

Asked what TDUers will do differently next time, Halstead says, "We will prepare better and start earlier. We didn't challenge the leadership immediately when they told us to go home instead of picket. We did not know our rights. Next time they tell us to go home, we'll tell them we can demonstrate at the picket line.

"Your strongest point is before the strike, in terms of getting members to participate. You need to say to people, 'Would you rather be at a rally for an hour or two or on strike for a month or two?'"

Secondary Boycott, Sort Of

"THIS GUY AND HIS BUDDIES IN THE UFCW got an email, and they threw up a picket line in support of locked-out West Coast dockworkers in front of a Payless Shoes somewhere in Minneapolis. That's the kind of support we got—in a landlocked state, no less," says Vance Lelli of International Longshore and Warehouse Union Local 23 in Tacoma, Washington.

All over the country in the late summer of 2002, as the ILWU negotiated a contract with big West Coast shippers and stevedoring companies, environmentalists, peace activists, anti-globalization protesters, community organizers, and unionists demonstrated in front of Targets, Home Depots, Wal-Marts, Payless Shoes, and other corporate members of the West Coast Waterfront Coalition. The WCWC was a lobbying group of these large retailers and of shippers interested in cutting their costs by weakening the longshore workers union. The WCWC lobbied the Bush administration to prevent any kind of disruption on the docks, which could mean getting a Taft-Hartley injunction against any strike or lockout.

By picketing and leafleting WCWC companies, the ILWU's supporters sought to educate people about the dockworkers' cause and its importance for the labor movement as a whole. "What Bush was threatening—to

As the ILWU negotiated a contract with big West Coast shippers and stevedoring companies in 2002, environmentalists, peace activists, anti-globalization protesters, community organizers, and unionists demonstrated to support them in front of Targets, Home Depots, Wal-Marts, Payless Shoes, and other corporate members of the West Coast Waterfront Coalition. The WCWC was a lobbying group of these large retailers and of shippers interested in cutting their costs by weakening the longshore workers union.

prevent any strike and use troops to move cargo—would have consequences far beyond the docks," says Jake Carton, organizer for Washington State Jobs with Justice (WSJwJ). "It could have seriously weakened the right to strike for all workers, like when Reagan broke the PATCO [air traffic controllers] strike."

Supporters around the country couldn't all get to the West Coast docks, but they could try to influence the big retailers to back off their campaign against the dockworkers. And, in at least one case, they succeeded.

Solidarity Strategy Targets Consumers

Technically speaking, for the ILWU to advocate that its members and other workers picket, boycott, or refuse to handle the goods of its employers' customers would constitute a secondary boycott, which is illegal under the Taft-Hartley Act. To avoid the appearance that the union was advocating anything close to a secondary boycott, the AFL-CIO, Jobs with Justice, and a number of local support groups, including Friends of the Harbor in Los Angeles and Friends of Labor in the Bay Area, organized the solidarity actions against the WCWC. Washington State Jobs with Justice was particularly active in developing the anti-WCWC strategy.

"We decided on a broad consumer strategy," says Carton. "We wanted to bring the struggle to storefronts as opposed to the CEOs. We refined the strategy over time. We had to get a sense of which WCWC companies operated in cities where JwJ has chapters. Then we had to figure out not just store locations, but where we could have access to customers. That's how we arrived on Payless. By asking activists in other cities, we learned that Payless had storefronts on streets, instead of private malls where we might be kicked out and away from interaction with customers.

"Unlike other retailers such as The Gap, Payless had not been inoculated from protest. The Gap was used to anti-sweatshop protests, so when we originally tried a protest at The Gap, management came out with a canned press release stating how worker-friendly and environmentally friendly they are. Payless, on the other hand, had to figure out how to respond to our protests. On one of our national days of action, we had about 35 protests at Payless stores around the country. Not long after, the CEO agreed to meet with officials from the AFL-CIO, the Teamsters [which represented workers at Payless warehouses], and the ILWU. He then sent a letter to the WCWC saying he did not support its position of asking for troops to run the docks."

To get things started, Carton and his fellow WSJwJ activists took the dockworkers' cause to the national JwJ leadership. "We spoke to the national field reps and the various coalitions they work with around the country. We explained the implications of the ILWU situation. We demonstrated that this was not just a West Coast issue. We then asked if they could devote time to the struggle."

Within a few weeks, WSJwJ had won enough support to coordinate several national days of protest. The AFL-CIO also provided help, in the form of money, people, mailing lists, phone trees, and lobbying politicians to support the ILWU.

"Once we reached critical mass in understanding the importance of the struggle," says Carton, "we had a series of conference calls every week or two to develop the strategy. That's how we set the targets and the dates. Then, after each protest, we would debrief to find out what worked and what didn't, what got under their skin, where were the best places to find foot traffic, how to rankle the other tenants in a shared retail location. Then we could plan the next protest with people borrowing tactics from each other."

Assessing Success

The discussions also helped the group get its point across more clearly. "We talked about how to relate the longshore employers' attack on dockworkers to what the WCWC companies were doing to workers in our communities," notes Carton. "We discussed how to get the media to care about the issue. The WCWC was trying to exploit the terrorism scare to turn public opinion and the administration against the dockworkers, so we demanded to know why it was a matter of national security how quickly Wal-Mart could stock its shelves. What does that have to do with terrorism?"

JwJ coalitions around the country helped bring people out. "We have an infrastructure of thousands of people who have signed 'I'll be there' pledge cards," says Carton (see Chapter 13). "We have volunteers with experience doing phonebanks, people who expect to get called. Locally, we have a phone tree with 300 people, so we can activate a high level of organization."

That organization produced the largest labor demonstration in Seattle since the anti-WTO protests of 1999. "We had a march and rally with over 2,000 people," says Carton. "It was a great public display against bringing troops in to run the docks. We marched at rush hour past major arteries, creating quite a traffic jam."

Electronic Solidarity Newsletter

UNIONISTS IN WASHINGTON, D.C. have noticed a surge of solidarity activity over the last few years. Protest crowds are bigger. Picket lines are larger. Politicians get bombarded with more emails. "We don't claim credit for it, but the Union City electronic newsletter has helped," says Chris Garlock, coordinator of the Union Cities Program for the Metropolitan Washington Central Labor Council. "Some issues pop up fast and don't make it on the general radar. In the past, nobody would come. Now we get at least a few dozen people."

Union City is a free, twice-weekly email message that goes to about 8,000 supporters. Every Monday, it lists upcoming events, rallies, demos, pickets, labor concerts, anything in the area with a labor connection. "Except meetings," says Garlock. "We had a fight at the beginning, because everybody wanted to include them, but we didn't want to bog down the calendar, and we wanted to emphasize action."

The Monday message sometimes includes brief background stories about upcoming events, as well as reports on past actions. "We put out the information; it's up to them to decide to attend," says Garlock. "We don't pressure them. If you want to know the labor movement in D.C., you have to be on the Union City list."

Because of the huge number of union staff jobs in Washington, the Wednesday message lists jobs available. "We added a separate message because we felt job announcements weren't appropriate for the mobilizing message," says Garlock.

Links in Union City's messages allow readers to send emails and faxes to politicians, editors, and corporate executives. When the newsletter promoted an effort to keep a community hospital from closing, the head of the hospital told the *Washington Post* he had received "zillions of emails." Garlock says it was probably a few hundred but notes, "Even 100 feels like a lot. They have a disproportionate effect."

GetActive, an expensive web-based service that the AFL-CIO has made available free to its affiliates, makes the electronic activism possible. If your local doesn't know about GetActive, try your international, your state federation, or your central labor council. Smaller organizations that can't afford GetActive can try www.mail-list.com.

Garlock suggests that if you are choosing between building a website and starting a newsletter, "do the newsletter. People have to come to a website, but email comes to them. You can always do the website later."

For more on electronic organizing, see Chapter 20. Ways to build up an e-list are on page 315.

Solidarity Schools

by Paul McLennan

IN THE EARLY 1990s, members of the New Directions Movement, a reform caucus within the UAW, realized that, like most union members, they lacked organizing experience, did not know the history of their union, knew virtually nothing about the economy, and understood little about the potential role of the labor movement in society. Their union did not help. The UAW, like most unions, focused its training on the mechanics of unionism—filing grievances, keeping union records, and lobbying.

So the caucus set up "schools" where rank and filers could learn the history of the union movement and develop strategies to transform their union. What began as a school for one union reform movement quickly grew into a multi-union educational project. Solidarity Schools were born.

Schools were held in different regions of the country, drawing rank-and-file activists who wanted to learn from fellow union members who had stood up at work. In 1993, the Workers Education Center (WEC) was established as a nonprofit institution (501c3 in the U.S. tax code) to provide "training for union activists who want to win battles in the workplace, the political arena, and the global economy."

The concept of the Solidarity Schools was heavily influenced by two earlier efforts to encourage grassroots/rank-and-file strategic thinkers—Highlander Folk School (founded 1932) and Brookwood Labor College (founded 1921). Both schools brought together leading radical intellectuals and workers from many different backgrounds. Proudly flouting Jim Crow segregation laws, Highlander insisted that black and white people live, eat, and learn side by side. It was here that folks like Ella Baker, Septima Clark, and Rosa Parks developed many of the civil rights movement's strategies.

Solidarity School Sample Agenda

8th Annual Massachusetts Jobs with Justice Solidarity School

Building the Links:
How can we learn from each other and build a stronger movement of working people.
October 30-November 2, 2003, Cape Cod, Mass.

Thursday Night, October 30

5:30 pm — Dinner and registration
7:00 pm — Introduction to the school
7:15 pm — Global Film Festival!
   Workers' struggles and victories from around the world
9:00 pm — Reception

Friday, October 31

7:00-8:30 am — Breakfast
9:00 am — Welcome to Solidarity School
   Goals, Agenda and Setting Working Groups
9:30 am — *The War on Workers in our Daily Lives*
   Participants "name the moment" and the specific economic reasons behind the intense corporate assault on working people, then start tracing it through our four campaigns: immigrant rights, global justice, health care, and the right to organize.
10:45 am — Break
11:00 am — Working groups analyze the war on workers and workers' response in the four campaign areas
12:00 pm — Lunch
1:00 pm — *Power Analysis*
   Working groups map the most powerful forces opposing us (in immigration, globalization, health care, and labor organizing) and then look at the forces on our side. Where are we stronger and where are they? How can we adjust our campaigns, themes, and messages to build a broader movement and win on our issues?
3:00 pm — Break
3:15 pm — Pooling the working group discussions and drawing lessons for our movement
4:45 — Quick evaluation of the School so far: what's working, what to improve
5:00-6:30 pm Dinner
7:00 pm — *Lessons from Organizing Around the World*
   International speakers describe ways they won victories on health care, global justice, etc. in their countries. Discussion: how is this different from the way we're organizing here?
9:00 pm — Dance, relax

Saturday, November 1

7:00-8:30 am — Breakfast
9:00 am — *New Strategies for Organizing*
   Leaders and activists from different movements guide us through a critical examination of their organizing models. How are they keeping people involved over time, developing rank and file leadership, and building a broader movement? What can we learn from them?
10:45 am — Break
11:00 am — *Beyond Slogans...*
   Why aren't we reaching people whose interests we share? "Deep messaging" is a way to rethink our campaigns so they broaden our movement.
12:00 pm — Lunch
1:00 pm — *... Messages that Build Movements*
   Working groups apply the morning's lessons to our campaigns. How can our messages neutralize our opponents' appeals, strengthen our own, and broaden our base?
3:00 pm — Break
3:15 pm — *The Strategies We Use and the World We Want*
   We'll look at the strategies we use and the messages that resonate over the life of a campaign, then start a dialogue about how we can integrate our different struggles into a broader movement for social justice. Are we projecting a world that working people want to join? What are the obstacles to getting people active and in the leadership of our organizations?
4:45 pm — Evaluate the training so far
5:30-7:00 pm — Dinner
7:00 pm — Dance and relax around the bonfire

Sunday, November 2

7:00-8:30 am — Breakfast
9:00 am — Working groups sum up the progress they made and present to the whole group
10:15 am — *The Big Picture: Winning Real Victories*
   What have we learned at Solidarity School? What new organizing models and skills are we going to try? What can we learn from different models of organizing that can strengthen our own? How can we make Jobs with Justice stronger and more useful for our different struggles? How can we make our movement powerful enough to win?
11:30 pm — Evaluate this year's School and ask what people want next year
12:00 pm – Lunch

Costs and Registration

Costs for the full four days including food and lodging are $190. Some day rates and limited low-income scholarships are available. For information or to register call Jobs with Justice at 617-524-8778, email jwj@massjwj.net, or go on the web at www.massjwj.net.

Brookwood lasted only 16 years but trained many future organizers of the CIO, including UAW New Directions members Victor and Sophie Reuther.

What To Include

Solidarity Schools operate on several levels. Political education, skill building, and problem solving are all involved. So are cultural interaction, strategic planning, and rank-and-file activism. The content varies from school to school, but the basic idea is to use popular education to draw out lessons from people's experiences, apply what they are learning to a real situation (strategy and tactics), tackle the different kinds of oppression that divide, and use music and theater to unite. Over the years, several principles have anchored the Solidarity Schools:

1. An interactive approach where everyone is encouraged to teach and learn on a basis of equality, regardless of their skill level or job title.

2. Co-sponsoring organizations, to expand the audience. Labor Notes and Black Workers for Justice, in addition to local host committees, have co-sponsored Solidarity Schools.

3. A central belief in developing leaders for rank-and-file control of unions and community organizations.

4. Creating a safe place where participants may speak freely and are challenged to consider new ideas and options.

Seven elements have become the basis for any school: history, personal experiences, economics (both U.S. and global), building solidarity through diversity, labor-community alliances or community-based unionism, strategic planning sessions devoted to real-life problems/campaigns, and a healthy dose of cultural and fun activities.

The schools talk frankly about challenging the system rather than individual problems. Issues that divide are tackled head on, whether it is race and gender issues or the global North/South divide. To increase the scope of discussion, schools have included participants from Canada, Mexico, and South Africa.

The first night of each school is spent getting to know everyone's personal history and their reasons for coming. By the end of the weekend, people will hopefully see their local struggles in a global context. People learn from the experiences of those from different unions and get support for the direction they have taken. Facilitators who can generate discussion are carefully chosen. Much of the weekend is spent on developing problem-solving and strategic planning skills.

One of the principal organizers of the Solidarity Schools in the 1990s, Jerry Tucker, believes the need is as great today as when they were founded. "Workers are not unwilling to fight injustice at work and in their communities," Tucker says, "but they need tools, strategies, and solidarity-based examples to work with. This is especially true against the backdrop of today's international situation, where U.S. workers are under attack by their own government at home while being asked to blindly support its aggressions abroad. We need critical education and a vision of global solidarity to counter this assault."

Schools continue annually in Massachusetts, sponsored by the local Jobs with Justice chapter. The WEC will help activists in other areas to organize Solidarity Schools.

Planning a Solidarity School

• The first step is developing a host committee responsible for finding a location, handling logistics, and outreach. The larger and more inclusive the host committee, the better turnout you will have. In Massachusetts, Jobs with Justice makes sure the school is connected to ongoing local campaigns.

Without an existing coalition or organization, you might have to create a host committee. Has there been a living wage campaign in your town? Who participated? Is an organizing drive taking place? Contract campaign? Has an employer announced massive job cuts? What community struggles are happening? Immigrant rights groups and a bus riders union have been sources of host committee members. The key is to give local activists a space to strategize about their issues. Sometimes the letterhead host committee may be large, but the actual working body much smaller. Once you get going, a good source for host committee members is past attendees.

• Plan ahead and allow enough time. A host committee may take three to five months to create. It will require phone calls, visits, letters, and/or short presentations to various organizations or their leaderships.

Once you form a host committee, allow at least six months for planning the school, especially if folks from outside the city or country are invited. Recruitment takes time, since many unions or community groups have internal processes that must be respected. Let invitees know that schools are most successful if participants come with at least two other people from their organization.

• The host committee plans the content of the school. Some committees have selected a theme to focus on throughout the weekend, such as strategies for organizing new members into unions. Other host committees have looked at local burning issues and developed sessions to tackle each of them. See the agenda on the previous page for an example.

An interesting mix of speakers and panels, experience sharing, skill development, interactive pieces, cultural presentations, and fun is essential—go light on the talking heads. In addition to expertise on their subjects, presenters should have experience encouraging participation, summarizing discussion, and keeping things moving. An ability to put an issue in its larger economic and political context is also helpful. Facilitators should reflect an appropriate balance of race, gender, age, and industry. Often, facilitators can do better by working in pairs.

A Massachusetts Jobs with Justice Solidarity School.

Massachusetts Jobs with Justice has developed a short facilitators guide. (See Resources at the end of this chapter.)

• Raise money for scholarships, since many of the potential participants may have no institutional backing or may be low-income. A subcommittee can be formed to apply for grants, seek donations from individuals and organizations, hold fundraisers, and get in-kind donations.

• Find a location where interruptions won't stand in the way of reflection and thinking. Retreat centers or summer camps in the off-season are possible sites. Find one that offers everything in one package. Things to consider are: price, distance from the city, accessibility, childcare, needs of the physically challenged, breakout space, and on-site staff for emergencies and problems. Plan for any translation needs.

Massachusetts Jobs with Justice has returned to the same site for five years, in part because the camp has ping-pong tables, basketball courts, and a soccer field. A Saturday night lakeside bonfire with dancing, singing, and talk is a tradition.

'Meeting the Challenge' Cross-Union Committee

by Paul McLennan

BASED IN MINNEAPOLIS/ST. PAUL, the Meeting the Challenge Committee (MTC) is a network of rank-and-file union activists who seek to reinvigorate the local labor movement through education and cross-union solidarity. The group's main activities are strike support, monthly educational forums, picnics, labor arts celebrations, informational mailings, an annual conference, and participation in various social movements, including those for immigrants' rights and against state budget cuts and war.

MTC emerged from support work for Austin, Minnesota-based UFCW Local P-9 in its strike against Hormel in the 1980s. A core group of activists met weekly during the strike to organize fundraising, recruit for picket lines, and promote the boycott of Hormel. After the strike, the group continued to meet to discuss union strategy, education, and activism. Some in the group became officers in their local unions.

Often called upon to speak in public, rank-and-file P-9 leaders and support activists set up a speakers bureau and trained other rank and filers to present at local union meetings and other forums. This became the St. Paul Labor Speakers Club, which held monthly meetings about the direction of the labor movement.

In 1992, this network of activists organized a conference on "meeting the challenge" of labor-management cooperation programs. Some 500 rank-and-file activists told their personal stories, learned from each other's successes and failures, and developed strategies to deal with their employers.

Struck by the success of the conference, on the one hand, and the unwillingness of official labor organizations, such as the state AFL-CIO and the city central labor bodies, to undertake such work, on the other, the conference organizers decided to form an organization for the primary purpose of holding annual conferences that would not shy away from controversial issues. They called this organization the "Meeting the Challenge Committee."

Their conferences have ranged in attendance from 100 to 600 people. They deal with local fights such as the St. Paul public employees' campaign against privatization in 1999 and the University of Minnesota clerical workers' fight for a fair contract in 2003. But organizers also bring in speakers from successful local struggles elsewhere in the country so that Twin Cities workers can learn from their nuts and bolts. These speakers have included an organizer of the Puerto Rican general strike against privatization, a community organizer from the Los Angeles Justice for Janitors movement, organizers from the American Postal Workers Union's drive to organize private sector workers, and a leader of the Harvard clerical workers' union.

All this while, the St. Paul Labor Speakers Club has continued its monthly educational programs at the St. Paul Labor Center, where it has been granted free use of a room by the St. Paul Trades and Labor Assembly. One forum highlighted leaders from SEIU Local 113, preparing for a strike of 6,000 workers against nine hospitals in the Twin Cities area. Sometimes movies are shown, or there is a guest speaker on labor history. Other programs have included debates between Greens and Democrats and a discussion about the Labor Party.

MTC's solidarity work goes beyond turning out for picket lines. When Pepsi drivers struck, MTC facilitated cooperation between Teamsters and UFCW locals. MTC has protested a seminar organized by a union-busting law firm, picketed sweatshop-made clothing at Kohl's department stores, and turned out participants for rallies at the State Capitol in support of immigrant rights and against budget cuts. MTC also built labor's participation in marches against the war in Iraq.

Druing the 2004 Meeting the Challenge conference, clerical workers from AFSCME Local 3800 received the Solidarity Award for community outreach before, during, and after their strike at the University of Minnesota.

Building the cultural side of labor activism has been a highlight of MTC's work. The group has organized labor and the arts celebrations, supported the performance of labor plays, collaborated with the Friends of the St. Paul Public Library on an annual program called "Untold Stories," which brings labor history events to library branches around the city, and, with the Twin

Cities locals of the American Postal Workers Union, helped to create the Solidarity Kids Theater.

In 2000, MTC worked with jazz composer-saxophonist Fred Ho to organize an Immigrant Workers Cabaret that brought together 600 rank-and-file workers and their families for a night of immigrant music and dance. The 2002 MTC Conference linked to a local hip-hop poetry program, organized in conjunction with local poets and cultural activists of color.

MTC has a steering committee of individuals from the Newspaper Guild/CWA, Teamsters, United Transportation Union, AFSCME, CWA, Sign Painters, IBEW, National Writers Union, IAM, AFT, Postal Workers, and UFCW. The committee meets monthly to discuss ongoing activities within individual unions, plan for forums, and organize solidarity actions. The committee works closely with the St. Paul Labor Speakers Club, helping to define programs and build audiences for their activities.

Postcards, flyers, e-lists, e-calendars, and the local labor press promote MTC's activities. Both the monthly meetings of the Labor Speakers Club and the annual Meeting the Challenge conference are promoted in the pages of the Twin Cities' two labor newspapers, the St. Paul *Union Advocate* and the Minneapolis *Labor Review*, as well as the labor webpaper, www.workdayminnesota.org.

A typical mailing for a monthly forum goes out to more than 1,000, with attendance usually around 50. Activities and mailings are funded by solicited donations from local unions and individuals, usually for each activity as it happens. The St. Paul Labor Center, a UFCW hall, and Macalester College donate their spaces for events.

The base of MTC's support has come from four local unions, TDU, and individuals from other unions. Locals kick in $150-$200 for annual conference expenses.

For the conferences, a planning committee is organized each year made up of self-selected members and leaders of local struggles. The need to develop more diversity in the planning committee is an ongoing problem the group is trying to rectify. A student/labor connection has developed over the years, providing MTC with the resources of a friendly academic institution, such as free meeting space.

The MTC network has earned a reputation as a place where rank-and-file workers can go with problems their union leadership refuses to address. While not initiating struggles, MTC can use its mailing list and mobilize support to make things happen.

These efforts can present an alternative to the leadership of some unions and the state federation, which sometimes see MTC as a threat. MTC has been outspoken in its opposition to cooperation programs and has strongly supported union reform movements. In response, the local Teamsters Joint Council, the IAM, and the state AFL-CIO have contacted local unions that have endorsed MTC's annual conferences and urged them to withdraw their endorsement or any financial help. The MTC committee disagrees about how openly and explicitly to respond to this intimidation. As yet, it has just continued to do what it does.

MTC does not consider itself an alternative to the local central labor body. Since a Jobs with Justice chapter does not exist in the area, MTC functions as a JwJ-like organization, but without official AFL-CIO endorsement. This gives MTC more independence, especially in its support of rank-and-file democracy.

Drivers Organize for Area-Wide Contract

HERE IS AN EXAMPLE of how rank-and-file workers in different locals of the same union in the same industry can work together to increase their power against employers.

Employers in the ready-mix concrete and concrete block industry in the Minneapolis-St. Paul area had sliced up their workforce into many different groups under many different contracts. At some employers as many as seven different contracts covered workers doing exactly the same work. Making things more difficult, three different Teamsters locals that represent concrete drivers in the area had not cooperated with each other in clashes with these employers.

Activists in Two Locals

John Gaither and Bob McNattin, drivers for two of the larger companies in the industry, are members of Ready-Mix Drivers United for a Better Contract. This rank-and-file caucus aimed to nudge the Teamsters locals to coordinate their bargaining and create a single, area-wide contract for all 450 unionized ready-mix drivers in the Twin Cities region. Gaither is chief steward at Aggregate Industries for Local 221, a 2,000-member construction local based in Minneapolis. McNattin drives for Cemstone and is a steward for St. Paul-based Local 120, an 8,000-member general local where Tom Keegel, Teamsters International secretary-treasurer, is president. The third local, 160, is a general local in southern Minnesota.

"I have been on the elected bargaining team in Local 221 for the last four or five contracts," says Gaither. "The union would not let us see the other contracts. You'd go to the bargaining table and the employer would say, 'Why should we pay you $25 an hour when Local 221 has a contract doing the same work for $21?' How can you respond? How can you prepare for that if you can't see the contracts?

"For the last ten years, I have made motions that we negotiate contracts together, but each time my motion was ruled out of order or ignored. I have looked at contracts from other plants, which I got from employees or stewards, and I've compared contracts to see the type of wording and the benefits and the wages, and it is frustrating to see stuff that we should have or vice versa. We're in the same local, with the same business agent. We were being whipsawed, and the union was allowing it. In fact, the BA read me the riot act and threatened to bring me up on charges when he found out I had the contracts.

"Finally, we had enough people at a meeting, yelling at the BA that we want to negotiate for everyone in the industry, that they agreed to let us have the contracts in each local. So Local 221 gave me 15 contracts covering three employers, and we got contracts from the BA in Local 120."

McNattin, a member of Teamsters for a Democratic Union (TDU), had done similar agitation in Local 120. He summed up the problem: "Without an area-wide agreement, when one group goes on strike, the rest of us haul mud [concrete] into the area."

Local Activists Come Together

In the spring of 2003, McNattin made up a flyer announcing a meeting at a local Legion Hall to talk about coordinated bargaining for ready-mix drivers. He invited Rich DeVries, a TDU activist and union organizer, to speak, since DeVries had experience negotiating area-wide contracts.

"I distributed the flyer at different worksites," says McNattin. "I went to Apple Valley [another company] and talked to the steward. At Aggregate Industries I talked to a forklift operator and mechanic, and they were excited. In Minneapolis, I went to the drivers' break room and a guy grabbed some flyers and took me outside. He made sure the flyers went all around.

"That meeting was in May 2003 and 46 people showed up on a beautiful spring Sunday. They came from all the different companies and all the different locals. We agreed that an area-wide contract was a good idea. We did a button, Ready-Mix Drivers United for a Better Contract. We also did a version on the website we started, www.readymixdrivers.net. Everybody was excited."

Subsequent meetings during construction season were not as well attended, but over the next year a core group of 10 to 15 workers, including McNattin, other stewards, and eventually Gaither, continued to meet. They went through each of the contracts covering ready-mix drivers, picking out the best language from each to create an ideal contract.

Brad Slawson, Sr., acting president of Local 120, came to one meeting in late November. He denounced the workers for meeting at the Legion Hall instead of the local union hall. He also attacked the meeting as "just more TDU bullshit," says McNattin. The workers, who had not affiliated with TDU, argued that the three locals had not supported their work, so they had to meet elsewhere. In response, Slawson agreed to have a meeting for interested workers from all three locals at the Local 120 hall. He even sent out an announcement about the

Making Rank-and-File Contacts

You might reach out to rank and filers at another workplace for many reasons. Maybe you work for the same company but in different plants or different locals or different unions. Maybe their company supplies yours, or vice versa. Maybe they don't have a union yet and you think they should be in yours. Maybe you face a common problem, such as an upcoming contract, outsourcing, or pollution in your city. Maybe management is trying to whipsaw you—playing one local against the other to press for concessions. For power, you need unity.

How do you begin? Hopefully, your union officials are in communication, but this tends to be the exception, not the rule. In any case, it can't hurt for rank and filers to communicate as well.

• One place to meet other rank and filers is at a union hall. To discover whether another facility has a union, call the AFL-CIO Central Labor Council. The Yellow Pages under "Labor" lists many unions. Use Internet search engines, typing city and company name and the names of likely unions.

• Many workers are in daily contact with other plants or offices in the company system, plus vendors and customers, through the course of their work. Use such phone, email, and personal contacts. Be discreet.

• Simply go to the other workplace before or after work and talk to workers coming and going, just as professional organizers do. At some companies you can walk into the building, go to the cafeteria, sit down, and talk. Or look for a seniority list near the time clock, and get names to make calls later. Try a nearby restaurant, coffee shop, or bar for lunch or right after work.

• Be bold. If you see the company jacket or a group of likely people, walk over and introduce yourself. This is easier if you have a particular issue to talk about, such as an upcoming contract.

• Hand out leaflets at company entrances or put leaflets under windshield wipers in parking lots. Wear company or union jackets or caps that will identify you as a group. "Fellow Acme Employees: Do you want a decent contract? So do we. We are a group of employees from the Oak Ave. office and members of Steelworkers Local 55. Call Chris at 312-555-9999 (home) or email rankandfile@etc."

• Company drivers who go back and forth between offices and plants making deliveries can deliver messages. Ask the driver to deliver the message to the steward.

• See Chapter 20 on using email, list-serves, online discussion groups, web pages, and other Internet tools to build solidarity.

meeting on Teamsters letterhead with signatures of the presidents of all three locals.

"Unfortunately, Slawson filibustered that meeting," says McNattin. "We got 125 people from all the locals and each company to attend. But he talked for an hour and 45 minutes. If there had been open discussion of the pros and cons of coordinated bargaining and an area-wide standard, it might have carried on into the break rooms. But that didn't occur. It was just another 'all b.s.' local meeting. It fed into the apathy."

Looking back, McNattin would do things differently. "I would not let someone filibuster another meeting. I should have stood up and said, 'Point of order. Your own rules for this meeting were that everyone has a right to speak. You are dominating the meeting. Sit down and let us speak.' We had the power and didn't use it."

Questionnaire as Organizing Tool

Despite the setback, the rank and filers kept meeting. Getting workers from Local 160 to attend was difficult. Local 160 officials were afraid of offending Slawson and Keegel, who had hinted that they would push to merge Local 160 into Local 120. The Local 160 officials instructed all members, especially stewards, to avoid Ready-Mix Drivers United for a Better Contract.

Nonetheless, the group began an organizing push in the winter of 2003-2004 to prepare for spring contract talks. Multiple contracts at Cemstone and Aggregate Industries, covering about half the ready-mix drivers in the area, were to expire on April 30, 2004. "This was a big opportunity for us," says McNattin. "We were trying to get common language and common expiration dates. We were going for a two-year instead of a four- or five-year contract, to get in phase with a large branch of Cemstone which is also in Local 221."

"We distributed a questionnaire to all the members," says Gaither. "'What would you like in the contract?' So they all had a chance to submit issues and demands. They also got to know that we were mobilizing. The locals refused to help us, but then they were forced to because we won control of the bargaining committees."

Using the questionnaire and talking to workers on the job, members of the group developed enough contacts that they were easily elected to the bargaining committees for both Aggregate Industries and Cemstone. The Cemstone committee had members from both Locals 120 and 221.

Joint Bargaining

Controlling the bargaining committees was a big step, but it did not give the rank and filers complete control. Under union rules, local officers, in this case Slawson, did the negotiating. Still, for the first time, the bargaining committees began to meet jointly to come up with common demands. Ready-mix Drivers United for a Better Contract continued to meet, too, helping prepare bargaining team members for the joint meetings and for negotiations.

Slawson agreed with the joint bargaining committee to seek a single contract for the area. To avoid conflict, the committee agreed that seniority lists should stay separate. The Local 120 contract with Cemstone, the strongest in the industry, would be the template. The union would delay negotiations at Aggregate and insist that it accept the Cemstone contract. In negotiations, Slawson told Cemstone that the union would extend pickets to all its locations in case of a strike, whether or not their contracts had expired. Slawson also agreed to reach out to Local 160 to bring Apple Valley under the area contract.

"All that happened because of the organizing we did for a year prior to bargaining," says McNattin. "The union leadership was dealing with an organized and informed membership. This was the path of least resistance for them."

Area-Wide on its Way

Negotiations went pretty much as planned. The union reached a master agreement with Cemstone. Drivers at Aggregate authorized a strike and held out for complete parity with Cemstone in vacation, holiday pay, sick days, and floating holidays. Local 120 leaders convinced Local 160 to join the master agreement and their contract expiration date was modified to match the master agreement. The union then targeted Apple Valley to complete the area-wide agreement. It "cannot be far behind," says McNattin.

The next step is to organize the non-union ready-mix companies in the area. "The metro-area agreement should go a long way toward bringing new drivers to the Teamsters," concludes McNattin.

Resources

- New Directions Workers Education Center. The WEC no longer initiates Solidarity Schools itself but can offer technical assistance with planning and running Solidarity Schools and developing specific "fightback strategy" educational conferences. Contact Jerry Tucker, 940 Oak Knoll Manor Dr., St. Louis, MO 63119. Email jtuckernd@earthlink.net.
- Facilitators guide for Solidarity Schools. Free from Jobs with Justice, 3353 Washington St., Boston, MA 02130. 617-524-8778. jwj@massjwj.net. Website: massjwj.net.
- St. Paul Labor Speakers Club, 411 Mahoney St., St. Paul, MN 55102. 612-696-6371. rachleff@macalester.edu. www.urww.org/LaborSpeakersClub.
- *Navistar: Promise and Betrayal,* by Anne Pick, 2003. 35 minutes. When the Canadian Auto Workers struck the Navistar truck plant in Ontario, strikers and flying squad supporters kept replacement workers from entering, stopped concessions, and stymied management efforts to transfer some work to Mexico. Available from CAW, 205 Placer Court, Communications Dept., Toronto, Ontario M2H 3H9. 416-495-6548. cawcomm@caw.ca. $10 Canadian postpaid.

Action Questions

Because union solidarity can take so many forms, the first questions you want to ask are about your goals. The next set of questions concerns the strategy you will use to achieve those goals.

1. Are you raising support for your own cause or for another group of workers?

2. Is the goal relatively short-term, such as a strike, a contract, or organizing? Or is the goal relatively long-term, such as reforming a union, building a rank-and-file group, or creating an area solidarity network? What can you do to have short-term and long-term solidarity reinforce each other?

3. What sort of resources do you have now: people, money, experience?

4. What kind of support is needed: money, material support, volunteers, attendees, advice, publicity, public pressure?

5. What kind of educational work needs to be done to alert people about the issues—leaflets, meetings, conferences, media work?

6. How will you make your initial contacts with the workers you need to reach? Visits, email, existing union structures?

7. How can you involve other workers in action? Demonstrations? Pickets? Social events? Fundraising? Boycotts? Wearing buttons? Speaking and voting at their union meetings?

8. What can you ask different people to do? Can some devote more time than others? Can some take more risks, such as being disciplined or getting arrested? Do some have money or expertise they can donate?

9. What are the limits of what you can expect from people? Can you expect massive turnout to events or must you plan something smaller?

10. What organizations or ongoing struggles can you turn to for help? Have you built connections with these people long before you need them?

11. How confrontational is your solidarity strategy? Will you need people to shut down plants or get arrested? Or is your strategy based on public pressure or education?

12. How can you institutionalize your work? Can you create a group that meets regularly? Can you put on a set of events, such as rallies, educational events, conferences, picketing, and direct action that will build a culture of solidarity in your company, city, or union?

13. Does your local have existing relationships with other locals or unions? What are they like? Do you share news, contracts, strategy? If you are in the same industry, does management try to play you off against each other? Do the locals or unions try to coordinate bargaining or other activities to counter this whipsawing? Could your union initiate such coordination?

14. What about the local central labor body? Does your local send delegates? What happens there? Is it possible to work through the central labor council to establish contacts between locals?

15. What about setting up an informal group of union activists or leaders who get together to discuss problems and support strikes? Who would you call first?

Authors

Aaron Brenner is a labor historian, researcher, writer, and editor in New York City. He has written about international labor solidarity, union reform movements, and rank-and-file rebellions by Teamsters, telephone workers, and postal workers, and is the editor of *The Encyclopedia of Strikes in American History.*

Paul McLennan is a retired member of Amalgamated Transit Union Local 732 and active in Atlanta Jobs with Justice.

Notes

1. This story comes from Gene Austin, "Beyond Buckets: A Plant-Gate Collection that Builds Solidarity," *Labor Notes*, January 2001.

2. See N. Renuka Uthappa, "Two-Tiered Grocery Contract Leaves Anger, Questions," and Chris Kutalik and N. Renuka Uthappa, "What We Can Learn From the Grocery Strike," *Labor Notes,* April 2004; Joel Jordan, "A National Struggle Is Needed," *Against the Current* 108 (Jan./Feb. 2004), p. 3; Kelly Candaele and Peter Dreier, "Lessons from the Picket Line," www.alternet.org/story.html?StoryID=18029.

On the Troublemaker's Website

See www.labornotes.org for two more solidarity how-to stories:

• Forming a multi-union council at a single employer.

• Forming an organization of local presidents that remains independent of the national union structure (in the American Postal Workers Union).

15. Organizing New Members

by Aaron Brenner

Strategic, Comprehensive, Rank-and-File Organizing

THE NEED TO ORGANIZE the unorganized is obvious. Only thirteen percent of workers belong to unions, and in the private sector not even nine percent are organized. As union density has fallen, the labor movement has lost influence. Unions must grow if they are to wield any clout with employers or politicians.

But there are other, more human, reasons why unions must organize. "For the very first time it felt like we had the power." "I'm just less afraid." "There's another world out there we didn't know about—the union world, where you get some respect." "The union is not just about money. It's about dealing with and preventing injustice." These are the thoughts of workers at the San Francisco Marriott Hotel, who fought for 13 years to organize and win a contract. They demonstrate more than any statistic why organizing is essential.

AFL-CIO leaders have emphasized the need to organize since they came to power in 1995. Yet international union leaders have been unable to stop the decline in union density. They point to a multitude of reasons: employer opposition, runaway shops, deindustrialization, globalization, technological change, anti-union government policy, restrictive labor law, media hostility, pro-business culture, and the way unions are structured.

No question, the atmosphere for organizing is extremely hostile. Yet unions do win over half of NLRB elections. Organizing is possible. Kate Bronfenbrenner and Robert Hickey, researchers at Cornell University's School of Industrial and Labor Relations, go so far as to say, "It is too easy to blame the global economy, labor law, and employer opposition for organizing failures, when in fact many unions continue to run weak and ineffectual organizing campaigns and have mostly themselves to blame for their organizing failures."[1]

Workers want unions. In poll after poll, majorities say they would vote yes in a free and fair election. And workers do join unions. Even more could join if unions ran better comprehensive campaigns.

Bronfenbrenner and Hickey studied hundreds of organizing drives and identify ten organizing tactics that work:

1. Adequate and appropriate staff and financial resources
2. Strategic targeting and research
3. Active and representative rank-and-file organizing committees
4. Active member-volunteer organizers
5. Person-to-person contact inside and outside the workplace
6. Monitoring union support and setting thresholds for moving ahead with the campaign
7. Issues that resonate in the workplace and the community
8. Creative, escalating internal tactics involving members at the workplace
9. Creative, escalating external tactics involving members outside work locally, nationally, and/or internationally
10. Building for the first contract during the organizing campaign.

Unfortunately, no union uses all of these strategies. Few use more than a couple. If they did, they would win more organizing drives. Bronfenbrenner and Hickey found that the more of these strategies a union used, the more likely its organizing drive would win. In fact, in the one percent of campaigns that used eight of these strategies, the rate of victory was a hundred percent.

The conclusion, say Bronfenbrenner and Hickey, is that unions must run comprehensive campaigns that integrate multiple tactics and activate workers. The importance of comprehensive campaigns holds true no matter which industry unions try to organize, no matter the size of the employer they face, no matter how mobile and global the company they confront, no matter how hostile the company acts, no matter what type of workers they

More Organizing Tactics

FOR MORE ON ORGANIZING new members into unions, see these stories:
- Linen workers strike for recognition, in Chapter 11, Corporate Campaigns.
- Cintas workers' corporate campaign, also in Chapter 11.
- The Interfaith Workers' Center helps workers choose and organize a union, Chapter 17.
- Using health and safety to help organize a union among immigrants, Chapter 7.
- A community organization and the UFCW join forces to organize immigrant meatpackers, Chapter 16.

are organizing, and no matter how diverse or homogeneous the workforce is.

Does this mean comprehensive campaigns always win? No. But they are far more likely to succeed than the campaigns most unions run today.

Thinking Strategically about Organizing

Before unions start running comprehensive campaigns, they need to think strategically about targets. Unions should put their organizing efforts where they can make the most of the leverage they have against employers, and increase it. This means building union density in an industry through a long-term, big-picture plan. Planning and coordinating this kind of organizing is a task for international unions, something too few of them do. But local unions can also develop strategic plans for organizing within their jurisdictions and within their areas, and within the overall plan of the international, if it has one. We discuss how in the next section.

Even as unions think about the big picture of organizing an entire industry, they need to do the hard, slow, nitty-gritty work of developing rank-and-file leaders at target employers, so workers can learn to be leaders in their organizing campaigns. The examples in this chapter demonstrate just how important this rank-and-file perspective is to success.

It's hard, though, to graft a pro-rank-and-file approach to organizing new members onto a union where members are either inactive or ignored. As our section on member-organizers illustrates, unions can improve their success rates by combining their member education and leadership development programs with their organizing. Drives are more successful when current members are involved. Moreover, while organizing, member-organizers learn how to do strategic targeting, research, list building, problem identification, one-on-one discussions, house-calls, public speaking, and other leadership skills. In the process, they become leaders who can both organize new members and mobilize current ones. A rank-and-file organizing strategy also means recruiting women leaders and leaders of color. This is a strategic priority for building a labor movement that can respond to the working class as it really exists.

As the examples in this chapter demonstrate, unions who plan on organizing new members usually must build alliances with other unions, community groups, political leaders, and/or clergy *before* they begin a drive. In practice, this means offering concrete solidarity to the struggles of other workers and community organizations long before calling on them to support organizing.

Another strategic question is how the union seeks recognition. Since World War II, most unions have sought recognition through NLRB elections. The hurdles that employers can use to blockade this process have led more unions to seek card check recognition, where the company agrees to recognize the union after a certain number of workers sign union cards. We look at both these options in this chapter. We also give an example of surprise mass action to win recognition, and of striking for recognition, the most common way to win a union before World War II. For another example, see the story of the ABC Linen workers in Chapter 11.

Who Organizes and How?

There are many ways to organize workers, but virtually all of them rely on personal contact between "organizers" and workers. Organizers might be union staff, member-organizers from existing union workplaces, or rank and filers in the target workplace. Each has strengths and weaknesses, and the best campaigns use all three.

Effective staff organizers have experience in campaigns and knowledge about the industry. They often know what works and what doesn't, how to focus the issues, develop leaders, research the employer, conduct assessments, and roll with the employers' punches. The best organizers have experience in overseeing how all these aspects work together in a comprehensive campaign. They can educate, advocate, and inspire. What they often lack is intimate knowledge of the details of work and life for the workers at a particular company. And they often do not share the same ethnic, racial, religious, or cultural background.

Member-organizers are current or retired union members from other shops. They know the industry, the rhythm of the work, and why they want to be in the union. They have lived the same life and speak the same language as the workers they are organizing. Sometimes they may live in the same communities and have neighbors, friends, and family working in the workplace that's being organized. Often, they have organized their own workplaces. Workers like these can speak about the employer and the union with an authority that no outside organizer, no matter how dedicated and talented, can match.

Rank and filers in the target shop have many of the same advantages as member-organizers. They understand their co-workers, and they are the ones with the most on the line, the ones with the fire in the belly to bring the boss to heel. What they usually lack is organizing experience. But rank and filers have something just as important: the potential to organize their co-workers on the job. Only rank and filers can be there to face the boss in a captive-audience meeting, defend a co-worker abused by a supervisor, or lead a group to protest a foreman's pronouncement. Only rank and filers can build the union on the job, before and after it wins an election.

Rank and filers are important for one more reason: they are the lifeblood of powerful unions. Organizing should launch a "virtuous circle" of activism, by turning rank and filers into workplace activists who grow into union organizers and leaders who turn more rank and filers into workplace activists.

In what follows, we tell stories that illustrate successful organizing strategies, including some that have launched a virtuous circle of activism. These stories are aimed at local unions who want their unions to grow—and grow strong.

Strategic Targeting

by Gene Bruskin and Aaron Brenner

MANY LOCAL UNIONS organize "hot shops." Organizers wait for workers at a local company to call, then the organizers and the workers meet. If the workers are angry ("hot") enough, the local launches an organizing drive. This method of choosing organizing targets can sometimes add members to the local, but it's not the best way to increase workers' power vs. employers, either for the local or for the labor movement as a whole.

Hot-shop organizing is most problematic when it takes place in an industry unrelated to the union's core jurisdictions. The union expends resources where it might be able to win elections but where it lacks the density and experience to bargain and represent workers effectively. Even worse, this kind of organizing diverts precious resources from industries where the union already has members and needs to build greater power.

A more promising approach to organizing is strategic targeting. Here, a union develops an overall plan to organize targets it chooses. It focuses its resources on shops that will increase its economic strength in its core industries and expand its political influence. Sticking to its primary jurisdictions allows a union to exploit its bargaining leverage either directly through already-organized units or indirectly through unionized customers and suppliers. The goal is 100 percent unionization in its industry, and the union has to think about how to get there.

One example of strategic organizing is UNITE HERE's national campaign to unionize Cintas (see Chapter 11). The union has organized a third of the laundry industry in the last five years, but Cintas represents the industry's "800-pound gorilla." For UNITE HERE to deliver sizable wage improvements for laundry workers, it must organize Cintas.

Two other examples are discussed in this chapter: HERE Local 2 in San Francisco has been organizing the city's hotels one by one, bringing them under a master contract that is eliminating the ability of non-union hotels to undercut conditions at union hotels. As union density increases, Local 2 has more leverage over non-union hotels. Eventually, it could have enough resources to engage in the same kind of strategic organizing in another of its core jurisdictions: restaurants.

CWA recognized early that unionized telephone companies were opening non-union wireless subsidiaries, which threatened the union's power in the industry. To end this threat at SBC, the second-largest phone company in the country, CWA District 6 ran a five-year campaign in five states and won neutrality, card check, and then a union for workers at the SBC subsidiary Cingular Wireless.

In these three examples, each union recognized that non-union employers in its core industry threatened both working conditions and the union's economic and political power. Each developed a plan that marked its targets' weaknesses and its own strengths. The goal was to organize on a large scale. Each union "thought big," figuring out how to go after multiple targets owned by a company, by involving the international, other locals, or other unions. Then it executed that plan through a comprehensive campaign that drew on those strengths, including organizers, current members, political clout, and community connections. In two cases, the union organized thousands of new workers, while in the UNITE HERE case the struggle continues.

International union leaders should initiate and guide strategic planning for organizing, but as the last two examples demonstrate, locals and regions can organize strategically, too. That's what we focus on here.

Developing a Plan

In developing an organizing plan, a local evaluates the non-union companies in its core sectors, creates a series of targets, and prioritizes those targets. It assesses its financial and personnel resources, in order to understand its own strengths and limits. And it considers the possibilities for support from community organizations, religious groups, and politicians.

Building on a Previous Defeat

DURING THE AMERICAN POSTAL WORKERS Union organizing drive at East Coast Leasing, an over-the-road mail hauler in Greensboro, North Carolina, "several workers came forward and said, 'I was talked out of voting for the union last time and I'm not going to let that happen again,'" says Mark Dimondstein, the APWU organizer on the campaign.

One of those workers was Mark Williams, an ECL driver who is now president of the local. "The company dispatcher told me our wages were set by the Service Contract Act, so the union couldn't do anything to change them, that the union was just a bunch of outside people who wanted our dues and would eliminate our seniority. I'd only been on the job seven months and didn't know any better, but those were all lies.

"The owner of the company had said, 'We are family,' and promised to improve wages and conditions. But once we voted out the union, ECL started to cut time off our runs [essentially a cut in pay]. It left a bad taste in our mouths. This was maybe seven years earlier, but we still remembered. We weren't going to let it happen again. Fool me once, shame on you. Fool me twice, shame on me."

Workers who can speak from experience are a huge advantage in an organizing drive. Look for them.

Once a local has an overall organizing plan, it researches target companies to understand their strengths and weaknesses. The Internet makes such research easier, so no local should be organizing a company it knows nothing about (see the Appendix on Researching Employers).

Strategic targeting does not mean a local never organizes hot shops, but it does mean that it evaluates calls from hot shops in terms of how well those shops fit into its overall strategy.

Here are some suggestions and questions to help you develop an organizing plan.

Selecting Targets

Unorganized units: Start where you already have some strength—in workplaces where the local represents some workers. What are the unorganized units at the company? Do you have the nurses, but not the techs or service workers? Do you have the back of the store, but not the front? The skilled, but not the unskilled? How can current members help organize the other units?

For example, nurses at Fletcher Allen Hospital in Burlington, Vermont organized into AFT Health Care. Then they helped organize the hospital's licensed practical nurses. Then all the nurses joined in to help the service workers organize.

Core industries: What are the non-union targets in your local's core industries in its geographical jurisdiction? Think of your company's competitors. You can find names and locations of companies on state government business websites, at the local chamber of commerce, on websites run by industry trade associations, in Dun and Bradstreet reports (on CD or through online subscriptions at libraries), and at business information sites, such as www.corporateinformation.com. Information on nonprofit companies can be found in their tax filings at www.guidestar.org.

The APWU, for example, traditionally limited itself to representing workers in the U.S. Postal Service. But it started organizing private mail haulers and private direct mail processors, because these non-union companies could undermine wages at the Postal Service, where, by law, wages must be comparable to the private sector.

Related targets: What targets can you find among the suppliers and customers of the local's organized units? Examples here might include a grocery union organizing food-processing workers and vice versa, or an auto union organizing parts manufacturers.

Company Profile

Corporate information: Who owns the target? What else do they own and where? Is it union or non-union elsewhere? Can you go after multiple units/locations of the same company at the same time, possibly with other locals or unions? Is the company shrinking or growing? Profitable or struggling? Is it vulnerable to import competition or to larger companies making the same product? Is it a critical player in the local/regional market?

This information might be found at the company's website; in the company's filings with the U.S. Securities and Exchange Commission (SEC), www.sec.gov; on business information websites, such as www.hoovers.com or www.corporateinformation.com; through subscriptions like Dun and Bradstreet; and from general searches done on www.google.com or www.newslink.org.

Company size: How big is the target? Big enough to be worthwhile? Too big for your local's resources? Will the local be able to service it?

Labor relations history: Has any union attempted to organize the target? What happened? Were unfair labor practice (ULP) charges filed? Does the target have any wage and hour violations? This information is available from various government sources, such as the websites and publications of the National Labor Relations Board, the Department of Labor, the Federal Mediation and Conciliation Service, and the Equal Employment Opportunity Commission. The Food and Allied Service Trades Labor CD, available at www.fastaflcio.org, brings much of this information together in one easy-to-use place. Other sections of the AFL-CIO, including the Building and Construction Trades Department, have similar resources on their websites.

Contractability: What will it take to win recognition *and* a first contract at the target? What is the company's Achilles heel? The fight for a first contract starts from the beginning of the organizing campaign, and workers need to be educated from the start that winning recognition is only one step, and is often much easier than getting a contract. By law a company must recognize the union if the union has a majority of the workers. But if it simply refuses to bargain, the worst penalty it faces is a piece of paper telling it to bargain in good faith. The only way a union gets a company to sign a contract is to make the cost of not signing greater than the cost of signing.

Road map: What will the union need to win? Strong worker actions? Boycotts? Corporate campaign? You need a map for why and how the company will eventually sign a first contract.

Target Workers

Issues: Why would the workers at the target want to organize? Better wages? Safer workplace? Ultimately, your success will depend on how well you address these questions, but you will not know the issues until you start talking to workers or place a "salt," a pro-union person who takes a job at the target. However, you can obtain some information in advance about company benefits at www.freeerisa.com, safety and health issues at www.osha.gov, and sometimes wage levels and other valuable information on the company's own website. To compare pay, wages by occupation and location are listed at www.bls.gov/bls/blswage.htm.

Ethnic/racial/gender makeup: Who works at the target? Do you have staff and members who speak their language and know their culture? Do the workers have community and religious organizations that might support the union? (See Chapter 16—Bringing Immigrants into the Movement.)

Finding workers/leaders: Most good organizers have developed ways to meet workers in targeted plants, such as salting, leads from existing and former members and their families, visits to workers' local hangouts, and running license plates (not legal anymore in most states). Often workers can supply lists of names. Internet sites such at www.theultimates.com allow you to run names and get addresses and phone numbers or do the reverse. Registries of licensed workers such as nurses, listings at a local tax assessor's office, and voter registration lists from state and local governments all allow you to check names against name and address lists.

Local Evaluation

Resources: What kind of organizing resources does your local have: staff, member volunteers, and money for lost time for members? Is help available from your international or central labor council? Do those resources match what's needed to win recognition and a first contract at your targets?

Progress measurement: How will the local judge its progress on each organizing drive? What milestones must be reached before a campaign can move forward? Will the local know when to give up?

Once it understands its core industries, the companies it's up against, the workers it's targeting, the issues involved, and the extent of its resources, a local can produce an overall organizing strategy that prioritizes targets, plans for the use of resources, and establishes goals by which the steps of each organizing campaign can be measured. Then it's time to do the actual organizing.

Building a Workplace Committee

ORGANIZING DRIVES usually start by putting together a committee of workers who will build the union among their co-workers. Ideally, the most active, respected, and eloquent leaders among the workers form this committee. The trick is to find those leaders and convince them to support the union.

Ellen Norton and two other organizers with SEIU Local 2020 helped build an organizing committee among the 1,800 service, maintenance, and technical workers at North Shore Medical Center, which has one hospital in Lynn and another in Salem, Massachusetts. Norton is a staff organizer, but volunteer member-organizers and rank and filers at the workplace being organized can also run the activities, she suggests.

With the aid of organizers, the committee can initiate a series of activities that involve more and more workers in fighting for the union. Through this process, committee members gain confidence, build their influence, and recruit new rank-and-file leaders to expand the committee and the network of support among the workforce.

Starting Small

"We start with our initial contacts," says Norton. "Some people have called the union to complain. Some are fed up with management and want to organize. Some have a relative in the union. We meet with them and talk about the job, what's going on, why they called, and what they want to see changed. We want to learn the major issues.

"We talk to them about what the union is, what it does, and how having a voice can impact their life at work. Then we talk about how the boss will campaign against the union. We do not pull any punches. We tell them they might get harassed or fired for trying to organize.

"We ask our contacts to identify potential committee members. Whom do they trust? Whom do they talk to when they want the facts about what is happening at work? As we talk to interested people, we have them go through a list of workers in their department, put together work schedules, and identify people who should be involved. This gives us some idea of their knowledge about their work and their co-workers. Then we ask them to bring a few people to a meeting.

"We start with small meetings. At smaller meetings, interested workers can ask questions and make suggestions. It's less intimidating than big meetings, and they don't have to fight for attention. They see a union organizer and rank-and-file union supporters face-to-face.

"It's important to organize department by department, so organizing committee members are not overwhelmed thinking about the entire hospital. They can concentrate on their own department. But we don't have department meetings until we have successful smaller meetings.

"Sometimes, potential committee members cannot get people to meetings. They are too cautious or they are not really liked by their co-workers. If that becomes apparent, we might have them take an organizer or a rank-and-file union supporter to the hospital to introduce them to other potential committee members in their department.

Leadership Responsibilities

"At meetings, we look for workers who can answer co-workers' questions," says Norton. "We observe the dynamics in the room. Who responds? Who defers to whom? Who understands the union? Who understands what the boss is doing? Is everyone mentioning a worker who is not present? I want to meet that person.

"We also look for people who are good judges of their co-workers. How well did they describe their co-workers' interests and concerns before they brought them to the meeting?

"As the campaign progresses, leaders must understand what the union is, how it works, and the plan to build it in their hospital. They need to be well versed on how decisions are made within the organization, how dues work, how strikes happen, and the process of negotiations. They must be able to teach their co-workers these things and prepare them for what management might do or say.

"To help with this, we do trainings on what to expect during the campaign and how to handle it. We explain how rank-and-file workers can take over the employer's captive-audience meetings, how to challenge management when they provide false information about the union. We may have a mock meeting and role-play. We also save anti-union literature from previous campaigns at other hospitals and review it with the committee so they can respond when their hospital uses it.

"As the committee comes together, we start with more tangible tasks. Committee members might get co-workers to circulate a petition, sign a union card, or wear a union button. Then they might get their co-workers to take actions, such as approaching the employer in a group with a demand. Through these actions, workers build their leadership skills.

"We constantly build the committee throughout the

Workers and Organizers

WHAT IS THE RELATIONSHIP between staff organizers and the workers they organize? Who leads and who follows? Who makes the decisions, the organizers or the workers? Here's how one organizer answered those questions on one organizing drive.

"Mostly it was workers talking to workers," says Mark Dimondstein, lead organizer on the APWU's campaign to organize East Coast Leasing, a mail hauler in Greensboro, North Carolina. "They'd meet in hotels where they laid over. Since most workers had questions about the union—dues, operations, negotiations—the workers would set up meetings with the organizers. They'd tell us where to meet and who to talk to. We didn't tell them. It was a pretty decent example of worker empowerment.

"The organizers had a background role. Our job was to encourage and educate workers to talk to each other and build the organization. We told them that if they weren't going to do it for themselves, we would not go forward: 'If you won't have a committee, we won't do it. You must be identified. If you are ready, we are.'"

Over three months of mostly one-on-one meetings, the workers and organizers built a committee. "The organizing committee had a very methodical approach," notes Dimondstein. "They kept a list of workers, did mailings, and met regularly, usually on Sundays, to review their progress and give updates, who they talked to, what their reactions were, if they were still on the fence, how to move them to the union side. They would invite people at relay points to breakfast or lunch meetings in small groups. Organizers would come to some of those meetings, so the union had a presence, so the workers knew we took it seriously. Workers need be able to look the union in the eye."

Organizers Have the Overview

Dimondstein is being modest about the organizers' role in the East Coast Leasing campaign. While he is right to emphasize workers' self-organization, he is downplaying the crucial role the staff organizers played, and indeed the role they play in most successful organizing drives.

APWU organizers had a strategic overview. Long before the ECL campaign, some APWU officers and members, including Dimondstein, recognized that in order to deal with the Postal Service's contracting out, APWU could and should represent workers in the private mail industry. They convinced the union convention to vote several million dollars for organizing. Dimondstein became a national organizer to help locals do the organizing.

APWU organizers made critical interventions in the ECL campaign to help the workers think strategically. So, for example, when it came time to bargain their first contract, the workers' negotiating committee took future organizing into account. See the box "Bargaining While Thinking Organizing" later in this chapter.

APWU organizers had industry knowledge and knew how to find answers to important questions. Thus, when the company insisted that the Service Contract Act limited the wages and benefits ECL employees could receive, they did research to demonstrate that this was false.

Finally, APWU organizers understood how to run a comprehensive campaign, as defined at the beginning of this chapter. For example, they suggested that ECL workers produce flyers with pictures and statements of support from the mayor, members of the city council, clergy, and other union leaders. "The community support campaign was important," says Dimondstein. "We drew on contacts built by existing APWU officials and members. Workers feel more secure when they see such people coming forward to support their rights."

In the ECL campaign APWU staff organizers did two things. They led and they built leaders. Not coincidentally, that's what ECL workers went on to do too. Several of them became local union leaders and helped organize other private sector postal workers.

campaign. We might give one committee member unsigned union cards but another co-worker brings the signed cards back. That's a potential committee member. Who responds during and after captive-audience meetings to soothe workers' fears? They are potential committee members. Who gets their co-workers to wear buttons, come out to leaflet, or march on the boss? They are committee members.

Committee in Action

"In the early stages there are no regular committee meetings," says Norton. "Instead, committee members concentrate on their departments, putting together small meetings to get more people involved. Once things start moving forward to an election campaign, the committee typically meets once a week.

"We concentrate on the largest departments first, since they can turn the election and that is where management concentrates its anti-union efforts. For departments where we don't already have contacts, we will do home visits to find committee members. This is a last resort. We don't like home visits, especially early in the campaign, because they get buzz going and alert management. We prefer to make contacts from department to department within the hospital."

SEIU Local 2020 tries to build a committee that is at least 10 percent of the unit, which would be about 180 people at North Shore Medical Center. At the least, they want the committee to cover 60 percent of the departments.

Once the committee comes together, it puts together a calendar of events leading up to the election. The calendar usually includes a petition, button days, and informational pickets, an activity each week to keep the campaign moving.

Involving Current Members

"Where possible, we try to take advantage of current union members," says Norton. "Several workers at North Shore have second jobs where they are in our union. They might not have experience with a previous organizing drive, but they can tell co-workers it's a lie when management says union dues are $1,000 a year. They can explain what the union does, what's expected of workers, and what to expect from management. They are invaluable, especially since organizers are sometimes seen as salespeople who cannot be trusted.

"The union also has a formal program that publicizes the importance of organizing and the need for member-organizers and provides training. We have many members involved on many levels of organizing. They help organizers get into worksites. They work with organizing committees, run informational meetings, do home visits, make phone calls, and do site visits. Some come out on internships and work with staff organizers. We even have 'flight teams' who 'fly' to help a campaign wherever it is."

The Laborers' Eastern Region Organizing Fund turns members into professional organizers, and also encourages members to volunteer on organizing drives.

Members As Organizers

MANY SUCCESSFUL ORGANIZING CAMPAIGNS involve organizers who are union members, not professional organizers. Why? Because "members make the best organizers," says Byron Silva, a coordinator for the Laborers' Eastern Region Organizing Fund (LEROF), which has been organizing mostly immigrant asbestos-removal workers in Delaware, New Jersey, and New York. "They understand what workers are going through and can communicate with them. They've done the job and know what it's like. Asbestos workers will listen to someone who has worn the mask."

Here we look at two ways to use member-organizers. LEROF has a formal education program aimed at moving members off the job and into full-time organizing. In the process, current members organize new members. Another union, AFSCME Local 3299, has an internal mobilizing program that develops members who lead their co-workers in on-the-job action and then participate in external organizing. In both cases, the unions devote a good deal of time, people, and money to developing member-organizers.

LEROF: Education To Organize

LEROF takes a two-pronged approach. The union turns members into professional organizers, and it also encourages members to volunteer on organizing drives.

LEROF runs a regular three-hour class to teach members about the union. "The topics include the history of the union, politics, labor law, ULPs [unfair labor practices], and the external factors that affect the union, such as the political backlash since Reagan," says Silva. "We also do a negotiation exercise where members learn how the union deals with management."

The class is taught at all of the 35 locals in the Eastern Region, which includes Delaware, New Jersey, and New York. Shop stewards must take the class, and business agents encourage all members to attend. Translation into Polish, Serbo-Croatian, and Spanish is available to accommodate the construction industry's diverse workforce.

From the three-hour class, LEROF picks two of the most active and interested members to participate in organizing training. Over two days at a local hotel, these members learn more about the union, labor law, and organizing techniques. They learn about grievances and contracts. They do role-plays, taking the parts of organizers and potential members. If the union has a picket nearby, the members attend. And they do a real house visit with an organizer, to get a taste of talking to potential members.

The two-day course runs on Fridays and Saturdays and LEROF pays attendees for the first day, when it is a lost day of work. During the course, instructors watch and rate the workers. Do they listen enough when they act as organizers in the role-plays? Do they answer questions about labor law correctly? Can they handle anti-union sentiments from potential members?

Top-rated members are hired as full-time organizers, working first with experienced organizers and then leading campaigns themselves.

At some point in their first year, full-time organizers attend "a ten-day boot camp," says Silva. "It goes into organizing in depth, with hands-on work. Members follow trucks to find sites to organize. They make daily house-calls. They learn how to use the Internet and how to do research on companies. They train to speak publicly and how to use labor law."

The ten-day boot camps are held around the country where the union has high-profile organizing campaigns in progress. The new organizers help on these campaigns, leading picket lines, handbilling, and doing house-calls. They also learn to handle the large inflatable rat that has become construction workers' universal symbol of an anti-union employer.

The boot camps include additional classes, taught by instructors from around the country, on labor law, membership mobilization, leadership development, union history, new immigrants, the changing economy, and political action.

Members who complete the three-hour class and/or the two-day workshop but are not chosen as staff organizers are still encouraged to work on campaigns. These member-organizers call workers, make house visits, provide translation, and mobilize for strikes, demonstrations, and other job actions.

Member-organizers also help identify unfair labor practices, prevailing wage violations, OSHA abuses, and other employer violations, which the union then publicly exposes to pressure the contractors and their clients. The union uses ULPs as the basis for strikes against employers that are resisting the union. The law allows these strikes and strikers cannot legally be permanently replaced.

So far in four years, the LEROF program has developed 35 members into organizers and added several thousand members to the Laborers' Eastern Region. For more on LEROF's organizing, see Chapter 16.

AFSCME Local 3299: From Internal to External Organizing

At AFSCME Local 3299, member-organizers develop out of the local's constant internal organizing efforts. New leadership at the local, which represents 17,000 service and patient care workers at all nine campuses of the University of California, has been trying to revitalize

Member Action Team members in AFSCME Local 3299 crowd the first day of bargaining at the University of California. Management threatened to have the workers arrested.

the local by mobilizing members to confront their bosses on the job.

"For workers to take ownership of the union, they have to take action together," says President LaKesha Harrison. "We don't file many grievances, even when we can. Instead, we try to solve our problems through action."

The local sets up Member Action Teams (MATs), each with eight to 20 members, at every worksite. One MAT member is the team's organizer. MATs are workers' first line of defense when problems arise on the job. In one example at UCLA, 20 groundskeeping workers marched to the office of the head of facilities with a petition demanding that the department cut excessive management and alleviate short-staffing. For the first time, management agreed to meet with the workers and address their concerns.

MAT organizers get their teams to union meetings, keep them informed about the union's activities, sign them up for political action, and meet with them one-on-one to learn their concerns. They encourage their team members to attend training sessions to learn about the union, practice one-on-one communication skills, and brainstorm ways to improve their workplace.

MAT organizers receive regular training on such topics as mobilizing members for action, contract bargaining, political action, grievance filing, and house visits. They work with MAT captains, who are responsible for leading a number of MAT organizers. Together, organizers and captains plan and coordinate MAT activities. At UCLA Hospital, for example, MAT captains and organizers among the respiratory therapists organized a series of actions—wearing stickers, distributing leaflets, and a petition with 200 signatures—that restored the workers' overtime bonus system.

MAT organizers and captains across the UC system meet regularly to share experiences and receive more training.

"Sometimes members ask who elected these MAT leaders," says Harrison. "There is no election. They are appointed, but they virtually appoint themselves. MAT leaders are the people who do the work, who mobilize their co-workers, get them to meetings, make the phone calls, distribute the leaflets, and have their co-workers' trust."

How does Harrison find such people? "We look for the natural leaders," she says. "We talk to people in a unit. We ask them who they talk to when they have a problem. Who do they trust? Who organizes the social events, the lottery, the events after work, the potluck? One person's name usually keeps coming up over and over.

"But the person who jumps up and says 'I'm the leader' is usually not the real leader. They just want to be the union person, the person with the information, the one who saves the day. But leadership is not about doing things for other people. It's about getting them to do things for themselves."

To separate the posers from the true leaders, Harrison uses little tests. "We ask a potential MAT leader to bring four people to a meeting or get a bunch of flyers out or sign members up for the political action program," says Harrison. "They do these things and they become the MAT organizer. Often, they've done this stuff already. They're already trying to be helpful, because they're natural leaders."

The development of MAT organizers and MAT captains eventually produces candidates for Local 3299's lost-time organizer program. These are workers who take time off from work to organize new members into the union. The program has been particularly successful in organizing workers at the University's many subcontractors. Since lost-time organizers often perform the same work as workers at the subcontractors, they can relate to the non-union workers and explain exactly how the union can help.

In their 2001 contract, Local 3299 won the right to take workers off the job for up to 90 days. Lost-time organizers attend a three-day AFL-CIO Organizing Institute training and two Local 3299 organizing classes. Then they work with lead organizers for the first two or three weeks of their assignments. They participate in campaign planning, house calls, meetings, protests, and every other organizing activity the union does.

Several lost-time organizers helped organize food-court workers at UCLA. One result of their efforts was more lost-time organizers, who went on to organize even more subcontract workers. "Mirna Martinez worked at the Taco Bell in the food court," says Harrison. "She was the first person to sign up as a member, the first union member at Taco Bell in the world. She understood the fears of her co-workers, who were mostly Spanish-speaking immigrants like her. With Mirna, we organized everyone at the Taco Bell and then everyone at the food court."

The food court workers became UCLA employees and members of Local 3299, with much better benefits and wages. Then, says Harrison, Mirna Martinez became a lost-time organizer on a successful campaign to organize workers at other campus subcontractors. "Mirna can say to the janitors at the museum or the parking attendants at the stadium, 'I was where you are a year ago, no benefits, no union. I know what it's like to come to America. I took the chance with the union. You can, too.' Her passionate personal testimony is very persuasive."

Kim Carter, who runs Local 3299's lost-time organizers program, cites several keys to success. First, "a strong internal structure gives you a pool of leaders to draw upon and makes sure that your union keeps operating at the unit level if you pull a leader out to go organize."

Second, you have to figure out the right criteria for a good organizer. "It's not the loudest person," says Carter. "It's the person with the demonstrated commitment to the union and to organizing."

Third, "you have to be brutally honest about what's expected of external organizers," Carter says. "They have to work very hard and they cannot be looking for a union job that takes them away from organizing. We start most lost-time organizers on 30-day trials. Either we extend the term or send them back to work."

Finally, a lost-time program is not cheap. The union must have the money to commit, as well as the people.

"Our goal as leaders is to identify other potential leaders and train them to reproduce themselves," concludes Harrison.

Mass Action at Iroquois Trucking

AGAINST SMALL, LOCALLY BASED EMPLOYERS, especially those who are vulnerable when Teamsters honor a picket line, a single mass picket can compel a company to recognize a union. In the case that follows, the Teamsters used such a threat by picketing not their target company, but its client. The legality of this tactic is dubious. The Teamsters were ostensibly picketing the trucks of the target company; only they were doing so *at* the client company, which is legal under the NLRB's "common situs" standards. However, they were hoping all trucks and all client company workers would honor the pickets, a possibly illegal example of a secondary boycott. In this case, the tactic worked and had no legal repercussions.[2]

Starting Socially

When Teamsters Local 705 sent Rich DeVries to Kankakee County south of Chicago to organize quarry drivers, it was too late in the construction season to organize any kind of workplace action at a non-union shop. So DeVries organized an end-of-the-season picnic for current union members. "We sent an invitation to all the members," says DeVries. "We also sent invitations to quarry workers who were members of the Operating Engineers and Laborers unions, with the permission of their local union leadership."

DeVries also started house-calls to members, to introduce himself and get to know them. Most of each visit was purely social. "If you cannot engage in the most rudimentary social contact with co-workers, you cannot expect them to follow you in struggle," says DeVries. "You have to develop their trust. The single most important part of organizing is listening to and hearing your co-workers. If you cannot hear them, they will not take the time to hear you."

The one question DeVries asked during house-calls was: "Who should I talk to about what's going on at work?" It was his way of identifying the natural leaders at each workplace. These would be possible member-organizers.

About 60 people showed up to the end-of-the-season picnic in the parking lot of the union hall in late October. "We stood around on a drizzly day drinking beer and talking about the season," says DeVries. "We also talked about the organizing we were going to do and how we would need everyone to be ready to help. We asked everyone to put together phone lists of people they could mobilize for a job action, whether or not they were in the union."

Over the winter, as DeVries continued house-calling members and building the phone tree to over 400 people, he settled on Iroquois Trucking as his organizing target. The company was double-breasted, with about half its workers in the union subsidiary and the other half non-union. That caused resentment among the union workers and made many want to help the organizing drive.

DeVries and several member-organizers began meeting with the Iroquois drivers, tracking them down at truck stops and fuel pumps. Through one-on-one and small meetings they collected union representation cards from a majority.

"The Iroquois drivers were afraid they would be fired when management found out they were organizing," says DeVries. "So we looked for a way to have our current members help them and keep them safe."

Mini Mass Action

DURING AN SEIU LOCAL 73 DRIVE among cafeteria workers at the University of Illinois at Chicago, member-organizers were having trouble finding potential organizing committee members at one satellite cafeteria. "So organizing committee members at the main cafeteria organized to all meet outside the satellite cafeteria at the end of a shift," says Tom Burke, a member-organizer.

"We had 20 workers there to talk to the 15 workers on the shift. The message was clear. 'We are organized. We are together, and we want a union.' That helped, and we convinced a majority to support the union."

Creating a Crisis

After about five months of organizing both the current members and the Iroquois drivers, DeVries set the date for a job action designed to force Iroquois management to recognize the union. And all the Iroquois drivers would have to do was stay in their barn.

DeVries sent word out that all phone tree members were to meet at 4 a.m. on a given morning in front of the Vulcan Materials quarry. The quarry produces dolimitic limestone, which is used for high-quality concrete. It was sure to be in demand on the day of action.

Before the day, DeVries won pledges from members of the Operating Engineers and Laborers who ran the Vulcan quarry that they would not cross any Teamsters picket lines.

"We had talked to the Laborers, Electricians, Operating Engineers, and Teamsters in Kankakee County," says DeVries. "They understood that there would be a recognition picket line at the Vulcan quarry. They knew that their physical presence at 4 a.m. would lead to solidarity that would put the Iroquois management on the defensive."

On the day of action, 400 workers, risking the loss of a day's pay, showed up and parked their cars along the road to the quarry, three hours before it was due to open. "We told the managers of the quarry that we would picket any trucks from Iroquois," says DeVries. "A few minutes later, the superintendent of the quarry showed up. He called Iroquois and said, 'Are you going to sign a contract or not, because I have several hundred Teamsters here blocking the quarry.'"

At the same time, the Iroquois drivers back at their barn, communicating with the union via radio, told management that they would not drive to the Vulcan quarry. "It was their first concerted activity," says DeVries. "All they had to do was say, 'No, we're not walking into the hornet's nest over at Vulcan.'"

If Iroquois management had refused to recognize the Teamsters, there would have been a virtual general strike in construction that day, since so many drivers were at the Vulcan quarry. "There would have been no drivers to drive for the other companies," says DeVries. "That would then get the employers' association motivated to do something."

Not only did Iroquois management agree to recognize the union even before the quarry opened, it signed the industry pattern contract before the end of the day.

Striking for Recognition

SOME OF THE BEST-KNOWN STRIKES for recognition were those carried out by the SEIU's Justice for Janitors campaign in the early 1990s.[3] In Los Angeles, 2,000 janitors and their supporters ignored the NLRB election process and struck instead. They disrupted business as usual in the swank Century City business district with a series of confrontational demonstrations, targeting a huge multinational cleaning contractor. They won a contract.

But most modern strikes for recognition have targeted smaller employers without deep pockets. We've placed this book's most inspiring example of a recognition strike in Chapter 11—Corporate Campaigns. The union, UNITE, turned a strike against a stubborn small employer into a full-fledged local-level corporate campaign. Please see that story for a detailed example of a recognition strike that pulled out all the stops.

Usually, though, a recognition strike works best as in our example below, when the union has the employer over a barrel and the conflict does not turn into a drawn-out battle.

Strike Talk

Automobile Mechanics Union Local 701, a Machinists (IAM) local, represents mechanics in the Chicago area. In the late 1990s and early 2000s, dozens of mechanics at several dealerships came into the local by going on strike. Walking off the job, they forced their employers to recognize and bargain with Local 701. In each case, as soon as organizers made contact to discuss the merits of the union, they started to prepare workers to go on strike.

These strikes for recognition worked largely because auto mechanics were scarce. When they walked out, finding replacements was difficult.

Local 701 has been around for some 50 years, so it was well known among mechanics. The union usually made contact with a non-union shop through word of mouth, often through an ex-union member who ended up working there. An organizer then set up a meeting with the mechanics to discuss the union. Mechanics were most concerned about benefits and wanted access to Local 701's health and welfare and pension plans. Other issues included work assignment and having a daily guarantee of pay.

The union worked to get overwhelming support among the mechanics through meetings and discussions. Once the local had the required support, including having the workers sign union cards or a petition, union reps went to the dealership and informed management that the local represented a majority of the workers. They offered a voluntary recognition letter for the manager to sign. If he refused, the union reps announced a strike and the mechanics closed up their toolboxes and walked out.

Most of the strikes lasted only a few days, but one strike at a Cadillac dealership lasted several weeks. Some of the mechanics got jobs at other dealerships, causing the Cadillac dealer to worry that he would be unable to find skilled replacements. The strike ended when the owner agreed to a non-NLRB card check, which the union easily won. Once the dealership certified the union, the business agent presented the owner with the union's contract and said, "Now we are on strike for a contract." In another couple of hours the workers had a contract, which they approved on the picket line.

The IAM could win these strikes for recognition and the pattern contract because:

- They had overwhelming support in a relatively small workforce.
- The companies could not move their production elsewhere.
- The skilled workforce could not be easily replaced with scabs.
- An industry pattern contract existed, so owners recognized that they would not be subject to higher costs than their competition.

Salts Get the Union Inside

SALTING is the practice of sending pro-union workers (salts) to work for non-union employers for the purpose of organizing. A pro-union worker on the job can give the campaign a head start. Ideally, salts are skilled organizers who can unify workers and lead them in workplace activity against the boss. Or they may simply gather information about a workplace for external organizers: who are the workers, are they willing to unionize, how is the employer vulnerable?

Salting is used most in the building trades; IBEW members are its acknowledged masters. Unions draw salts from their employed members, members' relatives, former and laid-off members, and retirees, as well as professional organizers. The AFL-CIO's Organizing Institute has trained many salts, including some pro-union college students.

Overt or Covert?

There are two types of salts: overt and covert. Overt salts do not hide the fact that they are union members when they apply for a job. Covert salts keep their union sympathies under wraps, at least until they are settled in.

The reason to use overt salts is to demonstrate that the employer discriminates against union members and sympathizers by refusing to consider them or refusing to hire them. If an employer discriminates, the union can file an unfair labor practice (ULP) charge. The union can then use the ULPs as leverage to push the employer to recognize the union or to raise wages. For small and medium-sized employers, ULPs are expensive to defend, as much as $55,000 per charge, says David Williams, director of the Organize Indiana Project at Indiana University Division of Labor Studies. If a union wins at the NLRB, employers can be liable for a big chunk of back pay and be forced to hire the salts. The costs are so high that the Associated Builders and Contractors offers its members "salting insurance" to covers legal fees and back pay.

Michael Lucas, a longtime IBEW official and now a union consultant, runs a seminar that explains salting tactics, particularly for the building trades. See "Resources" at the end of this chapter.

Recruiting Salts

Getting union members to work non-union is not easy, especially when they are highly skilled workers who make considerably more working union. This opposition can be overcome with education about the contribution salting makes to protecting industry conditions.

"The idea of salting was hard to sell to the rank and file," says Jerry Crangi, an organizer with International Alliance of Theatrical Stage Employees (IATSE) Local 15 in Seattle. "Early on they said, 'You guys want us to work non-union?!' Once they saw it worked to build the union, people said, 'Wow!'"

Some unions, like IBEW, pay their salts the difference between the union and non-union wage. IBEW Local 46 in Seattle runs weekly salting classes for members. The education starts with a history of the union's dominance in construction electrician jobs, reasons for its decline, and the importance of salting to organize the industry again. The legal rights of salts to engage in protected activity are covered. Members who take the class sign a salting agreement and get forms to make weekly reports if they are hired on a non-union job.

Although many unions use them, Jeff Lohman, international rep for IBEW District 6 in the Midwest, advises against salting agreements: "It is just more paper, and the boss can use it in an anti-salting case," which is a claim before the NLRB that the union is salting just to harass the company. NLRB officials have decided in favor of companies on a few occasions.

IATSE Local 15 offers a different incentive to recruit salts. "Local 15 operates a hiring hall. People work on a dispatch list that combines seniority with hours worked the previous year," says Aaron Gorseth, a salt and organizer with the local. "There are 600 on our dispatch list. The higher you are on the list, the more work you get. To motivate workers to salt, we offer double credit hours for every hour worked as a salt, up to 500 in a year."

Unions that don't have a hiring hall system like IATSE's could bring members out on leaves for union business.

IATSE and IBEW try to send their most-skilled members as salts. Such workers get more respect, both from co-workers and from the company, which may even give them crew-leader positions. Having highly skilled workers among the union supporters increases union leverage when bargaining with the company for representation or a contract.

Educating Salts

Sheet Metal Workers Local 20 in Indianapolis recruits salts out of its apprenticeship program. For six months during the program, every apprentice must work as a salt. The program is funded by an assessment on all members' pay, 30 cents an hour from journeymen and 15 cents an hour for others, which totals about $1 million a year.

The program starts with five days of classroom training using the Construction Organizing Membership Education Training program. COMET provides a brief history of the labor movement and explains why unions need to organize now and how members can contribute. "It's pretty old stuff, but it works," says Michael Van Gordon, retired head of salting for Local 20.

Local 20 introduces apprentices to salting with three main lessons:

1. Salts must be model employees. Most workers know little about unions and what they do know is usually wrong, so salts have to prove that they are not gangsters or lazy.

2. How to get a job. This involves evaluating a company for its potential to be organized and presenting a credible job application. "They make the calls to check your references now," says Lohman, "so you have to have a good story that checks out, or one that can't be checked out. I have no problem with lying to employers, since I know they will break the law to keep from hiring a union worker. And workers understand what you have to do to get hired. They don't hold it against you." Local 20 has a worksheet to help apprentices put together their application materials.

3. Report regularly to the union's salting coordinator: a job application report, a callback log sheet, an interview log sheet, and a daily salt log. (For samples, see "Resources" at the end of the chapter.) The forms tell the organizers what the salt is doing and how the company operates. They also provide a record of the salt's activity and the company's reaction, which can be used to support a ULP charge, and they force the salt to evaluate what he or she is doing, thinking critically about the way forward.

After Local 20 apprentices find work as salts, they have six months to contribute to an organizing drive before they return to their apprentice program. This short time has reduced the effectiveness of Local 20's salting, says Van Gordon. But the program is still valuable because it "helped us organize ourselves. Members have a deeper appreciation for belonging to a union because they have been through the program. Most have no experience and don't understand what it is like to work non-union. They think they make their money because they are so highly trained, but the program demonstrates they make their money because of the union. That is the primary benefit."

A Good Salt

The best candidates for salting are members from the same industry who know the culture and etiquette of the workplace. Once hired, a salt's first task is to gather information: names of employees, home addresses, phone numbers, shift times, schedules. Map the workplace and identify leaders. To do these things, a salt must build relationships with fellow workers.

Gorseth describes the personal skills of a successful salt: "The most important thing is being able to read people's personalities, to relate to them as individuals. You need to get information about people before you start organizing activities like house-calls. Observe the workers; get to know them really well. And know your job really well. If you don't, shut up and ask someone.

"People like to be acknowledged and respected for their skills, like to display knowledge. It gives you a chance to strike up a conversation. You have to get past the attitude, which some skilled workers have, that non-union workers must be unskilled or incompetent."

Tim Scott, a former salt and current organizer who uses salts in human services workplaces for UAW Local 2322 in western Massachusetts, says salts need to know when to lie and when to tell the truth. "The struggle with salting is being able to form relationships and gain trust. That can be tricky if you are undercover. You do not want to be deceptive, but you have to be. You can get around it by being quiet until you find people you can come out to. Then you make it clear why you did not tell them earlier why you are there. It's partly a matter of timing about when you are truthful. It's about relationships with people, and that's tricky."

Scott has two suggestions for landing a job: "It's often better to go in as a temp worker," since companies scrutinize temp workers less than permanent workers. "This works especially if you are just gathering information."

And if you alter your resumé, find people who will back up your story. "A former supervisor at a clinic agreed to support the lie that I was a caseworker and not an MSW [with a master's degree]. In another case, we got a cheap cell phone and created a phone line for a phony landscaping company."

Stay On for the Campaign

Scott salted at the YWCA of Western Massachusetts, which runs a number of human services facilities. He chose the YWCA because he knew several people who worked there. "I had met with the people I knew and we had put together a committee with leaders at six of the organization's eight sites. But nobody knew anybody from the teen-runaway residential program. It was one of the largest sites and we had heard it was one of the worst, with one of the worst supervisors."

Scott got a job there as a relief staff worker, filling in for other workers out sick or on vacation. "I stayed undercover at first and tried to identify potential leaders that organizing committee members from other sites could contact. That happened fairly easily, and we found a couple of people willing to join the organizing committee. Right before they were contacted by the committee I identified myself, so they would not be shocked about being contacted."

Even though the organizing committee was up and running, Scott kept his job as a relief worker. "Management found out I was an organizer, but they did not fire me. It was helpful for me to be on site, since many workers were nervous about the union and I could give them information and support. There was one key captive-audience meeting, and I was there. The supervisor came in with a consultant and they started an anti-union dog-and-pony show. I did not want to be aggressive, so whenever they said something not true about the union or out of context, I raised my hand and respectfully disagreed. They started attacking me and that worked against them, because people felt sympathy for me and heard my arguments. That helped bring undecided people to support the union."

Soon after, YWCA workers voted in the UAW.

'Kids' Join Dockers To Defeat Powell's Books

"YOU DON'T EXPECT a group of middle-class white kids to organize a union, but that's what we did," says

Michael Powell's reputation as a paternalistic employer who fostered a friendly and nonhierarchical work environment took a hit during the union organizing campaign.

Mary Winzig, member of ILWU Local 5 at Powell's Books in Portland, Oregon. In fact, the 400 "kids" who run one of the biggest bookstores in the world did just about everything right to win their representation election and their first contract.

Powell's Books is an institution in Portland. It has a downtown main store, Powell's City of Books, and half a dozen other stores scattered around town. The stores carry millions of new and used, paperback and hardcover books—all together on the same shelves—many of which are virtually impossible to find elsewhere. The store is open 365 days a year and its staff is extraordinarily knowledgeable about books. Book lovers everywhere make pilgrimages to Portland just to go to Powell's.

Powell's reputation is partly due to its owner, Michael Powell, who is well known as a book lover, a benefactor for local charities, a city booster, and a liberal community leader. Before the union drive, he had a reputation as a paternalistic employer who fostered a friendly and nonhierarchical work environment.

Many of the workers at Powell's are current or former college students, some of whom have been politically active on their campuses. Many do not expect to be at Powell's for long, but quite a few have been there for years. They come to Powell's for many reasons, but most of them love books.

The Boss Ignites the Drive

Like so many other organizing drives, this one began with a boss's act of provocation: an email from Powell's in August 1998 announced zero-to-three percent raises, based on merit. "That was the straw that broke the camel's back," says Winzig. "After restructuring our jobs, imposing teams, and taking away our control over sections of the store, all without our input, we were fed up."

The same night as the email, Marty Kruse, a longtime Powell's employee, talked to dozens of co-workers and got 13 of them to come to a bar near the main Powell's store downtown. The group discussed what to do. "Once the drinking started we had all sorts of ideas: strike, quit, release animals in the store," says Winzig. "Eventually we decided to unionize."

The next day, the group contacted the local Jobs with Justice chapter, who suggested they talk to the International Longshore and Warehouse Union (ILWU). The group also contacted the United Food and Commercial Workers and the Industrial Workers of the World.

"We didn't know what we were doing," remembers Winzig. "We invited organizers from two different unions—the UFCW and the IWW—to a meeting on the same night. We didn't know they competed. We thought the union movement was like one big union. But they gave their spiels, what their unions could do for us. They gave interesting talks, but neither fit. The IWW's politics were in line with the majority of the workers who are on the left, but we knew it would be a huge fight and the IWW didn't have the resources.

"The United Food and Commercial Workers seemed logical," continues Winizig. "But some of us had negative reactions to the UFCW after working at Fred Meyer [a local grocery chain]. Plus, they started right away talking about initiation fees and dues."

The group eventually decided on the ILWU. "We were really impressed by the history of the union," says Winzig. "It was one of the first unions to come out against apartheid and it went on strike in defense of Korean activists. It had organized bookstore workers in San Francisco. Plus, they were going to let us be our own local, not fold us into another local."

Building a Committee

The next step was a few meetings of 15 to 30 union supporters at the Longshore hall to chart the workplace: who worked where, on what shifts, and their sentiments toward the union. This also meant charting the company's warehouse and the half-dozen stores around the city. Then, with the help of ILWU organizer Michael Cannarella, the group began face-to-face meetings with their co-workers.

"We kept it small, hoping to sign up as many people as possible before the word got out," says Winzig. "We warned everyone that that once management knew about the union a fierce anti-union campaign would begin. That gave us credibility when the campaign actually happened."

There was no formal organizing committee, just those who really wanted to put in the time, a group of about 30 people representing most of the company's worksites. They met at all hours to accommodate all the shifts, often after the stores closed at 11:00 pm. They held regular Friday night meetings that began with questions and answers for new people to learn about the union. Then they got down to the business of assessing the union sentiment of each worker and discussing who would talk to whom next.

The worker-organizers developed different ways to communicate their union message. "We tailored how we got the information out," says Winzig. "Face-to-face meetings were the most important. There's no shortcut to creating relationships. But some people are shyer and might need to read instead of talk. Some will talk at work; others want a phone call. We did the work. Then we constantly tested to see what workers were willing to do—buttons, t-shirts, bringing others to a meeting, union cards."

The union had to overcome three obstacles within the workforce: fear, cynicism, and elitism. "People were scared of everything—the hell you know vs. the hell you don't know," says Winzig. "They were worried about how they would be treated by management, about losing their health care, about paying dues, about 'big, bad longshoremen.' Many thought unions were corrupt.

"Some thought they were too good for a union. 'I'm a professional; I'm not blue-collar.' They thought they could manage management themselves—rugged individualists. One of the best arguments we came up with for them was, "What about the others, the people who cannot speak for themselves?"'

Facing Down the Boss

Once managers learned about the organizing drive, they held non-mandatory meetings to warn against the union. Sometimes supporters used these meetings to promote the union. Michael Powell then spoke up and wrote a series of letters to each worker attacking the union. He claimed it would poison Powell's unique culture and undermine the workers' professionalism.

Luckily for the union, the letters grew less formal and their lack of seriousness insulted the workers. The letters also grew less accurate, calling the ILWU the International Longshoremen's Association (ILA—the far less democratic East Coast longshore union). Powell cited the salaries of ILA leaders as evidence the union was just after dues. "We used that against him by showing he was out of touch and that upper management made as much, if not more, than the ILA leaders he cited," says Winzig.

Still, the management campaign scared workers. Many believed they would be better off on their own or figured they were not long for the job anyway.

Union supporters started wearing buttons. "That was a huge deal," says Winzig. "I carried my button in my pocket for the longest time. Then Billy Bragg came in and wore one. That gave us a huge boost. We got many community people, authors, and musicians to wear them. And we got celebrities, like [author] Ursula Le Guin, who lives in Portland, [musician] Utah Phillips, Michael Moore, and [the Green Party vice-presidential candidate] Winona LaDuke, to write letters to us and Michael Powell supporting the union. We put all the letters in a book in each lunchroom so everyone could read them. That made it much less scary to be identified as a union supporter."

A bowling party with ILWU President Brian McWilliams gave the union a human face and demonstrated that a large union cared about a relatively small group of workers. Other social events helped get the union message across. "One mistake we made—at the urging of the union—was doing house-calls," says Winzig. "We got such a huge negative reaction about meeting people at their homes that we gave up after a week. Instead, we asked people to meet at a neutral place, like a coffee shop."

Winning the Election

By March, a majority of the workers had signed union cards, so the ILWU filed for an election. "We held a rally on the day we filed," says Michael Parker, who worked in the Powell's warehouse. "We had everyone, including community supporters, sign a huge poster, which we marched into Powell's office."

The election polarized Portland. "The media coverage was all negative and very personal," says Parker. "It was all about what the union was doing to Michael Powell, this great benefactor of the community." To counter the media, the union sought community support. Jobs with Justice helped. Informational pickets and leafleting told Powell's shoppers about the issues, while rallies, t-shirts, and button-wearing gave them a way to demonstrate support. The rallies took place in front of Powell's, often at lunch or on Saturdays when workers and supporters could come and the store was crowded. Workers, supporters, and ILWU officials spoke.

"We tried to meet with politicians," says Winzig, "but they wouldn't touch us. Powell gave them too much money."

The vote was close, 161-155. "We won because we took people to the polls," says Winzig. "We called them up and if they hadn't voted we drove them to the polling place." But that was only half the battle.

Bargaining Bogs Down

The election was in April, but bargaining didn't start until September. "We wanted to take a little break," says Winzig. "The organizer thought we were burnt out and there were too many hurt feelings. But it was a mistake to wait so long. We lost momentum. There was time for people to lose their anger. But nobody quit and we eventually got the momentum back."

The contract campaign followed on from the organizing drive. The union had to reach out to the large number of workers who had voted against the union. "We went back and talked to everyone about what they wanted in the contract," says Winzig. "We did surveys and we held a huge meeting to discuss our demands. We made it clear to everyone, even the anti-union workers, that they were welcome to express their ideas. That won a few of them over. It helped, too, that we never used name-calling or other attacks against anti-union workers during the campaign."

The workers elected a bargaining team of 12 people, with representatives from each location and each type of work. "The large team threw off Powell's lawyer," says Parker, who was on the team. "Plus we invited every worker to come to the bargaining sessions whenever they wanted. It was one thing for us to say what Powell was doing. It was another for them to see it themselves."

Bargaining dragged on for a year as the two sides fought over every issue—wages, benefits, scheduling, job definitions, breaks. The bargaining team met every Sunday night to plan bargaining. "Everyone was invited to those meetings," says Parker. "We wrote most of the contract language from scratch, because we had people who understood each job."

Multi-Faceted Campaign

Over the year of bargaining, the union engaged in dozens of actions. When management fired the original union supporter, Marty Kruse, supposedly for shoddy timekeeping and attendance, the union organized a ten-minute walkout later in the week. "Firing Marty completely undermined Powell's liberal reputation and demonstrated the power realities," says Parker. "Here was a union activist fired. It convinced many formerly anti-union workers to support the union."

Some campaign actions were small. "One day we took our coffee break in the third-floor reading area and had a reading of the children's book *Click Clack Moo* [about farm animals that go on strike]," says Winzig. "Another day we read *Confessions of a Union Buster*. We also had 'Chalk-Outs,' where a bunch of us would write about the contract struggle on sidewalks in front of the store and elsewhere downtown."

Other actions were larger. "At our Valentine's Day rally in front of the main store, we held a mock wedding in which a huge puppet of Michael Powell married a huge puppet of Larry the Longshoreman through the contract," says Winzig. "Then we delivered a valentine, signed by workers and supporters, to Powell's house. The Carpenters' convention was in town that day and we spoke to them. They voted to walk out and follow us to the rally. We had huge puppets, drummers, and we closed down the streets."

Through a petition drive held outside the stores, workers started asking shoppers to sign a pledge to boycott Powell's if the union asked. The union thought that if negotiations dragged on into a second Christmas season it might be able to gather enough pledges to hurt the company with a boycott. It didn't come to that, but the pledge turned out to be a good tool for telling people about Powell's intransigence at the bargaining table and building support for the union.

Several times during the campaign, the union filed unfair labor practice charges against Powell's for intimidation, surveillance, or unfair dismissal. Then the workers went on strike for a day or two to protest the ULPs. By striking against ULPs, "we knew we could not be replaced," says Winzig. "These were not full strikes, because we did not push to get every single worker out and we did not actively ask shoppers to honor our pickets. Instead, they were informational pickets and we had people sign the boycott pledge."

Adds Parker, "Small actions like these, the strikes, the rallies, the leafleting, add up. You are at a retail establishment where everything is visible. It can have ripples. It can hurt the bottom line."

May Day Turning Point

A May Day march and rally, organized by the city's left, turned into an enormous momentum builder for Powell's workers. The city mobilized large numbers of police, who overreacted to the marchers, arresting many, beating some, and herding the rest through the streets. In the disarray, "everyone marched to Powell's to support one of our ULP strikes," says Winzig.

"Plus, May Day was the first day of the ILWU convention, which was in Portland that year. As members, we went and told them about our struggle and they voted to join our pickets. So we led Brian McWilliams and 500 longshoremen through the streets of Portland to Powell's.

"A few cops tried to stop us a block from the store, but McWilliams simply pointed at the Powell's workers in front of the store and said, 'Those are our people. You can try to stop us, but there are 500 of us and only a few of you.' The cops just stepped aside and we marched on the store.

"The next day, we were still on a ULP strike, so 40 of us marched into the ILWU convention to a standing ovation. They passed around bags and delegates put in money for a hardship fund for those of us who lost time on strike or got fired. On the final day of the convention, the delegates joined us again for a rally and ring around the store.

"Having the union support us like that was amazing," concludes Winzig. "I'll never forget it. It demonstrated how strong the union could be and convinced a lot of workers to support us."

The May Day rally scared management, but movement at the bargaining table really accelerated after Jobs with Justice organized a Workers' Rights Board of politicians, intellectuals, and community leaders to assess the struggle at Powell's. Eight workers, including many who had been opposed to the union, testified at a public hearing about working conditions at Powell's. The board's findings went against Powell's and board members tried to meet with Michael Powell. "He saw these people as his class," notes Winzig. "He finally listened to them."

A week later, the union received a realistic wage proposal. After a few face-saving sessions with a federal mediator, the parties agreed to a contract. The ratification vote: 293-37.

Asked the lessons of the struggle, Winzig says, "We built relationships with workers who wanted to know 'who would care for me more, my co-workers or management?' They saw us listening, trying hard, admitting our mistakes—house-calls, waiting too long to bargain—which management never does. They saw us having fun. We made a lot of friends. We watched many people find their voices and learn that democracy doesn't have to end at the workplace door. That changes you forever."

Read more about Powell's workers on the job in Chapter 3—Shop Floor Tactics.

Vermont Nurses Reach In to Each Other and Out to the Community

THE JUSTICE FOR HEALTHCARE WORKERS CAMPAIGN (JHWC) is a coalition of Vermont health care workers, health care unions, and community activists that is leading a combined struggle for health care workers' rights and better health care for everyone. Central to the struggle is a strategic plan to organize all the health care workers in the state. Read about how unions work together to organize industry-wide on the Troublemaker's website, www.labornotes.org.

Here we describe a successful JHWC effort to support a union drive by nurses at Fletcher Allen Health Care in Burlington. These 1,200 nurses at the largest hospital in Vermont won with a two-pronged campaign: solidarity on the job and community support. We describe both their drive for recognition and their equally important next step, the campaign for a signed contract.

Considerable resources went into both prongs of the campaign. The union, AFT Healthcare, a division of the American Federation of Teachers, dedicated nine organizers with roots in the Burlington community to the drive, while a group of experienced labor and health care activists associated with the Justice for Healthcare Workers Campaign and the Vermont Workers Center provided crucial strategic and logistical support for the nurses' external solidarity efforts.

Among the nurses, a personal approach was key, says Martha Ahmed, an operating room nurse and union leader. "We have a motto. We meet anyone, anytime, anywhere. We still do, even after winning the union and one of the best contracts in the industry." By meeting with more than 670 nurses, union supporters built an organizing committee of more than 250 active members. "We had committee members on every floor, every unit, every shift," says Ahmed.

The large organizing committee laid the foundation for the comprehensive campaign. With so many nurses involved, some could dedicate their efforts to mobilizing the community, political leaders, clergy, and other activists.

For this work, planning ahead gave the nurses an edge, according to Jan Schaffer, Vermont/New Hampshire AFL-CIO director, who helped on the Fletcher Allen campaign. "Sometimes the community campaign is done in a panic at the last minute and things go badly. In this case, the AFT, with the support of the AFL-CIO, the Vermont Workers Center, and the Justice for Health Care Workers Campaign, built the community campaign into its strategy from the very beginning. They made it clear to the workers that in addition to the internal organizing they were doing they would have an extra task."

In the organizing campaign and in the contract campaign that followed, the combination of continual organizing, participatory organization, escalating tactics, and community involvement led to victory for the Fletcher Allen nurses.

Internal Organizing

Nurses at Fletcher Allen had tried to organize a union several times before, so there were some union supporters within the workforce. This group included nurses who worked second jobs at Copley Hospital in Morrisville. The Copley nurses had organized with AFT and later switched to UNAP. Since they were familiar with an organizing drive, the Copley nurses were similar to salts. They were the first contacts for AFT Healthcare organizers, and together they began meeting face to face with as many nurses as they could.

"We provided information about the union, answered questions, and asked for a verbal commitment," says Andrew Tripp, an organizer with AFT Healthcare. "Meetings were held all over town and on the phone. We did a few house visits, but with nurses' odd schedules, most of them felt more comfortable setting up something near work."

As in SEIU's drive at North Shore Medical Center, once workers voiced support, activists and organizers gave them small tasks to help build both the union and their confidence. These tasks included getting other workers to small meetings with organizers and setting up their own face-to-face meetings.

"The small meetings were the foundation of everything we did," says Tripp. "We had meetings with 670 nurses who gave us a verbal commitment to the union and we got 672 yes votes out of about 1,000 cast in the election. We held larger meetings only once a month."

"Small meetings build stronger commitments to the union," says Schaffer. "New people are more likely to come to a small meeting that includes a friend or co-worker they know. And at that meeting they are more likely to participate than at a large meeting where their presence has little impact. You cannot have a conversation at a large meeting. But you can in a small meeting, and you can build a relationship."

Small meetings were particularly helpful in a huge hospital where nurses worked on many different schedules and could not all meet at the same time.

Through these one-on-one and small-group meetings, the nurses built a network of supporters in every department of the hospital and on each shift. They also built the organizing committee, which was open to any nurse who wanted to participate. The committee met regularly, usually once a month, to discuss the state of the campaign and plan its next steps. These meetings gave nurses the chance to hear what nurses in other areas were doing and how they were coping with management harassment.

The next steps involved moving workers from their private support for the union to public demonstrations of their commitment. "The nurses got two blank books, wrote quotes in them about why they supported the union, and signed their quotes," says Tripp. The books became organizing tools. Union activists took them around the hospital to demonstrate the growing support for the union and to get more nurses to put their quotes in the books.

"After the books, the nurses made huge posters proclaiming support for the union," adds Tripp. "These had nurses' pictures and signatures." The nurses left blank spaces on the posters for new supporters. The posters were taken around the hospital and posted at meetings where new supporters could add their pictures.

When support grew large enough, the organizers broke out buttons and stickers. "We thought management might prohibit us from wearing the buttons," says Ahmed, "but they had encouraged us to wear United Way buttons in the past, so we knew that that established our right to wear buttons."

Face-to-face meetings personalized the union and

created a dense organization that allowed the workers to start acting like a union long before they won recognition. "We built an organization where workers took to heart the notion that when there is a problem, you organize a response to it," says Ahmed.

To act like a union and defend themselves against management, the nurses set up a steward system, creating one steward for every ten supporters. Union supporters in each unit voted for temporary stewards, who received training from union organizers. The temp stewards then met regularly with their fellow nurses, informing them of their right to support the union and act collectively to achieve it.

Whenever workers met with management, stewards attended in support, again asserting their right to concerted action. They passed out "Weingarten rights" cards, informing nurses of their right, when confronted by management, to have a witness present. This was important because management was holding constant one-on-one and group meetings to denounce the union and harass nurses for expressing their commitment.

By acting like a union even before they won recognition, the nurses increased their chances for success, as Kate Bronfenbrenner and Robert Hickey found in their study of successful organizing drives.[4]

External Organizing

Fletcher Allen was the second largest employer in Vermont at the time of the organizing drive (it's now the largest). Its chief executive was well connected with the state's leading politicians and businesspeople. With their considerable resources, hospital managers had already beaten several union drives and planned to beat the AFT.

Knowing their opponent, AFT Healthcare, VWC, JHWC, and the AFL-CIO started mobilizing community support even before the organizing drive started.

The coalition began by training nurses in outreach techniques. "Community outreach can be fun," says Schaffer, "but you cannot let the internal organizing go. We did not want to pull the best people away from the internal organizing to do the external work. So we trained a group of nurses whose specific job was to do outreach. We trained them how to talk to clergy and politicians. We did role-plays, showing them what it's like to talk to Senator Leahy or Governor Dean. They learned that it is hard to pin down politicians and how to get them to make a commitment.

"The nurses needed to be prepared to talk very specifically about health care issues. They needed to explain the problems with mandatory overtime and short-staffing. They had to be able to say, 'This is what it means when we are short-staffed, if we have three patients instead of two, if we have to go out and buy our own thermometers.' So we practiced talking to each other, to figure out the best way to make the arguments, to demonstrate why it is better for the community—the hospital's patients—to side with nurses than with the hospital."

Training was not all the nurses needed. They also needed a strategy for using community pressure. "We tried to map the community," says Schaffer. "Where are the pressure points? Who can exert leverage against the hospital?" Surveying Fletcher Allen's position in the community, the nurses came up with outreach activities to which JHWC members lent their contacts, experience, and time.

One of the nurses' first efforts was a petition demanding a "free and fair" election. This countered the hospital's anti-union campaign, which included hiring an anti-union law firm. But the issue of a free and fair election wasn't just an "internal" issue. The nurses argued that patient care was being sacrificed to pay for management's $1 million anti-union drive, so the community had a real interest in stopping it.

Nurses and their allies took the petition to the meetings of other unions and community groups and into the streets, and eventually gathered more than 1,000 signatures. They then delivered the petition to management, which, predictably, ignored it. The petition had the effect of alerting the community to the issues and helping the internal organizing drive by convincing nurses that many other people supported their cause.

Since state and federal government agencies regulate hospitals, nurses looked for ways to exploit this regulation to pressure management. With the help of JHWC, they researched Fletcher Allen's finances and found inconsistencies that suggested the hospital was stealing hundreds of millions of dollars from the state and several federal agencies. JHWC gave its information to state authorities and, after the state's investigation turned up fraud, publicized the hospital's criminal activity, which undermined the credibility of management's anti-union campaign.

The nurses testified about conditions at Fletcher Allen before several state regulatory hearings, including one at the state legislature. Again, they made the point that union-busting took money away from patient care and that the hospital's anti-union "captive audience" meetings took nurses away from patients.

By demonstrating that unionization would improve not just the working lives of nurses but also the lives of the thousands of Vermont citizens who would be Fletcher Allen patients, the nurses won endorsements for the union from Senator Patrick Leahy, Governor Howard Dean, Burlington Mayor Peter Clavelle, and Congressman Bernie Sanders. All of them wrote to Fletcher Allen demanding neutrality in the election. Religious, community, and union leaders also sent letters. Some letters and editorials were published in local newspapers. Nurses were buoyed by the widespread support they received.

The JHWC knew it had some leverage with several of the politicians. "There is a layer of Democratic politicians who ask for labor's support, but avoid the issues," says Hal Leyshon, who was president of the Burlington Central Labor Council. "But they were won over to coming out publicly in support of the nurses by the numbers they saw on the informational picket lines, by the numbers at community meetings, and by the positive support they saw in the media. And we pushed them. We made it clear to Dean, who was considering a run for President, that he couldn't even speak to [AFL-CIO President] Sweeney if he did not hold a press conference and say that if he worked at the hospital, he would support the union. We gave him the transcript and he read it. He didn't want to. Remember, he had worked at Fletcher Allen [as a doctor]. But he gave in to the pressure from the local and national AFL-CIO leadership and the strength of the rest of the community campaign."

The combination of long, hard, face-to-face organizing, a big committee, escalating activity, and community involvement led to a nearly 2-to-1 victory in the October 2002 vote. With the victory, the union chose the number 5221 for its local, as in Local 5 "2-to-1."

Huge Bargaining Team, Open Negotiations

In about one third of victorious elections workers fail to win a contract within two years of recognition. Since Fletcher Allen management was not going to give in easily to the nurses' contract demands, the union had to step up the fight.

Within a month of the election, the union had trained 150 elected stewards. "They were trained to fight grievances on the floor by organizing a response," says Tripp. "Management committed plenty of ULPs [unfair labor practices] but we did not file a single complaint with the Labor Board. Instead, the nurses organized. They met with management and then took action when they got the wrong answer."

"If small-group meetings didn't work, we went back with 50 nurses," says Ahmed. "We'd wear buttons and stickers. When managers refused to move equipment from the halls, we called the fire marshal, who cited the hospital. We had all sorts of bad equipment, which we put stickers on to indicate that it needed repair. It got so bad they couldn't start up rooms because they didn't have enough equipment. Then management tried to staff units with nurses on overtime. We were already doing 15 or 20 hours a week. So we started to refuse overtime unless they paid us double time."

For contract negotiations, "we set up a negotiating team with 50 members," says Ahmed. "They communicated with every shift, all the units. They signed an agreement to act in unity at the negotiating table, with no disagreements in front of management. They also agreed to open all negotiating sessions to all nurses. The minutes of every bargaining session were distributed to all the nurses."

"A big committee was really useful," says Tripp. "The team had people who understood the technical aspects of each area of the hospital, so they could counter management claims. During in-depth discussions about staffing ratios or the physical grouping of clinical specialties on the floors, committee members proved management wrong time and again and demonstrated that they had much more knowledge of the actual day-to-day operation of the hospital. When management insisted that a policy had always existed, nurses with 20 or 30 years at the hospital could point out that things had been different in the past. Workers almost always know what happens at work to a greater level of detail than management."

Small meetings continued. "We discussed every proposal in small groups and in large meetings with the negotiating team," says Ahmed. "All the demands were discussed and ratified in those meetings. So was our plan of action."

As negotiations dragged on, the union developed an escalating plan of action counting down to a strike deadline. It began with wearing stickers and red scrub tops and posting yard signs that read, "Nurses care. Does Fletcher Allen?" Then came informational pickets, a 30-day strike notice, radio ads, a petition in support of a strike if necessary, one-day strikes, and an indefinite strike. The union did everything in its plan except strike, and the nurses came within hours of walking out.

The nurses also continued their community outreach. They insisted that patient care was still the central issue. "Fletcher Allen is the biggest hospital in the state," says Tripp. "Sooner or later, virtually everyone in the state will use its services. Underpaid, overworked nurses are a threat to everyone's health."

"We testified on a number of bills during the con-

Bargaining While Thinking Organizing

"BARGAINING TO ORGANIZE" usually means that a union demands the employer not stand in the way of organizing new workers—by, for example, remaining neutral or accepting card check recognition (see next page). But we came across another kind of "bargaining to organize" that every union should consider.

When APWU members at East Coat Leasing (ECL), a private mail hauler in Greensboro, North Carolina, sat down to bargain their first contract, they were already thinking about organizing. "They knew that they would not survive if they did not contribute to the organization of other private sector postal workers," says organizer Mark Dimondstein. "So they fought for things that would promote unionism in the industry.

"ECL workers might have benefited most by better health or pension rights, but they decided to split the pie thinly into many different areas. This way, they got very small increases on many items, but they established their right to improvement on all items. They had three weeks vacation after ten years, but they changed it to eight, establishing that they could improve vacation rights. They made small changes in wages, layover pay, health, and other areas.

"They did this so they could show non-union postal workers that once you have a union, doors start opening. They built a contract that would attract all types of non-union postal workers, those who care about vacation but not about layover pay, and vice versa."

tract campaign, including one on whistleblower protection for nurses who expose illegal hospital practices," says Ahmed. "We also testified before the health and welfare committee of the legislature about the disarray at the hospital, which receives public funding."

As the tension mounted between the union and management, the nurses had to refine their strategy, especially with religious leaders. "Clergy had no trouble supporting the union during organizing," says Schaffer, "but when it looked like the nurses might strike, they hesitated. They were worried about the impact on patients, but they also hate conflict. They tried to mediate and reconcile the two sides. But the nurses wouldn't back down. They raised the level of tension and forced people in the community to take sides. Their determination and their continued message about patient care convinced many religious leaders that the best way to avoid the strike was to pressure management to accept the nurses' reasonable demands. A high-level delegation, including the Episcopal bishop, the head of the United Church of Christ, and a rabbi met with Fletcher Allen management. We don't know exactly what they said, but given the circumstances their message had to be supportive of the nurses."

The same was true with phone calls to management from Dean and Leahy during the contract campaign. "These people—the politicians, the religious leaders—they all know the top executives of the hospital," says Schaffer. "To divide that group was important. Hospital management saw that the community, even its top leaders, was holding them accountable."

The community demonstrated active support for the nurses on several occasions. On Good Friday, a manager fired a member of the bargaining team. On Sunday, the community inundated the CEO's home with phone calls. On Monday, the bargaining team marched out of the negotiating session and sat in at the CEO's office. On Thursday, the nurses and their community supporters "brought fire"—a candlelight vigil—to the CEO's house. On Friday, the fired nurse was reinstated.

In the days leading up to the strike deadline the community joined nurses for informational pickets and a rally of nearly 1,000 people, which was quite large for a small community like Burlington.

As it had in the organizing campaign, the combination of continual organizing, participatory organization, escalating tactics, and community involvement led to victory. Nine months after their election, the nurses won one of the best contracts in the industry, according to the union. It included raises, no mandatory overtime, guaranteed nurse-patient ratios, and a ban on being forced to cover units where they lacked certification. These last features were victories not just for the nurses, but also for their patients—the community that supported them.

CWA Wins Neutrality and Card Check, Defeats Double-Breasting

IT'S CALLED DOUBLE-BREASTING: opening a non-union subsidiary to undermine the union at the parent company. Trucking companies are famous for it, but it happens in many industries. In telecommunications, the practice is rampant, especially as telephone companies move into new markets, such as wireless communications and data service, or contract out old ones, such as Yellow Pages.

The Communications Workers have been fighting double-breasting by telecom companies for two decades, with some successes and some failures. This is the story of success at SBC, where CWA combined member mobilization, continuous bargaining, organizing, legal pressure, and political leverage to win neutrality, card check, and then unionization for workers at Cingular Wireless, a previously non-union SBC subsidiary.[5]

The CWA began its effort in 1992 as a regional campaign to unionize Southwestern Bell Mobile Systems (SBMS), the mobile phone subsidiary of Southwestern Bell and the predecessor company to Cingular Wireless. The union's campaign then followed the mergers and acquisitions that transformed Southwestern Bell into SBC, the second largest telephone company in the coun-

Neutrality and Card Check

A *NEUTRALITY* AGREEMENT is a contract between an employer and a union in which the employer agrees to remain neutral during the union's organizing efforts. Some neutrality agreements severely restrict management behavior by enumerating prohibited activity and providing penalties for violation. Weaker agreements simply state an employer's intent without specifying the meaning of neutrality or any sanction for violating the agreement.

Most neutrality agreements limit what the union can do to disrupt the workplace, as well as any attempts by the union to coerce workers into joining the union. Many include binding arbitration to resolve disputes.

In a *card check* agreement, the employer agrees to recognize the union when a set percentage of workers signs membership cards. Card check agreements can be complicated, spelling out in detail how cards must be collected—how quickly, by whom, who counts the cards, which workers are eligible.

Card check agreements eliminate the need for NLRB recognition elections, which have become extremely difficult to win. During such elections, employers can delay the election on technical legal grounds and intimidate, cajole, harass, bribe, or otherwise influence workers to vote against the union.

Neutrality and card check make winning union recognition easier, but they do not make building a strong union automatic. Organizers and rank-and-file activists still must mobilize the new members to raise hell if they are to win a decent first contract.

try. Among the companies now part of SBC are Southwestern Bell (Arkansas, Kansas, Missouri, Oklahoma, Texas), Pacific Bell (California and Nevada), Ameritech (Illinois, Indiana, Michigan, Ohio, Wisconsin), Southern New England Telephone (Connecticut), and Cingular Wireless, now 60 percent owned by SBC and 40 percent by Bell South. The campaign continues as the union organizes the last remaining non-union workers at SBC.

Neutrality and card check (see page 227) were and still are central planks in CWA's strategy to organize non-union telephone subsidiaries through "bargaining to organize" with the parent companies. The union has brought a wide variety of pressures to bear to convince management that it's better off signing a card check agreement. These tactics were simultaneous, ongoing, and mutually reinforcing, but to simplify the discussion we will treat them one at a time.

Strategic Vision and Education

Over the course of the 1990s, CWA District 6, which includes Texas, Arkansas, Oklahoma, Missouri, and Kansas (the territory of Southwestern Bell), developed an increasingly comprehensive approach to organizing SBC's non-union subsidiaries. The first step was recognizing the industry trend toward mobile communications, which meant employment at SBMS was growing while jobs at SBC were shrinking. As they understood the extent of the shift, CWA regional leaders initiated a debate about the need to organize SBMS, with the goal of convincing local leaders and rank-and-file activists to participate in making SBC wall-to-wall union.

To stimulate the debate, every meeting or conference in the district—including leadership schools, the women's conference, local presidents' meetings, organizing retreats, and local union meetings—discussed the need to organize SBMS. At all these meetings, officials and members talked about the wireless industry, which companies owned which franchises, the types of jobs in wireless, industry profits, and the difference between a store (wholly owned) and an agent (independent).

A strategy group within the district came together. It investigated any angle that might provide a leverage point with the company, including cellular tower regulations, regulatory legislation, service standards, safety, and the community impact of company operations.

District staff also conducted organizing schools on wireless for CWA locals. Since the CWA has an active member-organizer development program, more than 700 rank-and-file activists attended these schools between 1992 and 1997. Most of them went on to participate in organizing wireless workers, with and without neutrality and card check.

As part of its wireless education program, the union got hold of an anti-union manual from the company's union-busting consultant. The union distributed the manual and other anti-union material to locals, alerting them to the company's tactics and firing up the rank and file.

Management opposition to unionization at SBMS played a big role in convincing rank-and-file activists to help the organizing efforts, says Danny Fetonte, area director of organizing. "Here they were telling union workers how important it was that management and the union work together to build the company, and then they were bringing in union-busting lawyers to prevent us from organizing wireless workers."

A consensus on the need to organize SBMS quickly emerged, but debate continued on tactics. At one end of the spectrum, some CWA activists were reluctant to use political and legislative leverage that might hurt SBC, slow its growth, and jeopardize jobs. At the other end of the spectrum, some wanted all-out war against the company. Debate over how much to resist and how much to cooperate with management, particularly in the legislative and regulatory arena, continued throughout the SBMS struggle. In practice, the union both resisted and cooperated.

Continuous Bargaining

During bargaining with SBC in 1992, CWA managed to win a weak neutrality agreement that covered all SBC subsidiaries except SBMS, which insisted on negotiating its own separate neutrality agreement. This agreement with SBMS did not specify card check recognition, but it said the company's position would be neutral and it granted union access to company property. In practice, SBMS violated the neutrality agreement by hiring a union-busting consultant, training supervisors in anti-union methods, holding captive-audience meetings, and transferring workers to dilute union strength within bargaining units.

SBC had several programs in which workers and/or union reps would meet with management to discuss various issues—productivity, staffing, work rules, training. Using each of these encounters as an opportunity, the union turned every meeting with SBC management into a forum on neutrality at SBMS. "Management would hold a meeting to talk about productivity or some other issue, and workers would demand to know why they should cooperate when SBMS management was violating the neutrality agreement," says Fetonte.

The union leveraged its relationship with SBC to help specific organizing campaigns at SBMS. During a 1992 union election at SBMS in St. Louis, management announced a captive-audience meeting. CWA Vice-President Vic Crawley called SBC's CEO to object to the meeting, while a CWA District 6 political action officer did the same with SBC External Affairs. The union officers negotiated successfully for the presence of a union representative at the meeting. "I think we would have lost the election at that point if we had not been able to show the mobile workers that we had some power through our relationship with the parent company," Crawley says in the union's history of the campaign.

During 1995 contract talks with SBC, CWA raised the issue of neutrality at SBMS, citing specific violations of the 1992 agreement. As a result, SBC management pressured SBMS managers to improve the neutrality agreement, so that it included mechanisms for the mediation and arbitration of disputes. CWA still did not have card check recognition, and the company continued to violate the agreement, but now the union had another avenue to pressure the company: arbitration.

Using the NLRB

In 1994, during an organizing drive in Abilene, SBMS management made three anti-union temp workers permanent, and the union lost the election by two votes. The union had evidence that management had made illegal promises during the campaign, and it filed unfair labor practice charges against the company. With pressure coming from SBC management—angry at its increasingly tempestuous relationship with the union—SBMS management settled the ULP charges by agreeing to card check recognition for the 25 workers in Abilene.

Under the agreement, CWA would wait 18 months to begin organizing again in Abilene and would then have 60 days to get 60 percent-plus-one of the workers to sign membership cards. The agreement also locked the bargaining unit on the earliest date appearing on the cards signed and turned in to the American Arbitration Association. Freezing the unit meant the company could not pack the workforce with anti-union workers. This language represented a strong precedent, and the union built upon it in future campaigns. The Abilene workers won union representation through card check in July 1996.

Where CWA could not build open-and-shut ULP cases or clear violations of the neutrality agreement, it used the discovery process of NLRB and arbitration hearings to expose the company's anti-union campaign. Through the hearings, the union obtained managers' descriptions of training they received on how to present CWA negatively and how to thwart a union drive, the interviews they had with a union-busting consultant, and the records they kept on each employee's union sympathies.

By demonstrating anti-union activity at SBMS, the union built a case it could use to educate and mobilize existing CWA members at SBC and potential members at SBMS. The information also allowed the union to demonstrate to the public the hypocrisy of SBC's claims that it wanted a partnership with the union. Finally, the information helped the union negotiate increasingly better neutrality agreements by facilitating the introduction of language prohibiting more aspects of the company's anti-union effort.

Mobilization

Over and over, CWA members and officials protested management opposition to the union at SBMS. In 1993, angered at managers' refusal to reach a contract with new members in St. Louis, local officials arrived at an annual SBC company-union reception wearing red t-shirts that read "Contract Now."

The next year, CWA locals in Dallas set up informational pickets and passed out flyers in front of several National Auto Cellular outlets that resold SBMS service. SBMS was furious. Not only did the company threaten to sue CWA for a secondary boycott, it faxed maps and directions to an SBMS retail sales outlet as an alternative site for CWA pickets. A few months later, to avoid a repeat performance in front of its new stores offering both local and wireless service, SBC offered CWA card check for the stores in Houston, Austin, and Beaumont. The terms were the same as the Abilene agreement, except that the union needed only 55 percent-plus-plus-one for recognition.

In 1995, 200 union members marched in front of SBC corporate headquarters in San Antonio, demanding that SBC adhere to its neutrality agreement at SBMS. In January 1997, another 200 CWA members from around the state converged on Abilene in support of that unit's contract fight and to push for card check at other locations. The union wanted to show that it would support even the smallest group against the company.

Of course, the union held many smaller demonstrations and protests in conjunction with local organizing campaigns, part of the union's regular organizing strategy.

Political Action

SBC comes under the regulatory scrutiny of the Federal Communications Commission, the Federal Trade Commission, the Justice Department, dozens of state public service commissions, and hundreds of municipalities. The company is constantly asking federal, state, and local agencies and legislatures for approval to raise rates, introduce new services, run cable, or acquire a company.

The company counts on CWA, which has a certain amount of political clout, to support its legislative and regulatory agenda. This gives the union a source of leverage. As SBC fought for favorable laws and regulatory agency decisions, especially for mergers and acquisitions, the union took a carrot-and-stick approach, sometimes withholding and other times offering support, in exchange for the company's agreement to neutrality and card check.

In 1994, J. D. Williams, president of the Texas CWA Local Presidents' Conference, wrote a public letter to his fellow presidents suggesting that CWA withhold support for SBC legislation if SBMS did not agree to the union's latest neutrality proposal. The letter sparked a frenzied response from SBC External Affairs, which offered to help the union.

Switching to the carrot, the union mobilized 5,000 members, at company expense, to support SBC in a joint lobbying day at the Texas legislature. The union brought up its demand for neutrality and card check at the joint planning meeting for the lobby day, but did not threaten to withdraw support. The union also brought 200 members to a San Antonio City Council meeting to oppose plans to lease out a city-owned fiber optic ring to a Canadian consortium. This would have increased competition for SBC, which, the union argued, had provided good-paying and stable jobs for city residents. Together, the union and company defeated the plan.

SBC's proposed merger with Pacific Bell in 1997 provided the union's greatest opportunity for leverage. The merger faced opposition from the California Public Service Commission, and CWA's influence was pivotal in winning approval. In exchange for union support, the company negotiated a new neutrality and card check agreement that applied to all of SBMS and to all other SBC subsidiaries.

The agreement, which largely still applies, requires 50 percent-plus-one signed cards within 60 days for recognition, freezes the bargaining unit on the earliest date on the cards turned in to the American Arbitration Association, allows workers to transfer between subsidiaries, and establishes that CWA and SBC agree to support each other before legislative and regulatory bodies unless each determines such support to be in conflict with its interests.

As SBC merged with additional phone companies, CWA made sure the agreement applied to the new companies. As a result, the agreement covers workers in the West, the Southwest, the Midwest, and the Northeast, virtually everywhere SBC or one of its subsidiaries has a presence.

Organizing with Card Check

From 1992 to 1997, under the weak neutrality agreement, CWA organized 500 workers at Cingular Wireless. From February 1997 through 1998, 5,000 more joined the union, and in 2004, the CWA represented 21,919 Cingular workers nationwide. CWA has organized several thousand more workers at other SBC subsidiaries, such as those that handle DSL, Yellow Pages, and data communications.

Asked what's different about organizing under a card check agreement, Seth Rosen of CWA District 4 says, "The threshold is lower. Without the agreement, it takes a very high threshold of anger to keep workers jumping through hoops of fire while rocks are being thrown at them."

Rosen also notes that under the agreement "every card counts. Without the agreement, one or two workers might sign cards at a given worksite, but when the election comes they back down under the tidal wave of co-worker and company opposition. With card check, if a majority of workers wants the union it does not matter how that majority is distributed among the workers."

In CWA's District 4, which includes Indiana, Illinois, Michigan, Ohio, and Wisconsin, the union won area-wide bargaining units for Cingular Wireless workers, including both store workers, who have been less enthusiastic for the union, and call center and technical workers, who are more likely to be supporters. Other districts in California and the South did not win area-wide bargaining units, and many stores there remain non-union.

In all the campaigns, CWA member-organizers were the main activists organizing the new members. "These were folks who did similar work," says Rosen. "Call center workers from SBC talked to Cingular Wireless call center workers, and technical workers from SBC talked to technical workers at Cingular, and the new members went into existing locals with similar workers."

Felicia Jones helped build the committee at the Cingular call center where she works, in the Chicago area. "We had a series of meetings before the drive started," says Jones. "We talked about the process, how it worked, the benefits of the union. Then we formed teams. When the drive started, I handed out cards and explained to workers what it was about, the benefits of the union. If they did not sign, I pursued them a second and third time, asking them why they wouldn't sign. If I could not get in touch with them, I asked a team member to talk to them. It was a lot of one-on-one conversations.

"Lots of people were collecting cards. We worked with Celia [a CWA organizer], going through the list of workers. It went very smoothly." Jones later became a member-organizer on drives at Verizon Wireless (which failed) and SBC Yellow Pages (which won).

Is Card Check Too Easy?

The benefit of card check—no employer fear-campaign that scares workers into voting no—should be weighed against a possible cost to the union in the future. Erin Bowie, a CWA organizer in the Northeast, points out that it can be harder to mobilize workers to take action in a card check drive. When the company remains neutral, "there's no anti-union campaign to get people angry."

Most organizers who've lived through an NLRB election against a vicious management will take card check any day. Still, Bowie says of the CWA's new Cingular units, "There are fewer activists. This is not a situation where the workers have had to fight for a union and fight for a contract. CWA has had a friendly relationship with Cingular. I am from the phone company, and it's not like that there. It's combative. At Cingular there is a totally different mentality. Part of it is because of how the organizing is done. That is a disadvantage of card check. But is it better to organize or not? We've faced fierce opposition at Verizon Wireless and haven't organized anyone."

Bowie thinks the union's lack of creativity, not card check, is mainly to blame for the lack of activism among Cingular workers. "Sales reps at Cingular *are* angry about the changing sales goals the company imposes. There is not much willingness to mobilize around the issue, but we have to figure out how to motivate those sales reps. Most of the locals in the Northeast are phone company locals. The locals just expect the aggressive phone company worker mentality, and we haven't figured out creative ways to get the Cingular workers involved. We are just starting to get them involved in the locals, involved in training, and connected to phone-company people, so they can see that Cingular and SBC are the same company. This is harder where the Cingular groups are in their own local, isolated from the phone company people."

Bowie's suggestions point to the way to use card check. Getting workers into the union is not enough. While collecting signatures, organizers need to run a comprehensive campaign that employs all the tactics we have talked about to energize and mobilize workers for a first contract and beyond.

Everything but the Kitchen Sink: HERE's 13-Year Campaign Beats the Marriott

IT TOOK WORKERS at the San Francisco Marriott Hotel 13 years to win a union and a first contract. Their story demonstrates how difficult it is to organize in today's legal and economic environment, but it also illustrates how a comprehensive campaign carried out by workers and a union willing to persevere can win.

Card Check Recognition and Neutrality

In the late 1980s, Marriott Corporation bid to build a new hotel as part of San Francisco's Yerba Buena convention center. As part of the approval process, the city's Redevelopment Agency heard comment on the company's bid. Hotel and Restaurant Employees Local 2 demanded that the agency require the hotel to agree to card check recognition and neutrality in any organizing attempt by the nonsupervisory staff.

With 10,000 members, Local 2 is one of the most militant unions in San Francisco and it often mobilizes members for a variety of causes. This time, the pressure paid off when the Redevelopment Agency made card check recognition and neutrality part of its agreement with the Marriott.

But after the hotel opened in 1989, Marriott campaigned actively against HERE's organizing. It took six years of legal wrangling before the company finally agreed to abide by card check and neutrality, under the supervision of a court-appointed "Special Master" named John Kagel, an arbitrator who would settle disputes as the two sides carried out the agreement.

"During that time, we organized other hotels and won better contracts for our members, including a better master hotel contract for the city," says David Glaser, an organizer who led the Local 2 campaign and is now with the International. Glaser and other Local 2 officials were convinced that card check/neutrality was the only way to win a union at the new hotel. "Marriott had never signed a union contract. An NLRB election was out of the question. We would never have won. They had already intimidated many workers into opposing the union. And even if we had won, they would have contested it and dragged it out forever. With card check, we had a very good shot at recognition, and having recognition makes a contract fight possible."

The 18-page agreement detailed what each side could do, describing company neutrality and limiting the types of attacks the union could make on management. It specified that management would have a two-week period for mandatory meetings, at which it could describe the neutrality agreement without arguing against the union. Local 2 was given 18 months to win recognition by getting a majority of workers to sign cards.

"The crucial mistake [for Marriott] was settling the case," says Glaser. "They should have kept up the legal challenges, but they clearly believed their own rhetoric about workers being 'Marriott associates,' loyal to the company. What's more, they really were neutral, which was stupid, because the agreement said that if they broke the agreement, the agreement could only be extended six more months. They should have fired people willy-nilly, since there really was no punishment for breaking the agreement. But they believed the people loved them."

Marriott's captive-audience meetings began in February 1996. "Under the agreement, we received tapes of every meeting," says Glaser. "We were outraged when we first heard them, and we filed charges with the Special Master, who agreed that the company spokesperson went beyond the definition of neutrality. But once we calmed down and started listening to the workers, we discovered that the things that upset us did not upset them. They wanted the boss to say, 'The union sucks' or 'The union is fine.' But their attorney was restrained and legalistic. He infuriated the workers with his legalese. So management lost its credibility during the one shot it had to communicate an anti-union message, and that gave us the opportunity to tell the workers that it would be the union, not the company, who would give them a straight answer."

The legal settlement and the captive-audience meetings validated the union. "We [the five organizers on the campaign] could show up on the sidewalk outside the Marriott," says Glaser. "We could be in the workers' faces. We could say, 'We heard about the meetings, let us tell you about the union.' We turned their frustration about the captive-audience meetings into a way to talk to them."

Organizing One by One

The Marriott workforce included housekeepers, kitchen staff, restaurant and banquet personnel, telephone operators, and bell staff. Dozens of countries were represented, including China, Philippines, Eritrea, Ethiopia, Russia, Mexico, and Guatemala. Housekeepers were largely Filipina and Chinese women, while dishwashers were predominantly Latino men. Workers in the "back of the house"—those who do not interact with customers—were overwhelmingly immigrants. The "front of the house" tended to employ more native-born workers, but was still quite diverse. Chinese were the largest group, followed by Filipinos, Latinos, whites, and African

Americans.

To communicate with the workforce, all five of the Local 2 organizers were at least bilingual, speaking English and either Mandarin, Cantonese, Tagalog (the Philippines), or Spanish. They translated all written communications into Spanish, Tagalog, and Chinese, while all meetings were simultaneously translated into Spanish and one of the Chinese dialects.

The organizers began with Marriott workers who were already Local 2 members, those who had second jobs in unionized hotels. "There were 50 Local 2 members out of about 800 at the Marriott," says Glaser. "Forty-seven of them were actively pro-union. They had good experience at their union jobs. They knew Local 2 was an aggressive, democratic, grass-roots union that had won improved contracts in the hotel industry over the last ten years. They knew that they were not in this alone, that if we held a demonstration many people would show up, maybe even the mayor. They could explain how the union worked and how our comprehensive campaign could win."

Only about five or six of these members were active on the organizing committee, however. "Most of them had two full-time jobs, so they didn't have enough time," notes Glaser. "But they did support the union drive."

Laura Barrera, a housekeeper, was not a Local 2 member, but her husband had been in the local for 25 years. "I was familiar with the union and with the advantages and benefits that come with being a union member," she says.

Beginning with the Local 2 members or contacts like Barrera, the organizers asked supporters among the workforce to talk to the people they trusted the most. "They would say, 'You met with management, now meet with the union. Give me your phone number and I'll give it to the union.' And they would try to get their co-workers to agree to a call from the organizers. We wanted active approval, no cold calls."

Barrera describes how she worked. "I began to take people from the hotel down to the union hall to learn about the union. Sometimes I took four people, other times six people, and the staff and I would sit down and talk to them to make them conscious, to educate them about what a union is, so that they wouldn't be afraid. We did this for two months, and every day I took down three, or four, or five people. One time I took down ten, but every day I took some people."

Committee Grows

With five organizers doing one new visit and one repeat visit each day—usually in coffee shops or sometimes workers' homes—the union was seeing 25 new potential members a week. The exact number of workers in the bargaining unit had not been settled, but the organizers figured they needed 400 signed union cards to be safe. "We were doing visits at a fast clip," says Glaser. "We were enlarging the organizing committee, which expanded the number of people who could get phone numbers."

The organizing committee met every week to discuss their progress. Workers reported on their efforts—who they talked to, who was interested in the union and who was not—and co-workers and organizers made suggestions. Organizers also used the meetings to explain how the union worked (structure, elections) and the benefits of a contract.

As the committee grew and the one-on-one organizing dragged on, workers became anxious. "Workers just want the company to stop its harsh treatment," says Glaser. "They want to win and they want to do it sooner rather than later. We explained how hard this was going to be. We argued that we were not ready to move on. We said, 'We'll move to the next stage when we do more visits.' We put it on them to get more names, more phone numbers, and more approvals for phone calls. We insisted that they view themselves as the union in terms of the organizing work."

The organizers and the organizing committee assessed the mood in July. "Things were going well," says Glaser. "The boss was silent, and the number of written questions management was getting from workers [which management had to share with the union under the agreement] was tiny and some of them were pro-union. Management seemed to be oblivious to us."

So the organizers suggested a survey. "The organizing committee did the survey," says Glaser. "They asked all their contacts, 'If you had a union card would you sign it?' If the answer was yes, they would ask, 'Why would you sign?' If no, 'Why not?' Then they reported their results to the committee meeting."

The survey had a dual purpose. It was a way to gauge support for the union and "to test the talent of the committee," says Glaser. "Did they have the ability to hear and persuade their co-workers? Lots of organizers don't listen. The most effective are present in a conversation. People are pro-union for different reasons. Good organizers hear who they are talking to and explain the union from where they are at."

The next step in the campaign shook up the committee, but it also solidified the workers' commitment. "We told the committee that we would take their photographs

It took workers at the San Francisco Marriott 13 years to win a union and a first contract.

at the next meeting," says Glaser. "We explained that we would use the photographs for a leaflet when we passed out the union cards. The employer was going to attack us and we needed the leaflet to show scared workers that we would stand up to the employer.

"This was the hardest thing we asked the workers to do during the entire campaign. They would talk to people and come to a meeting every week, but they were afraid to display their union support in such a public and permanent way. We explained that we would not hand out union cards until they put their pictures on the leaflet. We explained that union supporters had to display confidence to their co-workers. The committee signed union cards that week, but we had to delay the photographs a week."

Once the photographs were done and the leaflet was ready in Spanish, Chinese, Tagalog, and English, the committee planned the distribution and collection of union cards. "We, the organizers, said we would not get workers to sign cards," says Glaser. "We explained that this was a task for the committee. It was an example of how they were the union."

The committee picked a Thursday, when it thought it could get through the weekend before a management counterattack and when it knew committee members would be working. "The committee had about 60 people coming to meetings at that time," says Glaser. "It was not ideal. You want 90 or 150, but things were going well and the boss had been silent. The committee is never as big as you want, so you have to make a judgment."

As it turned out, the committee's timing was perfect. The workers collected signed cards from a majority of the bargaining unit in eight days. "All of us who were in the committee were very strong," says Barrera. "The union gave each of us cards to get signed. They gave me 15. Some signed and some didn't sign because they were afraid. One person was going to tear up the card, but I told her she had to give it back, because I had to return every card to the union, signed or unsigned."

The union turned in the cards to the Special Master in August 1996, was certified in September, and began contract negotiations in November.

Contract Talks Stall

The company took a hard line in bargaining. "They were sophisticated," says Glaser. "It was not clear for ten months that they planned to break the union."

The union prepared for bargaining by holding departmental meetings where workers hammered out their demands. "We asked people what they wanted to fight for," says Glaser. "Lots of new people stepped forward and became leaders. And these were not the people who had led the organizing committee. It was a great opportunity to consolidate and supplement the rank-and-file leadership."

A bargaining committee chaired by the Local 2 president did the negotiating. The committee, which grew out of the organizing committee, caucused regularly to work out differences, but it spoke with one voice, through the president, in front of management. "Lots of workers participated in bargaining, which was open," says Glaser, who was the union's note taker. "If we were talking about housekeeping, 25 housekeepers attended. On some occasions, workers would speak about their jobs.

"Overall, more than 150 workers attended bargaining sessions, some multiple times. They got to see how creepy the boss was. Marriott was represented by an attorney who was arrogant and nasty. They could see managers and human resource people. It was chilly, ugly. It took courage to attend bargaining in front of people who could make your life miserable.

"It was a great opportunity to train the leaders and rank and file about the union and about what they were facing in bargaining month after month. It hardened workers toward management and strengthened their determination to win."

In January 1997, two months after negotiations began, Marriott raised the wages of all non-management, non-union employees, including engineers, salespeople, and front desk clerks. Then in June, it made a dramatic benefit proposal to the union, including domestic partner coverage and lower medical co-pays. The union refused, since the offer was not as good as the master contract that covered most of the union hotels in the city.

The union had made it clear from the beginning that it would not accept a contract whose total costs came in below the citywide master contract. "If it did," says Glaser, "other employers would demand the same. The union was flexible on how the cost was structured, to meet the demands of Marriott workers, but the total hourly cost could not be less than the master contract."

Since management had not come around on basic demands, such as seniority, or on specific demands such as the tip structure in the banquet room or the number of rooms housekeepers had to clean, few workers thought management's offer worth accepting. As the contract fight dragged on, in fact, workers' demands grew. "They said, 'We've held out this long, let's get everything we want,'" says Glaser.

Bargaining sessions continued intermittently, but progress was excruciatingly slow. "Management would make fun of us and laugh at us," says Barrera. "They would say, 'Why should we have you clean fewer rooms than you are now? Why would we do that?' When our union president saw that they weren't really negotiating, he stood up and said, 'Well, if you're not going to negotiate, then we're going,' and we walked out."

Surveying for the Next Step

With no progress in negotiations, the union began to step up the pressure on the job. The bargaining committee decided to survey the workers to see if they would wear buttons in support of the union's demands. When they were sure it would be an impressive showing, they started wearing the buttons and trying to get more workers to display them.

Then they did a survey to see if workers would participate in demonstrations. When the answer was yes, the workers started demonstrating in front of the hotel once a week to demand a decent contract.

The committee also began house visits to workers who had not yet come out in support of the union. Many of these workers were immigrants, quite a few in housekeeping, who were afraid they would be singled out and possibly turned over to immigration authorities. With the lowest pay and some of the hardest work, they were also more vulnerable to management buy-offs.

With the house visits and the surveys, the committee laid the groundwork for an escalating series of activities to win a good contract. "We were constantly talking to people about why the next step would be necessary," says Glaser.

Defeating Decertification

In the fall of 1997, management began a full-bore decertification campaign, attacking the union in a series of captive-audience meetings. Several workers wore anti-union buttons, criticized the union, and distributed a petition for decertification.

Union workers countered by "going nose to nose with anti-union people on the job," says Glaser. "There were verbal exchanges and confrontations. It was very tense. They had the power of the boss behind them, and the union workers had to work hard to maintain their organization and morale."

"A supervisor from the housekeeping department was the leader of an anti-union group," says Barrera. "These people talked against the union, they called us all sorts of names, they used the worst sort of language, and they gave us the finger.

"When we began to wear union buttons, each with a different slogan demanding seniority, or benefits, or childcare, or retirement benefits, they put on buttons saying, 'Union Fuera' (Out with the Union). But we were not intimidated because we knew what we were fighting for."

Union workers attended the decertification committee's meetings and picketed. They also confronted management during the captive-audience meetings. "Union people stood up and defended the union," says Glaser. "They took on the HR person and said, 'You are committing an 8a1 and an 8a3 violation [referring to the clauses of the National Labor Relations Act]."

The company filed its decert petition in December 1997, but an election could not take place as long as there were outstanding unfair labor practice charges before the NLRB. The workers had filed dozens, so many that it had become something of a joke among the workers.

"Over the years during the contract campaign, the workers took over the cafeteria a dozen times," says Glaser. "Often, they would announce the filing of an unfair labor practice charge. There got to be so many that the workers organized a raffle to guess the correct number of times the Labor Board would charge the company with breaking the law. And 18 months later, they actually awarded a union jacket to the worker who guessed right. It was something like 72 charges against the company."

To protest the massive number of ULPs, union workers started wearing buttons: "Marriott—Not Above the Law."

Corporate Campaign

The decert campaign put an end to bargaining for what turned out to be 20 months. But even when bargaining resumed, the company would move only slightly, and then refuse to meet for months at a time. The union began to transform what had been a comprehensive organizing drive into an all-out corporate campaign.

Through fall 1997 and spring 1998, close to 100 workers testified before the NLRB about abuses at the San Francisco Marriott. The battle before the Board and the courts took many twists and turns, but the union was successful in two ways. First, it forced Marriott to make back payments of roughly $1.5 million and to give wage and benefit increases to workers—after it had given these improvements to the non-union, non-management workers at the hotel but not the union workers, which is a form of illegal discrimination.

Second, the union forced the company to give vacation pay to workers who had not received it when they left the company. The company also had to change its national vacation policy. As an added benefit, union success before the NLRB seemed to prompt Marriott to resume bargaining.

The union attacked Marriott's business practices. San Francisco Marriott workers testified before various government agencies around the country that regulated local development projects. They argued that government concessions should not go to a company that violates labor law. In Boston, Denver, Houston, San Jose,

Fighting the Fear of Being Fired

IT'S ALMOST A GIVEN that management will retaliate against workers they perceive as leaders of a pro-union campaign. How can the union help deal with the fear this creates? In one HERE organizing drive in Virginia, a community-based organization called the Tenants and Workers Support Committee found a way.

Jon Liss of the Committee recalls: "A worker named Toribio Alvarenga got fired because management videotaped him coming to the Committee office for a meeting. The next day the company asked him for names of who else was present, and he said no. He was fired.

"Toribio filed charges with the NLRB, and eventually he settled for full payment of his back wages (but no job reinstatement). We called that a victory. So we blew up a photo of him with the $21,000 check, put it on the back of a pickup truck, got a megaphone, and drove around Latino working class neighborhoods. We used this to show that yes, you can fight the hotels and win."

Sacramento, and Oceola, Florida, workers' testimony contributed to decisions to deny Marriott permits for development of large convention center hotels, the main profit generators for the company. "They were going to build 60,000 rooms and we stopped 6,000," says Glaser. "That's a big chunk of revenue."

The union kept up its weekly demonstrations and from the fall of 1998 began holding larger monthly demonstrations that included civil disobedience in the hotel lobby or on the street in front of the hotel. These attracted anywhere from 200 to 2,000 people, and local politicians, labor leaders, and community activists often attended. Monthly demonstrations were often called to coincide with union conventions, so delegates could march to the hotel in a show of solidarity. During one demonstration, 2,000 bicyclists, part of the pro-bicycle Critical Mass movement, blocked rush hour traffic in front of the hotel.

Scott Sjoberg, a banquet bartender/server at the Marriott, was arrested in front of the hotel at one demonstration and remembers it as "one of the most powerful moments of my life. The feeling of solidarity, sitting there as a group while hundreds of supporters cheered us on, was amazing."

Barrera felt the same way. "They arrested me four times. It was the kind of experience that matures you and makes you understand what you're fighting for. They arrested us and took us a few blocks from the hotel and wrote us up and let us go. They didn't scare me. On the contrary, I fought even harder."

On the job, the workers kept up the pressure. "On four or five occasions we took over the workers' cafeteria, and we carried out educational meetings right there," says Barrera. "We talked to the workers to raise their consciousness about the union, and to overcome their fear. We would take it over from 10 in the morning until the early afternoon, through the whole lunch period. We would hand out leaflets, talk to the workers, and sometimes we passed around cake. The first time we did this, a woman from the personnel department told us we would have to go, but we stayed."

"For the first time, we felt like we had the power over the Marriott," says Lisa Bettles, a food service worker, about that first cafeteria sit-in.

Union supporters continued to distribute literature, wear buttons, and talk up the union among their co-workers. Even though they had no contract, the workers started to act as if they did. They asserted their "Weingarten rights," which give any union worker the right to union representation during any investigative interview with management that could possibly lead to discipline.

"They disciplined two workers because one had punched out for the other, and they were going to fire them," says Barrera. "But we asked for a meeting with management, and we went right in there to talk to them, and they didn't fire those workers."

"The workers were increasingly aggressive in asserting their rights," says Glaser. "In fact, they expanded the meaning of Weingarten by not only acting as witnesses during meetings with Human Resources but by arguing against the discipline management wanted to impose. They moved from passive witness to active counselor and advocate. In effect, they were shop stewards running grievances."

Two-Day Strike

In the spring of 2000, with the busy summer and fall seasons approaching, the leaders among the union workers conducted a survey: were workers willing to strike? "We had discussed a boycott," says Glaser. "But we wanted our base to cut one more tie with the company in their hearts before calling a boycott, and nothing does that more than a strike.

"The crucial thing in a strike vote is turnout," he notes. "You often see overwhelming majorities for a strike, but how many of the eligible workers vote? We had over 50 percent turnout, which was terrific since workers had to come down to the union hall to cast their vote. More than 90 percent voted for a two-day strike."

To prepare for the strike, to be held in July, the organizers and the bargaining committee discussed the attacks they would face from the company and the divisions the strike could cause among the workers. "The dynamic of a picket line is different from a demonstration," says Glaser. "You have to be ready to go nose-to-nose with your co-workers a block and a half from the entrance to the hotel. But you also have to avoid obsessing over numbers. Everybody will look for his or her co-workers. If a department with 50 people has two people scab, they will obsess over those two, forgetting that they got 48 to honor the lines."

The company sent workers a letter threatening them with permanent replacement if they went on strike. Leaders confronted the fear this generated in four ways. First, they explained that the letter was almost certainly just a scare tactic, not the company's actual plan of attack. "If they are really going to fire you, they don't tell you beforehand so you can prepare some opposition," says Glaser.

Second, they explained how difficult it would be to replace the workers in just two days. The logistics of finding and training replacements in the few weeks before the strike would be expensive. Though the company could begin the process of recruiting replacements, it could not legally hire them until the strike began. Long before they could all be hired, the strike would be over.

Third, the union planned to tell management at the start of the strike exactly when workers would return. The short duration of the strike would mean that the company could not prove legally any economic necessity for permanent replacement. Finally, the organizers argued that the company would be less likely to carry through its threat if a large majority of the workers supported the strike.

So for two days in July, when all the hotel's rooms and banquet space were occupied, hundreds of workers walked off the job and picketed. The turnout was good, but not complete. "About 40 percent [of the bargaining unit] signed in on the picket line," says Glaser. "Many did not come either to picket or to work. Many picketed but did not sign in. But it would not be accurate to say we had 75 percent active support. We were a majority, but we had to fight constantly to keep support."

The results of the strike were a mixed bag, given the number of scabs. Still, the committee felt it went well. "The staff were thrilled," says Glaser. "We thought it was one more demoralizing event for management. This was the end of the fifth year without a contract, without union staff ever having stepped foot on the property, and the workers were escalating the struggle in dramatic fashion. There's never a silver bullet in a struggle like this, but we thought it was a body blow."

The strike definitely had an impact, says Barrera. "The day after the strike, many were afraid to show up for work because they feared they would be fired, and we told them, 'Don't be afraid. Now you are more respected than before.' And that's the way it was. No one said a word to us, absolutely no one said anything."

Boycott

The strike also did just what the committee thought it would do: prepare the workers for a boycott of Marriott. "You receive a letter threatening that you will be permanently replaced and you see the dark side of management," says Glaser. "A strike is us and them. It's passionate. At the first meeting after the strike, the committee suggested a boycott. 'The company will lose money,' we warned. 'Management will say you are just hurting yourselves.' But there was no hesitation. The workers said, 'Screw 'em. Let's do it. We're ready.'"

The union announced the boycott of the San Francisco Marriott at a Labor Day rally in front of the hotel. Mayor Willie Brown, wearing a Boycott Marriott t-shirt, spoke out against the company. Few big companies honored the boycott, but several organizations, including the American Political Science Association, the National Association of Insurance Commissioners, and the Niku Corporation, moved their conventions elsewhere.

Staffers researched ways to pressure such groups to change their hotel plans. In the case of the insurance commissioners, the union threatened to oppose their re-election.

Church groups, community groups, and Coretta Scott King endorsed the boycott. To spread the word, workers did dozens of unannounced drop-ins to local businesses with ties to Marriott. One delegation of clergy, students, and workers protested at the offices of Wells Fargo in an attempt to get them to cancel a conference at the hotel. "They sat down, disrupted the office, and then left when the police arrived," says Lamoin Werlein-Jaén, a vice-president of Local 2.

Another delegation visited a local AIDS group. "The Marriott gave them free meeting space and sponsored the AIDS Walk," says Glaser. "We pointed out the hypocrisy of a company that tried to maintain a progressive image on the issue of AIDS but refused in bargaining to contribute a single nickel to the union's AIDS fund. We said the AIDS group should cut its ties to the hotel to expose this hypocrisy."

To complement the boycott, workers held a series of monthly 16-hour pickets targeted at a convention being held at the hotel. These pickets began at 6 a.m. with a "wake-up" song delivered via bullhorn and drum. They continued all day and into the night with leafleting, chanting, singing, music, marching, and mild harassment of hotel guests. "In addition to annoying customers and management, the day-long demonstrations gave workers, supporters, and other Local 2 members a way to participate in the struggle," notes Glaser. "The boycott is no good without its popular manifestation in demonstrations and other public acts."

Workers also organized a community hearing, hosted by the archbishop of San Francisco and the Bay Area Organizing Committee, a coalition of faith-based, union, and civic associations. Clergy presided as Marriott workers testified in four languages, before an audience of 800, about the abuse they had suffered at the hotel. Marriott management was invited but did not attend.

Settlement

In the fall of 2001, Marriott replaced its local negotiator with one from corporate headquarters. Over the next ten months, the union and the company engaged in intermittent and tedious bargaining, while the union continued its boycott and demonstrations. The parties reached a settlement along the lines of the industry master contract in August 2002.

Just what moved the company is impossible to say. "In a comprehensive campaign, you cannot point to one or two things that force the company to relent," says Glaser. "It is a cumulative process that brings management to the point where it says, "Let's make a business decision and put this thing behind us.' There will be a last straw, but you cannot know it until it happens. In this case, we still do not know what it was."

The boycott almost certainly had an impact. On the day of the settlement, managers handed over the names and phone numbers of four organizations that had promised to pull out if no settlement were reached. Combined, the organizations represented 23,000 room-nights, well over $2 million in revenue.

It probably helped, too, that John Wilhelm, president of HERE, and J. W. Marriott, Jr., chairman of Marriott International, developed a relationship in the aftermath of the attacks of September 11, 2001. Both testified before Congress about the state of the tourism industry and later met to discuss various issues. "We took that meeting as a sign they were prepared to settle," says Glaser. "But we got that meeting as a result of our fight."

In for the Long Haul: The Nonmajority Union Strategy

by Paul Bouchard

For years the biggest problem facing the International Union of Electronic Workers has been General

Electric. IUE's membership and resources have continued to shrink as the massive multinational has frustrated every attempt to organize the growing union-free portion of the corporation. In 2003, only 14 percent of the workers at GE factories were union-represented. During bargaining, company officials boasted that in four years that number would be down to 9 percent.

Clearly, the IUE needed to do something different to organize GE. In 2001 we merged with the Communications Workers (CWA), which had experience in using nontraditional approaches to organizing at both IBM and Microsoft. An analysis of GE's union-avoidance program led CWA organizers to conclude that the company was not organizable using the traditional tactics based on winning an NLRB recognition election.

In the past, IUE organizers had been quickly pulled out of failed GE campaigns and redeployed to other projects. After building close relationships with organizers and seeing them on a daily basis, local organizing committees went for months without contact from "the union" after campaigns ended. CWA realized that these efforts had reinforced GE's portrayal of the union as a "third party" interested only in gaining dues-payers.

CWA's solution to the challenge of GE was to adopt a nonmajority union organizing strategy, to be called *Working At GE*, or WAGE. WAGE was intended to build union awareness and knowledge of the power of collective action slowly, over a long time. The goal of winning an NLRB-supervised recognition election would be completely de-emphasized. This required a leap of faith by IUE-CWA leaders and by leaders of Local 201, based at GE's jet engine plant in Lynn, Massachusetts. Local 201 hired me, out of a Lucent Technologies plant that was being shut down, as a full-time organizer. They accepted a "go slow" approach that would demand growth and participation by the workers.

The first WAGE committee coalesced in 2002 around the remnants of a local organizing committee that had just lost an NLRB-supervised election at GE's newly acquired Johnson Technologies Plant in Muskegon, Michigan. Soon, CWA and IUE-CWA organizers were distributing WAGE newsletters at non-union GE plants around the country. The first newsletters were simple—explaining WAGE, telling about the committee in Muskegon, encouraging workers to mail back the business reply card for more information.

By year's end, a WAGE committee was formed at the nearly 800-worker GE Aircraft Engine/Global Nuclear Fuels plant in Wilmington, North Carolina. The workforce in Wilmington is 60 percent white and 40 percent African American. Another committee was formed at the 150-employee GE Industrial Systems plant in Somersworth, New Hampshire. Both plants are three-quarters men and one-quarter women, and, as at all GE factories, workers are mostly 40 or older with 15 or more years of service. Interest in WAGE was also building at other GE plants, like the one in Auburn, Maine.

In theory, each WAGE committee is a grassroots, self-help organization that meets regularly to assess problems facing workers on the shop floor and designs strategies—using any available means—to pressure the company to change its behavior. Those means could include using the law, negative publicity, community pressure, shop floor agitation, and shop floor collective action. While the WAGE program's short-term goal is to solve problems by using workers' rights to collective action

GE's Union Avoidance Plan

No GE manufacturing facility has been organized since 1987, but not because of lack of effort. GE's union avoidance plan is both simple and effective. Appealing to individualism and self-interest, management tells workers at every opportunity that they are getting the same wages, benefits, and treatment as a unionized worker, without having to pay dues. At contract time, GE passes along union-won improvements as if they were a gift from a benevolent employer.

Non-union plants maintain an array of procedures to address workplace problems and resolve individual grievances. Workers most often turn to the plant human resources director, whom they are encouraged to view as their advocate. Grievances can be brought before a Peer Review Panel, usually made up of three workers and two managers, or workers can take advantage of the plant manager's "open door" policy and take the problem directly to him. All are advised that they can contact their division headquarters if they are not satisfied with the answers they get locally.

Not surprisingly, these procedures are less than effective. Even when the Peer Review Panel finds in favor of an employee, management simply sets aside the decision. Workers who avail themselves of the "open door" policy often find themselves in even more hot water, for going over their boss's head. And the response at the corporate level is that the employee should be dealing with the problem at the local level.

When workers do try to organize, GE flies in a team of trained union-avoidance experts to manage the situation. Unpopular plant managers are quickly transferred. Supervisors are schooled in how to appear more open, attentive, and understanding. Mandatory employee/management meetings begin immediately. Workers are immersed in an atmosphere of care and concern and lavished with free pizza, doughnuts, and coffee. Superficial problems are addressed and apologies are offered for having made the mistake of "not listening."

Although GE does not have a record of firing union activists (only a handful of cases in 30 years), those who try to organize soon find themselves on the outs with both management and their fellow employees. When the campaign fails, they are often left isolated, ostracized, and reluctant ever to get involved with organizing again.

under Section 7 of the National Labor Relations Act, its long-term purpose is to teach workers they can improve their lives by joining together. By doing so, our aim is to create an environment in which winning a union recognition election is a possibility. In essence, we are helping workers to become a union even before they have a contract.

When WAGE theory was put into practice, it quickly became evident that we could not easily undo the effects of relying for years on other tactics. Workers in nonunion plants such as the Wilmington facility were used to organizer-led, NLRB-election-type campaigns. They immediately saw WAGE as something less than a full commitment.

Similarly, when workers in Somersworth were approached with the idea of converting a failed card-signing effort into a WAGE committee, few initially agreed to be involved, and committee members there still have little faith in their ability to make changes at work. Consequently, I have come to see the biggest challenge facing an organizer trying to establish a nonmajority union in the wake of an NLRB election campaign as "uneducating" workers and overcoming everything they thought they knew about organizing.

A Different History

This was not the case in Auburn, Maine, however. Auburn GE workers had no prior history of election campaigns and were not burdened with preconceptions.

Established in the late 1960s, the GE factory in Auburn employs about 210 people, of whom perhaps 180 are eligible for representation. Workers stamp, grind, machine, and plate parts for circuit breakers in a noisy and smoky environment that leaves them grimy and exhausted by the end of their shifts.

These workers did not rush to embrace Local 201 when we started handing out WAGE newsletters at the gate. Local 201 organizing committee members Jim Tilden and John Berini, both machinists in the Lynn Gear Plant, leafleted Auburn four times in 2002 and received little response at first. After a while they began to be recognized by workers on their way into the company lot. A handful of cards was received at CWA headquarters in Washington, not enough to form a WAGE committee.

But in December 2002, management announced that five of every employee's vacation days would be taken and used as plant shutdown days. Disgruntled Auburn workers began sending back cards from the WAGE newsletter and contacting us through the WAGE website.

"The vacation day takeaway drove everything," says WAGE committee member Ray Dargie. "We wanted to control our own vacation time."

We reached out immediately to all our new and previous contacts and invited them to meet at a restaurant near the plant to discuss the new policy. Nearly three dozen workers showed up at three meetings that day. Years of pent-up frustration spilled out as worker after worker told the same stories. Most agreed it was time to do something about it, but without any past organizing activity, there was no great demand to sign cards and go for an election. When I talked about the NLRB election process and then introduced the WAGE concept, no one asked why we were going to build WAGE instead of just trying to win an election.

GE Auburn was a "hot shop" if ever there was one. In the past, the IUE would have deployed a raft of organizers to Maine to build a committee and file for an election. But because both the CWA and the IUE-CWA division within the union had committed to building WAGE, I would be the only organizer traveling to the location this time. Instead of mapping the workplace, assessing the workers, and getting them to sign cards, we all focused on the problems the workers faced and tried together to find ways to make changes.

This took discipline and understanding from top union leaders and the leaders of Local 201. The workers themselves would have to do the heavy lifting. The union wasn't "out there" somewhere; it was right there at each meeting and whenever the workers on the shop floor volunteered their time, energy, and skills to advance their mutual cause.

How WAGE Functions

Workers can join WAGE as either "members" or "supporters." Members pay dues of $10 a month and are IUE-CWA members with voting rights. Since most of the WAGE committee's activity occurs at the local level and no committee has attended an IUE-CWA convention, they haven't yet been able to use this right to vote in a meaningful way. WAGE members attend meetings, plan strategy, and carry out issue-oriented campaigns. WAGE supporters do not pay dues but participate in activities in the same way that voting members do.

Building a nonmajority union is a piecemeal business, dependent on workers mobilizing themselves around a particular issue and finding a creative way to prevail. By winning little victories through their own

Members of Auburn and Somersworth WAGE committees at Local 201 IUE-CWA contract rally.

efforts, workers gradually learn that they have power through collective action independent of their national union, the courts, or labor law. At Auburn, an issue was presented to us on a silver platter.

Ken Townsend, who had worked at the plant as a toolmaker for over 20 years, was one of the reservists called to active duty after September 11, 2001. When he returned to work a year later, his job had been eliminated; he would be downgraded to a production job at lower wages. Management finagled the move so that it didn't violate the laws protecting reservists' jobs while they are called up to active duty.

Ken took his problem to his boss, the human relations manager, and the plant manager, who all said they would do nothing. Co-workers surmised that Ken was being paid back for years of being independent and outspoken. Some even said he deserved it.

Ken's name came up at all the early WAGE meetings as an example of how GE could shaft an employee and get away with it. While GE was in technical compliance with the law, its actions clearly violated the law's intent and were viscerally immoral. This issue became the perfect opportunity to put the WAGE theory into practice.

With patriotism at a fever pitch, the Auburn WAGE members decided to shine a public spotlight on GE's mistreatment of armed forces members. They wanted to bring the entire workforce into the fight, whether WAGE supporters or not, and use the threat of public humiliation to change management's mind.

The committee's first step was to draft a letter to Maine's U.S. senators. Circulated at the plant, the request for help was signed by 130 of the 180 potential union members, transforming it into a collective action. "Most people were happy to be doing something about it, happy that we were doing something rather than just talking about it," says Tom Casey, now the WAGE committee's vice-president.

Like a strike or many other job actions, the letter's greatest effectiveness was as a threat: the committee printed it in the monthly WAGE newsletter, together with a promise to mail it if management didn't back down.

Within a week Ken's job grade was restored and he soon received a check for back pay. The committee had engendered a great sense of empowerment on the shop floor. The members had demonstrated that the WAGE strategy could be applied in practice.

Involvement in the Contract

The Auburn WAGE committee and the other committees around the country soon found themselves involved in the union's 2003 GE contract campaign. For the first time, workers at union-represented GE plants reached out to their counterparts at the non-union plants and asked them to get involved in the fight for a better contract. They attempted to complete the circle left broken by GE for many years—we are all GE employees and what we bargain for benefits you. Why not help us bargain a contract that benefits us all?

The WAGE committees became a two-way conduit for information about what was going on during preparations for bargaining. They circulated surveys to their co-workers about bargaining issues. Representatives from the WAGE committees joined bargainers at the table in New York City, made presentations about health care cost containment, pensions, and organizing rights, and participated in the talks.

These representatives then reported back to their co-workers. When the contract was settled, WAGE members in Auburn and Somersworth passed out the same detailed contract summaries that we used in Local 201.

Training Stewards

Nonmajority unions rely on tackling workplace issues for forward movement and growth. In the lull following the Ken Townsend victory and the contract settlement, problems became apparent. What does the committee do when there are no obvious issues to take on? What if none of the issues are clearly winnable? What if the issues do not engage the interest of the committee or the rest of the workers?

Working with the experienced activists at Local 201, we discussed and developed a way to create an institutional role for WAGE supporters and members. The intent was to train them to take on the role of "stewards" on the shop floor—resource people—and for them to transmit what they learned to other employees. We hoped that this would establish the WAGE supporters as shop floor leaders, while waiting for the next actionable issue, and would create a visible ongoing organization.

The training was carried out by labor educators from the University of Maine at Orono. Nearly 20 WAGE members and supporters attended the two sessions and learned about state and federal labor law, worker's comp law, the Family and Medical Leave Act, the Americans with Disabilities Act, and other federal anti-discrimination laws. Since the training, says Jill Starbird, WAGE committee president, "people come to me with all kinds of questions. If I can't answer them on the spot, I know where to get the answers."

The centerpiece was training WAGE stewards to become "Weingarten" representatives who would be available to accompany co-workers when management called them in for an "investigatory interview." "Weingarten rights," named after a Supreme Court case, give union-represented workers the right to have a steward present during any questioning that could lead to disciplinary action. In 2000 the NLRB extended Weingarten rights to all non-management workers, whether union-represented or not, and for a short time, all workers could demand that a co-worker be allowed to accompany them to an interview.

When the NLRB reversed itself in mid-2004 and took away Weingarten rights for non-union workers, it cited concerns about a non-union representative's lack of training. This concern had already been addressed in Auburn, and similar training will hopefully become part of labor's effort to restore Weingarten rights for all workers.

We Jump the Gun

WAGE activists from around the country met during the quarterly GE-IUE Conference Board meeting in late 2003. The Conference Board is a meeting of all the IUE-CWA locals working under the master contract with GE. At this meeting, an IUE organizer asked two members of the Auburn WAGE Committee when they were going to stop "screwing around" and go for an election. Tom Casey politely but firmly told him that their WAGE committee would go for an election when they were ready. But pressure to push for elections in Auburn and elsewhere was growing within the IUE-CWA.

We made the decision to see whether the Auburn WAGE Committee could become the basis of a local organizing committee. The usual pre-card-signing activities began: "mapping" the workplace, reaching out to potentially supportive workers, assessing the level of support. Soon, it became clear that while workers were comfortable with WAGE and liked the work the committee was doing, they were not ready to sign cards and hold an election.

Our activity sent a clear message to local and corporate GE management and they responded as they would during any organizing effort. The union avoidance experts came in and an "anti" committee was formed. Management and its cronies circulated hostile and divisive literature and rumors sprouted that customers were withholding work from Auburn because they feared union activity was hurting quality and productivity. As happens in every NLRB election organizing campaign,

Advice for Building a Nonmajority Union

- Make the decision whether to use the nonmajority union route based on a careful analysis of your sector, your union's history in the sector, and your resources for sustaining a long-term plan.

  Some of the factors that influenced the IUE-CWA, for example, were: the employer's expertise in defeating traditional drives, a history of failed attempts by ourselves and others, the centrality of GE to our union, and the CWA's experience in nonmajority-type organizing at other employers.

- As much as possible, take the issue of moving to an NLRB union-recognition election off the table. Focus on building the nonmajority union.

  It may take years of hard work, by the workers themselves, to build the support and understanding needed to overcome all of the obstacles to winning an election. By contrast, larding on union resources and trying a mad dash to the promised land of an election and a contract creates a much more immediate goal. Given the choice of years of hard work to create fertile ground for winning an election or a few months of frenetic, but probably unsuccessful, activity, people will choose the shorter and less daunting option every time.

- Design issue-oriented campaigns so that they involve all of the workers, not just committee members and supporters. As many victories as possible should be attributed to all of the workers.

- Take credit for any victory, no matter how small or how tenuous the connection to the committee's activities—it's usually true! Committees often overlook the changes they are making or attribute them to other causes, including the employer.

- Bring the nonmajority activists together with rank-and-file union members at every available chance. Create a partnership between the established local and the nonmajority group. The local's organizing committee members should be involved consistently.

- Show respect for the corporate programs that workers at non-union plants are accustomed to, such as bogus problem-solving procedures or ineffective joint health and safety "teams," while pointing out their flaws and presenting a vision of how it could and should be done. Workers become defensive when their institutions are attacked, regardless of their true nature. It takes time to break this loyalty down.

- Create a real organization. Nonmajority unions should collect dues that help fund their activities. There should be leadership elections and shop floor stewards. A newsletter is indispensable and should be published frequently and routinely. The organization should draft a mission statement and bylaws and should adhere to them.

- Train members and supporters in subjects relevant to union members, just as a union local would. This information helps to make activists the "go-to" people on the shop floor. What activists learn during training should be made readily available to everyone. Copies of resource information should be advertised and on hand if a co-worker wants to read it.

- Be patient. It takes time to establish a nonmajority union. If we take the attitude that "we'll give it three months and then we're out of here," we simply duplicate the mistake made by unions when they shut down campaigns after failing to get enough signed cards. At Auburn, we knew we couldn't be impatient and we went ahead and were impatient anyway. Resist knucklehead pressure.

- Have fun. If the committee is all about struggle and sacrifice, workers will tire of it. Hold social events—picnics, outings—and invite the entire workforce.

- Although a staff organizer should plan on spending most of his or her time building a nonmajority union, remember that the goal is to work constantly toward creating a self-functioning, autonomous organization. Help create means for activists to communicate among themselves, rather than through you.

tension and anxiety were ratcheted up and workers were soon driven into opposite camps.

We tried to chalk it up as a learning experience, rationalizing the failed attempt as an opportunity to expose the workers to a real anti-union campaign with no lasting damage done. What had really happened, however, was not quite so benign. We had changed the fundamental dynamics the Auburn committee operated in and squandered the advantage we had had in building WAGE at a location with no election history.

WAGE activists began complaining about the hard time they were getting from some of their co-workers. Many co-workers were no longer willing to take and read WAGE literature, and meeting attendance dropped. Some of the elected WAGE leaders expressed unhappiness with the inability to change things quickly and began to openly doubt the committee's ability to succeed. More spoke about the need to win an election and get a contract rather than focusing on changing how the company acted and improving conditions at work.

Perhaps the most unfortunate effect of the premature election drive was to stunt the potential for expanding the committee. Before, workers were open to hearing about WAGE's work, getting involved in some of the efforts, signing petitions, and circulating literature. After the election drive fizzled, many who were once sympathetic now refused to talk with committee members, read literature, or attend meetings. The process had become nasty and divisive.

On the other hand, says Starbird, "it was good for us to see how the shop panicked. Maybe it was premature, but it drove home the point that WAGE and trust had to be established before an election could succeed."

Jury Is Out

The work at GE Auburn is ongoing, as it is in Muskegon, Wilmington, and Somersworth. To a great extent, we are making up the program as we go along, trying to head off some problems before they arise and to react to others. The question whether WAGE or other nonmajority union programs can endure over time and lead to NLRB-recognized unions with contracts is far from settled. Given the hostile climate facing workers who try to organize through the NLRB, some unions are even asking whether nonmajority unions are a sufficient end in themselves, provided they are largely autonomous and self-sustaining.

When Local 201 originally committed me to work on the WAGE program, it was with the understanding that WAGE would take a day or two a week and that we would have plenty of time to also pursue organizing of local GE vendors and other targets. It quickly became apparent that building and supporting one WAGE committee was not a part-time task. Rank-and-file organizing committee members from Local 201 have done wonderful work in plugging the gap, but their ability to spend time at distant GE factories is necessarily limited.

Fortunately, CWA reimburses locals for 75 percent of the salary paid to an organizer hired directly by the local. CWA has also picked up all of the cost of supporting the WAGE program, including the organizer's full salary while working on WAGE, lost-time wages paid to local organizing committee members, and printing and transportation costs.

WAGE members and supporters around the country are presented with evidence at every opportunity that they are not alone in their work. The national WAGE newsletter features updates on what is going on at the different locations. Conference calls allow them to talk with each other. Despite these connections, workers quickly begin to feel on their own when taking on GE. The overarching organization must be systematic and dependable and can't take time off.

Local Victories

Agitation has led to some victories at non-union GE plants around the country. WAGE activists in Decatur, Alabama got a safety eye-wash fountain moved from a position where it would be mostly useless in an emergency to a better location; they had warned management they were willing to take the problem outside the factory to OSHA or the local media.

Workers in Somersworth got the company to back off their plan to shorten their work week to four days and keep them from filing claims for reduced wages, simply by threatening to organize. WAGE activists in Wilmington restored premium overtime pay in departments where it had been eliminated by conducting a coordinated refusal to work more overtime.

And the Auburn WAGE Committee has made many improvements in health and safety conditions by pointing them out in their newsletter and routinely following up at weekly safety meetings. "For the first time, we have a group of people in the plant who stick together," says Tom Casey. "You can depend on them."

But the hold GE has over its employees is not to be underestimated. Workers reflexively turn to bankrupt problem-solving methods like the Peer Review Panel even though they have been shown to be ineffective time and time again. Workers hear and obey the call to take what the unions provide without paying dues, to let someone else do the work for them, because making change themselves is hard and often uncomfortable.

The changes needed for workers at non-union GE shops—to become aware of the power of collective action and of the need to join with all GE workers if they are to maintain the standard of living they are accustomed to—will not come overnight. This is what we said when we introduced WAGE in 2002. At that time CWA Vice-president Larry Cohen committed to do this "for as long as it takes."

To make it happen, we have to fight the urge to put aside what 15 years of organizing without a victory tells us. That would be to rush into elections before workers have a complete understanding of what building shop floor power, and unions, are all about.

Resources

- *Reaching Higher: A Handbook for Union Organizing Committee Members,* by Richard Bensinger, 2002. Easy-to-read, comprehensive look at the process of organizing a workplace and the role of organizing committee members. Available in Spanish. Order from James Bowers, Organizing Resources, PO Box 126, McLean, VA 22101. 800-935-2937 x02. orgresources@aol.com. $12.95 plus $5.95 shipping. Quantity discounts available.
- *Blueprint for Change,* by Kate Bronfenbrenner and Robert Hickey, 2003. A study of which strategies have made for the most effective organizing. Order from Labor Notes, $10 includes shipping.
- IWW's Online Guide to Salting. Information for those who want to organize under cover. Tips on how to get hired and what to do when hired or if fired, and a checklist of responsibilities as a salt. www.iww.org/organize/strategy/salt.shtml.
- Salting Resources Toolbox website. Links to NLRB cases on the legality of salting, worksheets for salts and organizers to keep track of salting activity. From Organize Indiana, www.labor.iu.edu/organizeindiana/res-salt.htm.
- Seminars on salting: Michael Lucas, former IBEW official, 703-754-8330.
- *Organizing and the Law,* an organizer's guidebook to the law that governs organizing rights and the union recognition procedure. Out of print, but being revised by one of its co-authors, Judy Scott, SEIU's General Counsel. Should be available late 2005. For information on the book, write to Scott at 1313 L St. NW, Washington, DC 20005. Include your email address.
- *Organizing to Win: New Research on Union Strategies,* edited by Kate Bronfenbrenner et al. Organizing in changing industries, involving members and allies, building a framework for sustainable organizing. Cornell University Press, 1998 (paperback). $19.95.
- *On nonmajority unions*: See *Labor Notes*' three-part series in July, August, September 2002 (www.labornotes.org/archives/toc/toc02b.html). Read about the attack on Weingarten rights in *Labor Notes* August 2004 (www.labornotes.org/archives/toc/toc04b.html) and about a conference of nonmajority unions in *Labor Notes* October 2004. See Chapter 20 for a different kind of nonmajority union, the CWA's Alliance@IBM.

Action Questions 1

SUCCESSFUL ORGANIZING involves rank-and-file activists at the target company, member-organizers, and staff organizers. Some of these questions apply more to one group than another, but since they are aimed at getting started, everyone involved can think about them.

1. Does your local have a strategic organizing plan? Does the plan build the local's power within its core jurisdictions? Does it accurately assess the local's resources? Does it have a realistic set of benchmarks so the union can measure its progress? Are the targets realistic? Will success at one target lead to success at others? Does the plan involve current members? Does it require cooperation with other locals or other unions?

2. Do you have an organizing target? Can you see ahead to how to win a first contract? Can you mount a comprehensive campaign that includes all the different pieces, including a rank-and-file organizing committee, member-organizers, escalating tactics, community involvement, and a first-contract campaign? Will you be able to represent the workers effectively?

3. Do you know the target's labor relations history? Do you understand its corporate structure or its place in the government structure and its financing? Who are its executives and how might they be targeted? Do you have union workers in one part of the company or a related company? Who are its customers and suppliers and are they unionized? What are the employer's vulnerabilities?

4. Can you relate to the workers at your target? Do you have members and staff who speak their languages? Do have any relationships with their community and religious organizations? Have you met any workplace leaders? What specific needs do the workers have?

5. What are the issues at the target workplace? Does your local have the expertise to address workers' specific concerns (such as particular kinds of injuries or pension questions)? Does your union have programs that address workers' needs, such as citizenship classes or GED?

6. How will you judge your progress? What goals must you meet before moving on?

7. How might member-organizers contribute to organizing your target? Do current members have contacts at the target? Do they work for the same or a similar employer? Do they speak the same language or live in the same neighborhoods? Can they form a local union organizing committee to meet regularly and help the rank-and-file committee at the target company? Can they help with research, building a contact list, or getting community organizations involved?

8. Describe the target workplace. How are the workers distributed? Which have more leverage against the boss? Which are more upset about conditions? Can you get a list of names, addresses, and phone numbers?

9. Who are the rank-and-file leaders? Who do workers turn to when they have questions or concerns? Could one of them organize a social event to discuss workplace issues and the union?

10. What community organizations might support your organizing? Do current members or rank and filers at the target belong to churches or community organizations that might help? Do you have contacts with politicians who might voice support?

11. How can you use media? Has management done something blatantly unjust or are there health and safety or environmental practices that might interest media?

12. Can you use salts at your target? Do the salts have the right experience and skills? Have you trained them? Will they be overt or covert? Do you have procedures in place to track salts' work? Do you have the legal skills and resources to file ULPs if your salts are refused a job or fired because of their union affiliation?

Action Questions 2

IF YOU ARE A NON-UNION WORKER who wants to organize your workplace, you should call several unions who might represent workers in your industry and talk to them. Here are some questions to ask.

1. Who does the union represent? How many of its members do what you do? How many are in your industry? Do workers at your employer's competitors belong to the union? Does the union have a plan for increasing union density in your industry?

2. If you join, will they expect you to pay dues and initiation before you win a contract? If so, how much?

3. Would your workplace have its own local? Or would you become part of another local? If so, how big is the local? What kinds of industries and services are in the local? Would you still have separate meetings for your industry, company, or workplace?

4. Does the constitution guarantee you the right to elect your own stewards and other representatives?

5. Can you get copies of the international's constitution and the local union bylaws?

6. How many people come to union meetings? What committees are active? How can a rank and filer join a committee?

7. Can you get copies of current contracts for similar workplaces?

8. What is the union's policy and practice on concessions? On labor-management "partnership"?

9. Can you get copies of LM-2 forms showing the officers' salaries and union expenses so you know how the union is run? (If the union will not give them to you, that's a bad sign, but you can get them on the web at http://union-reports.dol.og/olmsWeb/docs/formspg.html).

10. Will they let you come to a local union meeting? Can they arrange for you to meet a group of rank and filers from one of their workplaces?

11. Do the stewards and the executive board represent the racial and gender make-up of the local? Is the civil rights committee or women's committee active? Is translation available at meetings if necessary? How does the union feel about negotiating clauses of importance to gay and lesbian members?

12. What is the attitude of top leaders and local leaders toward disagreement within the union? Are there safeguards for members who speak out? Are their democratic rights protected?

Authors

PAUL BOUCHARD is a former skilled tradesworker and union member at AT&T and Lucent Technologies who is now Organizing Director for IUE-CWA Local 201.

AARON BRENNER is a labor historian, researcher, writer, and editor in New York City. He has written about international labor solidarity, union reform movements, and rank-and-file rebellions by Teamsters, telephone workers, and postal workers, and is the editor of *The Encyclopedia of Strikes in American History*.

GENE BRUSKIN is secretary-treasurer of the Food and Allied Service Trades division of the AFL-CIO and co-convener of U.S. Labor Against War. He was a local union leader for ten years, an organizer and campaign coordinator for various local and national unions, and Labor Director for the Rev. Jesse Jackson for two years.

Notes

1. Kate Bronfenbrenner and Robert Hickey, *Blueprint for Change: A National Assessment of Winning Union Organizing Strategies*, Office of Labor Education Research, New York School of Industrial and Labor Relations, Cornell University, August 2003, p. 38.

2. According to labor attorney Ellis Boal, any attempt to block not only the trucks of the target company (Iroquois) but all traffic to the client company's (Vulcan's) site, in order to pressure the "neutral" client company to pressure the target company to sign a contract, is grounds for either the target or client company to sue the local for treble damages and to discipline those involved in the action. Had the blockade been limited to target company (Iroquois) traffic only, it would have been legal and protected under the NLRB's "common situs" standards. Had the union made no explicit or implicit demand on the client company or other employers to pressure the target company—possibly a difficult position to sustain at the NLRB or in court—again there would have been no secondary liability.

Any worker at the client company honoring such a line would assume the status of an economic striker. He or she could ask the company to be assigned other work. The company would have the option of replacing him or her with a scab willing to cross the line, but not of firing him or her. This would apply to the workers whether or not they were unionized. However, if a client company worker were unionized, the contract might preclude the workers from honoring picket lines. Traditionally, Teamster contracts, for example, do allow members to honor picket lines. So check the contract.

Curiously, the courts have a more advanced position on this question than the NLRB does, and have found good sympathy strike language in union contracts where the NLRB did not. Organizers should look at not only the contract but also the bargaining history.

3. *A Troublemaker's Handbook*, 1991, pp. 192-194.

4. *Blueprint for Change,* p. 21.

5. For more details, see "CWA at Southwestern Bell: Five Years to Card Check," July 1997, available from the CWA; and Erin Bowie, "The CWA's Experience: A Tale of Two Card-Check Agreements," *Labor Notes*, April 2003.

On the Troublemaker's Website

• Unions need to work together for new members, not compete. The Justice for Healthcare Workers Campaign has a strategic plan to organize all health care workers in Vermont. Go to www.labornotes.org.

16. Bringing Immigrants into the Movement

by Teófilo Reyes

IMMIGRANTS ARE RESHAPING THE COUNTRY, and by implication the labor movement. Over 30.5 million immigrants live in the United States, or about 11 percent of the population—the largest share since the 1930s. Immigrant labor has long been crucial in harvesting the nation's food, but the astounding growth of immigrant labor in construction, hotels, health care, building services, and manufacturing means that unions must organize immigrants if they hope to remain relevant.

This realization has forced a dramatic turnaround from labor's historical stance of trying to keep immigrants out of the country. Thanks to both rational self-interest and the mobilization of many unions and their members, in February 2000 the AFL-CIO officially supported a broad amnesty for undocumented workers and now sees itself as a leader in the fight for immigrant rights. A serious fight to change immigration laws is one key to building labor's credibility among immigrant workers, who are often leery of unfamiliar bureaucracies offering to improve their lot.

On the flip side, native-born workers on the lower rungs of the economy are finding that employers prefer those they can exploit more ruthlessly. A concerted effort to improve the conditions that immigrants face will ultimately lead to improvements for all workers.

But, as the stories in this chapter indicate, organizing immigrants often means a broader idea of organizing. Where unions have declined to tread, "workers centers," based in immigrant communities, have stepped in to fill the gap.

In this chapter we will discuss how unions can change the culture of their locals so that workers who are new to this country can be active and accepted members. We will look at how some unions have addressed immigrants' particular problems related to their legal status and to the post-9-11 crackdown on immigrants. We will look at union recruitment strategies in immigrant communities, including the importance of lasting relationships with religious and community organizations. We will show some steps for organizing in a multi-ethnic, multilingual workforce.

Many of the most inspiring labor struggles of the last ten years have involved immigrant workers. You can read about immigrant workers organizing new unions (Chapter 15), fighting for job safety (7), in contract campaigns (8), on the shop floor (3), in corporate campaigns (10), and training new leaders (21). See especially Chapter 17 on workers centers and "Dealing with Language Differences" in Chapter 19.

What's in It for 'Us'?

by Dan La Botz

NOT TOO MANY YEARS AGO, Ironworkers Local 272 in Miami was a tiny, all-white local with fewer than 100 members and no apparent future. Today it has 1,200 members, a third of whom are white, a third African American and black immigrants from Haiti and Jamaica, and a third mostly-immigrant Latinos, reflecting the local workforce. The local has become a force in the local construction industry and is still growing.

What happened?

The answer begins in 1992, when member Dewey Tyler ran for business manager, the local's top officer, as a reformer promoting union democracy. "Winning" was a relative term, however. What Tyler acquired was leadership of a local with only 72 active members and no staff. But Tyler also had a vision. By targeting contractors he increased the local's size more than six-fold and in 1996 hired his first organizer, Dave Gornewicz.

Gornewicz says, "It was mainly white males at the time, and we decided that in order to reenergize we needed to organize the non-union workforce that was almost totally minority." Tyler and Gornewicz got their executive board to read John Sweeney's book, *America Needs a Raise,* with its emphasis on organizing.

Having convinced the board, Tyler and Gornewicz turned to educating their members. Gornewicz traveled to the AFL-CIO's George Meany Center for a "train the trainer" course to learn how to present new ideas, and the pair used a training manual and video from the AFL-CIO

Building Trades Department in a one-year program called COMET—Construction Organizing, Membership, Education, and Training. The material describes the effects of declining union density on wages and benefits and discusses ways to reverse the trend.

The patient approach paid off. By the time the local voted, in 1997, on whether it would transform itself into an active organizing union that reached out to Latino and black non-union workers, the vote was 145 for and 15 against. "A year earlier, it probably would have been reversed, if we hadn't done the education," says Gornewicz.

But getting members to agree—in principle—that the local would reach out to non-union immigrant workers was just a first step. Long-lived union policies had to be revised and engrained attitudes had to change.

The construction trades have a long history of viewing non-union workers of any race as "rats," scabs to be driven off the job. When the "rats" are also black or Latino immigrants, hostility to non-union workers gets intertwined with racist attitudes. Since Florida is an open-shop state, where crews of union and non-union workers might be working on different parts of the same construction job, the anti-rat attitude wasn't winning any new members. Moreover, since union members weren't supposed to take jobs with non-union companies, there was little opportunity to talk with and recruit the non-union workers. All of that had to change.

"We introduced amendments to our bylaws, including the ability to send members to non-union jobs without penalty, as long as they are under the direction of the leadership," Gornewicz explains. Other bylaws changes created a funding mechanism for organizing, with members agreeing first to give up five cents an hour, then ten, enabling the local to accrue as much as $9,000 a month. The money compensates members who work as "salts," paying the difference between their non-union and union wages. It also compensates for lost time testifying at the Labor Board, pays volunteer organizers who make night visits, and covers expenses such as phones, leaflets, and posters.

The changes enabled the union to use local members in its organizing drive, which was crucial to its success. "Professional organizers don't have the access to the non-union workforce that the workers do in the field," Gornewicz explains. "With a change in the attitude of treating workers as brothers, not enemies, we could identify the skill level of workers on the job. A person may have the skills of a second-quarter apprentice, or he may be a journeyman, and wages are related to those skill levels. So we were able to identify them in the field by our ironworkers, and then approach them with an opportunity to join the union."

Workers whose skills had been evaluated were referred to union employers, who could be confident of what they were getting. And as the employers got more workers with reliable skills, they were encouraged to bid on larger jobs, slowly building the unionized sector's share of the total work being done.

"We had to educate the contractors we already had. They were under the belief that if we had 400 union members, that's all they had to work, so they were reluctant to bid more jobs," says Gornewicz.

The union grew from 5 percent density to 20 percent in just a few years. Still, old prejudices died hard. Local 272 went to work to make sure that its new immigrant members were welcomed.

"When race becomes an issue on the job,

Roberto Sanclemente's New Family

ROBERTO SANCLEMENTE, from Colombia, tells how he joined Ironworkers 272 and became an organizer for the local:

"I was working on a federal job, and all of a sudden this guy, a ceiling inspector, noticed how I was doing the job. He came to me and asked, 'How much are you making an hour?' I told him I was making $7.50. This guy tells me that I should go to the union.

"I tell you, I was afraid to go because the foremen always talked bad about the union. That's the way they keep the guys out. But I was getting sick and tired of the way they were treating me. The low pay. I said, 'The hell with this, I'm going to see what's good about the union.' I got over there and got a job, and since February 2000 I've been working with the union.

"I found that they offer you a lot of courses, if you want to take them. I always took the courses, one every two months or three months. They always had something going. Every time I wanted to go over there my co-workers would say, 'Hey, Colombian, how can you be so stupid that you still have to go to school? We're going to have a soccer game.' That was like a challenge for me. I kept going to school. They give you courses in constructing windows, welding classes, all kinds of things.

"One day Dewey Tyler asked me if I was happy where I was working. He asked me if I wanted to come to work with the union staff. I don't speak English that well, but I find my way. They had some people at the local that spoke Spanish, and they gave me a little test. They figured out that I had good experience, and they sent me to work right away.

"Now I go to the job site, to non-union jobs. We are trying to get them to sign contracts with the company. We organize bottom-up, and top to bottom. The bottom-up is to have someone working there like a secret agent, talking to the guys, getting them to join the union. If they all agree we create a committee.

"It's not only one guy working. It's all the guys together working. And we all care about each other. I really like my co-workers. They treat you like a family, as I always say."

the leadership will immediately go to the job and tell people it won't be tolerated. And members have been brought before the executive committee for violating that rule," says Gornewicz. When a worker of whatever race uses a racial slur against another, the union insists on an apology and will charge the worker who used the slur. In extreme cases, members can be expelled from the union and fined up to $2,500.

"We had an incident a while ago, and we filed charges," Gornewicz recalls. "The brother was brought up in front of the executive committee, and there you can decide for a trial by the board or by the members. He indicated he would apologize in front of the body, and they shook hands and gave each other a hug. We try to do that publicly."

The local also recognized the importance of quickly bringing immigrant members into leadership. Although Local 272's constitution requires members to have been in good standing for two years before they can be elected to office, there is nothing prohibiting the local from hiring its new immigrant members as staffers. "We have an apprenticeship director now that's Jamaican," says Gornewicz. "I have an organizer that's Cuban, one that's Colombian, one that's Puerto Rican, and the other one is a white guy. The apprenticeship director is also elected as recording secretary, and there's a new appointee to the executive board who is Cuban who is eligible."

The local now includes 110 apprentices and an additional small apprenticeship program in Naples, Florida. "When we began, we had only six or seven employers; now we have 100 employers both within and outside the local area," says Gornewicz.

Success converted the skeptics. "I will give you a quote from one of the early opponents," Gornewicz offers. "He said, 'I hated everything you guys are doing, but boy, do I love the results.' Our last contract had the largest wage and benefit increase in 20 years."

The First Hurdle: Coping with Documentation

by Dan La Botz

IMMIGRANT WORKERS WITHOUT DOCUMENTS face problems that can make everyday life miserable, keep them in marginal economic situations, and sometimes lead to brushes with the law, possibly jail, and deportation. For example, many cannot get a driver's license or open a bank account because they don't have acceptable identification.

Such workers want more from a union than the usual focus on workplace issues. They need help with day-to-day survival, and they want an organization that will fight for their most important long-term concern, legal resident status. That means organizers seeking to unionize immigrant workers must also build social support systems.

One model is offered by the Farm Labor Organizing Committee, which represents farmworkers in Ohio, North Carolina, Michigan, and Florida, including seasonal workers from Mexico. The union's associate membership program provides members with a union photo ID, and it is open to anyone, including family members and community members inclined to activism. FLOC also promotes official recognition of the *matricula consular*, an ID card issued by Mexican consulates to Mexican nationals. The city of Toledo has already accepted the *matricula*, opening the door for immigrant workers to open utility accounts or to get library cards. Now FLOC is pushing for other institutions—notably banks—to follow suit.

Indeed, banking access is one of the biggest hurdles facing immigrant workers. Mexican workers in the U.S. send $13 billion annually to their homeland, but millions are nibbled away through unnecessary charges. "First," explains Baldemar Velásquez, FLOC's president, "workers go to a check-cashing service, where they pay $10 to $20. Then they go to

In a vegetable processing plant in Ohio, a Mexican American woman sorts tomatoes grown in nearby fields. Many undocumented immigrants work on farms in this area. The Farm Labor Organizing Committee is building a social support system that helps them obtain ID while building a base for organizing.

Jim West/jimwestphoto.com

Basics of Welcoming Immigrants

by Dan La Botz

HERE IS SOME BASIC ADVICE for union officers and activists who are new to working with immigrant members.

You probably already know that immigrant workers want pretty much the same things any unionized worker wants. A decent job. A living wage. Respect and trust. Some measure of control over their lives.

The other thing you should know is: Don't presume to know anything. Forget stereotypes. Approach immigrant workers in an open, straightforward manner and see what you can learn.

Many immigrants may have as much to teach you about the labor movement as they have to learn. Some may have been involved in labor, political, or even revolutionary movements in their native countries.

Others may be professionals—doctors or teachers—but because of citizenship and licensing issues find themselves working in lower-skill jobs here. A surgeon becomes a taxi driver.

Here are some guidelines:

- Immigrants are the experts on their own community. If you wish to reach an immigrant community, you will need to have immigrants themselves involved in—and ideally leading—the effort.
- The immigrant community is not homogeneous. Upper class people or professionals have goals that conflict with those of blue-collar workers.
- Translate organizing materials into the appropriate language(s). Translate the union constitution and bylaws, contracts, health and pension plans, and the union newspaper, even though doing so may be expensive. Immigrant members cannot participate as equals without these tools.
- Provide translation at all meetings or conduct them in the workers' language. Translation can be a pain: cumbersome, time-consuming, boring, or irritating to those who are listening to remarks and responses (questions, anger, laughing) when they don't know what is going on. Make sure interpreters are sensitive to those issues and familiar with union terminology. Sometimes it may be advisable to temporarily divide groups and conduct separate meetings in different languages, but if you do, you should also hold joint meetings.
- Be sensitive to religion and customs. Be aware of days and times of worship and of religious or national holidays, to avoid scheduling conflicts. Be respectful of immigrants' dress and other customs. Even when you are "just kidding," you can drive members away from the union.
- Identify capable immigrant activists and promote them as stewards, committee members, and spokespeople. Immigrants will take the union seriously as their own organization to the degree that they hold leadership positions. Note, however, that immigrants will resent being pigeonholed as ethnic spokespersons—they must become leaders in the union at large, not just one of its enclaves.
- Respect immigrants' right to self-organization. Any minority group may encounter discrimination or misunderstanding that may cause its members to want to meet separately. Immigrants should be able to caucus as a group.
- Educate native-born members. Open discussion of issues like police harassment or racism may help other workers better understand the immigrant workers' problems.
- Immigrant workers can help us understand the global economy. When workers from southern Mexico explain that they came to the United States because of the collapse of their rural economy, American workers may learn more about NAFTA than they would in a year of union newspaper articles.

Western Union, which charges them $15 to $30 to send money to Mexico. They also lose money in the conversion rate from dollars to pesos, so they end up paying three times what they should."

FLOC arranged with a Toledo bank to provide members with free checking and debit cards, giving them access to ATM machines. "They send that card to Mexico and then call and give a family member the code so that they can withdraw the money at ATM machines there," Velásquez explains. "The transfer fee using the ATM card is $1.75, and you get the best peso exchange rate, so we're saving workers hundreds of dollars."

As Velásquez sees it, such services create a base for FLOC. The union's associate members pay $25 a year, he says, "while we're organizing them into a community of workers. We get them to participate in lobbying for workers' issues, such as amnesty. But the main purpose is to keep track of their worksites. Right now in Toledo we have two worksites where the majority are associate members, so we will go and ask for union recognition."

Dealing with No-Match Letters

ALTHOUGH LACK OF LEGAL STATUS does not technically prevent workers from exercising their right to organize, it does give employers the opportunity to threaten workers who do. The threat of a raid by Immigration and Customs Enforcement (previously the INS, Immigration and Naturalization Service) helps keep workers from protesting.

A more recent threat is the Social Security Administration, which has become more aggressive in monitoring phony Social Security numbers. When the SSA notices an error on a Social Security account, it sends a "no-match" letter to the employer stating that an employee's number doesn't match the administration's database. Although the intent of these letters is to ensure that employees' accounts are properly credited for the work they've done, some employers use the letters to threaten or fire workers.

According to Kim Wirshing of HERE Local 2 in San Francisco, no-match letters originally were sent directly to the affected workers. But because SSA wasn't getting responses, it began sending them to employers. While the letters warn that they are not evidence of immigration status and that employers should not take action based solely on them, some employers have used the no-match letters as weapons.

The first such case in his local, Wirshing said, was at a Travelodge at which eight people were fired after the employer received the letters. The local grieved and won at arbitration, with a ruling that the company reinstate the fired workers and make them whole. The hotel responded with a federal lawsuit seeking to vacate the award. That resulted in discussions with a court-appointed mediator, with the union deciding to settle for a monetary award and reinstatement of all workers who could show a correct Social Security card.

To prevent this from happening again, the local began negotiating with other employers, resulting in language with "the broadest protection for immigrant workers in the country," Wirshing contends. The agreement requires employers to notify the local as soon as they receive a no-match letter and gives employees up to a year to get documentation without loss of seniority. Moreover, a worker who takes up to two years to produce proper documentation can still reclaim his or her former job, although as a new-hire.

The language "gives people a window of opportunity to correct any issues they might have with work authorization status. It also requires the employer to talk to the union and to notify employees of their rights under that section of the contract," Wirshing says. In addition, the union set up a legal plan that provides free consultation with an attorney for members with immigration issues, and has used the arbitration decision to educate employers who still believe a no-match letter requires them to fire an employee.

The most recent no-match letters, Wirshing says, give the employer 45 days to report back to Social Security, creating the impression that employers who fail to meet the deadline will be penalized in some fashion. "Our position is that you are relieved of responsibility if you notify the employee," says Wirshing.

Teamsters Local 556, at a small frozen foods plant in Oregon, faced the firing of 40 workers because of no-match letters. The local responded by winning members the right to change their names or Social Security numbers without repercussions.

And it began an education campaign: "We train them and their stewards on what they should do if this were to happen again," says Vice-President Sandra Stewart. "Normally, when workers were called into the office and told that there was a no-match letter they would confess, instead of being quiet. Stewards know now how to deal with this issue." The union's work had a ripple effect at another of its units: when managers at the company next door received no-match letters, they didn't attempt to fire the workers.

Building a Coalition To Fight Intimidation

by Dan La Botz

EMPLOYERS NEED NOT WAIT for a no-match letter, of course; they can call the ICE (previously the INS) directly. In Seattle, when an employer promoted an INS raid during contract talks, a big response from the labor movement was crucial in defending both immigrant workers and the contract.

Shortly after the September 11, 2001 attacks, Lufthansa subsidiary Sky Chef, an airline caterer, contacted the INS while it was in negotiations with HERE. Justifying its actions as conforming to post-9-11 security measures, the company provided INS officials with Sky Chef managers' uniforms, then invited a dozen workers to a meeting so the disguised INS officials could arrest and deport them.

Fortunately, a group of community and labor organizations, working with the local Jobs with Justice chapter, had held a demonstration at the airport supporting the HERE bargainers even before September 11. So when the INS began a series of airport raids at Hertz, then at Host, and finally at Sky Chef, an existing coalition was in place and ready to respond.

JwJ organizer Jacob Carton, noting that a government agency like the former INS will respond to political pressure, explains that coalition members decided "to be more preemptive regarding future raids." The question, he says, came down to: "How could we do this in a way that would be noticed by everyone in the airport, get good media attention, and at the same time send a message that employers would be punished in the future for conducting themselves this way?"

JwJ and HERE started by contacting other unions, such as the International Longshore and Warehouse Union, fresh from its own battles around "domestic security," and the Machinists, who were in the middle of organizing the ramp workers—almost half of them low-wage immigrants themselves. JwJ went into high gear, reaching out to its established base through mail, phonebanking, and email. "We asked each of our member organizations to commit to bring two or three people and their organization's banner," says Carton.

Because organizing a demonstration in an area of high security—or any time you expect possible conflict with the police—is a great responsibility, Carton and other coalition leaders tried to plan everything in great detail: transportation, press relations, the march and rally, the speakers, the political points to be made. Nothing could be left to chance, no oversight permitted that might give opponents an opening for attack.

For example, a number of activist groups had fought for decades for the principle that airports are public spaces, with free speech and free press rights that each airport had to protect in its regulations. So the coalition formally requested a copy of those regulations, then wrote a letter using the regulations' language to request space for a public gathering. The coalition then asked for a meeting to walk the premises, explaining its desire to conform with the rules.

"We believed everybody had to know what was happening and to agree to it," Carton explains. "We are not opposed to civil disobedience, but that was not the plan for this demonstration. We sent the airport authorities a map so they'd have a full understanding of what we were doing. We had peacekeepers with cell phones and we gave the airport authorities their cell phone numbers. We had rally leaders who would make decisions if there were a crisis."

To eliminate parking problems and make it easy for the rally to start on time, the coalition decided that demonstrators should take the bus together to the airport. The group ride created a sense of solidarity even before the demonstrators arrived, which was an added benefit.

The coalition did advance publicity, which some media picked up on. The head of the King County Labor Council wrote a letter to the *Seattle Post-Intelligencer* arguing for INS reform and labor rights, and the Washington State Labor Council passed a resolution criticizing the INS and supporting immigrant workers, further adding to the pressure.

Organizers conveyed safety rules. "People had to be aware about the secure areas that should be avoided," Carton explains. "They had to be told that sticks would not be permitted in the airport, but that signs could be carried in and banners could be hung up. Some peacekeepers were assigned to help keep travelers on the escalators moving safely."

Because the demonstration was to be held in an atrium, organizers thought airport security might claim the rally was disturbing travelers there. So the coalition asked its seniors to come early to occupy all the atrium chairs. In that way no travelers would be there to complain, and the seniors wouldn't have to stand the whole time.

Laborers Rediscover Their Immigrant Roots

by Nick Robinson

When the Laborers realized their organizing was in need of a kick in the pants, the first opposition the union had to overcome was from its own members—especially when those members realized their union was proposing to spend a lot of dues money on foreigners.

Lost in that reaction was any sense of history. A century ago, the union grew because of Irish and Italian immigrants. By 1947 LIUNA could claim to represent 87 percent of all laborers. Today, that percentage is down to 16.

To reverse that trend, the International realized it had to decentralize its organizing efforts and give local organizers the room to respond to opportunities not easily seen from inside the Washington, D.C. beltway. But first it had to educate its activists. The answer was Volunteer Organizers in Construction Empowerment, a mandatory training program for all shop stewards and member-organizers.

The program begins with a three-hour Membership Orientation Program. "It shows members our history as a union and connects immigration, the changing workforce, and why it is so important for us to organize the immigrants of today," says organizer Ana Taveras. "It opens up members' eyes to what we could do, and it's very effective because more and more members are being mobilized. When we have a demonstration, our members are there."

The best organizers go on to a two- or three-day training done internally or in conjunction with the AFL-CIO's Organizing Institute or a local labor education center. A third and final step is an intensive, ten-day session that pulls in organizers from across the U.S. Designed to push participants out of their comfort zones, the first day ends with a videotaped one-minute speech in front of the class. Students learn about Internet research, hand-billing, house-calling, and developing volunteer organizing committees.

"On the tenth day," says Ana Taveras, "we go out to households with immigrant workers, and even if the new organizers don't understand the language, they have a feel. It really opens their eyes."

For Taveras, the connection between member-to-member organizing and a strong stance on immigrants' rights and legalization is immediate, obvious, and crucial. The Laborers have amended their constitution to advocate legalization for undocumented workers, prominently supported the Immigrant Workers Freedom Ride in 2003, and provide space in their magazine for immigrant members to be heard and to publicize their events.

"As an organizer, the first thing I tell people is, 'I'm an immigrant worker,'" says Taveras. "'I came here to better myself and my family, and I would never do anything to hurt you.'

"When we hire people from the rank and file, they are the best organizers. I work in demolition, so I know what it is to work in demolition. I can say, 'I'm an immigrant, I know what it is to come here, to live in a small apartment and have the responsibility of sending money home.'"

The demonstration took place on a Saturday in July, "and you better believe this airport was packed," Carton recalls. "When we marched in we did it two by two, farmworker-style, so we were a long snake. Just a long line of people walking for ten minutes through the airport, up escalators, past ticket counters, to the rallying place. As we turned in front of the counters everyone started chanting, and it made a tremendous noise. Everything in the airport stopped as our chant reverberated through the building.

"We had leaflets for travelers about the issue. What are travelers most concerned about? Probably safety. So we talked about it from the point of view of safety. Arresting and deporting workers who have been doing their jobs for ten years and had been doing them safely will not make the airport safer.

"Our rally had diverse speakers from different immigrant communities with different messages." These included the Hate-Free Zone of Washington, a local anti-hate crime group; the Asian Pacific American Labor Alliance; and the Latino Coalition. One speaker read a statement from the families of the detained airport workers: "Imagine that one day your husband or wife goes to work and does not return home, disappears, and you do not know what happened to them," she told the crowd.[1]

Since the rally, "we have had no INS raids at the airport that we know of," says Carton. That December, JwJ named Sky Chef its Grinch of the Year and delivered the award on the loading dock to an assistant general manager.

Multi-Ethnic Organizing in Asbestos

MANY IMMIGRANTS GET THEIR FIRST JOBS in the United States through contacts with folks from home who have arrived earlier. Often these jobs are at mom-and-pop employers, and often the owners are immigrants themselves. The nature of these industries makes forming unions a challenge.

The New Jersey asbestos abatement industry, made up of many small companies, is a case in point. The immigrant workforce speaks several languages, and many workers have ethnic ties to management. That combination all but assures the futility of a traditional organizing approach, of targeting employers one-by-one. Something different was needed.

Dave Johnson, director of the Laborers Eastern Region Organizing Fund, says that in 2001 organizers "targeted the entire industry—60 non-union contractors and 500 non-union workers—and used a non-NLRB election strategy. By targeting the industry as a whole, organizers sought to elevate standards and conditions across a significant share of the industry in a short period of time." The union allocated more than $600,000 and assigned 15 multilingual rank-and-file organizers for the task.[2]

These steps were possible because the Laborers International had restructured the way organizing was funded, creating independent regional organizing funds that would not be subject to political whims in Washington. Instead, locals kicked in money for regional funds, providing greater local autonomy.

Ana Taveras, an immigrant from the Dominican Republic and a Laborers member who worked in demolition, became a lead organizer on the asbestos campaign and currently coordinates all non-construction organizing campaigns for the Eastern Region. Success in the asbestos campaign, she stresses, hinged on individual

The Laborers used 15 multilingual rank-and-file organizers in the New Jersey asbestos abatement industry. The union printed newsletters in Serbo-Croatian, Spanish, and English.

visits with each existing member of the local. "One-on-one, through house visits, we informed them of the campaign, told them that we needed their support, and explained the impact of the campaign if successful. We identified some members that could help us, and brought them on as organizers for the campaign."

Because most of the non-union workers were from the former Yugoslavia or Mexico, the union began printing newsletters in Serbo-Croatian, Spanish, and English, with information about the Laborers local, how it was changing, and the different companies that had signed contracts. "Asbestos is like a community," says Taveras. "The workers know each other and the companies where they are working, so the word would spread fast."

The union opened a satellite asbestos-handling training school and offered free refresher courses taught in Serbo-Croatian. It identified potential member-organizers through its VOICE program—Volunteer Organizers In Construction Empowerment—which is mandatory for all shop stewards. The VOICE program failed to turn up an organizer from the former Yugoslavia, but the house visits eventually found three.

In this case, government regulations proved a big help. "The good thing for us is that asbestos work needs to be announced," Taveras explains. "The companies need to report with the health department when they go to work, where, how much they have to remove. That is public information, so we already knew what companies were operating where. You also need to have a license. We investigated and learned how many workers had a license to remove asbestos—and you have to keep renewing it every so often."

The union was able to dispel some of the workers' fears about the government. Although the majority were legal immigrants, those who were undocumented were afraid to apply for asbestos removal licenses because of their legal status, which is enforced at the federal level. "We told them that the license is from the state—the state decides if they can do the work. Explaining something as basic as that helped a lot," Taveras says. "There is a myth—they are told that they have to be citizens to join a union—we told them they had the right to organize."

Taveras says that in this campaign it wasn't much of an issue that the workers were from different ethnic groups, but that the organizers had to get used to different cultures. "With the Serbs, the problem was that their language and their culture were totally different to ours, so we had to try to relate to them. They would receive me, but even though I was the lead organizer they would always focus on the male organizers, even the workers who spoke English. They would direct their questions to him."

The campaign began in March 2001 with a house-calling "blitz" in which organizers visited more than 1,000 workers and obtained about 750 union authorization cards. In signing the cards, workers cited poor safety, few benefits, and employer failures to pay prevailing wages on public work.

The union then divided the organizers into groups of four and gave each of them a list of companies to attack, in a pressure campaign that lasted from April to November. "The companies saw that we were going up against all of them at once," says Taveras. "It had a huge impact because they didn't think we would do what we did. At first they thought we were just another union passing by, but they soon saw that we were serious."

Taveras describes the campaign as "bottom-up and top-down. Top-down is where you pressure the politicians. The bottom-up is the workers filing complaints with the Department of Labor, for example wage and hour violations."

Also bottom-up were the job actions and strikes against different contractors that occurred on a weekly basis. In one case, says Johnson, "unfair labor practice charges were filed with the NLRB after a group of workers—all Latino—refused to eat their lunch in the containment area where the asbestos is removed. The workers walked out in a concerted fashion and were fired later that day. The union filed charges with OSHA as well, because it is a violation to eat lunch in a containment area."

The union was quick to find contractors' Achilles heels and aggressively attack, publicizing legal violations at critical moments, such as during bidding, and thereby forcing a quick resolution. "We pressured them from all sides," Taveras says. "Asbestos is very delicate work, and many of the companies had a history of violations with OSHA, EPA, and the Department of Labor. We maintained pressure by calling those agencies and criticizing authorities because these companies had work at public schools. We put a lot of public pressure since asbestos is so harmful to the community."

The first high-profile targets were companies that wanted to avoid adverse publicity. One gave in and agreed to sign a contract almost before the large inflatable rats that construction unions haul to their demonstrations were fully inflated. The company that had hired East Coast Hazard, for example, tolerated a picket line for just 15 minutes before giving in, largely in response to pressure from clients and other institutions.

Johnson explains the process at one company, D&G Painting: "Researchers documented the prevailing wage violations, lawsuits, and other citations/liens in a comprehensive 'protest packet' which the union gave to the Department of Labor and other clients where D&G Painting was bidding for work. Organizers then planned a rally in front of the DOL building in Trenton. Over 200 workers and union members turned out. The rally featured three 25-foot inflatable rats placed on the lawn of the DOL. Several days after the rally, D&G signed a collective bargaining agreement and five Serbo-Croatian-speaking workers joined Local 1030."

The industry jumped from a 15 percent unionization rate to 65 percent. Eight months into the campaign, Johnson was able to report that Local 1030 had signed 44 asbestos abatement contractors to full collective bargaining agreements, with pay increases of $5 to $7 an hour, contractor-paid health insurance and pension plans, and improved safety.

And Taveras notes that the local also has been transformed. "The members are now committed to the growth of the local. If you have a picket line, you call and people are there from 12 to 6, and when they're done they say 'call me.' Before the campaign, no one went to the meetings; after the campaign they go to their meetings, they are there. I had a strike at my local, and they came to support us from 1030 even though it's not their local. And they came with picket signs, ready to make noise and everything."

To Organize a Union, Organize the Community

ANOTHER EXAMPLE of how unions can pick up a tailwind by organizing within an immigrant workers' community can be seen in Nebraska, where Omaha Together One Community teamed up with the United Food and Commercial Workers to organize four meatpacking plants. OTOC is a coalition of congregations and a project of the Industrial Areas Foundation.

Sergio Sosa, an OTOC organizer, explains that the group's first step, before they began working with the UFCW, was to set up individual meetings with people in their homes. The purpose was to get to know people, learn their histories, learn what their key issues were, and identify community leaders. Given the lack of unions in the region and workers' substantial fears about forming a union, it made more sense to find an existing issue to rally around—an issue, as it turned out, that had nothing to do with unions.

"Soccer fields were the first issue," Sosa says. "We began to organize a soccer league with 36 teams made up of immigrants from Mexico, Central America, and Sudan. We fought with the city to win playing fields, and

In Omaha, a community group, Omaha Together One Community, teamed up with the United Food and Commercial Workers to organize four meatpacking plants. Each plant had its own organizing committee. Although the committees were supported by four UFCW and two OTOC organizers, it was the committees that drove the campaign.

this showed everyone that together we could achieve things. Seven hundred people showed up to celebrate when we got the soccer fields."

Through the individual meetings, OTOC quickly realized that most of the immigrants worked in meatpacking plants and that virtually all had complaints about abusive working conditions, particularly about the speed of the line. Building on the momentum generated by the successful soccer field campaign, the coalition now started organizing committees in each of the plants and began studying how the plants were organized and how their power structure was laid out.

In order to educate workers about their rights and resources, OTOC arranged for speakers from the Department of Labor, OSHA, and other agencies. But it quickly became clear that this route would not solve their problems. Instead, says Sosa, "We needed to create power. Without power we couldn't organize anything."

That's when OTOC began discussing an alliance with organized labor. Its committees met in church basements and discussed various unions, ultimately deciding to invite the UFCW for a conversation. Sosa and other OTOC representatives had a preliminary meeting with UFCW officials, then prepared a list of more than 100 questions—eventually pared down to two dozen—for coalition leaders to ask Local 271 representatives. Afterwards, Sosa adds, "we made an evaluation to see what we had learned politically. We saw that we had to do it, that alone we wouldn't be able to confront the meatpacking plants. Some didn't like the idea and they left the committee and didn't return."

But deciding to create an alliance was the easy part. The harder chore was reconciling different organizing styles. For example, Sosa explains, "there were two different organizing models—house-calls vs. individual meetings. A house-call is like a salesman arriving to sell the union, and our idea wasn't to go and convince them to vote or sign a card—it was to learn their story, to learn what their interests were, and to pose the question, why do you want to organize?"

The key to organizing the plants, the new allies decided, was to identify potential leaders and to connect with people through their established social relationships: friends, families, people from the same town. Sosa explains: "Before launching any campaign, there has to be a strong committee so that its members can do the work. They make diagrams of the company to know where each worker is located—40 in a line. What are their names and what are the stories of each of them?"

By mapping out all the workers, their relationships, and their attitudes to the union drive, the organizers were able to quickly build support for the union. "If you meet the right leader who has influence with 18 people from this little town, those people talk to each other and it forms the social fabric," Sosa explains. "One of the leaders signs four friends, a brother signs his wife, the wife her friends. That way, in less than a month we have half the cards signed but the company doesn't know we are organizing."

In addition to identifying leaders, the organizing committee also mapped the relationships among workers at various plants. Sosa says, "In one family, for instance, Julio works in Conagra and Rosie in Nebraska Beef, one sister here, another over there. It wasn't only a campaign at Nebraska Beef, it was a question of organizing all of the companies. It was a campaign to organize four or five campaigns at the same time." Families and friends supported one another, helping remove the fear factor. This structure helped workers say, "because of love or solidarity, I am going to support the union."

Mapping the plants also gave workers a better understanding of how each company was organized. The workers analyzed their product, learned where it came from and where it went, and gained a greater appreciation of their own role in the process. "Someone organized the plant from top to bottom, so we learn to disorganize it," Sosa says. After the election and recognition, "then you reorganize the plant."

Each plant had its own organizing committee, and although the committees were supported by four UFCW and two OTOC organizers, it was the committees that drove the campaign: members got most of the cards signed, mobilized people inside the plants, and went to house meetings. Committee members also collaborated on a newsletter, *La Neta* ("The Real Deal"). One *La Neta* drawing, by ConAgra worker Jorge Ramirez, showed a worker chasing a carcass down the line in a little car, running over another worker in his haste to keep up, while the line speed control moved from "fast" to "faster" to "over the top." Instead of handing it out at the gate, workers took the newsletter inside. When a supervisor threw copies in the trash, committee members even went to the Human Relations Department to protest.[3]

A fundamental element of OTOC's organizing drive was an iron rule never to do something that others could do for themselves. But because action entails risks, OTOC also trained its leaders in risk assessment and how to ask essential questions: "How do you confront power? How do you confront management?"

In one example of such training, OTOC arranged a meeting with Governor Mike Johanns. Workers learned that "they didn't have to be so reverent with power, and could seek it out as a political ally," recalls Sosa. Indeed, they not only convinced the governor to support a workers' bill of rights, but after meeting with many public officials found themselves more at ease in speaking with people in power.

Those who stood out as leaders were pushed to speak in public, sometimes in front of 300 or 400 people. Workers spoke during mass, on Spanish-language radio, and eventually on the shop floor.

Organizing from the Pulpit

Five days before workers at a ConAgra plant were due to vote on joining the UFCW, workers took their campaign to the Spanish mass at St. Agnes Church.[4] Father Damian Zuerlein recognized the many ConAgra workers in the congregation and introduced the plant's union committee. "Speak about your struggle for justice," he urged them.

After the mass, a kill floor worker named Olga Espinoza urged workers who supported the union to come forward. "Don't be afraid," she urged them. "This is our moment. No one's going to stop us this time." After a few minutes, more than a hundred workers were on their feet, some with concern or fear on their faces, but all determined that secret support for the union would be a thing of the past. From that moment, Espinoza knew that "if we could stand up in the church on Sunday, we could do it in the plant on Monday."

The test came three days later, at a mandatory anti-union meeting called by the company. A vice-president explained why unionization was a bad idea. But Espinoza, empowered by the show of support she'd marshaled at St. Agnes and armed with three questions she and her co-workers had prepared in advance, was ready.

She walked to the front and told the managers she wanted to speak from their microphone. She fired off the first question. "If you're so concerned about us, why haven't you fixed the place where Tiberio fell and was hurt?" she asked. "Are you waiting for someone else to get hurt too?"

The Human Relations Director took the microphone. "She told us she couldn't answer the question right there," Espinoza recalls, "but that she'd give the answer to anyone who came by themselves to her office later on. No one liked that, and we began chanting, 'Now! Now!' Then they told us there wasn't any more time for questions and to go back to work. We just hooted them down."

Two days later, workers voted for the union, two to one.

The company later credited the mass with having turned the tide. They weren't far wrong. Although the organizing campaign was built on many, many months of patient mapping and networking, the mass was a deciding moment in which the workers—through their culture and religious faith—found a sense of safety and security that couldn't be broken by normal anti-union tactics. Moreover, it was a visible symbol of something deeper: a long-term coalition between the union and a community-based organizing project.

As the new union members prepared for bargaining a first contract, sometimes normal union procedures got a face-lift. The UFCW brought in its standard survey of 60 questions, but the worker committees wanted something more. "We wanted to ask some things that weren't there," remembers Sosa. Instead, they went back to the beginning. "The idea was to make individual meetings so that each person could talk about the problems they faced."

Overcoming 'Divide-and-Conquer' Racism: Koreans and Latinos

ONE OF THE UGLIEST YET MOST COMMON TACTICS used by employers trying to keep immigrant workers under their thumbs is to fan racial and ethnic divisions—not just between immigrants and native-born but among immigrants themselves. In Los Angeles' Koreatown, a workers' center is uniting Korean and Latino immigrants against their common employers. Korean Immigrant Workers Advocates has founded two types of worker organization, including an independent union, to deal with the problems of both groups of immigrants.

KIWA was founded in 1992 originally to give voice to Korean workers, to balance the power wielded by Koreatown's business owners, and to challenge stereotyped images of the community. KIWA Director Danny Park explains, "From the mainstream's view, the Korean American community was seen as a model minority built on successful small businesses. But there's always workers working for these businesses, and their working conditions are horrible."

KIWA's initial approach was to deal with workers' problems individually, helping them file for disability or workers' comp, for example. It also offered English classes and seminars on workers' rights, and its staffers wrote letters to employers and met with them on behalf of aggrieved workers. If a dispute couldn't be resolved at that level, KIWA would pursue claims before the state labor commission or in court.

Yet such piecemeal services allowed the same problems to recur year after year. So KIWA decided to tackle workers' issues on an industry-wide rather than complaint-by-complaint basis. Its first target was the restaurant industry, where long hours and substandard wages were common and the Department of Labor estimated that 97 percent of employers were not in compliance with labor law.

During four years of organizing waitresses, cooks, busboys, cashiers, and dishwashers and targeting restaurants for boycotts, KIWA helped create the Restaurant-workers Association of Koreatown. In one campaign at a Korean barbecue restaurant, for example, seven people went on a hunger strike, and there were daily pickets during lunch and dinner. RAK grew to 240 Latino and Korean members, with two paid staffers and a workers' board to monitor restaurant compliance with labor law.

"The huge fight was with the Restaurant Owners Association," Park explains. RAK won agreements that allowed the group to monitor all the member restaurants and to give workers' rights seminars to employees. The association agreed to print and post a labor law poster, in Korean and Spanish, on each member's premises to inform workers of their rights, and it created a $10,000 fund to compensate workers denied their proper pay.

When individual workers came to RAK or KIWA with problems, the group would take up issues that they could generalize, Park says. They would "pick out a really good fight or unique issue so that fighting this publicly would help restaurant workers in the whole industry win their rights, and also get out the message to the owners that this kind of violation cannot be happening." Sometimes KIWA called for boycotts of individual restaurants to make their point.

KIWA found that it was mostly Latino workers who were bringing the complaints—and this caused friction with some in the Koreatown community. "Korean community organizations would say to us, 'You call yourself *Korean* Immigrant Workers Advocates,'" Park recalled. "'Why are you representing Latino workers and bringing trouble to Koreatown and beating up on your own fellow Koreans?'"

KIWA responded in two ways, Park says. Leaders would say: "As a Korean organization, we clean up our own community. It is better that a Korean community center like KIWA is pointing this out, rather than a Latino community organization doing it. And whether they are Latino or Korean, they are workers; you have this legal obligation to treat them right."

When one targeted employer brought in the INS against the workforce, he broke a basic immigrant community taboo. "A lot of our community suffers because of the INS," Park explains. "Seventeen percent of Korean workers in the whole country are undocumented, and in Koreatown it's more. The Korean community really didn't like what the owner did, calling the INS, so we won that campaign.

"Afterwards we did an extensive survey to see if we'd made any improvements. We found that something like 60 percent of the restaurants are now abiding by labor law"—a huge improvement from the three percent figure of before.

Independent Union in the Markets

Employers tried to divide and conquer again during KIWA's ongoing effort to organize workers in Koreatown's big supermarkets, which have much larger workforces. KIWA's first target was Assi, a family-owned supermarket with other markets on the East Coast and two wholesale warehouses. Its Koreatown market employed 160 workers, half Korean and half Latino.

Assi market workers were making minimum wage and fighting for overtime. "Their workload was really heavy compared even to other Korean markets in Koreatown," Park says. "The workers who worked in different markets said it was two times harder than in other markets."

At first, KIWA encouraged Assi workers to set up a meeting to talk to the owners, but the owners refused. Workers decided to establish the independent "Immigrant

Workers Union" and fight for recognition; they elected a president and board members. Worker leaders and KIWA organizers began doing house visits to other workers and organizing trainings on unions and labor law.

Once the campaign surfaced, the United Food and Commercial Workers approached KIWA but, Park says, "people felt that in our community, a mainstream AFL-CIO union coming in to organize" wouldn't do too well. KIWA, by contrast, had been in the community for over 11 years. The workers held open the possibility of partnering with the UFCW or another union in the future, but first wanted to win a few of their own victories "so that they would be on better ground to talk to a union about how to work out a partnership," Park says.

A march through Los Angeles' Koreatown targets two companies: Assi Market, for fighting its Korean and Latino employees who are organizing the independent Immigrant Workers Union, and Forever 21, for refusing to accept responsibility for the sweatshop conditions in which its clothing is produced.

The organizing drive went public after the workers filed for an NLRB election in November 2001 and it attracted widespread support, with 97 community organizations signing on. That proved especially helpful because many of the workers were undocumented. "Anything that has to do with civil disobedience we have to stay away from," Park notes, "so our militancy is very limited. Some of the militancy comes from the community supporters."

Still, Park says, the workers themselves did "basically everything except a strike. They wore union buttons and union t-shirts to work and gathered petitions signed by all of the workers." When one worker was fired for taking his lunch break at the assigned time despite being told he'd have to continue working, "the workers got pissed off and on the same day, same time, all of them walked out to the street and took a ten-minute break and then all of them went back at the same time. They wanted to prove that the market couldn't operate. So the manager says, 'Okay, okay, we'll schedule your time better.' Break and lunch time is now written into their daily schedule."

One technique union supporters used to prepare themselves to confront management was role-playing, where workers would play both sides. "The Assi market workers have done a lot of delegations, getting managers to sit down with them, a lot of accountability sessions," says Park. "Role-playing helps them get into that mode of expecting what the other party would say. After a year, Assi workers are very good at it.

"When you play both roles you really understand what the other people are going through, how they're feeling. Without the role-play, you think just *you* are in fear when you talk to the managers, but when you act a role-play on the manager's side, you see he's also fearful and uncomfortable. By going through it, it gives the workers much more confidence. They think: 'Maybe this is something that I could do. It's not hard just on me, but on the manager as well.'"

Bridging the Language Gap

KIWA staffers help the Korean and Latino supermarket workers bridge the language gap. Many KIWA organizers are either trilingual or bilingual, and KIWA is used to conducting meetings in two or three languages, using translation equipment. Park has found, however, "that even without being able to communicate, the workers know each other well. One set of workers would evaluate the other set of workers, and it came out very accurate. Latino workers would say, 'These persons are really cool, they're really supportive of the union.' And the results were all true, and vice versa."

Assi hired a union-busting firm, and the March 2002 union election resulted in a tie. While the NLRB dithered over 15 challenged votes, Assi campaigned among its Korean employees, saying that the Immigrant Workers Union would be run by Latinos—and that Korean workers should be loyal to Assi's owners.

In August Assi upped the ante: citing Social Security "no-match" letters, management put 56 workers on "disciplinary indefinite suspension." Of the 56, four were

Korean, the rest Latino. "Starting that morning, the fired workers launched a boycott," Park says. "The workers inside who supported the union came out to support them during their breaks and after work. For the first three or four months, workers picketed the market eight hours a day, seven days a week," then reduced the picket to four hours a day. A year later, the picket was still continuing.

Supportive customers, meanwhile, responded by paying with pennies, or by shopping and then returning the groceries. Supporters packed Assi's parking lot with their cars to prevent shoppers from parking, or drove around the parking lot for hours on end honking their horns. "The fired workers and community supporters have basically chased around the owner," Park adds, "doing actions in front of his church, going into the church, surrounding the owner through the whole service. Going to his house and giving leaflets to the neighbors on Christmas, New Year's. Creative actions."

Two lawsuits are pending, one claiming $2-$3 million in back wages for workers who weren't paid overtime, the other charging discrimination against Latinos.

Meanwhile, the Assi workers decided not to wait for the NLRB to rule on the challenged votes, and filed to dismiss the election results. "The workers felt, why go through this whole hearing process, where even if we win Assi will appeal and then it could get dragged out another two or three years," Park says. Instead, the workers are reorganizing themselves either to have another election or to pursue an alternative means of getting recognition, such as card check organizing or a community-held election.

Although some of the fired workers had to move on for financial reasons, 15 or so die-hard pickets continue to walk the line and in doing so have provided a rallying point for the wider community. "A lot of community organizations and supporters have played a huge role in fundraising, a lot of passing the hat within different organizations, organizations matching funds, holding house parties," Park says. "Workers started up a temporary co-op—a car wash—where worker leaders would call up supportive organizations and tell them, 'We are going to wash your staff and members' cars, we will be coming on certain days.' It serves as a strike fund."

When 70,000 southern California UFCW members at the major chain supermarkets went on strike against health care concessions in October 2003, the Immigrant Workers Union and KIWA knew they had to be there. After all, one of their main demands was that Korean markets raise their standards to match those of the mainstream markets. They translated customer flyers for Korean customers, did outreach to the Korean press, and joined strikers on the picket lines.

Helping Garment Workers Help Themselves

THE SOUTHERN CALIFORNIA GARMENT INDUSTRY is the country's largest, comprising retailers, manufacturers, and contractors. A complex system of subcontracting creates lengthy production chains in which companies at the top of the chain shrug off responsibility for those at the bottom, resulting in low wages and notorious sweatshops for as many as 120,000 garment workers.

Yet traditional unions represent less than one percent of the garment workforce. "The union model doesn't fit in this industry," explains Kimi Lee, a Korean American daughter of garment workers. "The factories have 20 to 30 workers and it is all these little mom-and-pop shops that open and close. The life span of a factory is only a year." Indeed, the needle trades union, UNITE HERE, "has made it very clear that they are not organizing garment workers," having witnessed the flight of so much garment production abroad.

Still, the garment industry, Lee says, "is not just going to disappear. It is a $30 billion a year industry." Companies need orders filled quickly to meet the demands of quick-changing fashions, so local production will continue. To meet the needs of tens of thousands of women workers who are often ignored, community organizations and workers centers including KIWA, the Coalition for Humane Immigrant Rights of Los Angeles (CHIRLA), the Asian Pacific American Legal Center, and Sweatshop Watch came together to found an alternative organization. The Garment Worker Center opened in 2001 with Kimi Lee as the first director; a year later it became a membership organization, run by an elected workers' board.

From the beginning, the center determined it would provide more than a bandage. Workers who came for help—almost invariably because they were owed wages and were fired—would have to agree to be part of the process: the GWC was not going to serve as a collection agency. "We only help workers that agree to help themselves," Lee explains. "We do not do it for them. So a worker must be willing to be very active in their case, go to the factory with us, make sure that they are a part of the whole thing. We talk to them about the bigger problem of the garment industry, and exploitation, and sweatshops.

"If they say 'no, just help me get the money,' then we don't take them as cases. We refer them to other places and say, this center is about workers helping themselves. The majority do stay, and we have all these different activities for workers to plug in and help each other."

Workers whose cases are accepted by the center are required to sign an agreement that commits them to attend workshops and to communicate regularly with the center. During weekly drop-in hours, workers volunteer to talk to their peers about their cases and give advice. "We have 75 active leader workers here at the center," says Lee. "We have 150 paid members, but more than half of them come at least once every other week. Dozens of workers come every week, come to our workshops and volunteer. They're peer mentors, they do the health trainings." Lee estimates that more than 400 workers came through the center in its first couple of years.

One is Agustina Mondragón from Guerrero, Mexico, who became involved with the Garment Worker Center when her employer stopped paying her. Now she's a two-year *veterana*, working as a counselor for other garment workers. Mondragón says, "We've learned our rights, learned the law. We have a right to a minimum wage because it's the law and they are breaking the law.

"Some people said that if you didn't have documents you couldn't demand your rights. I'm learning that I do have the right to the salary I am owed, my time worked. So it has been very useful.

"Besides, we also learn about globalization, about health, what is important as a worker, as a head of household, as a partner, everything. I help workers who come in for the first time, counseling them so they aren't afraid."

"It's not just that they come here for a little bit and once their case is settled they leave," Lee says. "It's more of a long term—we're all in it together. Members are accountable to their peers, as opposed to staff saying, 'You said you'd come, where were you?' There's a level of accountability to which our members hold each other."

In its recruitment, GWC has made use of the immigrant community press. "When we first opened," Lee recalls, *"La Opinion* and a lot of the Spanish press came by, the *Chinese News*. Newspapers would write stories and at the bottom say, 'If you're a garment worker, if you need help, call this number.'" After GWC helped the first workers, there was a "balloon effect where more and more workers would tell their friends or their co-workers, and more workers would come. Now we have groups of workers coming in, 10 or 15 at a time from the same factory.

"It's just amazing to me that workers work six days a week, crazy long days, then come for five hours and sit through a globalization workshop, or come and protest two hours in the sun, and bring their children. And they don't have that much free time. They take the bus here. There's all these things that they give up so that they can be a part of the center's activities."

Workshops on health and safety and labor law are supplemented by topics determined by member interest: nutrition, domestic violence, sexually transmitted diseases, self-defense. GWC often calls on other community organizations with expertise to teach the workshops, and some GWC members have been trained to teach about health. Members also are encouraged to join committees, including a social committee, an education committee, and a retention and recruitment committee, which calls members with invitations to participate in GWC activities and which checks on their job situations.

Like KIWA, the GWC serves a multi-ethnic population: 75 percent Latino, 15 percent Asian—mostly Chinese—and about 10 percent Armenian and Eastern European groups. As a result, board meetings are held in Chinese and Spanish, although workshops are usually conducted in a single language. The Center tries to break down stereotypes that originate in the factories, where workers are divided by language.

Like KIWA, the Garment Worker Center serves a multi-ethnic population: 75 percent Latino, 15 percent Asian—mostly Chinese—and about 10 percent Armenian and other Eastern European groups. The Center tries to break down stereotypes that originate in the factories, where workers are divided by language.

"At our Chinese New Year's Party," says Lee, "we had maybe 10 Chinese workers, but 60 Latino workers came, and we explained what Chinese New Year's was, and the lunar calendar, the Chinese horoscope, and the workers really enjoyed it. They see each other in the factory, but they're never able to communicate. Here it has been more of a relaxed social setting."

GWC has joined forces with KIWA, CHIRLA, and the Filipino Workers Center to create the Multi-ethnic Immigrant Workers Organizing Network. "For all of us," says Lee, "the underlying problem is legalization. If these workers had their documents, they wouldn't be exploited as much as they are." MIWON uses May 1 as a public education and public pressure day, with annual marches in Los Angeles that started with a few hundred workers and now number in the thousands. "Workers stand up and say 'Yes! We're here, we're workers, and we're powerful.'"

Its activism has helped GWC make inroads against the garment industry's most abusive practices. In its first couple of years the center pursued approximately 140 complaints, the overwhelming majority for non-payment of wages, and won more than $1 million in back wages—more than had been obtained in government actions. It also developed a working relationship with the Department of Labor, which responded to the center's prodding by starting to translate official documents. "If you went to go file something, it was all in English," recalls Lee. "We finally got them to do Chinese—our staff does the translation for them."

Forever 21

Garment Worker Center leaders know that to change working conditions in the Los Angeles garment industry, more than worker education and pursuit of individual employers will be needed. So the Center is pursuing one major campaign that could help to set standards. The target company is Forever 21, a retailer geared to teens and young women. The campaign includes 50 workers who have worked in at least 25 different factories, a kaleidoscope of shops that come and go, some shutting down completely, some merely changing names and others moving—but all working on the Forever 21 label.

The goal, besides obtaining back wages and penalties, is to get the retailer to adopt stricter policies for its contractors. "Forever 21 does 95 percent of their production in the U.S., and we know the majority of it is probably here in L.A.," Lee explains. "They're a huge company—they have about 150 stores and they're opening another 30—and they made $500 million in 2002. So for them to adopt some type of code of conduct or to admit they're responsible for the workers that are sewing their clothes would benefit thousands of garment workers in L.A. That's going to help shift the industry."

Forever 21 offers plenty of targets for complaint: "rats and cockroaches in the buildings, no bathrooms, no clean water to drink, no break time, no overtime, not being paid minimum wage, all of the very typical sweatshop conditions," says Lee. To pressure the company, GWC launched a public campaign involving students, churches, and other community groups, with a combination of speaking tours and weekly actions at Forever 21 stores. A national speaking tour visited student groups and churches in seven states.

One mid-level manufacturer for Forever 21 accepted a consent decree that included payment of back wages and penalties, as well as training for workers and their subcontractors; the company also agreed to allow workers from different factories to have joint meetings so they could compare wages and working conditions, and agreed to post a hot-line number for reporting violations.

Resources

• UNITE HERE's resources for stewards. See www.unitehere.org/resources/stewardres.asp, under "Immigrant Member Issues." Specifically, see "What To Do in a Raid."

• "Contract Provisions that Protect Immigrant Workers," negotiated by SEIU Local 1877 and HERE Local 2. www.calaborfed.org/resources.

• AFL-CIO: "What Unions Should Know about the Legal Rights of Immigrants" and "Getting to Work," a study of programs to teach immigrants language and job skills. www.aflcio.org/issuespolitics/immigration.

• National Employment Law Project, 55 John St., 7th floor, New York, NY 10038. 212-285-3025. www.nelp.org. Under "Publications," see "Social Security No-Match Information and Employer Sanctions: What Advocates Need to Know," "Social Security No-Match Letters: Top 10 Tips for Employers," and "Guide to Drafting Day Laborer Legislation." See also "Social Security No-Match Letters: Fact Sheet for Workers," www.nelp.org/docUploads/pub155%2Epdf. NELP has many other resources as well.

• National Network for Immigrant and Refugee Rights. Coalition of immigrants, religious, community, and labor organizations. 310 8th St., Suite 303, Oakland, CA 94607. 510-465-1984. nnirr@nnirr.org. www.nnirr.org.

• *Voices from the Front Lines: Immigrant Worker Organizing in Los Angeles*, by Ruth Milkman and Kent Wong. Translated into Spanish by Luis Escala Rabadan. Bilingual book on some organizing campaigns that have helped to build the labor movement. 2000. UCLA Center for Labor Research and Education, Box 951478, Los Angeles, CA 90095. 310-794-5982. www.labor.ucla.edu, jamonroe@ucla.edu. $10.

Organizations in this chapter:

• Garment Worker Center, 888-449-6115, www.garmentworkercenter.org.

• Korean Immigrant Workers Advocates, 213-738-9050, www.kiwa.org. KIWA's restaurant survey is at www.kiwa.org/e/rc6surv.htm.

• Sweatshop Watch, www.sweatshopwatch.org.

Action Questions

1. What is the composition of your workplace? How does it compare to the local workforce in your industry? Are there clear fault lines between those who work in union and non-union shops? Do you clearly see the need to organize among immigrants?

2. How do your members feel about organizing immigrant workers? Do they resist the idea? What resources does your international have to educate members about the need to organize immigrant workers?

3. Do you know the countries, cultures, religions, and languages of immigrants in your union and community? Do you take these differences into account in your meetings and social activities? Are there community organizations that your union could reach out to? Do you have a presence among immigrant communities?

4. Do you know the history of immigrant workers in your local and industry? Why and how did they come to your community? Do you know anyone who was a union or community activist before they came to the States?

5. Do you translate union documents and meetings as necessary?

6. What steps can you take to improve the quality of life of immigrant members outside the workplace? Do

they have ready access to banks, utilities, and other services?

7. What other issues are important to immigrants outside the workplace? How else can the union have a positive impact?

8. Is there a visible movement supporting immigrant rights in your community? Is your union part of it? It should be!

9. Are immigrant communities aware of your union's stance? Do you talk to local immigrant and community media about what your union does or resources it makes available?

10. Immigration raids are often used to intimidate workers, and rarely to disrupt production. Do you suspect local employers have called in tips on their own employees? What actions can your union take to prevent raids at union and non-union workplaces? Do you have an emergency response ready in case one occurs? Are workers (and employers) educated on how to respond?

11. Are local authorities a help or a hindrance?

12. For many reasons, workers sometimes give inaccurate information on their job applications. Do you have contract language to protect workers if they have to change their personnel information? Do you educate workers and employers about what to do with no-match letters?

13. Are you taking advantage of immigrant members' network of relationships? Do immigrant members play a leading role in developing and implementing organizing plans?

Authors

DAN LA BOTZ wrote the first edition of *A Troublemaker's Handbook* in 1991. He is an activist, teacher, and labor historian based in Cincinnati, where he writes frequently for *Labor Notes*. He was a founding member of Teamsters for a Democratic Union in the 1970s and wrote a book about that movement, as well as books on unions in Mexico and Indonesia. He is editor of the monthly web publication *Mexican Labor News and Analysis*.

TEÓFILO REYES, a former director of Labor Notes, is an organizer for the Transnationals Information Exchange, which brings together worker activists in North and South America, Europe, Africa, and Asia. He facilitated the formation of the National Coalition for Dignity and Amnesty for Undocumented Workers and serves on the board of the Coalition for Justice in the Maquiladoras and the Executive Committee of Labor Notes.

NICK ROBINSON is a former student-labor activist at Miami University and Labor Notes intern. He is now a volunteer organizer with the Montpelier Downtown Workers Union and the Vermont Workers Center.

Notes

1. Andrew Block, "Labor charges that INS helped squelch Sea-Tac organizing campaign," *Real Change News*, August 8, 2002.

2. David Johnson, "Model Organizing Campaign Doubles Union Membership in Nine Months," *Labor Notes*, May 2002.

3. David Bacon, "The Kill Floor Rebellion," Labor Notes July 2002 archives, www.labornotes.org/archives.

4. The story of the Mass and the captive audience meeting comes from David Bacon, "The Kill Floor Rebellion."

On the Troublemaker's Website

"Aumento Ya! PCUN's Fight To Raise Wages in the Strawberry Fields," by Teófilo Reyes. Strawberry pickers in the Northwest struck for a raise—at harvest time. The action was organized by Pineros y Campesinos Unidos del Noroeste—PCUN (Northwest Treeplanters and Farmworkers United). Go to www.labornotes.org.

17. Workers Centers

by Dan La Botz

IN THE LAST TWO CENTURIES workers have organized in many ways to support each other on the job and in our communities. Unions represent one form of working class organization, but not the only one. After all, the goal of organizing is not merely to build unions: it is to increase the power of working people on the job and in society.

This requires finding models that fit the needs of particular groups of workers. This chapter will highlight the emergence of workers centers. We are focusing on these projects because of both *how* they are organizing and *who* they are organizing.

Workers centers are labor organizations, but they are based in the community rather than in a particular workplace. Most have arisen among low-wage immigrant workers employed in industries that present sizable barriers to unionization: garment work and other small, low-wage workplaces with high turnover; housecleaning; day labor in construction and other jobs.

These centers play the dual role of fighting for rights on the job and of giving immigrant workers a voice in a society in which they have come increasingly under attack. Because their members are usually people of color, workers centers are always dealing with racism and discrimination as part of their members' daily experience. Often a majority of their members and leaders are women.

According to researcher Janice Fine, who has studied workers centers across the country, the centers have arisen in "generational waves" as new groups of immigrants have arrived and needed to create ways to negotiate with the larger society. Their successes include developing strong leaders and strong allies in the larger community, winning checks for thousands of workers cheated out of their pay, and changing the way the media and the public look at immigrants.[1]

Because of their relatively small size and their typical constituencies, Fine says, workers centers have been more effective at bringing political pressure to bear through community organizing strategies than at "economic intervention" through actions based in the workplace. Workers centers can be seen as "part of a newly emerging immigrant infrastructure," filling a void where most unions have failed to organize.

Steve Jenkins of the Make the Road by Walking workers center in Brooklyn says, "In the big picture, we're not really changing power dynamics between workers and their employers on the job. What we are doing is creating a group of more politically conscious workers who will be able to play a role in changing the balance of forces when the opportunity presents itself. The creation of local power bases in immigrant communities is one of the most important functions that workers centers are currently serving." In several of the examples in this chapter, however, workers did exert enough power to change employers' behavior, up to and including forming a union.

A typical workers center does some or all of these activities: train leaders, teach classes in English and in basic workplace rights, provide legal representation to recover unpaid wages, organize workers to pressure employers, work for immigration law reform, and speak on behalf of its constituencies to government agencies and legislators. Workers centers vary greatly in their structure and functioning, but they tend to be looser and more experimental than unions. Most have a board and various committees. A little over two-thirds of the 40 centers Fine surveyed have 500 members or fewer, with the other third having 500 to 1,000.

Fine adds that most workers centers treat membership "as a privilege attained through participation" rather than simply through receiving the cen-

Working Class Traditions of Organization

Working people have always organized in the face of hardship. One early form of worker organization was mutual aid societies, organizations that provided aid to the families of workers facing tragedies like a death or injury on the job. Working people have also organized educational groups, from the simplest study circles to workers' universities that taught labor economics and organizing and promoted visions of alternatives to a society organized for profit.

Immigrant workers, who were pivotal to the earliest struggles for industrial unions in the United States, have a long history of organizing community centers. In the early nineteenth century, German immigrants established Turnvereins, athletic and social organizations which sometimes functioned as meeting places for union activists. Italian activists brought with them the tradition of the Casa del Popolo, the People's House, a center for working class people. In the early twentieth century many immigrant groups were organized through foreign language branches of the Socialist Party or the Industrial Workers of the World (IWW).

ter's services or attending one of its events. Along with membership come specific responsibilities and duties. These sometimes include paying dues, though less than half of the centers Fine surveyed require dues. Most are dependent for funding on foundations and grant money.

Some workers centers are wary of what they see as unions' hierarchical practices and know-it-all attitude; others work closely with unions despite friction that results from different ways of functioning. Despite these tensions, workers centers are part of the labor movement, and should be welcomed by unions not as rivals but as allies in building a movement for social change.

With their focus on leadership development, their promotion of solidarity among workers from different workplaces, and their openness to creative tactics, workers centers have much to teach unions about democracy and participation. Workers centers function in the languages that their constituencies speak; stress the education of new leaders among women and people of color; educate workers about their rights, labor law, and the principles of collective action; and challenge existing labor laws and the political climate in which anti-immigrant policies flourish.

For this chapter we have chosen as examples some campaigns carried out by six workers centers in Chicago, New York, and Rhode Island. Workers centers are also featured in Chapters 16 on Immigrants (Korean Immigrant Workers Advocates, Garment Worker Center, Omaha Together One Community), 11 on Corporate Campaigns (the Coalition of Immokalee Workers), and 21 on Developing Leaders (DARE).

Our case studies showcase six examples of what workers centers do: workers' rights education; fighting for unpaid wages; hooking workers up with unions and helping to democratize a local; forming workers' cooperatives; and organizing day laborers.

Workers' Rights Education

A PRESSING CONCERN among immigrant communities is ensuring that people know their rights, on and off the job. The Chicago Interfaith Workers' Center, which is a project of the Chicago Interfaith Committee on Worker Issues, is getting that vital information out. Director José Oliva visited workers centers around the country in the late 1990s, looking for a model that would best suit the needs of the workers he was organizing among. He returned from that trip convinced that strong ties to unions were critical.

The Interfaith Committee already had a history of working with the labor movement (see Chapter 13). As one of the first steps in moving the workers who sought help toward unions, the Center published a simple manual about labor law and workers' rights under various laws—anti-discrimination, health and safety, wages and hours. "We had lots of information that no one had ever thought to put together in a simple form," says Oliva. "If you wanted to know about wages and hours you had to call the Wages and Hours Division for information that was written for lawyers. We decided that we would put together a small, comprehensive guide."

The manual that the Center produced included information from OSHA, the Environmental Protection Agency, the NLRB, and the Illinois and U.S. Departments of Labor. It was printed in English, Spanish, and Polish. In 1998, the Center started distributing the manual, largely through churches. Soon after, they began to get calls from workers saying, "I read your manual and it says here that after 40 hours a week I should get overtime—that's not happening in my workplace."

The Center referred these workers to the Department of Labor (DOL), without thinking what this meant in practice. In only a matter of time they learned that workers who went there didn't get help, because the hours were only 9 to 5, because of language difficulties, or because undocumented workers were simply afraid to enter a government building. So the process of filing a legal complaint was basically inaccessible.

Creating a Clearinghouse

This experience led the Center to step in and see what it could do to open up the process. Oliva says, "We created one simple form and we proposed it to the government agencies—OSHA, NLRB, EEOC, USDOL, and Illinois DOL. It's a standard form that we use in Chicago now, a single form that all government agencies can use. Workers come in and give us their complaints. We help them fill out the form. It goes to a clearinghouse person in the government, who then sends it to the right agency.

"We were able to get them to create that position of clearinghouse person, someone who works at the middle level to make sure grievances go to the right department. Then a person from that agency contacts us, and we function sort of like case managers to help the workers. They have only a few Spanish-speaking investigators, so with our help it is possible to deal with a greater volume of Spanish-speaking workers."

Getting the various government agencies to agree with the idea of one form was like pulling teeth, Oliva says, and took more than two years of persistence. Activists at the Center found the process incredibly legalistic. "All of these different agencies see their job as reducing caseloads," he says. "They take the position that they can't really enforce the law, so they only try to go after highly visible cases to use as an example.

"We basically raised the argument: you can work with us and we can help you access these communities and function as a bridge for you, or you can work against us and we will shed light on how screwed-up this process is for workers."

The relationship that the Interfaith Center established with government agencies became formalized as the Chicago Area Workers' Rights Initiative. They now send about 20 forms per month to the government's clearinghouse person. Oliva estimates that three-quarters of those who fill out forms are Latino immigrants, 15 percent are Polish, and 10 percent are native-born.

Meanwhile, the Center's organizers are constantly

A Brooklyn workers center's campaign won $65,000 in back wages and better conditions for workers at MiniMax, a local retailer.

looking for places to give workshops about workers' rights, such as at churches and community centers. Oliva says he describes legal rights and then has the participants break into groups. "Each one gets a scenario for a workers' rights problem, and they pick a 'steward' who will inform the other groups of what their problem was and how they solved it. By doing this, we get people to think democratically—they're electing someone who will represent them—and to think of collective forms of resolving problems.

"We talk about, 'What does the law give us and what does the law not give us?' The law doesn't give us vacations, raises, benefits, job security. Once they list all that, I ask, 'Is there a way we can get this?' Then the real dialogue begins. There is always someone who knows what a union is and people with both positive and negative experiences. It's a great forum for them to learn from each other." For more on the Interfaith Center's work with unions, see below.

Fighting for Unpaid Wages

ONE OF THE MOST COMMON PROBLEMS facing immigrant workers is non-payment of wages. Dealing with employers who frequently do not speak their languages and who are often impossible to track down makes immigrant workers vulnerable to some of the worst kinds of violations.

Brooklyn Workers Win Back Pay Plus Future Protections

by Betsy Esch

Make the Road By Walking, a workers center based in the Bushwick section of Brooklyn, has become known in its community for its success in winning unpaid wage cases. Through the center's Workers Justice Project, workers have been able to win back wages for themselves and sometimes wage increases and protections for other workers.

Unpaid wages are completely typical in the industries where people in Bushwick tend to work, such as construction, garment, and small-scale commercial operations. In the garment industry, bosses tend to cut corners by paying by the week and ignoring overtime hours. Less legitimate firms will pay workers with checks that aren't funded.

Deborah Axt, an attorney who works with the Workers Justice Project, says Make the Road has been effective because of the willingness of workers themselves to take action. "Protest is what works," explains Axt. "When people feel like there is a chance of winning, they will take risks. We've been able to develop a group of workers who have confidence in the power of collective action. When new people are exposed to this it gives them confidence, too. It's almost always people who are fired, so they can't get retaliated against. But even those who do still have their jobs almost always get fired.

"We typically start with a small action in which a delegation of workers will go to the boss and present a demand letter. We hold demonstrations. Often we have several of these kinds of small campaigns going at once, so sometimes people have to 'wait their turn' for us to be able to focus on their problem.

"People are obviously nervous about immigration issues. In low-wage immigrant workplaces there is often a mix of people with and without papers. So a threat that affects your neighbor will scare you even if your situation isn't quite the same. Sometimes people say they are scared because they are undocumented. But the real issue is that people are scared because the boss has all the power. And for undocumented workers, the fear isn't so much about what will happen to them if they engage in action; it's that they have no recourse if they are retaliated against.

"We had one case involving a local retailer. A small discount department store in our neighborhood called MiniMax owed back wages to eight workers, all of whom were women. When they came to us none still had their job."

Axt explains that beyond their personal demands, the workers wanted to ensure that current MiniMax employees did not suffer the same abuses they had. "In this case they were owed $90,000 in back wages, but they were also demanding sick days, break time—basic protections for the current workers."

Planning the Campaign

The Workers Justice Project has weekly meetings, which is where the campaign begins. These meetings are typically attended by 40-60 workers. A core group of 20 consistently attends, and are joined by new people or others involved with specific campaigns. At those meetings, says Axt, "we set up a volunteer committee of workers to plan the campaign with staff."

For the MiniMax campaign, workers drew up a list of demands and filed a lawsuit. At the same time, they held a series of protests, kicked off by a Mother's Day demonstration. "One of the big issues was that some of them had been fired for not being at work when their child was home sick," explains Axt. "We organized a Mother's Day protest around the theme that women shouldn't have to choose between being mothers and workers."

As the campaign continued, they also held a Halloween protest, with costumes, and a Christmas protest where Santa came to denounce the employer. Typically, says Axt, "we'd have a reasonably big protest once a month, with a few people leafleting around the store more regularly."

When the employer agreed to meet with the workers, each worker explained one of their demands. With some persuading from his attorneys, the employer agreed to work something out. Axt notes that in these campaigns, "it's impossible to separate litigation from organizing. We negotiated everything together—the back wages and the workplace demands. The judge thought it was weird—she just wanted to settle the back wages. But we explained this case was about much more than that.

"We won $65,000 in back wages. More importantly, though, was that the women were organizing to change the conditions of the workers who are there now. We were able to win paid sick days, an FMLA kind of coverage, and a public posting of legal and workplace rights. We were demanding assurances that people not be fired if they had to miss work.

"And we now have a core of members who are very sophisticated. They recognize that it is legitimate to drive an employer out of business. They reject the idea that any job is better than no job. And they also know that as workers they do have power, bosses need them. So if one shop closes another will open, the job losses won't be permanent. We have members who have been involved in campaigns at five different employers.

"Our activist leaders know that even when you win a campaign, in itself it doesn't change the conditions of work in any structural way. People see that and draw conclusions about the limits of what is possible inside this economic and political system."

Embarrassing the Boss

The Workplace Project is a workers center based in the Latino community of Hempstead, Long Island. José and Adelardo Garcia came to the Project seeking help with an unpaid wages case. Because this is such a common problem, the center has a routine way of handling these situations.

In this case the Garcia brothers were working for a construction contractor named Mike Pasquaretto who had refused to pay them. Says Director Nadia Marin Molina, "We start a campaign by calling the employer and then following up with a letter. The employer usually says, 'Okay, I will pay you,' but then they don't. So the campaign really starts then, when a group of workers visits the employer to demand that he pay the unpaid wages. The whole group goes to visit the employer, even if it is not their own case. Pasquaretto refused to pay.

"When that happened we knew we were going to have to start a collective, direct action campaign. We made a leaflet which explained that Pasquaretto owed more than $7,500 to these workers. We went to his house and passed it out to all his neighbors and encouraged them to call him expressing support for the workers. In many situations this is what causes the employer to respond to us; they begin to take us a little more seriously.

"Pasquaretto was still not responding, so we decided to hold a demonstration in front of his house. We brought signs and were chanting, which brought even more attention from his neighbors. He came out and insulted the workers and tried to get the police to arrest them. In some ways that is one of the best parts of protesting. The employers almost always call the police and tell them to arrest the workers. But the police invariably tell the employers that the workers have a right to protest as long as they stay on the sidewalk and follow the regulations.

Teacher Assistants DARE To Organize

by Sara Mersha

In 1999, a group of mostly Latina teacher assistants working for the Providence School Department decided that after years of working at minimum wage with no benefits, they weren't going to take it anymore. They decided to organize with DARE—Direct Action for Rights and Equality—a grassroots, multiracial, multilingual community organization in Rhode Island. After over a year of fighting, the teacher assistants won their demand to be hired permanently, with double the wages, full family health insurance, dental coverage, pensions, and union membership. This is how we did it.

Our main method was to be *in the face* of the decision-makers, wherever we could find them. We used actions—surprise visits to decision-makers' offices by groups of workers and supporters. We used "accountability sessions," where we asked the target to meet with us. We testified at public meetings, and we used the press.

The teacher assistants' fight grew out of a larger living wage campaign for the city of Providence that DARE and Rhode Island Jobs with Justice began in 1999. Several of the early DARE leaders of the living wage campaign were "temporary" teacher assistants who had been working for the School Department at minimum wage for three, four, or even five years. At the beginning of that campaign, a DARE member who was a permanent teacher assistant brought Sara Gonzales, a temporary assistant, into the DARE office. Sara had been unjustly fired after working for the school department for three years.

DARE organized a small group of members to go with Sara, along with some press, walk straight into the office of the boss who had fired her, and demand her job back. This boss was clearly not used to workers confronting her like this, and called the police, who threatened to arrest all of us. We decided we didn't want to get arrested at that point, but got a meeting later that day with the Superintendent of Schools. We presented the situation, and Sara won her job back.

At a public hearing, a teacher assistant explains, based on her family budget, why a living wage is needed.

Sara walked out of the meeting energized from that victory, and ready to fight for more. "I got my job back," she said, "but I still only made minimum wage, no benefits, and there were a lot more in my same situation."

Sara organized a house meeting the next week, inviting other teacher assistants to come talk about their situation together. Twelve came to that first meeting, and decided to join DARE and create a subcommittee of DARE's living wage campaign.

We did research and found out that the School Department had an agreement with the union that represented the permanent teacher assistants. That agreement said that after teacher assistants worked 60 consecutive days, they would automatically be made permanent. But the School Department would call temporary teacher assistants on their 59th day and tell them they couldn't come in to work, making them start all over again the next day.

Accountability Session

The committee created a Teacher Assistant Bill of Rights and presented it to the new Superintendent at an accountability session. Months went by, nothing happened, and when the committee tried to go back to the Superintendent, she had us meet with the Human Resources Director. He agreed to some of our demands (like training), but had no power to agree to the last and most important, permanent jobs. Frustrated with the administration's unwillingness to do anything, the committee started targeting the School Board, first testifying at each board meeting, then doing actions with press at board meetings.

Deyanira Garcia, one of the teacher assistant leaders, made the racism and sexism behind the situation clear when she testified, "It's not a coincidence that those of us who never get made permanent are women of color." The School Board finally started noticing us and recognizing that they needed to change the situation. That's when the union that represents permanent teacher assistants finally got involved. We had some meetings with the union, then the union had some meetings with the School Department. This resulted in an agreement to make teacher assistants permanent the next school year.

When the School Department failed to make teacher assistants permanent by the date they had agreed to, we were right back in their faces, bringing allies from Jobs with Justice and state representatives along to pressure the School Board to live up to this agreement.

At the very next School Board meeting, they started the permanent hiring. Two months later, all of the more than 100 teacher assistants in our situation were permanent! This victory was just the beginning. Two of the teacher assistants became DARE board members and one became a staff organizer. And the teacher assistants inspired bus monitors in a similar situation to organize: they won the same level of pay and benefits as permanent monitors.

The Chicago Interfaith Workers' Center has helped workers choose a union, meet with organizers, and negotiate the terms of their joining.

"That angers the employers and gives the workers a lot more courage. They see the police enforcing their rights; sometimes the police even try to convince the employer he should pay.

"In this case even that didn't work! We asked the Attorney General of New York to look at the case. The National Employment Law Project helped us to pressure the Attorney General's office to take the case. NELP helps us calculate amounts owed in back wages by taking into account not just the amount owed but overtime and penalties.

"Finally they came to the negotiating table. Pasquaretto's attorney told me that if it hadn't been for the protests and the leafleting they wouldn't have negotiated. Taking away their ability to abuse workers in secret is really important."

Bridging the Gap from Workers Centers to Unions

THE CHICAGO INTERFAITH WORKERS' CENTER has helped workers choose a union, meet with organizers, and negotiate the terms of their joining. Director José Oliva tells how a group of Latino construction workers organized.

"In November 2002, a couple of workers came in to see us. They worked at ANSCO, a construction company that buys and rehabs dilapidated buildings in a part of town that's gentrifying. They hire immigrant workers and pay them $6 an hour for work usually done at $12 non-union, and $16 to $30 by union workers. These workers were doing carpentry, drywalling, painting, and very high-end, high-quality work.

"It was also very risky work, such as asbestos removal with no protective equipment, and electrical work with no training and no protective equipment. A worker told us a basement was flooded and they were doing electrical work in a situation that was almost suicidal. A couple of workers fell off a second-story window because they had no straps. That's the kind of conditions they were exposed to. They were working 50 or 60 hours with no overtime.

"One of the workers had heard one of our workers' rights workshops at his church, and he had told the others. They were just trying to find out what their rights were. I explained to them that there were laws—wage and hours, OSHA—but I also said, maybe you should think about organizing if you want long-term change. This is the same story we tell every worker that comes in here. If this affects more than just you, talk to your co-workers and bring them in here so we can host a meeting and you can talk about your problems."

So the original couple of workers went back to work and talked to their co-workers. The next time they came back to the Center, there were 30, a third of the workforce. "We started talking about all the options," recalls Oliva, "and every time we mentioned unions they said, 'No, no. Unions just take your dues and steal your money.' At that point it was clear that we needed to have an in-depth discussion about the labor movement in this country. Most of them come from other countries, and they are often describing the labor movement back home. Not to say unions here don't have problems, but these workers have often seen extreme examples of corruption."

'Be a Union'

Oliva explains that the Center doesn't just try to push workers into a union but rather helps them figure out how to organize themselves into a union. "We try to get workers prepared to create a union, not to just passively join the union. Instead of 'joining a union,' we talk about 'becoming a union.' We don't say 'become part of a union' but rather 'be a union.'

"We work with workers to help them interview the union. The workers want to know about the union, and the union wants to know if the workers are serious. We helped them carry out a mutual interview, in both directions. At that first meeting we host it, we facilitate and moderate it, because we have a relationship."

Oliva convinced the construction workers that they should at least talk to a union to see what it had to say. "When we work with workers seeking to organize, we describe the unions, and give the workers some information. We respect the idea of jurisdiction, but we wouldn't always recommend that workers just follow jurisdiction, especially if the union is not democratic.

"In this case the Carpenters had a very open and new approach to organizing, and had some interesting proposals. The Carpenters said, 'This is how we would run the campaign, this is how you would be involved.' It was a fit, exactly what the workers were looking for.

"So for the second meeting we met at the Carpenters' hall. It was the first time that workers had been inside a union hall, and that gave them a more accurate perspective of what the labor movement is like here. Immediately a strategy was developed out of that meeting.

"ANSCO went ahead and fired three of the core leaders, but what we didn't expect is that when they fired them, all the workers walked out—which wasn't part of the strategy. These workers had cell phones, and they contacted the other two buildings, and the workers walked out at all three sites. We immediately organized a press conference and got religious leaders out there. We filed a barrage of claims, OSHA, EEOC, and Wage and Hours, and the Carpenters filed a bunch of unfair labor practices with the NLRB.

"At that point the campaign came to a head. That was a Saturday, and on Monday we had a prayer vigil at the home of the owner, who was Jewish. This was during Passover, and we had several major rabbis come out with members of their congregations to join the workers. That prayer vigil pushed the owner to reach an agreement. He called his lawyers and they called the Carpenters' lawyers.

"This was obviously one of those super-successful and very fast campaigns. This is the model, though it doesn't always work this well."

Cleaning Up a Company Union

As union activists know, having a union doesn't necessarily lead directly to being able to stand up to the boss. In some cases, union members come to workers centers seeking strategies for getting representation from their union. Oliva gives an example of that scenario.

"We were contacted by a group of workers from Wheaton Plastics. These workers had a union. They were members of Local 221 of the Glass Moulders and Plastic Workers Union, AFL-CIO. But the union wasn't doing much for them: the president of the union was the brother of the owner of the company. The workers came in and they had complaints about the company, but they complained more about the union because, they said, it did nothing for them.

"We have a clear philosophy about working with unions. First, we don't ever refer workers to a union that doesn't have a good standing with us. Second, when we deal with a union we always work through the union first. We do it internally and do it in writing, before we go anywhere else.

"So we did all of that in this case. We contacted the union, and the head of the union informed us that he was the brother of the owner of the company, and he told us we were barking up the wrong tree if we thought he would do anything against his brother.

"We went back to the workers and explained the situation. We said, 'Well, first, it doesn't make sense to decertify the union, because what you have is better than nothing.' At least they had some basic provisions: vacations, annual raises, a minimal health care plan.

"But, we said, if you want, we can provide you all the guidance and the training to help you run an effective electoral campaign when the next union election comes up in one year. We will help every way we can to get you the control of that local. The workers had a lot of discussion, and decided they wanted to get rid of their current officers and elect new ones from among themselves."

The workers center supported the workers in their campaign to elect new officers—and when the election came, they won. "Now they run it,' says Oliva. "The new president of the local is now on the steering committee of our workers center. The company now hates the union, and the old leadership is very unhappy. But that's the way it should be, no?"

Cooperatives

FACED WITH THE TASK of organizing the unregulated and fragmented world of domestic work, the Workplace Project started from the principle of collective action: they helped start the Unity Housecleaners Cooperative (Cooperativa de Limpieza de Casas Unidad). In starting their co-op the women wanted to establish a way to seek out their own jobs, set their own standards, and collectively distribute the jobs among themselves. The co-op is run by a coordinating committee with committees on finances, publicity, rules, and education.

A worker cooperative is a business where the workers are also owners. In the ideal situation there will be profits at the end of the year, which are divided among the workers in addition to the wages they are paid.

Setting the terms of work is especially important in jobs where employers routinely expect total flexibility. Often domestic workers think they are being hired for one thing and the employer insists on another. Nadia Marin Molina from the Workplace Project says that often "you will be hired to clean the house and then the employer will tell you to watch the kids, or walk the dog or mow the lawn. Co-op members know it's important to be very clear about what you will do and how long you will work."

The co-op members set the prices and terms of work, which means that they are able to share work assignments fairly and negotiate wages without having to pay fees to agencies. Ten percent of their earnings goes to the co-op.

Unity Housecleaners is able to charge about $15 per hour. Molina says that opposition to paying domestic workers a living wage is one of the biggest obstacles they face. "Some people think $15 is too high; they say that is what a university graduate is paid. And they can almost always find someone to work for less, so this is a real challenge for us. Not just finding jobs but finding stable jobs." The co-op also wants to bring in childcare workers.

The education committee gives a class on house cleaning, trains new members on what a co-op is, and coordinates English classes. It has also organized training on breast cancer and domestic violence prevention. The co-op therefore not only is a way to take control of working conditions but also creates a community group and a place for women to come together.

★ ★ ★

Because so many immigrants, especially those without documents, work as day laborers, organizing day laborers is one of the most common projects that worker centers take on. Here we discuss two workers centers in Chicago that take different approaches. The Day Labor Organizing Project focuses on workers at small temporary agencies, and the Latino Union has organized both agency workers and those who get their jobs day by day on the street corner.

The Latino Union and Day Laborers

by Dan La Botz and Teófilo Reyes

JOSÉ LANDAVERDE, a Methodist minister and Salvadoran immigrant who had worked as a day laborer in Houston, helped found the Latino Union (or in Spanish, Union Latina) to bring an end to the abuse day laborers faced from employers and police in Chicago. Says Landaverde, "Day labor is a system of slavery, because you get up at five a.m., unsure where you are going to work, worried whether you can feed your children, and worried that you have to pay the rent. That is already enough to worry about.

"Later you need to worry about the police harassing you if you look for work. Later you worry if the person who hires you will pay you or not. Later you worry that you can't stand up for your rights because the laws are all stacked against you. Then there is the language barrier. You have everything against you. The only thing in your favor is your life."

The Latino Union is a member of the National Day Laborer Organizing Network. "We are a membership organization," explains Landaverde. "The day laborers pay a dollar a year to be members, and they fill out their membership cards and receive an ID."

"It was a group of women day laborers who actually founded the organization," explains Jessica Aranda, who worked as an organizer for the group before becoming its director. "The women were being charged for rides by a temporary agency, and sometimes the agency would charge them for hard hats or other materials. There was a lot of sexual harassment. The workers organized protests at many of the agencies and shut many of them down, at least temporarily, and also attracted a lot of media attention during 2000 and 2001. Then, joining with other organizations, we were able to pass state legislation to regulate the agencies."

Challenging the Temporary Agencies

The work started with the Latino Union having visibility in the community around day-to-day issues. Says Aranda, "At that time José Landaverde was leading the organization. He would help people read their mail, make a phone call, or help with consumer services. People came in and used the office because we had those bilingual services.

"With that visibility in the community, people realized that if they had labor issues they could come talk to us about those problems as well. People started coming from the temporary agencies saying, 'I tried to cash my check, but there were insufficient funds. They make me pay for transportation and pay for safety equipment. They are forcing workers to cash their check at the temp agency for a fee. There is sexual harassment and discrimination.' At first we were helping people case by case, but gradually we realized that this was a more systemic problem.

"We started to involve workers in the organizing process. We would say, 'Instead of just talking to me about your individual case, bring others with you so we can start talking about doing something together.' We said that we could possibly get their check paid individually, but it would probably just happen again tomorrow. We used popular education methods. We would have a meeting and have everybody in the room tell his or her story, and then they realized that it was larger than just one person's story.

"The workers suggested that we call the Spanish media—two major networks that people watch all the time, and the newspapers. They decided to organize a protest in front of the agency, to bring the issues to the attention not only of the surrounding community and the media but also to the other workers who were inside.

"We showed up at several of the agencies with signs and bullhorns. We had people tell their stories in a press conference fashion. Then we would march in a circle in front of the agency, flyering people who were coming in and out. The reactions varied. Most of the temporary agencies wouldn't talk to the press, and they would close their doors for a day.

The Latino Union in Chicago has worked to organize street corner day laborers.

"But the point is that they were forced to shut down for a day. At first people were skeptical of what was going on, but the people telling their stories on the outside resonated with everyone there, and then people would join us, coming out from inside the offices."

Need for Legislation and Regulations

The Latino Union's demonstrations led to meetings with agency owners. Aranda says, "Once we met with the owners we realized how entrenched the temporary agencies industry was within the structure of manufacturing and business in Chicago. Many of them donated to local politicians. So we realized that we had to be more systemic in order to get the day labor issue on the map. We decided to formulate legislation. These agencies were completely unregulated."

The Latino Union joined with other Chicago organizations working on the day labor issue, such as the San Lucas Center and the Pilsen Workers Center, and together they got the politicians to take up the proposed legislation. "All the media attention and highlighting the egregious abuses that were taking place really made it attractive to local politicians, who could champion this issue," says Aranda.

"State Representative Miguel Del Valle pushed the state legislation. The goal was to create a system of licensing and to outline rules of conduct for a temporary agency: provide an adequate space to wait for work, no charge for transportation, no charge for safety equipment, no forcing workers to cash their checks at the agency. We also won a city ordinance with the support of the aldermen."

After winning the regulations, the Latino Union continued to offer services to the community: English as a Second Language programs and a government program that provides gas and electricity subsidies to low-income people. "Those programs are our outreach arm into the community, so people become familiar with our organization and learn our mission," says Aranda.

Street Corner Day Laborers

The Latino Union's next project became the organization of street corner day laborers. "The corner day laborers can be invisible if you don't know what you're looking for," says Aranda. "Throughout the United States there are workers who stand and wait on the corner for an employer to come by and offer them a job. This is a tradition that comes from Latin America.

"They wait for employers at three main places: McDonald's, Dunkin' Donuts, and a hardware and lumber store such as Home Depot or Lowe's. The workers wait for jobs mostly in construction, landscaping, and moving. In Chicago there are about ten principal day labor corners, each with about 75 to 200 people rotating out of that corner.

"The workers are mostly immigrants. Here in Chicago the two largest groups are Latinos— Mexican, Guatemalan, and Ecuadorian—and Eastern European, mostly Polish, but also Czech. There is a poor group of Mongolian workers as well.

"Workers congregate at some corner, early in the morning, and the employers drive up. Workers congregate around the employers' vehicles, and negotiation takes place around what kind of job and wage. On the corner, whoever will go for the least amount of money will get the job. Then they jump into the car and are taken to the worksite.

"The biggest problem we see is theft of wages. Employers have an advantage of being anonymous to the workers, so after the job is done, some refuse to pay. Another problem is that employers put workers in very dangerous situations. These workers perform the most dangerous demolition and construction work. The employer doesn't feel any accountability in terms of safety training or a safe environment, so we see a lot of permanent workplace injuries. One of our leaders fell from a roof because he wasn't secured. He was left permanently blind in one eye.

"Police harassment is another issue. Many local businesses and residents don't want workers congregating in the area. Workers are often confused with loiterers or with people with some purpose other than looking for work. There are also problems with exposure, dehydration, and frostbite during the harsh winters."

Establishing a Center

Day laborers are difficult to organize because they are transient and undocumented, but on the other hand, says Aranda, they are at the same place every morning. "The first step is to go and stand on the corner with them, in order to establish trust," she says. "We may help them with translation with the employer, while not interfering with their normal business."

As the Latino Union organizers heard about the abuses, they helped workers to recover stolen wages by visiting or calling employers or writing letters. Out of those activities, a first group of leaders was formed.

"The next step was to facilitate some sort of election and the creation of a representative body," says Aranda. "Then the elected leadership talked to other workers about what they wanted to do. Workers who had had experiences from other places in the country, from California or Texas, talked about the idea of a democratically run workers center.

"So we've created the Albany Park Day Labor Co-op, and we plan to have a physical space, a community center where workers can wait for work. We don't yet have the physical space, but we have built the organizational infrastructure.

"When we describe this, we like to avoid the word 'hiring hall,' so we just say 'a community center' where workers can congregate in the morning. This will take the whole issue of being out on the street in the cold out of the equation. At that location workers can also agree to establish a minimum wage for different types of jobs and a fair system for distributing the jobs. So instead of a race to the bottom, it's workers working cooperatively to get jobs."

José Landaverde explains that even before the co-op has a building to operate from, different workers are in charge of security, communications, cleaning, and contracts with employers. "We have an intake form where the day laborer puts his name and the contractor puts his name, or we just write down the license plate. And the day laborer with three co-workers negotiates with the contractor the amount of money that the person will go to work for.

"If the worker doesn't want to use the process, they are told: if you go negotiate your terms by yourself, do two things. Don't charge less than our established rate, and write down the license plate number and the name of the contractor. With that data we have enough to find them if the day laborer cuts a finger or gets in an accident. With that data we can establish a claim with a lawyer for workers' comp, or with the Department of Labor if they didn't get paid. The contract committee is in charge of that.

"The publicity committee is in charge of distributing flyers and of promoting the work. On a street corner anything can happen—some people drink, sometimes use different substances, so the security committee is there to make sure those kinds of things don't happen.

"Job distribution is based on points that workers receive for their participation in the campaign," Aranda explains, "and those with the most points are assigned the first jobs that come into the co-op. So those who are participating the most have the most opportunity to get a job. This is for now, until we have a physical space." In the meantime, members meet weekly to create a strategy for fundraising and encouraging local lawmakers, residents, businesses, and the police to support the co-op.

Divide and Conquer

In Chicago, as elsewhere, race, gender, ethnicity, and immigrant status are used by employers to divide workers. Dan Giloth of the Day Labor Organizing Project says: "The day labor agencies follow immigrant neighborhoods. Black neighborhoods are completely shut out. The companies discriminate by gender and by race. The African American and white workers get frustrated, because they show up earlier and earlier, but get passed over.

"What this does structurally is to divide immigrant workers from African American, white and Puerto Rican workers, so there is this real friction. Sometimes the workers buy into the employers' argument that African Americans, whites, and Puerto Ricans aren't good workers. In part the immigrants are 'good workers' because they don't complain about their hours. So African American, white, and Puerto Rican workers start to resent these workers."

DLOP tries to overcome this divide simply by getting immigrant and non-immigrant workers to talk to each other, says Giloth. "You've got to get people together and get them to tell stories. You can't really do it with high-minded rhetoric about unity. You have to find whatever common ground there is—and usually there is quite a bit around unpaid hours. You've got to hook people into the fight together. Once they've gone through something like a direct action or press conference, there tends to be a certain camaraderie, and that's one of the things we've learned. Don't try to persuade them out of their prejudices, but commit them to this action with that person."

DLOP has also filed EEOC complaints against temp agencies for discriminating against certain classes of workers. One of the temp agencies, Trojan, had to close down after a disgruntled African American dispatcher quit and took the company's records to DLOP. In other cases DLOP has trained salters to do civil rights testing. Giloth explains: "We choose people by race or gender, train them, organize evidence of violations, and develop class actions."

Working with Unions

When workers come to the office who want to organize into a union, as often happens, the Latino Union refers them to the Chicago Federation of Labor or to the appropriate union. Relations between the unions and the Latino Union, however, have not always been smooth. Some unions have seen the Latino Union as organizing cut-rate workers. But Landaverde says that when a union asks for a Social Security number, or insists the worker go to a GED class, or demands a $500 initiation fee, it is excluding many day laborers.

The Latino Union looks for opportunities to collaborate with the unions. For example, says Aranda, often employers whose workers are on strike will try to replace them with day laborers. "We had a situation with the Teamsters," she says, "where the company went to the day laborers to find replacement workers to do garbage collection.

"But an important part of our democratically run workers center is the educational program. While the workers are waiting, they can receive education, such as ESL classes, talks about their rights as workers, and get information about ongoing workers' struggles. So through our education program, we informed them about the Teamsters strike.

"We didn't have anyone cross the Teamster picket lines. Once they knew, they really felt solidarity with the terms the Teamsters were asking for."

The Day Labor Organizing Project

ACCORDING TO DAN GILOTH, an organizer for the Day Labor Organizing Project at the San Lucas Workers Center in Chicago, until workers centers began organizing, "there was no enforcement around racial and gender discrimination, unpaid overtime, illegal fees. They figured out that nobody's watching." The workforce DLOP organizes is diverse, about 60 percent Latino immigrants, 35 percent African American, and 5 percent white or Puerto Rican.

Day labor is, of course, unstable. Maria Gonzales, a former day laborer who is now a member of SEIU Local 880, explains, "They can be sent anywhere. It can be garment, toys, candy, the Chicago Auto Show. They go to the offices on a daily basis. At times they get sent to work for a week or a month, and other times they get sent to work for a day and then don't get work until the following week or are never sent to work again."

The Project uses "salters" to dig up information about abuses by the temp agencies. Gonzalez, who volunteers with DLOP, explains, "We give the workers a stipend to go to agencies where they aren't known, to ask for work. They go as worker-detectives, and that is how we have gathered a lot of information.

"Sometimes they even get a camera to take pictures; they've brought reports that the bathrooms aren't working, or that it's not a factory but an empty and unhealthy warehouse.

"Even if they don't get sent to work, they still bring us reports about the agency—if the agency discriminates against women, or what ages they prefer to send to work. Each time they go as a detective, they get $30."

DLOP has used this information to force audits of six day labor agencies, has won over $200,000 because of illegal charges for transportation, and has even shut down some abusive agencies.

DLOP also does "hits" on agencies to bring a lot of pressure to bear quickly. At the Trojan Labor agency, one of the worst violators, says Giloth, "they were charging people 3.5 times the state limit that can be charged for transportation to the worksite. The state limit was three percent of gross—at minimum wage that would be $1.25. But this agency was charging $4-$5 to get to the worksite, and they were making people sign a waiver that they were not hurt, signed at the beginning of the day, only in English. 'I agree to waive my right to state cap on what I can be charged on transportation. I agree I didn't get hurt.'

"Legally it wouldn't stand up, but it was psychological. We sent in about 40 community people and demanded a meeting with the owner." Because of the community mobilization, "the owner dropped the transportation fee from $4 to $1.25 and dropped the waiver. We won some things early on that gave us some credibility.

"Our general plan for these actions is:
- Take over the office.
- Get the owner on the phone, or demand to meet with him, then or in 24 hours.
- Bring community leaders in to support a negotiating committee of workers.
- If they blow us off, hit their client companies."

Giloth argues that it can be more effective to hit a high-profile client company—those who are using the temp agency's services. "Very often workers work, and the day labor company says, 'The client company didn't send us your hours.' They tell the worker, 'you have to get the paperwork.' They try to fatigue the worker into giving up, and even if it works only one in ten times, they get a lot of profit.

"Ron's day labor agency was working at Marshall Field. We went to Ron's and they blew us off, so we took 60 people and we got inside Marshall Field's Human Resources office. We demanded to speak with their general manager, and after some resistance he came down. He got on the phone to Ron's, and he transferred all our pressure and anger and noise to Ron's: 'Why are people working here and not being paid?' We made him the good guy. Needless to say, those people got paid within an hour." Checks that had been lost for months were suddenly found.

Stopping Scabs

DLOP has helped several Chicago unions stop temp agencies from providing scabs. In one case, the Project and the United Electrical Workers worked together to investigate a day labor agency that was sending scabs to break a UE strike. As it turned out, the agency didn't have a valid license and was overcharging for transportation. The UE organized a protest at the agency and threatened to take legal action over the violations. The agency, afraid of publicity and legal action, stopped providing scabs.

The Project has also trained unions on how to "salt" an agency, that is, to send in volunteers to seek jobs there and look for dirt. On one occasion two locals were on strike at the same time. Giloth explains: "We worked with them to train salters. The Teamsters and UE sent salters into the agencies that were doing the scabbing, but they cross-salted. They couldn't go into the agency that was breaking their own strike, because they would be recognized when they were sent to work, so UE members went to the agencies being used to break Teamster strikes, and Teamsters went to the agencies being used to break UE strikes."

Gonzáles explains how organizers also dissuade workers from scabbing: "We go to the temp agencies and we tell the workers that if they get hurt working as scabs, no one is going to defend them. The workers on strike are defending their jobs, and if an outsider comes in, well, there have been a lot of problems. People get beat up, or worse things happen. No organization is going to help them if they are scabbing."

As a result of its help for the unions, the unions have also helped the Day Labor Organizing Project. Giloth notes, "Unions helped us defend the Illinois day labor law when it came under attack. They also helped to pass a local ordinance supporting day laborers, and signed letters of support." DLOP helped to draft that precedent-setting day labor ordinance.

Thinking longer-term, DLOP would like to see a code of conduct for temp agencies. They would pressure clients to use only agencies that had signed the code.

Resources

For a list of 133 workers centers and their contact information, compiled by Janice Fine, go to the Troublemaker's section of www.labornotes.org.
• National Day Laborer Organizing Network, which includes workers centers around the country. www.ndlon.org. Includes links to research on day laborers. Information in English and Spanish about starting a day laborers workers center at www.ndlon.org/issues.htm.
• Janice Fine, *Building a New American Community at the Edge of the Dream: Immigrant Worker Centers*. Economic Policy Institute, $17.95. 800-374-4844. www.epi.net. Published spring 2005.
• Articles by Jennifer Gordon, founder and former executive director of the Workplace Project in New York: "Immigrants Fight the Power," *The Nation*, January 3, 2000. "We Make the Road by Walking: Immigrant Workers and the Struggle for Social Change," *Harvard Civil Rights-Civil Liberties Law Review* (1995).
• "Organizing, advocacy, and member power. A critical reflection," by Steve Jenkins. *Working USA* 2002, Vol. 6, No. 2, 33 pp. Request an email copy stevezjenkins@yahoo.com.

Action Questions

1. Is there a workers center in your city? What types of workers (by industry or sector) does it represent? If this center represents immigrant workers, what countries or regions are they from?

2. Do any of your members come from these countries or regions? Or do they at least speak the same language?

3. What types of campaigns is this workers center involved with? Are there campaigns, in either your community or industry, that you could work on jointly?

4. Does your union have any resources to offer the workers center, either in general or for particular campaigns? For example, could the union help by turning people out for protests? Or by providing office space or use of copiers or printing equipment?

5. Would it be useful to hold a hospitality day and invite workers center staff and members to come to your union hall to meet people over lunch or dinner, in order to build good will?

6. Could your union or the central labor council work with the workers center on a strategy for dealing with the recruitment of replacement workers during strikes?

Authors

BETSY ESCH teaches history at the University of Illinois at Champaign-Urbana.

DAN LA BOTZ wrote the first edition of *A Troublemaker's Handbook*. He is an activist, teacher, and labor historian based in Cincinnati, where he writes frequently for *Labor Notes*. He was a founding member of Teamsters for a Democratic Union in the 1970s and wrote a book about that movement, as well as books on unions in Mexico and Indonesia.

SARA MERSHA is executive director of Direct Action for Rights and Equality in Providence, Rhode Island.

TEÓFILO REYES, a former director of Labor Notes, is an organizer for the Transnationals Information Exchange, which brings together worker activists in North and South America, Europe, Africa, and Asia. He facilitated the formation of the National Coalition for Dignity and Amnesty for Undocumented Workers and serves on the board of the Coalition for Justice in the Maquiladoras and the Executive Committee of Labor Notes.

Notes

1. Janice Fine, "Non-Union, Low-Wage Workers Are Finding a Voice as Immigrant Workers Centers Grow," *Labor Notes*, August 2003. Fine directs the Economic Policy Institute's National Immigrant Workers Centers Study. She was interviewed by N. Renuka Uthappa for this chapter in August 2004.

18. Reform Caucuses and Running for Office

by Aaron Brenner

THIS CHAPTER IS ABOUT REVITALIZING A LOCAL UNION. It is for members who are dissatisfied with their leaders and feel they can do a better job. It tells how to build influence and contest for power in the local.

This chapter has two important lessons. First, getting elected is not the ultimate goal. The goal is increasing the power of workers to fight management at the workplace and beyond. This may or may not require running for office. If it does, winning and keeping control of a local works best when it arises from and then encourages a fight with the boss. Second, democracy is power. This is not just a moral issue. Members' control of their union improves their ability to confront management and win. This second lesson is so important that *Labor Notes* published an entire book about it, *Democracy Is Power: Rebuilding Unions from the Bottom Up* (see next page).

The two lessons are mutually reinforcing, as the groups discussed here demonstrate. These groups organize against management first. They want to accomplish things at work—better pay, more control over their work—but their officials, or something about the way their union operates, is in the way. So they run for office

Why Democracy?

Union democracy is essential for the simple reason that members have the fundamental right to control their own organization. It's their union, so they have the right to run it.

But democracy is essential for another reason: because democratic unions are more effective for building power in the workplace and in society. Why is this so? Because members are the ultimate source of a union's power, and democracy is the best way to galvanize members.

Members who have a voice and a vote are more likely to take the union seriously, offer suggestions, and answer leaders' calls for mobilization. They are more likely to develop into new leaders, and broader leadership means more good ideas percolating through the union, less reliance on a few increasingly burdened people, and greater capacity to inspire members to action. With broader leadership, collective decision-making, and greater participation, democratic unions are more likely to fight intelligently, with more energy, and with deeper commitment than undemocratic unions. Even with its mistakes and inefficiencies, democracy is potentially more powerful than any other arrangement.

True, democracy takes work. Most workers aren't storming the union hall doors, seeking democracy for democracy's sake. If someone else could do it for us, if a benevolent-dictator leader could pound the table and get us a good contract, most of us would prefer that route. The problem is that no union leader is powerful alone. Officials have no leverage against employers if they cannot mobilize members and their supporters in the community to disrupt business as usual. The "let George do it" model simply does not work.

So what is union democracy? At a minimum, it is a set of written rights and rules that establish procedures and institutions through which members run their union. Rights include, among others, the right to free speech, to free assembly, to participate in union activity, to vote on contracts and union policies, to protection for minority groups, and to run for office. Rules regulate elections, meetings, financial disclosure, information distribution, and debate. Rights and rules allow member participation and leadership accountability.

Making democracy real means more than honoring those rights and living by those rules, however. Unions can go further by encouraging a democratic culture. They can open the union paper to opposing views, sponsor debates on issues, give all members access to membership contact information so it is easier to campaign for change, and encourage members to challenge leaders and offer alternative ideas. Rules may need to be changed to create ways for members to exercise leadership from below. This could include stewards' councils and officers who stay on the job.

Building democracy is not easy. But it can be done, as the examples in this chapter illustrate. Our book *Democracy Is Power* (see box on next page) has more.

or campaign to change the bylaws. At the same time, they recognize that the best way to build shop floor power is to involve as many members as possible in actions that challenge management. This builds their group's influence within the union and helps them get elected. So, by acting as shop floor leaders even before they are elected and by leading workers against their employers, these activists increase participation, democratize the union, win local office, and increase members' capacity to win on the job and in the community.

There are no simple guidelines for when to start a local reform group. In the most obvious cases, incumbent leaders are uninterested in or hostile to building an aggressive, active, inclusive union. That's why you need a group. In other cases, local officers might just need support, new blood, or better ideas. In such cases, you can still build a network of active members to help the union take on employers, but you are not contesting to run the local. Our focus here is on those situations where the union cannot be changed without new leadership.

The examples in this chapter offer suggestions for how to start a caucus, how to run a contract campaign from the rank and file, how to fight for or against union rule changes and restructuring, how to run for office, how to overcome a trusteeship, and how to build a union presence on the job before you win office.

Starting a Rank-and-File Group

IF YOU AND YOUR CO-WORKERS don't have enough power on the job, and your local officials are useless or worse, a good example to learn from is Teamsters for a Democratic Union (TDU). For nearly 30 years, TDU has fought to build a rank-and-file movement for a stronger Teamsters union. Although TDU is a national group, its strength lies in members who organize themselves at the level of the local union, sometimes as rank and filers and sometimes winning office. TDUers played a key role in making sure the government's 1989 intervention to oversee the union led to one-member-one-vote elections for national officers. Even after the TDU-backed Ron Carey slate took International office in 1992, the group kept building from below. Its network of experienced members lay behind the union's impressive victory in the 1997 UPS strike, and today it enables rank-and-file members to keep fighting to take back the union from the hapless leadership of James P. Hoffa.

We talked to TDU national organizer Ken Paff for advice about how to start a local group or caucus that can lead a fight to strengthen the union. Paff has been a labor activist for more than 30 years. He is most familiar with the Teamsters, but his suggestions apply equally well in other unions. Our focus here is on actions to take within the union, but equally important for building your group is on-the-job organizing. You will find many suggestions for creative actions that rank and filers and stewards can lead later in this chapter and in Chapter 3.

Analyze the Power of the Local

"The first thing to do is learn your local," says Paff. If the local represents just one plant or office, map out how many workers are in each department and what they do. Which workers have the most power to disrupt operations? Which workers have the most opportunity to meet other workers?

If the local has members at multiple locations, put together a list of those locations. You have a legal right under the Labor-Management

Essential Reading: *Democracy Is Power*

Democracy is vital to rebuilding the labor movement. Not only does this book explain why, it tells you how.

Democracy Is Power describes democratic approaches to contracts, grievances, communications, and the relationships between leaders and members. It explains ways to instill a democratic union culture that promotes participation and solidarity. And it offers guidelines for the practical parts of democracy, like elections, bylaws, and holding good meetings.

• Why does democracy matter? Why do some unionists say it doesn't?
• Where does apathy come from and how do we overcome it?
• What makes a good membership meeting?
• How to put democracy to work in bargaining and on the job
• Being effective at union meetings, from the floor
• Election procedures, union structures, and bylaws: Which ones work? Suggested bylaws
• How inclusion and equality aid democracy
• Once you win: pulling together a leadership team, rebuilding the union around the members, dealing with opposition
• Mergers: Is bigger better? Local autonomy vs. national coordination
• What's democratic in international elections and conventions?
• Leading a membership meeting, including hints for using Robert's Rules of Order
• Simplified Rules of Order.

To order *Democracy Is Power: Rebuilding Unions from the Bottom Up,* go to www.labornotes.org/bookshelf, or email business@labornotes.org. Call 313-842-6262, fax 313-842-0227, or send $17 plus $4 shipping to 7435 Michigan Ave., Detroit, MI 48210.

Reporting and Disclosure Act to review all the contracts on file at the union hall, and those will tell you which units are in the local and their wage rates and contract language. To review contracts, you might have to make a written request to the union for an appointment.

"You can also look at the LM-2," says Paff. "This is a financial report filed annually by all U.S. union locals (except those composed exclusively of public workers) with the Department of Labor. They are filed by March 31 for the previous year. The LM-2 gives local size, when the next election is, how much money the local has, officers' salaries. It's easy to do and helps you learn the ropes about the union." To get an LM-2 for your local, go to http://union-reports.dol.gov/olmsWeb/docs/formspg.html or to www.biglabor.com.

Learn your local bylaws and be familiar with your international union's constitution. If you need help interpreting these documents, contact the Association for Union Democracy (see page 280).

"Using this information," says Paff, "try to assess where you stand as a potential political force in the local. If you are a handful of people, you'll have to reach out to others before you can take any action. Who has the clout in the local? Is there one shop or department that is bigger than all the rest? Is your group well represented in that shop or department? Do you have any stewards in your group? Are stewards elected? Are members of your group popular? Do they know everyone? Do they know the different cliques on the job? Can they speak to a range of people? Does your group have the potential to involve all the different nationalities represented?"

Intervening in a Union Meeting

One of your group's first "political" activities may be intervening in a local meeting. People who care about the union are likely to be there, and those are the people you want to meet. Participating at the meeting can be a regular activity for your group, a way to get and keep people involved. And by intervening, your group can shake things up and get political debate going in the local.

"In many local unions, meetings are poorly attended, because members feel nothing happens there," says Paff. "Sometimes a rank-and-file group can start 'making things happen' at the meetings, and in the process draw people to come. In a Teamsters local of 3,000 members, for example, 60 members might normally be there. A group of 10 can have an impact, if they are organized.

"The first time you go to a meeting, however, don't just get up and give a speech challenging the leadership. Listen to what other members are saying. What are their concerns? Maybe there are others who agree with you. Make contacts. You can make a proposal later. It's not the first step. The first thing is outreach. You have to have a small group, even a few members, working together.

"Talk to people one-on-one. Look them in the eye. You can't organize with just an email list. You must be with people and talk with them to get them involved."

A common mistake many groups make is to have one spokesperson, says Paff. "We like to have several

TDU has long fought for fairer pensions. Above, members of the Central States Pension Improvement Committee met at the 2003 TDU convention. At right, TDU helped Kroger bakery workers in Detroit who were denied pensions.

people be prepared to speak. Make a plan. If you are going to make a motion, say on a contract proposal, have it written down so you can refer to it if you get flustered. Everyone should have a copy of the motion. Have a pre-meeting and talk things over. Who will make the motion? Who will second it? Have multiple people ready to do both.

"Advertise what you are going to do in advance. There's no advantage to surprise. Talk to members before the meeting; draw them in. Get things out to the members, not only to make your group transparent, but also to make union meetings that way. Tell people there will be a motion on the pension plan. Ask them to come support the motion. Put it out in writing. Get them to sign a petition in support of the motion."

Once you speak or make a motion in a union meeting, you can talk to people afterwards and ask them what they thought. Look for people outside your group, in workplaces where you don't yet have contacts. Invite them to a meeting. Ask them to bring their workmates.

"Take names," says Paff. "I don't know how many times I've heard a member say, 'I gave them my name and phone number.' You want *their* name, address, and phone number. Take other information, too, if you can get it: their shop, shift, days off. Keep building that information. Everyone you have met, talked to at the plant gate, who has donated money, who has bought raffle tickets. Keep this information. You are building a list that is going to be critically important, and you may want to computerize this information."

Building the Group

As you establish a core group, learn about the local, and do outreach, you will learn about the issues that concern members, that are positive, that you can be out front on and involve other people in. You may want to pick an issue and put out a leaflet describing the problem and how you think it can be solved. See Chapter 3 for do's and don'ts of establishing a shop floor newsletter. Many reform caucuses, including ones described in this chapter, have made a name for themselves by having a regular publication. The successful newsletters always concentrate on what's going on at work rather than just discussing union politics.

Think of *actions* that can build your group's influence in the union. Many of these can take place at work, where your group can talk to members one on one. See, for example, in Chapter 3, how TDUers in Local 556 built a member-to-member network and fought management harassment. A campaign to support a particular grievance might be a way to solve an on-the-job problem and build your group. Use flyers, petitions, meetings, buttons, and group visits to the supervisor.

Local TDU chapters sometimes hold classes on issues that the union is not addressing, such as rights under the Family Medical Leave Act. "This shows that you can do things without holding office," says Paff. "You can hold a class on how to be on a negotiating team, which flows into having a rank-and-file negotiating team. You can push to change the bylaws to have the negotiating team be elected, and then run to be on it." If you do not have these skills, you can find help (see Resources at the end of this chapter).

A common TDU activity is a campaign to change local bylaws. You might want the right to elect stewards, for example. This will involve writing the bylaws amendment, getting signatures in support, and submitting it to the local. Each step is an opportunity to organize support. Get members to sign petitions, distribute flyers, ask people to come to union meetings, and organize carpools to get them to the meetings.

Activities like these build a rank-and-file group's confidence, expand its network of contacts and supporters, test its strength, and give it a reputation for effectiveness. They also help keep the group together, says Paff. "And that's very important for sustaining a movement and giving it a visible face where people can turn when they have questions, because there will be ups and downs. The local group should be an active force, an educational force, not just an election slate."

The idea is to get members moving, test reactions, do some education, find allies, perhaps change some rules, and win some victories. If your group is successful in these steps, you may well be strong enough to contest for office as well.

Transit Workers Caucus Runs Contract Campaign

RANK-AND-FILE ACTIVISTS do not have to control their local to run a contract campaign and shape the outcome of negotiations. This is what members of the New Directions caucus did inside the 38,500-member Transport Workers Union Local 100 in New York City in 1999.

Through nearly 15 years of organizing the New Directions group had built influence, pushing to make the local more militant and more democratic. By 1998, the group was strong enough that it nearly won control of the local. Its candidate for president, Tim Schermerhorn, a subway train driver, won more than 49 percent of the vote, and its candidates for the board won 21 of the 45 slots.

This success gave the group influence in a union that has the power to bring New York City to a standstill. Most Local 100 members work for the Metropolitan Transportation Authority, operating and maintaining subway and bus systems. They include drivers, conductors, car cleaners and maintainers, mechanics, token booth clerks, track maintainers, and station cleaners and repairers. About three-quarters are African American and Latino.

After its election successes in 1998, New Directions returned its focus to fighting the Transit Authority over the 1999 contract. "What New Directions did during the contract campaign was take the focus away from the union and put it on the TA," says Marc Kagan, who was a train car maintenance worker. "We did not say, 'The union is about to sell you out.' We said, 'We want to fight the TA harder.' If you set the standard for how to fight, it forces the leadership to tail along just to hold the membership, and it forces them to give you certain openings."

"Everything we did in 1999 was based on previous work," says Steve Downs, a train driver who also sat on the union executive board. "We had already intervened in several contract campaigns, only this time we had more influence. We pushed the idea that we had to start a year before the contract expired and take a no-givebacks position and educate around it. Our slogan was 'End a Generation of Givebacks.' We suspected Willie James, the local president, would not fight. Yes, we could put forward contract demands, but demands are easy. What is the strategy to win them? That's where we felt the leadership would fail.

"We thought the best tactic was to let the leadership know that a concessionary contract would be rejected by the members. The next election would be in 2000, so the leadership's future depended on the contract they negotiated."

New Directions' no-concessions message was popular, given the union's recent history. "Workers saw the 1996 contract as a fiasco," says Kagan. "It had a one-year wage freeze and it instituted workfare, which let welfare workers do car cleaning in exchange for their welfare checks. Workers were angry, too, at the TA's duplicity. It had demanded the wage freeze to deal with its supposed revenue shortfall, but right after we received our lump sum payment the news came out that the TA had a big budget surplus. So it was payback time."

Mobilization vs. Public Relations

The contract was set to expire December 15, during the holiday shopping season and right before the huge millennium celebration—a crucial time for subways and buses that gave the union maximum leverage. For his version of a contract campaign, in the spring James contracted with Hank Sheinkopf, a Democratic Party consultant, to run a public relations campaign for the union. James held a referendum to approve a special assessment of $60 per member to pay for the PR push. New Directions opposed the assessment, arguing that the campaign was too limited and moved the focus away from mobilizing members on the job and toward influencing political hotshots, which wouldn't work.

"We won and the assessment was defeated," says Downs. Still, James did not give up on public relations. "Late in the summer, he contacted Corporate Campaign, Inc., headed by Ray Rogers," says Downs. "Rogers met with New Directions to make sure we were on board. We told him we would support a corporate campaign depending on how it was organized: it should be run by the division officers and the executive board members,

Members of the New Directions caucus picketed outside union president Willie James's fundraiser in April 2000.

not just the top officers. That would give it more than public relations value. It would help us organize members to fight. He agreed. He said he wanted demonstrations and members involved. But when the proposal came before the board, it did not include any of the things we had pushed for, so we opposed it and lost.

Rogers ran a PR campaign, but it had little impact.

"As our alternative to the PR campaign, we said the local should organize actions on the job, big demonstrations, slowdowns, strike preparations, and links with other city unions whose contracts were expiring or had expired, to have a common front against the city and the TA. There had not been a local-wide meeting since the early 1960s." Mass meetings would fire up the members, prepare them for any actions, and send a message to the Transit Authority.

New Directions members did not merely call for Willie James to implement their strategy. They put the strategy into practice on the job. One way was through their newspaper. For years the group had published *Hell on Wheels*, a newspaper that members looked to for information they were not getting from the union: coverage of grievances, negotiations, protests.

"We put out the paper more often during the contract campaign, and we frequently distributed leaflets," says J.P. Patafio, a bus driver and later a *Hell on Wheels* editorial board member. "We had contacts in each barn. We'd meet with them and they would distribute the paper in the barn. Within each barn, we'd make sure to cover each tour [shift]. We encouraged them to put it in people's hands, not just leave it on tables, and make sure that members were discussing and talking about it. We knew the leadership would have their own propaganda, so we had to get the information out about the productivity and health care givebacks the TA was demanding." Money for printing came from New Directions members and supporters within the union.

Another New Directions tool was on-the-job action. "We had a long-range approach that focused on generating activity in the workplace," says Schermerhorn. "Most of the activity came from RTO [Rapid Transit Operations], the folks who run the trains. That's where most of the New Directions people were. Besides talking up the contract in small meetings, we would try to start slowdowns and job actions around other issues. We would give people ideas. 'This is how you slow down the train and this is how you use the rules to cover yourself.'

"We were doing this for years, long before the contract campaign. That way people could learn how to do the actions, know all the rules so they could get away with it, and get better at it. As you get closer to the contract expiration, people see that they are affecting the system. They start to get excited and it generates a momentum of its own."

Using its influence on the board, disarray among the officials, and the restiveness of the rank and file, New

Directions got the union to hold a series of demonstrations in October and November at MTA headquarters and at the governor's New York City office. "New Directions built the demonstrations and they were huge, probably more than 10,000 at the MTA," says Downs. "James was drowned out with chants of 'Strike! Strike! Strike!' We also used the dates of the rallies as days for major disruptions on the subway. We organized slowdowns, which were uneven. But they happened, and they were noticed by the MTA and the membership. The *Daily News* reported a spike in late trains and other problems we created as part of the slowdown."

"The leadership had not an inkling of how many people would show up to the demonstrations," says Kagan. "We knew. We worked. And the anger of the membership forced the leaders to agree to our demand for a mass meeting. It helped, too, that there were splits among the top leaders, so we could put together a majority of the board on some issues. Not on big issues like the contract or a strike, but on smaller issues like holding a mass meeting."

Mass militancy provoked a response from Mayor Rudolph Giuliani. Strikes by public workers are illegal in New York, but that wasn't enough for a control-obsessed mayor worried that threats of a transit strike would disrupt holiday shopping and the millennium celebration. He secured an injunction promising to arrest and fine $25,000 any transit worker who even mentioned the word "strike." "That definitely put a chill on things with some members," says Schermerhorn.

Mass Meeting

By early December, it was clear that the leadership would not build for the mass meeting, scheduled for December 14, the day before the contract expired. "It was up to us," says Downs. "We convinced enough people on the executive board to force James to put two New Directions members on staff to work full-time to organize the meeting." To accommodate workers on different shifts, there were actually two meetings, in the morning and in the evening.

"The turnout was huge, probably 4,000 at the morning meeting and more in the evening," says Downs. "This was the first time in a generation there had been local-wide meetings. At the morning meeting, Vice-president Gil Rodriguez got up to announce that Mayor Giuliani had gotten an injunction against the local and he was ordered to read it to the meeting, serving everyone with the injunction. He read the injunction, stayed for some discussion, and then left. We took over and ran the meeting, which we had not been prepared for. Perhaps we should have been prepared. It was very chaotic. People were incensed. The sentiment was, 'Forget Giuliani.'"

"People came to vote to strike, even if they weren't sure they actually wanted to walk out," says Schermerhorn. "There was some disagreement among New Directions people about what to do. Making a strike motion could lead to arrest under the injunction, and we knew we could not do much from jail. Having a leader arrested would feel like a defeat, but I felt like not having a strike vote would be a worse defeat. So I ran up to the fourth balcony and made the motion: if the TA made no acceptable offer in the next day, we should strike." The voice vote was unanimous.

Schermerhorn had publicly violated Giuliani's injunction. And, interviewed by CNN outside the hall, he violated it several times more. "The only reason I wasn't picked up by the police," he says, "was that the police were still without a contract themselves, and they didn't want to arrest me. A detective told me that when they sent him to my work location three days in a row after the strike meeting. That's not the kind of solidarity you can expect from the police."

"Between the morning and evening meetings, New

Some Legal Rights Inside the Union

Your Rights at Union Meetings. You have the right to attend union meetings, to feel safe and secure while you are there, and to address the meeting, subject to the rules of parliamentary procedure. If the chair rules you out of order, you have a right to appeal the ruling to the body, and have the vice-chair step in to count the vote.

Your Right To Form a Caucus. Union caucuses are not dual union movements. They are not illegal. They are not disloyal. A person cannot be removed from a union position because he or she is a member of a caucus.

The reason is that a caucus is not a separate union seeking to come in and represent workers to the employer. A caucus supports the union and works to strengthen it. It does not seek itself to bargain with management. Rather, it seeks to make the union do that job better.

You have an absolute right to hold a caucus meeting or demonstration. You have an absolute right to picket the union hall. You may bar hostile persons from your meeting, including even union members.

Do not be deterred by threats of libel or slander suits because of something you said in a meeting or a leaflet. In the union context, to prove a case against you it must be shown that when you said it or wrote it you knew it was false or probably false.

But be careful about statements you make. It is better to discuss issues, not personalities. Though you may be protected legally, irresponsible statements will not move things forward.

Directions board members went to the Hyatt hotel where the negotiations were taking place," says Downs. "We insisted that James leave the negotiations and refuse to negotiate with the gun of an injunction to our heads. We lost the vote on the board and James kept talking."

"I went to the evening meeting," says Kagan. "The officials didn't even show up. So New Directions ran the meeting. Steve comes out and holds up the injunction. The members shouted, 'Rip it up! Rip it up!' and he ripped it up. That was a great moment. Then we opened up the floor. There was discussion and then we made another strike motion, which passed overwhelmingly. Then we closed down the meeting. We kept hearing rumors of a settlement and we wanted to be at the board meeting to keep James from passing the settlement without us. In retrospect, that was a mistake. We all should have marched across town to the Hyatt. That would have put pressure on James not to sell out."

Downs agrees. "We just went to the union hall to wait for the outcome of negotiations. Looking back, it would have been better for everyone at the mass meeting to talk about what we could do. Then we could have marched to the negotiations or into the subway and prepared people in the case of a strike. I don't think a wildcat was feasible, but we could have been out there to intensify the slowdown in the final hours of negotiations."

Long- and Short-Run Momentum

James reached a settlement with the TA early the next morning. It included serious concessions on work rules and health care. New Directions board members voted against the settlement, but lost, and the proposal went to the members in a mail ballot.

New Directions launched a "vote no" campaign. "The money was more than we expected," says Downs, "but health benefits and job conditions were major concessions that still haunt us."

New Directions kicked off the "vote no" campaign with a march across the Brooklyn Bridge that same day. Officers from the Track Maintenance Division, which was chaired by Roger Toussaint, a New Directions member, had gotten a parade permit to march across the bridge that day in case the local was on strike. The previous afternoon at the board meeting during negotiations, "Toussaint had called on James to refuse to negotiate with the injunction hanging over our heads," says Kagan. "He said the union should call in all the expressions of solidarity from every union in the city and get them to join transit workers in a march across the bridge to surround City Hall. This big show of solidarity would give us a gun, too, against the city's injunction. Of course, James and his supporters on the board dismissed the idea of breaking off negotiations. So New Directions held the march, which was pretty small, just New Directions and its strongest supporters. We passed out our first 'vote no' leaflets."

Despite New Directions' opposition, the contract was approved two to one. "People felt we could not get anything better," says Downs. "The Christmas season had passed. The good leverage was gone. And they were right, in a way. We did not have a good answer to the question, 'Okay, we vote no. Then what?' We had lost the momentum."

New Directions had lost the momentum of the contract campaign, but its organization was as strong as ever. "People felt sure that we won better wages in the contract because of the activities of the membership, which we led," says Downs. "The MTA thought things would get out of hand and that James could not control the situation, and people might walk off the job. That was our leverage."

New Directions' contract campaign boosted its prospects in the long run. "The mass meeting was a turning point," says Patafio. "The leadership didn't show up. We ran the stage. From then on, it was only a question of time before we won the local."

"People saw us as the leaders of the contract fight," says Kagan. "You have to be seen as someone who can run the union, not just as someone who can criticize. During the campaign, we filled that role. The message that came through was, 'We would be doing this job better—we would have gotten more—if we were in charge.'"

Less than a year after ratifying the contract, Local 100 members voted overwhelmingly for the New Directions slate headed by Roger Toussaint.

New Directions' victory resulted from years of persistent hard work, culminating in the 1999 contract campaign. Lessons from their work include:

• A regular publication with news members couldn't get anywhere else established the value of the group. Handing it out was a way to talk to members and get new people involved.

• The long-term focus on activity on the job trained large numbers of workers in using their leverage where it counted.

• The group agitated around not just a set of demands for the contract, but a strategy for how to win those demands through rank-and-file action.

• The group's contract campaign slogan addressed members' major concern—concessions.

• The group tried to involve rank and filers in every aspect of the campaign, mobilizing for demonstrations, pushing for on-the-job actions and strike preparation, proposing solidarity with other unions, and demanding a local-wide meeting.

• The group used its numbers on the executive board to pressure officials, getting them to call the first local-wide meeting in a generation and forcing board votes where officials had to go on record.

• The group did what the union should have done during the contract campaign, getting information out to members, building the demonstrations and local-wide meeting, organizing slowdowns, running the local-wide meeting, and holding a strike vote.

• The group should have been better prepared to deal with the local-wide meeting and its aftermath.

Carpenters' Grassroots Rebellion

DURING THE 1990s top leaders of the United Brotherhood of Carpenters (UBC) restructured their union from a network of small- and medium-sized locals to a series of large regional councils. Leaders said they needed to consolidate power to match the regional and national contractors who have come to dominate the construction business. The consolidation, they said, would improve the union's ability to bargain and to organize, especially among the immigrants hired by the growing portion of non-union contractors.

As a result of the restructuring, locals lost virtually all their power. Locals could no longer spend money on officer salaries or on attorneys, only on clerical staff. In essence, all they could do was hold meetings and elect delegates to the regional councils, which now handled contract negotiations, grievances, and job referrals. Each regional council's executive secretary-treasurer had the power to hire and fire all business agents, organizers, and representatives. Members no longer voted on their contracts or directly elected their representatives.

Carpenters around the country were furious, but in New England, home to 27,000 union carpenters in 26 locals, they were furious and organized. A group came together to resist the restructuring and restore their democratic rights, calling themselves Carpenters for a Democratic Union. So far, their successes include the restoration of members' right to ratify their contracts and the election of their candidate to head New England's regional council. Here's how they did it.

Building on Local Tradition

Carpenters Local 33 in Boston has an active membership. "We attend meetings and know what's happening in the union," says former steward Jim McDermott. "We have active stewards. We get high turnout for elections. We picket when a job doesn't pay the prevailing wage. It is a historical thing. We have big market share in the area, built by guys who came before us. We want to preserve that."

"The union argued that we had to go regional to counter the contractors' regionalism," says Michael Cranmer, a carpenter in Local 33. "That made sense to me. But I questioned why it was necessary for rank-and-file carpenters to lose their right to negotiate their contracts and select the leaders who represent them."

The creation of the New England Regional Council of Carpenters (NERCC) threatened to cripple Local 33's activist traditions by undermining its decision-making power. It also threatened carpenters' wages and working conditions. Long-time elected business agents, organizers, and representatives were removed and replaced by officials beholden to the new regional council executive secretary-treasurer, David Bergeron. These new officials controlled job referrals, contract negotiations, and grievances. They loosened rules to allow contractors to bring in carpenters from around the region rather than hire them from the local hiring hall. This increased travel for everyone and increased competition for jobs in Boston, where pay is higher. While it increased pay for carpenters who came from other areas to work in Boston, it forced Boston carpenters to leave the city to find work, where they received lower pay. The rules also meant that the members who mobilized to make sure a potential project was done with union labor were not necessarily the members who got the jobs. This set members against each other.

"The new rules create a divided loyalty," says McDermott. "Now carpenters are getting their jobs through contractors, instead of working out of the hall. That opens them up more to the influence of the contractor and less to the union.

"When word got out about the changes, a few of us, mostly stewards, met at a bar and talked about what we should do. We had all been active in local politics. We were not naïve. First, we all threw in a few bucks in case we needed a lawyer. Then, through word of mouth we got 50 or 60 people together. Those first few meetings were raucous; people vented. Then we came up with a plan for a group, Carpenters for a Democratic Union, with an executive board, a financial secretary, and a recording secretary." It was a volunteer group with no dues.

Soon, the group was too big to meet at a worksite, so they hired a hall to meet each week. "We had an evolving leadership," says Michael Cranmer. "We'd add one member from each of the locals that came on a regular basis. One person would be chosen by the group to lead each meeting. We used Robert's Rules of Order. We tried to conduct ourselves as we thought the union should be conducted."

The group talked to a lawyer and filed a complaint with the U.S. Department of Labor. The complaint claimed that since the regional council had taken over all the duties of the locals, it was required to hold direct elections for top officers, as the law requires of local unions. The Department of Labor rejected the argument, so CDU pursued a lawsuit, with Tom Harrington, a former Local 33 business agent, as the lead plaintiff. The Association for Union Democracy (see box, next page) helped CDU and filed a brief in the case.

Newsletter

The group started a newsletter called *CDU Update*, a one- or two-page flyer with news about CDU meetings, the lawsuit, and other CDU activities. "We'd run off a few hundred and hand them out at job sites," says McDermott. "We had pretty good relations with other trades, so it was not hard to get laborers or ironworkers to drop them off at other sites."

"We put together a petition calling for one member, one vote," says Susan Cranmer, a UBC member, CDU's first recording secretary, and Michael's wife. "We went to every local and every meeting. Usually somebody would know somebody from the local, who would ask the president to put us on the agenda. Then we addressed the membership, talked to the people going in, and got them to sign the petition. There are 26 locals in the region, and we hit most of them."

"At those meetings we would talk about changes in the council, the loss of our right to vote and our right to representation," says McDermott. "We made it clear we weren't against the locals' business agents. We argued that the locals should have the right to vote to keep him there. This was a big issue, since many BAs had been removed. We asked them to pass resolutions, sign the petition, and run delegates who would support our campaign for one member, one vote.

"The first few times we traveled, we took a bunch of people. We rented a bus to go to Springfield, Massachusetts. Other times it was just a caravan of cars. Sometimes we'd show up with 45 people and there would only be 20 members at the local meeting. So we decided to tone it down. We didn't want to appear like bullies from Boston. Just a few of us would go after that."

CDU also took its message to the public. "We marched in parades in South Boston, the St. Patrick's Day parade," says Susan Cranmer. "We talked to lots of labor leaders and politicians. We protested at the Carpenters' convention in Chicago."

"We had a sign campaign, like those political lawn signs," says McDermott. "We plastered the area. It was like a contest between the members to see who could get the most signs up and in the best locations. They were on bridges, overpasses, telephone poles, job sites. Some are still up, six years later."

To raise money CDU held a party with music and charged admission. The group also raffled off a pick-up truck. "I don't recommend that one," says Susan Cranmer. "The logistics of trying to get the dealer to sell the truck at a reasonable price and then sell the tickets was an all-out effort. It worked out, but we were lucky."

The group produced t-shirts and sweatshirts with slogans like "One Member One Vote" or " CDU: Union Carpenters Demand the Vote." "We did them in safety orange, so they could be worn as safety vests," says McDermott. "This was during the Big Dig [the huge tunnel construction in downtown Boston] so we sold a lot of them. We made two or five dollars on each. We also had signs and bumper stickers for the different trades within the union, 'Union Pile Drivers for Democracy,' 'Millwrights Demand the Vote.'"

Rank-and-File Resource: Association for Union Democracy

AUD is a nonprofit organization that promotes union democracy as a means of strengthening the labor movement. It provides education, legal assistance, and practical advice to members on their democratic rights to free speech, fair elections, due process, and, where appropriate, fair hiring. It reports on battles for democracy in its bimonthly *Union Democracy Review* and on its website, www.uniondemocracy.org.

Where necessary, AUD litigates to protect and expand members' rights. It encourages members to be active in the internal life of their unions. It gives special attention to unionists who are battling corruption and to workers of color and immigrants who face discrimination.

Here's an example of how AUD helps workers who have been forgotten by their leaders. In the spring of 2002, a group of New York City bus drivers who provide para-transit service for the elderly and disabled contacted AUD. Their union, Amalgamated Transit Union Local 1181, had not held a para-transit meeting for three years, and it did nothing to address workers' grievances, stop management's speed-up, or protect seniority rights.

AUD conducted a series of workshops on workers' rights and strategies for organizing against management and within the union. These strategies included a newsletter, petitions, building a rank-and-file coalition, and running for office.

Drawing on skills they learned from AUD, New York City para-transit bus drivers led a successful strike in the spring of 2004.

Combining the skills they learned at AUD with their own inventiveness and determination, the Drivers' Coalition got one of their members elected to the negotiating committee, saved the job of another member who was unfairly fired, and led a successful strike in the spring of 2004. During the strike, union officials did virtually nothing, but Drivers' Coalition members organized the picket lines, talked to the media, and reached out to other unions for support. Only a handful out of 1,000 drivers crossed the line. The strike won higher wages, a 401(k) plan, more paid time off, and the conversion of many part-time jobs to full-time.

Union members should contact AUD with questions about their democratic rights or when they need technical or legal assistance enforcing those rights. See Resources at the end of this chapter.

Going International

Through its website, its activities at the national convention, and word of mouth, CDU developed a small national reputation among carpenters upset about changes in their union. With AUD's help, CDU organized a national conference in Boston in 2000.

A hundred carpenters from reform groups in Boston, San Francisco, Atlanta, Philadelphia, Chicago, Tacoma, New York, and other cities came to share experiences and debate options. The attendees decided to form Carpenters for a Democratic Union International (CDUI) and elected a steering committee with representatives from each of the 13 regions attending.

So far, CDUI has been mostly a loose network of activists around the country. Several websites have been started to facilitate communication and debate among carpenter activists, including www.ranknfile.net, which reports on pro-democracy reform efforts, tracks the activities of UBC leaders, and provides links to sites of interest, including legal decisions affecting construction workers and UBC board minutes.

Working within the System

Soon after CDU's formation, members began attending regional council meetings. Delegates to the council are elected from the locals every three years. They elect the executive secretary-treasurer (EST), who wields virtually complete power in the region. When CDU began, about 50 of the 133 delegates also held appointed staff positions. Since they owed their jobs to the EST, they were unlikely to vote against him in the council.

At first, CDU had to stay outside. "We would go out and picket the meeting," says Michael Cranmer. "The regional council would hire police to prevent our getting too close. There was a bridge across the turnpike to the meeting hall, so we made sure all the delegates had to go through a gauntlet of us to get to the meeting. We were told we could not attend, but we petitioned. They invited one member to come down and speak to the delegate body."

It wasn't long before CDU got more members inside. "In 1998, a slot opened up for one of the delegates from Local 33," says Susan Cranmer. "There was an interim election and we won. The next year, there was an election for all 14 delegates from Local 33. We ran a slate and won all 14."

Local 33 activists then helped other locals elect pro-democracy delegates. "For the campaigns, we made posters and helped people write letters," says Susan Cranmer. "You can do mailings to the membership, so we made sure everyone had access to their local's list in a timely fashion and that they understood all the rules. We made sure that every member got letters from us and we made sure CDU members brought the delegate elections up at work and discussed it with people."

CDU's work paid off. In 2002, they elected enough council delegates to elect a new executive secretary-treasurer, Thomas Harrington, the lead plaintiff in the suit against the UBC. Though CDU does not yet have the power to alter the regional council structure, Harrington has pledged to operate as democratically as possible. He has also vowed to continue his suit against the union with the aim of forcing the council to operate as a local, with direct secret ballot elections for officers every three years.

For more on Carpenters for a Democratic Union, see articles at www.uniondemocracy.org/UDR.

Running for Office

"ELECTIONS ARE NOT JUST ABOUT WINNING OFFICE," says Ken Paff. "They are about mobilizing members to take control of their union." Before you run, read TDU's *Running for Local Union Office: How to Use Election Campaigns to Build Member Involvement and Transform Our Union* (see Resources at the end of this chapter). Its advice applies in any union.

"We judge our success not just on whether we put our people in office," says Paff, "but also on how well we get members involved in the process, generating

Elections are not just about winning office. They are about mobilizing members to take control of their union.

ideas, participating in debate, taking initiative, engaging in action. A union does not get better just because the right people get elected. It gets better when members understand their collective power and start exercising it, not just to turn out ineffective or corrupt officials but to fight for their rights at the workplace."

So with that in mind, how do you get elected?

Prepare Yourselves

Running for office is not the place to start. In the section "Starting a Rank-and-File Group" earlier in this chapter, we talked about activities to build your group's influence. "As you do these things over the course of a year or so," says Paff, "gather some support, and build a group that is not just one clique of 40-year-old white guys from one loading dock, you are also testing yourselves. Who is sticking with it? Who can you rely on? Who is holding up under pressure? Who is just trying to get a union job? Who can bring out supporters? Who talked big but only brought himself, and nobody from his shop sat with him? Once you have found out who is for real, you will be in a position to think about mounting a campaign for office.

"We emphasize the platform more than the candidates," says Paff. "What do you stand for? We always put rank-and-file power up front: elected negotiating committees, steward networks, steward education, contract campaigns that involve members, reliance on membership initiative, drawing members into the union. The platform should also be specific about issues you'll address on the job, such as eliminating two-tier, electing worker reps to a safety committee, how you'll win grievances."

Once the group has agreed on a platform, a committee can write it up in leaflet form. The committee should be broader than the candidates, since other members will have good ideas too.

Early campaign leaflets should invite members to get involved. "Make it about opening up the union," says Paff. "Next you would have some issue literature, taking up hot-button issues and your platform for change. Some of the best literature is targeted to one shop or department, perhaps signed by stewards or activists that people there know. 'We're supporting the Members for Change slate because…'

"Ideally, your group has leaders who can form the core of the slate," says Paff. "But you can be shopping for members to fill out your slate while you are campaigning, because you are open to new people and always doing outreach. We encourage candidates to schedule their vacation time for during the peak of the campaign, so they can talk to people full-time and get to all the shops."

Campaign Organization

A well-organized campaign, especially in a larger local, has a division of labor among the key leaders: a campaign manager, a fundraiser, a treasurer, someone in charge of printing and distributing literature, and, sometimes, a person in charge of watchdogging the rules and filing protests.

The campaign manager coordinates activity and takes care of the details so that candidates can spend their time talking to members. The fundraiser is essential to keep the money coming in to pay for the flyers and mailings.

"Somebody on your team should deal with election rules and observers," notes Paff. "In most Teamsters locals, the local executive board determines all election rules. But you can make a motion at a union meeting to have an elected election committee and democratic rules governing the election. If the officials rule your motion out of order, you still demonstrate your commitment to involving members in the process.

"You have the right, under federal law, to have observers involved in all aspects of the election, anything to do with the ballots. Having observers involved at the earliest stages of the process is not only a way to prevent or detect election rule violations, but also a way to mobilize and test supporters and get folks involved.

"In the Teamsters, challengers often have problems exercising their rights during elections, so members need to become jailhouse lawyers of a sort. But we have a 90/10 rule. If you are using more than 10 percent of your time to file election protests and less than 90 percent to campaign one-on-one, then you have broken the 90/10 rule. You need to be a watchdog, but don't let it become dominant in your campaign." If you need help with election procedures and protests, the Association for Union Democracy can help.

Campaigning

"Campaigning is outreach to draw people into one-on-one conversations," says Paff. "Literature is what you hand people, but mainly you are talking to them, building contacts, getting all the different people—black, white, old, young—together.

"We stress one-on-one, because that's how you build commitment. I always hear about the organizer who goes to the plant gate and hands out leaflets and all the people say, 'We're with you.' And when she comes back she says, 'That shop is 100 percent behind us.' Oh yeah? How many names and phone numbers did she get so we can call them to turn out the vote? How many are wearing a campaign button? How many have a campaign sticker on their lunch cooler? How many have put up a hand-written leaflet on the bulletin board supporting the rank-and-file slate? How many are collecting money for you? How many are openly campaigning for you in the shop? These are some ways we judge how well we are doing.

"This is part of aiming high and building a culture of solidarity. You are trying to draw out leaders, get them involved in the campaign, in the union. They are the ones who will carry the shops. They will also help you keep building your list."

In large locals with several shops, a mailing to reach all members is critical. This may not be important in a local within one workplace. Where it is important, you will need to mail at least once to every member of the local. If you cannot afford such a mailing, you are probably not a serious candidate.

You have the legal right to mail to every member as many times as you want. The union does not have to give your group the membership list, but it must mail to the list if you provide the literature and the money. You also have a legal right to do targeted mailings. These are mailings to specific shops or to specific areas sorted by zip code, say a mailing just to the Acme plant members, aimed at their issues.

Mailings, general and targeted, are best done at the end of the campaign. The more mailings you can afford to do, the earlier you can start sending them.

Countering the Opposition

"When rank-and-filers challenge established incumbents, 'experience' is often the biggest issue," says Paff. "Teamster incumbents usually have a leaflet about the challengers that says something like, 'Number of contracts bargained, 0; number of arbitrations won, 0; number of strikes led, 0.' Down at the bottom is a big zero for the total. The International has produced a formula leaflet like this. It has some effect, but only where officials have credibility.

"Sometimes incumbents have experience, but it's negative experience. They have negotiated bad contracts. They have not defended members on the job. They have let pension benefits disappear. We talk about what it takes to be a good union official: guts, knowledge of the contract, and honesty, which we have plenty of. We say we will hire experts if we have to. And we run our campaign professionally and produce literature and conduct ourselves in a serious way. That helps address the experience issue."

The Big Push

Campaign activity "should build to a peak right before the vote, what we call the GOTV [Get Out The Vote] weeks," says Paff. "It's not just who has the most support, but who turns out the vote. That's why you want the large list, to get people to endorse the slate with a name and phone number. Then, right before the election, you phonebank. In the Teamsters, many of the locals use mail ballots. We call up. 'Did you vote yet? Did you get a friend to vote?' Then a week later, we call again, since they usually have two or three weeks to vote.

"In a walk-in vote, it's slightly different. You need your supporters to bring people down to the hall. You mobilize them to mobilize the members.

"When you get to the GOTV period, concentrate on your strongest shops. You are done convincing, so you are not going to have much success turning out people from your weaker shops. In your strongest shops you can turn out the most people. If the opposition doesn't turn out the same percentage, you win."

Because you may have to file election protests and seek a new election, do not let your campaign organization collapse when the election is over. Discuss in advance with your supporters that they should be prepared to continue campaigning if necessary.

Presumably, your group will continue, win or lose. Discuss in advance what action you will take next. Consider issuing a statement, so your supporters know what to expect.

Winning, of course, brings a different set of questions. In the next sections, we learn how to answer some of them.

Organizing New Members Fuels Fight for Rank-and-File Control

SOMETIMES, a small taste of rank-and-file power is all workers need before they start mobilizing for more. That is what happened in Service Employees (SEIU) Local 36, which represents 4,500 building maintenance workers in the Philadelphia area. Local 36 rank-and-filers learned how to confront management on the job, organize new members, run their own union, take on an undemocratic trusteeship, run a rank-and-file slate, and ultimately win control of their local.

Union reformers sometimes concentrate too much on the fight at the union hall, which far fewer members care about, instead of the fight on the shop floor. Reformers in Local 36 avoided that pitfall. Their story illustrates how struggles against the boss can create organization that eventually produces new union leaders.

Organizing Current and New Members

When Paul Scully was hired in July 2002 as Local 36 organizing director, most members and the International agreed that organizing suburban building workers would help win good contracts for building workers throughout the Philadelphia area. The question was how? Scully and his team of organizers, supported

SEIU Local 36 rank-and-filers learned how to confront management on the job, organize new members, run their own union, take on an undemocratic trusteeship, run a rank-and-file slate, and ultimately win control of their local.

by Local 36 VP Denys Everingham, started mobilizing members who worked downtown to pressure their employers to recognize the union in the suburbs. Local officers, including President Michael Russo and Secretary-Treasurer Brenda Brisbane, opposed the new approach, but could not stop it.

Scully used the local's member-organizer program to pull downtown workers off the job for eight weeks at a time and put them to work organizing current and new members. These member-organizers, staff organizers, and stewards began holding regular building meetings to discuss members' concerns, the first time this had been done in years. Then they started regular job actions, with the intent of addressing members' direct concerns, building solidarity among members, and training them to organize in the suburbs. In other words, mobilizing members to solve their own problems was a way to prepare them to organize new members. As it turned out, it was also a way to prepare them to fight for control of the local.

"We met at the Clothespin, a statue across from City Hall, every Wednesday at 2 p.m., and then went to a workplace for some kind of action," says Chris White, a staff organizer for Local 36. "We called it the Purple Storm, because everyone wore purple SEIU t-shirts. One time, we handed out biohazard flyers at the Gallery shopping mall food court. We were warning customers that the company had laid off so many union cleaners that it was impossible to keep the mall sanitary."

"There was a girl who was sexually harassed by a supervisor for six years," says Yvette Spence, a cleaner who organized for the local. "We made flyers saying, 'You have a pervert working in your building.' We went to the building with the flyers. We stood outside chanting. The supervisor lost his job that night and never came back. We had another rally at an Aramark building downtown, because the workers complained it was so hot when they turned off the air conditioning at night. We bought 1,000 pounds of ice and dumped it in the lobby. They kept the air conditioning on after that."

Workers' interest in the union skyrocketed. Bimonthly membership meetings ballooned from 20 or 30 to over 400. More workers volunteered to be stewards. Organizing activity increased. The organizing team, including the member-organizers, led several strikes at suburban buildings, which led to new contractors signing on to the union's suburban contract. It was a virtuous circle: activity generated small victories, which generated interest, which generated more activity, which generated larger victories.

The new militancy alarmed Russo and Brisbane, who tried to mobilize the board against the organizing program. As conflict escalated in the spring of 2002, Russo went on sick leave and eventually resigned.

Rank-and-File Takeover, then Trusteeship

A struggle to replace Russo followed. Everingham, the VP, was to serve in Russo's absence, but the final decision on who would become president fell to the executive board. Brisbane wanted the presidency, and she controlled the executive board. However, under the constitution, the president called board meetings. Without Everingham's approval, Brisbane held a board meeting. Everingham and several dozen rank-and-file activists, including many who had participated in the member-organizing program, attended the meeting to let the board know they preferred Everingham for president. Brisbane and the rest of the executive board abandoned the meeting, so Everingham used her powers as acting president to remove them from office for dereliction of duty.

"A stewards committee ran the local and trained a leadership structure," says White. "They fired the business agents. It was all rank-and-file workers and some staff. The staff's credibility came from the fact that we had listened to the workers and organized to fight for things they wanted."

The new Local 36 leadership continued the job actions and suburban recruitment. But their experiment lasted only five weeks. Brisbane and her supporters did not give up. At a local meeting attended by SEIU International reps, they disrupted the proceedings and provoked violence. The disarray in the local gave the International a reason to impose a trusteeship.

Wyatt Closs, former special assistant to SEIU Secretary-Treasurer Anna Berger, was named trustee, along with two deputies.

"We thought they would come in and straighten out everything and help us run the union," says Spence. "They came in and brought their own people from New Jersey and New York. They were traveling every day and we were paying them. We were running the union. We were winning grievances. But Wyatt had his own agenda. He hired who he wanted." Some old and new staff were dismissed, including Scully.

Within months, the trusteeship became a disaster in the eyes of many rank and filers. They opposed Closs's decision to move the union to plush new offices, his union-funded SUV, and his six-figure salary.

Elba Mercado, a janitor, was upset with the way Closs handled organizing and bargaining. "I was an organizer for the union," Mercado says. "Wyatt thought I was a 'Dumb-o-Rican.' He thought I just cleaned toilets. He sent me to organize in the suburbs, mostly Mexican workers. He didn't know I can speak and write both languages. We pulled a strike out there. I stood in the middle of the street. Trucks did not go in or out. We struck for two days, and then Wyatt sends them back to work because the union couldn't pay strike pay. The people knew that and they were still willing to stay out on strike. But he sent them back and half of them lost their jobs."

Anger against Closs ballooned when he negotiated a concessionary master agreement covering 2,200 janitors and engineers. They saw new premiums for family health coverage, which had been free, and big increases in their medical co-pays.

Mercado began talking to people about how to get rid of the trusteeship. She and Delbert Franklin, a janitor, wrote a public letter to SEIU President Andrew Stern. They signed it "United for Power Committee." As a result, they got a meeting with International Secretary-Treasurer Berger, which went nowhere. "She called me a nobody," says Mercado. "That's fine. We let them think we are nobodies."

Underground Organizing

It became clear that Closs would run for president. After secretly securing Everingham's commitment to run against him, Mercado started building an "underground group" in the summer of 2003, shortly after the master agreement ratification and her letter to the International. She kept it secret for fear that if Closs knew there was significant opposition he would prolong the trusteeship and delay the election.

"We made sure we had African Americans, Polish, Hispanics, Liberians, everyone who opposed the contract he forced on us," says Mercado. "That's how I started it. Then when he called the election, we had a coalition of people just waiting for the moment.

"We talked to people at work, asking them about the contract, getting information about how they felt, and they were mad. We asked, 'If there is an election, what would you do?' We had the people, so we kept going. We looked for leaders who had the mouth, who had no fear in them. Many had fear in them. They are followers, not leaders.

"I donated my house for the length of the campaign," says Mercado. "We met every Saturday. We had about 25 people, very strong people. We discussed the buildings. We had charts. If a building was split, one of us would take off from work and meet the people at the building at lunch or on break. We stood out in the rain. We got phone numbers. I got a computer and put in all the information.

"We wrote flyers and took more time off to hit the buildings with the flyers. We didn't go in the buildings. The election rules said you cannot campaign during work hours. Wyatt violated the rules. He went in all the time. We didn't. One member would take the flyers in during a lunch break and people would read. Wyatt went in and never got people hot. We never went into a building, but we got people hot. It took our time, our money, our vacation, our gas, our sacrifice."

Nasty Campaign

The union announced the December 13 election on November 7, 2003. Closs fielded almost a full slate for president, secretary-treasurer, and 23 executive board slots. Everingham's slate, which Mercado dubbed the Philly Home Team, included rank-and-file candidates for every slot except secretary-treasurer. Wayne McManiman, a building engineer, had announced his independent candidacy for that job, along with a slate for every position but president. The Philly Home Team decided not to try to merge with McManiman's slate for fear that a slate headed by two white people would be open to attack by Closs, who is African American. "That was a mistake we made," says Mercado. "Wyatt turned everything into a racial thing anyway." "We should have merged our slates," adds Everingham.

Closs campaign material charged Everingham and McManiman with running racist campaigns. One leaflet portrayed Everingham as a snake, says Spence. A Closs press release said, "Everingham and her partner McManiman, both white, carefully went after immigrant, white and Latino members with the subtle message that an African American could not win for them. With many Americans predisposed to embrace racist beliefs, few words were needed to get the message across. The whites came out by the dozens."

The charges of racism did not stick, because the Philly Home Team and the McManiman slates both had African American majorities. The Philly Home Team had representatives from virtually every ethnic group in the union. African Americans dominated the Closs slate, which had no Caribbean or Eastern European candidates. Spence, a Trinidadian, summed it up, "Blacks, Latinos, immigrants from Africa, the Caribbean, Poland, Albania—we all joined together because we know that Denys and Wayne will fight for all of the members. Wyatt sent a lot of mailings out against Denys, but those mailings couldn't convince us to change what we know in our hearts."

On the day of the election, the Philly Home Team mobilized. Mark Zommer arranged for buses to bring workers from a Polish neighborhood. Mercado and others arranged carpools for workers in a heavily Latino area. Several buildings with African American majorities organized car pools to vote for the Philly Home Team.

Everingham and McManiman won with 60 percent of the vote, but only six of their candidates won positions on the executive board. Their two slates had split the vote, allowing many Closs slate members to win. Fearful that the divided board would be a problem, Everingham prepared for a contentious first board meeting. "But it turned out that people want to move on," she says.

Meanwhile, Mercado and other rank and filers did not stop meeting. "We meet about every three weeks," she says. "We are waiting to see what the executive board is going to do for the members. If they don't do the right things for the people, there will be a rumpus. We won't keep quiet."

CDU Becomes the Union; Then Wins the Union

IN NOVEMBER 2003, the Caucus for a Democratic Union (CDU) won control of the California State Employees Association (CSEA), a hybrid labor organization representing 140,000 workers, including administrators, office and clerical workers, nurses in state hospitals, librarians, agricultural inspectors, janitors, food service workers, and social service workers. The victory was 11 years in the making, but what follows is not the story of CDU's victory. Instead, we focus on what CDU did to create and grow a rank-and-file group inside an undemocratic union with hostile leadership.

CDU succeeded because it did the things the union should have done: 1) it mobilized workers to fight for their rights on the job, 2) it organized new workers into the union, 3) it ran contract campaigns, 4) it lobbied and protested to influence the state legislature, which set workers' wages and working conditions, 5) it kept members informed with personal contact and a newsletter, and 6) it built new leaders. It also succeeded because a core of dedicated and persistent activists sustained over the long haul an organization with a clear purpose and a democratic structure.

CSEA's Complicated Structure

CSEA is an unusual union. It combines elements of a traditional union—it is Local 1000 of SEIU—with elements of an employee association and a retiree group. CSEA represents four distinct and somewhat autonomous state employee groups.

First is the Civil Service Division (CSD), representing rank-and-file state employees. It is the largest unit of CSEA, with over 90,000 workers, and is the largest source of funds for the union's budget. It is divided into 55 District Labor Councils, or chapters, each with elected officers. CDU originated in this division, which is the most militant part of CSEA.

The other groups represent workers in the California

State University system (CSU), the Retired Employees Division (RED), and the Association of California State Supervisors (ACSS).

CSEA is governed by a 25-member board of directors. The board has four statewide officers, two officers each from CSD, CSU, RED, and ACSS, and 13 regional directors elected by members in all four divisions. The four statewide officers are elected by a General Council of delegates, similar to a union convention, which meets every two years. Delegates are elected by the members of each division. CSD delegates also elect their four division officers.

CDU's task of reforming CSEA was made both easier and more difficult by the complex structure of the union. On the one hand, there are many opportunities to run for office and stewards are self-selected. Thus, activists had many opportunities to speak out and organize, often from positions of authority as chapter officers, division officers, delegates, or stewards. On the other hand, the union structure gives retirees and supervisors the ability to block the desires of the majority in the Civil Services Division. Through control of the board, these groups retained control over the daily operations, hiring and firing, and finances of the entire union.

Provoked into Organizing

CDU was founded in 1992 during a contract fight. Republican Governor Pete Wilson insisted on concessions from state employees, and CSEA leaders accepted his demands. However, in the Civil Service Division's Bargaining Unit 1, six of the seven elected bargaining team members refused to recommend the proposed contract to the unit's 40,000 professional administrative, financial, and staff services workers. So CSEA's president (the top elected position) and its general manager (the top staff position) ousted all but one member of the bargaining team and signed management's offer. The officials also expelled from the union the resisting bargaining-team leaders, who took their case for contract rejection to the members.

Some of the ousted bargaining team members decided to organize rank-and-file resistance. Two of those expelled, Cathy Hackett and Jim Hard, had considerable experience as union activists. Hackett, a budget analyst, had chaired the Unit 1 bargaining team for seven years and had participated in organizing new members. "We had a huge network in the Employment Development Department, lots of active people," she says. "That was our base."

In addition to several years of service on the bargaining team, Hard had worked with Teamsters for a Democratic Union in the vegetable canneries around Sacramento. "I had worked as an outside supporter, doing leafleting and going to meetings," says Hard. "I had seen how TDU argued that it was hard to solve problems on the job if the union was blocking members' participation and education."

While fighting their expulsion from the union, Hackett and Hard joined a group of 33 other CSEA members from around the state and founded CDU in Sacramento. It was directly modeled after TDU, committed both to the restoration of rank-and-file power in the union and fighting for workers on the job. The group adopted bylaws, including dues, yearly statewide meetings to set policy and program, a statewide steering committee, a caucus newspaper called *Union Spark*, and area chapters.

CDU also drafted a rank-and-file bill of rights, which called for the direct election of officers; a fair grievance procedure; an end to employer and union discrimination against women, people of color, gays, lesbians, and transgendered people; decent contracts; freedom of expression; and membership authority over the union. The group also committed to build a union that organized new members and mobilized the public in support of public services.

The bill of rights gave activists a set of goals and activities to organize around, while the CDU structure provided mechanisms for planning and coordinating those activities throughout the union. This structure kept CDU activists connected to each other, motivated, and focused on a clear set of priorities that they had collectively established.

Building CDU by Being the Union

CDU activists built their organization mostly by talking to people, but they also communicated their message by setting up literature tables outside state office buildings to collect names and phone numbers and distribute flyers about particular issues, such as defending activists against expulsion or fighting concessions. The group held public events of interest to state workers, like forums on workers' compensation. "That was the first step—to articulate the problems we saw and expose the opposition," says Hackett.

Getting workers to join CDU "was just like organizing," says Hard. "We spoke one-on-one with activists about the need to change the union. Fundamental is to target who you are going after. We went after stewards, the union's activist core. We took anyone, and we have many members who are not stewards, but our focus was on stewards."

In a victory that was 11 years in the making, the Caucus for a Democratic Union won control of the California State Employees Association. The caucus continues to meet monthly.

"They are the organizers and the leaders," adds Hackett.

"As people became active in the union, usually as stewards, we told them about the factional situation and asked them to join the caucus," says Michael Rubin, who worked for the Department of Social Services in Oakland. "I did some steward training, so I would talk about being a reform caucus member during the training. In my experience, CDU was a hard sell if they were not already active in the union. The caucus only made sense if you were trying to accomplish something. The union's undemocratic nature became apparent once people became involved. So we would bring people to a board of directors meeting so they could see what was going on, how they were messing with the Civil Service Division."

Democracy was not the only issue. One of the first things CDU did was "mount a campaign against takeaways," says Hackett. "After we were kicked off the bargaining team, we organized and got our supporters elected to the new bargaining team. We said, 'You should never agree to these types of concessions.' The government would not offer anything but takeaways and our supporters would not agree, so there was no new contract for four years, until a new governor [Gray Davis] took office and we had won control of the Civil Service Division in 1996." Working under the old contract was not ideal, but it prevented takeaways and represented a victory under the harsh circumstances.

CDU members made it their mission to know their contracts inside and out. "I was on the bargaining team for ten years," says Rubin. "So we got points because nobody knew the contract as well as we did. People would call me to ask about the contract. They got to know that I was a member of the reform movement and that we knew the contract better than the officials."

CDU members were active in every aspect of the union, including contract campaigns, lobbying, union elections, state government elections, and grievances. In fact, they were often the only union presence on the job. "The old guard didn't have worksite meetings, no flyers, no leaflets, and few bargaining updates," says Rubin. "Workers said, 'The union never talks to me. Where is the union, anyway?' We held meetings. We did the things that a union needs to do to have any credibility whatsoever. And we constantly asked people to join us.

"So when people looked to see who was active and who was doing the everyday work of building the union, they saw CDU people. That gave CDU credibility, whereas officials who were not part of the reform movement were not active in building the union."

As they built credibility as rank-and-file leaders, CDU members built their caucus. In Sacramento they held monthly CDU chapter meetings and they met intermittently in other areas. "Yearly meetings were also important, because they set the agenda for the group statewide," says Marangu Marete, an operations research specialist in Sacramento. "Everyone knew the priorities and CDU leaders had to hold to the agenda, because they were accountable to the group."

"We started getting members at $25 per year and sustainers at $25 per month," says Hackett. "Eventually, we got people to sign up for automatic withdrawal from their checking accounts, which was important because renewals are hard to maintain. We kept a renewal list with us, so at meetings we could ask people for renewals. We also passed the hat at every meeting."

Raising money was crucial to pay for the regular publication of *Union Spark,* other literature, buttons, posters, mailing, and travel.

Running for Office

CDU's strategy was to consolidate a base and then expand. First, the caucus focused on Bargaining Unit 1, where it had started. After establishing a strong base of support, demonstrated by having lots of stewards in the caucus and getting some members elected to chapter office, the group branched out to the rest of the Civil Service Division. Once members had a base within the division, they ran in regional elections, which included candidates from other divisions.

CDU started running candidates immediately after its formation. "We ran slates of candidates in as many local chapters (DLCs) as possible," says Hard. "No one in CSEA had seen a slate of candidates before CDU. We ran for bargaining representative first. Over time, we ran slates for chapter offices, convention delegates, and eventually division office."

CDU also campaigned to change a rule that allowed each chapter president to appoint her chapter's delegates, if nobody ran. The group felt that the rule discouraged people from running. "We felt we needed to organize around running for office, to make it less bureaucratic," says Hackett. "But we are state workers. We know a lot about bureaucratic processes. So we filed a lawsuit, arguing that because the union was incorporated they were required by law to have delegates directly elected. We did not win the case, but the union changed the bylaws at the convention.

"You have to prioritize. You know you will not win at first. But you are good soldiers, out there to publicize what you stand for, put statements in union publications, or make a speech at a convention. That gives you visibility. You have to have consistency, so people know you are serious. Even though you don't win, you look at incremental gains: more votes, more members, more participation in the caucus. Target small elections where the voice of a few people can make a difference."

Over time, CDU activists won more elections. It got to the point where "few caucus members were without union office of some kind, whether it was stewards or bargaining team members or chapter officers," says Rubin. "That increased our visibility 1,000 percent."

Visibility helped build the caucus, which recruited enough people to expand its structure with volunteer statewide organizers and regional organizers. "People started coming to meetings and the network developed everywhere in the state," says Rubin.

In 1996, CDU won control of the Civil Service Division, with Hard becoming president, Hackett vice-president for finance, and CDU members in the other two top offices. This gave CDU considerable organizational resources, but because CSEA's board of directors still controlled most of the purse strings and the hiring and firing within the division, CDU's power to implement its vision of a more militant rank-and-file union was limited.

Defending Activists and Activism

CDU activists faced disciplinary action from their officials. Over the years, Hackett and Hard were expelled from the union three times and each time they won reinstatement. "We had a lot of education," says Hard. "Cathy has a master's degree, I have a bachelor's. We could defend ourselves by reading the rules and the law, but we did a bad job to begin with and lost our unfair labor practice charges. We did better once we were coached by an attorney who had worked for the Public Employment Relations Board. He gave us the right language. If you don't have much capability to do the reading and the analysis, you will need outside help. And if you cannot find a free attorney it is prohibitive to get legal advice. But you can consult with Labor Notes or AUD."

Early on, the hostility of the leadership actually helped CDU. "They spent all their energy fighting us, instead of ignoring us," says Hard. "They fought us directly, which spurred people to find out about us. They gave us attention on their website and in their newsletters. People who saw problems with the union figured we had something to say and would seek us out."

CDU also faced opposition from the union staff, even after winning division office. CSEA staff members are not directly responsible to elected officials, even in district labor councils. Rather, they are responsible to the general manager and regional managers, who are appointed by the board of directors. As long as opponents of CDU controlled the board of directors, they instructed the managers to instruct the staff to oppose whatever CDU officials did, such as trying to organize new members or run contract campaigns.

To get around the staff, CDU officials in the Civil Services Division innovated. "We didn't hire any staff," says Hackett. "We knew we could use union funds to finance different things, so we used money for union leave instead of more staff. The old guard and staff refused to honor union leave, but we got it in the contract. We got people off the job and started teaching them about organizing, instead of just filing a grievance."

CDU officials in control of the Civil Service Division made winning new members a priority. By convincing non-member state employees to join CSEA, CDU built the union *and* its own strength. "We had one delegate to the General Council for every 100 members," says Rubin. "By organizing 10,000 new members over several years we added 100 new delegates from the division. That gave us more influence over the union."

By 2003, CDU had won enough delegates to control the General Council and elect its slate to the top offices of the entire CSEA.

Long-Term Success

CDU has enjoyed tremendous long-term incremental success. "We have met every month in Sacramento for 11 years," says Hackett. "We still meet. If you have standard meetings and a publication and a standard agenda you are trying to accomplish, and if you show consistency over time and show people this is the way to be a stronger union, then it makes sense to them, especially if the union is saying nothing about those things."

"One reason for our success is that we had a publication that we put out consistently and that was pretty well distributed, with hundreds of distributors," says Rubin. "Another reason is that people were devoted. The core group, including Cathy and Jim, was incredibly solid and dedicated. People would get up in the morning and distribute flyers before work and then again after work. They just kept at it."

Resources

In addition to *Democracy Is Power* (see page 273) and the websites mentioned in this chapter, see:
• Association for Union Democracy, 104 Montgomery St., Brooklyn, NY 11225, 718-564-1114, aud@igc.org, www.uniondemocracy.org. AUD's website has a great deal of information about enforcing your legal rights within the union. You can sign up for monthly email updates or the bimonthly newsletter *Union Democracy Review. How to Get an Honest Union Election,* by Herman Benson, is $6.
• Websites run by rank-and-file reformers in many, many unions: for links, go to AUD at www.uniondemocracy.org. See Chapter 20 for detailed advice on setting up a website yourself and for information on your legal rights to dissent within the union (page 307).
• Teamsters for a Democratic Union. Publishes monthly *Convoy-Dispatch* newspaper, $30/year. PO Box 10128, Detroit, MI 48210. 313-842-2600. www.tdu.org. tdudetroit@tdu.org.
• *Running for Local Union Office.* $10 from TDU. www.tdu.org/Store/store.cgi.
• *Rank-and-File Rebellion: Teamsters for a Democratic Union,* by Dan La Botz. Verso, 1990. The stories of TDU members. $17 postpaid from TDU.
• *The Transformation of U.S. Unions: Voices, Visions and Strategies from the Grassroots*, Ray Tillman and Michael Cummings, eds. Lynne Rienner Publishers, 1999. An anthology of experiences with and arguments for union democracy. $22.50 from Labor Notes.
• U.S. Department of Labor public disclosure site. Annual reports filed by unions, employers, and labor consultants, disclosing their financial activities. www.union-reports.dol.gov.

Action Questions

The following questions focus on the practical aspects of building a caucus and running in elections, but they are ultimately aimed at revitalizing your union by increasing member involvement and increasing workers' power on the shop floor. That's why two questions in the back of your mind should always be: how do we get more people involved in our fight, and how do we increase our power at the workplace?

1. What is the relationship between the union and your management? Who runs things for management? Who is management regularly in touch with at the union? How do they get along? Buddy-buddy? Corrupt? Hostile? Cordial? Respect?

2. What are the offices of the union and who holds them? Do you know their salaries?

3. Are there members who do not hold office but who play an important role in running the union? Are there international or district officials who play a role in your local? Retired officials? What about an out-of-office caucus or clique? Are there politicians, mobsters, or employers who play a role?

4. Have you sat down and talked to the important individuals and groups in your union (both the formal and informal ones)? Do you know what makes them tick? They will be your allies or your opponents, so you had better understand them.

5. Take a large piece of paper and draw a flowchart showing the power relations within the union. Put the most powerful figures in the center and draw lines showing how power, money, information, and other resources flow.

6. Chart the membership. Who works where? What are their phone numbers, addresses, work locations, shifts?

7. What are the most important issues on members' minds? Contract issues? Shop floor issues? Industry issues, like contracting out or deregulation? Discrimination? Lack of union democracy? Do all the members care about the same things? What are the three most important issues? Write up these issues as if you were going to put out a leaflet to the membership about why you are going to run for office.

8. Have you talked to workers in all departments? Women and men and all racial and ethnic groups? Do you need to conduct a survey to find out what members think?

9. Do you have a copy of your constitution and local bylaws? How many members go to union meetings? What happens at them? What important individuals or groups are at the meetings? Does the union publish a newspaper? Is it open to anyone?

10. What are the rules governing elections? Who is eligible to run for office? What is the time frame for filing? What is the procedure for nomination? Do you need to get petition signatures or have seconds for nominations? Are there experienced members who can help answer these questions?

11. Is running for office the best way to achieve your goals at this time? Would it be better to work in some other way, such as on a union committee? Or should you form a caucus to build a base and think about elections in a year or two?

12. If you are going to run for office, should you form a slate, a temporary group of allies running for office on a common ticket? Or should you form a caucus, a formal group, like a political party in the union, committed not only to running candidates but to long-term political goals?

13. How will you choose candidates? Will individuals simply volunteer or will the slate or caucus collectively decide? How will you make sure your slate fairly represents men and women, the different ethnic, language, and racial groups, different departments and job classifications?

14. How can you raise money for your campaign? How much will you need? Who will be the fundraiser? Who will be the treasurer?

15. What personal sacrifices will have to be made? How much money will candidates and supporters donate? Will candidates have to take vacation time or leave of absence to campaign? Could people who declare for office be disciplined or fired? Has all of this been discussed with spouses and families? Should spouses be asked to become part of the core campaign group?

16. How will you publicize your campaign? Make up a list of media you want to contact. Do you have a union printer lined up? What combination of leafleting, email, website, and phonebanking will you need? Do you need a union mailing company?

17. Who will be the campaign manager?

18. Make a tentative timeline for the period until the election, including time to build your slate and get out the vote.

19. How can you ensure the election will be honest? Is there an election committee that your supporters can run for? Check your bylaws to become thoroughly familiar with election procedures. Who will you recruit as observers?

20. How will you prepare for losing? Will you have a leaflet announcing that your caucus will keep working to strengthen the union?

21. What will be the first thing you will have to do when you take office? Negotiations? Committee appointments? Financial housecleaning?

Author

AARON BRENNER is a labor historian, researcher, writer, and editor in New York City. He has written about international labor solidarity, union reform movements, and rank-and-file rebellions by Teamsters, telephone workers, and postal workers, and is the editor of *The Encyclopedia of Strikes in American History*.

On the Troublemaker's Website

"Running for Union Office: Your Legal Rights." www.labornotes.org.

19. Running Your Local

by Robert Hickey

"WHEN YOU WIN UNION OFFICE," points out Teamsters Local 96 President Bill Gibson, "the pressure to go along and get along is intense."

It's easy to look at the mound of paperwork on your desk and get sidetracked. Officers who win election by promising to reform the local, get members involved, and do a better job than the incumbents often experience a big "gulp!" when they take the oath of office. It's a lot easier to say what someone else is doing wrong than to install a whole new culture in your local. "I remember the first time I picked up a gavel at our convention." says Jelger Kalmijn, president of a statewide CWA local in California. "I thought, 'Okay, now we won, what's next?' The transition from opposition, fighting for membership participation, to being in charge and responsible for the progress of the union was abrupt and unnerving. The skills, tactics, and collective effort to run a union on a program are different from those used to fight for that program, even though the vision does not change."

How can officers avoid the traps set by management or by years of business-union tradition? Officials who are most successful and who avoid burnout often have two key qualities: an ability to develop new leaders to share the work and a commitment to bigger goals. They know that it's not just about their local union; they have a vision that keeps them keeping on.

They also understand that times change. Most unions operate under the same organizational models that have been in place for years. What worked in 1940 may not be as effective today. The union may need to develop new structures, new alliances, and new approaches. This chapter will offer some ideas on how to involve members and build a broader leadership base, so that officers don't go it alone. And we will talk about stepping back and making a long-range plan to win your goals.

"I ran with a goal of giving members more of a say and more information," says Kalmijn. "We do put out a lot more of that now, but that doesn't necessarily translate directly into more participation. It's a long process to change an engrained practice where people don't participate, and don't expect to participate, and don't expect their participation to make a difference, when our employer does everything possible to make that not happen. There's no silver bullet solution."

No silver bullets, but the ideas in this book should help.

Much of the fun stuff that's part of leading a local is not included in this chapter, however. Contract campaigns, organizing new members, shop floor actions, strikes, developing new leaders, dealing with the media, setting up a website—all those topics are covered elsewhere in this book. To find them, look in the table of contents or the index.

In addition, Labor Notes has a whole book devoted to running your local smoothly, democratically, and inclusively—*Democracy Is Power*. We won't repeat here the wealth of information available there (see the box below).

This chapter covers strategic planning, budgeting, communication and setting up member-to-member networks, working officers, using lost time, stewards committees, managing staff, dealing with language differences, promoting new leaders through a junior executive board, election debates, and keeping the big picture in mind.

It all begins, of course, with having a plan.

Making a Strategic Plan

WHAT IS STRATEGIC PLANNING? It sounds like a subject for business school, not a union. And in fact the concept of strategic planning was developed by businesses

---

More on Running Your Local

Labor Notes' book *Democracy Is Power* is the Troublemaker's Handbook for running a strong union. In *Democracy Is Power* you can find:
• Why democracy *concretely* contributes to making the union stronger against management
• What leadership means in a union setting
• How to get members to participate
• Building racial and gender equality within the union
• Democratic election procedures
• New officers' checklist
• Which are better—elections or appointments?
• What size local works best?
• National conventions
• How to have a good union meeting
• Leading meetings well
• Hints on using (and changing) Roberts' Rules
• Suggested bylaws

To order, see the ad at the back of this book.

such as General Electric. But all too often unions simply react to management initiatives. Strategic planning for unions means analyzing your situation to develop long-range goals, and then working out the specific steps to get from here to there.

Unions can't use the same top-down, by-the-numbers, profit-oriented planning method that businesses rely on, though. We need a model based on union values and democratic procedures. For example, it might not be cost-effective, in the short term, to organize new members, but organizing new members needs to be part of every union's strategic plan.

Done right, strategic planning is a tool for building the union. The planning process forces members to assess their strengths and figure out ways to overcome their weaknesses. Instead of playing the hand that the employer deals, we bring our own deck of cards to the game.

The past 25 years have been difficult for unions. Our employers are constantly changing the rules, and unions have been slow to develop strategies to meet these challenges. For example, when the Steelworkers faced tough contract negotiations with Phelps-Dodge in 1983, the union followed traditional collective-bargaining practices, including a militant strike. But Phelps-Dodge, with help from the Wharton School of Business, implemented a long-range plan to keep operating during the strike and bust the union.[1] In the 1980s this sad scenario was repeated many times.

But we learned from our struggles and losses. Unions started developing strategies to add to the traditional forms of solidarity, strategies that could disrupt the new structures of corporate power. In 1989-1990, the Mine Workers at Pittston faced the same threat of permanent replacement and the same hostile Labor Board as the copper miners at Phelps-Dodge, yet they won their strike. The difference was that the union had analyzed the company and the industry and had developed a winning plan.[2] Steelworkers at Bridgestone-Firestone and Teamsters at UPS also won victories because they took the time to develop a far-reaching strategic plan.

In addition to helping unions win, planning also:
• Provides a systematic method for setting priorities.
• Builds members' involvement and ownership of the union's plan of work.
• Helps train activists and develop leaders.
• Creates accountability and a framework for measuring performance.
• Encourages members to think about the long term.

Union strategic planning must be democratic to succeed. If members do not participate in the process, it will be much more difficult to convince them to carry out the new strategies, and the plan will not reflect the experiences of the members on the ground. Leaders should bring members in through surveys and small group discussions. Democratic planning is especially important if the plan calls for shifting resources or for changing long-standing organizational set-ups.

A Mission and Vision

The first step is to agree on the union's mission and vision. The mission statement serves as the moral compass by which you set your course and judge your actions. It should describe the basic purpose, values, and activities of the union. New leaders of Teamsters Local 556, for instance, described in Chapter 21 on Developing Leaders, agreed that their mission was to organize low-wage food-processing workers in eastern Washington and Oregon and to shift the balance of power from employers to workers in their region.

Building from the mission statement, you then state your vision of the future. What does the society and world that you are struggling to create look like? Think about more than winning a few more grievances. What larger results do you want to achieve as a union?

Analyze the Environment

The next step is to analyze the environment in which you work. Your approach should be realistic and unafraid of self-criticism. One simple tool is called the "SWOT analysis," standing for Strengths, Weaknesses, Opportunities, and Threats. In small groups, members brainstorm to create a list of the current strengths and weaknesses of their union. Opportunities and threats focus more on the external environment: potential sources of strength or weakness created by the employer, the community, or other factors outside the local.

	SWOT Analysis	
Internal environment	Strengths	Weaknesses
External environment	Opportunities	Threats

In filling out the chart, don't focus on which box a particular issue fits in. It may belong in more than one. Instead, describe why a particular characteristic of the union is a strength or weakness. For example, although new leadership might be a weakness because of lack of experience, its new energy and greater diversity can be a plus. Similarly, some threats may also provide opportunities. The introduction of "just-in-time" manufacturing, for example, creates serious speed-up. At the same time,

Five Steps in Strategic Planning

1. Articulate the union's mission.
2. Analyze the environment.
3. Set goals.
4. Develop an action plan.
5. Monitor, evaluate and modify.

because it is more vulnerable to disruption, it can give unions bargaining leverage. The point is to think through each issue carefully.

Strategic Research: Understand Your Employer

Researching your employer is an essential element of planning, but research doesn't stop when the first plan is made. You will need to constantly update the information you have about the company or agency, the industry, allies, and other stakeholders. Understanding how corporate power is structured and how it flows is essential to developing counter-strategies. (See the Appendix on Researching Employers.)

Knowing how your employer generates revenue and makes a profit is not always straightforward. For example, during the five-year campaign to bust a lockout by Crown Central Petroleum in Houston, oil workers learned that the company's profit center was not the refinery where they worked but the retail gas stations hundreds of miles from the picket line. So their union, the Paper, Allied-Industrial, Chemical & Energy Workers (PACE), focused on building a boycott of gas stations by cultivating relationships with hundreds of allies.

Through research, the union then learned that Crown had found a new source of revenue, Norway's state oil company, Statoil. PACE reached out to the International Federation of Chemical, Energy, Mine and General Workers' Unions and to the Norwegian oil workers union to put leverage on Crown. The union not only broke the lockout but preserved the national bargaining pattern in the oil industry.[3]

Companies have their own strategic plans, and figuring out how to block or stall the corporate business plan is an essential part of strategic research. When the Crown Petroleum workers learned that their CEO planned to take the company private, the union launched a campaign to block the takeover, which added pressure to end the lockout.

Finally, research must extend beyond the boardroom to look at the political and social context. Who are your potential allies in the community? Are there political opportunities to increase your bargaining power? SEIU spent years developing a political strategy to create a legal "employer of record" in California for workers who took care of patients in their homes. At the same time, the union organized the homecare workers in the community. As a result, over 76,000 homecare workers became SEIU members in southern California.

Assess Your Union's Power

Another part of strategic planning analyzes the union itself. This analysis should include a review of how the union operates, its strengths or weaknesses within its industry or company, the extent of member participation, and the quality of community and political alliances. The union's current structure and allocation of resources may not match the goals you are beginning to formulate in the planning process.

- *Union density:* How many of your employer's suppliers and customers are unionized and how many at the company itself? Where is your bargaining power? Where can you organize to increase density and power?
- *Leadership:* Do you have a program to educate members and develop more leaders? How representative of the workforce is the current leadership? How are decisions made and carried out?
- *Allocation of resources:* Does the union have an operating budget? It is surprising how many locals base expenditures on the previous month's trustees' report. Budgeting should be part of the strategic planning process, not an afterthought. How are priorities determined?
- *Current activities:* What is the state of the union's organizing drives, political action, contract bargaining, and enforcement?
- *Appropriate structures:* Unions are debating whether and how to reorganize along industry lines. The emergence of industrial unions required a similar difficult transformation 70 years ago. Whether it involves a top-down reorganization to create sector-based unions or a bottom-up effort by locals to set up networks at the same employer or in similar professions, strategic planning requires you to analyze and perhaps adjust the structure of your union.

In Chapter 14, Union Solidarity, we gave an example of how rank-and-filers organized to overcome weak organization. Twin Cities concrete drivers were scattered in three different Teamsters locals with a slew of different contracts. A rank-and-file committee agitated successfully for one master agreement and pressured local officials to set up a joint bargaining committee and go for common expiration dates and common language.

Research Your Community

Another part of strategic planning analyzes where power lies in your community. In a multi-union campaign in Stamford, Connecticut,[4] AFL-CIO lead organizer Jane McAlevey explained how the campaign approached the question of power in that city: "Who were the powerful forces and why? Which would be allies and which would be obstacles? How could you enhance the power of our friends and neutralize that of our opponents? The idea was to measure power two ways, first in absolute terms, but also in relation to goals. Just like you 'chart' workplaces as a crucial step to organizing, you need to 'chart' real leadership and power in the community to understand how to hem in the boss."[5]

In Stamford, the unions and community groups identified all the powerful actors in the city and then rated them as either potential allies or likely adversaries, creating a map of the local power structure. This map identified strategic alliances and likely obstacles. While this approach is particularly useful for public sector unions and for local employers where power is locally or regionally based, unions facing global companies can expand the analysis to include international allies and adversaries.

Identify Goals

Your mission and vision statements describe the ultimate goals of your work, but you also need short-term and long-term goals that serve as milestones on the way. SMART goals provide a good road map:

Specific: Be as specific as possible. Instead of "get more members involved," a better goal would be "recruit ten new members to the volunteer organizing committee" and "investigate state of the member-to-member networks in Departments A and C; recruit and train new point people as necessary."

Measurable: How do you assess progress? Having specific goals makes it easy to tell when you've met them.

Attainable: Be ambitious but realistic.

Relevant: Goals must be relevant to the members and the organization. Unions have been at the forefront of many living wage campaigns, for example, but making such campaigns relevant to existing members often requires specific strategies for educating them and getting them involved.

Timely: Goals should have a fixed timeline, such as "Complete classroom training for new volunteer organizers by February 15. Complete field training program by April 30."

If you think of everything that you might want your union to achieve over the next year, your list might be too long. If you can't do it all, you need to select the most important goals. Given resources, member support, and obstacles, what is the chance of success? How long will each take to accomplish? How big an impact will achieving this goal have on your members?

How To Make It Work

- Use an external facilitator: Bring in someone from outside who is experienced in progressive movements and union values. Facilitators include university-based labor educators, community organizers, or staff from the international union's education department. Don't hire a corporate consultant.
- Leave the union hall: Get the planning process away from the constant pressures of daily life. Turn off the cell phones and pagers. Provide food.
- Don't wait for the crisis: You don't want to begin your planning after the contract has expired and the union is already on strike.
- Get a commitment from the leadership: Strategic planning often involves risk for elected leaders, who may fear a critical assessment of the union. If the union agrees on a bold new plan, it will shake up old habits and old alliances. But leaders have to be willing to follow through with the necessary resources, or strategic planning is not worthwhile.

Develop an Action Plan

An action plan is as simple as deciding *who* is going to do *what* by *when*. A detailed action plan should include:

- Objectives: What are the intermediate steps to achieve each goal? Define victory carefully and in detail.
- Tactics: Which would be most effective?
- Resources and budget: Do you have the people and the money to carry out these actions?
- Allies: Who can you get to help?
- Specific actions/tasks: What is the "to do" list for the campaign?
- Person responsible: Who is responsible for making sure each task is completed on time?
- Employer opposition: How will the employer react?
- Internal obstacles: Will there be internal opposition? What other obstacles will you face?
- Structure and accountability: Who do the activists report to?
- Timeline: When will each task be completed? When do you plan to achieve your goal?

Monitor, Evaluate, and Adjust

Schedule regular evaluations as part of the action plan. Pick dates and reassess; don't wait until things start to get off track to start monitoring. Build accountability into the plan's structure. The world changes in unpredictable ways, so the plan must have the flexibility to adjust to new events. For example, in the campaign against Crown Central Petroleum, PACE turned what had been a campaign focused on the CEO into a broad-based effort to build a boycott. Summary reports should be sent to all the participants in the planning process so everyone can collectively assess and take responsibility for progress on the plan.

Even the best strategic plans do not guarantee success. But if we understand the threats and opportunities we face, and adjust our strategies accordingly, we are much more likely to win.

Budgeting by Program

AN IMPORTANT PART OF STRATEGIC PLANNING is assessing your resources and creating a programmatic budget. All too often, unions operate without a budget to guide spending. Instead, members and officers wait for the balance sheet at the end of the year, when the money is already spent, and then discuss whether the money has been used wisely.

What's more, the line-item accounting model that most unions use reinforces poor budgeting practices and leaves little room for democratic input. Line item reports (which are required by most financial reporting forms, including the Department of Labor's "LM-2") have no way to show whether the local is spending its money on what it considers important. You can see what you spent on office furniture, but not what you spent on an organizing campaign.

Programmatic budgets, on the other hand, provide for democratic input and for strategic allocation of the members' dues. Instead of thinking in terms of the traditional reporting lines—salaries, office expense—you create a budget built around specific programs and campaigns. How much do you want to spend on your contract campaign? How much on new organizing? How much on education?

A steward education program, for example, might include expenses for staff time, materials, lost time for the stewards, and meeting space. In the line-item model, these expenses would be grouped with staff time, lost time, and meeting spaces used for organizing and contract bargaining—it would be impossible to see how much the steward education cost. Programmatic budgeting forces the union to specify its core activities and allocate its resources based on those priorities. Then at the end of the fiscal year, you compare the budgeted expense with the actual expense for each core activity, and evaluate the result.

A meaningful budgeting process should be tied to the union's overall strategic plan. Without a strategic plan, most locals simply continue to spend money as they have in past years. They make changes only if the bottom line turns sour, and usually just cut staff rather than adjusting activities. If you use a programmatic budget, it's easier to make appropriate spending cuts when necessary and still keep moving toward your goals.

Consider the traditional LM-2 format versus a programmatic budget:

Sample LM-2 Statement B: Receipts and Disbursements

Receipts

Dues	41,497
Fines	0
Assessments	2,500
Per capita	8,987
Sales of supplies	542
Interest	168
Sales of fixed assets	5,500
Total Receipts	**50,207**

Expenditures

Officers	10,662
Employees	15,507
Per capita	8,987
Office & administrative	12,458
Education and publicity	580
Purchase of investments and fixed assets	1,500
Total Disbursements	**49,694**

Just about the only thing you can learn from this report is that the union received more money than it spent. Even salaries for specific individuals provide no information about which programs and campaigns those staffers actually work on.

Traditional line-item reports are still a useful tool, but they should support a budgeting process, not replace it. Although the bottom line of actual income and expenditures will be the same, the program-based budget

Sample Programmatic Budget

	Budget	Actual	Difference
Organizing program	212,150		
Cintas	79,900		
Organizer 1.5 FTE*	60,000		
Printing	1,200		
Clerical .5 FTE	12,500		
Legal	5,000		
Meeting space	200		
Lost time	1,000		
Rosewood Medical	132,250		
Organizer 2.5 FTE	100,000		
Printing	2,500		
Clerical .5 FTE	12,500		
Legal	14,500		
Meeting space	750		
Lost time	2,000		
Education program			
Steward training			
Staff .25 FTE			
Clerical .10 FTE			
Materials			
Meeting rooms			
Lost time			
Food			
Staff training			
Staff .25 FTE			
Contract campaign			
Survey			
Lost time 2 wks FTE			
Materials			

* FTE means "full-time equivalent"—one staff salary.

allows officers and members to see whether the union is putting its money where its mouth is.

Steps to create a programmatic budget:

• *Start with available information.* Existing financial reports do provide useful information. Translate them into a program-based budget as much as you can. Look at reports over several years to identify trends and cyclical fluctuations. Outline current union activities by specific programs. Break down each major area of activity—organizing, training, and so on—into its component parts. Staff time, administrative costs, and other expenditures can be associated with the appropriate program.

• *Create a strategic plan.* The budget should be driven by this plan, which will include assessing current capacity, setting priorities, and allocating both financial and non-financial resources. If, on the contrary, the local allows last year's line-item reports to determine union activities for the next year, it runs the danger of letting the balance sheet determine what the union does or does not do. The union's strategic goals should guide the budget process, not the other way around. Certainly a realistic budget will constrain expenditures, but union priorities should be a political decision by the members and leaders rather than one for the accountants to decide.

• *Get more CPA for your buck.* Most accounting firms also have financial planning services. If the local is already spending money for annual and quarterly reports, you might be able to get this expertise for little additional cost.

- *Don't worry about management.* Unions sometimes fear that open debate about finances will let the employer learn the intimate details of the local's bank account. But employers already know exactly how much money the union has: they write the dues checks, read the LM-2 reports, and monitor union activities. The members are the only people left in the dark.
- *Include non-monetary resources.* The union movement would not exist without voluntary contributions of time and resources. Whether it is volunteer members working in an organizing drive, or community allies working a union phone bank, acknowledge these resources in the budget. For example, if the contract campaign needs ten coordinators and the union can pay two on lost time, the budget should also acknowledge the eight volunteer members who will be recruited (though it won't assign them a monetary value). This allows a more accurate plan of work.
- *Make multi-year forecasts.* Resource allocation may look very different in a contract year. In fact, preparing for big contract fights requires multi-year financial planning.
- *Be flexible.* Something will happen to disrupt the budget plan: an irate employer will sue the local, or layoffs may reduce the membership. If you have a plan, it is easier to keep the money focused on your key programs.

Communication

A MEMBER-TO-MEMBER NETWORK, described below, is the local's most important means of internal communication, but other methods are essential too. Whether you are an officer of a small or a large local, you should see communication—both internal and external—as one of your central jobs.

Communication is two-way. Don't wait for the phone to ring or for members to come to you. Find ways to have one-on-one conversations—not just a quick back-slapping hike through the plant but time for a more focused exchange (attending committee meetings won't do the trick). And then don't do all the talking yourself, but listen.

An open door policy sounds good, but officers can quickly become overwhelmed with calls and visits. The "open door" can actually shut the door on member involvement by letting a few people monopolize your time, while other people and projects slip through the cracks. It's better to schedule your day so that some blocks of time are not interrupted. Schedule specific times for visits with members in the workplace or at the hall.

Most union communication is reactive, putting out a flyer to members when there is important news, or responding to a call from the media. This piecemeal approach is inefficient and ineffective. The local needs to have structures in place for a regular flow of communication, with coordination between the internal and the external messages. What you say in flyers and what you say in press releases should have a consistent message, so that you are not reinventing your theme every time you communicate with a different audience.

Communication Director

Someone needs to be responsible for thinking about the big picture of union communication. Put someone in charge who does not have a boatload of other duties. You don't want to appoint the person who's also preparing contract language or dealing with 50 grievances; that person will likely end up saying, "If I have time, I'll type up a newsletter when I get home tonight." The communication job deserves as much attention as the local's other work. Depending on the local's size and resources, the communication director may be one of the elected officers, a staffer, or a rank-and-filer who works part-time for the local.

Duties of the communication director can include:

- Creating and maintaining the member-to-member network, including recruitment and training of volunteers and coordinators.
- Developing materials for the network, such as flyers.
- Working closely with officers to make sure everyone is on the same page in terms of message and talking points.
- Training members. Different types of training are appropriate for different members: active listening skills, one-on-one speaking, small- or large-group public speaking, dealing with reporters, writing for members or for the press. Seek help from the international or a local labor-studies program.
- Producing the union newsletter or newspaper. If your first instinct is to run a photograph of the president handing a check to a member who won an arbitration case, you're off base. Newsletters should have quotes from the members, run pictures of the members, and highlight the activity of the members. The newsletter committee or member-to-member network can gather stories about member activities, pose questions to members to get feedback, and recruit members to write. See the Troublemaker's web page for some hints on creating a lively newsletter.

The most faithful reader of the union newsletter and leaflets is probably the boss. Sometimes union leaders use the fact that "the information will fall into the wrong hands" as an excuse not to communicate. Don't worry about that; you want the boss to get the message. Make sure it is loud and clear.

- Soliciting email addresses, maintaining the union's website and email communication. Email, instant messages, and websites are great if used in coordination with traditional methods. See Chapter 20 for much more on this topic. Survey your members: how many regularly use the Internet and email? Organizers all too often feel they have been communicating ("I've tried to reach him several times now"), when all they've done is clicked. Know the limits. Email works well for co-workers who are constantly online and are comfortable using it, but never assume that just because you've sent an email, it's been heeded. We still need to look each other in the eye and talk.

This is a hefty list of duties. The director is responsible overall but should work with a committee of members and with staffers as needed. Remember that focusing on the member-to-member network is the most important task. In too many cases the priorities are reversed: officers focus on putting together great newsletters and flyers, but then don't have the capacity to get them throughout the shops.

For the director's external communication tasks, see Chapter 22, Dealing with the Media.

How to Develop a Member-to-Member Network

MANY UNIONS HAVE ADOPTED this simple method for a two-way flow of communication: the local recruits volunteers who commit to talking one-on-one with every member, inside the workplace, both on a regular basis and when the network is "activated." At most, each volunteer should be responsible for ten members.

When setting up the network, organizers should build on the informal networks that already exist and on whom people see in the course of their work (see "mapping" in Chapter 3). Recruiting volunteers who naturally interact with the members of their assigned group helps make the system work.

A smaller number among the volunteers will act as coordinators. Say your workplace has 50 people on each of three shifts. The local would recruit five volunteers for each shift, each of them agreeing to be in touch with ten co-workers. One of those volunteers would take on extra duties as the shift coordinator.

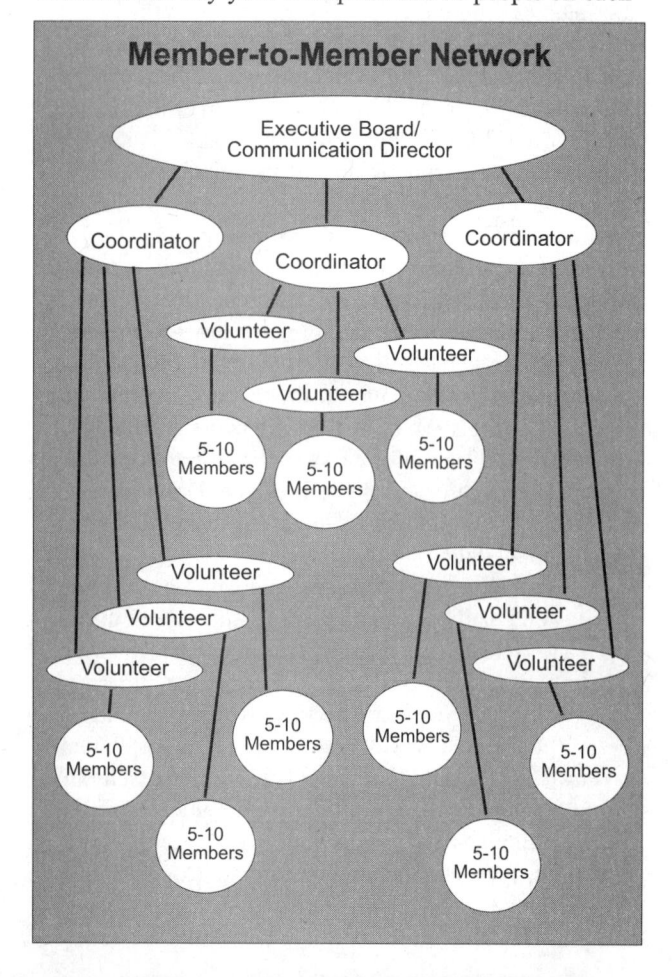

The three shift coordinators then need a way of communicating with each other, as well as with the local's overall communication director. The director should be in charge of getting out the information to and talking directly with the shift coordinators. The shift coordinators can call regular meetings—which can be very brief—of the volunteers on their shifts. The volunteers, in turn, pass out written information and speak directly to their ten buddies. They both provide and receive information.

What might activate the network? Say grievances are piling up on a certain issue, and the stewards council wants members to show management their concern. Or new equipment is about to be introduced, and the bargaining committee wants members to be alert for speed-up. Information about management's doings, changes in the international union, threats to the industry that the union should be responding to, legislative issues—all can be subjects for the network to disseminate. As discussed in other chapters, activating the network is the first step in shop floor campaigns, ranging from wearing stickers to organizing a lunchtime rally that brings in the media.

At the same time, the network must work bottom-up. Officers should be part of the network and make it a point to meet with members in formal and informal settings. They should regularly seek information through the network: How is the new system for job transfers working? Has supervisor Jones shaped up since the union forced management to slap his wrist? And the volunteers should be pro-active about asking their co-workers for their concerns. The volunteers bring that information—such as, "everyone wants to know why we gave $1,000 to the sheriff candidate"—to the shift coordinators, and so on from there.

Member-to-member networks are often ramped up during a contract fight and allowed to atrophy afterward. Instead, the structure needs to be continually and immediately available; put it up on a wall chart and in a database. Don't worry that you will be creating "make work" or idle communication. The employer will provide plenty of grist for the union communication mill.

How do stewards fit into the network? Few workplaces have a one-to-ten stewards ratio, so the network should complement the steward structure. It may be that stewards make the most natural shift coordinators, or it may work better to recruit different members for that job—and get more folks involved. There are no hard-and-fast rules. In any case, the network must work hand in glove with the stewards and set up regular channels for doing so. Avoid turf wars.

For more on a member-to-member network, see "AFSCME Local 3299: From Internal to External Organizing," in Chapter 15, and "Building a Member-to-Member Network" in Chapter 3 (a network created by rank-and-filers that eventually replaced their officers—with themselves).

Part-Time Officers, Lost Time, and Rank-and-File Stewards Committees

by David Pratt

EVEN WITH THE BEST INTENTIONS, union officials can lose a sense of what it is like to be a regular working member of the union. The officers and staff become a group unto themselves, separate and above the membership. Or the officers may try to do all the work themselves and forget about involving the members. Three ways to avoid this trap are for officers to continue working part-time in their regular jobs, to set up a stewards committee to oversee staffers' work, and for the union to supplement the officers and staff by taking members off the job to work for the union temporarily.

Officers Who Stay on the Job

One large local whose elected officers continue to work part-time in their regular jobs is a statewide CWA local, the University Professional and Technical Employees at the University of California. The local represents 11,000 researchers, museum scientists, electronics technicians, machinists, animal technicians, scene technicians, environmental health and safety techs, social workers, pharmacists, and clinical lab scientists. President Jelger Kalmijn, who researches the genetics of alcoholism at UC San Diego 40 percent of the time and works for UPTE the rest, explains, "Our preference is to keep an identity with the unit, the issues and challenges they have day to day. We want one foot in the workplace."

In such a large local, with chapters at 12 campuses throughout the state, the difficulties of being a part-time chief officer are immense, as any president can imagine. UPTE officers say it's worth it. Kalmijn says, "I have much more legitimacy as a union leader because I live under the conditions I'm responsible for negotiating. The officers are part of the life the members live.

"I also have a much better understanding of the pressures of the workplace, because I'm under those same conditions, in a very personal way. If you're off the job for 20 years there's not much difference between you and a person from the outside. The officer becomes more related to their union job than to the employer. Health benefits, the salary structure, parking—we pay $72 a month for parking—ergonomic issues: our officers are experiencing these and know what matters to members.

"When I get back to my UC job it's a relief. It's not the same as some unions, where people are looking to get off the job because they hate their work. With our kind of work, most of us do like our jobs."

To get the work done, UPTE's part-time officers do lots of delegating and use lost time to take members off the job to work temporarily for the union. Each chapter has campus-level officers who can use lost time. The union has negotiated an arrangement whereby the university continues to pay the officer's entire salary—and the

Members of the University Professional and Technical Employees/CWA at UCLA march to the chancellor's office. Despite representing 11,000 members, officers of UPTE still work part-time at their university jobs.

officer continues to receive service credits—and the union reimburses the university for the percentage of time spent on union work.

After serving on the statewide bargaining team in one set of talks, Kalmijn opted not to be a regular member of the team next time around. "When you're in bargaining you have to focus on that and shut down other activities," he explains. "Management doesn't send decision-makers to the bargaining table anyway. When the real decisions are made, at the end, they send in their higher-ups. It's better for the union to have a higher level [the president] to send in too."

For UPTE officers, working part-time has another benefit. Staying off the job for years could make it difficult to get back into their fields because of rapid technological and other changes. Similar considerations may apply for workers in other jobs, such as the skilled trades.

Stewards Committees

Another University of California union, the independent Coalition of University Employees, representing clericals, also functions with non-full-time officers. The statewide union has full-time staffers who handle grievances on some campuses, but they are accountable to a rank-and-file stewards committee as well as to officers, and the local relies on stewards to handle grievances up to and including arbitrations.

"Initially, we had no money, so it came from necessity," says Claudia Horning, who was CUE's president while working in the UCLA library. "Then, when we did have money to hire staff, we kept the model because it works. The newer folks just assume that rank-and-filers can do everything, and if they do assign work like this to staff, they assume staff should be accountable to and directed by members.

"At UCLA, our stewards committee has helped develop a sense of accountability for both the stewards and for staff who do grievances. The staff and the stew-

The Coalition of University Employees' stewards committee has helped develop a sense of accountability for both stewards and staff.

ards committee meet weekly; only members vote. We talk about cases, give each other advice, and decide how to proceed. Both stewards and staff feel like they have backup. With multiple people 'watching,' we can sometimes catch patterns that lead to mini-organizing campaigns—things that an isolated steward might not pick up on.

"It's worked quite well, in part because we've been very lucky in our staff, in terms of their competence and their integrity. But I think having the stewards committee in place would end up working even if we're less lucky in the future. Neither staff nor rank-and-file stewards are able to cut deals independently or without the knowledge of the committee. It keeps everyone honest, and the whole local benefits.

"Making stewarding a collective experience and developing accountability takes more work on the front end. A local has to commit time to it and figure out creative ways to share information. Sometimes it can be frustrating for more experienced stewards, who feel like they know what they're doing, to have to explain what they're doing and why to inexperienced stewards. But if they don't do that, they can slip into bad habits, and newer people don't have the opportunity to learn from their experience.

"It helps to keep re-stating the goal. At UCLA, we have every new steward sign a pledge that includes the idea of accountability."

Does any strategy guarantee against falling into a "servicing model" of unionism? Not necessarily, according to Horning. "It turns out it's just as easy for rank and filers to slip into that mode, or to allow staff to do it. It helps to keep examining your practices in some conscious, regular way, and to force committees to regularly explain their functioning to larger groups of members."

Using Lost Time

One way to boost participation and stretch the local's resources is to use lost time. Although the union has to pay members' wages when they come off their regular jobs to work for the union, this is a relatively inexpensive way to supplement full-time staff. Of course, it means you have to negotiate such union-leave provisions into your contracts. Locals use lost time in several ways:

• As part of an orientation program for activists, to give them insight into the workings of the union and help train them for future leadership positions. Each participant might spend some time in bargaining, arbitration, executive board meetings, organizing drives, and political action.

• In organizing drives, where motivated rank and filers can be extremely effective.

• To greet and help orient new members.

• During bargaining: to help build contract campaigns or set up strike funds and picket rosters.

• To boost campaigns against difficult employers. For example, after a contract is signed, the union may need to organize to make sure new language is enforced. Activists on lost time can help members understand the new contract, organize grievance campaigns with petitions and surveys, or track violations. For these kinds of campaigns, it's often best to train and use certain members repeatedly rather than having a large number barely get their feet wet.

• For political activity, such as phonebanking, testifying at public hearings, or attending legislative conferences.

• To lead solidarity activity. For example, the Civil Service Employees Association (AFSCME), which represents public employees throughout New York State, has a solidarity strike force that leaders activate as needed. Strike force members leaflet, beef up picket lines, help build turnout for rallies, do plant gate fundraising or food drives, or work with media contacts or religious or other support organizations. In a large local, solidarity opportunities can arise frequently, and a strike force can keep a core group active. Smaller locals that have fewer internal opportunities can use a strike force to work with Jobs with Justice or do other cross-union solidarity work.

Avoid Lost-Time Pitfalls

Unions should use lost-time programs selectively, as an addition to ongoing rank-and-file involvement, not as a substitute. If members get the message that they shouldn't do union work without getting paid, the lost-time program is having the wrong result. In an active union, the amount of work is too great for staff, full-time officers, and lost-timers to accomplish it all—and if they could, that wouldn't strengthen the union. Members who do union work on lost time should continue to volunteer time as well. This can be one of the requirements for participation in the program.

Work that is time-sensitive, such as mobilizing members during a contract campaign, may be well suited to a lost-time arrangement. Members on lost time can also coordinate the activity of volunteers.

In general, work on union committees should be for volunteers, and committees should be open and meet when members can attend, not during working hours, although this may mean that staff will have to help carry out committee work. Volunteers are also best for the role of member-organizers during organizing drives. Here the volunteer aspect is part of the message—that regular members are willing to devote their own time to build the union.

Make sure the lost-time program does not become a patronage system for political or personal friends. If the program is weighed down with self-serving or ineffective participants, members will view it with cynicism. Select activists on their merits, in a way that is transparent and fair. Clear guidelines for pay, length of time off the job, evaluations, and supervision are essential. So are clearly defined goals for their work.

Don't expect new lost-timers to function without training and guidance. Allocate staff or officers' time for educating them and for managing the lost-time work so that it runs smoothly, and figure such time into the program's budget. Since the lost-time program involves a great deal of training, make sure it is integrated with the local's education program. Steward training classes, for example, can serve a dual purpose.

AFSCME Local 3299 at the University of California provides an example of integrating volunteer activism with lost-time work. As described in Chapter 15 on Organizing, the local has Member Action Teams (MATs) that function at the workplace to keep members informed and confront management. In the MATs, workers develop their skills as organizers and communicators. Some then receive training in recruiting new members into the bargaining unit. When needed, these new member-organizers become temporary full-time staffers on lost time.

Leading and Managing Union Staff

FOR MOST TROUBLEMAKERS, fighting the boss comes naturally. Being a boss does not. Leading and managing union staff is often a challenging and sometimes a painful experience. Nevertheless, an elected official usually faces the dual roles of being both a union leader and an employer, whether the staff consists of one part-time secretary or a dozen organizers and service reps. Recognizing staff management as a distinct and important function of union leadership does not mean the local simply acts like a business. To the contrary, union leaders who try to build a social movement without good personnel practices are more likely to create a dysfunctional mess than an effective organization.

Do I Have To Be a Supervisor?

Managing union staff is often an unwelcome part of an officer's job. We want to be out of the office organizing non-union workers or leading a contract campaign. Instead, we feel stuck dealing with problems among the staff. Although leading staff can be hard work and takes a lot of time to do well, it's not a distraction from leading the union. In fact, leading and motivating staff to carry out the union's mission is one of the most important jobs of an elected official.

Consistency is critical. For example, some unions have organizing programs that assume high levels of turnover and rapid staff burnout. They don't mind having organizers work 80 hours a week for a couple of months. If that's your plan, why bother investing in training? If, however, you have a different model where you want to retain staff, you need to have a training program that will develop the necessary skills.

Staff Motivation

It takes more than money. If your motivation plan is nothing more than "we pay you good money so you gotta work harder," you're unlikely to motivate anything but resentment. Start by sharing why you got involved in the union. Instilling a sense of enthusiasm in others begins with explaining what motivates you.

Build a unified vision. What are we fighting for? Day-to-day union work can feel like drudgery. Making sure that the work of the union is founded on a clear vision of creating a better world for working people is the cornerstone of staff motivation. At the same time, elected leaders must recognize that staffers see their jobs as both a calling and a job. You have to let them give voice to both sides of those concerns.

While elected officers and the membership ultimately decide the direction of the union, having a voice is critical to staffers' motivation. People are more committed to programs they helped to create.

Accountability to the Mission

A union administration ought to have a platform of issues that it campaigned for and that members elected it to accomplish. As explained above in the section on strategic planning, the union should capture its goals in a mission statement that will guide the officers' and members' efforts as well as the work of the staff.

When reformers are elected to office, they will often make significant changes in goals for the union and in the way the union functions to achieve those goals. When staffers are accustomed to a prior administration's way of operating and have political agreement or loyalty to the old ways, this can create problems. They may balk at shifting from a business-union way of operating to a member-involvement model.

Having a mission statement makes it clear to all what is expected. It sets a standard. One way to provide some accountability is to ask staffers to sign an agreement to follow the mission statement and the implementation steps designed to accomplish the new goals.

If you want to retain staff, you must give them training opportunities to help them succeed in carrying out the mission. Performance evaluations are also important, using standard evaluation tools that involve members.

But no administration should have to retain disloyal or unmotivated people who are not showing they can perform. Sometimes new administrations will determine that the staff from the prior administration will be in the way of progress, because their loyalty or their ability to shift gears is not there. When staff unions are involved, it is even more important to establish what behavior is not in line with the mission.

Support staff—those who keep the union office running—may or may not have taken the job out of dedication to the union cause, but they play a critical role. They are the ones whom members can always reach, and their interactions with members affect how members view the local. They deserve the respect that all staff deserve; they should be part of the life of the local and receive training in advanced skills, as necessary.

Employment Policies

It is a serious mistake not to have a written employment policies manual for staff. Having written policies reflects not whether the executive board trusts staffers but rather its commitment to follow good personnel practices. At the same time, your job as a manager of staff does not end once you have handed out the policy book. A policy manual should support the following goals:

• The tone of the organization. If the leadership wants the union to be more like a social movement than an insurance club, the employee handbook can help set this tone. Include the union's mission statement and explanations of what motivates the executive board and other activists to work so hard for the cause.

• Rules and policies. Expense reimbursement procedures, paid time off, and other employment policies should be spelled out. The handbook should be reviewed at least once a year to address any needed changes or to incorporate staff feedback.

• Firm stance against discrimination and harassment. Make it explicit that such practices not only violate the law but are also contrary to basic union principles and will not be tolerated.

• Keeping elected leaders accountable for treatment of staff. Once the policies are written, follow them.

Does Managing Staff Seem Too Easy? Just Add Internal Politics.

Like any other organization, unions are rife with politics and personalities. While these two sources of conflict often overlap, it is important to see the distinctions. Internal union politics are as certain as death and taxes and usually involve substantive differences over the direction and activities of the union. In contrast, personality conflicts tend to be more about individuals' characteristics.

Still, personal disputes that are allowed to fester can seriously undermine the organization and lead to splits in leadership. These problems need to be addressed early on. Staff may not become best friends, but the union can avoid an apolitical civil war.

The leadership team should figure out who is the person who can best handle people and deal with personal issues—a person who has good mediation skills and who takes the time to hear both sides of the dispute. You must have a recognized process in place, clear steps the local can take to intervene in personal disputes. Two approaches are possible: You can say "both of you get over it or get out." Or you can invest more time and energy to intervene.

Dealing with substantive political differences, on the other hand, is a central part of the local's personnel management. Staff jobs are inherently political. Elected officers are empowered to hire staff to assist them in carrying out the duties of their position. In some locals, administrative and other support personnel have traditionally been isolated from internal politics and regime change. But usually it is impossible to avoid the impact of internal politics on employment practices.

Political loyalty trumps other personnel management considerations. Regardless of whether the staffer is a good or a bad representative, appointed staff members who campaign against elected officers should be fired. Private disagreements are common and healthy in a democratic organization, but it is undemocratic for appointed staff to undermine elected officers.

The reverse situation is usually more difficult. How do elected officers tell a political supporter that he or she is just not doing the job? Training and support can help that person succeed, but if not, you shouldn't keep a dead-weight loyalist on your staff. Clear and fair practices can help ease the pain of separation or help the person find other effective roles within the organization.

Being a Good Staff Manager

Elected officers all bring different strengths to the organization. If the principal officer is not good at managing staff, he or she needs to delegate this job to someone who can perform this important leadership function. In the same way, senior staff who were appointed to supervisory positions because of their skills as servicing reps or organizers also need training and support in developing staff-management skills. Organizing and contract campaigns are difficult, but leading and managing staff can feel a whole lot harder.

We've all had experiences with good and bad bosses, and we can apply these experiences to managing staff. We know, for example, that organizations function better when leaders value and respond to employee input. While staff will not have the final word on how union policies are implemented, their feedback and ideas should be taken very seriously, since, if they are doing their jobs right, they are in close communication with members. Staff should have various avenues for input, including day-to-day interaction with the officers in an informal setting, as well as more formal settings like staff retreats.

Do not use memos or emails as the primary form of communication with staff. Officer-staff communication should include staff meetings, one-on-one conversations, informal chats, written memos, and formal evaluations. Sometimes we all just need to vent, and scheduling one-on-one conversations is critical.

Making sure that the work of the union gets done is, of course, central. The type of accountability procedure you establish depends on skill level, political importance, and nature of the assignment. Sometimes union leaders can give staff complete autonomy to get the work done. In other cases, the assignment demands close supervision. In either case, union leaders need to have a system for assessing and adjusting the work.

A good accountability mechanism falls somewhere between the extremes of "do it my way or else" and "I'd rather you like me than criticize your work." Building mutual trust and respect is different from making others like you personally. The expectations of the assignment and the program for assessment should be made clear from the beginning.

Decisions about how staff build members as leaders (and don't take over that function themselves) are also critical. Having this discussion up front helps staff understand their role and makes clear to members their own responsibility to take leadership.

One of the worst mistakes union leaders can make is to ignore accountability problems. The labor movement cannot afford dead weight. At the same time, they can't expect staff to succeed without giving them feedback and the additional tools and resources they need. Trying to have accountability without training is like telling staff to run a race without conditioning. Training and development programs show that the union is committed to helping staffers succeed.

Even though the union's staff is committed to the cause, money matters. Highly charged emotional issues of value and respect are tied to compensation. Fairness and consistency are critical to the compensation plan. The more layers of staff and skill levels there are, the more important it is to have a clear compensation schedule and stick to it. While it may not seem like a big deal to delay a one-percent raise for six months, the message that such a delay sends to staff members is highly negative. Some unions have a policy that raises for the staff are tied to raises for the members: if the members get a three percent raise, so does the staff.

And last, have some fun together. Union work is intense and stressful. You may think you already spend too much time with staff at work, but it is important to build camaraderie outside the union hall.

What About Staff Unions?

The debate over staff unions will rage on for years to come. Both sides can point to plenty of horror stories. Whether it's a principal officer acting like a dictator or a slave-driver, or business agents bargaining to protect their union Town Cars, objecting when members do lost-time work for the union, or campaigning against elected leaders, there is plenty to criticize.

For union leaders, whether or not the staff forms a union is ultimately not their choice. While on a personal level it might be natural for an elected officer to view staff unionization as an act of disloyalty or a personal attack, such reactions can only lead to deteriorating relations. Progressive staff management skills are important whether or not the local has a collective bargaining agreement with its staff. The point of good management practices in unions is not to keep them "union-free," but to build the union and strengthen the labor movement.

Structures that Train Leaders

by Marsha Niemeijer

IN 2004 International Longshoremen's Association Local 1422 in Charleston, South Carolina began an experiment with a "junior executive board," to train future leaders. "Everyone is concerned about the future of the union," says President Ken Riley, "because we know that the current leadership are all in the same age group, 40-50 years old."

Ken Riley.

The five junior board members are elected in the same way as the regular ten-member board. They attend board meetings, although they do not vote, in order to develop the skills to one day run the local themselves. Their duties are to take notes, observe, and make suggestions.

Junior members are expected to attend all union events or union/community support events. "They should be among the first ones to volunteer and rally the troops," says Riley. "There should be junior executive members on any bus going somewhere for the local." They also elect a delegate to meetings that the local participates in, such as the Dock Marine Council or the Longshore Workers Coalition (a reform group in the international union) and are expected to give reports.

A provision for a junior executive board can be added to the local bylaws.

SEIU Local 616 represents 9,000 homecare workers who come from many countries. Translation of meetings into Spanish, Chinese, and Farsi is essential. The homecare workers also meet monthly in language/ethnicity-based caucuses to discuss contract issues, union business, and broader labor movement topics.

Organizing a Candidates' Debate

When the 2003 local elections were at hand in Local 1422, rank and filers initiated a petition calling for a debate. "The petition was overwhelmingly supported," says Riley. "Not one of the 27 or so candidates could ignore it, for fear of losing credibility.

"It was a huge debate. We asked two members to moderate. Each candidate was asked to give a two-minute opening talk, and then we opened it up to questions from the floor. About 300 members attended, and they asked question after question from the microphone. The debate started at 7 pm and at 10:30 pm we finally cut it off. We ran out of time for closing statements from the candidates.

"The debate was a really good weeding-out process. A lot of candidates were running for office on popularity or on their family's name. They had no idea of their job function and they didn't have a good grasp of the industry. When they got tough questions, they couldn't answer in an articulate way. They were exposed.

"The other benefit is that the members were put in a position to think about leadership—what does it take to be a good leader for your union—in a more serious way. As a result, the vote for our elected officers was much more of a quality vote.

"I also think that it is yet another way to increase participation in the union. I saw people at the microphones that I hadn't seen anywhere else. When members have an opportunity to voice their opinion, it means that their opinion matters. An election campaign then becomes more than just casting a vote. Some people told me they felt that the debate allowed them to help shape other members' opinions about the leadership. The debate continued for days after that evening.

"A lot of the issues that were brought up had to do with the contract. Other questions focused on the way the union should be run. Our membership is now realizing that we all have to be actively engaged in making sure we grow new leaders, because if we don't, everything we've invested in becoming a militant local will come crashing right down."

In this case, the debate worked in favor of the incumbents. But rank-and-file members running against an entrenched old guard might also want to make a motion at a union meeting to have a candidates' debate.

Dealing with Language Differences

by Kay Eisenhower

SEIU LOCAL 616 REPRESENTS 9,000 homecare workers in Alameda County, California. These workers don't have conventional workplaces, as they assist the elderly and disabled in their own homes. They also come from many countries and cultures, with little in common other than being low-paid and ignored for many years by the labor movement.

Language is one of the biggest challenges to overcome if these union members are to participate fully in their union's life (Local 616 has 14,000 members overall). Chinese, Spanish, and sometimes Farsi translation services are essential, though expensive. Membership meetings of the Homecare Chapter are conducted in both English and Chinese, with simultaneous translation into Spanish. The translation equipment, consisting of headsets and microphones for the translators, cost the local around $3,500 for 22 sets. Naturally, it takes longer to conduct meetings in several languages. Farsi translation is usually done with an individual translator because there are fewer Farsi speakers (Farsi is spoken in Iran, Afghanistan, and India). Either way, it's a lot of whispering.

Homecare organizer Ivan Ortega acknowledges, "People's tolerance level takes a while to build up. But we announce at the beginning of the meeting that we are translating into several languages and ask members to be patient. There's no other way that the non-English speakers can participate equally." Bilingual union staff or members provide the translations. When necessary, the local hires professional translators as well, although they have a rough time with the union lingo.

Local 616's homecare members meet monthly in language/ethnicity-based caucuses to discuss contract issues, local union business, and broader labor movement topics. These three caucuses are conducted strictly in the language of their members: Spanish for the Comunidad Hispana, Chinese for the Chinese Homecare Family, and English for the African American Homecare Committee. A current project of the Chinese Homecare Family is setting up workshops at a local Chinese senior residence hotel to try to work out issues between workers and consumers of homecare services.

When the local does training on workers' rights, immigrant rights, how to work better with difficult consumers, or how to navigate the In-Home Support Services bureaucracy, it's usually done by language group. Leadership training, on subjects such as how to run meetings and organize co-workers, is done in smaller groups and includes all the language groups together, using the simultaneous translation equipment. The local executive board's monthly meetings are also conducted in three or four languages, using the equipment.

Union leaflets are produced in multiple languages. Local 616's experience in this area was very useful in a 2004 ballot campaign to support public health care services. Local members campaigned in Oakland's Chinatown and distributed election materials in multiple languages to urge voters to support Measure A. We reached parts of the community we had never worked with before, which was critical to our election victory.

It might seem that English classes would be an obvious help for this local, but Local 616 has found that it's not that simple. When the local set up English as a Second Language (ESL) classes, it had an instructor from the local adult school or community college come to the union hall twice a week. Using the hall was important to increase attendance and allow workers to feel at home. But for these workers, who have constantly changing schedules, it is difficult to keep to regular classes, and a workforce with several different languages and different literacy and English levels makes it hard to teach effectively. ESL teachers say that five classes a week are needed, which was not practical for our members.

Although ESL classes can be a valuable service for members, they are not a substitute for involving members before they learn to speak English. Locals should take all of these factors into account when considering how to integrate workers who speak many languages.

Keep Your Eyes on the Prize

by Jane Slaughter

WHAT QUALITIES MAKE FOR GOOD UNION LEADERS? The list is a long one. Officers who do best by their members are often those who keep in mind labor's broader goal of a just society for everyone—not just the next grievance or contract. These leaders also find that keeping "the big picture" in mind keeps them energized and in touch with why they wanted to be union leaders in the first place.

The big picture usually means getting involved in coalitions that expand the local's goals and horizons, such as those for health care reform, environmental causes, the rights of immigrants or minorities, democratic reforms in the international union, or living wage campaigns. Reasons to get involved include:

• Such work serves the local's basic purpose of representing members. Cleaner air, stopping police harassment—these are concrete improvements in members' lives, as well as those of other community members.

• Making allies stands the local in good stead when it needs partners for its own fights (see Chapters 12 and 13).

• It's a way to get more members involved. Some who've never been interested in union meetings or making waves in the workplace might have experience in community-based campaigns or want to get their congregation on board to fight for health care reform.

• Movements educate members about how society works and put them in touch with people who have a vision of how it could work better.

• Knowing the score and having a vision makes activists more willing to stick around for the long haul. They don't give up after the first defeat.

"Our officers know how to branch out," explains Gloria Lum of Letter Carriers Branch 294 in New York City. "We are part of Labor Notes and other efforts to reform the labor movement. We worked closely with the Association for Union Democracy, having them help us set up education programs. We've gotten involved in APALA [Asian Pacific American Labor Alliance] and learned a lot at their conferences. This is the only way to grow and expand and stay energized, by being part of other good efforts to build the labor movement."

Branching Out

Patty DeVinney is president of CWA Local 1168, one of the largest health care unions in Buffalo. Her local consciously goes on the offensive rather than simply responding to the latest management-caused emergency. "It would be easy to fall into the mode of functioning where you spend the whole day dealing with this crisis and that crisis," says DeVinney. Instead, she and other officers go out and educate community and union groups about the crisis in health care.

When she does, says DeVinney, a registered nurse, "I feel much more inspired and more at peace with myself. I feel I'm going in the right direction. People

CWA Local 1168 works aggressively to educate the Buffalo community about the crisis in health care.

need that, especially now. We in the labor movement are constantly getting slammed. To keep going, to remember *why w*e're doing it is very important."

Local 1168 has participated in a living-wage campaign for low-wage city workers and belongs to Jobs with Justice. The local sends members to national conferences of JwJ, Labor Notes, Universal Health Care Action Now, and Families USA. But officers see a special role for the local in educating community groups and other unions about the causes of the health care crisis.

Local 1168 and Jobs with Justice have developed a PowerPoint slide presentation that shows graphically the forces opposing quality health care. DeVinney uses it to argue for a single-payer national health care system. The local has given talks to a wide range of Buffalo-area groups—seniors, churches, unions, students, nursing classes—and presented a workshop at a national JwJ conference and the CWA national convention. "People are very, very appreciative to get the bigger picture of what's going on in health care," DeVinney says. The local uses a "train the trainer" program to teach both local members and community people how to share the information as well.

Local 1168 helped JwJ put together a delegation to study the single-payer system in Canada, right across the border. DeVinney wants her local to play a specific role within the health care reform movement, "debunking the myths about Canada, like waiting lists. When people say it doesn't work in Canada, we can describe what's really going on."

Sometimes progressive union leaders get too wrapped up in such "outside" work, as individuals, and don't try to bring the members along. If they neglect the more mundane aspects of leading the local, they may find themselves unelected. This isn't a problem in Local 1168, since "the way health care dollars are distributed has a huge impact on our members' working conditions," DeVinney explains.

Bringing It Back

Local 1168 sees national conferences as a way to remind members and officers of the big picture. When the local sends members, though, they understand they are not getting a union-paid vacation. They're required to submit reports. Cori Gambini, an area vice-president for a unit of nurses, represented the local at the 2003 Labor Notes Conference. The benefits to the local, she says, were both practical and intangible.

One workshop taught her how to mobilize members for a contract campaign and how to make information requests of management. "When I came back," she recalls, "I took all the information I had and put my own package together with highlights from each workshop, from my notes. I gave a report for the executive board.

"Then when we went to do surveys for bargaining demands, I pulled out my notes, and we didn't use only a checklist kind of survey, like we might have. We had the members write in what they wanted, as we'd learned at Labor Notes. And we appointed a research committee to research wages and working conditions in different hospitals across the nation."

Equally important for her functioning as an elected leader, Gambini says, was "the people you're surrounded by at the conference. When you get all of us together, everybody gets really motivated—you feel like you can walk out of there and just knock the walls down. You are knocked down so many times by management, and your own membership sometimes. We inspired each other."

So how do the Local 1168 officers make sure that they build big-picture work into the local's plan of work?

• They budget for the big picture. The annual budget includes funds for training and outreach to other unions, physicians, and health care advocacy groups.

• They help elected leaders educate themselves. When new bargaining committee members were elected, DeVinney sent them a list of sources on pensions, overtime, and health insurance.

• Since the local was founded they've received a bundle of 50 copies of *Labor Notes* every month, which they distribute to stewards and executive board members. At board meetings DeVinney points out articles that are particularly relevant.

• They're conscious about training new leaders. In 1999-2000 the local gained over 2,000 new members when an existing employer merged with another health care provider. They made sure that new leaders were among those sent to educational conferences.

• The local puts rank-and-file members in charge of four crucial areas: political action, organizing/mobilizing, health and safety, and communications. Each of these four activities is led by members who are on lost time three days a week. One of the organizer-mobilizer's duties is to be the local's liaison to Jobs with Justice.

Other Benefits

DeVinney believes the local's effort to educate the community about health care reform has not only enhanced the local's reputation in the Buffalo community, it has increased members' confidence to act in the workplace. "When people feel they have a better handle on what's going on, they are freer to start speaking on issues," she says. "The reaction is, 'There's so much more to this than I ever thought. And there are groups out there doing things that I can see myself as part of.'

"They're able to articulate what the issues are, versus just complaining. At meetings regarding staffing in the hospital, they're more likely to stick to their guns and identify what the problem is and what the solutions are."

The health care activism helps in organizing new members, as well; in 20 years the local has grown from 800 nurses to 4,500 health care workers in all job titles.

How can locals make sure they are part of a larger movement and a larger vision? As part of its strategic plan, the local should collectively decide its priorities for work outside the confines of the shop floor and the union hall. These should be specific: not "build a stronger labor movement" but "initiate a contract-campaign support committee on the Central Labor Council," for example. Money should be budgeted. Education programs should bring members on board, and there should be ample opportunities for members to be active in coalitions.

And how can individual officers make sure they don't get buried under the local's other important work?

- Budget in time to work on your local's big-picture goals, on a daily or weekly basis. Make a commitment that you will do this work no matter what.
- An "open door" policy can allow random interruptions to blow the local's priorities off track. A better idea is to set aside some time when you don't take phone calls or visits, and then build time for direct contact with members into your schedule.
- Delegate, delegate, delegate. Every day the local receives a barrage of requests by mail and by phone. Put someone else you trust in charge of making decisions on what is a priority and what can wait or be tossed.
- Prioritize top-notch training for stewards and encourage direct action on the shop floor (see Chapter 3). If members can't get their problems solved without calling the hall, officers' time will be eaten up with putting out individual fires.
- Get more hands on the plow. Use lost time and the other methods discussed in this chapter and in Chapter 21 to build more leaders.

Resources

- *CWA Local Officers Resource Manual*. Available free from Steve Early, c/o CWA District 1, 100 Tower Office Park, Suite C, Woburn, MA 01801. 781-937-9600. Lsupport@aol.com.
- *UE Leadership Manual*. Focuses on involving and training more activists. United Electrical Workers, One Gateway Center, Suite 1400, Pittsburgh, PA 15222. 412-471-8919. ue@ranknfile-ue.org. $75 plus $5 shipping.

Authors

KAY EISENHOWER was a co-founder of SEIU Local 616 in Alameda County, California in 1973 and a board member and officer for many years. She does advocacy work to support the local public health care safety net.

ROBERT HICKEY is a labor educator and Ph.D. student at Cornell University. Before attending Cornell, he spent ten years as a Teamster dockhand and organizer.

MARSHA NIEMEIJER staffs Labor Notes' New York office, where she covers longshore workers, telecom workers, and Canadian and European labor, as well as international economic issues. She has worked with the Transnationals Information Exchange since 1995 and helps coordinate international and cross-border programs for TIE and Labor Notes.

DAVID PRATT is an organizer for Teamsters for a Democratic Union.

JANE SLAUGHTER is the editor of this book.

Notes

1. Kate Bronfenbrenner and Tom Juravich, "Out of the Ashes: The Steelworker's Global Campaign at Bridgestone/Firestone." *Multinational Companies and Global Human Resource Strategies*, William Cooke, editor. Quorum Books, 2003.
2. Dan La Botz, *A Troublemaker's Handbook*, Labor Notes, 1991, pp. 112-114.
3. Robert Hickey, "Preserving the Pattern: Membership Mobilization and Union Revitalization at PACE Local 4-227." *Labor Studies Journal*, Spring 2004.
4. This tool was developed by Anthony Thigpen, a long-time community organizer in southern California and founder of Action for Grassroots Empowerment & Neighborhood Development Alternatives (AGENDA).
5. Jane McAlevey, "It Takes a Community: Building Unions from the Outside In." *New Labor Forum*, Spring 2003.

On the Troublemaker's Website

Read more about ILA Local 1422, described above. The local is famous for its fight to defend the "Charleston 5" in 2000-01. Read about that campaign, plus how a reform group took over the local, the union's outreach to the Charleston community, and its involvement in a reform movement within the ILA. By Dan La Botz.

"How a Local Newspaper Can Get the Membership Involved," by Mary Baird.

Go to www.labornotes.org.

20. Troublemaking on the Home Page

by Matt Noyes and David Yao

THE INTERNET has created a whole new world of communication and interaction for workers. While electronic communication will never displace person-to-person contact at worksites or union halls, it is certainly augmenting unions' efforts to educate and organize. The days when a workforce lived in the shadow of the factory are long gone. When a union's membership is dispersed by geography and by different shift times and worksites, or when the demands of work and family life are barriers to union participation, a well-maintained electronic link can keep workers in touch with what they need to know about the state of the war with their employers.

This chapter has two parts: first, advice for rank-and-file union reformers and second, guidance for local unions using the Internet. Much of what we say applies equally to both, and we tried not to be repetitious, so we urge you to look for what you need in both sections.

Rank-and-File Reformers and the Internet

MANY UNIONS WERE SLOW to move into cyberspace, and then created websites that resembled official union publications, giving the official line but offering limited information and little interaction.

Rank-and-file unionists, on the other hand, took to the Internet like fish to water, at home in its democratic, free-speaking, do-it-yourself culture. No wonder: the Internet provides an ideal environment and powerful tools for much of what activists do offline. You can get your hands on information and resources, share that information with others, network and communicate with co-workers, and finally turn it all into action offline.

Cyber activism is not a substitute for "real world" activism—the hard struggles on the shop floor, in the union hall, and on the streets. But the Internet offers a valuable space for critical thinking, education, and democratic participation. And once people get talking and participating, the step to action is easier to take.

How can rank-and-file workers use the Internet to organize for democracy and power on the job and in the union? One of the most popular and effective organizing tools is the rank-and-file website. These independent sites reflect the priorities of their authors, from personal diary pages to industry-buff sites to pages of ranting posted by the disgruntled. Then there are the troublemaking sites, the ones designed to get workers involved in collective action on the job and in the union. Here are basic guidelines for building such a site, with illustrations from websites online in early 2004.

A Few Design Basics

Have a home page. This is crucial from an organizing point of view. The home page is where you explain what you are doing and try to get the visitor involved. It should show people what's available on the site and how to get to it.

Put high-priority content "above the fold." The key part of the home page is the section that fits into most people's screens without scrolling. Part of this area is used for site navigation (links to other pages on your site), part for the name, description, and contact information, and part for content—the information most important for people to see.

Tip: Do not make a home page that is more than three or four times as long as the area above the fold. Many people will not have the patience to scroll all the way down. (Articles and documents can be a little longer, because people know that what they can't see is a continuation of what they are looking at.)

To decide what goes above the fold, think about your

Where's the Website?

Websites come and go. All the sites used as examples here have undergone changes, and some are no longer in existence.

To see the sites as they were at the time this chapter was written in early 2004, go to the very useful Internet Archive Wayback Machine (www.archive.org/web/web.php) and type the URL printed in this chapter into the search box. (For example, to see the Bartenders for a Stronger Union website, enter www.vegasbartender.org.) You will get a list of archives.

To find the sites as they are today, or to find other sites by rank-and-file members of the same union, go to the frequently updated links page on the Association for Union Democracy website, www.uniondemocracy.org.

Technology is evolving too, so some specific references or tips may become out of date. For technical advice, consult the resources list at the end of the chapter.

goals for the website. What information is central to your mission, and what is secondary? If your focus is on action, don't fill the area above the fold with general news about the industry you work in, or big photos or logos.

If you want to educate, agitate, and organize, then make sure that there is a little of each above the fold. You can do this by placing links to pages with those contents; by taking a sentence or two from items you want people to read and then giving a link to follow for the rest of the story; or by making a "what's new" list that has items from each category. Make sure to focus on the most important current tasks and campaigns, especially the time-sensitive issues—an upcoming action or meeting that people must act on now.

You also need to think about your audience. Discuss with co-workers what they would like to see. Listen carefully to what people say on the job, in the union, in forums and discussion lists.

Stay current. People don't want to keep visiting a site that still talks about "upcoming" events from last year. Having time-specific information on the home page helps show that the site is alive.

Have a clear navigation system that is the same throughout the site (same list of navigation links, same names, same location on the page, same design and layout). The most common approach is to use three types of navigation links:

1. Basic navigation along the top of the page—typically, "home," "contact us," "about [your group's name]," "links," "search this site," and links to main content pages such as "upcoming events" or "the forum." The "contact" and "about" links should lead to pages with more detailed contact information (including a form for people to write to you), and a more detailed description of your site and its mission.

2. In the left column, a list of links to the site's contents. Put the high-priority items at the top of the list.

Cyber-Democracy: Your Legal Rights Online and Offline

SOME AUTOCRATIC UNION LEADERS have responded to Internet free speech by trying to shut it down. Fortunately, members have legal rights that protect internal union activity, including activity that takes place online. This summary from the Association for Union Democracy describes your rights under a federal law, the Labor Management Reporting and Disclosure Act (LMRDA), as they apply to online activism.

It is illegal for the union or the employer to retaliate against you, or threaten you, for exercising your rights under the LMRDA. (The LMRDA applies to private sector union members and some federal employees, and includes union bodies that represent a mix of public and private sector workers. Public sector workers often have the same protections in other forms, through state laws or regulations, or through case law.)

1. The Right To Participate in Your Union

You have the right to participate in union affairs, including meetings and elections. This means you have the right to participate freely (subject to reasonable rules) in official union chat groups or discussion lists. You have the right to run for office, which means equal access to union publications for campaigning—including union email lists, websites, listserves, and email publications. You have the right to distribute election campaign material to the union's list (complete or partial) of member email addresses.

2. The Right to Essential Information

You have the right to certain types of information—financial reports, contracts, constitution. Some of this is available online, but you do not have the legal right to force the union to make the information available online.

You are free to publish and distribute, in print and electronic form, on flyers, websites, and email lists, the information in these reports and documents. Do not be intimidated by a union attorney who threatens to sue for copyright infringement.

3. The Right to Free Speech

Your right to free speech about union affairs (in the union and in public) is very broad and includes email and web speech. You are free to: criticize (or praise) union policies, officers, staff, or candidates; discuss union policies and issues; write about, sing about, and draw cartoons about union representatives; complain, protest, demand, and advocate.

4. The Right to Free Assembly

Your rights to organize with your co-workers are very broad. You can form a committee or a caucus; meet on or offline without official union permission or participation; set up a website, discussion list, newsletter, chat room, or other online publication or forum; limit access to all or parts of your site to members of your committee; link to other websites, organizations, and unions (including your own); take collective action to influence the union (online pickets, PDF flyers, email petitions, and websites).

Note: Be careful not to represent yourselves, your group, or your website as official union representatives if you are not. Do not use computers or other resources that belong to your employer, or to the union. In union elections, an employer—anyone who employs at least one other person—is prohibited from contributing to a candidate or a campaign.

Contact these organizations for help:

Association for Union Democracy, 104 Montgomery St., Brooklyn, NY 11225, 718-564-1114, aud@igc.org, www.uniondemocracy.org.

Public Citizen Internet Free Speech Project, www.citizen.org/litigation/briefs/IntFreeSpch/index.cfm.

These links need not be to sections of your site with generic titles (like "Documents"). It's helpful to the reader to link to specific pages (for example, "our Oct. 15 letter to management about overtime violations"). It is good for content deep in your website to "bubble up" to the home page.

3. On a content page, use the left column for links to items on that page. (These are called anchor links.)

Bottom line: a visitor to your site should always know where he or she is and how to get to the other parts of the site. If not, it's like you are just walking up to co-workers and dumping boxes full of disorganized papers in their laps.

Guide people to the material they need. Make your links specific and descriptive. For example, instead of "Events," name the link "Local meetings and campaigns: Nominations next month, Carlson's picket next Thursday." Or make separate links to each event.

If your site has more than ten pages, include a "search this site" box on every page.

For all links off your site, give a short description of the site you are linking to and the full URL. Check these links regularly; dead links are a turn-off. Be sure to say whether a link means you endorse the site or not. Most Internet users know that linking to a site does not imply you agree with it, but your opponents may try to make this claim.

Use your priorities, and the needs of your audience, to decide who to link to. Long lists of links can feel like a waste of time and make it harder for people to understand what you're trying to accomplish (are you trying to be an online encyclopedia?).

Tell people who you are:

The Conscience of 294. An unofficial website for the members of Teamsters Local 294, Albany, New York. Short and sweet. www.co294.com/.

The Barking Dog / El Perro Ladrador / Ang Asong Kumakahol. An unofficial newsletter put out by Caroline Lund, a member of UAW Local 2244 at the NUMMI plant in Fremont, California. geocities.com/abarkingdog/. The site title makes an effort to reach out to Spanish- and Tagalog-speaking workers.

"DUES NEWS" ADVENTURES IN SOLIDARITY (CWA Loco 9510), THE WEB SITE FOR THE REST OF US (The Good, the Bad, the Ugly & the Indifferent)... owned by Mike Drake, Member & "Defrocked" Shop Steward of CWA Loco 9510, Orange County, California. www.mindspring.com/~drakester/. Some descriptions give you a flavor of the website and its sponsor.

Build a division of labor. If someone else already has a great list of all the grievance settlements from your local online, or links to all the locals in your union, or a lively discussion board, link to them. By adding links that make use of existing resources, you are building community and connections among activists.

Be creative, but respect the low-end users. Graphics, video, animation, audio, and music are fun and entertaining, and creativity and humor are important organizing tools. Draw on members' talents to make the website more interesting, funny, provocative. But keep these rules in mind:

1. Don't let graphics, splash pages, and other creative touches become hurdles the user has to jump over to get to the content they are looking for. For example, do not add an extra welcome page before the home page.

2. Make sure the user feels safe and in control. Involuntary gizmos like pop-ups and even voluntary items like cookies can make users feel like the site is out of their control, or that someone is spying on them.

3. In general, use a few simple graphics on most pages, and collect larger or more advanced files—like photos, songs, and video—in a gallery or special multimedia page that users can choose to open or ignore.

Tell People Who, What, and Where You Are

It seems obvious, but many rank-and-file sites fail to do this. Why make people search all over, or guess who you are? On the home page, at the top, the site should tell the visitor what the site is about, who it is for, who puts it out, and where they are located. (This is also helpful to search engines and people linking to your site, who often quote your description in their link text. You can use this description as a "meta tag" to help search engines identify you.) In the description, make it clear that your site is "not an official union publication."

Include the site name and a one-sentence description on every page, since people may not enter your site via the home page.

Tip: Get a good domain name for your site, something short and easy to remember. (To see if a domain name is available go to "Who is": www.networksolutions.com/en_US/whois/index.jhtml.) You don't want to be stuck with the long cumbersome names that free website hosts assign. Compare Bartenders for a Stronger Union's domain name—www.vegasbartender.org (and clever email address, Heybartender@vegasbartenders.org)—with this monster for Plumbers and Pipefitters Local 787 Members for Democracy: www.mountaincable.net/~namrik/ualocal787mfdver04001.htm. Try putting *that* on a t-shirt or leaflet.

Have a specific audience in mind for your site, one that matches your organizing goals. If you are organizing on the local level, for example, your site should speak primarily to your local members. What you post and the priority you give items should speak to the top interests and concerns of the people you are hoping to work with. Include the audience in your description: "the unofficial forum for members of Local 787, United Association of Plumbers and Pipefitters."

Put contact information front and center. Give your email address at least, and phone, fax, and address/post office box if possible. The email or phone number of individual activists that workers can contact is best.

What if you want to be anonymous because of fears about retaliation? To avoid being identified by someone doing a "who is" lookup, there are anonymous domain registration services available: domains.aplus.net/anonindex.php. You can also set up an anonymous email account. The downside of anonymity is that it is harder for interested workers to get in touch with you and it weakens your credibility—"these people aren't even willing to stand up for their views and they want me to stand up to the boss?" Another option is to openly identify the site's owner but to include messages and articles by anonymous writers.

Say What You Stand for and How You Plan To Get It

In addition to the brief description of your purpose, you should have a concrete **mission statement**—what you stand for, the specific changes you want to make, and how you think they can be accomplished. This is one of the most important items on your site. It helps people assess you and your intentions. The mission statement should be specific—do not just promise to be good people and do good things. Give a brief summary of your mission on the home page and have a link to the full statement.

Work with others. The site can become a place where collective discussion and planning takes place, not just the record of one person's gripes or his or her individual master plan for solving the union's problems. Like a print newsletter, a website can help a group define itself and keep its focus. It takes work to operate this way, but the site will be stronger and more representative and the group will learn how to handle debate and come to a decision.

Keep the web steward accountable to the group. This can be tricky. Web stewards get pretty involved in their work, and it's hard to hold back and let the group make key decisions, especially if you are in a hurry to add or change something. The group also has to be careful not to micromanage what is, after all, someone's volunteer work. But the group should decide big issues— such as whether to support a proposed contract or who to back in a union election.

This is not to say that individual websites are a bad thing or that reformers should avoid using them. In some cases, as in the Carpenters, IBEW, and United Association of Plumbers and Pipefitters, there is a network of sites and discussion forums run by individuals that form a kind of collective project. This format allows for maximum freedom on the part of the web stewards without losing track of common issues and projects. You may want to be a piece of a larger network of this type.

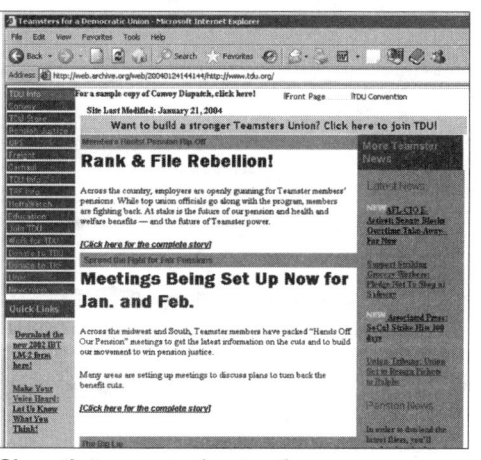

Show that you are about action:
Teamsters for a Democratic Union—the largest and best organized union reform group in North America—does a good job of showing that its members are about action. The left column on the TDU home page lists TDU's priority campaigns: Pension Justice, UPS, Freight, Carhaul. Each link leads to a separate page about how members are organizing and suggestions on how to get involved.

The most important items in these sections are included in the central features column, which uses clear and compelling headings for two stories about members organizing against a pension rip-off. Additional links to key items are found in the Quick Links and Latest News boxes. Repetition of links in this way does no harm. Make sure to use the same description so people who have seen the item once don't waste time going there again. www.tdu.org/index.html.

Show that You Are about Action

Focus on what people are doing to solve the problems. There is a lot of complaining on the Internet, just like in the union hall or workplace. It's good to provide space for some of that (like in a forum or bulletin board), but to move from complaining to organizing, you need to talk about what is being done to make a change. This helps people see that something can be done, that there are people who are trying to do it, and that they can help. Report on job actions, petitions, pickets, or other actions. Give action items top priority. Follow the "70 percent positive" rule: don't let your criticisms and complaints take up more than 30 percent of your website. (People posting to your forum or bulletin board may break this rule, but your own posts should not.)

Give people a way to get involved in the actions that your group has planned. If it is an event, tell people how to get there, what to expect, how to help organize it. If it is a petition, give people a copy of the form or a contact person to get it from. Use discussion lists, forums, or surveys to talk about possible plans. (You can save confidential details for private conversations or closed discussion lists.) This gets people to participate in planning strategy and you can get a feel for how much support there is for a proposed action.

Provide tools for members to take action where they are—petitions, draft grievances, flyers and handouts, stickers they can print on label paper, pictures and posters, newsletters—anything people might want to use on the job or at a union meeting. (Don't just send people off with an NLRB complaint form, though.) Note: make your group available to discuss the problem—there may be a great organizing opportunity hiding in a small complaint.

Follow up on your actions with reports, photos, discussion, and next steps. This is part of the focus on action. Post photos of an action or event. This can give people a picture of what it looks like to get active. Celebrate your hard work and recognize the efforts of people who made an event a success.

One way to keep the focus on action is to put up a campaign website, like Mike Watson's *One Man One Vote* site for IBEW members (communities.msn.com/OMOV), "dedicated entirely to the passage of the Amendment to institute a direct election of International Officers of the IBEW to assure that the individuals who work for us are accountable to us by the rank and file election of their positions."

Problem: one key democratic principle is inclusion and equality—

the title of these activists' site makes it sound like they're not interested in having sisters participate. By contrast, the *IBEW Rally* page specifically recognizes the efforts of the brothers and sisters who participated in that rally: www.angelfire.com/cantina/ibewrally/index.html.

Give People Information and Ideas They Need

Publish information that people need to solve problems—legal rights, how to enforce them, grievance procedures, hiring hall procedures, pension rights—or link to it. Provide information the union officers should be providing but aren't—the contract, the constitution, union meeting times and locations, minutes of past meetings, contract proposals, side agreements, election timelines or rules, grievance forms. Don't stop pushing union representatives to provide this information, but if they won't, do it yourself.

Labor Notes (www.labornotes.org) publishes online several stories from each print issue. Link to articles that are relevant to your members, or *Labor Notes* is glad to give permission to post them on your site, with credit and a link.

Provide or link to *accurate* information. Do your best to get the facts and be honest about what is fact and what is opinion. Don't give advice you're not sure of. Check with people you trust or with organizations like Labor Notes or the Association for Union Democracy. Build your own list of trusted sources, including other rank-and-file websites.

Help people understand the material you provide. Use Frequently Asked Questions, an advice column, or forums to answer members' questions. Recruit a few designated "forum leaders" who will respond. Put a form on your site for members to ask questions. Summarize key information in one-page handouts people can print and distribute.

If you link to material on another site, look for the most accessible material. For example, the Association for Union Democracy (www.uniondemocracy.

Publish information that people need:
Electrician Mike Ryan provides information for new IBEW members on issues like working in a local, traveling to other locals for work, and participating in union meetings. www.miketryan.com/contents.html.

Rank and File Advocate in TWU Local 100 in New York City features executive board reports by an activist on the executive board. www.rankandfileadvocate.org.

CWA member Mike Drake provides union meeting schedule and location information and suggestions on how to participate in meetings. He also gives his own description/commentary on past meetings. Dues News, Adventures in Solidarity www.mindspring.com/~drakester.

Mike Rose's Las Vegas Bartender links to the Labor Notes book *Democracy Is Power*, the ACLU web page on workplace rights, the Steward Update website, and the text of the Federal Monitor's report on HERE corruption. www.vegasbartender.org.

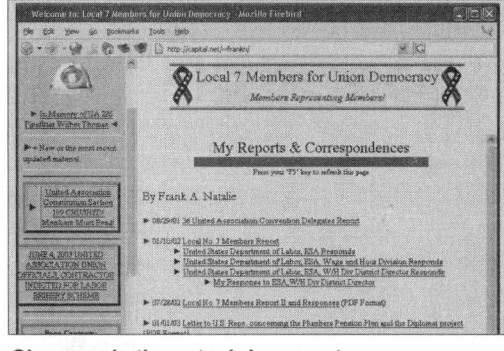

Give people the actual documents:
Frank Natalie's Members for Union Democracy site shares his and others' correspondence with the union and the Department of Labor regarding contract and dues issues. capital.net/~frankn.

Ken Little's Carpenters for a Democratic Union International page promoted a nationwide debate on the future of the union movement by publishing a document outlining the plans of the New Unity Partnership in the AFL-CIO. www.Ranknfile.net.

The Road Drivers Organization, for Teamsters, has an NMFA (National Master Freight Agreement) Library that includes contracts from all over the U.S. www.yellowfreightdrivers.com.

Tip: Union constitutions and bylaws, contracts, side agreements, and many other documents are public information that can legally be reproduced and distributed, including on websites. Do not be intimidated by a union attorney who threatens to sue for copyright infringement. Contact the Association for Union Democracy: www.uniondemocracy.org.

org) publishes the text of the Labor Management Reporting and Disclosure Act but also a plain language guide to the act that offers realistic advice. You can link to both.

Give people the actual documents. Publish the full text of the contract, including side letters, the union constitution, official correspondence on important issues. If officials refuse to let members see the full contract before a vote, or give out financial information, show that it is possible and valuable to share information.

However, do not bury people in a hundred documents. Prioritize. People will not want to wade through your 13 letters to the Department of Labor. (Note: when posting a document, try to post it not just in PDF format, but also as html. Many people who will look at a document online will not download a PDF file—fear of viruses, or just impatience.)

Link to other key materials and resources, such as government agencies and public interest groups. When linking, use targeted links straight to the page you need, not just the home page. Give phone numbers and URLs for government agencies. Give people a sense of what they are likely to encounter if they do contact the agency. *The Steward for Human and Labor Rights* gives Teamsters and other unionists interested in bringing an NLRB charge both information on how to do that and an analysis of the weakness of NLRB enforcement. www.thesteward.net/frame.html.

Show Them You Are about Democracy

Question authority. Have a little attitude—this is your union. Question your officials, demand the full story, don't be put off or blown off. Name names and challenge your opponents to explain their views or actions. And remember, what goes around comes around. Be prepared to have your own authority questioned.

Hold leaders accountable. List their contact information so people can call them directly. Tell how officers voted on issues of interest. For example, the *Castleton*

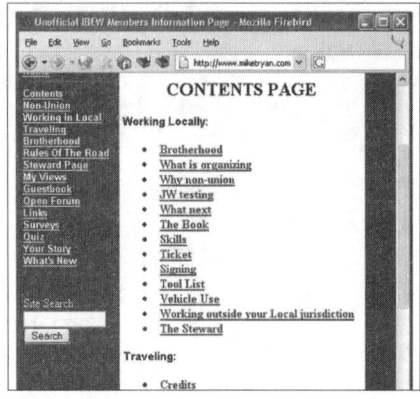

Chronicle website (members.fortunecity.com/atu726//index.htm) has a frank report card on ATU Local 726's officers and stewards: "Shop Steward Ziyad Shakoor [gets a] "D"—Who? Ziyad was never in the office before he was elected. You need to give him a break because of this but Ziyad is more than often MIA. Always asks someone else for the answer. When he works L/R he always tells you to come back tomorrow. Hasn't been seen in the office for weeks." You could put a link to such a section on your home page: "How're They Doing? See Our Union Reps Report Card."

Practice what you preach. Encourage frankness and honesty in forums and bulletin boards. Discourage "flaming" and personal attacks (though it is important that people feel able to name names). Do not overreact to bad behavior. It is understandable that many frustrated union members who finally find a forum to speak freely come out swearing and fuming. Offer friendly advice and feedback. Show that it is possible to disagree strongly without treating the other person like the enemy of all humanity.

Link to the opposition. Post correspondence to and from your opponents. Link to opposing websites. Always link to the official union websites and to any useful information they publish. Show your confidence in members' ability to judge for themselves. You want your supporters to be with you because they understand and agree with you, not because you are the only people they know about. Rival slates in the Coalition of University Employees linked to each other on their campaign websites: www.geocities.com/cuepower/.

Links to the employer's website and some employer-friendly websites can help members "know the enemy." It is part of the culture of the Internet to link to anything useful. But think twice about linking to organizations that may share some of your criticisms of your union, or provide useful information, but actually want to do away with unions altogether. If you choose to link to a group like that, make it extremely clear to your visitors that you oppose its mission.

In addition to a regular message board, TWU Local 100 member Ed Kehoe's *Local 100 Emails* website posts "all the emails that float around the Local 100 membership network." www.voy.com/142528/.

The *Carpenters Jawin'* discussion forum is open and unrestricted—a space for members to say whatever they want, which may include all nature of vituperation and discrimination as well as reasoned argument and mutual aid. The key to the list's longevity is a relatively stable group of members who write frequently.

Help people understand the material:
IBEW Minuteman's "Ask Eddie" page takes questions and provides practical answers on legal and union problems. A typical answer begins like this: "Your first course of action should be to raise 7 minutes of holy hell at your union meeting and get your point across!" ibewminuteman.com.

Note: *Jawin'* uses a typical forum disclaimer: "The views expressed in these articles are those of the submitter, who is solely responsible for the content. Jawin' does not endorse any of these views, Jawin' makes no guarantee of the accuracy, validity, correctness, or completeness of any information on the Jawin' Website, and is not to be held responsible for any of the content provided in the submitted articles." http://angry.at/jawin.

Build bridges and practice solidarity. Make sure to include issues that affect each part of the workforce. Do not let anyone play you against your fellow workers: high seniority vs. low seniority, craft vs. craft, black vs. brown vs. white. Make it clear that you are for a union of, by, and for all the workers. Translate documents into other languages, highlight issues of concern to particular groups in the union like low-seniority workers or particular trades, recruit people you are trying to work with to write to the discussion forum. This is not just part of being strategic—avoiding divide and conquer—it is a basic democratic principle. More reform groups need to embrace this principle in their websites.

HEARDNY provides legal rights info in English and Spanish for HERE members. www.heardny.org/main.htm.

32B-J Yes We Can/Si Se Puede, a website for SEIU members in the New York metro area, includes on its home page links to letters and flyers in English and Spanish, and an article from the local Spanish-language newspaper. This is only a start for a local with a large Spanish-speaking membership, but it was ahead of the official union site in this regard. www.32bjyeswecan.com/index.html.

There are many sites for women in nontraditional trades. One great list is *Women in Construction.* Building trades activists should link to such sites and promote them. members.tripod.com/%7Ebarbijo/hers.html.

Build Your Group

Help people find each other. Isolation is a major obstacle for people who want to make changes. Your website can help them connect to other activists in their area or work location. List the contact people or create an activist directory that people can access by emailing you and asking for contacts in their area. There is also networking software, used by companies like *MeetUp.com,* that some union members have used to organize meetings in their areas.

Do the grunt work of building an organization. Use the website to collect names, emails, addresses, phone numbers, and other relevant information. Set up a database—a computer address book can work for this—and be careful to put in *all* the information you gather. The information you collect this way is often the most up-to-date and accurate and can be crucial in election campaigns or other mobilizing efforts.

Follow up on website contacts with direct personal contact. Make a phone call, meet the person after work, invite him or her to a meeting. Have a contact system—if workers on a particular job contact you, have a person on that job they can get in touch with. The Carpenters for a Democratic Union International website—www.ranknfile.net—has a link titled "Contact steering committee members in your area" that leads to a long list of activists, with contact info. Be sure to make such information easy to find.

In the California State Employees Association, the Caucus for a Democratic Union contact page is organized by region, with phone numbers and emails for contact people. www.unionspark.org/main.htm.

J.D. Walker's website for Greyhound bus drivers has a great guest book with a series of questions that get the visitor into a conversation about the union. Walker then responds personally to each entry, basing his comments on visitors' responses to the form. See users.adelphia.net/~jdw1043/index.htm and click the guest book.

Open source: Got a great guest book format? Did you find a good free bulletin board program? Know someone who wants to start a website in your union? Follow the spirit of the Internet (at least the good side of it) and share your know-how. Frank Natalie of UA Local 7 Members for Democracy has helped others start MFD sites by simply copying the code for his site and passing it on. That way people can change the content and the design to suit their local needs, without having to re-create the site from scratch. It also gives the MFD sites a similar look and feel. Of course, you can also just view the source code for a page you like and learn from its html.

Local Unions on the Internet

INTERNET COMMUNICATION HAS OBVIOUS ADVANTAGES for unions: it's inexpensive and fast, both for routine purposes and for crisis mobilization. Interactive features can collect information and responses from members and newcomers alike. Online bulletin boards give workers employed by the same company or in the same industry a channel of communication they never had before.

As more workers are plugged into the Internet, their increased access to information potentially includes more access to union information. And as the Internet replaces television as the medium of choice for an increasing number of Americans, unions have an opportunity to step up and speak for labor's side of the story in the face of the corporate media "content providers."

The following sections give advice on how to:
• Build a local union website (most of the advice on rank-and-file websites, earlier in the chapter, applies here, too).
• Use it to reflect your values and further your goals.

The Nuts and Bolts of Building Your Own Website

THERE ARE TWO BASIC WAYS TO CREATE A WEBSITE—by using a web design software program that requires only basic word-processing cut-and-paste skills, or by writing and editing your own HTML code (HTML is the computer language of web-building). Most beginners use the cut-and-paste software, but if you know HTML you have more design choices.

The software programs look and operate like desktop publishing programs, so if you can use those, the web software is easy to learn.

If you decide to write the HTML code directly, using Wordpad or another text editor, you have more control over what you produce. This route demands the most of you as a designer—you have to learn the code and how to use it to get the right effects. You will also want to keep up with changes in the code itself. People who write HTML swear by it, but many experts use design software to do their coding, or work in both.

One great resource, if you know how to use HTML, is just viewing the source code of websites you like. You can do so while visiting the site by clicking on View on your browser toolbar and then clicking on Source. You can copy ideas, but if you want to copy the exact code it's best to get permission, whether or not you see a copyright logo.

There are many web design programs available. They are constantly updated and new software appears all the time, so it is difficult to recommend a particular program. A few, like Microsoft's FrontPage, come bundled with the computer's basic software. You don't have to pay for additional software and the software may be supported by the manufacturer. To find the best and most powerful software, look for what the professionals are using. Programs like Dreamweaver, for example, will cost you money, but may be worth it.

The most useful tool for learning about the advantages and disadvantages of different software programs is the Internet itself. The Webmonkey website provides reviews and information on leading programs. A Google search will also turn up reviews and discussions of software. And you can simply ask fellow web stewards what software they recommend.

- Use email for communication and for online action.
- Use the Internet as part of mobilization efforts.
- Set up online bulletin boards for members to use for discussion.

Building a Local Union Website

Survey your members. Before building a new website or upgrading an existing one, do a survey—in person, at meetings, or through your existing email lists. Sample questions:
- How often do you access the Internet?
- How often do you visit the website of the national union (or other relevant labor group)? What information there do you find useful?
- What types of information would you like to see added to our website? (Give choices, such as news about my employer or industry, grievance forms, etc.)
- What other labor or job-related websites do you find useful?
- Do you have high-speed access through cable or DSL, or slower dial-up modem? (To accommodate the latter you'd want more text-based content on your site.)
- Would you rather get news from your union through our website, or monthly emails, or both?
- Is your email text-only, or can you read HTML messages and/or open file attachments such as Word or PDF?

Consider whether you want to grant "members only" access to a portion of your site. If you have an open shop you may not want to give away information to non-members, and you may want to keep the prying eyes of management away from online discussions. You can safely assume that employers will be scrutinizing any union websites. Another consideration is federal campaign laws, which consider union political endorsements on websites to be a campaign contribution, unless access to that portion of the site is restricted to members.

However, setting up a password system adds another layer of effort for site visitors. A union that puts its democratic workings up for public display is one that can generate a greater degree of trust.

Decide who will design it. If you build it yourself, the good news is that the tools have gotten much better for do-it-yourselfers, and modern software lets union webmasters add to and update content with simple word processing cut-and-paste skills. Linda Guyer, president of Alliance@IBM/CWA Local 1701 and designer of its website at www.allianceibm.org, says that unions don't need to spend thousands of dollars to pay an outsider: "You can do a website real cheap. All you need is someone with a PC, the time, and the software."

If you need to hire an outside designer, the Washington Alliance of Technology Workers/CWA Local 37083, or WashTech, is a good referral source for finding web design specialists who are union members, at contact@washtech.org or 206-726-8580.

Eric Lee, founder of the Labourstart web project (see International Solidarity, below), offers web design and consulting services at www.ericlee.me.uk.

Carol Simpson DesignWorks for Labor and Non-profit Organizations is a union shop that offers labor cartoons and web and print services at www.cartoonwork.com, where you can view samples of their website work.

Other unionized companies that will design and host your website are Unions-America.com, UnionSites.com, and Web Networks at web.net. You can view samples of their work online. While an Internet search will locate a variety of non-union firms that claim to specialize in union websites, there is a lot of turnover in the field and the results are not always impressive.

Whether you build it yourself or not, visit many sites to see which appeal to you in style or content. If a site's design appeals to you, contact the webmaster to find out who built it. Volunteer web designers, who are often just members with computer skills, usually will share software information or even web templates with other unions.

Choose a website host. Many Internet service providers give you free website hosting as part of your service package and will often offer tutorials and pre-made templates to help you get started. The three unionized design firms mentioned above, Unions-America.com, UnionSites.com, and Web Networks, also host sites. The best ways to choose a host are to compare features and costs, use resources like the Webmonkey site (hotwired.lycos.com/webmonkey) to get independent information, and ask your friends and fellow activists what they are using and how they like it.

Free website hosting providers, such as Geocities, may require advertisements and have other drawbacks, like being non-union.

Find out if there is a plan for your entire union to coordinate its web efforts. In 2003, the Canadian Union of Public Employees began free website hosting for all of its divisions, locals, councils, and committees, as explained at www.cupe.ca/www/webhosting. The person responsible for a local website's content doesn't need to know HTML or any other computer language. Simple cut-and-paste word-processing skills and the password to the "back end" of the site are all that are needed to create web pages. In addition, CUPE members can get a free (ad-free, spam-free, and fee-free) web-based email account, as well as other services like chat, message boards, and online actions.

If your international union is creating such a system, it's important to push for a policy of local autonomy. CUPE reserves the right only to remove something that contravenes libel laws, that would hold the union in contempt of court or leave it open to criminal prosecution, or that would contravene CUPE's Equality Statement.

The Service Employees' Locals Online has a similar system for locals to set up sites, using a variety of different looks, or templates. There are several Locals Online manuals posted at www.localsonline.org/guides/index.cfm. The Locals Online User's Manual for Website Administrators has information about web design principles and an interesting inside example of how to manage a website. The Locals Online Web

Planning Guide is an exercise aimed at involving local staffers in the website planning process.

Use online resources for planning your website. The single best online guide for unions is the CWA's Guide to Establishing and Maintaining Local Websites, also known as the CWA Web Manual, at www.cwa-union.org/about/local_web_manual.asp. It's a thorough treatment of most of the practical considerations, although the advice and tools it offers, such as the news feed, are designed for CWA locals. It offers less direction on content than this chapter attempts to.

Labourstart has an online guide to "Building better trade union websites" at www.labourstart.org/webhelp.shtml. Labourstart also sponsors an online forum for web stewards, which is the first listing on the Labourstart Web Forum page at www.labourstart.org/cgi-bin/UltraBoard/UltraBoard.pl.

Consider the possibilities of video. The Coalition of Immokalee Workers (CIW), for example, which is seeking higher wages for Florida farmworkers who pick tomatoes, has used video footage on its website (www.ciw-online.org) of scenes from its hunger-strike campaign against Taco Bell. Site visitors can choose from a number of short video clips (short clips are easier to download), showing a rally at Taco Bell headquarters in Los Angeles, music and speeches by supporters, and solidarity actions in two other cities. The CIW site uses free, open-source Quicktime software.

The IAM international's website (www.goiam.org) uses the "newsroom" format for many of its videos, whereby one or two talking heads give commentary on breaking news. It's more dynamic than seeing the same words in print, but less compelling than other videos on the site of workers at rallies.

Publicize your website. Put the address in your newspaper, on fliers, on bulletin boards, even on t-shirts. Include the address of the website in all your emails, especially if you can customize your "signature." UFCW Local 789 maintains a website, www.targetunion.org, for organizing Target retail workers, and has placed signs with that web address around Target stores—once on a bike parked at the store's bike rack.

Content for a Union Website

A union's web presence can reflect the degree of its commitment to grassroots, militant, democratic unionism.

Give organizing a prominent place. Highlight organizing on your website's home page, and link it to the organizing web page with an eye-catching button. Labeling a link "Get A Union Where You Work" or "Need A Union?" is more attention-getting than simply "Organizing."

An organizing web page typically answers questions about joining a union, such as why, how, the risks, and

On your website, use photos of members in action. Pictures of picket lines or rallies convey the message that a union is action-oriented and encourage non-participants to join future mobilizations.

advantages. If you want to avoid the "dues-for-service" model of business unionism, then be up-front about the need for workers to organize themselves. ILWU Local 19's "So you want to unionize?" web page at www.ilwu19.com/organize/unionize1.htm lists ten tasks for the workers to accomplish, relegating union staff to the role of advisors.

UFCW Local 1001's organizing web page at www.ufcw1001.org/need_a_union adds a column on the right side of the text with photos of several local members, identified by name and workplace. Above the photos are quotes from each worker describing, from their own experiences, the benefits of belonging to Local 1001. Such testimonials are more persuasive than an abstract pitch to join.

Local 1001, which is based in Bellevue, Washington, has gotten many leads from its website, from people all over the country. While distant leads are referred to other locals, web contact led the local to its biggest organizing win—adding 1,800 new members at Sacred Heart Medical Center in Spokane, the first hospital in that city to gain union representation. Peter Diaz, the local's organizing director, recalls, "When we walked into our first meeting with the workers they were already reading our literature from the organizing page of our website."

Use photos of members in action. Pictures of picket lines or rallies convey the message that a union is action-oriented and encourage non-participants to join future mobilizations. UFCW Local 1001's website uses many photos of members, and none of officers. "That was a conscious decision," says Diaz. "All of our literature has our members being the face of the union. On the other hand, we're considering adding the pictures of two of the officers, because the members want to know that their dues money is paying for a staff that works for them. It's a delicate balance."

UFCW Local 789, which does substantial outreach

on the Internet, has a "Meet our organizers" feature at www.ufcw789.org/organize.htm with photos and quotes that personalize the individuals that prospective members would be contacting.

Invite members to participate. The home page of the Coalition of University Employees (CUE), representing clericals at the University of California (www.cueunion.org), has a button labeled "How You Can

> Ever wondered what you can do to help support CUE? Here are a number of ideas. If you have more, please contact CUE!
> • Join the Contract Support Network
> • Write letters
> • Display a poster
> • Attend a meeting or a rally at your local campus
> • Become a union steward!

Help."

Publicize meetings, agendas, correspondence, and bargaining reports. This encourages participation and tells members what issues are being addressed. It also shows that your union has an open and democratic process. The CUE website has bargaining reports for every session of the latest contract negotiations, at www.cueunion.org/bargaining/reports.php, plus every bargaining report since CUE's first negotiations in 1998. The website tells where and when the statewide executive board meets, with agendas that tell the time each item will be discussed.

Make it easy for workers to contact the union. Display phone numbers and email addresses for officers, stewards, staff, or committee chairs, indicating what shifts and areas each handles. You should list email addresses only for those who will check their messages frequently. If you solicit online responses, make sure that someone is designated to respond promptly. Tell how to contact your web steward, to answer visitors' technical questions.

Make demands of your employer. Would it be beneficial to put union contact information on your employer's website? The University of California at Santa Barbara lists "Union & Employee Organizations at UCSB & Their Representatives" at hr.ucsb.edu/Labor/unionreps.htm. The same page also links to the full text of the collective bargaining agreements.

Offer resources such as contract language and grievance forms. The Pacific Northwest Newspaper Guild/CWA Local 37082 lists the contracts for all of its bargaining units, with their expiration dates, at www.nwguild.org/contracts/index.php.

The CUE website offers a collection of leaflets produced by different CUE locals across the state, for other locals to borrow or modify (for example, "Why Are Clericals Important to Students and Faculty?") at www.cueunion.org/resources/locallit.php. There are printable posters, petitions, and sample letters of support for CUE's efforts on the How You Can Help page at www.cueunion.org/events/action.php.

Show solidarity with other workers, other unions, other struggles. The Canadian Union of Public Employees (www.cupe.ca) lists all "Strikes and Lockouts" affecting CUPE members. It also has a prominent "Action Centre" with links to online campaigns such as "Act now for quality childcare."

Two of the most useful links for solidarity are Campaign for Labor Rights (www.

Using the Internet To Promote International Solidarity

IN AN ERA OF GLOBAL MARKETS, some unions are starting to educate their members about the struggles of workers outside the U.S.

The best web source for international news about workers' struggles is Labourstart, www.labourstart.org. You can easily link your site to Labourstart, which displays dozens of stories from around the world.

Labourstart offers a frequently updated free news wire service that displays five global news headlines on participating websites. You can easily put this news service on your site by copying and pasting one line of code onto your web page. Information on how to do it is at www.labourstart.org/lnw.html.

Another Labourstart service, ActNOW Wire, is similar. Adding a line of code to your website displays a list of international action campaigns in defense of workers' rights. To do so, go to www.labourstart.org/actnowwire.shtml.

Clicking on any of the links described above brings the viewer to an explanation of the campaign and a simple way to send customized or form letters to the targeted authorities.

You may want to offer information about international connections that are more specific to your members. For a good example of a website that makes internationalism very concrete, see the United Electrical Workers' international solidarity page at www.ranknfile-ue.org/international.html.

In addition, the UE has a separate site devoted to the topic, www.ueinternational.org. The site explains why international solidarity is important to UE members, tells of the alliances the UE has forged with unions around the world, and provides current solidarity news. There are explanations on how to connect with "sister shops" owned by your employer in other countries and quotes from workers on their experiences with cross-border solidarity.

Constantly improving translation tools like Altavista's Babelfish (babelfish.altavista.com/babelfish/) can help your international visitors read your website in many languages.

campaignforlaborrights.org), which promotes specific action campaigns, and Labourstart (www.laborstart.org).

The AFL-CIO's home page (www.aflcio.org) features the "Working Families e-Activist Network" with action links (mostly U.S. legislative issues) and a sign-up for email action alerts. Contact the web stewards of these sites for the technical info on how to have their action links displayed directly on your site.

For links to websites highlighting struggles in your area, check the websites of your state or county labor federation or Jobs with Justice chapter. If they don't have a feed for local action alerts, ask them to set one up.

Avoid corporate ads. Your website should reflect your values alone. Don't dilute your message by placing your website with a host that pushes intrusive ads on your viewers.

It's a different matter, though, to display links to sellers of products with a social conscience: sweatshop-free, "fair trade," and union-made goods. Examples are at: www.nosweatapparel.com, www.transfairusa.org, unionshop.aflcio.org, www.sweatx.net, and www.northlandposter.com.

Action Questions: Websites

Most of the suggestions earlier in this chapter for building a rank-and-file site apply to a local union site as well.

1. Does the home page tell at a glance who you are, who you represent, and what your goals are?

2. Does it encourage viewers to get more involved, with clearly labeled links such as "Join Our Union/Rank-and-File Group," "Take Action Now," and "How You Can Help"?

3. Is there an easy and obvious way for visitors to sign up for future communication by email?

4. Do you use photos of members in action to give depth to your descriptions of what you do?

5. Does your site offer tools to facilitate participation, such as downloadable grievance forms, fliers, and contracts in multiple formats (HTML, Word, PDF files) for wider access?

6. Does your site make the workings of the union transparent? In other words, does it explain how to file a grievance, how to take action outside the grievance procedure, and how to participate in union meetings and elections, with the constitution and bylaws available for reference?

7. Does every page give access to contact information for officers, committee members, or activists, along with an explanation of their jurisdictions or assignments?

8. Do you have relevant labor news feeds or someone assigned to do frequent postings to your site, to keep viewers coming back for fresh information?

9. Do you have accessible links to other labor websites that promote values of solidarity, democracy, and grassroots action?

10. Do you offer access to "horizontal" communication among members and activists, through moderated discussion groups or online forums?

11. Is the "back end" of your site easy to use to add or change content, with more than one person trained to do so?

12. Does your Internet host force you to carry commercial content on your site, which degrades your message and annoys visitors?

13. Have you registered your site with the various search engines, using the "meta tags" you believe will attract the visitors that you want to your site?

Use Email for Fast and Cheap Mass Messaging

You can communicate with small numbers of workers, stewards, or activists through group lists you set up on the address book of whatever email program your computer uses. For large groups, you need a mass email program, called a "listserve," through an Internet service provider.

To build your mailing list:

1. Put a line for email address on any form where you collect address and phone information, such as a union card or a meeting or picket line sign-in sheet. (But don't automatically add them to your list; see #4.)

2. Take sign-up cards for your newsletter or emailing wherever you go—meetings, pickets, demonstrations.

3. Put a link on your website or in any email you send that allows people to sign up for your emailings. Several web-based services, including GetActive, make this easy.

4. Never send the mailings to people without their permission. Send them an introductory message first that invites them to subscribe, with a sample copy. Explain that they will get well edited, well presented information, and say how often. They won't get harassed.

If some groups of workers don't have email access—and that is more common in lower-paid jobs, and with immigrants and workers of color—devise a plan so that no group is excluded. You might arrange for computer access and training for activists and do extra recruitment of workers from groups with financial, cultural, or language barriers. Print copies of your email messages for workplace bulletin boards and distribute them through your member-to-member network. Getting the message out to all members is the important point, regardless of how you do it.

Where workers use email as part of their job, the union can negotiate the right to use work email addresses to communicate with members. For example, the Society of Professional Engineering Employees in Aerospace gets updated work email addresses for its members at Boeing as part of its weekly data requests to the company.

However, emails to work addresses have the obvious downside of being readable by the employer. Treat them as you would a public posting, and never send confidential information. In addition, work addresses are completely worthless in a strike situation. SPEEA had to scramble to collect home email addresses during its strike against Boeing in 2000.

Action Questions: Email Lists

1. How much of your membership or target audience has access to computers and actively uses email?

2. What do you hope to accomplish by using the Internet to reach members, and what would be the advantages over how you do things now?

3. Is your union or group building its database of email addresses in every way possible, including website and paper form solicitations?

4. How do you plan to make use of the email list (e.g., action alerts, meeting notices, monthly newsletter)?

5. Can your list be easily used to reach just certain categories, for example activists versus non-activists, by work location, employer, or job classification?

6. How much time is used to set up, maintain, and send to your email lists? Are the results worth it?

7. Do your emails have an interactive feature, asking for membership feedback or action?

8. Do you ask recipients to forward your emails, or print them out to pass along to others, or do you use a tell-a-friend feature to expand your list?

Use Online Campaigns To Mobilize

Many nonprofit groups use GetActive (www.getactive.com/getactive/index.html) and similar programs to generate emails and faxes to Congress, the President, corporate CEO's, and other decision-makers. To participate in an online campaign, users must first register their email address and other information. They can also sign up for future alerts, choosing among various issues that interest them. The AFL-CIO has made GetActive software available free to all of its affiliates.

The software makes it as simple as hitting "Reply" to an email to generate a response. Or you can send an email to your list with an Internet link leading straight to the online campaign. If the campaign is aimed at Congress or state legislators, the responses are automatically directed to the representatives for each individual's state and district—no need for anyone to look them up. Since responses are routed back through the GetActive software, campaign organizers can tally the number of responses and where they came from.

Generate mail. SEIU Local 775 in Seattle, which represents 28,000 home health care workers, started using GetActive in 2003 as part of its campaign to win raises from the state legislature. During the six-month legislative session, the campaign generated 25,000 phone, email, and in-person contacts between supporters and legislators. Ten thousand of these contacts were generated by email from the local's list of 2,000-3,000 members and supporters.

Local 775's officers believe the online actions played a role in the campaign's success. Funding for home health care worker raises became the issue that deadlocked the state budget process in the legislature. The 75-cent increase that finally passed was the largest one-year raise ever for these workers.

In some cases, an online campaign by itself can make a difference. Eric Lee, founding editor of the Labourstart news service, says, "Labourstart's own experience with online campaigns—which we have documented—shows that in a number of cases (such as the Sydney Hilton Hotel, Ashland in Norway, Samsonite in Thailand, and most recently, BAT in Burma) we have been able to persuade giant corporations to change their policies, recognize unions, negotiate contracts, and even pull out of a country—with the support and participation of thousands."

Mobilize and inform members. In 2003 the Unity@Verizon campaign, conducted by the Communications Workers, used an email database to help mobilize members for a contract campaign. Kris Raab of the CWA Research Department tells how the database was built: "We had an existing database we'd been building for years for all CWA, and got the names where the Verizon field was checked. We contacted the big locals we already knew had an e-list. We sent email bulletins to all 50,000 on the CWA list, asking them to sign up for the Unity@Verizon campaign. That list includes all local presidents, and they forwarded on the messages. Every paper flier we passed out had the website address, www.cwa-union.org/verizon, which had a pop-up ad for visitors to sign up.

"The most effective way we built the list was distributing a paper sign-up form, which we passed out at meetings. People are good at contacting folks at work and at meetings, but there's not always a computer there that they can use. It's easier to have someone sign a piece of paper there and then, rather than having to go home, remember to turn on the computer, find the website, etc.

"We ask for email addresses on membership forms and anything else we can think of. To get a response we ask, 'What do we have that people want?' One CWA local was successful at getting email addresses while preparing for a strike by asking for the addresses on the form for strike benefits."

Unity@Verizon newsletters were emailed to a list that grew to 18,000 addresses. As bargaining heated up, the frequency increased from weekly to more than once a day. A typical message might include a bargaining update, a mobilization update, and photos and reports from rallies and other actions around the country. The "In Solidarity" column featured email letters of support from Verizon workers and customers, as well as other unions. There was also a box with links leading directly to the Unity@Verizon website, which had most of the new material:

> Visit Unity@Verizon on the web for more:
> - Mobilization photos
> - Solidarity messages
> - Updates from regional bargaining tables
> - Past Unity@Verizon email updates

Other stories were "Following the Work" (reports received from members on "how contracting out often wastes time and money"), "Ivan Buried Under a Blizzard of Faxes" (reporting that supporters had generated 15,000 faxes to Verizon's CEO), and "Scabs-R-Us" (identifying

The CWA worked hard to build a database of members' email addresses to mobilize members during the 2003 contract campaign at Verizon.

contractors who were helping Verizon to train scabs and seeking reports of specific locations and of other contractors). Each of these stories was interactive in some way, reporting on member feedback and soliciting more responses.

The Unity@Verizon newsletters are all available at www.unionvoice.org/cwa_unity_verizon/all-msgs.html.

Recruit and mobilize supporters. Unity@Verizon was primarily a member-based campaign. To escalate pressure on the company, the CWA launched a second campaign, Fairness@Verizon, asking the public to "join the community campaign against corporate greed at Verizon." At the website, supporters could add their names to those supporting the union, and Verizon customers could authorize the CWA to switch them from Verizon to unionized AT&T service, if necessary.

This tactic, said Raab, especially upset the company. "Doing this online was easier than doing paper pledges. Plus it got us a lot of publicity. So it was useful from a media angle and for pressuring the company. It also gave us an electronic database of supporters to ask things of, if we wanted them to make calls or send email."

Fairness@Verizon asked supporters to send faxes to Verizon CEO Ivan Seidenberg, calling on Verizon to keep jobs in local communities. Fifteen thousand faxes were generated from online responses through GetActive software, which cost the CWA about $2,000. "Faxes are annoying and harder to block than emails," Raab says. "It cost more money from GetActive, but it was worth it. We know we annoyed him."

On the overall success of the campaign, Raab reports that "we reached folks we'd never have reached except electronically. It made it easy for people to write to us—for example, the letters of support we published on the website. We got much more material sent to us than we actually used.

"We got great feedback from the locals. We are geographically dispersed, and it helped folks in small offices feel like part of a much bigger thing when they'd see militant photos from different states.

"We had the equivalent of one-and-a-half people working on the campaign full-time. We could commit the resources because our surveys have shown that there's a high rate of computer use among CWA members. We also did a survey of our campaign participants, which showed that 20 percent of them were forwarding on our email bulletins. Another 20 percent were printing them out and posting them on bulletin boards."

The lessons of the online portion of the CWA campaign at Verizon are:

- Building a database of email addresses is the fundamental first step for doing online campaigns.
- The most reliable way to get email addresses is the non-electronic way—in person, with pen and paper.
- Email is a more active way than a website to get your message out, although a website can be a valuable additional resource that emails link to.
- Online campaigns can be a quick way of garnering support and media attention, if you are already in a high-profile dispute with an employer and have built a database of supporters.

On a cautionary note, the Internet is not an electronic shortcut for mobilizing. Unions should avoid de-emphasizing traditional forms of in-person organizing where there are direct routes for contacting members. There can be no substitute for the kinds of on-the-ground actions the CWA engaged in against Verizon, including working to rule, picketing 100 Verizon wireless stores, and many local rallies. See Chapter 10.

In one dramatic example, email by itself was able to trigger an action by striking workers. Members of the Society of Professional Engineering Employees in Aerospace (SPEEA), who work for Boeing, are almost all computer users, given the nature of their jobs. The bulk of SPEEA's membership is in one area of western Washington state.

Using email alone, SPEEA was able, during its successful strike in 2000, to generate a picket line of 500 people in six hours to disrupt an unannounced meeting of the Boeing board of directors at a local hotel.

Normally, of course, you would not want to rely on the Internet for turnout. In this case, the union's members were in a state of mobilization for the strike and checked their email frequently for strike news. As instant messaging becomes more commonplace on cell phones as well as computers, unions will want to consider the tactical possibilities for quick mobilizations.

Set Up Online Group Discussion

In the business union model, officers alone discuss and decide what's best for members. Grassroots unionism, which empowers members to make decisions for their common good, requires broad-based, democratic discussion. Email and the Internet make possible such discussions across barriers of time and distance, using listserves (email discussion lists), bulletin boards (also called message boards or web forums), and weblogs (compilations of messages or information that one or many users can add to). Online discussion can take on proposed contracts, mergers with other unions, and union election campaigns, among other things.

The key to successful discussion groups is clear rules for participation and conduct, such as banning messages that disrespect other members. Groups of any size might also benefit from a moderator to screen out messages that violate those rules. It also helps to have an unofficial moderator who can help keep the discussion constructive by maintaining an even disposition and contributing reliable facts.

List-serves. In a group discussion listserve, messages sent to the listserve's email address are relayed to everyone on the list. The downside is that recipients may cancel if your volume is more than they want to receive. Some listserves offer a digest option where all messages are bundled into a daily, weekly, or monthly digest.

The strike by the Pacific Northwest Newspaper Guild against the *Seattle Times* in 2000 is an example of how email discussion lists bolstered the resolve of striking workers. Group email lists developed spontaneously among the strikers, until they grew into a listserve with a moderator. Columnist Paul Andrews wrote, "When nerves frayed or spirits flagged, someone always came up with an encouraging email to pass around. The mailing list provided an instant, no-holds-barred forum for airing frustrations as well as testing membership sentiment. Strikers got to hear each other out in ways not possible even in group meetings. In the process they got to know one another better and build a communality in purpose..." ["How the Internet Sustained a Strike." Full text at www.unionrecord.com/final/display.php?ID=1934.]

CUE maintains a listserve called CUE-Activist, for for "stewards, activists, or CUE members who just want to listen in to the union discussion. Grievance advice is sought and given, ideas about CUE and other unions shared, and CUE members from all over participate."

"It helps shape union policy in that those members who are elected officers get to hear non-elected members' opinions," says Debbie Ceder, who maintains CUE's listserve. "However, I feel not enough members participate to get a true sense of the majority. When true policy issues arise that the elected leadership feels need widespread input, we either set up a survey online and/or mail paper surveys or ballots to the membership to ensure that everyone gets the opportunity to speak their mind."

Bulletin boards. An online bulletin board allows users to view current and previously posted messages whenever they choose, a format with some advantages over listserves. However, a bulletin board is dependent on people remembering that it exists and being motivated to use it. Display a link from your website to your discussion area, whether it's on your site or not.

During the 2000 *Seattle Times* strike, an email discussion group developed spontaneously. "When nerves frayed or spirits flagged," wrote columnist Paul Andrews, "someone always came up with an encouraging email to pass around."

Some formats allow you to separate discussions into different forums and even different topics. A good example can be seen on UFCW Local 789's website for retail workers by following the "Forum" link at www.youareworthmore.org. There are over 20 forums, with such titles as "How do you feel about unions?" and "Dollar General—The place where Dollar General workers meet to organize!" Within each forum there are topics, such as "Safeway Strike" and "Why is there no boycott of Safeway?" This allows viewers to quickly find the issues that interest them without wading through messages on unrelated topics.

Concerns. The official union movement, with some exceptions, has not jumped at the chance to promote member-to-member electronic communications on union websites. One concern has been fear of opening up the union to lawsuits for potentially libelous statements made on its website. Legal rulings, however, have generally protected site providers from liability in such cases; see the resource list at the end of this chapter.

Another fear is that online forums will be used as a soapbox by perpetual malcontents or critics of union policies. But the advantages of increased discussion outweigh any downside. Officers and rank and filers alike can know much more about what's concerning their members. An officer who fears online discussions might as well fear membership meetings.

In some cases, outright anti-union types have tried to disrupt union forums with negative posts, under the cloak of anonymity. If that happens, and you are a membership organization, you can require online registration so that only members can post messages. It's also easy to set up your online discussions to make access entirely "members only." Members register at the site and are approved by the site caretaker, who uses a membership list to cross-check.

Whether or not you have your own listserve or discussion board, you can provide links from your website to other discussion groups. This can be useful to a union that wants to encourage free discussion of strategies and tactics—including secondary boycotts or job actions that would violate a no-strike clause—in a forum that the union is not responsible for.

To set up a bulletin board, listserve, or weblog, ask your current website host what options are available. You might want to consult with unionized firms that do this kind of work, such as web.net or Unions-America.com.

Or have your discussion group hosted by Labourstart Web Forums. The service is free to unions and rank-and-file groups, and there are no ads. All messages on the forums are readable by the public. Some forums restrict posting to registered users. The rules of use are simply agreement that "racist and sexist language will not be tolerated here." Write to ericlee@labourstart.org for details. Follow the "Forums" link from the Labourstart home page at www.labourstart.org to view them.

Perhaps the most popular way to set up labor discussion groups has been to use the free service offered by Yahoo. There are hundreds of Yahoo groups listed under the "Union" category, and hundreds more listed under "Labor." Many are specific to members of a local or craft; some can be reached through a link from a local's website. A directory of the labor groups is at finance.dir.groups.yahoo.com/dir/Business___Finance/Labor. The downsides of Yahoo are the pervasive advertising and the fact that unionized alternatives are now available.

Locals that Rely on the Internet

Organizers at **UFCW Local 789,** based in South St. Paul, Minnesota, started their website for retail workers at www.youareworthmore.org. and subsequently launched specialized sites for employees of Target (targetunion.org) and Borders Books (bordersunion.org). Their online forums allow for unorganized workers to vent their frustrations, compare experiences, and question co-workers about company policies at different stores. A union staffer moderates the discussion, occasionally joining in to supply information. The aim of the websites is to engage and ultimately unionize some of the 20 million workers in the non-grocery retail sector.

"Ask the Rep!—Fast answers from a union rep" is a site feature that allows workers to post questions about their problems and find out what their rights are on the job. A union rep answers these questions daily. This initial contact starts the process of building relationships, and the local has started several organizing efforts from online contacts. The first such successful drive organized workers at the Minneapolis Borders in 2002.

The local does traditional on-site as well as online organizing, doing unannounced walk-throughs at local stores to hand out union flyers. For example, Local 789's Action Squad of member volunteers did a "Borders Blitz," handing out bookmarks to workers and customers at the unorganized stores. The bookmarks advertised the bordersunion.org and youareworthmore.org websites.

Local 789 also takes advantage of the speed of the Internet to keep members informed in great detail about contract negotiations. During grocery contract talks, leaders emailed the minutes of bargaining sessions to their list of activists, who posted them at work. The minutes were also put up on the local's website. During negotiations with Borders Books, the local president reported, "Every shred of communications is online at BordersUnion.com. All of the negotiating notes posted. We have live video streaming of customers, commentaries, and even parodies of the negotiation talks."

Organizer Bernie Hesse says, "The more information you give people the better. People were glued to it. Total transparency (in negotiations) builds strength." He noted that company officials get very upset when remarks like "the workers aren't worth what they're paid" are posted the next day for the very same workers to see.

Alliance@IBM/CWA Local 1701 is a union for IBM employees, functioning with nonmajority status. It started after IBM announced a pension cut in 1998. Alliance@IBM grew from online contacts, website sign-ups, and in-person meetings. It has lobbied extensively on pension issues and on the offshoring of IBM jobs from the U.S., and organized a presence at stockholder meetings to speak up for worker rights.

IBM employees started four discussion groups on Yahoo! in 1999, ibmunion and ibmpension, and later, ibmemployeeissues and ibmretirees. Alliance members now moderate these groups. The forums have posted tens of thousands of messages and are heavily visited by IBM workers, as is the local's website, www.allianceibm.org.

IBM has some 150,000 employees in the U.S. in hundreds of locations, none of them unionized. There are Alliance chapters in many of the larger workplaces, where volunteer organizers do the traditional work of leafleting and recruiting in person. However, an estimated 30-40 percent of IBM employees work from home or are mobile, without a fixed workplace. The two paid staffers would be hard-pressed to hold together a far-flung organization without electronic tools.

Most of the local's 6,000 members joined online. There are two kinds of members: subscribers and voting; the latter pay dues of $10 a month. Both receive a quarterly print newsletter and more frequent email newsletters. Joining a union online counts as signing a union card for NLRB election purposes, but Alliance@IBM has not yet been in a position to start an organizing drive.

WashTech, a union for high-tech workers, also relies on its website (www.washtech.org), email lists, and online discussions. WashTech (Washington Alliance of Technology Workers) joined CWA in 1998. Washtech has voting, dues-paying members in the hundreds, and subscribers that have numbered as high as 13,000.

Washtech has tried two organizing drives, one at Amazon in Seattle and one among Microsoft "permatemps"—temporary employees who had worked for the software company for years. Both drives ended when company moves closed the targeted work areas.

Both Alliance@IBM and WashTech have succeeded at connecting on a regular basis with thousands of interested workers. The obvious challenge they face is figuring out how to turn interest and discontent into power.

Pitfalls and Potential for the Future

As the WashTech and Alliance@IBM efforts show, electronic organizing is not a cure-all for the labor movement. First of all, many workers lack computer access and training, particularly immigrants, people of color, and those stuck in low-wage jobs. And second, even when the workforce is wired, the Internet is not a substitute for face-to-face conversations at workplaces and union halls. Email lists should never provide an excuse to cancel or de-emphasize membership meetings, stewards councils, or similar assemblies.

Third, if electronic communication is used as a tool just for union staff and officers, it can widen an information gap between "insiders" and the membership.

What does the future hold for the Internet and labor? The Internet has already shown its potential as an information disseminator, a mobilization resource, a forum for discussions, and, to an extent, a tool for organizing workers. Using the Internet is clearly not just a question of technology and efficiency; it's also a question of goals. Will it be used to advance militancy, democracy, solidarity, and organizing?

What should labor want from the Internet? To borrow from the controversial Samuel Gompers: MORE. More workers online. More discussion and democracy in unions. More alternatives to the current cable company and Internet "content providers" with their pro-business information flow. More pro-labor video content readily accessible to working class households. More international solidarity. More unionized Internet employers. More outreach efforts bringing organizing victories.

Resources

A few suggestions to get you started:

Specific to labor (besides the many references cited in the text):

• Labor Notes, www.labornotes.org, works to bring activists together by publishing a monthly magazine, books, and pamphlets and holds a large conference every two years. A place to learn about the struggles, strategies, and solutions within the labor movement today. Selected articles from the magazine are available online. A Troublemaker's section of the website contains practical stories like the ones in this book.

• The Association for Union Democracy, www.uniondemocracy.org, maintains a list of rank-and-file websites and has information on union democracy that activists are encouraged to copy and distribute.

• A collection of essays with many how-to tips: Arthur H. Shostak's *CyberUnion Handbook: Transforming Labor through Computer Technology*, M.E. Sharpe, 2002 (www.cyberunions.net).

• xpdnc.com, which bills itself as "the most comprehensive human-retrieved labor directory on the web."

• *Legal Perils and Legal Rights of Internet Speakers*, an outline of a speech by attorney Paul Alan Levy regarding Internet free speech. It contains legal citations, links to relevant websites, and other resources, www.citizen.org/documents/InternetlegalrightsoutlineV2.pdf.

• Annual LaborTech conferences, a forum for labor media activists to learn, link up, and organize: www.labortech2004.org.

• www.labornet.org: U.S. labor news.

• For an insider's story of organizing co-workers over the Internet, see *www.allianceibm.org: Real-World Experiences of Online Organizing*, a paper by Linda Guyer of Alliance@IBM/CWA, at: www.allianceibm.org/docs/TUC/AllianceIBM_paper.htm.

Technical stuff:

• Website design and tools: Webmonkey (www.webmonkey.com) and www.useit.com. Peachpit Press's "Visual Quickstart Guides" on major software and html. Nielsen Norman Group, www.nngroup.com, for website usability advice and discussions.

• Information on blogs (web logs): Weblogs Compendium—www.lights.com/weblogs/hosting.html.

• Reviews and info on broadband (high-speed connection) service providers: www.dslreports.com. For info on dial-up providers: www.thelist.com.

• Companies that provide Domain Name registration: www.icann.org.

• Starting your own discussion list: www.egroups.com; www.topica.com; www.listbot.com; groups.yahoo.com.

Authors

Matt Noyes is Internet coordinator for the Association for Union Democracy, telecommuting from Tokyo, Japan. His writing on use of the Internet for union democracy can be found on the AUD website (www.uniondemocracy.org) and in *The CyberUnion Handbook*, Arthur Shostak, editor.

David Yao is a chief steward for the Greater Seattle Area Local of the American Postal Workers Union, and a member of Labor Notes' Policy Committee. He writes for *Labor Notes*.

21. Developing Leaders

by Tony Perlstein

THE UNITED FARM WORKERS have a saying, "Every worker is an organizer." In other words, everyone has the potential to lead.

But how do we move from doing our jobs the way the bosses want to making change in our workplaces and communities?

How do we learn to work together to make change?

How do we increase the number of workers willing to take responsibility for our unions?

How do we assure that we have new leaders with different ideas, who do not simply clone the leaders we already have?

How do we make sure that our unions survive and grow when we are not around?

This chapter discusses ways unions can recruit, train, and sustain rank-and-file leaders.

In the labor movement, you can ask five people about leadership and get five different responses, ranging from "the leaders lead and the workers follow" to "there are no leaders." Here we assume five things about developing leaders:

1. We want leaders whose goal is to involve others in the fight for social and economic justice. We are not looking to create charismatic individual heroes or martyrs.

2. Anyone can develop skills and strengths to help build our movement.

3. First-hand experience is a powerful learning tool.

4. People can learn from each other.

5. People learn and "develop" differently.

Some of the examples in this chapter may seem geared toward officers who are in a position to create formal leadership programs. But the lessons apply to anyone trying to build a group, perhaps in a non-union workplace, a dissident caucus, or a community organization. For more lessons related to developing new leaders, see Chapters 2, 3, and 18 on Basics of Organizing, Shop Floor Tactics, and Reform Caucuses.

This chapter starts with some basic principles of educating leaders and then shows how they were implemented in one Teamsters local in Washington state. Next Sara Mersha, a leader of a workers' community organization, tells about her group's formal leadership training programs, and Tim Dean, education director of SEIU Local 2020 in Massachusetts, does the same. We finish up with some resources.

What Is a Leader?

Leaders help others see and make change. Leaders look at problems and suggest solutions that make sense to people. They motivate and energize others. Good leaders have vision, listen to others, and stay open to alternatives.

Becoming a leader does not necessarily mean becoming a full-time officer or staffer. Unions often pull their most talented organizers out of the workplace, leaving a leadership void at work.

The future of our movement depends on increasing the number of leaders with vision.

"Many unions just train the stewards to handle grievances," says Tim Dean. "Steward training alone will not create the next generation of activists. Developing leaders is a long-term project.

"The benefits may not be clear in one year or even two. You don't know who is going to emerge, who will take the skills and put them into practice. Part of a union's job is to create a space to come back into, to find out what we did right or wrong."

Create a Plan

Just like an organizing drive or contract campaign, leadership development needs its own plan. Without a plan, training new leaders will inevitably drift to the bottom of the list. Other priorities such as grievance time limits and meetings will always occupy us unless we make the time to think about and train leaders.

Recruiting, training, and sustaining leaders must be a deliberate part of everything we do, from workshop planning and grievance handling to contract campaigns and organizing drives. Activists should ask these questions about every grievance, every contract fight, and every conversation: *How can this involve more people? How*

Every year four to five hundred members of SEIU Local 2020 attend the local's leadership development programs, such as the Worksite Leadership Academy.

does my action increase someone else's sense of power and responsibility? How does this build our organization?

One officer cannot train a new generation of leaders alone; the entire organization needs to be on board. Start by making a plan at a retreat or in a situation where existing leaders have come together to make long-term plans. A good education plan for existing leaders and potential leaders might begin with the following elements, with a timeline to work on them:

Make a recruitment plan. Who gets to decide which members will be trained? Will they be chosen by the current leaders or by the members? Will they be those who self-select, for good or bad reasons? What happens if somebody new, with a strong position different from that of the current leadership, emerges? Will he or she get "developed"? No one right answer fits all organizations, but the leadership team should have answers in mind beforehand.

- Identify existing shop floor leaders and potential leaders. Map the workplace and make charts to track their activity and involvement.
- Assess prospective leaders' level of commitment, skills, and potential. Ask what it will take to get these potential leaders more active.
- Identify campaigns that have potential to recruit new leaders and challenge existing leaders: grievances, contract fights, health and safety campaigns, political campaigns.
- Plan a conversation with the potential leaders you have identified. Ask yourself and others: What moves these leaders? What do they care about? What difference will their involvement make? What fears do they have? What are they committed to already? Practice the conversation in which you talk to the member about these questions.

Make the training hands-on. Leaders develop best in a structure that gives them real responsibility and provides support and feedback. A formal, stand-alone training program is a terrific way for leaders to gain confidence in a safe environment without the boss, but leadership training should include hands-on experience, too.

Training should include practice in talking with co-workers, making plans, and, preferably, dealing with forces outside the union—mainly the boss. This hands-on experience can be in handling grievances, working on a contract campaign, planning a demonstration—whatever real-life work the union is engaged in.

The basic learning structure is: the leader-in-training identifies a problem, makes a plan, acts on the plan, and then talks with others about what happened.

Have a clear structure. Having a well-defined structure that people can plug into helps them get active. Having clear goals helps them see why they are doing the task at hand, and having a clear plan helps them see how to get from A to B. People are more likely to take the first step to involvement when they see a path to achieve what they want, and when they see other people with a commitment to attain those goals.

Mentor and support. Follow-up and mentoring are critical. One-on-one support and feedback help us learn from our mistakes and triumphs and keep us motivated when we're not together as a group.

Challenge each other. In evaluating with new leaders why they succeeded or failed on their commitments, challenging and pushing one another is part of the process. We should not be reluctant to challenge each other to think differently, work efficiently, and become stronger people. We want to take on challenges that we're not sure we're up to. We can do this when we trust that the other person's challenges and criticisms come from shared goals and the desire to help us be better leaders.

Work as a group. While one-on-one discussions are important, group meetings—and action—are part of learning to be a leader too. Get people in the habit of making decisions together in regular leadership meetings; this builds the individual's accountability to the group. Group action increases our sense of movement and connection. See Chapter 19 for an example of a "junior executive board" designed to train future leaders.

Keep the vision. How do we keep our leaders involved over the long haul? How do we train long-distance runners who will get to the finish line? Inspiring, long-term goals help leaders stay active. Our vision serves as a reminder of where we want to be, of the kind of world we want to create.

"We need people with skills who have a vision of justice," says Sara Mersha of Direct Action for Rights and Equality. "We need people who can identify and understand the systems that affect us. By connecting to the bigger picture we become more effective in our daily organizing. The political gives our organizing heart."

New Local Leaders Train Even More New Leaders

FROM 2000 TO 2003, I worked for Teamsters Local 556, a 2,500-member union of low-wage, mostly immigrant Latino, food processing workers in Washington and Oregon. The leadership of our local had led a rank-and-file rebellion in one meatpacking plant and took office without prior experience. (For more stories from Local 556, see Chapters 3 on Shop Floor Tactics and 8 on

---

The Learning and Organizing Cycle

1. As a group, identify a goal or problem to work on.
2. Make a plan to solve the problem or achieve your goal.
3. Act on your plan.
4. Meet with others to figure our what worked and what didn't.
4. Start the process again based on what you learned from steps 1 through 4.

Contract Campaigns.)

From the beginning, part of our vision was to deepen our local's leadership base. We said we would make the training of stewards and mentoring of activists a priority. We often talked about it more than we actually did it.

We were in office a year before we could make a real plan. We had disagreements on the executive board. We were all overwhelmed with work. But the great thing in our local was that the leadership core believed that active members made the union strong, so the conversations always centered on how to involve more people and how to get more people to take responsibility.

Setting Goals and Making a Plan

We joined ENLACE, a low-wage, cross-border workers' organization made up of local unions and community-based organizations. ENLACE staff help affiliates with strategic planning and campaigns. We asked them to work with us on a leader recruitment plan. In the first session, we agreed on the mission of our local: to organize low-wage food processing workers in eastern Washington and Oregon and to shift the balance of power from bosses to workers in our region. We were able to look honestly at where we had been successful and where we had not.

It became clear that although many more workers were participating in union events and we were recruiting and training people, we were not doing it in a systematic way. People were slipping through the cracks. For example, we would help a workplace leader organize co-workers to come to an event. Then we wouldn't follow up. We'd get caught up doing something else.

So in the next session, we talked about how many activists we would need in order to have a solid communication structure and how many we would need for the union to effectively challenge a large employer like Tyson IBP, our largest.

We drew up a huge list of members, showing their level of participation in the union and their relationships to other workers. We separated them into concentric circles. In the inner circle were the most committed leaders. The next ring included people who had shown some level of commitment and who we thought could lead others, but still needed to be more committed, and so on. The goal was to get people to move toward the center circle, bringing the second tier of active leaders into the first tier.

We mapped out the relationships: who in our inner circle could talk with and move a person in the second tier? In some cases it was staff, in others it was the members who had the relationships. We tailored our message to individuals and thought carefully about each person: What did he care about? Why had she shown interest in the union? What did he fear?

We thought about the best way we could help those people face their particular challenges and deepen their commitment. We had specific tasks for people to work on, such as a grievance investigation, a contract campaign at one employer, or our health and safety campaign at another. We were figuring out the relationships we had and how to deepen them.

Two workplace leaders, Arturo Aguilar and Sandra

From the time they took office, the reform leaders of Teamsters Local 556 had a vision of deepening the local's leadership base. Arturo Aguilar, left, and Sandra Stewart are workplace leaders who became leaders of the local.

Stewart, are examples of our process at its best.

Arturo showed leadership on the slaughterhouse floor when he acted as translator for his co-workers. He and others from the union would go as a group into the office and argue with management. Arturo also participated in most of our meetings and trainings, taking on more responsibilities each time, leading discussions and planning. He helped organize large demonstrations around safety, arguing with supervisors and managers over the slippery floors.

But most importantly, Arturo brought others to the table with him. As a result of his commitment, Arturo joined other co-workers in our strategy sessions. Eventually he was elected to the executive board.

During contract talks at LambWeston/ConAgra, Sandra Stewart, a quality-control worker on the day shift, made midnight runs from the bargaining table to the plant to inform key leaders there about negotiations. During one fight over putting a respect-and-dignity clause in the contract, management claimed no one in the plant cared about respect—the bargaining committee, they said, had forced members to sign a petition demanding the respect language.

So Sandra and others on the committee inspired members to go in groups to the bosses and hand them their petitions. The employer looked silly as teams of workers marched to the boss, holding the petitions they'd signed, with no committee members present. Sandra later spent time on staff as a union representative, and then returned to the plant as a chief steward and vice-president.

DARE Connects Skills with Long-Term Vision

by Sara Mersha

DIRECT ACTION FOR RIGHTS AND EQUALITY (DARE) is a member-run community organization in Providence, Rhode Island. We help workers organize in their workplaces (see Chapter 17, Workers Centers), for a living wage, and for police accountability in their communities. Members and leaders are mostly working people of color, immigrant and native-born.

DARE tries to create a group of people who can move our struggles to the next level, who have the capacity to do more when the time is right. We have four goals for leader development:

1. Have people learn from each other. Everyone who comes into our organization brings valuable skills and experiences. We help people figure out what their skills are so that they can teach them to others.

2. Help people identify the other skills they believe they need in order to feel confident enough to win change.

3. Help people make connections between their oppressions and have a bigger vision for our organization. The bigger vision gives hope and energy.

4. Develop paid staff, member organizers, and member activists from within DARE. Members connect with their community members and co-workers better than an outsider can. This is the only way to develop the large numbers of leaders that we need to build a powerful movement.

We have two formal leader training programs, the DARE Leadership Institute (DLI) and Apprenticeship for Member Organizers (AMMO). DLI is a six-month program that combines monthly workshops on organizing skills—recruitment of members, door-knocking campaigns, action training, and public speaking—with political education, mentoring with experienced DARE members, and working on a project.

We offer two workshops a month. Participants are required to attend at least one, have weekly talks with their mentor, and work on a campaign or project connected to the workshops. Once everything is completed, participants receive a $50 per month stipend for the six months.

We work political education into the skills training. It's no coincidence that people of color are in the lowest-paid jobs in our economy or are unemployed. Our work is undervalued and our members will have to deal with racism within unions and in other areas of their lives. We help people recognize the role racism plays in our society so they can struggle against it.

For example, we have held workshops on "Working with the Media" and "Fear Factor." In the media workshop, a Jobs with Justice organizer showed how to get our message out through press releases and letters to the editor. Participants could write one or the other. In "Fear Factor," participants learned how our government creates a climate of fear to justify the expansion of police, prisons, the military, and war. For their projects, participants could read an article and answer questions or attend an upcoming rally against increased prison and military spending.

We ask members to talk in a group about their experiences with public speaking—what their fears are. We watch a video of a famous speaker such as Malcolm X. Then we watch a video of a DARE member speaking in public and evaluate what the person did well and what could be improved. Then we ask people to practice their own speech in front of the group, and give them honest feedback.

Another workshop starts with participants using a wall-sized map of the world to place where their ancestors came from. They talk about how and why they or their families came to the United States. Participants then form small groups and are given a short description of a struggle in black or Latino communities. They create a short skit to act out this struggle in front of the rest of the group. Through this process, the group sees that communities of color have much shared history of struggle.

The last part of DLI is building a relationship between experienced leaders and newer members, paired up. The purpose is to develop relationships within the organization and share what people know, but some people click and some don't. We are still figuring out how to give the mentors more support.

AMMO is a ten-week part-time organizing training program, more intensive than DLI. We focus on recruitment and contact work, campaign research, and fundraising skills. We usually have three people at a time in the program, each working on a different campaign. Participants, who are paid for 20 hours a week, set goals for what they want to learn. We see a big change once members finish this program; they take on much more responsibility within the organization.

Leadership Training, from Basic to Advanced

by Tim Dean

SEIU LOCAL 2020 IS A UNION of health care workers in Massachusetts with about 10,000 members and 100 contracts. For us education means creating opportunities for members to learn from each other and give each other support: *everyone teaches, everyone learns.*

Every year 400-500 workers attend our leadership development programs: Basic Stewards Training, Stewards College, Leaders-in-Training, and the Worksite Leadership Academy. We also have on-demand workshops that address everything from contract campaign planning to strike prep to building the union at the workplace. We design these on-demand workshops with union reps and members to meet their needs. And we have a separate Worker Education Program, funded by grants, that provides English as a Second Language instruction, a high school diploma program, and reading, writing, and computer skills.

Our six-hour Basic Stewards Training covers the

fundamentals of being a steward, legal rights, and grievance handling techniques. New stewards pick a work problem and practice interviewing, grievance prep, and hearing presentation.

Stewards College covers topics that need more attention, such as taking on a toxic boss, organizing around grievances, creative actions, creating communication networks, diversity in the workplace, and the FMLA. The sessions take place on four Saturdays, and if stewards attend all four, they graduate with a certificate and get a union jacket. While as education director I have the main responsibility, the college is co-facilitated by rank-and-file leaders and union reps. We use role-playing, small and large group discussions, drawing, and skits. We do the College three times a year.

Leaders-in-Training

Our Leaders-In-Training program takes place on one full work day per month for eight months. Those chosen for the program get union-paid release time and are expected to attend every session. The themes include: defining a worksite leader, chapter building and internal organizing, labor history, public speaking, strategic planning, running union meetings, dealing with problems at work, globalization, political organizing, lobbying, and "race, citizenship, and immigration."

Some of the sessions are co-facilitated by staff and former LIT's or by guest presenters. For example, our local's political director co-facilitates a session on politics; guest presenters have done pieces on globalization and the war in Iraq; former LIT's co-facilitate the Race, Citizenship and Immigration workshop.

LIT's are expected to assess their worksites and develop projects that build the union there. The projects are reviewed in class throughout the year. Brian Johnson, for example, used what he learned about escalating tactics to lead a contract campaign at Boston Medical. "Each week we would do something different," he says. "As we went along, more people were willing to get in the fight. People saw that as we went along we got stronger."

In the spring, we do graduation, with diplomas and a union jacket for each graduate. We then do an "LIT Re-Union" once a year to bring together all the graduates and continue the process. The "Re-Union" is organized and facilitated by graduates of the program.

Worksite Leadership Academy

Our Worksite Leadership Academy (WLA) is jointly run with other SEIU locals, which helps build member-to-member solidarity. SEIU is a union of health care workers, state workers, building service workers, and allied industrial workers. They can't be stitched together unless members really understand the problems and strategies of other members. As Harriet McCausland from Provident Nursing Home says, "Having other locals there gave us different viewpoints on how to take on members' problems." The WLA develops a cross-local network of activists who can be brought into any number of union activities, from political work to recruiting members for other training programs.

We use the real problems and real obstacles that participants face to stimulate the learning process. For example, participants from our North Adams chapter developed a work plan that included writing and distributing a newsletter. Hispanic women participants developed a separate event, Dia de Conversación (Day of Conversation), aimed at building participation of Spanish-speaking women.

Iliana Zorilla-Cruz from Allied Health helped plan and facilitate the Dia de Conversación. She's a shop steward, executive board member, and graduate of the Stewards Training, LIT, and WLA programs. "In the Dia de Conversación we used an exercise called 'the wall,'" she says. "We posted a picture of a wall and identified the different issues we faced at home, work, and in our community. Then we discussed strategies and tools we could use to solve these issues through the union."

Much of our work is in small groups. For example, in one workshop, participants start out by defining what "the American dream" means to them. Using the outline of a tree (the "trouble tree"), they then discuss the reality of the dream and post the problems as the "leaves" of the tree. The immediate causes for these problems, such as government budgets and policies, are posted on the trunk. Participants are then asked to think about and discuss the "root causes" (cultural, economic, structural, and political) of these problems and post them on the roots of the trouble tree. Then they discuss the role the union can play in dealing with the problems they've identified.

In "Making Meetings More Effective," we have people draw a good and a bad meeting, then have the group post the pictures and explain them. Participants work in small groups to draw roadmaps of what they need to do before, during, and after the meeting. The roadmaps are then posted and compared. We also go through a checklist to evaluate our own union meetings, what works and what needs to be improved.

On the last day we bring it all together through "Making a Plan." We have participants identify goals for their worksites and begin to work on a plan. Of course, they don't implement the plan without going through the process with other leaders at their workplaces. Our goal is to understand that learning leads to action and action takes planning.

Elements of a Good Program

A good leadership development program has some essential elements:

• Make it participatory ("popular education"). Role-playing, drawing, theater, and critical discussions all draw on the knowledge workers bring with them.

• Track the graduates. We keep a record and reps know who has attended which program. This knowledge tells us who wants to be active.

• Mentor and coach. The job of the mentors is to encourage participants, bounce ideas around, and help them keep focused. Mentors can meet regularly with the members or on an as-needed basis. It is not a supervisory role.

• Bring leaders back together. We do "Re-Unions" to reconnect the graduates, do more training, and evaluate current education programs.

• Have graduates facilitate parts of the program they've already done. Worker-trainers are vital, particularly for language issues and diversity.

• Create work-plans for members as part of the training. Follow up to see if their goals are met. Without this crucial step that has members follow through on what they've learned, we risk losing connection with them.

Leo Robinson speaks in a stop-work meeting at ILWU Local 10. This longshore union tradition, in which the job is closed down once a month, makes it easy for everyone to attend the union meeting and helps build rank-and-file leaders.

Union Traditions Build Leaders, Too

THIS BOOK MAKES THE ARGUMENT that unions can't be strong unless they're strong in the workplace. That's where members can feel and exercise some power over their daily conditions of work. What can unions do to create dozens and hundreds of leaders *on the job*? So far we've talked about programs for developing leaders in a formal way, but even more important are solidarity structures and union traditions that encourage rank-and-file members to stand up for themselves.

One union to learn from is the International Longshore and Warehouse Union. The ILWU's hiring hall system makes it more powerful against the employers and also creates a "classroom" that trains rank-and-filers what it means to be a union member.

In the 1930s, longshore workers forced the employers to accept union-run hiring halls. To this day, workers come to the halls for work, and companies have to use the workers dispatched by the union. Workers even elect their own dispatchers. The old-timers created a union culture and work rules that have been passed on for several generations.

"Every morning we can put in two or three hours extra just to pick up a job. Nobody minds the extra time because they see what it means to be together," says one longshore worker in Los Angeles. "The hall is a daily reminder that the company would still be picking its favorites if it weren't for the union dispatch hall."

During their daily visit to the hall, workers spend time talking about what the employers are doing, safety conditions, the condition of equipment. Sometimes the dispatchers or union officers will stop the dispatch to talk about a problem at work or to announce a solidarity event. The union provides racks for members to put out meeting announcements, newsletters, and campaign leaflets.

New members learn about the contract at the hall. A worker will say, "The company tried to do this or that to me." Someone else will say, "That's against the contract." Another worker will whip out the contract, and they'll find someone in the hall who has more experience.

On the Job and at the Hall

Not all unions can create hiring halls, of course. But some ILWU locals have further procedures that other unions could try (these practices vary from local to local):

• "Stop-work meetings": once a month the job is closed down for a union meeting. This makes it easy for everyone to attend. Some locals even fine members if they miss.

• A system where members must attend stewards council meetings if they want to move up from "B-card" to "A-card." ("A-card" workers have more freedom to choose jobs and are guaranteed a yearly wage.) Members can also get credit for going to rallies, picket lines, and other union events.

• Workshops that every worker must attend on how to be a union member, parliamentary procedure, the constitution, the contract, safety, and union history.

• Executive board meetings open to the members.

• A rule that full-time officers can serve only a certain number of years before going back to the job.

• A contractual holiday to commemorate "Bloody Thursday," a day crucial to the history of the union. In 1934, several workers were murdered by police during the longshore strike that became the San Francisco general strike.

• A tradition of one-day strikes in support of other workers' struggles. "I'll never forget when Nelson Mandela came to San Francisco to thank supporters," says one ILWU member. "He closed by saying that most of all he wanted to thank the longshore workers who boycotted this one ship in the 1970s. He told us that many of the movement leaders had been jailed and the movement had hit a low point, and then they got word that in San Francisco the longshore workers had refused to unload a South African ship, in solidarity. 'It gave us our second wind,' he said.

"The B-cards learn the history, then they get involved, they're looking for things to do, because they understand that it's bigger than them, it's bigger than me. An injury to one is an injury to all. It really makes us bigger than our component parts."

Resources

• ENLACE, an organization of workers centers, immigrants unions, and organizing groups in North America. Does training on strategic planning and developing a strong, democratic leadership. 320 SW Stark, #410, Portland, OR 97204. 503-295-6466. http://communitiesunitedforpeople.org/. ENLACE has produced "A Standard for Evaluation," a user-friendly guideline for organizations to evaluate their work and their functioning. www.enlaceintl.org/articles/Literature/AStandardforEvaluation.html.

• *UE Leadership Manual*. Focuses on involving and training more rank-and-file activists. United Electrical Workers, One Gateway Center, Suite 1400, Pittsburgh, PA 15222. 412-471-8919. ue@ranknfile-ue.org. $75 plus $5 shipping.

• *Organizing for Social Change: A Manual for Activists in the 1990s*, by Kim Bobo, Jackie Kendall, and Steve Max. Midwest Academy. The leadership development chapter is pages 86-93. Order from Seven Locks Press, P.O. Box 25689, Santa Ana, CA 92799. 800-354-5348. $23.95.

Action Questions

1. For what purpose do you want new leaders to come forward? What is your organization's vision?

2. How will you develop a group vision that will keep folks motivated? With existing leaders? New leaders? At a retreat? At a meeting? In one-on-one conversations? How will your day-to-day work fit into the larger vision?

3. How will you create opportunities to develop new leaders? What fights, grievances, issues will move people into action and teach them new skills?

4. What practical skills do your potential leaders say they need?

5. Many people are afraid of taking a leadership role—either because of the boss, or because they are nervous about making fools of themselves in front of their co-workers. But they probably won't come right out and tell you they're afraid. How do you have the conversation that can help you understand what's holding them back? What are the ways you can address their fears? (Some answers are baby steps—small activities that build confidence—working with the member to prep for the activity, and debriefing afterwards, giving good feedback.)

6. Who gets to decide which people get trained in leadership/organizational skills? Will potential leaders be chosen by the current leaders? By the members? Or will it be those who self-select, for good or bad reasons?

7. What happens if somebody new, with a strong position different from that of the current leadership, emerges? Will he or she get "developed"?

8. What do you do when you realize you've targeted the wrong person? Or maybe the person self-selected and no one respects him or her? How do you move such members into less crucial activities without alienating them?

9. What happens when your leader-building activities are successful, more people start to take on leadership roles, and an existing leader starts to get upset (threatened by the possible erosion of his/her base)? How do you convince the leader that building new leadership is a good thing? How do you convince your new recruits not to back away?

10. What do you say to a newly recruited leader who doesn't follow through on what she or he promised to do? How do you provide support as well as accountability?

11. How can you create opportunities for new leaders to reflect on what they have learned and experienced? Do they have someone with experience whom they can talk with on a regular basis? Are there other role models? Are there group events and regular meetings?

12. Can you create opportunities for leaders to learn from each other and work with each other?

13. When you put on workshops and classroom activities, can the targeted leaders help in creating them and have a role in how they run? Will there be opportunities to use what they have learned outside the workshops? Will folks be challenged to rethink what they already believe?

Authors

TIM DEAN has been a member of SEIU for 27 years, six as a rank-and-file hospital worker, 13 as a union representative, and eight as education director for Local 285 and now Local 2020.

SARA MERSHA is executive director of Direct Action for Rights and Equality in Providence, Rhode Island.

TONY PERLSTEIN is a member of the International Longshoremen's Association, where he is involved in a rank-and-file reform effort. He has worked as an organizer and union representative for several locals, including the Teamsters and HERE.

On the Troublemaker's Website

To help staffers at a large public sector local learn how to identify, educate, and mentor new leaders, labor educator Lynn Feekin used group-discussion exercises that present common problems. With modification, the exercises could be used by anyone who's trying to pass the torch. Look for "leadership development exercises" in the Troublemaker's section of www.labornotes.org.

22. Dealing with the Media *by Andy Zipser*

EARLY IN MY JOURNALISM CAREER, when I was still naïve in the ways of the world, I worked for the Myrtle Beach *Sun-News* in South Carolina. The rest of the newsroom worked on the glitzy seaside strip known as the Grand Strand, but I had been hired to open a one-man bureau in Georgetown County, some 30 miles and 100 years to the south. I soon decided I had much the better deal: dirt roads, hardscrabble tobacco farms, walled-off compounds of middle-class whites living in so-called "plantations," the unforgettable stench of a paper mill, a pre-Civil War downtown of handsome buildings yellowed by the smoke pouring out of the adjacent steel mill.

It was the steel mill that most provided the kind of drama a young reporter lusts after. Everything about it was outsized, from the mountains of scrap metal piled outside, to the roar and heat of the furnaces inside, to the burly, begrimed men who transformed all that tumult into endless rolls of thick steel cable. So when the steelworkers went on strike, I was like a moth to the flame. What could be more journalistically satisfying than to explore the issues that had forced a shutdown of one of the county's economic pillars? I anticipated walking the picket line while interviewing steelworkers, visiting with their families to learn what hardships they now had to endure, confronting company officials with the evidence I had unearthed of their unreasonableness. Nothing this raw ever occurred on the sun-soaked sands of Myrtle Beach.

It also didn't happen in the pages of the *Sun-News*—and not because of censorship. The steelworkers on the picket line wouldn't talk to me, referring all questions to the local's leadership. The leaders, meanwhile, had retreated into the union hall, from which I was barred. When finally I managed to buttonhole someone of significance, after days of hanging around like a lost puppy, he took momentary pity on me. Look, he said, we have no interest in talking to anyone from your paper. Nothing personal—it's just that whatever we say gets twisted. We know they hate unions up there.

The result was a series of token stories, based largely on press releases from both sides. And guess what? When it comes to press releases and spin management, corporations—with their professional communications staffs—have it all over unions. In the court of public opinion, the steelworkers never had a chance.

What's the Lesson?

THE GEORGETOWN STEELWORKERS had reasons for their attitude. The *Sun-News* was in fact "anti-union." From my editor's point of view, unions were bad for business in an area of already high unemployment and low wages. When a textile plant announced it would be relocating to Myrtle Beach from New York City, the editorial staff was warned not to write about the reason behind this windfall: a union organizing drive up north. The new local jobs would pay only a fraction of New York wages, but hey—their loss, our gain. No sense in fanning resentment or spreading union talk locally, possibly scaring off the company before it ever set up shop.

Approaching the media is much like an organizing drive. First, you have to figure out who the players are and decide who's already an ally, who's potentially reachable, and who is not going to reward your efforts, no matter how hard you try.

But what the Georgetown steelworkers didn't appreciate is that newspapers are not monolithic institutions. Like unions themselves, newspapers are staffed by people with a wide-ranging mix of attitudes, philosophies, ambitions, and work ethics. To dismiss all journalists as anti-union or as sensationalizing grandstanders is to fall into the same trap that some reporters fall into when they categorize union members as rednecks or racketeers. Not only are journalists more diverse than union members often acknowledge, some are actually sympathetic to working people and are willing to go to bat for them—even if that means arguing with an editor who feels otherwise. But they won't win those battles without the right kind of ammunition.

What the Georgetown steelworkers also didn't appreciate is the importance of public understanding of the issues that cause labor-management confrontations. Strikes, organizing drives, or other union campaigns can generate immensely more pressure on an employer if they're reinforced by community support, which can include boycotts, messages from customers or suppliers, or public pronouncements by clergy and elected officials. Public perception also affects the way law enforcement responds to union actions and the way the media cover such events. If the union is not communicating its position clearly and openly, public response will be defined almost entirely by the union's corporate opponents.

At the *Sun-News,* the editor who banned mention of the textile plant's reasons for relocating would have been hard-pressed to impose a similar blackout on an article describing the steelworkers' grievances. The steelworkers, after all, were already members of the community. Their families and friends subscribed to the paper, bought goods from the paper's advertisers, filled pews and school desks alongside the families and children of other *Sun-News* readers. A reporter armed with great quotes and ample local color would have won the space to tell their story—if the steelworkers hadn't played into the anti-union camp's hands.

Laying the Groundwork

WHILE UNIONS DO THEMSELVES A DISSERVICE by shunning the press, it would be a mistake to assume that the correct course is simply to throw open the union hall doors. For the truth is, some reporters *are* sensation seekers or ideologically driven ax-grinders.

An even greater truth, however, is that many more reporters are lazy or overworked or just plain ignorant. That means they're prone to taking shortcuts or to accepting too much at face value, and it means they make dumb mistakes. How often, for example, have you seen the AFL-CIO referred to as a union? Similarly, references to "union bosses" or other negative clichés are much more often signs of knee-jerk writing than of a hidden anti-union malice. Such mindless shorthand deserves to be challenged in a constructive manner, but labor usually views it as proof that the media are out to get them. And to clam up. Which is self-defeating.

Approaching the media therefore has to be viewed much like an organizing drive. First, you have to figure out who the players are and decide who's already an ally, who's potentially reachable, and who is not going to reward your efforts, no matter how hard you try. Second, you have to devote your time to the first two groups and educate, educate, educate. And third, you have to settle in

A Multi-Union Communications Campaign

by Justin Jackson

CONTRACTS FOR 250,000 WORKERS in Los Angeles County expired in 2000—and by coordinating their efforts, L.A. unions got their message out.

Neal Sacharow, then communications director for the L.A. County Federation of Labor, AFL-CIO, explains that contracts expired for a wide range of public and private sector workers. High-visibility strikes by Justice for Janitors, the Screen Actors Guild and AFTRA, bus drivers and mechanics, and L.A. county workers, along with tense negotiations between teachers and the board of education, gave labor an opportunity to put out messages that could complement each other.

"Through the County Fed," says Sacharow, "we created a group of 'labor communicators.' It was a committee made up of local union staff in charge of communications, or they were assigned by their leadership because the union didn't have a full-time communications director."

With one "communicator" per local, the media committee spread key messages about the contract fights both to media and to members. They used joint press releases, news conferences, and press briefings as well as union newsletter articles and leaflets. Beginning four months before the contract campaigns started, communicators developed the messages along with contract campaign and strike leaders. In bilingual media training for rank-and-file members, they role-played talking to reporters and helped with techniques for delivering pithy sound-bites. They represented the unions at rallies and picket lines and directed reporters to these well-trained rank and filers.

The media committee became the conduit for communications with journalists. "When we handed out press kits they included all the media contacts from all the different locals," says Sacharow. "When we issued press releases, we would coordinate it so as few different ones would go out as possible. If a local needed to send out its own, it clearly did. But we also made sure that umbrella messages were included that communicated the importance of these fights to the greater well-being of L.A.'s communities. Reporters often get hung up in the specifics and technicalities of contract negotiations, and we wanted to make sure they looked at the big picture as well."

The committee even developed a self-check method to improve its work. "We would review print and video clips on a weekly basis and evaluate the effectiveness of our media outreach," Sacharow says. "That helped us refine our messages."

Overall, says Sacharow, the effort showed "how unions can create 'media synergy' through their Central Labor Council. We showed how all these different bargaining issues related to the overall welfare of L.A. County. It allowed each union to create its own specific messages as well. There was message discipline but no message authoritarianism."

for the long haul. What you're doing is building a relationship, and that's not something that will happen overnight or that can be switched on like a light bulb the next time you have a crisis.

Sound like a lot of work? It is, but it's something corporate America learned long ago—and the payoff is visible every time you pick up a newspaper or turn on the TV news.

Employers have professional public relations staffs that can smother a crisis with their own perspective, of course, but they do so much more to enrich the soil. Reporters are wooed with lunches, gifts, and ready access to top executives. Editors are invited to business roundtables, receive honoraria as guest speakers, and often serve on various community boards. Company speechwriters supply op-ed pieces acclaiming the virtues of free trade or deregulation. Corporate-sponsored fellowships and seminars teach journalists the economic ropes from a pro-business perspective.

Most union activists, meanwhile, do none of this—then wonder why they find themselves fighting an uphill battle just to establish that their point of view is legitimate.

Even national unions, much less small locals, don't have the resources to match the corporate full court press. But here's a secret: all that lavish attention isn't really necessary.

Most reporters—not all, but that's why this process begins with triage—want to do a "good" job, which in their view means providing fair, even-handed coverage of issues important to their community. Many got into the profession because they wanted to make a positive difference in the world, and they understand that reinforcing power and privilege doesn't contribute to that impulse.

Some significant number even embrace the principle that it is a journalist's job to afflict the comfortable and comfort the afflicted. These are the folks you want to reach, and they'll be as responsive to a respectful, professional overture by a labor activist as they will to the soft soap of a Fortune 500 CEO.

Inventory

Begin by conducting an inventory of the media in your area: newspapers, radio, television. Don't overlook community weeklies, business and trade journals, or ethnic publications. Many cities also have so-called "alternative" weeklies, which may be receptive to covering labor issues sympathetically.

In addition, in larger cities look in the phone book (both white and yellow) or use an online search engine like Google to sniff out the local bureaus of non-local newspapers, newspaper chains, or wire services. These include the Associated Press, Bloomberg and Reuters, and, less frequently, Gannett, Knight Ridder, the *Washington Post,* and the *New York Times.* The *Wall Street Journal,* to cite one example, has 15 domestic bureaus, so if you're with the United Auto Workers, it's helpful to know that the *Journal* has a bureau in Detroit.

Do the same inventory with television, and don't neglect cable outlets like CNBC and CNN. Keep in mind that except for all-news radio stations, virtually none of the other stations will have their own news staffs.

Next, start reading, listening, and viewing so that you can identify the particular reporters who might cover your issues. Don't expect to find reporters whose only assignment is labor—there are only a handful of those left in the U.S. But many business journalists are responsible for reporting on industries that employ organized labor. If it's unclear who's covering which "beat"—journalistic slang for a specialized coverage area—call the news desk and ask who's reporting on your industry or company.

At smaller newspapers, most TV stations, and almost all radio stations, there may be too few reporters for such well-defined beat coverage and you'll have to deal with "general assignment" reporters. (Indeed, at the very smallest newspapers you may end up talking to the editor.) This will be a mixed blessing.

On one hand, you'll be working with someone far more ignorant of your industry—and perhaps of business basics—than a regular beat reporter. That means you'll have to do a fair amount of hand-holding, providing basic education about the complexities of your issues. But on the plus side, you'll probably be reaching someone who's been less brainwashed by a management perspective. And while a beat reporter might be anti-union, leaving you with few options for sympathetic coverage, the odds are there will be several general assignment reporters who might work on stories that concern you, multiplying your odds of finding a receptive ear.

In those few cases in which it's clear a beat reporter has been co-opted by the dark side, search for alternatives. Although business reporters cover most news affecting labor, working class issues transcend the confines of the business page. "Lifestyle" or "Living" sections delve into working women's issues, childcare, health care, and "quality of life." Metro sections, religion pages, and entertainment sections are other potential outlets for labor issues. The entertainment section, for example, may include book, television, movie, or theater reviews that could deal with labor issues. It may take a bit of creative thinking, but there's usually a way to forge a connection.

Once you have your list of journalistic candidates, you can begin separating them into those who already seem receptive to labor's message, those whose sentiments are unknown, and those on whom your efforts will be wasted. Ask around among other union members. Most reporters will fall into the middle group.

Start with your "receptive" group, then move on to the unknowns. Call each in turn, identify yourself, and say that you're handling media relations for your local. Ask the reporter if he or she would be the appropriate person to receive press releases and other materials from your organization, and if not, who would be. Ask what format the reporter would prefer—mail, fax, or email—and get all appropriate contact information.

Then invite the reporter to lunch.

Care and Feeding of the Media

ALL REPORTERS EAT LUNCH. And virtually all reporters love having someone else pick up the tab, partly because most of them aren't paid much, partly because, quite frankly, it feels like stroking and most people like to be stroked. A lunch invitation means an opportunity to get out of the office on somebody else's dime, since this is the one kind of "favor" the news media uniformly allow. From your perspective, meanwhile, it means undivided access to a reporter in a neutral setting where you can do two things: deliver some basic information, and assess the person sitting across from you.

Pick a mid-priced, relatively quiet restaurant that's readily accessible to the reporter—walking distance is best. Time is a reporter's most precious commodity, so don't squander it. Bring a packet of information, including:

- Who you are—how many and what kind of workers you represent, where they work, what they contribute to the local economy. Charts and graphs may be useful here: these folks always feel pressed for time. If there have been recent news stories (in any medium) about your organization, address any inaccuracies in an even-handed way that sets the record straight.
- Organizational structure—where your unit fits within the union hierarchy, how the leadership is chosen and its terms of service, who the locally available leaders are and how to contact them.
- The "state of the union"—an assessment of the challenges and issues you're facing, such as an organizing drive or negotiations. If you're mid-contract and labor-management relations are peachy, say so and emphasize that you're simply establishing good media relations. If there are tensions or the possibility of upcoming confrontations, describe those too, in as even-handed and informative a fashion as possible. Your purpose here is to give the reporter a heads-up that will result in more well-rounded coverage down the road.

Your information packet can also include head-and-shoulders glossy photographs of union leaders (color is more versatile, but black-and-white will do), together with brief biographies of each. Don't try to cram too much information into the bios: think of them as signposts for a reporter looking for experts in various situations, which may be broader than your own organization's activities.

If, for example, one of your local officials has economic expertise, highlight it. The potential payoff is a telephone call seeking comment the next time the White House unveils a new tax plan. If one of your officials has visited someplace interesting, such as Iraq, highlight that, too: that fact may spark a feature story, resulting in more exposure for your organization. In all events, keep the bio short and snappy.

The packet must also include the names of primary and secondary media contact persons, with telephone numbers, email addresses, and cell phone numbers. These contact persons should be willing to take calls at almost any time of the day or night—not because reporters will be in the habit of calling all the time, but because when a reporter needs answers or quotes he or she needs them *right now*.

Most important, make sure whatever you include in this packet is accurate, mistake-free, and professional in appearance. Typos, factual misstatements, amateur graphics, and shoddy production values will send a message of incompetence and exaggeration—one that will stand out even more starkly when contrasted with the slick materials generated by the opposition. Details matter—like the difference between "its" and "it's." If there's no one among your membership with the appropriate editing and graphics skills, ask for help from other union sources, such as central labor councils or your international. If that's a dead-end and you have the money, look for a local graphic arts shop and see what you can negotiate on a consultant base.

If all else fails and you're on your own, keep it simple! One- to two-page statements of straight text—black ink on white paper only, please—are perfectly acceptable. For the technical details, follow the same rules that you would for a press release. Don't try to impress the reader with big words or fancy language—get to the point, and once you've made it, move on.

The lunch itself should be informal and as personal as circumstances permit. This is your opportunity to put a human face on an abstraction—"organized labor"—that is as foreign to most reporters as "investment banking" or "ecumenical councils." Worse yet, if the person sitting across the table has any notion of what a union is, it probably resides in a mental bin filled with such oddities as "communists," "gangsters," and other social pariahs. It's your job to puncture the layers of misconception and present yourself as a knowledgeable and helpful source for future stories and background information.

Assess the Press

At the same time, this is your opportunity to begin assessing the intelligence, trustworthiness, and needs of the reporter facing you, and to begin planning how best to strengthen your relationship.

Does the reporter pretend to know it all, or will he or she readily admit ignorance and seek information? The second variety is both rare and a blessing. The first should ring an alarm bell, suggesting that future stories will be error-filled and the odds of getting timely corrections near nil. Some reporters in this category might be diplomatically steered in the right direction, but it's best to maintain a strictly business-like relationship, with no off-the-cuff or "off the record" comments, and with as much information as possible conveyed in writing to diminish the error rate.

Find out what piques the reporter's interest. Is he or she a number-cruncher who feels most at home looking at balance sheets and statistical studies? Or is the reporter more of a history buff, intent on tracing the root causes of events? Does he or she brighten at the thought of talking to rank-and-file members and their families about their working lives? Or does the reporter seem more interested in gaining access to union leaders for one-on-one interviews? Whatever the answers, you should strive to provide that kind of information and access in the future: winning a reporter's interest is half the battle of obtaining the kind of coverage you want.

Finally, try to learn a bit about the reporter's work-

Speaking to Reporters

by Gregg Shotwell

THE RELUCTANCE OF UNION OFFICIALS to speak to reporters works to the advantage of reformers and dissidents. Whether it's in the *Wall Street Journal* or *Labor Notes,* a story requires conflict. Without a conflict, it's not a story, it's an infomercial, a dud. So reporters need us for an opposing point of view.

Union officials generally don't trust reporters, but then, a lot of them don't trust workers either. Reporters are workers. They have a job to do, and they would like their work to be respected. If we want our message to reach a wider audience and gain legitimacy, we should foster a friendly rapport with the workers whose job it is to tell the story we want told.

How can union dissidents interest the mainstream media? A UAW reformer tells his story.

I don't believe reporters intentionally burn their sources. Reporters need contacts; they can't do their job without them. Treating contacts respectfully is just good business. I've never been misquoted. Sometimes I've said some stupid things, but I have never been misquoted. "Misquoted," and "taken out of context" are weak excuses. It's our responsibility not to be "misquoted."

A good way to make sure that you are not misquoted is to think in advance what message you want to convey and how you want to say it. Then repeat that key phrase, that quotable quote, to make sure the reporter catches it. For instance, if your union officials are about to agree to two-tier wages, you might repeat, "Equal pay for equal work is a fundamental union principle." Stay on target. If you ramble on, the reporter may quote something you said, but not what you would have preferred.

When General Motors said it would spin off its Delphi parts division in 1999, our plant manager invited a reporter from the *Grand Rapids Press* to tour our Delphi plant. He took her on a well-chaperoned tour. Later I sent her an email including some excerpts from my shop floor newsletter, *Live Bait & Ammo.* She was happy to meet with me and hear a different point of view. I put her in touch with a number of other rank-and-file members. When the article appeared, we got as much space as the company officials, and she even plugged *Live Bait & Ammo.*

During the 2003 auto negotiations Julia Bauer, a reporter from the *Press,* called me. She didn't know me; she had pulled my name out of a file created by the previous reporter. Since she was new, I gave her a lot of background information. I sent her articles on the auto industry from my archives. She appreciated the heads-up. She told me that union officials wouldn't return her calls, and that made it difficult to write a balanced story. She quoted me accurately, and she plugged *Live Bait & Ammo.*

Fill the Gap

In those same 2003 negotiations, the International UAW hid behind a curtain of silence, but those of us who were agitating for a fair contract and full disclosure stepped in to fill the gap. We contacted reporters and told them our points of view. Aspects of the contracts that had passed unnoticed in previous negotiations were exposed. For instance, "COLA diversion," a device for giving cost-of-living raises back to the company, was explained in detail. Most rank-and-file members only found out because of the press coverage. The margin of ratification was lower than usual, because members were better informed and had more questions.

At my own local, where the president delayed the ratification vote long enough for the membership to evaluate and debate, we voted the contract down two to one. Reporters were calling me and asking why. I explained that we opposed the two-tier supplement for new-hire Delphi workers because two-tier destroyed solidarity. I called one reporter back on a cell phone when I got to the plant. I told him, "I just heard a quote that will clinch your story." I put my co-worker, Dave Fowler, on the line, and told him to repeat what he had just told me: "At least we will be able to look the new-hires in the eye and say we tried our best to do right by you."

After the contract was ratified, two of my co-workers received their 25-year UAW rings. They wrote a letter to UAW President Ron Gettelfinger, saying they were too ashamed to wear the rings. They felt betrayed by the union leadership. The letter would have gone in the shredder at Porkchopper Headquarters, spiked without a whimper, except I called a reporter from the *Grand Rapids Press,* and she wrote their story and put their pictures on the front page of the business section. She didn't put words in their mouths or spin the story; she let them tell it in their own words.

We made a point of thanking her for that, but the reason there were no "misquotes" was that these workers weren't talking out of both sides of their mouths. Shoot straight and you won't have to make up excuses and pass blame.

ing situation. This can vary tremendously, requiring a wide range of possible responses from you. When I was the editor of a weekly newspaper in Port Jefferson, New York, the entire editorial staff consisted of just me and one part-time reporter. That meant that when the local teachers went on strike, I had to take photographs of picket lines, interview strike leaders, seek school board comments, and write news and "color" stories. Every little bit of information that was shoveled my way was a god-send, and any roadblock or delay was fatal.

On the other hand, when I worked at the *Wall Street Journal* I had a virtually unlimited expense account and gobs of time for truly big stories, didn't have to worry about taking pictures—and had an extraordinarily demanding group of editors looking over my shoulder. The pressure on me then was to deliver exclusivity, access to high-level decision-makers, and insightful— rather than merely descriptive—coverage.

If anything, those contrasts are even more pronounced today. Reporters at smaller dailies and television stations are poorly paid and overworked. Entry-level reporter pay at newspapers with less than 10,000 circulation runs a little over $20,000; for "experienced" reporters at dailies in the 30,000 to 50,000 range, it's about $31,000. For those wages, reporters are expected to churn out as many as 30 stories a week—which may explain why these publications average complete staff turnovers every 15 to 36 months. On the other end of the scale, reporters at the *New York Times* and other top-tier publications start at a minimum of $60,000, with some pulling down twice that amount. Their workload, when measured by numbers of words, is a fraction of what is churned out by their lesser peers—but it has to be of much higher quality and has to beat out competition that most smaller news outlets don't face.

One of the more important differences among newsrooms involves story assignments. In some news organizations, reporters must generate most or all of their own story ideas. This is especially true of beat reporters, who are expected to be experts in their specialty areas. In other newsrooms, editors generate many of the story ideas that reporters are then expected to pursue.

If the reporter you're wining and dining is the kind who's expected to come up with stories, so much the better. If not, you may have to lift your sights and have a second lunch, with the section or managing editor. (Television news producers are notorious for reading local newspapers to find out what they should be covering, while most radio news is of the "rip 'n' read" variety, in which announcers simply summarize the day's headlines. That's one reason this chapter is skewed toward newspapers.)

In chatting with your lunch guest, ask the other questions that will help you better meet that reporter's needs. What are his or her deadlines? Does the reporter want to receive background papers on your union and its struggles? Press releases? Meeting notices? What format— email, fax, postal service—is best? By asking these questions, you will communicate your desire to make the reporter's job as easy as possible. And believe me, in a world of competing voices and time demands, that's an invaluable message.

Off the Record

ONE OF THE MOST HAZARDOUS MINEFIELDS any news source navigates when talking with reporters is defined by such phrases as "off the record, "not for attribution," "deep background," and similar euphemisms for "let me tell you this without getting myself into hot water." How do you know which magic phrase is appropriate?

In a word, you don't. Many reporters don't know what these catch-phrases mean, either. Accept a guarantee that your comments are "off the record" and you might get burned, not out of malice but because you and the reporter have different ideas of what's been promised.

"Background" used to mean that a reporter was being told something solely to increase his or her understanding of a situation; such comments were not intended for publication. "Not for attribution" told a reporter, "you can use this in print, just don't link my name to it." "Off the record" meant "you can use this if you can get someone else to confirm it, but you didn't get it from me."

So how do you determine what the reporter means when he or she invokes one of these magic phrases? Ask. Get a specific definition of your agreement. Better yet, don't agree to any such arrangements until you've established a trustworthy relationship. In all other circumstances, expect that anything you say is fair game and may show up in print or paraphrased in a broadcast.

Tape Recording

You get a call from a reporter and start chatting about your union—but unknown to you, you're being taped. Is the reporter under any obligation to warn you?

More often than not, no. While some states make phone tapping illegal without the consent of both parties, in a surprising number of states such taps are perfectly legal if only one party has given consent—which in this case would be the reporter.

The great majority of reporters who tape their calls don't have a malicious purpose in mind: they're simply trying to ensure the accuracy of quotes. They may also be seeking documentation in case the source claims he or she was misquoted.

Remember that anything you tell a reporter is grist for the mill. Choose your words accordingly.

One final anecdote to drive the point home, this time from the other side of the Great Divide. Read the financial press and you'll soon realize that one of the most frequently quoted analysts is Hugh Johnson of First Albany. Any time the market hiccups there's a sentence or two from Johnson explaining just why the Dow zigged instead of zagging, or why interest rates dipped.

Now, First Albany isn't an investment brokerage on the same plane as Merrill Lynch or Morgan Stanley, and Hugh Johnson isn't a hot-shot money manager like Peter Lynch. But Johnson is a great schmoozer: he must meet a different reporter for lunch nearly every day, he distributes his business cards and First Albany materials liberally, and he's always available. Need a quote on deadline? Johnson will answer his own phone, he speaks in sound bites, and he never makes a reporter feel like he's asked something stupid. The result is a media presence out of all proportion either to First Albany's financial significance or to Johnson's insights.

Yeah, Yeah, It's a Lot of Work...

Yes, it's all a lot of work. Worse yet, its payoff may not be all that great. Some reporters (although not many) won't accept your lunch invitation, in which case you should send them your information packet anyway, then follow up with a phone call to ask many of the questions you would have asked over a hamburger—and maybe to offer a second lunch invitation. Of those you do meet, some will prove to be hacks or drones or ideologically appalled by the principles you represent. And even when you find a sympathetic ear, in two or three years that reporter may be moving on and you'll have to start all over again with his or her replacement.

Small wonder, then, that many union activists never undertake this kind of painstaking networking. But just as a union organizer can't march onto a shop floor and spark an organizing drive by waving a placard, a labor activist can't expect favorable—or even neutral—coverage of a work action or an organizing drive unless the ground has been prepared. Long odds or not, this is work that must be done.

Ken Riley, head of the longshore local in Charleston, South Carolina, ILA Local 1422, relates how one reporter kept writing that dock workers were all making $100,000 a year. "We invited him down," Riley remembers, "telling him we were going to have a press conference. When he got there we closed the doors and said, 'Look, you pick out any five or ten members on the list and we will get you their pay statements. We also want you to go to work for 10 or 12 hours a day, on containers stacked five feet high.' We told him what we were upset about, and we got him focused.

"He then asked us, 'Can you help me? Can you give me the stories first, so I can get them in the paper before they appear on TV?' So we said yes, we could do that, and we did, and he never ran any more stories about how much our members made."

Although that story had a happy ending, the problems it illustrates would not have occurred if there had been a pre-existing relationship between the longshore workers and the reporter. The reporter would have known how much the workers earned and would not have regurgitated company propaganda; the union would have known the reporter's deadline needs and could have helped him meet them.

When the Crisis Hits

OKAY, BUT LET'S BE REAL: most unions haven't done the spadework before they find themselves in a crisis that draws—or should draw—a media spotlight. What then?

Much of the foregoing would still apply, but within a compressed time frame. You still should prepare and distribute a press packet of background information about the union and its members, but supplement the general information with more targeted facts and figures relevant to the dispute. You still should provide the media with contact names and numbers, together with a list of leaders and their bios. You also should consider giving the media contact information for rank-and-file members who can speak knowledgeably about the situation but can humanize it, too.

But the most crucial difference between the more generic media approach and a crisis-driven one is that in the second case you have to shape a simple message that captures the essence of your position. The message has to be shared and clearly understood by your members, so that they can articulate it without hesitation when a microphone is thrust in their faces. Most of all, it has to be one message only. Multiple messages can be confusing—especially on broadcast media, which may devote no more than 15 to 30 seconds to a story—and will detract from your main point. Worse yet, if multiple messages are in conflict they practically invite a counterattack from your opponents or from the press itself.

It Has To Look Good

To catch the eye of the press, use eye-catching visuals. You're much more likely to make the news if your action looks unusual; that's why so many unions have invested in giant puppets and balloons. For ways to add to your visual appeal, see Chapter 4.

Verizon workers in Boston protested the company's job-cutting plans with a "Who Will Be Next?" roulette wheel and a ringmaster. Another time, "Scrooge" drove up in a stretch limo, accompanied by two members in turkey costumes, to protest Christmas-time layoffs. And Verizon workers have visited the company's lawyers with one guy dressed in a shark suit.

A classic example of the press going on the attack occurred during the 1994-1995 baseball strike, which forced the season to end without a World Series. Virtually all labor disputes are framed by the media as two-sided conflicts between labor and management, with management typically given the white hats. In the baseball strike, however, neither side succeeded in formulating a clear, simple message to summarize its position. The result? The media came up with their own summary, characterizing the strike as a squabble between millionaires and billionaires—inviting a pox on both houses.

In addition to being simple, your message has to resonate with a public that is nearly 90 percent non-union, doesn't understand a lot of labor's shorthand (what the hell is a ULP?), and often can't identify with your issues. "Most unions' media message is far too insider and obscure," claims Craig Merrilees, director of AFSCME Local 3299, a statewide local of 16,000 blue-collar and hospital workers in the California university system. "Stop thinking about the message as being about your union. Think instead about speaking to the general public."

For example, Merrilees says, an emphasis on preserving job security might backfire in an economy where most workers have none. "Job security is an alien concept to most workers who aren't in a union. It's not likely to resonate with most folks, mostly because they don't understand it or are resentful," he explains. "They're likely to see the union people as special, privileged, sometimes spoiled and selfish people who don't understand what most workers have to put up with. Or we think a strike is inherently fascinating, for instance, but not always, unless we amp it up a little bit.

"The slogans and the signs that people carry are really important. Many of the signs that we use in union pickets are Greek to the general public. They sometimes have nonsensical phrases like 'Mercy Hospital Unfair to Workers' or 'ULP strike.'"

On the other hand, Merrilees adds, a union can shape its message to specifically address consumers in its industry. When his local was negotiating in 2000 with University of California hospitals, one of the biggest problems it confronted was chronic short-staffing—an issue that quickly struck a public nerve when workers couched it in terms of deteriorating patient care rather than complaints about their workloads. "People talked about how patients get neglected, face injuries and even death if staffing is so short they can't devote the time that patients need," he recalls.

As such advice suggests, the importance of framing the right message can't be overemphasized. It also tends to repel many activists because it seems simplistic (which it is) and too much like sloganeering (which it also is). Yet the radical right has shown how effective the right slogan can be: "right-to-work," "paycheck protection," "free trade." All these labels put organized labor on the defensive. If the best defense is a good offense, we have to become just as creative in our own thinking.

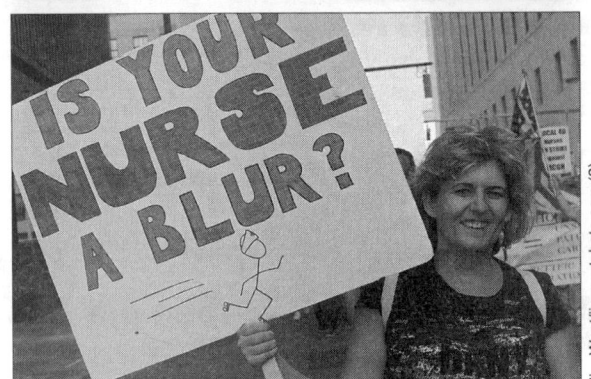

Get the Members Talking

THE EMPHASIS ON MAKING SURE MEMBERS UNDERSTAND and convey the message runs counter to common practice in most unions, where rank and filers are told to refer media inquiries to an official spokesperson. That makes sense if leaders aren't communicating with members, who therefore don't have a clue, but it also reinforces a perception that unions are closed, secretive societies. It also presents the union as anti-democratic, which then feeds into the notion that uninformed reporters are likely to fall back on anyway—that labor disputes are really fights between corporate bosses on one side and union bosses on the other, with union members merely the duped draftees.

It's the human dimensions of labor strife that make such stories attractive to journalists, but you need real human beings for that. "No one wants to hear officials—people can dismiss them as partisan," observes Frank Halstead, a warehouseman and member of Teamsters for a Democratic Union, who drummed up support for the southern California grocery strike in late 2003. "The labor movement was trying to do what it could to mobilize support for the workers, but the union didn't have the rank and file talking to the press. The UFCW not doing that hurt in terms of countering the companies' huge media barrage."

For Halstead, a much better road map was provided by the 1997 strike against UPS, when "you constantly heard rank-and-file union members sharing their stories of why they were fighting." Indeed, the UPS strike is a textbook example of how to develop a unified message

These two rank-and-file union members did a great job of making their messages clear and simple.

that is then amplified by thousands of union members who have shared in its development, and who therefore can tell it consistently and confidently (see Chapter 9).

Rand Wilson, who planned much of the Teamsters' media campaign for the strike, says that a union's media campaign will necessarily be "a reflection of the strength of the membership's unity and involvement. To the extent that members are united and involved, press work is relatively easy. If your union is weak and not well organized, and people are not urged to speak up and be involved, it's not going to be a good media campaign."

Which reinforces our point about avoiding mixed messages. If labor leaders are telling reporters that health insurance is their top issue, while their members' real beef is low wages, or if leaders tell the media that the main goal is x but tell their members they won't settle a contract without z—that's a recipe for confusion.

"The most important communication," Wilson suggests, "is the communication that occurs between members. It's what people are saying to one another and their families that becomes the truth. If people are all talking about money and you're saying 'This is about quality care,' the media are savvy enough to pick up on that."

Of course, good internal communication doesn't occur overnight. It requires just as much preparation to establish as do external press relations. Teamster leaders started planning their campaign two years before the contract's expiration, concluding from membership surveys and meetings that a primary bargaining goal would be converting part-time jobs to full-time ones. In addition to meeting members' needs, the issue was correctly seen to be photogenic, with strong media appeal and resonance for a growing number of part-time U.S. workers.

The campaign itself was launched 13 months before contract expiration, with communication to the rank and file a high priority. By the time the strike began, picketing Teamsters who were approached by reporters knew the issues and were persuasive with the public.

Nor should discussion of your issues be restricted to your own ranks. Community allies who can affirm your point of view multiply the effectiveness of your message. "If at all possible, get other voices to join you," Wilson counsels. "If you're a nursing home aide, see if you can get the voice of a resident into the story. If you're a bus driver, get a passenger."

In addition to demonstrating the value of advance planning, the UPS case also illustrates how the threat of a strike at even a highly visible company like UPS may be slow in attracting media coverage. Unless there's picket line violence or some other catchy visual, most media that haven't already been plugged into your union through earlier relationship-building won't pay much attention. The issues seem too complex and difficult to explain; or the company may be in a position to hurt the newspaper or station financially if it feels coverage is biased against it; or the conflict may seem too much like insider baseball. There are lots of reasons why you might get the cold shoulder. Initially.

But like a snowball rolling down a hill, media attention gradually will feed on itself. The impending Teamsters strike, says Wilson, "wasn't on the mainstream media's radar for a long time, but slowly and surely membership involvement began to engage the public. First local weeklies and local dailies in small towns began to catch on, then the trade press, other print media, and eventually, of course, TV and radio. But this was built up very slowly over a long period of time."

Putting It All Together

MOST HOW-TO GUIDES on press relations start by telling you what resources and internal processes you need, then move outward to discuss the media themselves. This chapter has reversed the order for two reasons: first, because it was written by a journalist who has seen the newsgathering process from the other end; and second, because it makes more sense to understand the task in front of you before you select your tools.

Which brings us to the "you" addressed throughout this chapter. Who must "you" be, to do a good job? What tools, talents, and resources will you need? Where can you turn for help?

As should be evident from the sections on laying the groundwork and care and feeding of the media, you'll need time and energy and a bit of a salesman's, or missionary's, sense of purpose—and that means within your organization, too, because you'll have to convince other members that such work should be more than an afterthought. A union that merely maintains a list of media fax numbers and sends a press release in moments of crisis is wasting its time. I know—I was the vice president of such a local.

Ideally, your union will recognize that having a "communications director" is as important as having a mobilization coordinator or director of organizing. Indeed, the communications director's job is similar to both these positions: it entails membership mobilization to come up with a unified message and media "organizing," or networking, to produce results.

But because media outreach also requires communicating your union's goals and values to the public, you'll need to have the confidence of both your leadership and the rank and file that you can do so accurately. That might mean forming a committee to discuss what issues should be made public and how best to respond to outside criticism.

Ideally, as well, you are someone who already has a media background, or at least is familiar with the various forms of media and contemporary media issues. The most pressing of these is the trend toward media consolidation and corporatization, which affects your ability to get favorable coverage. These trends are also of great concern to journalists, who have to contend with multi-skilling and other "efficiency" trends that are transforming their work into little more than information processing. So you may find, as you reach out to the journalists in your community, that you have far more in common as workers than as news subject/news reporter. You can learn more about these issues at www.newsguild.org, www.mediareform.net, and www.reclaimthemedia.org.

On the other hand, if you don't have a media background, don't despair. Union members with organizing experience are usually good communicators, which, together with attention to detail, are the two qualities most needed in this position. What you don't know, you'll pick up, and you already know your core subject matter—organized labor, your union, and your members' issues—better than any reporter you'll be contacting.

Resources

- The International Labor Communications Association is an AFL-CIO affiliate with membership open to union communications directors and newsletter editors. Although most ILCA programs are aimed at improving internal union communications rather than media outreach, its leadership is trying to broaden its scope, and individual members may have the expertise—and willingness to share it—that you need. www.ilcaonline.org or 202-637-5068.

- The AFL-CIO's George Meany Center for Labor Studies in Silver Spring, Maryland from time to time offers media courses for union members. If what you're after isn't currently available, ask what you can do to get what you need. The Meany Center is responsive to demand, but it has to have a minimum level of interest before it can offer a course. View course offerings at www.georgemeany.org. 301-431-6400.

- *Grassroots Journalism,* a handbook by reporter Eesha Williams, describes itself as "a practical manual for doing the kind of news writing that doesn't just get people angry, but active." It's a pretty good primer for anyone dealing with the media. Apex Press, 2000, $22.95, www.cipa-apex.org.

- FAIR (Fairness and Accuracy In Reporting) provides an invaluable critique of media biases and manipulation for anyone trying to get a deeper understanding of the corporate press. FAIR, 112 West 27th St., New York, NY 10001. 212-633-6700. www.fair.org.

- For broad coverage of journalism issues and news, look for the *Columbia Journalism Review* and the *American Journalism Review,* probably available at your public library. Or browse the Romenesko blog on the Internet, a favorite of many journalists, to keep a finger on the journalistic fraternity's pulse. Go to www.poynter.org/column.asp?id=45.

Action Questions

1. What are the media outlets in your area? Are there any newspapers other than the local daily? Do any of the national newspapers or magazines have bureaus? What about trade journals, business publications, alternative weeklies? What television and radio stations in your area ... local news coverage? Any cable outlets? ... e there any reporters at the news media you've ... o cover labor or unions? Are there any who ... ur particular industry or company? Which local reporters write about workplace and family issues?

3. What are the phone numbers and email addresses of the reporters you've identified? What are their deadlines, and what kind of material will they be most interested in receiving? Which ones seem sympathetic, and which ones come across as hostile or condescending?

4. Have you prepared a basic press kit about your organization? Does it contain information about your members, what kind of work they do, and what they contribute to the local economy? Does it provide short bios of your leaders? Glossy head shots? Most important, does your press kit provide reliable contact information for a reporter trying to reach your organization's communications director?

5. Has your organization discussed the importance of having a disciplined relationship with the media? Does it have a communications director? Does it have an organized system of deciding what will be communicated to the media and of ensuring that the members understand and can communicate the message? Is there an organized system for responding to media inquiries?

6. Does your membership know and understand your organization's approach to the mass media? Does the leadership understand and support your organization's media relations?

7. Do you know who within your organization has media experience? Do you know which members are web-savvy? Which ones can write well? Which ones have graphic abilities or know how to take pictures?

8. Who are your natural allies in your community? Which ones have media experience and might be willing to speak (or write or call) to the media in support of your issues? Do you have reliable contact information—phone and fax numbers, email addresses—for each one?

Authors

JUSTIN JACKSON is a graduate student in history at the University of California-Santa Barbara and a member of UAW Local 2865. He conducted most of the interviews for this chapter.

GREGG SHOTWELL belongs to United Auto Workers Local 2151 at Delphi in Coopersville, Michigan and to the UAW Solidarity Coalition (http://hawk.addr.com/uawsc). He writes a shop floor newsletter, *Live Bait & Ammo.* Find him at www.greggshotwell.net.

ANDY ZIPSER is editor of *The Guild Reporter,* the newspaper of The Newspaper Guild-CWA. He has worked for community weeklies, the "alternative" press (*New Times,* in Phoenix), the *Wall Street Journal,* and *Barron's.* He is a vice-president of the International Labor Communications Association.

On the Troublemaker's Website

SEE WWW.LABORNOTES.ORG for "How To Write a Press Release," by Andy Zipser, and for a sample union press release.

23. International Solidarity

by William Johnson

WHEN WORKERS IN ONE COUNTRY help workers in another, that's international labor solidarity. For over 150 years, workers have built solidarity across borders for mutual defense. They share experiences and information and create international labor organizations for the good of workers everywhere.

International solidarity can take many forms. Workers visit each other's countries to learn about conditions and discuss common problems. Unions have organized campaigns to free union members held in jail by repressive governments and have organized strikes in one country to help workers in another.

In a world economy dominated by multinational corporations, international solidarity is more critical now than ever before. "Outsourcing" and "offshoring" have become part of labor's vocabulary. Connecting with unions in other countries is key to countering this trend.

International solidarity work can also help you develop ties with workers in your own country, since you have to work with others to be most effective. As you research an employer's international activities, you may learn things about its domestic activities too, such as plants you weren't aware of.

We focus here on what rank-and-file activists and local union officers can do. We'll start with an overview of how to get started. You'll find where to go for help and the five "don'ts" of solidarity diplomacy. We'll tell you how the U.S. government lost its popularity in the Third World, and why some of our national unions have a reputation for arrogance. You'll then find examples of:

• getting support from co-workers at your same company, in another country.

• building support for Mexican workers employed by a U.S.-based multinational.

• setting up a speaking tour and a longer visit for unionists from abroad.

• building an ongoing union-to-union partnership.

• being part of the global justice movement.

How To Begin International Solidarity

by Dan La Botz

SUPPOSE YOU LEARN THAT YOUR EMPLOYER, a multinational corporation, plans to do something that will harm union members where you work. You want to know whether management's actions are local or whether they represent part of a new international strategy. For example, is the strategy to outsource all U.S. production? Is the company building non-union sister plants? How are employees in other countries treated and how might they help? Are unions mounting an effective response anywhere else?

Where do you begin?

Look for information within your company and union.

• You probably have a good sense of where your products go and where the suppliers to your facility are located—just look at the shipping labels. You want to know about the chain of production, about the shipping, warehousing, and final destinations of parts and products. Where are the weak links? Who could cause the company problems? Do an Internet search (see the Appendix on Researching Employers). Many companies have maps of where they operate; others proudly list the companies they supply.

• Are there members in your local who are natives of the country where you seek contacts? There's a chance they have company or union connections there.

Contact international labor organizations (see the box on the next page).

• Ask your international if it has relationships with unions in these other countries. See if your international will help you contact the International Trade Secretariat that your union belongs to.

• Contact the AFL-CIO Solidarity Center.

International Labor Organizations

by Dan La Botz

Official Organizations:

• The International Labor Organization (ILO), a part of the United Nations, is a tripartite organization made up of government, employers, and union officials. The ILO formulates international labor standards in the form of Conventions and Recommendations. With these it sets minimum standards of basic labor rights, such as the right to organize and bargain or against child labor, but it has no power to enforce them. The ILO plays no role in organizing international solidarity. www.ilo.org.

• The International Confederation of Free Trade Unions (ICFTU) has become the largest and most important international labor organization, made up of 215 labor federations in 145 countries, with some 125 million members. While it can be a vehicle for international labor solidarity, it is also a bureaucracy of bureaucracies, so rank and filers and local union officers cannot expect to get its attention, though their international union might. www.icftu.org.

• International Trade Secretariats (ITSs) bring together national unions that are involved in the same industries, such as food, chemicals, metalworking, or transportation. The ITSs differ greatly in their commitment to international solidarity. Some of the most active are the International Metalworkers Federation (IMF) at www.imfmetal.org/main/index.cfm, the International Federation of Chemical, Energy, and Mine Workers Unions (ICEM) at www.icem.org, and the International Union of Food Workers (IUF) at www.iuf.org/en. These three ITSs sometimes head up international campaigns, and local unions may be able to get their ear.

• The AFL-CIO Solidarity Center in Washington, D.C. maintains Solidarity Centers in Africa, the Americas, Asia, and Europe. They are funded by the AFL-CIO, the National Endowment for Democracy, the Department of Labor, the Department of State, and the U.S. Agency for International Development. The Centers have done some important solidarity work, such as the campaign in the 1990s to free Indonesian union leader Dita Sari from prison. However, the AFL-CIO Centers in some countries attempt to promote American models of unionism or to direct local campaigns. Both American and foreign unionists have been critical of the Center's close connections with the U.S. government. Contact the Solidarity Center to see what possibilities exist, and leave other options open. 1925 K Street, NW, Suite 300, Washington, DC 20006. 202-778-4500. www.solidaritycenter.org.

Unofficial Organizations:

International solidarity organizations have grown up around specific regions, industries, groups of unions, or particular problems. Here are some examples; if you investigate a particular situation, you will find more.

• The International Dockworkers Council (www.idcdockworkers.org) was created by unions to organize solidarity on the waterfront when the official ITS, the International Transport Workers Federation, failed to do the job.

• The Coalition for Justice in the Maquiladoras (CJM, www.coalitionforjustice.net) is a tri-national coalition (Canada, Mexico, and U.S.) of religious, environmental, and labor organizations working to improve conditions for workers in the maquiladoras. CJM's board includes representatives from unions in all three countries.

• The Transnationals Information Exchange (TIE, www.tieasia.org/TIEnetwork.htm) helps build cross-border networks to exchange information and strategies, with an aim to build common projects. TIE organizes conferences for workers in a variety of industries including auto, retail, chemical, and garment. TIE operates in North and South America, Asia, Europe, and Africa, with representatives in Malaysia, Russia, the Netherlands, the U.S., Germany, Brazil, and Chile. TIE's work with the workers of the Bayer Group multinational is described later in this chapter. TIE is very accessible to workers and local unions.

Other Resources:

Campaign for Labor Rights, the "Grassroots Mobilizing Department of the U.S. Anti-Sweatshop Movement." 1247 E St., SE, Washington, DC 20003. 202-544-9355. clr@clrlabor.org. www.clrlabor.org.

International Labor Rights Fund, www.laborrights.org.

TIE-Asia (see above) works in Malaysia, Sri Lanka, Bangladesh, Thailand, and Indonesia.

China Labour Bulletin, P.O. Box 11362, General Post Office, Hong Kong. 852-2780-2187. web@china-labour.org.hk. www.china-labour.org.hk.

Chinese Working Women Network, Room 216-219, Lai Lan House, Lai Kok Estate, Cheung Sha Wan, Kowloon, Hong Kong. 852-2781-2444. cwn@cwwn.org or exco@cwwn.org. www.cwwn.org.

New Trade Union Initiative, uniting independent Indian unions with a democratic perspective. B-137 Dayanand Colony, First Floor, Lajpatnagar Part IV, New Delhi, India 110024. Phone 91-2621-4538. Fax 91-2648-6931. newtuinitiative@yahoo.co.in.

South Africa Labour Bulletin, PO Box 3851, Johannesburg 2000, South Africa. salb@icon.co.za.

See "Using the Internet To Promote International Solidarity" in Chapter 20 for more sources of information and for how to connect with "sister shops" owned by your employer in other countries.

In general, going through union bureaucracies is a frustrating experience, since they tend to follow protocol. Union bureaucracies in other countries are just as daunting as those here, and you may initially encounter distrust from union activists abroad, so finding a direct contact will require persistence and humility. It's worth trying the official channels; you may at least pick up some information.

Contact unofficial, independent organizations.

Such networks of activists exist to do solidarity work with Mexico, Central America, Africa, and Asia. For example, for the U.S.-Mexico border region, contact the Coalition for Justice in the Maquiladoras. If you want help from an Asian union, check with TIE-Asia. Labor Notes may be able to put you in touch with the right activist network.

Members of UNITE picket a retail GAP store to protest the sweatshops that are used to produce clothing sold by the chain.

welcome investment that creates jobs, they understand that the incentive is cheap labor.

• Some activities of U.S. unions have been questionable. In the past, the AFL-CIO and U.S. international unions worked with the U.S. State Department and the CIA to eliminate nationalist or leftist unions in other countries. They sometimes cooperated in political movements and even in coups to overthrow governments. While the AFL-CIO has put some distance between itself and the State Department, U.S. labor organizations still have a reputation for thinking they know what's best for workers in other countries.

Language and Culture. Many unions will have some English speakers at the higher levels, but most local officers and rank-and-file workers will not speak English. Interpretation is an art, and it is very much based in an understanding of the country's culture, society, and politics. Ideally, you want an interpreter who has a feel for the labor movement.

You should of course be sensitive to issues of lan-

How To Approach Unions Abroad

When you approach a union in another country, whether to ask for help or to offer it, you should do so with some humility and tact. Workers abroad have their own unique histories, problems, laws, and customs. While they will usually be friendly and helpful to you as an American worker, you should understand that many people around the world have reservations about the United States. Why?

• Our government has been involved in political and military interventions around the world, including overthrowing democratically elected governments (in Guatemala, Chile, Iran, and the Congo, for example). Many people in other countries fear and resent the United States government (though usually they will not hold that against you).

• U.S. corporations' plants in other countries often pollute the environment, exploit labor, and interfere in politics. While the people of Mexico, for example, may

Diplomacy

When you work with unionists from abroad:

• Don't assume that you or your union knows how to organize better than they do.

• Don't offer to send organizers to their country or say your union should have the right to organize them.

• Don't assume their contracts and grievance procedures are like ours.

• Don't do anything to suggest you want their jobs returned to the U.S.

• Be aware that many cultures value civility and human relationships over speed and efficiency, and put far more emphasis on politeness, process, and consensus than we do in the U.S.

guage, religion, and ethnic or national customs when dealing with people from another country. Be respectful, tolerant, and flexible.

Poverty. Most nations in the world are poor. The United States, with 5 percent of the world's population, controls at least 25 percent of the world's wealth. Millions of people around the world live on less than a dollar a day. When we seek or offer help, especially to nations in Latin America, Asia, and Africa, we should remember that we will usually have a lot more resources than they do. A genuine solidarity relationship based on fairness will mean that the richer partner will often pick up the tab, without embarrassing the other.

A proud record. At the same time, other countries often have much more solidarity-conscious, militant, and politically sophisticated unions than we do. For example, throughout 20 years of military dictatorships (1964 to 1984), some Latin Americans had to go underground to form unions. During the last ten years, workers in Latin America have organized many general strikes against international trade agreements, against privatization, and against their own governments. In Bolivia, they drove the president from office through massive protests. We have a lot to learn from unions in other countries.

Independence frustrated. In some countries the government protects company unions, and workers find it hard to form independent unions because of legal barriers. Sometimes the best unions will be those that are not "official."

Repression. Workers in some countries face serious repression by employers, the police, and the military. The most extreme example is Colombia, where over 4,000 unionists have been killed since 1986 by employers' thugs, the police, or death squads linked to the military. When workers face such terrible levels of repression, they may have to create both legal, public organizations and also underground ones. We should be discreet and follow their guidelines for making contact and arranging visits.

★ ★ ★

As employers globalize their operations, international contacts within your company or industry can be crucial. In the following story, Trudy Manderfeld describes how her union cultivated international contacts in its fight against a plant closing, and then maintained those contacts beyond the campaign.

Solidarity within a Multinational Company

by Trudy Manderfeld

IN NOVEMBER 1999, United Steelworkers Local 12273 in Elkhart, Indiana got the word that the Bayer Corporation would close its Elkhart plant. Of the 550 good-paying jobs that would be lost, 380 were union. The closing would be done in stages and would be completed by December 2002.

Bayer operates worldwide with headquarters in Germany. Its 120,000 employees make diagnostic equipment, chemicals for agriculture, plastics, prescription drugs, and over-the-counter medications like aspirin, Alka-Seltzer, and Aleve. Of its 50 U.S. plants, only six are union.

Bayer had come to Elkhart in 1978, when it purchased the Miles Laboratories plant. At the time, Bayer promised the community that the company would always keep the manufacturing site in Elkhart and continue to use the name Miles Laboratories, famous as the maker of Alka-Seltzer. Thus, even though signs of a plant closure had been evident for a while, everyone was devastated when the announcement was made. As president of the local, I had to do something.

On the surface our local seemed to have little leverage to force Bayer to stay, or to at least treat our jobless workers generously. It was time to locate some pressure points. We identified three advantages.

One was the relationship that I had established with Bayer workers in Germany. Although we had only exchanged emails up to this point, that had laid the foundation for closer work.

The second was the considerable damage done to Bayer's reputation by much-publicized corporate scandals—price-fixing, Medicaid fraud, and impure chemicals.

Third, we had recently established contacts with a German newspaper, *Bayer Danger,* devoted to reporting on the dangerous aspects of Bayer's products and corporate behavior. *Bayer Danger* published an article I wrote detailing the situation at Elkhart and the lies Bayer had told our union and community.

The First International Labor Organization

by Dan La Botz

International labor solidarity has a long history. In the 1850s, English construction unions reached out to workers in France and Belgium, asking their support against scabs from the European continent. In the 1860s, during the Civil War in the United States, unions in England sent messages of solidarity supporting the Union government of Abraham Lincoln in its struggle to abolish slavery. Those English union officials also contacted a German economist living in London, Dr. Karl Marx, and asked his help in putting together some sort of organization to build international solidarity.

Out of those efforts, in 1864, came the International Workingmen's Association, also known as the First International, an alliance of unions throughout Europe. Later the IWA established some chapters in the United States. It worked to reduce international scabbing, build international support for organizing and strikes, free jailed unionists and other political prisoners, promote legislation such as the ten-hour day, and establish labor parties.

Corporate Campaign

Quickly the local organized a committee to develop a corporate campaign involving the community, local colleges, the media, other unions, and contacts in Germany. Accustomed to reaching out to the community, we formed a broad campaign committee that included members of the Communications Workers, the Machinists, and the International Brotherhood of Electrical Workers. Our goal was to stop the closing or, at the very least, to apply pressure for a fair settlement and let Bayer know we were not going to go quietly.

We also included labor studies professors at Indiana University in South Bend and a professor from Notre Dame. The local had strong community support from the small business association, local mall officials, and McDonald's. They were as outraged as our workers were because of Bayer's broken promises. These broken promises made it easy for us to keep our story in the media.

We raised money by selling buttons, bumper stickers, t-shirts, and barbecued chicken on street corners. A local television station helped us make a commercial and aired it during prime time. The mall's marquee advertised our demonstration and march planned for January 30, 2000. McDonald's offered free coffee for all demonstrators, and the community set porta-potties along the route and offered hot chocolate. A local radio station joined the march while playing the Alka-Seltzer theme song ("plop-plop-fizz-fizz, oh, what a relief it is").

In the run-up to the demonstration I traveled to Germany to meet with Bayer union workers, who held public hearings to publicize our situation and my visit. I was hosted by a group of progressive rank and filers, a caucus within the union, who had been active in TIE (see "International Labor Organizations," above). They pulled together workers from Bayer plants in Germany and organized community meetings to discuss how our struggles were connected. They also passed out flyers at their plant gates, covering over 20,000 workers. Groups from Germany sent letters of solidarity and support to Local 12273, which were read at our January demonstration.

Before I left I had contacted the Washington office of the international trade secretariat for chemical workers, the International Federation of Chemical, Energy, and Mine Workers Unions (ICEM). They gave me the name of an ICEM official in Hanover, Germany. We met, she felt me out on my goals, and then set up a meeting with one of the union officials.

Although it was a pleasant meeting, we ultimately disagreed on strategy: he suggested that I stop writing for *Bayer Danger,* and he did not approve of the caucus's leafleting. Both would only enrage Bayer, he said. This official did, however, volunteer to speak with Bayer about giving us an early retirement package. The caucus's fighting approach was more in sync with what our committee thought had to be done.

Despite our efforts, the plant closed on Bayer's schedule, but members of Local 12273 left with their heads held high. We were able to negotiate language allowing workers close to retirement to fill the gap until they could collect their pensions, as well as other benefits such as money for college and health care for all members. We could not have achieved these results without the community support and the international pressure from our links to the German Bayer workers.

Ongoing International Network

My participation in the networking continues even though the plant has closed, and it has made a difference. At the 2001 Labor Notes Conference in Detroit, several U.S. locals, the German union, and a Canadian local all exchanged contracts. This has been invaluable, since Bayer routinely lies about its contracts.

Our international networking also led to stronger ties among unions in the U.S. For example, the Bayer plant in Berkeley, California, represented by the ILWU, was told that no Bayer plant had a cost-of-living benefit. Through this contract exchange, the California local was able to expose Bayer's lie.

In another case, Bayer tried to implement a "behavior-based" safety program (see Chapter 7), designed to pit worker against worker on the plant floor. Through the sharing of information and contract language among plants we were able to stop the worst aspects of this program.

In 2001, right after the anthrax-in-the-mail scares, Bayer announced that employees would be getting their paychecks in the mail. The union plants in the U.S. collectively filed grievances with the National Labor Relations Board. Paychecks were once again given out on plant floors.

The networking continues, and our Bayer group is now part of the larger European Pharmaceutical and Chemical Network that involves workers from seven other companies. Just as Labor Notes connected Bayer workers in this hemisphere and Germany, TIE helped start the European Network. This network meets annually and includes workers from Switzerland, Germany, Belgium, Turkey, India, France, and the U.S. These conferences deal with the problems we all have in common—threats of plant closings, downsizing, and outsourcing, as well as creative contract interpretations by the companies.

In 2003 Bayer decided to sell off part of a division, affecting plants in the U.S., Germany, and Belgium. In the U.S. they told the union that the workers in Germany had taken a wage cut. Through the network, which met at a TIE conference, the truth came out, and the plants in Belgium and the United States entered into an exchange of information during the negotiations over the results of the sale.

★ ★ ★

A campaign to support workers abroad can also be useful for workers here at home. Here is an example of a North American solidarity organization that supported Mexican workers while also teaching U.S. workers about the value of solidarity.

A Corporate Campaign To Support Mexican Workers

by Judy Ancel

WHEN I WAS ELECTED TO THE BOARD of the Coalition for Justice in the Maquiladoras in 2000, I had no idea that within a few months I'd be strategizing on a major corporate campaign and agonizing over the firing of hundreds of workers.

CJM is a coalition of organizations in the U.S., Canada, and Mexico. Our members include orders of nuns, unions from all three countries, and organizations of current and fired maquiladora workers in Mexican border towns. I was representing our local Kansas City group, the Cross Border Network, which was formed in 1997 by labor, human rights, and religious activists.

At CJM's annual meeting in Tijuana in May 2000, Eliud Almaquer and Silvia Martinez came to ask us for help. They had worked at the U.S.-owned Duro Bag Company in Rio Bravo, Tamaulipas, 15 miles south of the border at McAllen, Texas. Duro made gift bags and its primary customer was Hallmark.

Eliud and Silvia told us that Duro had fired an elected workers committee for attempting to have a voice in contract negotiations between the company and their corrupt union, an affiliate of the Confederation of Mexican Workers (CTM). The workers, they said, had many grievances, ranging from bug-infested food and filthy bathrooms to sexual harassment and abusive bosses. Workers had lost fingers, they said, when their machines had no safety guards.

Firing the committee touched off a walkout by hundreds of Duro's 700 workers, who demonstrated around Rio Bravo. They went back after the company agreed to reinstate the fired committee, but Duro was dragging its feet.

In a struggle like this, CJM's advantage is a diverse membership, positioned to build solidarity in a variety of ways. This is essential, since the companies have a truckload of tools of repression and are often aided by police and the government. Our corporate campaign strategy had to bring pressure on different targets simultaneously.

Building a Web of Solidarity

CJM set up a coordinating committee of its members to support the Duro workers. This included the Authentic Workers Front, or FAT (Frente Auténtico de Trabajo), an independent Mexican union; several other workers' rights organizations from Mexico City; maquiladora worker organizations from nearby Rio Bravo; the AFL-CIO; and several activist groups from the U.S. and Canada. We later recruited the Paper, Allied-Industrial, Chemical and Energy Workers International Union (PACE), which represented Duro workers in the U.S. We agreed to do some research and get back together in a teleconference to develop the plan.

Within a month, however, about 300 second-shift Duro workers walked out and set up strike banners. The company accused them of conducting an illegal strike and imprisoning management in the plant (a false charge), and the police broke up the picket line, beat workers, and arrested seven people. One was an American, a member of the Cross Border Network who was there in solidarity. Meanwhile, over a hundred workers were fired, and the first shift, intimidated by the repression, failed to walk out.

We immediately publicized this repression internationally, using CJM's email alert list and contacting our member organizations to send out alerts to their mem-

Glossary

Maquiladoras: Low-wage factories in Mexico or Central America that import raw materials or parts, assemble them, and export the assembled products, usually to the U.S. The plants are usually owned by foreign companies, most often American.

North American Free Trade Agreement (NAFTA): On January 1, 1994, NAFTA turned Canada, Mexico, and the U.S. into one free trade area, lessening restrictions on the trade in goods and services among the three nations. Though side agreements on labor and the environment were incorporated into NAFTA, these have had little to no effect. The U.S. has lost over half a million manufacturing jobs since its passage, and results have been equally disastrous in Mexico, where, for example, the availability of cheap U.S. corn has devastated farmers. NAFTA allows corporations to sue governments for policies that interfere with *expected* profits.

Free Trade Area of the Americas (FTAA): The FTAA is currently being negotiated among all of the countries of the Western Hemisphere (except Cuba). It is essentially an expansion of NAFTA.

World Trade Organization (WTO): Established in 1995 and based in Geneva, the WTO specifies and enforces rules for international trade. It is specifically dedicated to free trade. Its rules cover not just goods and services but intellectual property (ideas, patents, inventions).

Under the WTO, member countries can sue other countries for passing laws or regulations that "restrict" trade by, for example, imposing environmental or labor standards. The WTO's workings are largely secret, and the public has no say in electing its officials or in its policies. Historically, the WTO has been anti-worker and anti-environment. For example, it has disallowed laws that would have banned products made with child labor.

Sources: United for a Fair Economy; www.ftaareferendum.org/nyc/Glossary/Glossary.html.

bers. We issued press releases that began to generate media interest. We helped arrange for lawyers to file charges at Mexico's labor board for reinstatement, and we raised bail. Dozens of workers moved to what would become a ten-month tent city (*planton*) in Rio Bravo's main plaza.

With legal support from the FAT, the Duro workers filed papers to found their own independent union. With support from maquila worker organizations in Nuevo Laredo and Valle Hermoso, the workers campaigned tirelessly to pressure Tamaulipas Governor Tomás Yarrington to grant the registration (*registro*) for the independent union. The workers literally followed Yarrington from one appearance to the next with banners and chants. In Mexico a union must be registered with the government in order to file for a recognition election. Thus gaining union representation often requires workers to fight both the government and their employer.

Outreach to U.S. Unions

At the same time the workers were struggling for their *registro*, we were extending the web of solidarity to U.S. unions. The AFL-CIO put us in touch with PACE, who put us in touch with the local at Duro's headquarters plant in Ludlow, Kentucky. PACE officials also offered to help by raising the firings with Duro management.

When we called President Dave Klontz of PACE Local 5-0832 in Kentucky, we didn't know what kind of reception we'd get. After hearing what Duro had done in Rio Bravo, Klontz said, "Oh, I believe you, that's how they treat us here. How can we help?"

Over the next eight months the local and the International helped the Rio Bravo workers in a variety of ways, including inviting Duro workers to PACE regional meetings, where they could build solidarity and raise funds.

CJM sent out many email alerts, asking its supporters to send money to the workers and letters to Duro management and high-ranking Mexican elected officials, demanding reinstatement of the fired workers and recognition of the new union. We generated so many letters that Conciliation and Arbitration Board officials begged the workers' lawyer to call off the letter-writing.

A highlight of the campaign was a forum held by an independent labor federation, the UNT, or National Workers Union (Unión Nacional de Trabajadores). It met in Reynosa, just northwest of Rio Bravo, and heard testimonies about the violations of labor rights at Duro. Hundreds attended. They included members of the telephone workers union, social security workers, Duro workers, and two PACE local officers from the U.S.

Finally, Governor Yarrington agreed to grant the Duro workers their *registro*, which would allow them to file for a *recuento*—a vote for the right to negotiate a collective bargaining agreement. It was the first *registro* for an independent union issued in that state in 70 years.

Hallmark: Care Enough To Do the Very Worst

The CJM coordinating committee knew from the start that we would have to target Duro's customers—and especially Hallmark, the Rio Bravo plant's largest purchaser. We thought that publicizing the contrast between Hallmark's cuddly image and the cockroaches in the cafeteria might force Hallmark to pressure Duro to respect the workers' demands.

We started by obtaining a copy of Hallmark's Supplier Code of Conduct. At first their spokespeople denied they had a code; then they said we couldn't have a copy. So we decided that the best way to talk to Hallmark was to go public with our accusations, in talks we gave around town. Sure enough, we got a call from Hallmark's purchasing department, saying they'd give us the code and talk with us.

We promptly translated the code for the Duro workers. It called for respect for the workers' right to organize, decent health and safety conditions, and other provisions Duro had routinely broken. In a meeting with management we explained the problem and were told they would perform an "audit."

Predictably, Hallmark's audit was a sham. They said they'd found only a few bad chairs and some sanitary problems they had forced Duro to rectify. Everything else was fine. One worker told us that the auditors never asked about labor rights, and that management knew just whom Hallmark was interviewing, since the interviews were done at the plant.

We turned up the heat. We demanded that Hallmark tell Duro to shape up, but Hallmark said they would not interfere in another company's business. Just before Christmas 2000, the Cross Border Network held a couple of demonstrations in front of Hallmark's classy department store in the Plaza district of Kansas City. We held up pictures of the shanties that Mexican workers live in and called it the "Hallmark Hall of Shame."

By February 2001, we were organized enough to take the campaign international, with the help of the Campaign for Labor Rights' email alerts (see the box on page 340). We planned Valentines Day demonstrations against the "corporation with no heart." The alerts helped us recruit students, kids (who sneaked around stores stuffing our flyers in every card and bag on the racks), nuns, skateboarders (who blocked access to a store for hours), and many others. Twenty-six demonstrations were held at Hallmark stores from Monterrey, Mexico, to Vancouver, British Columbia. We got media coverage in all three countries. But Hallmark didn't budge. In the end, they quietly cancelled their contract with Duro, as the CTM union had threatened.

Through CJM members in Washington, D.C., we got a letter from 43 congressmen to Mexican President Vicente Fox, urging him to schedule a "free and fair election" and stop the intimidation.

The constant pressure of the workers themselves, a large demonstration organized by CJM and allied unions in Mexico City at the federal labor board, the letters, and the corporate campaign finally forced the Mexican government to announce in mid-February that the *recuento* would take place in two weeks, on March 2, 2001.

At the end of February, the PACE local in Ludlow invited two Duro workers to company headquarters and hosted a press conference demanding a fair election. They got great media attention, but Duro tried to fire Dave Klontz and intimidated the local into not sending observers to the *recuento*.

Recuento

Earlier, in 2000, a number of U.S. and Canadian unions had pursued a case under NAFTA's labor "side accords," seeking fair elections in Mexican unions. The Mexican government promised to promote the use of secret ballots in *recuentos*. Despite this, the labor board announced that at Duro the vote between the two unions would not be by secret ballot.

Members of the Duro workers independent union demonstrate outside the plant in March 2002 as their fellow workers inside are put through a fraudulent union representation election.

By this time the discredited CTM union had found a substitute: the CROC, a notoriously corrupt union known for its intimidation tactics. CROC thugs flooded Rio Bravo, following workers around, tearing up their signs, threatening and harassing them.

Meanwhile, CJM assembled about 25 election observers from Mexico, the U.S., and Canada, including a representative of the Canadian paper workers union, CEP. These observers, however, were kept out of the plant by management and the Conciliation and Arbitration Board. The only observers allowed in were five fired Duro workers, representing the independent union, and their lawyers; they felt so intimidated that they wondered if they'd survive the day.

The observers estimated that CROC had about 75 thugs in the plant. The second shift was held captive overnight in the plant without sleep. In the morning, each worker was individually escorted to vote by CROC thugs, running a gauntlet of more thugs and then having to declare their preference out loud, in front of management. Not surprisingly, only four voted for the independent union. All four were fired the next week.

Going after the Gap

But the Duro workers refused to settle or drop their cases at the labor board. A lawyer from another CJM member organization took over the cases. The workers kept meeting and started organizing others. By then, virtually all the workers had been replaced by illegal temps, who knew nothing of the original organizing campaign.

Then, in the fall of 2002, as the labor board cases approached conclusion, the workers got word that Duro's big new customer was Banana Republic, owned by Gap Inc. Several CJM board members active in the Interfaith Council for Corporate Responsibility had worked with Gap's corporate responsibility people before, and they helped us arrange a meeting.

Meanwhile, we arranged a pre-Christmas tour for Carmen Julia Silva, one of the fired workers, of six cities in the U.S., which rekindled letters to Duro. We also gathered letters and delivered them to the Mexican consulate in every city we visited. We kept the heat on Duro but used the threat of targeting Gap as a way to keep them negotiating.

Gap, it turned out, was a much better target than Hallmark. Unlike Hallmark, Gap was publicly traded (stockholders could thus apply pressure) and it had been hit before with consumer campaigns. Maybe we just got lucky, and Gap decided it was easier to pressure Duro, since the company had other worries at the time. Gap told Duro to do the right thing.

Victory?

Finally, in May 2002, Duro agreed to pay full severance pay as required by law, plus all back wages and raises since spring 2000. It came to $185,000 for about 20 workers. As far as CJM knows, this is the first time a company in Mexico has actually had to pay for its violations. But the workers had also wanted full reinstatement to their jobs, with back pay, so they could keep organizing. Mexican law, however, doesn't require that, even if the workers were fired illegally.

Duro was a difficult target. Most of its facilities in the U.S. were non-union, and the union at the Ludlow headquarters was not strong. The idea of international solidarity was new both to them and to the Duro workers, who took months to okay the demonstrations against Hallmark. The greatest problem, however, was that the resources needed to support and sustain an effort to win an independent union in a maquiladora are huge, and in Mexico these resources are lacking.

Some CJM members could see only defeat in the Duro struggle. The workers got fired. They got blacklisted, and they lost the *recuento*. There will be no new union. But that's not how the workers see it.

The workers' group went on to form an organization called DUROO (Democracy, Unity, Respect for the Organization of Workers) in May 2003, and opened a workers center in Rio Bravo. DUROO is collaborating with other groups along the border and helping other maquila workers get organized.

Sometimes we don't measure these struggles in unions won. We measure them in the transformation of people's lives and consciousness. The Duro struggle activated and educated working people across North America who campaigned and saw broad solidarity emerge in three countries.

Throughout, the women workers drove the struggle

with their persistence and refusal to give up. As they camped out in the tent city, some collected wild herbs to eat. One worker's child died because of delayed medical treatment, and another's house was robbed of documents and burned down by arsonists. Most of the workers were blacklisted and couldn't find work in either Rio Bravo or Reynosa. Still they kept on.

As Carmen Julia Silva said, "I think that if we don't struggle for what we believe, we go through this world without leaving a footprint."

★ ★ ★

One of the tools used during the Duro struggle was bringing workers from Mexico to meet with workers in the U.S. Meetings between workers from different countries show each how much they have in common and how much they have to learn. Our next two stories are about hosting visitors from other countries.

Organizing a Solidarity Tour

by Dan La Botz

SHARON WALLACE ORGANIZED A SOLIDARITY TOUR in 2002 for the Palestine General Federation of Trade Unions. Wallace explains, "The idea was not to have top union leaders come and talk to the top labor leaders here, but for Palestinian labor activists who are out there in the factories and in the streets to come talk to their counterparts here." The Palestinians hoped to educate American unionists about their view of the Middle East situation and to get support for their struggles as unionists in the midst of war.

Wallace sent an email letter to lists of union activists throughout the U.S., asking who would be interested in working on the tour. The response was "unbelievable," Wallace says, and she arranged for visits to 22 cities.

Wallace adopted an approach we could call the "self-organized tour." In each city where there was interest, activists created a local committee to sponsor the tour and chose a point person to be in touch with her. "They organize within their city, plan their event and provide local transportation, lodging, and meals on the ground, and they also help raise funds for the delegation's visit," Wallace explains. "So each city had its own sponsors, and each city selected its point person."

With people in each city taking responsibility locally, Wallace could concentrate on the international arrangements. "That is the nightmare," says Wallace. "How do you get them out of their country and into this one? You're talking work on this 24/7 because of the time differences. We had to negotiate by long distance, in Arabic, in the middle of the night. We had to get them out of Gaza. And getting visas after 9-11 is a nightmare."

Tour coordinators will want to find knowledgeable people with language skills and with experience dealing with the bureaucracies of both the other country and the U.S. State Department. While making arrangements for Palestinian workers is far more complicated than arranging tours for workers from most other parts of the world, you will usually need to have an expert on board.

One City's Experience

In the San Francisco Bay Area, Wallace's contact was Michael Eisenscher, coordinator of the local Labor Committee for Peace and Justice, which formed shortly after 9-11.

To build the local Palestine tour committee, Eisenscher says, "We reached out to organizations in the anti-war movement, in the labor movement, in the Palestinian communities, to other groups doing Middle East solidarity work, to Jewish Voice for Peace, and to the Middle East Children's Alliance. We then formed a committee of representatives of these organizations, and each of the groups planned their own events. But they also did joint publicity and helped to build one another's events."

The committee set up meetings with local labor organizations. "Publicity was done throughout the Bay Area labor movement with email announcements, flyers, phoning, and announcements at meetings," Eisenscher says. "We had one event with the San Francisco Labor Council and one event with SEIU Local 1877, the janitors local—there is a whole group of Yemeni janitors. We also did a forum in Oakland at the headquarters of SEIU Local 250. It was not sponsored by the union, but officers were present to welcome the delegation and present them with union t-shirts and other mementos."

Eisenscher explains how he attempted to interest union activists or officials in sponsoring these talks: "Most people aren't aware that there is a labor movement in Palestine. We talked about the crisis confronting working people in Palestine, the humanitarian crisis, and what the union movement's role is in dealing with that." Eisenscher believes that while many union leaders "may not be prepared to step out publicly on the issue, they do want to open up a conversation about the issues and expose their members to different points of view." You will, of course, have to tailor your "pitch" to the specifics of the countries involved.

At the Event

"We had to use interpreters, and that's where our relationship with the Arab and Palestinian communities came in handy," Eisenscher explains. "A Palestinian trade unionist in the Bay Area acted as an interpreter, and that was helpful because he understood both the language and the union issues." Many solidarity activists have found out the hard way that an interpreter who doesn't know union lingo can add unneeded confusion.

Organizers should try to have literature in both English and the speakers' native language. For example, for a Colombian tour, have literature in English and Spanish.

The impact of your tour is magnified if you can get media coverage. Since most mainstream media are not overly interested in labor issues, Eisenscher suggests seeking out particular sympathetic reporters and offering them an interview. (See Chapter 22.)

Fundraising is crucial. Eisenscher says, "Our fundraising was not only to defray the costs of the event but also to give them money to take back to Palestine. We're talking about a movement that needs very basic things, like computers. We helped them get a video camera and a digital camera." Besides passing the hat during the event, you can solicit donations from executive boards. Having the visitors stay with local union people saves money and builds bonds between the visiting activists and their hosts.

One additional function that tours serve is to build a foundation for future work. Out of that Palestinian workers' tour in 2002 the Palestine Labor Support Committee-USA-Canada was established, to maintain solidarity in the future.

Long-Term Visit Builds Sister Union Relationship

by Steve Early

IN JUNE 2002, CWA national convention delegates adopted a resolution condemning "Plan Colombia." This $2 billion U.S. military aid program has strengthened the political and military forces that are murdering unionists in war-torn Colombia. CWA urged the AFL-CIO to "offer relief and sanctuary in this country to Colombian trade unionists under imminent threat by paramilitary death squads."

Hector Giraldo

The AFL-CIO Solidarity Center's 2002-2003 sanctuary program enabled 20 Colombian unionists to spend a year in the U.S. They first studied English at the AFL-CIO's George Meany Center near Washington and then lived and worked elsewhere in the country under the sponsorship of local unions and central labor councils.

In fall 2002, CWA District 1, Massachusetts Jobs with Justice, and SEIU Local 615 took advantage of the AFL-CIO program to sponsor one of those Colombians in Boston. During his stay, Hector Giraldo, a municipal union organizer from the city of Medellín, educated hundreds of union members and others about a sister union far away and created bonds of solidarity that carry on.

During the first part of Giraldo's stay, he helped organize Spanish-speaking members of Local 615 for a month-long, city-wide "Justice for Janitors" strike. SEIU provided financial support, and the rest of his funding came from CWA's "Union to Union" International Solidarity Fund. Every year, District 1 locals in New Jersey, New York, and New England are asked to contribute 10 cents per member to this fund.

Throughout Giraldo's visit, he was a highly effective roving ambassador for grassroots labor internationalism. As a result of his meetings and personal contacts with hundreds of CWA members, District 1 locals raised over $32,000 in 2001-2004, almost all of which went to support his union, SINTRAOFAN. As part of this grassroots fundraising effort, CWA members in upstate New York paid $20 for commemorative metal bracelets—made in Colombia and with Giraldo's name on them.

At every stop on his speaking tour, Giraldo's plea to "stop Plan Colombia" was accompanied by a moving personal story that resonated with union members. In his home province of Antioquia, the then-governor (now Colombian president) Álvaro Uribe had led the drive to privatize municipal services. In Colombia, when public sector unionists oppose privatization, they risk being killed: private contractors who hope to replace public workers with their own non-union employees hire paramilitary thugs to do their dirty work.

"Our union is fighting for economic and social rights and against free trade agreements," Giraldo explained. "Because we are fighting, we are the targets of paramilitary violence. My union president was assassinated in front of the workers, with seven bullets. Then they said they were going to kill me, so I had to leave Colombia.

"Your tax money is being used to kill union members. It isn't used to open schools or hospitals—or even stop drugs. It's for helicopters and weapons."

Giraldo took this message to CWA union halls and social events, central labor council meetings, steward training sessions, Jobs with Justice conferences, and state AFL-CIO meetings in Massachusetts, Vermont, Connecticut, Rhode Island, New York, and New Jersey. He met with editorial board members at the *Boston Globe*, did radio and newspaper interviews, spoke to community and student groups—like national and regional meetings of the United Students Against Sweatshops—and appeared at a Labor Notes fundraiser.

On his trip home, Giraldo and his co-workers were accompanied by an American labor delegation that included local officers who had arranged meetings for him. In a report to CWA members distributed in November 2003, Giraldo and SINTRAOFAN's president reported on the progress they had made in rebuilding the union since his return.

District 1 helped sponsor production of a 25-minute video about Giraldo's visit. You can learn more about the situation in Colombia from "Hector Giraldo: Trade Unionist." Email julieerosenberg@comcast.net. $5 for VHS; $10 for DVD; plus $3 shipping.

A Model of International Solidarity: The UE-FAT Strategic Organizing Alliance

by Dan La Botz

THE RELATIONSHIP BETWEEN the United Electrical Workers (UE), a small U.S.-based union, and the Authentic Labor Front (Frente Auténtico de Trabajo—FAT) is a model for building international long-term solidarity. FAT (pronounced "faht") is a Mexican federation of unions, peasant organizations, worker cooperatives, and urban poor people's groups. Since 1992, the UE and the FAT have promoted member-to-member exchanges, supported each other's organizing drives and strikes, and worked together to oppose international trade agreements.

The UE-FAT Strategic Organizing Alliance is a mutual support pact based on these principles:
- The two organizations treat each other as equals.
- The relationship is mutual and reciprocal; that is, each helps the other.
- Each organization takes the lead in its own country.

While these principles might seem obvious, they were a departure from the experience of many Mexican unions in their relations with U.S. unions. Here are some of the projects the UE and FAT have carried out together:

Worker-to-Worker Exchanges

These visits to each other's countries involve education about the economy, labor law, and union organizing. Most important, in the words of General Electric worker Dave Kitchen, "This work has helped our members develop an understanding that it's not workers against workers. They understand that the workers in Mexico are simply being taken advantage of and that the more we can work with them to raise their standard of living, the less of a threat they are as low-wage countries. No one deserves to be treated any less than we are treated here.

"We lost our DC Motors division to Mexico," says Kitchen, who is plant steward at UE Local 506 at GE's Locomotive Works in Erie, Pennsylvania. "We didn't have an alliance with the FAT then, so we didn't hear much about General Electric's operations in Mexico, or for that matter, any place else.

"After the UE established the relationship with the FAT, we have sent at least three delegations to Mexico on investigative trips to see how Mexican workers work and to tell them how we work, to see how they live, and to tell them how we live. We also sponsored some FAT members to visit this local and make a presentation to our members."

One result of developing these relationships was better information about the corporation. "Since then," says Kitchen, "we know pretty much when General Electric opens a plant, closes a location, how many employees they have, what they do, the status of that plant, whether they are doing well or not so well, whether they are union or non-union, and that's a result of our international work. It's that simple."

FAT Helps UE Organizing Drive

During the early 1990s the UE won two organizing drives at industrial plants in Milwaukee. Word of those victories spread to workers at the Aluminum Casting & Engineering Company (AceCo) foundry, the largest employer of Mexican Americans in the city. Most AceCo workers were immigrants, many of them recent arrivals. African Americans, whites, Latinos of various nationalities, Hmong, and Laotian workers were employed in the plant. A group of workers became interested in organizing a union—but not one of them was Mexican American.

The UE contacted the FAT, which sent Roberto Valerio to Milwaukee. Working with the UE organizers and Mexican workers from the plant, Valerio leafleted at the plant gate and visited workers in their homes. UE organizer Terry Davis wrote, "Within a few days the effect of the 'Mexican connection' could be felt in the plant. Valerio could explain the differences between a rank-and-file union like UE or FAT and the corrupt government-dominated unions some of the Mexican workers had encountered at home. He could relate to rank-and-file workers and understand their concerns about the INS or strikes. Simply by being there, he embodied the principle of cross-border solidarity."

Valerio handed out a leaflet in Spanish and English with a personal message: "I feel proud to see my countrymen demanding their union rights. And it's moving to see workers of all races and nationalities joining forces. Keep on, brothers and sisters. The way to the future is the union."

Valerio's presence encouraged the Mexican workers. Régulo Ruíz, who worked in the plant, remembers, "I would tell the guys, if he can come all the way from Mexico to help us, you should be able to come to a meeting three blocks from your house." Mexican workers began to put on UE buttons when they went to work.

When the ballots were counted, the UE had won. At the union hall, Mexican, Puerto Rican, African American, and white workers joined in celebrating their victory.[1]

Financial Aid

Some UE locals have implemented voluntary check-off contributions for the FAT. One is Local 896, representing graduate-student employees at the University of Iowa. Labor Solidarity Chairman John McKerley explains, "Members fill out a form asking their employer to make an additional dues deduction, which goes to our national office, which, in turn, sends it on to the FAT."

How does McKerley get his fellow workers to contribute? "I and other UE members from my local have visited Mexico, and we have met with FAT members. I talk about our experiences meeting FAT-affiliated workers who work in the bathrooms in the Mexico City produce market, and how they were working to get respect and fair treatment.

"I explain that the workers we're supporting are some of those who most desperately need the help. The $12 per year that our members give can go a very long way in helping these workers win a modicum of respect and dignity."

UE Local 896 has also attempted to steer some business to FAT-organized shops.

"We've been exploring getting a FAT-affiliated shop to produce some lapel pins for us," McKerley says. "This will be a promotional tool for our union, so people see our union logo, and it's another way to support the FAT."

More International Ties

The UE-FAT relationship has benefited the UE in unexpected ways, notes Robin Alexander, UE's director of international affairs: "We have assisted each other in making connections with other unions. We have introduced the FAT to unions in the U.S. and elsewhere, such as the Zenroren confederation in Japan, and they have done that for us in Mexico and other countries.

"For example, many Canadian and Quebecois unions don't much like U.S. unions, but our relationships with some unions in Canada are far stronger because we got to know them through the FAT. Our alliance with the FAT gave us credibility, and allowed us to develop our own relationships. We now have a close working relationship with CISO, the International Workers Solidarity Center of Quebec, and with some of its member unions."

Lessons from the FAT-UE Experience

The UE is a national union, but many U.S. local unions have established special sister-union relationships with locals abroad, much like sister cities. What can they learn from the FAT-UE experience?

• Solidarity relationships need time and shared experiences to develop. Be patient. Take some time to develop an understanding of each other's histories, values, and objectives.

• Look for opportunities to show solidarity on many levels, from financial support and solidarity statements, to organizing and strike support, to international trade issues.

• Worker-to-worker exchanges, especially involving workers from the same company or sector, promote mutual understanding and aid in developing strategies. Brothers and sisters in other countries can teach us skills we can use here.

• Make a commitment for the long haul. It will bring future benefits that you cannot now imagine.

Organizing with the Global Justice Movement

by Steve Hinds

Many union members were first introduced to the global justice movement when union members, students, and environmentalists hit the streets of Seattle in late 1999. They were protesting the World Trade Organization, a promoter, enforcer, and symbol of corporate-friendly globalization policies. Over and over, the "Teamsters and Turtles" protesters explained that they weren't against trade or exchanges among countries. Rather, they wanted to stop corporations' freedom to invest, pollute, and exploit anywhere they chose, halt the worldwide race to the bottom, and prevent antidemocratic institutions from governing the world economy.

The politics and customs of some of the young global justice protesters were unfamiliar to many union members. Their loosely-structured "affinity groups" looked vastly different from union functioning. But they agreed on a lot, and some unions are continuing to build on such alliances.

We'll tell here how one Seattle local made the Teamsters-Turtles alliance real in the streets, and then how a Massachusetts central labor council has educated members, coalition partners, and the public.

Seattle Teamsters and the WTO

Bob Hasegawa, who was then president of Teamsters Local 174 in Seattle, says, "Our shining star was what we did around the WTO meetings. We were at every worksite telling our members what globalization and WTO were all about.

"Our message was different from what the Teamsters International was trying to sell, though. They were talking about globalization very narrowly as a threat to American interests—a very nationalistic approach. We saw globalization instead as a threat to democracy—not just here, but all over the world. People were at risk of losing the democratic processes they use to make decisions for themselves.

"We were talking to our members about how the WTO can be used to overturn environmental laws, how there's no transparency in the process, and how decisions are being made by corporate appointees instead of by democratic bodies around the world. The trend and future threat was that power would continue to be consolidated away from the people and toward corporate interests.

"It can be tough to get members involved, regardless of the struggle. Multiply that with getting them involved in struggles outside their immediate self-interest and it's really difficult. It was our consistent educational work that seemed to pay off. The members responded to the message.

"Our local was one of the first to join a community coalition that met regularly to do bottom-up organizing for the protests. It included environmental, Ruckus Society, and student activists. I had imagined that today's young people did not have a strong interest in political action, but I felt better about the future after seeing that work.

"The big labor rally during the WTO protests was during the day on a Tuesday—tough timing for many of our members. We brought 400 picket signs, and we ran out right away. We estimated some 600 members were there."

The local used a very visible symbol of the union presence. "To help make the community aware of Teamsters' support," says Hasegawa, "we brought out our big gun—the huge 174 truck with our local number on the side. During strikes it had been our mobile strike headquarters. It was a meeting space, a base of operations, and we loaded it with sound equipment. We'd park the truck and everyone would know it was a central rally spot. We even managed to park it directly across from the hotel where the WTO meetings were taking place—right in the thick of the battle."

Local 174 leaders were able to give leadership to inexperienced demonstrators. One night when police

The North Shore Labor Council, which represents workers north and west of Boston, and New England Jobs with Justice sent a diverse delegation to the 2001 protests against the proposed Free Trade Area of the Americas in Quebec City. They were joined by tens of thousands of young global justice activists and Canadian unionists from the public and private sectors.

tear-gassed and pepper-sprayed innocent bystanders, local residents were enraged and took to the streets by the hundreds. Local 174 Staff Director Steve Williamson, wearing Teamster colors, called a street meeting and discussed with the people what was going on and how they should respond nonviolently. Staffer Mike Brannan grabbed a bullhorn and led the neighborhood in chants.

Brannan says, "Teamster co-workers and I took food and coffee to the vigil/protest at the King County jail. There had been over 600 arrests during the demonstrations. We set up a table and had it stocked with food for over four hours. The people were grateful to the Teamsters, and thanked us repeatedly. It was a small but great moment, like so many during the week where solidarity ruled and I was so proud to be in the labor movement."

The local had also planned to turn its union hall into a hostel for activists who needed a place to stay during the WTO events, and to hold evening activities for debriefing and socializing. That plan was unfortunately nixed by the International.

Globalization Education

The North Shore Labor Council, which represents 18,000 workers north and west of Boston, for years has educated both members and the community about globalization and free trade. Council President Jeff Crosby, who is also president of a big IUE-CWA local at General Electric in the area, says, "In 1993, we had the campaign against NAFTA. In 1999, we sent 12 people to Seattle, which was widely reported locally. In 2000, we had a community hearing about the increased outsourcing to many countries from our area, including GE's defense work.

"We had elected officials at the hearing and our congressman spoke to us by phone from Washington. We had personal testimony from GE workers and other workers whose work had gone to Mexico. The unions had made it a major issue in the congressional election in 1996 and we dumped a pro-NAFTA Republican and brought in an anti-free trade Democrat.

"This was all part of a consistent campaign, repeated over years, to win community support for GE workers, who a lot of people had seen as somewhat spoiled."

When unionists and global justice activists planned a big mobilization against the Free Trade Area of the Americas negotiations in Quebec in 2001, the labor council prepared another series of educational events. In a two-part training for union members, city councilors, students, and other community leaders, workers testified about how their industries had been affected by globalization. The training was co-led by a labor educator from the University of Massachusetts.

"We used creative ways to make our points," says Crosby, "including a role-play where people had to portray workers, city councilors, and lawyers in three cities. They were all trying to convince a multinational to invest in their town—one in Lynn, Massachusetts, one in the southern U.S., and one in Mexico.

"The training got people to see that free trade is not just about 'my job going to Mexico,' but globalization is the context for all our jobs. So letter carriers talked about the attempt by UPS to sue the Canadian postal service because their 'monopoly' was a constraint on free trade. The carpenters talked about poor immigrants being forced across borders and undercutting their standards. Bringing the public sector and building trades into the anti-globalization fight was something new."

After several months of that kind of education, the labor council built a delegation of 35 people that traveled to Quebec City for the protests. This diverse group included a city councilor who was also an IBEW member, letter carriers, manufacturing workers, and community and health care activists. All of them took vacation time and paid for themselves, although CWA paid for the buses.

"It was a terrific mobilization," says Crosby. "As we saw in Quebec, this is a movement that has room for everybody. And when our plant was threatened again with layoffs, because of GE's outsourcing, we had a ready ear in the community, because we had already been working with them for ten years."

Action Questions

Basic facts about the employer:
1. Do you work for a multinational company?
2. Where is it headquartered?
3. Where else, both in your home country and abroad, does your company employ workers?
4. How is your workplace affected by corporate globalization? Outsourcing, trade policies, immigration to the U.S.?
5. Map the chains of production of the good or service you produce. What subcontractors provide the inputs for your work? Where are they located, and who owns them?
6. What do you know about the wages, hours, and working conditions of the workers who come before you on the production chain?
7. Does your company have a corporate code of conduct for outsourcing?
8. Where does the good or service you produce go next? Ask the same questions about the workers there.

Strategic questions:
9. How dependent is your employer on particular suppliers or customers? Do you see any ways that this could give you leverage against your employer?
10. What changes would need to be made (even if these seem hard to imagine right now) to make globalization more beneficial or less harmful to your members?

Information you'll need to develop a campaign:
11. What languages are spoken by the workers you need to ally with? Does anyone in your workplace speak this language? Can you find interested contacts in your community who speak the language?
12. Are any of your co-workers from the country you're working with? Does your union have formal or informal relations with a union in this country?
13. What do you know about unions in the country you're working with? Have they historically been tied to the government?
14. Is there an existing organization that does international solidarity work with this country (such as TIE or CJM)?
15. Are there any groups in your area that do international solidarity or global justice work, say at universities or in religious organizations? Do their current interests overlap with yours? If not, can you see a way to make a connection?

Authors

JUDY ANCEL helped found the Cross Border Network for Justice and Solidarity. She is a board member of the Coalition for Justice in the Maquiladoras and director of The Institute for Labor Studies, a joint program of the University of Missouri-Kansas City and Longview Community college.

STEVE EARLY is an international representative in CWA District 1.

STEVE HINDS teaches math in the City University of New York's adult literacy program. Previously, he was an activist in the New Haven Federation of Teachers (AFT Local 933), and before that an organizer with the United Electrical Workers (UE).

WILLIAM JOHNSON joined the Labor Notes staff in 2003 and covers SEIU, teachers, and the public sector. His writing has appeared in *Z*, *The Nation*, and *Counterpunch*.

DAN LA BOTZ wrote the first edition of *A Troublemaker's Handbook*. He is an activist, teacher, and labor historian based in Cincinnati, where he writes frequently for *Labor Notes*. He was a founding member of Teamsters for a Democratic Union in the 1970s and wrote a book about that movement, as well as books on unions in Mexico and Indonesia. He is editor of the monthly web publication *Mexican Labor News and Analysis*.

TRUDY MANDERFELD retired as president of USWA Local 12273 and as a Bayer worker. She now concentrates on building the Bayer international network and on getting the college degree she has always longed for. In 2001 she received a Labor Notes' Troublemaker Award.

Thanks to MARSHA NIEMEIJER for conducting interviews with Jeff Crosby and Bob Hasegawa.

Note

1. This account is adapted from Terry Davis, "Cross-Border Organizing Comes Home: UE and FAT in Mexico and Milwaukee," *Labor Research Review* #23, pp. 23-29.

24. Troublemaking for the Long Haul

by Jane Slaughter and Dan La Botz

IN THIS BOOK YOU'VE READ about scores of people who are organizing with their co-workers, against tremendous odds, to take control of their work lives. It's not easy. The employers and the government have been bearing down on us, and it takes all we can do to hold our ground. But some, as you have read, have even been able to push back.

We can learn from these troublemakers. What we can learn most of all is that when ordinary workers act together, they have the power to turn the tables, organize by the hundreds of thousands, and beat corporations at their own game.

When you're doing your day-to-day work—handing out a leaflet, talking to your co-worker, going to the union meeting, signing the petition—you can't really see how you fit into the big picture. You're too close. To learn from this book, and from our own work, we need to step back and get some perspective, to look at what's happened in the past and what's happening in other workplaces. Think of the kind of painting that's made up of many tiny dots. When you're up close, those dots hardly look like anything at all. But when you back away, you find that together they create an impressive picture.

A workers' movement is like that painting. It is made up of millions of little actions that, added together, create a bigger whole. The leaflet you help to write, the group grievance you circulate—they are part of that process of shifting the balance of power, of making history.

In Mexico there is a saying, "Traigo mi granito de arena," that is, "I bring my little grain of sand." Each of us is bringing our little grain of sand to the anthill—or better, to the construction of a great pyramid, to our project of making a better world. What you are doing every day as you start that conversation at work, or show a new worker how to tell the boss to get lost, is bringing your little grain of sand. Sometimes it feels like you are banging your head against a wall—but you shouldn't lose sight of the great project you are engaged in.

When movements

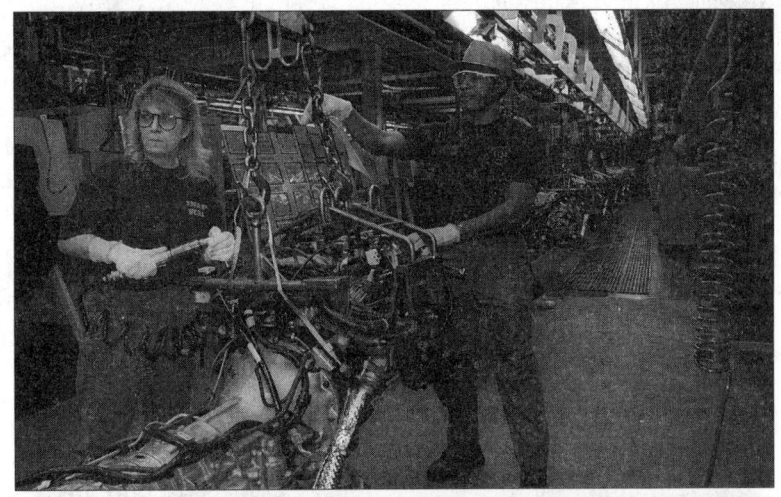

From top: workers at DaimlerChrysler's Jefferson North Assembly Plant; a class on making flyers and newsletters at Labor Notes' conference on "Troublemaking in Troubled Times"; the Immigrant Workers Freedom Ride at a rally in Detroit.

prevail, when they make changes that matter in a nation's economic structures, in its political system, in its culture, they succeed because of the small changes that grow from the bottom up. When we think of the great labor movement victories of the 1930s, we think of John L. Lewis, head of the CIO. But Lewis was pushed forward and pushed up by the thousands of workers involved in the sit-down strikes and the mass picket lines at the auto plants and the steel mills and the Woolworths, each bringing their own grain of sand.

When we think of the civil rights movement in the 1950s and 1960s, we think of Martin Luther King, Jr., but he was pushed forward and pushed up by ordinary African American maids and field hands and factory workers, and by black teenagers who stood up to police beatings, police dogs, and fire hoses.

When we think of the United Farm Workers winning contracts for farm workers in the 1970s, we think of their leader, Cesar Chavez. But Chavez was pushed forward and pushed up by Mexican American field hands who laid down their hoes and struck and picketed and boycotted.

Every one of those movements was created by all the someones who went up to another worker and said, "Would you like to know for yourself?" "Would you like to *do something*?"

No Rose-Colored Glasses

It's hard to be optimistic right now. Employers are determined not to let unions in, and to sap them where they are in, and they have almost every politician in the country on their side. Management uses the threat and reality of outsourcing to make workers afraid to fight. And instead of creating a unified strategy for organizing the 87 percent of the workforce that's not in unions, unions compete with each other and fail to galvanize their own members to recruit.

Employers are demanding—and usually winning—concessions on a scale not seen since the 1980s. Two-tier wage scales and health care cuts are chief among them. The difference this time, from the last big era of concessions? Far less fightback against the givebacks. We see lots of contract rejections by the rank and file, who are sometimes asked to re-vote until they give in, but there are fewer strikes, more resigned acceptance. And some union leaders seem to believe that the next concession they make will somehow be the last, that the bosses will be satisfied.

If You Think This Is Bad

It's grim. But think about the last great period of labor upheaval, in the 1930s, and how bleak workers' prospects seemed then. Workers were laid off by the millions and unemployment reached 25 percent. The companies ran the factories with an iron hand; foremen demanded kickbacks for jobs. Every worker knew that outside the plant, hundreds of men and women were lined up, waiting for his job. When workers protested, police on horseback beat them back with clubs. There was no Internet to spread the grassroots word; most workers didn't even have telephones. There was no guaranteed right to organize until 1935.

Yet in 1934 workers began to organize combative strikes that would bring millions of workers into unions. The Big Three auto makers were the Wal-Mart of their day. The Ford Motor Co., in particular, maintained a network of workplace spies and beat up on organizers. Ford looked as invincible as Wal-Mart does today. But starting with clandestine one-on-one meetings and escalating, over years, to an enormous walkout, workers forced Ford to recognize their union.

How Movements Are Built

WHEN A GREAT TURN-AROUND TAKES PLACE, it often comes with surprising suddenness and swiftness. The 1930s strike wave seemed to begin overnight. The civil rights movement of the 1950s and the 1999 demonstrations in Seattle against the World Trade Organization caught most observers by surprise. But movements do not appear spontaneously, out of nothing. The ground has been prepared by years of spadework, by person after

Where Should We Be Organizing?

Instead of the scattershot, each-union-for-itself approach that prevails today, unions should be coordinating and setting priorities. We should be undertaking massive campaigns in sectors of the economy where workers are potentially the most powerful. Some examples are:
- the choke points of distribution (dock workers, truck drivers, railroad workers)
- the choke points of the information infrastructure, such as computer repair workers
- vital services (sanitation, transit, health care)
- manufacturing. Workers here are linked to each other and to workers abroad through production chains.

Management's insistence on "just-in-time" production means that what happens at one workplace is quickly felt elsewhere, and workers' power is magnified.

Just as important, we need to build on the successes of workers who've already shown a willingness to fight, and organize there as well. When they go into action, these workers help to create the sense of a working class movement in society and can help show the way to others who may be more fearful. Recent examples are nurses, who've struck against forced overtime and for safe staffing, and immigrant hotel workers, janitors, and asbestos workers (see Chapters 15 and 16).

person bringing a grain of sand.

The upheaval of the 1930s was prepared by years of different kinds of organizing in the 1920s and early '30s. AFL unionists and Wobblies, immigrants who were skilled machinists, Farmer-Labor Party members, working class socialists and communists on the shop floor, all worked for years in their own ways. They won reputations as trustworthy leaders. Some of them kicked off the strike wave, and others were there to lead it when it spread to their factories.

Likewise, the civil rights movement grew out of long-term work by the NAACP, African American churches and community groups, and Southern radicals and liberals. Rosa Parks was not just a tired woman on a bus; she was part of a group of trained organizers who had made a strategic decision to take on Jim Crow.

And if "Teamsters and Turtles" collaborated in the Battle of Seattle (see Chapter 23), it was because some years before, Teamsters for a Democratic Union members had reformed the Seattle local, and because environmentalists had been standing against the logging companies for decades.

Swift change can also be spurred by a new economic or political context. The Depression drove workers to want unions, for example. The election of Franklin Roosevelt gave them a sense of hope.

At the same time, change must seem both necessary and possible. Desperation is seldom the goad to action, and more seldom the prod to successful action. The first of the great strikes of the 1930s began not at the bottom of the Depression but in 1934, just when the economy seemed to be improving a little. Workers may have felt it necessary to act before, but had not seen a way. In 1934, they struck in Toledo, Minneapolis, and San Francisco.[1] Their victories inspired other workers to believe that they had a chance to win too.

Movements grow fastest when they move from victory to victory. When the bus boycotters in Montgomery won in 1956, the civil rights movement spread like wildfire. When the winds shift, the little movement we lead today can become an important and powerful one tomorrow. Victory turns slow, incremental change into an express train.

Troublemakers Lead

TODAY, once again, working people know that the deck is stacked, but they don't know what to do. Most don't have the experience of being in a big fight with the boss, and they don't know that they can win. This is where troublemakers come in. What troublemakers do best is to lead. They lead day to day, by example, and they try to give their co-workers a glimpse of the bigger picture—what workers and the union movement can do. We hope that you've learned something about that picture—the picture made up of many tiny dots—from reading this book.

Of course, not everyone who should be leading in this way is doing so. Many of our elected leaders are

What Do Troublemakers Need?

It's easy to get discouraged or burnt out when you're taking on the boss. Our movement needs long-distance runners, leaders who can sustain themselves over years. (In Chapter 15, read about an HERE organizing drive/first contract fight that took 13 years.)

If you are a troublemaker, you need:
- A job you can do and live with. Take care of yourself at work. Have a life.
- A long-term view that helps you roll with the punches.
- An overall strategy for your goals that fits well with your day-to-day work.
- To pick your fights. Don't be a lone wolf.
- To treat co-workers with respect. Don't take it out on your allies.
- To recognize that everyone can play a different role. Ask co-workers to make the contribution that's possible for them. Start where people are.
- To respect your opponents within the union. Don't hold grudges. Welcome those who come over to your point of view.
- To spread the burden, take a load off, involve more members, train new leaders, be a mentor.
- To study labor history. This is how you learn that workers have always fought back. People give up because they think their co-workers will never change. But then they do.
- To involve your family in your union work.
- To be part of a network of people who share your outlook. Join Jobs with Justice and the Association for Union Democracy. Read Labor Notes. Call us and ask us for contacts in your union, industry, or community.
- To get your batteries recharged at Labor Notes conferences every other year. After the 2003 conference, Phyllis Walker, president of an AFSCME local in Minneapolis, said, "It's an opportunity to let our members get firsthand experience that this is definitely a movement and that they're part of something much larger."

And Cori Gambini, vice-president of a nurses union in Buffalo, said, "When Labor Notes gets all of us together, everybody gets really motivated—you feel like you can walk out of there and just knock the walls down."

Do's and Don'ts for a Strong Labor Movement

DON'T:	DO:
Accept two-tier wages.	Practice solidarity. An injury to one is an injury to all. Bring younger workers into the movement (they may be voting on your pension).
Shrug off management's outsourcing, lean production, tech changes, or speedup ("You can't stop progress." "Management rights.").	Insist on bargaining over every change that affects workers' conditions. Take collective action on the shop floor. Work safely and carefully; the job you save may be your own.
Think the union lives at the union hall.	Make the union alive in the workplace with member-to-member networks, stewards councils, and actions that everyone can join in.
Make concessions to keep the peace.	Think long-term to how you will fend off concessions. Who do you need to ally with? Who do you need to organize?
Try to salvage only your own health care benefits.	Build a movement for a single-payer national health care plan.
Use a "catch who you can" approach to organizing new members.	Target industries in a coordinated fashion, in a way that builds union density and thus power.
"Organize" by promising the boss you won't make waves.	Get current members involved in organizing. Use the models described in Chapter 15.
Put all your eggs in the political basket. Trust politicians.	Build a movement that's a force to be reckoned with no matter who is in office.
Support right-wing politicians in exchange for short-term gains for your members.	Make political choices that will benefit all workers, union and non-union.
Go it alone.	Make the community's issues your issues.
Go it alone.	Act in solidarity with other workers' struggles. Join the picket lines. And don't be afraid to ask for help.
Go it alone.	Welcome immigrants. They are ambitious, brave, and savvy, or they wouldn't have taken the risk to come here.
Go it alone.	Connect with others in your union who want to make it stronger and more democratic.
Go it alone.	Seek out international solidarity—give it and get it.
Go it alone.	Connect with others who share your vision of the labor movement and of society. Come to Labor Notes and Jobs with Justice conferences.
Run the union like an old boys' club.	Bring in everyone (or kick down the door). Workers who have to fight racism, sexism, homophobia, or anti-immigrant prejudices can make the toughest union activists too.
Do it yourself. Burn out.	Involve new leaders constantly. Pay special attention to younger workers. Tell them what you know. Work yourself out of a job.
Say "we've always done it this way."	Use creative and fun tactics to make more members want to join in.
Get lost in the details.	Make time for coalition work and the big picture. Remember why you got involved in the union.
Spend each day putting out fires.	Make a strategic plan. Lay a foundation for the future.
Think of current members only.	Have a vision for all workers.
Be a fraidy cat.	Take risks, be bold. Think big. Make no small plan.

taking concessions without a fight and giving lip service to organizing. They don't know how to energize their members, and some of them don't want to. These hapless leaders will keep struggling in vain to find an easy formula for success until they start trying to defeat the bosses, instead of cooperating with them.

Other union leaders know the stakes, and some of them are thinking big, with a strategy for organizing and a long-term approach. Where these leaders sometimes fall down is on the question of how to build enough power to carry out their ambitious plans. They want the labor movement to be bigger and more powerful, with higher wages and more union clout in politics. These leaders often seem to forget, though, that worker power is achieved only by exercising that power, not by cutting deals.

Their vision may see the workers as the supporting cast, while the union officials and staffers are the real power players, the stars. This approach makes it harder for them to achieve their bigger numbers. If the union doesn't offer potential recruits an organization that wins good contracts and belongs to members, where's the incentive to join?

What Does the Labor Movement Need?

IN THE CHART ON THE PREVIOUS PAGE, we've offered some ideas for discussion and debate. We think it boils down to a) member ownership vs. a top-down approach and b) acting like a union instead of a junior partner to management.

You read about the reasons for member ownership in Chapter 18: Unions have no power without their members, and democracy—member ownership—is the best way to galvanize members. With more leaders at all levels, member-run unions are more likely to fight intelligently, with more energy, and with deeper commitment than top-down unions. Leaders look over their shoulders, and the rank and file are there. Unions were created in the first place because workers knew their interests were opposed to bosses'. Acting like a union means the hardheaded understanding that it's us against them, and committing to solidarity on our side of the class line. It means seeing every interaction with management as an opportunity to gain power for working people.

Teamsters and Turtles collaborated in Seattle to oppose the World Trade Organization.

Leaders and Rank-and-Filers

The labor movement needs a healthy, respectful, two-way relationship between elected leaders and members. Most union members are not straining at the bit to take on their employers, bursting with great ideas and just held back by shortsighted officials. Sometimes rank and filers get active only *after* a bad contract has been bargained, and then only long enough to come to the ratification meeting and vote it down.

On the contrary, elected leaders who want to confront the boss too often find that it's a struggle to get members involved. One local president, quoted in Chapter 19, said, "I ran with a goal of giving members more of a say and more information. We do put out a lot more of that now, but that doesn't necessarily translate directly into more participation. It's a long process to change an ingrained practice where people don't participate, and don't expect to participate, and don't expect their participation to make a difference, when our employer does everything possible to make that not happen."

Whose responsibility is it to change unions into member-run organizations that take on their employers? It's leaders' responsibility because they have the authority to begin organizing members at work, to show how to pull off on-the-job actions, to open up the union, to build from members' connections in communities. And it's rank and filers' responsibility, where their leaders are not doing this, to start the long, difficult job of approaching their co-workers, taking small steps, and constructing a new kind of union.

How Do We Make Progress?

THIS BOOK INCLUDES SCORES OF TACTICS and dozens of strategies. They're not guaranteed to produce victory. Sometimes the employers are stronger than we are, and they win. Or we win a round, but it's only round one.

Troublemakers have to be in it for the long haul. It took CWA Local 1037, for example, seven years and a huge array of tactics to reverse the privatization of the Department of Motor Vehicles (see Chapter 6). And sometimes, says President Hetty Rosenstein, "even the victories are lopsided." What keeps people going despite the reversals, she says, is the belief that activism works. "You have to have lots of examples of successes, which is why the *Troublemaker's Handbook* is so important."

What the ideas in this book should produce is an organization that's stronger for the next fight. At the end of the day, what we want from each union fight (besides triumph) is:

- *Lessons learned.* We want to be smarter about the way the world works, about the forces we're facing, about what it will take to win. We want tactical learning and big-picture, aha! learning.
- *A stronger organization.* Did we build personal connections of trust? Did we put in place structures and alliances that can be used again? Have more leaders stepped forward? Each fight should build off the last.

Here's an example:

In 1999, members of Teamsters Local 556 in Pasco, Washington, who work for one of the largest food companies in the world, pulled off a wildcat strike after their contract expired. Many of these immigrant meatpackers had joined Teamsters for a Democratic Union (TDU), but they didn't control their local, and in fact their union officials did nothing to help them win.

Still, the rank and filers got the strike made official, marched through town, held Mass on the picket line, demanded a USDA investigation, and received overwhelming community support. In the end, their officials forced a concessionary contract on them.

TDU organizer David Levin, who helped the workers out during the strike, wrote:

> *Workers had lost the strike, but built a union in the process.*
>
> *"We didn't win what we wanted in the strike—in fact, I lost my pension—but I don't regret it,"* said Flaco Pereyra. *"I see it as something beautiful that happened. We sent a message to the company and the union officials that we weren't the same ignorant workers they'd known for years. We weren't going to stay quiet. We were going to fight."*
>
> *When workers returned to the plant, activists organized a march. They parked their cars on the picket line and marched into work together, chanting, "The union is back!" Once inside, they immediately organized a job action. Management had to re-issue new knives and equipment, since workers had left their tools in a heap the day they walked out. Workers concealed and shuffled their reissued equipment, creating chaos and delaying the start of work.*
>
> *"For me the strike wasn't a defeat. It was a step we had to take,"* said Maria Chavez. *"The company needed an example and we gave it to them. The only thing they used to say to us was, 'If you don't like it, there's the door.' But after the strike they saw us differently. This plant of theirs, so powerful, we all saw it could be brought to the floor if we used our power to shut it down. With all their machines and supervisors and money, the company couldn't do the work without us."*
>
> *And Maria Martinez—who later became the local's secretary-treasurer—says, "We knew the way the strike ended wasn't because of us. We were strong enough to carry it on."*

These rank and filers went on to take over their local, build member-to-member networks in the plants, run contract campaigns, ally with the community over food safety, join the Immigrant Workers Freedom Ride, and work for legalization of immigrants. They're still fighting their employers' attempts to bust the local—but they have a lot of ammunition. (See Chapters 3, 8, 16, and 21.)

Think Big

THIS BOOK HAS CONCENTRATED on transforming unions and fighting in the workplace. More is needed if working people are to be a force in our country once again. We need to think of the labor movement not just as union members but as everyone who works or who needs the power of workers on their side.

When workers have power in the workplace and through their unions, we also have the potential to join forces in the community and in society at large. Through coalitions we can win political battles and stop accepting whatever pro-business candidates the Democrats nominate. Ultimately we need to escape the two-party trap and run candidates of our own.

We cannot, however, become such a political power without rebuilding our movement from bottom to top. We begin in the workplace, and through organizing new members, and through workers centers, and through reforming our unions. There is no short-cut.

In the end we will transform our country because, as "Solidarity Forever" tells us, "When the union's inspiration through the workers' blood shall run, there can be no power greater anywhere beneath the sun."

You who are painting your dot in the picture, you who are bringing your grain of sand to the building of a new labor movement, you are the ones who are making the difference. When our country builds a new culture that puts working peoples' needs at the center of our concerns, you will be the ones to do it.

You are part of something bigger than yourself. Be proud to be part of the scrappy side of the labor movement. Be proud to be a troublemaker.

Authors

JANE SLAUGHTER is editor of this book and has worked with Labor Notes since 1979.

DAN LA BOTZ wrote the first edition of *A Troublemaker's Handbook* in 1991. He is editor of the monthly web publication *Mexican Labor News and Analysis*.

Note

1. *Labor's Untold Story,* by Richard Boyer and Herbert Morais. United Electrical Workers, 1955.

25. Resources

by Peter Ian Asen

THE RESOURCES below are ones that are general or cut across several categories. You will find many more resources in the preceding chapters, listed toward the end of each chapter. For example, Chapter 7 includes health and safety resources. To find advice for stewards, see Chapter 3 on Shop Floor Tactics. To find help in enforcing your democratic rights in the union, see Chapter 18. And so on.

We haven't included every possible item. Please send us your favorites for listing in *Labor Notes* magazine's monthly Resources column. Write to labornotes@labornotes.org or call 313-842-6262.

The Troublemaker's page on our website, www.labornotes.org, will be an ongoing source of new information. Please send us ideas for that page too.

Organizations

We have not included local or national unions or workers centers. Locals can be found through directory assistance, the Yellow Pages, or web searches. Every U.S.-based union with a website—national or local—can be found on the Biglabor website at www.biglabor.com/everyunion.html. To locate unions in your area or to connect with locals in your international, go to http://biglabor.com/lorsform.html. The AFL-CIO website has links to most of its member unions and many locals, at www.aflcio.org/aboutunions/unions, or call 202-637-5000. To find workers centers, see the list on our website.

Education

For a list of all the university-based labor education centers in the U.S., with contact information, see http://laborcenter.berkeley.edu/publications/stateoflabor.pdf, starting on page 121.

Center for Popular Economics. Teaches economic literacy to activists involved in social change. Offers individualized economics training sessions to unions and other labor and social justice groups. P.O. Box 785, Amherst, MA 01005. 413-545-0743. www.populareconomics.org. programs@populareconomics.org.

Highlander Research and Education Center. Residential popular education center and research organization that has been bringing together workers and others involved in social justice projects since 1932. 1959 Highlander Way, New Market, TN 37820. 865-933-3443. www.highlandercenter.org. hrec@highlandercenter.org.

Labor Notes/Labor Education and Research Project. Publisher of this book—"putting the movement back in the labor movement" since 1979. Publishes monthly *Labor Notes* magazine, see below. Holds large biannual conference that brings together activists from all unions and several countries, for practical knowledge-sharing and a dose of inspiration. Helps workers in the same union or industry get in touch with each other. Call to find out about upcoming Labor Notes events, including ones in your area. 7435 Michigan Ave., Detroit, MI 48210. 313-842-6262. www.labornotes.org. labornotes@labornotes.org.

Organizing Institute. Run by the AFL-CIO. Teaches organizing techniques through classroom and field training. Three-day trainings are held around the country. Some are specialized for those bilingual in

English and Spanish; African Americans; Asians and Pacific Islanders; LGBT workers; or young workers. www.aflcio.org/aboutunions/oi.

United Association for Labor Education. Organization of labor educators. Runs an annual conference with the AFL-CIO and conducts annual summer schools for union women in four regions of the country. www.uale.org.

United for a Fair Economy. Education programs and other resources for combating deepening inequality. 37 Temple Place, 2nd Floor, Boston, MA 02111. 617-423-2148. info@faireconomy.org. www.faireconomy.org. In Spanish: www.economiajusta.org.

Workplace Fairness. Provides information, education, and assistance to individual workers and their advocates nationwide and promotes public policies that advance employee rights. Affiliated with the National Employment Lawyers Association (see below). 44 Montgomery St., Suite 2080, San Francisco, CA 94104. 415-362-7373. www.workplacefairness.org. info@workplacefairness.org.

The Work Site. Established by the American Labor Education Center. Free training materials and other tools for grassroots activism, plus resources for strategy and campaign analysis. Users can participate in forums on organizing and other topics. www.theworksite.org.

Communication

Canadian Association of Labour Media (CALM). Network of about 500 union publications. Provides members with monthly news and graphics packets, and a quarterly newsletter *(CALMideas)*. Gives workshops and has other resources for union editors. 76 Westmount Ave., Toronto, ON M6H 3K1, Canada. 888-290-2256. www.calm.ca. editor@calm.ca.

International Labor Communications Association. Provides resources, expertise, and networking for union newspaper editors and other communicators. The website carries articles from union newspapers that can be reprinted by anyone. ILCA works to encourage democratic labor media. 815 16th St. NW, Washington, DC 20006. 202-974-8039. www.ilcaonline.org. ilca@aflcio.org.

LaborTech. Annual conference that includes labor video, media, computer, and technology activists from the U.S. and around the world. P.O. Box 425584, San Francisco, CA 94142. 415-282-1908. www.labortech.org. lvpsf@labornet.org.

Progressive Technology Project. Grant program for unions and other social change groups looking to improve their technology capacity. Publishes electronic newsletter and other information on using technology to enhance organizing. 2801 21st Ave. S., #132E, Minneapolis, MN 55407. 866-298-6463 (in Minnesota 612-724-2600). www.progressivetech.org. info@progressivetech.org.

Union Communication Services. Publishes communications and educational tools for local union activists. Monthly news service, 12-15 pages of labor articles, feature stories, columns, and cartoons: $175/year. Monthly graphics packet, 30-40 labor graphics: $222/year. All by mail or web download. A labor book catalog, which includes materials published by UCS itself as well as others, is available in print or on the website. 165 Conduit St., Annapolis, MD 21401. 800-321-2545. www.unionist.com. ucs@unionist.com.

Workers Independent News Service (WINS). Gathers news by and about working people and creates programs and feature stories for commercial, public, community, and college radio stations. Offers training and assistance to unions and community groups in the technical aspects of reporting, radio production, and media relations. Subscriber service ($50/year for individuals; $120/year for unions with fewer than 1,000 members; more for larger unions) provides unlimited web access to WINS' short daily newscasts, as well as longer feature news and newscast scripts. Contact Frank Emspak, WINS, 414 Lowell Hall, 610 Langdon St., Madison, WI 53703. 608-262-0680. www.laborradio.org.

Legal Help

Association for Union Democracy. Helps enforce your legal rights within your union and offers organizing advice for building democracy. Has links to rank-and-file websites in many unions. Monthly email updates. 104 Montgomery St., Brooklyn, NY 11225, 718-564-1114. www.uniondemocracy.org. aud@igc.org.

National Employment Lawyers Association. Organization of employee-side labor lawyers. Website has tool that allows you to find a labor lawyer in your area. 44 Montgomery Street, Suite 2080, San Francisco, CA 94104. 415-296-7629. www.nela.org. nelahq@nelahq.org.

National Labor Relations Board. Access NLRB forms and publications on workplace rights, union elections, unfair labor practices. www.nlrb.gov.

Rights@Work section of the AFL-CIO website describes basic rights for union and non-union workers, such as health and safety rights, the right to overtime pay and family medical leave, and rights against discrimination, in English, Spanish, Chinese, and Vietnamese. www.aflcio.org.

Pressure Groups

American Rights at Work. Lobbying group that advocates for the right to organize a union. 1100 17th St. NW, Suite 950, Washington, DC 20036. 202-822-2127. www.araw.org. info@americanrightsatwork.org.

Labor Party. Political party started in 1996 to address the concerns of working people. Currently does not run candidates, but organizes campaigns around greater access to health care and higher education, and in support of the right to organize and other workers' rights. Publishes bimonthly *Labor Party Press,* free with membership. PO Box 53177, Washington, DC 20009. 202-234-5190. www.thelaborparty.org. lp@thelaborparty.org. *Towards a New Labor Law,* by the Labor Party's Debs-Douglass-Jones Institute, argues that the current body of labor law is wrongly grounded in the commerce clause of the Constitution, and must be fundamentally changed for workers' rights to be upheld. Available at http://campaignforworkerrights.org/paper.html.

National Alliance for Fair Employment. A network of organizations concerned about the growth of part-time jobs, temping, and subcontracting. 33 Harrison Ave., Boston, MA 02111. 617-482-6300. www.fairjobs.org. info@fairjobs.org. The NAFFE membership list at www.fairjobs.org/about/alpha_org.php contains a wide range of organizations working on many job issues, with contact information.

Pension Rights Center. Advocates for pension rights, publishes easy-to-understand explanations of pension laws. 1350 Connecticut Ave. NW, Suite 206, Washington, DC 20036. 202-296-3776. www.pensionrights.org. pensionhelp@pensionrights.org.

U.S. Labor Against the War. A coalition of union members and leaders working to oppose the war in Iraq. The site provides current headlines and information. www.uslaboragainstwar.org.

Regional Organizations

Black Workers for Justice. Supports organizing in the South, including among non-union workers. 216 E. Atlantic Ave., PO Box 1863, Rocky Mount, NC 27801. 919-977-8162.

Project South. Holds two-day trainings called "Building a Movement: A Popular Education Retreat" that strategize about building a movement for social and economic justice. Held in Atlanta and Washington, D.C. every few months, and elsewhere around the country. 9 Gammon Ave., Atlanta, GA 30315. 404-622-0602. www.projectsouth.org. general-info@projectsouth.org.

SouthWest Organizing Project. 211 10th St. SW, Albuquerque, NM 87102. 505-247-8832. www.swop.net. swop@swop.net.

Think Tank

Economic Policy Institute. Pro-labor research group that conducts research on unemployment, job markets, effects of public policy on working people, trade and globalization, living wage and minimum wage, and more. Publishes biennial "State of Working America" report. 1660 L St. NW, Suite 1200, Washington, DC 20036. 202-775-8810. www.epinet.org. epi@epinet.org.

Periodicals

See also Organizations, above, for their publications.

Dollars and Sense. Bimonthly review of economic issues, written in down-to-earth language. Publishes annual issue entirely devoted to labor. 740 Cambridge St., Cambridge, MA 02141. 617-876-2434. www.dollarsandsense.org. dollars@dollarsandsense.org. $27/year.

Labor Notes. Monthly magazine reports news and analysis about the labor movement that you won't find anywhere else: news from the grassroots, honest analysis of labor's shortcomings, debates over direction and strategies, practical advice for officers, stewards, and rank-and-file troublemakers. Selected articles available online. 7435 Michigan Ave, Detroit, MI 48210. 313-842-6262. www.labornotes.org. labornotes@labornotes.org. $24/year. Inexpensive bundles available.

Labor Studies Journal. Quarterly journal that publishes research about work, workers, labor organizations, and labor studies and worker education. P.O. Box 6295, West Virginia University, Morgantown, WV 26506. Published by the United Association for Labor Education (www.uale.org); free with UALE membership. All others, $45/year. Make checks to WVU Press.

Labor: Studies in Working-Class History of the Americas. A quarterly journal about labor history in the U.S., Canada, Latin America, and the Caribbean. Duke University Press, Box 90660, Durham, NC 27708. 888-651-0122. subscriptions@dukeupress.edu. $40/year for individuals.

New Labor Forum. Three-times-a-year journal for the labor movement and its allies to debate and discuss strategies. Website: qcpages.qc.edu/newlaborforum. To subscribe, contact Journals Customer Service, Taylor and Francis, 325 Chestnut St., Suite 800, Philadelphia, PA 19106. 800-354-1420 x216, or customerservice@taylorandfrancis.com. $31/year for individuals.

Our Times. Bimonthly, independent Canadian labor magazine. 15 Gervais Dr., Suite 407, Toronto, Ontario, M3C 1Y8. 800-648-6131. www.ourtimes.ca. office@ourtimes.ca. $25 Cdn /year.

Rethinking Schools. Quarterly journal dedicated to reforming public schools with a vision of equity and social justice. 1001 E. Keefe Ave., Milwaukee, WI 53212. 414-964-9646 or 800-669-4192. www.rethinkingschools.org. rethink@execpc.com. $17.95/year.

WorkingUSA: The Journal of Labor and Society. Quarterly journal discusses issues that relate to working people, union and non-union, employed and unemployed, in the marketplace and at home. Blackwell Publishing. 800-835-6770. www.blackwellpublishing.com. subscrip@bos.blackwellpublishing.com. $42/year for individuals.

Handbooks

Blueprint for Change: A National Assessment of Winning Union Organizing Strategies, by Kate Bronfenbrenner and Robert Hickey. Research shows which strategies are most likely to win union elections. 2003. $10 includes shipping. Order from Labor Notes.

Democracy Is Power: Rebuilding Unions from the Bottom Up, by Mike Parker and Martha Gruelle. What a democratic union looks like. How to achieve it. See more info about this book in Chapters 18 and 19. 1999. 256 pages. $17. Order from Labor Notes.

Education for Changing Unions, by Beverly Burke et al. Activities, ideas, and debate about union education. 2003. $24.95. Order from Between the Lines, 720 Bathurst St., Suite 404, Toronto, ON M5S 2R4, Canada,

800-718-7201. btlbooks@web.ca. www.btlbooks.com.

The FMLA Handbook: A Union Guide to the Family and Medical Leave Act, by Robert M. Schwartz. Second edition, 2001. $12.95. Work Rights Press, P.O. Box 391066, Cambridge, MA 02139. 800-576-4552. workrights@igc.org.

Labor Party's online guide to planning a house party. Created for its Just Health Care campaign, but useful for house parties intended to enhance all sorts of organizing efforts. www.justhealthcare.org/g_house.html.

Popular Education for Movement Building: A Resource Guide. Popular economic and political education for our times; includes workshops on "Welfare and the Global Economy" and "Health Care for All." $25. Available from Project South (see Organizations).

Power on the Job: The Legal Rights of Working People, by Michael Yates. Explained in a real-world context, with particular attention to the rights of women and people of color. South End Press, 289 pages, $26. Order from Labor Notes.

Starting with Women's Lives: Changing Today's Economy, by Suzanne Doerge and Beverly Burke. A facilitator's guide for a visual workshop to use with groups of women union members. $12. Order from Women and Human Rights Dept., Canadian Labour Congress, 2841 Riverside Dr., Ottawa, ON, K1V 8X7. 613-521-3400x202. womensmarch@clc-ctc.ca.

Stopping Sexual Harassment, by Camille Colatosti and Elissa Karg. Organizing and legal approaches. Real-life examples and tips, including getting co-workers on your side and dealing with unsympathetic officials. 115 pages. $9. Order from Labor Notes.

Teaching for Change: Popular Education and the Labor Movement, edited by Linda Delp et al., 2002. Experiences of popular educators in the labor movement. $20, includes shipping. Send checks payable to "UC Regents" to UCLA Labor Center, Box 951478, Los Angeles, CA 90095. 310-794-5982. jamonroe@ucla.edu. www.labor.ucla.edu/publications/index.html#change.

A Troublemaker's Handbook, 1991, by Dan La Botz. The advice in the original 1991 edition is still very much on target (though you won't find any web addresses). Similar in format to the 2005 *Troublemaker's,* with hundreds of winning examples. 262 pages. $17. Order from Labor Notes.

The Union Member's Complete Guide: Everything You Want—and Need—to Know About Working Union, by Michael Mauer. Union Communication Services (see above), 2001. $12.95.

Void Where Prohibited: Rest Breaks and the Right To Urinate on Company Time, by Mark Linder and Ingrid Nygaard, and *Void Where Prohibited Revisited,* by Mark Linder. Details workers' rights under OSHA in this regard. $9 each or $15 for both, from Labor Notes.

Working Smart: A Union Guide to Participation Programs and Reengineering (with *Strategy Guide*), by Mike Parker and Jane Slaughter. Explains lean production, the appeals of "employee involvement," why "quality programs" are really speed-up or job-loss programs. Strategies and contract language. Case studies from a range of workplaces. $15 plus $4 shipping. Order from Labor Notes.

Labor History and Analysis

[The first four books are analyses of strikes/lockouts in the 1980s or 1990s. All have excellent and detailed discussions of the strategies the unions used—and why they did or didn't work.]

The Betrayal of Local 14: Paperworkers, Politics, and Permanent Replacements, by Julius Getman. Chronicles an unsuccessful 1987 strike against International Paper in Jay, Maine, and the local's fight against both IP management and their international union. Cornell University Press, 1999. $18.95 paperback.

Hard-Pressed in the Heartland: The Hormel Strike and the Future of American Labor, by Peter Rachleff. Looks at the 1985-86 strike by UFCW Local P-9 in Austin, Minnesota. South End Press, 1992. $12 paperback.

Ravenswood: The Steelworkers Victory and the Revival of American Labor, by Tom Juravich and Kate Bronfenbrenner. Story of the Steelworkers' successful contract campaign at a West Virginia aluminum plant in the early 1990s. ILR Press, 2000. $17.95 paperback.

The Staley Workers and the Fight for a New American Labor Movement, by Steven Ashby and C.J. Hawking, to be published in 2005 by University of Illinois Press. See Chapters 10 and 11 of *Troublemaker's* for information on the Staley workers.

An Injury to All: The Decline of American Unionism, by Kim Moody. Analysis of U.S. unions from World War II through the 1980s. Verso, 1988. Out of print; check www.amazon.com or www.abebooks.com.

The Canadian Labour Movement: A Short History, by Craig Heron. James Lorimer Press, 1997 (updated edition). $24.95 Canadian.

Great Labor Quotations: Sourcebook and Reader, by Peter Bollen. Red Eye Press, 2000. $19.95.

Labor's Untold Story, by Richard Boyer and Herbert Morais. Classic history of the American labor movement from the 1850s to the 1950s. Published by the United Electrical Workers, 1955. Out of print, but check www.amazon.com or www.abebooks.com.

From the Folks Who Brought You the Weekend: A Short, Illustrated History of Labor in the United States, by Patricia Murolo and A.B. Chitty. New Press, 2001. $17.95 paperback.

The New Rank and File, edited by Staughton and Alice Lynd. Interviews with organizers of the 1970s, 1980s, and 1990s about their experiences. Cornell University Press, 2000. $18.95 paperback.

The Next Upsurge: Labor and the New Social Movements, by Dan Clawson. How unions and community organizations are working together. ILR Press, 2003. $17. Order from Labor Notes.

A People's History of the United States, by Howard Zinn. Perennial, 2001 (revised and updated edition). $18.95 paperback.

The Shadow Welfare State: Labor, Business and

the Politics of Health Care in the U.S., by Marie Gottschalk. Why the labor movement failed to achieve substantial health care reform in the 1990s. ILR Press, 2000. $19.95 paperback.

State of the Union: A Century of American Labor, by Nelson Lichtenstein. Princeton University Press, 2003. $29.95.

Strike! by Jeremy Brecher. A historical look at mass strikes from the late 19th century onward. South End Press, 1997 (revised edition). $22.

Taking Care of Business: Samuel Gompers, George Meaney, Lane Kirkland, and the Tragedy of American Labor, by Paul Buhle. Analysis of AFL-CIO leadership and politics over the last century. Monthly Review Press, 1999. $18.

Three Strikes: Miners, Musicians, Salesgirls and the Fighting Spirit of Labor's Last Century, by Howard Zinn, Dana Frank, and Robin D.G. Kelley. Beacon Press, 2001. $23.

The Transformation of U.S. Unions: Voices, Visions and Strategies from the Grassroots, Ray Tillman and Michael Cummings, eds. Lynne Rienner Publishers, 1999. An anthology of experiences with and arguments for union democracy. $22.50. Order from Labor Notes.

Unfair Advantage: Workers' Freedom of Association in the United States under International Human Rights Standards, by Lance Compa. An account of the violation of workers' rights and human rights in the United States. Human Rights Watch, 2000. www.hrw.org/reports/2000/uslabor.

The Unfinished Struggle, by Steve Babson. A concise history (224 pages) of the U.S. labor movement from the Great Railroad Uprising of 1877 to the 1990s. Rowman and Littlefield, 1999. $27.95.

Women and Unions, edited by Dorothy Sue Cobble. Essays by 40 activists and scholars on the relationship between women workers and organized labor. Cornell University Press, 1993. $21.95 paperback.

Workers in a Lean World, by Kim Moody. In-depth look at labor worldwide. Examines the strategies of multinational companies and the need for international cooperation among unions. Verso, 1997. $20. Order from Labor Notes.

Videos

For more videos, see the index.

Bread and Roses, by Ken Loach. Feature-length fictionalized account of an organizing drive of janitors in Los Angeles, led by undocumented Mexican immigrant workers and a white union organizer. Studio Home Entertainment, 2001. $24.98.

The Take, documentary by Avi Lewis and Naomi Klein. When employers in Argentina abandoned their factories after the economic collapse of 2001, many workers sat in and took control. The story of 30 auto parts workers who wanted to run their plant. See www.thetake.org for ordering info and theater showings.

Trade Secrets: The Hidden Costs of the FTAA, by Jeremy Blasi and Casey Peek, 2002. 16 minutes. $15. Explains concisely the potential impact of the proposed Free Trade Area of the Americas, as well as of NAFTA. Has 32-page discussion guide, $3. Global Exchange Online Store, 110 Capp St., San Francisco, CA 94110. 800-505-4410. store.globalexchange.org. storemaster@globalexchange.org.

Internet

The **Association for Union Democracy** website includes links to many rank-and-file reform groups. www.uniondemocracy.org.

The **Biglabor** website, run by Union Communication Services, offers new information every week: every U.S. union website; a labor song, quote, joke, and cartoon; steward tip and member tip; cool labor site; today in labor history. This site is an easy way to find your union's LM-2 form, which describes the union's expenditures and other basic information (see Chapter 18). The site can also be used to locate other unions in your area or other locals in your international. www.biglabor.com.

LaborNet: Aims to promote online communications for a democratic, independent labor movement. Includes online forums, links to labor news and resources, commentary, events calendar. www.labornet.org.

Labourstart. Labor news service maintained by a global network of volunteers. www.labourstart.org.

Solidarity Info Services. Publishes several electronic news lists for social justice activists. **Solidarity4Ever** covers a wide variety of issues and social movements, with special attention to Iraq, Palestine, and U.S. foreign policy. **LaborLeftNews** focuses on the labor and left movements, politics, economics, and business. **Labor4Justice** is devoted to the labor antiwar movement. Subscriptions are free, but a contribution to sustain the service is requested. Make checks payable to SolidarityInfoServices/OTC, 731 Oakland Ave., #6, Oakland, CA 94611. For more information or to request a subscription, write to sis@igc.org.

Workday Minnesota. Daily electronic labor newsletter and other resources. www.workdayminnesota.org.

XPDNC Labour Directory. World's largest labor link website. Links to other sites that cover everything from organizing drives and legal services to health and safety information and labor history. www.xpdnc.com.

Author

PETER IAN ASEN is a writer and labor activist based in Providence, Rhode Island. He is the former Managing Editor of the *College Hill Independent,* a joint publication of students at Brown University and the Rhode Island School of Design. His writing has appeared in *Labor Notes, The Progressive,* and *Against the Current.* He gathered most of the resources listed in the chapters as well as those here.

Appendix. How To Research Employers

by Stephanie Luce and Tom Juravich

WHETHER YOU ARE TRYING to organize your workplace or fighting demands for concessions, it pays to know your employer. Information is key to exerting pressure on an employer to settle a contract or recognize the union. You can find out, for example:

• How many workers are employed at your site and at subsidiaries and whether employment has been growing or shrinking over time

• What the company's business strategy is

• Whether there have been recent mergers or acquisitions that suggest the company's plans and what the key business relationships are

• Who the key players are both inside and outside the firm and whether the company has applied for tax breaks or permits to start business in another location

• Information to use as leverage on the company or its executives, such as violations of OSHA or environmental laws.

It's All Online

THE INTERNET has made researching your employer much easier. With the increasing resources available on the web, rank-and-file activists can conduct solid basic corporate research. A great place to start is the company website.

Enter the company name in a search engine such as Google (www.google.com). Many company sites contain a great deal of information, including financial statements and annual reports. We found a company site that included email addresses for all the supervisors. Some of these sites include so much material that you may have to spend time searching around. You might start with options such as "about our company" or "information for investors."

Of course, you don't want to rely solely on information provided by the company itself. Your next step is to find public sources that can provide both company and industry detail, such as Yahoo Finance, at finance.yahoo.com, or www.hoovers.com.

Use these to learn what investors have to say about the company, as well as to get detailed information about company executives and important facts such as whether the company is publicly traded on the stock exchange or privately held. Also learn the company's stock ticker code and Standard Industrial Classification code (SIC). These codes can help you learn more about the company and industry.

Although these sites offer some information free, you may have to pay for more details. Before you pay for information, though, use the libraries in your area. Talk to the reference librarian in the government documents and business sections of your public library or at your local university. Valuable databases that would be expensive for individuals might be available free at a public university or a library. These include Dun and Bradstreet's Million Dollar Directory and Lexis-Nexis. The latter allows an extensive search of domestic and international news sources. These database services can really turbo-charge your research.

If the company is publicly held (that is, it sells its stock to the public), then the Securities and Exchange Commission (SEC), a federal government agency, provides a wealth of information. The main document that companies are required to file with the SEC, the 10-K, includes a list of facilities, financial details, and information about management. The 10-K is filed annually, so if you need more recent information, check the 10-Q, which is filed quarterly.

For information on the board of directors, including the directors' compensation, examine the proxy statement. Proxies and 10-Ks are available through www.sec.gov and then "Search for Company Filings," or check www.reportgallery.com. Of course, financial statements can be tricky to read. John A. Tracy's *How to Read a Financial Report* (John Wiley & Sons, 1999, $19.95) will help you through it.

Private (non-traded) and foreign firms do not have to file 10-Ks, so finding information on them will take more work. Dun and Bradstreet reports are a great resource on privately held firms, but they cost real money.

Nonprofit companies must file different paperwork with the government, namely the "990," which is their tax exemption statement. Guidestar, www.guidestar.com, allows you to access 990s and other information on nonprofit employers.

If you request 990s directly, in person or in writing, nonprofits must provide them, as well as their past three years of 990 or 990-EZ records. If you make the request in person, they are legally required to give you the copies that day. If you make the request in writing, they have 30 days to fulfill the request.

Leverage Points

FOR OTHER USEFUL INFORMATION, check regulatory and other government agencies. Visit the Occupational Safety and Health Administration website, www.osha.gov. Search in the Statistics section and under "inspections" to find material on individual employers. (Remember that OSHA inspects only a small fraction of worksites each year, so don't be surprised if you don't find anything.) OSHA conducts planned inspections, as well as follow-ups to complaints. You can track these inspections online, including their outcomes and the penalties, if any.

The Securities and Exchange Commission site has records on fraud and tax compliance, at www.sec.gov/divisions/enforce.shtml (check Enforcement Actions). Environmental Protection Agency records are at www.epa.gov/enviro, although they are not easily searchable. The Environmental Defense Fund keeps a list of major polluters by region, at www.scorecard.org. Check any other regulatory agencies that may apply to your industry.

The Equal Employment Opportunity Commission does not have accessible data on all companies that have had charges filed against them. However, you can find a list of some Americans with Disabilities Act litigation at www.eeoc.gov/litigation (check the Litigation Settlement Monthly Reports). To see if you can find any press releases or other documents about EEOC charges, enter your employer's name in the general search at www.eeoc.gov.

In all cases involving federal or state agencies, you can also submit a Freedom of Information Act request to get more information. Directions on how to do this are usually on the agency's website.

To continue your search for points of leverage, enter the firm name in a search engine such as Google. It is amazing the dirt you can sometimes turn up. Many newspapers now keep their archives available online, so search the hometown paper of each subsidiary as well as headquarters. Other general news sites to check include PR Newswire, Bloomberg News, and *Business Week*.

Tax Breaks

IT MAY BE USEFUL to find out whether your employer receives tax breaks from the city, state, or federal government. Tax breaks or credits may come in a variety of forms, such as through TIFs (tax-incremental financing) or low-interest Industrial Revenue Bonds. Good Jobs First, a nonprofit research organization, helps track examples of corporate subsidies and tax break abuse. For useful reports on corporate welfare in selected cities and states, see www.goodjobsfirst.org.

Good Jobs First also tracks cities and states that are beginning to put tax-related information online. For example, at www.newyorkbiz.com/index.cfm, New York City posts documents related to companies asking for tax breaks, one week before a public hearing about the break. At www.dor.state.nc.us/publications/williamslee.html, North Carolina posts lists of firms receiving tax credits each year. At www.dor.state.nc.us/collect/delinquent.html, North Carolina also publishes a list of evaders of personal income tax as well as corporate and sales taxes. You may find your company or your supervisor on a similar list in your state.

A few states are far ahead of the rest in putting this kind of information on the Internet, but this may change in the next few years, so keep checking your state's Department of Revenue website. If the information is not yet online, you can sometimes get it easily and for free.

For example, the Massachusetts Office of Business Development, the state office that helps businesses locate in the state, provides a list of all companies in the state receiving TIFs and the number of jobs they promised to create in order to get the reduced local and state tax rates.

A number of federal tax credits are available to businesses located in federal "empowerment zones" or other designated economic regions. To find out whether your employer is located in a designated zone, go to hud.esri.com/egis/cpd/rcezec/ezec_open.htm. If you are in a zone, check to see if an annual evaluation report is available, listing the businesses receiving money from the Department of Housing and Urban Development. Much of this money goes to nonprofit social services, but a good deal also funds businesses such as hotels, retail stores, and restaurants.

Muckrakers

GENERAL MUCKRAKING RESOURCES include the *Multinational Monitor*, which archives information on multinationals and corporate abuse at www.essential.org/monitor/monitor.html. The nonprofit Investigative Reporters and Editors, Inc. (IRE) offers a resource center for those doing investigative reporting, www.ire.org/resourcecenter. You have to join to get full access to materials, which your union or community organization may want to consider.

The AFL-CIO has a section called "Eye on Corporate America" on its website, www.aflcio.org, which includes CEO salary data. Find out the political campaign contributions of corporate execs at www.opensecrets.org, under the "individual donor" search.

More Resources

- Data Center. Customized research on your company or on consultants. 1904 Franklin St., Suite 900, Oakland, CA 94612. 510-835-4692 or 800-735-3741. www.datacenter.org. datacenter@datacenter.org.
- Good Jobs First Corporate Research Project. Assists with strategic corporate research; website contains a guide to doing basic corporate research on the Internet and other tools. 1311 L St. NW, Washington, DC 20005. 202-626-3780. www.corp-research.org. pmattera@goodjobsfirst.org.

- University of Massachusetts-Amherst Labor Center. Conducts strategic corporate research, surveys, and other research for unions. See "Research" section at www.umass.edu/lrrc for examples of research projects. 418 N. Pleasant St., Suite B, Amherst, MA 01002. 413-545-5907. sluce@econs.umass.edu.
- "Manual of Corporate Investigations," from Food & Allied Service Trades, AFL-CIO. 202-737-7200. fast3@fastaflcio.org.
- *No More Secret Candy Store: A Grassroots Guide to Investigating Development Subsidies,* by Good Jobs First, 2002. A comprehensive guide to researching state and local subsidies and economic development agencies. Intended to support organizing against subsidy giveaways and in favor of accountability by subsidy recipients. www.goodjobsfirst.org/research.htm.
- The University of California-Berkeley Labor Center has links on how to research your employer:

"Corporate Research: An Online Guide," www.iir.berkeley.edu/library/blg/corprsch.html, and

"Strategic Research: Employer Analysis Questions and Resources," http://laborcenter.berkeley.edu/strategiccampaigns/research_bible.pdf.

- Several unions have put together their own resource lists for doing basic corporate research. AFSCME, for example, walks you through some of the steps. Go to www.afscme.org and then search for "Corporate Research."

Authors

STEPHANIE LUCE AND TOM JURAVICH teach at the University of Massachusetts Amherst Labor Center.

Index

Articles on the Troublemaker's website (at www.labornotes.org) are included in this index, as are the resources listed in this book. For example, a website article about a public employees' contract campaign is mentioned on page 107, so it is indexed here under "public employees" and "contract campaign." Similarly, on page 28 you'll find a manual on grievances, so that manual is indexed under Stewards training.

A

Absenteeism programs 73
Accountability session 111, 264, 297-298, 301
ACORN 158, 160-161, 177
Actors Equity 48
Adopt-a-family 125, 148
Advanced Practice Management 64-65
Affirmative action 51-52, 54, 56, 180
AFL-CIO 188, 195, 199, 204, 224-226, 292, 316, 340, 341, 345, 348
AFL-CIO website 40, 316, 360, 365
African American workers 18-20, 45-47, 51-57, 69-72, 152-155, 179-180, 181, 188, 191-193, 200, 234, 244-246, 269, 275-278, 283-285, 301-302, 349, 354-355
AFSCME 48, 298, 325
  Local 209 171-174
  Local 1184 51
  Local 1363 51
  Local 1488 83
  Local 1725 55-45
  Local 3299 25-26, 215-216, 299, 336
Aguilar, Arturo 17
Ahmed, Martha 223-227
AIDS 48, 236
Aircraft workers 21, 35
Alexander, Robin 350
Alliance@IBM/CWA Local 1701 313, 320, 321
Alliance for Sustainable Jobs and the Environment 183-185, 193, 194
Allied Industrial Workers Local 837 127-130, 143-148
Alvarenga, Toribio 234
Amalgamated Transit Union Local 726 163-164, 311
Amaral, Francisca 155
American Federation of Government Employees 48
American Federation of Teachers (AFT) 13, 40-42, 48, 223-227
  Local 933 84-86, 192
American Postal Workers Union 32, 35, 58, 207, 210
  Organizing in private sector 210, 211, 213, 226
Americans with Disabilities Act 44, 365
Ancel, Judy 344
Anonymity 27, 281
Apathy 1, 7
A. Philip Randolph Institute 58
April 4 National Student Labor Day of Action 170-171, 179-180
Aramark 179-180
Aranda, Jessica 267-270

Asen, Peter Ian 148, 359
Ashby, Steven 127, 140, 143
Asian American workers, 231-236, 254-258, 268, 302-303
Asian Pacific American Labor Alliance 59, 303
Aspen Foundation for Labour Education 168-169, 176
Associate members 246-247
Association for Union Democracy 105, 273, 279, 280, 282, 288, 307, 310
Association of Flight Attendants 134-135
Austin, Gene 196
Axt, Deborah 262-263

B

Baird, Mary 305
Ballot initiative 166-167, 180-181, 303
Banking services 246-247
Bargaining, continuous 61-62, 66-67, 74-77, 81, 83, 356
Bargaining, getting word out 100, 102-103, 104-106, 115-116
Bargaining, "mutual gains" 77
Bargaining table, members at 50, 95, 222, 226, 278
Bargaining tactics 95-96, 101-104, 106, 188, 204-206, 226,
Bargaining to organize 226, 228-229
Barger, Jennifer 188-190
Baril, Rob 191
Barking Dog 11, 27-28, 308
Barrera, Laura 231-236
Bartley, Aaron 175
Baseball strike 336
Bathroom, use of 17, 49, 362
Bayer Corp. 342-343
Benchich, Al 76
Benitez, Lucas 149-152
Bettles, Lisa 235
Biers, Carl 105
Bigman, Paul 183
Billboards 33
Bissell, Katherine 188
Black, Kathy 43-45
Black Studies 12
Black Telephone Workers for Justice 56-58
Black Workers for Justice 59, 361
Bleakney, David 23
Boal, Ellis 137-138
Bobo, Kim 187, 189-190, 328
Boilermakers union 21
Bondy, Ken 86-87
Bookstore workers 13, 179, 220-223, 320
Borer, David 134
Bouchard, Paul 236
Bowens, Alison 58
Bowie, Erin 230-231
Boycotts 36, 83, 148-152, 179-180, 236, 256
Brannan, Mike 351
Braxton, John 29, 101
Breakfast Club 54-56
Brenner, Aaron 61, 72, 120, 152, 162, 195, 208, 272
Bridges, Harry 12
Bronfrenbrenner, Kate 208, 242, 362

Brooks, Rick 64-65
Brookwood Labor College 200
Brotherhood of Maintenance of Way Employees 40
Brummett, Mary 148
Brummett, Richard 129
Bruskin, Gene 210
Budgets, union 293-295, 304
Bulletin board 12, 115, 319
Burke, Tom 217
Burn barrel 110
Burnout, avoiding 20, 355, 356
Burns, Joe 134
Butler, Margaret 179, 182, 183
Bylaws, changing 16, 275

C

Cagan, Steve 178-180, 182
Calgary and District Labour Council 168-169
California Faculty Association 37
California State Employees Association 285-288, 312
Calver, Andrea 170-171, 175-176
Campaign for Labor Rights 315-316, 340, 345
Campbell, Danny 98-100
Canadian Auto Workers 45, 86-87, 122-124, 196-197, 207, 350
Canadian Union of Public Employees 164-166, 313, 315
Canadian workers 21, 23-25, 45, 112-113, 122-124, 164-166, 168-169, 196-197, 207, 313, 362
Card check See Organizing new members
Carey, Bill 184, 186
Carey, Ron 98, 100, 113
Carney, Steve 131-133
Carpenters 222, 279-281, 311
  Local 33 279-281
  Local 218 53, 266
Carpenters for a Democratic Union 279-281, 310
Carter, Jimmy 152
Carter, Kim 216
Carton, Jacob 182, 198-200, 248-250
Cartoons 32-34
Casey, Tom 239-241
Casilli, Ric 105
Caucuses
  Black 54-57
  Women's 53-56
  Ethnic 303
Caucus for a Democratic Union 285-288, 312
Celebrities, support from 181, 222
Central labor council 48, 147, 162, 168-169, 188, 200, 330, 351-352
CHAOS™ 134-135
Chavez, Cesar xi, 48, 171, 354
Chavez, Maria 16, 358
Chicago Interfaith Committee on Worker Issues 188-190, 261
Chicago Interfaith Workers' Center 261-262, 265-266
Cholger, Al 182
Cintas 152-155, 173, 210
Civil disobedience, See Illegal tactics

Civil rights movement xi, 11, 354, 355
Civil Service Employees Association 298
Class size, reducing 181, 192-193
Clergy and Laity United for Economic Justice 189
Coalition for Justice in the Maquiladoras 340, 344-347
Coalition of Black Trade Unionists 59
Coalition of Immokalee Workers 148-152, 314
Coalition of Labor Union Women 43-45, 59
Coalition of University Employees 297-298, 315, 319
Coalition on Occupational Safety and Health 82, 87-89, 120
Coalitions 52, 88, 120, 141, 157-168, 170-175, 178-194, 248-250, 303, 330, 342-352, 357
  Cultural divide in 187, 188, 251, 257
Code of conduct for employers 258, 271, 345
Code of conduct for joint programs 62-63, 77
Cohen, David 73
Cohen, Larry 241
Cohen, Sheila 44
Colombian workers 348
Committee on Political Education 163, 166
Communication director 295-296, 330, 337
Communications, Energy and Paperworkers Union 112-113, 164
Communications Workers (CWA) 103, 131-134, 236-241, 290, 297, 314, 317-318, 320-321
  District 1 348
  District 6 210, 227-231
  Local 1037 9, 11, 12, 67-69, 93
  Locals 1101, 1102, 1103, 1400 131-134
  Local 1168 303-305
  Local 1180 40
  Local 1298 50-51
  Local 1701 313, 320, 321
  Local 9510 310
  Local 37082 315
Community support 68, 73, 88, 89, 94, 96, 133, 144-148, 148-152, 154-155, 157-177, 178-194, 222-223, 225-227, 235, 248-250, 251-254, 255-256, 280, 342-343. See also Strikes, community support for
  From customers/clients/patients 14, 65, 70, 84-86, 100, 154, 162, 163-164, 198-200, 256, 318
  Supporting community issues 72-73, 157-161, 163-164, 164-166, 166-167, 167-168, 171, 180-181, 183-187, 191-193, 196, 304-305
Concessions in contract, fighting 50-51, 93-95, 98-101, 109-110, 112-113, 113-114, 114-116, 127-130, 131-134, 143-148, 197-198, 275-278, 284-285, 286, 287, 317-318, 333, 354
Conference on Creative Organizing 42
Connecticut Center for a New Economy 191-194
Connor, Michael Ames 12-13
Construction Organizing Membership Education Training (COMET) 219, 244
Construction workers 53-56, 218-219, 244-246, 265-266, 279-281
Contraceptive equity 43-45
Contract campaign 50, 92-107, 109-112, 114-115, 116-118, 127-136, 162, 171-173, 191-193, 204-206, 222-223, 233-236, 226-227, 239, 275-278, 317-318, 330, 336
Contracting out, See Outsourcing
Cooperative, workers' 266-267, 269
Corporate campaign 93-95, 140-156, 173, 234-236, 342-343, 344-347
Costumes 36, 37, 263, 335
Convention, union 40
Council-o-meter 161
Crangi, Jerry 219
Cranmer, Michael 279, 281
Cranmer, Susan 279-281
Criminal prosecution 82
Crosby, Jeff 104-105, 109-110, 167-168, 351-352
Cross Border Network 344-347
Customers or clients, pressuring 142-143, 146, 148-152, 236, 251, 270

D

Damis, Kristi 99-101
Dargie, Ray 238
Database of member information 188, 189, 275
David Friedman, Ellen 5
Davis, Terry 349
Day laborers 267-271
Day Labor Organizing Project, 269-271
Dean, Howard 225-227
Dean, Tim 322, 325
Debate, union candidates' 302
Decertification 234
Deen, Aamir 179-180
Delphi Corp. 22-23, 333
DeMay, Pete 141, 153-155
Democracy Is Power 273, 290, 310
Democracy, union 124, 125, 272-289, 357
Demonstrations, planning 126, 248-250
De-skilling 1, 64-65
DeVinney, Patty 303-305
DeVries, Rich 205, 216-217
Dhermy, Art 130, 145
Diaz, Peter 314
Dimondstein, Mark 210, 213, 226
Direct Action for Rights and Equality 264, 325
Discipline, unfair 73
Discrimination 43-60. See also Chapter 16 on immigrant workers
  Against gay, lesbian, bisexual, transgender workers 47-50, 59, 98, 286
  Against women 43-44, 45, 54-56, 59, 264
  Disability 44
  Racial 45-47, 51, 54-57, 58, 59, 245-246, 260, 264, 269, 285, 325
Disinvestment 73
Ditz, Jeff 88-89
Diversity training 47
Domestic partner benefits 47-48
Domestic workers 266-267
Dorey, Dennis 23-24
Douglass, Frederick 13
Downs, Steve 276-278
Drake, Mike 308, 310
Drug testing 33, 77
Dubinsky, Joanna 72, 162, 170, 175
Dudley, Barbara 187
Dudzic, Mark 93-95
Duro Bag Co. 344-347

E

Eames, Steve 21
Early, Steve 102, 346
Earth First! 183-184
Education at workers centers 257, 260-262, 267, 268, 325
Education, union 40-41, 57-58, 62, 63, 70, 158, 166-167, 168-169, 200-203, 203-204, 214-215, 239, 244-245, 249, 280, 298, 303, 325-326, 350, 351, 359-362
Edwards, Dana 46
Eisenhower, Kay 13-14, 302
Eisenscher, Mike 347-348
Election, union, See Running for union office
Email communication 70-71, 99, 103, 196, 200, 295, 316-318
  Building an e-list 316-317
  As mobilizing tool 317-318
Emerich, Malcolm 142-143
Emerson, Ralph Waldo 66
Employee involvement 61-65, 74-77
English as a Second Language classes 87, 168, 254, 268, 303, 325
ENLACE 324, 328
Equal Employment Opportunity Commission 44, 261, 269, 365
Environmentalists, coalition with 158, 183-187, 350-351, 355
Environmental Protection Agency 82, 158, 251
Esch, Betsy 262
Espinoza, Olga 253
Essex County Community Organization 167-168
Estrada, Cindy 88
Everingham, Denys 283-285
Executive board, junior 301

F

Fahey, Joe 15, 101-102
Fairness and Accuracy In Reporting 338
Falicov, Anna 175
Families, participation of 35, 47-48, 70, 116, 143, 162, 163, 168-169, 204
Family Medical Leave Act 48, 263, 362
Farm Labor Organizing Committee xi, 36, 246-247, 354
Farm workers 48, 140, 148-152, 246-247, 259, 322, 354
FAT (Frente Auténtico de Trabajo) 344-345, 348-350
Feekin, Lynn 328
Feldman, Rich 44
Ferbel-Azcarate, Pedro 12-13
Fine, Janice 260-261, 271
Fire Department inspection 154
First Amendment rights 197-198
Flanagan, Mary 58
Fletcher Allen Hospital 223-227
Flight attendants 4, 98-101, 134-135
Flying squad 125, 196-197, 214
Flynn, Elizabeth Gurley 131
Food bank 125, 190
Ford Motor Co. 44, 86-87, 354
Foreign workers, See International solidarity
Forever 21 258
Fowler, Dave 333
Frank, Miriam 47, 48
Free trade 184-185, 186, 350-352
Free Trade Area of the Americas 184-185, 344, 351-352, 363
Fundraising 195-196, 245, 256, 280, 287, 347-348, 349, 362
Furst, Gillian 114-116

G

Gaither, John 204-206
Galpern, Pamela 131
Gambini, Cori 304, 355
Game show parodies 40-41
Gandhi, Mohandas 11
Gap, The 199, 346
Garcia, Deyanira 264
Garcia, Marisela 88-89
Garlock, Chris 200
Garment Worker Center 256-258
Gay, lesbian, bisexual, transgender workers, See Discrimination
General Electric 33, 74-77, 104-105, 109-110, 167-168, 236-241, 349, 351
General Motors 122-124, 137, 195, 333
George Meany Center 90, 244, 348, 388
GetActive software 200, 317, 318

Gibson, Bill 290
Giloth, Dan 269-271
Giraldo, Hector 348
Giuliani, Rudolph 277
Glaser, David 231-236
Glass Moulders union 266
Global justice movement 350-352
Global positioning systems 66, 78
Goldstein-Gelb, Marcy 87-88
Gonzalez, Maria 270-271
Gonzalez, Sara 264
Gornewicz, Dave 244-246
Gorseth, Aaron 219-220
Great Labor Arts Exchange 42
Gres, Liz 152-155
Grievances 9-10, 28-29, 73
Grievances, group 9, 85
Griffin, Mike 127, 130
Grocery workers 32, 97-98, 197-198, 254-256, 314-315, 319, 336
Guthrie, Arlo 13
Guthrie, Woody 13
Guyer, Linda 313, 321

H

Hackett, Cathy 286-288
Haitian American workers 94
Halstead, Frank 97-98, 197-198, 336
Hanley, Larry 163-164
Hansen, Gary 168-169
Harassment, dealing with 16-17, 22-25, 45-50, 54, 245-246, 268
    Sexual 45, 59, 267, 284, 344
Harbor/UCLA Medical Center 2, 18-20, 121-122
Hallmark 344-346
Hard, Jim 286-288
Hargrove, Buzz 123
Harrington, Thomas 279, 281
Harrison, LaKesha 215-216
Harvard University 7, 126
Hasegawa, Bob 158, 350
Haslam, James 182
Hate legislation 48
Hawking, C.J. 127, 143
Hawkins, Jeanette 129
Hawkins, Todd 54-56
Hayes, Alfred 13
Health and safety 21, 79-91, 117, 120, 135-136, 241
    Contract language 86
    "Behavior-based" safety program 81-83, 89, 91, 343
    Safer materials 86-87, 89
Health care benefits, fighting for 44, 109, 192-193
Health care reform 109, 304-305, 363
Health care workers 94, 303-305, 317, 325-327. See also hospital workers
Heiman, Kathleen 111
Henry, Sherman 51-52
HERE 170-171, 175, 179-180, 234, 248-250, 308, 310. See also UNITE HERE
    Local 1 188-190
    Local 2 210, 231-236
    Local 217 188
    Locals 34 and 35 191-193
Hereth, Ella 151, 171
Herzmark, Jay 83
Hesse, Bernie 320
Hessling, Brad 117
Hickey, Robert 208, 242, 290
Highlander Center 200, 359
Hill, Joe xi, 13, 31
Hinds, Steve 84, 146, 167, 178, 191, 350
Hiring hall 219, 269, 327
History, lessons from 3, 55, 108, 113, 123, 126, 131, 176, 200-201, 203, 260, 291, 327, 342, 354-355, 361, 362, 363

Hoffa, James P. 100
Horning, Claudia 297-298
Hospital workers 2, 13-14, 18-20, 39, 64-65, 69-72, 121-122, 166-167, 191, 193, 212-214, 215-216, 223-227, 336
Hotel workers 38, 188-190, 231-236
Hotline, telephone 115
Housing, affordable 188, 192-193
Huber, Sonya 157, 164
Huck, Gary 33
Huicochea, Fred 2
Hunger strike 68, 151, 173
Hunter Group 70-71

I

IBM 313, 320, 321
Identity card 246
Ilg, Ken 179
Illegal tactics 68, 110-112, 175, 192, 235, 277-278. See also Sit-downs, Wildcat strikes
Illinois Nurses Association 69-72
Immigrant workers 15-17, 87-89, 141-143, 148-152, 152-155, 168, 174-175, 179, 196, 214-215, 231-236, 244-259, 260-271, 283-285, 302-303, 323-324, 354, 355, 358, 360, 363. See also Latino workers, Asian American workers
    Eastern European immigrants 250-251, 257, 261, 268, 284-285
Immigrant Workers Freedom Ride 179, 190
Immigrant Workers Union 254-256
Immigration and Customs Enforcement (ICE) 247
Immigration and Naturalization Service (INS) 248-250
Indonesian workers 35
Industrial Workers of the World (Wobblies) 131, 221, 242, 260, 355
Information request 66-67, 77, 83
Ingalls, Barb 113-114
Insourcing 74-77
International Alliance of Theatrical Stage Employees 37, 219
International Brotherhood of Electrical Workers 217, 309-310
    District 6 219
    Local 46 219
    Local 827 56-57, 103, 131-134
    Local 109 62
    Local 2222 131-134
International Labor Communications Association 338, 360
International Longshore and Warehouse Union 86, 135-136, 158, 197, 198-200, 326-327
    Local 5 13, 220-223
    Local 19 314
    Local 23 135-136, 198
International Longshoremen's Association 221, 301-302, 321, 335
International solidarity xi, 37-38, 51, 86, 292, 315, 339-352, 363
International trade secretariat 340, 343
International Workingmen's Association 342
Interns 175-176
Interpreters 247, 303, 347
Iosbaker, Joe 69-71
Ironworkers 53
    Local 272 244-246
IUE-CWA 236-241
    Local 201 104-106, 109-110, 167-168, 237-241

J

Jackson, the Rev. Jesse 119, 193
Jackson, Justin 330
James, Willie 276-278
Janitors, Justice for 174-175, 179, 217-218,

348, 363
Jenkins, Steve 260, 271
Jimmerfield, Bud 86-87
Jirmanus, Lara 174-175
Job Preservation Committee 74-77
Jobs with Justice 52, 114, 143, 147, 174-175, 178-183, 186, 199-200, 201-203, 206, 264, 298, 355
    As training ground 182
    Ballot campaigns 180-181
    Chapter building 181-183
    Difficult questions 183
    Pledge cards 182, 200
    Structure 178, 181, 182
    Supporting contract campaign or strike 174-175, 179-180, 198-200, 223
    Supporting organizing drive 180, 221, 222, 223-227
    Workers' Rights Board 178-179, 181, 223
Johnson, Brian 326
Johnson, Dave 250-251
Johnson, William 2, 339
Joint labor-management program 61-65, 74-77
Jones, Felicia 230
Juravich, Tom 362, 364
Justice for Healthcare Workers Campaign 223-227

K

Kagan, Marc 275-278
Kalmijn, Jelger 290, 297
Kapanowski, Gary 44
Kehoe, Ed 311
Keith, Margaret 79
Kern, Jen 158-161
King County Labor Council 48
King, Martin Luther, Jr. xi, 11, 28, 56-57, 130, 151, 171, 354
Kitchen, Dave 74-77, 349
Klontz, Dave 345
Konopacki, Mike 33
Korean Immigrant Workers Advocates 254-256
Krehbiel, Paul 12, 17, 121-122, 177
Kruse, Marty 221-222
Kutalik, Chris 92

L

Labor Council for Latin American Advancement 59
Labor, U.S. Department of 21, 279, 340
Labor Employment Law Office 54
Laborers Union 214-215, 217, 249-251
Labor Heritage Foundation 42
Labor Management Reporting and Disclosure Act 273-274, 307
Labor Notes magazine 33, 147, 304, 355
Labor Notes conference 304, 343, 355, 356
Labor Party 93, 147, 203, 360, 362
Labor Speakers Club, St. Paul 203-204, 206
La Botz, Dan 9, 67, 97, 108, 126, 141, 166, 171, 178, 244, 246, 247, 248, 260, 267, 288, 305, 339, 340, 342, 347, 348, 353
Labourstart 313-317, 320, 321
Landaverde, José 267-269
Lane, Dan 129, 145
Latino Union 267-270
Latino workers 15-17, 18-20, 25, 69-72, 87-89, 95-97, 101-102, 141-143, 148-152, 152-155, 174-175, 191-193, 215, 231-236, 244-247, 249-258, 261-271, 275-278, 283-285, 302-303, 311, 323-324, 325, 326, 348, 354, 358
Laundry workers 141-143, 152-155
Leadership development program 57-58, 192, 193, 200-203, 297-299, 301, 304, 322-328
    Public speaking 325

Leaflets, right to distribute 6
Leaflets, use of 25, 26-28, 39, 65, 115-116, 142, 163, 195, 279
Leaflets, writing good ones 26, 35, 94, 100, 115, 144-145, 282
Leah, Tony 122-124
Leahy, Dan 185, 187
Lean production 61-67, 77
Lee, Eric 313, 317
Lee, Kimi 256-258
Legal rights 6, 16, 27, 28, 61, 66, 82, 83, 101, 105, 118-119, 128, 137-138, 197-198, 216, 218, 223, 224, 234, 235, 242, 254, 258, 262-263, 273-274, 277, 282, 289, 307, 360, 362
Lelli, Vance 135-136, 198
Lessin, Nancy 79, 81, 91
Levin, David 15, 358
Levins Morales, Ricardo 31, 32
Levy, Paul Alan 321
Leyshon, Hal 225
Libel/slander 28
Liss, Jon 234
Listening 7, 16, 18, 69-70, 186, 212-213, 217, 232, 274, 295
List-serve 319
Living wage campaign 158-161, 162, 172-173, 176, 181, 264
Living wage law 155
LM-2 form 274, 293
Lobbying, See Politicians, pressuring
Lockout 119, 185-186
  As union tactic 112
Lohman, Jeff 219
London, Jack 74
Longshore workers 86, 131, 135-136, 158, 197, 198-200, 301-302, 326-327, 335, 340, 354
Lost time 216, 283, 288, 297-299, 304-305
Luce, Stephanie 364
Lukaszek, Paula 54-56
Lum, Gloria 303
Lund, Caroline 27-28, 308
Luskin, Matt 160, 177
Luthens, Sarah 49

M

Machinists union (IAM) 45, 218
MacMeekin, Anne 196-197
Majors, Rick 23
Make the Road by Walking 260, 262-263
Manderfeld, Trudy 342
Manno, Rich 74-76
Mapping 189, 253, 324, 325, 326
  Body map 80, 89
  Workplace map 14-15, 79-80, 89
Maquiladoras 340, 344-347
March to Miami 184-185, 187
Marcum, Randy 171-174
Marete, Marengu 287
Marin Molina, Nadia 263, 265, 267
Marks, Kim 183-184
Marriott 231-236
Martinez, Maria 15-17, 358
Martinez, Mirna 216
MassCOSH 87-88
Master contract, establishing or matching 204-206, 233, 236, 250-251
Matricula consular 246
Maxxam 184
May Day 223, 257
Mazón, Eleuteria 154
McCafferty, Paul 20
McCall, Julie 31, 42
McCann, Sharon 49
McCarty, Tom 110
McCausland, Harriet 326
McClear, Sheila 43, 53
McDermott, Jim 279-280

McDonald, Linda 64-65
McGilp, Doug 114-116
McGreevey, James 68
McKenna, Paul 34
McKerley, John 349
McLennan, Paul 200, 203
McNattin, Bob 204-206
McWilliams, Brian 222, 223
Meatpacking workers 15-17, 34, 87-88, 251-254, 323-324, 358
Media, dealing with 51, 68, 70, 82, 85, 111, 115, 117, 150-151, 264, 267-268, 325, 329-338
Meeting the Challenge Committee 203-204
Mentors 323, 325, 326
Mercado, Elba 284-285
Merrilees, Craig 25-26, 336
Mersha, Sara 264, 325
Metalworking fluids 86-87
Metzger, Hanna 93
Mexican workers 344-347
Miami University 171-174
Midwest Express 134-135
Milling, Sue 45
Minnick, Debbie 162
Misich, John 64
Mission statement 291, 299, 309, 324
Mistakes, use of enemy's 21, 22, 71, 164-165, 221-222, 225, 228, 231, 239
Mondragón, Agustina 256-257
Montgomery, David 3
Moody, Kim 56, 362, 363
Moran, Tom 41
Mother Jones xi, 37-38
Mt. Olive Pickles 36
Multilingual organizing 215, 231-236, 250-251, 254-258, 302-303, 349
Multi-union council 207
Musgrave, Bil 67

N

Nagy, Gyula 160-161
Nailor, Bart 113
Natalie, Frank 310, 312
National Association of Government Employees 48
National Association of Letter Carriers Branch 294 303
National Day Laborer Organizing Network 267, 271
National Education Association 8, 110-112, 162
National Employment Law Project 258, 265
National Interfaith Committee for Worker Justice 187, 193
National Labor Relations Act 6, 16, 83, 118-119, 237
National Labor Relations Board 82, 118-119, 137-138, 229, 234, 255, 256, 261, 310, 343, 360
National Organization for Women 44
Navistar 196, 206
Needleman, Ruth 55
Neff, Roni 79, 81
Negotiations, open, See Bargaining, members at
Negstad, Lars 189-190
Network, member-to-member 15-17, 29, 95, 98-100, 117, 133, 215-216, 295
Neutrality, See Organizing new members (Card check)
New Directions (in TWU Local 100) 275-278
New Directions Movement (in UAW) 200-201
Newspaper workers 32, 33, 113-114, 315, 319, 329-335
Niemeijer, Marsha 15, 79, 95, 167, 301, 352
Newsletters, shop floor 26-28, 56-57, 89, 130, 253, 276, 279, 286

Newspapers, union 295, 305, 360
New Unity Partnership 310
NIOSH 90
No-match letter 247-248, 255, 258
Nonmajority unions 236-242
North American Free Trade Agreement (NAFTA) 344
Northland Poster Collective 32, 42
Northwest Airlines 4, 98-101
Norton, Ellen 212-214
Noyes, Matt 306
NUMMI 27-28
Nurses 2, 64-65, 69-72, 223-227, 303-305, 336, 354

O

Occupational Safety and Health Administration/Act, use of 82, 83-84, 88, 89-90, 251, 261, 364
O'Donoghue, Julie 32
Office and Professional Employees International Union 48
Officers, union, functioning of 290-305, 327, 357
Offner, Amy 126, 174, 175
Oliva, José 261-262, 265-266
Omaha Together One Community 251-254
Ontario Coalition Against Poverty 24
Ontario Energy Coalition 164-166
Operating Engineers union 217
Organizing Institute 216, 219, 359
Organizing new members 4, 5-8, 34, 87-89, 141-143, 152-155, 206, 208-243, 244-246, 249-251, 251-254, 254-256, 265-266, 283, 344-347, 349, 354, 356, 360
  Building a committee 212-214, 221, 223-224, 232, 238-241, 251-253
  Building from defeat 210, 229, 237-238, 241, 346-347
  Captive-audience meeting 213, 221, 228-229, 231, 234, 253
  Card check 153-155, 180, 218, 227-231, 231-233
  Choosing the right union 221, 243, 252, 266
  Community support for 222-223, 225-227, 235, 251-253, 255
  Hot shop 210, 238
  House-calls 214, 217, 222, 234, 251, 252
  Mass actions 216-217, 222, 223
  Members as organizers 209, 213, 214-216, 228, 230, 231-236, 238, 249-251, 283
  Making support public 214, 222, 224, 232-233
  Nonmajority union 236-242
  Recognition strike 141-143, 217-218, 266
  Relationship between staff and rank-and-file organizers 209, 212-214, 232, 233, 238, 240, 241
  Salting 218-220, 242, 245
  Small meetings 212, 221, 223-224, 226, 232
  Targeting 209-212
  Training organizers 214-216, 228, 249, 253
  Websites in 314
  Winning first contract 134-135, 211, 217, 218, 222-223, 226-227, 254
Ortega, Ivan 303
Outsourcing 74-77, 339, 349. See also Insourcing
Overtime ban 73, 74, 226

P

PACE 182, 292, 345-346
  Local 1-149 93-95
  Local 5-0832 345
Paff, Ken 273-75, 281-283

Palestinian workers 347-348
Palladino, Lenore 170
Paraprofessionals 41-42, 162, 264
Park, Danny 254-256
Parker, Bill 76
Parker, Michael 222-223
Parker, Mike 63, 76, 77
Parks, Rosa xi, 355
Part-time officers, 297
Part-time workers 117-120, 362
Passover 189, 266
Patafio, J.P. 276-278
Patterson, Lorell 147
Payless Shoes 198-199
Pearson, Bill 32
Pensions 48, 193, 361
Pereyra, Flaco 15, 358
Perkins, Julia 149-152
Perlstein, Tony 95-96, 322
Petitions 95-96, 100
Philllips, Toni 135
Phone tree 217
Picket lines 14, 35, 36, 48, 51, 97, 112, 115-116, 124-125, 184, 196-197, 197-198, 236, 345
Picket signs 35, 97, 115, 119, 336
Pineros y Campesinos Unidos del Noroeste (PCUN) 259
Plankenhorn, Royal 146
Plant closing 342-343
Plumbers union 54-56
    Local 7 310, 312
    Local 787 308
Political endorsements 26
Politicians, getting support from 25-26, 51, 88, 116, 225-226, 268
Politicians, pressuring 51-52, 68, 111-112, 158-161, 162, 163-164, 164-166, 358. See also Regulators
Pope, Sandy 103-104
Postal workers 23-25, 32, 35, 120, 207, 210, 303
Powell's Books 12, 179, 220-223
Pratt, David 84, 297
Press release 330, 332, 335, 338
Pride at Work 49, 59
Privatization 41, 67-72, 164-165
Props 36, 40
Public employees 6, 9, 12-14, 17-20, 25-26, 38, 40-41, 67-72, 107, 162, 163-164, 164-166, 166-167, 264, 275-278, 285-288, 328, 348. See also Postal workers, Teachers, University workers
Puerto Rican workers 269, 270
Puppets 37-38, 222

Q

Quality programs 22, 61-63, 77

R

Raab, Kris 317-318
Rachleff, Peter 35, 113, 362
Racism, See Discrimination, racial
Railroad workers 35, 40, 354
Railway Labor Act 98, 101, 134-135
Rainbow Foods 32
Ramirez, Jorge 253
Rank-and-file contacts, making cross-local 204-206, 279-281
Ratification procedure 104-106
Reardon, Dave 132-133
Reform caucus 192, 200, 204-206, 266, 272-281, 284-288, 306-312, 333, 338. See also Teamsters for a Democratic Union
Regulators, pressuring 155, 229-230, 234-235, 251
Relationships, as foundation for organizing 7, 13-14, 47, 49-50, 69-70, 187, 191, 195, 217, 219-220, 221, 223-224, 330-335
Religious groups, connections with 38, 151-152, 161, 162, 167-168, 187-190, 191-193, 227, 236 253
Researching employer 140-141, 211, 291, 364-366
Respect, contract language on 95-96, 324
Restaurant workers 254
Reuther, Victor xii, 201
Reyes, Teófilo 244, 259, 267
Rhode Island Hospital 64-65
Rich, Marc 37-38
Richardson, Charley 4, 62, 66, 77
Ridicule bosses 12, 31-34, 36-37, 39, 41
Riley, Ken 301-302, 335
Rizo, Ana 170
Road warriors 113-114, 146-147, 184
Robinson, Nick 64, 93, 172-173, 187, 249
Rogers, Ray 144-146, 276
Role-playing 188, 213, 225, 255, 330, 351-352
Rondeau, Kris 7
Rose, Lincoln 49-50
Rosen, Seth 230
Rosenstein, Hetty 9, 11, 67-69, 93, 357
Rovers, Bert 123
Rubin, Michael 287-288
Ruiz, Régulo 349
Running for union office 57-58, 172, 266, 281-283, 284-285, 287-288, 289
Russo, Monica 51-52
Ryan, Sarah 54

S

Sacharow, Neil 330
Sagovac, Simone 98
St. Juste, Jean-Carmel 87-88
Salting 270-271. See also Organizing new members
Samuel, Leah 158, 163, 168
Sanclemente, Roberto 245
Sather, Rick 32
Satyagraha 11
SBC 50, 227-231
Scabs, dealing with 97-98, 112, 118-119, 125, 173, 198, 235-236, 270-271
Schaeffer, Nicolle 172-173
Schaffer, Jan 224-227
Schermerhorn, Tim 275-277
Schools, teaching labor in 168-169
Schrimpsher, Emery 130
Schwartz, Robert 101, 118, 126
Scott, Tim 220
Secondary boycott 141, 148-152, 198-200, 229
SEMCOSH 88-89
Seminary Summer 190, 193
September 11, 2001 4. See also Terrorism
Service Employees International Union 48, 189, 292, 313
    District 1199 New England 188, 191-193
    Local 32B-J 311
    Local 36 283-285
    Local 73 69-72, 217
    Local 250 347
    Local 254 20, 174-175
    Local 509 48, 57
    Local 531 188
    Local 615 348
    Local 616 13-14, 302-303
    Local 660 2, 12, 16-20, 121-122, 166-167
    Local 775 317
    Local 880 160
    Local 1000 285-288
    Local 1199 51
    Local 1877 347
    Local 2020 48, 212-214, 325-327
Sexism, See Discrimination
Shareholder support 151-152
Sheet Metal Workers Local 20 219
Shipley, Linda M. 103
Shop floor organizing 2, 5-30, 31-32, 34, 36, 46, 49, 50, 64, 67, 69-70, 73, 84-86, 93-95, 98-100, 102, 112, 117, 121-122, 127-136, 154, 213, 215, 222, 232-235, 239, 241, 255, 266, 283-285, 295, 358
Shotwell, Gregg 22-23, 333
Sick-out 110-111, 121-122
Silano, Bruno 164-165
Silva, Byron 214-215
Silva, Carmen Julia 346-347
Sit-down or sit-in 23-25, 29, 51, 122-124, 126, 175, 180, 193, 363
Site visit, preparing for a 77
Sjoberg, Scott 235
Skidmore, Elizabeth 53-54
Skill levels and organizing 219, 245
Skinner, Mike 23-25
Skits 34, 39-41, 325
Slaughter, Jane 1, 61, 67, 77, 104, 303, 353
Slippery slope 75, 76
Slowdowns 29, 30, 67, 112, 276-277
Smith, Patricia 45, 50
Snitching 45-46
Social contract 191-193
Social Security Administration 247-248
Society of Professional Engineering Employees in Aerospace 110, 316, 318
Solidarity, cross-union 51, 69-72, 75, 113-114, 146-148, 155, 195-207, 243, 326, 330, 343
Solis, Joel 2, 166
Songs 31, 34, 38-42, 185
Sosa, Sergio 251-254
Southern New England Telephone 50-51
Speaking, public, See Leadership development, Union meeting
Speaking tour 113-114, 146-147, 149-152, 184-185, 346-348, 349
Spence, Yvette 284-285
Staffers, union, managing 299-301
Staff union 301
Staiger, Dave 64
Staley, A.E. Mfg. 127-30, 143-148, 362
Stamford Organizing Project 188, 292
Starbird, Jill 239, 241
Stewards 2, 10, 14, 15-16, 68, 86, 215-216, 225, 226, 235, 286-287, 296, 297-298
    Recruiting 17, 20, 216
    Rotating 20
    Training 19, 28-29, 239, 326, 362
Stewards council 17-20, 327
Stewart, Sandra 95-97, 248, 324
Stock analysts 94-95
Stock, David 86
Strategic planning 210-213, 290-293, 322-324
Strategize, how to 2, 5, 11, 14-15, 18, 35, 55, 70, 129, 140-141, 142-143, 145-146, 149, 150, 152, 159, 191, 198, 209-212, 225, 273-274, 330-331, 354
Street actions 34-35
Strikes 35, 50-51, 56, 68, 74, 93, 108-126, 135, 141-143, 173-174, 174-175, 190, 193, 197-198, 251, 280, 318, 344, 358, 362, 363. See also Picket lines, Picket signs, Road warriors, Scabs, Sit-down, Wildcats
    Community support for 109, 110-112, 116, 116-120
    For union recognition 141-143, 217-218, 266
    General strike 126
    Limited duration 93, 109-110, 110-112, 222, 235-236, 255, 327
    Unfair labor practice 118-119, 141-143, 222, 266

Strong, Curtis 55
Structures, union 279, 301
Student Labor Action Project 143, 170-171, 174-175, 177
Students, teaching about unions 168-169, 175-176
Students, working with 143, 146, 151, 170-177, 350
Supervisor, group visit to 2, 12, 13, 18-20, 51, 68, 96-97, 154, 263, 264, 270
Surveillance 67, 78
Surveys 57, 85, 95, 98, 103, 206, 232, 233, 254, 313
Swanson, Doug 107
Sweeney, John 187, 244

T

Taco Bell 148-152, 216, 314
Taft-Hartley Act 141, 146, 198-199
Tamarin, Harry 189
Taveras, Ana 249-251
Taylor, Frederick W. 67
Teachers 12, 37, 84-86, 110-112, 168-169, 179, 192, 264
Team concept 63-64
Teamsters 29, 32, 33, 63-64, 113, 116-120, 152-155, 270, 291, 350
  Local 120 204-206
  Local 160 204-206
  Local 174 4, 158, 350-351, 355
  Local 221 204-206
  Local 294 308
  Local 355 27
  Local 556 15-17, 95-97, 101-102, 248, 323-324, 358
  Local 572 97-98, 197-198
  Local 630 197
  Local 705 216-217
  Local 805 103
  Local 938 21
  Local 1145 114-116
  Local 2000 98-101
Teamsters for a Democratic Union 15-17, 63, 84, 95-97, 117, 197-198, 205, 273-275, 286, 288, 309, 336, 355, 358
Technology, bargaining over 61, 66
Teeley, Kevin 110-111
Telephone workers 50-51, 56-57, 112-113, 131-134
Tellier, Kathy 23
Telomen, Rodney 69-71
Temple University 44
Temporary workers 264, 267-271, 361
Tenants and Workers Support Committee 234
Tent city 151, 173, 174, 345, 347
Terrorism, as bogus issue 198-200, 250
Thompson, Paulette 111
Thompson, Wendy 45-46
Thomson, Joan 169
Toussaint, Roger 278
Townsend, Dorothy 51-52, 181
Townsend, Ken 239
Tradeswomen 53-56, 59, 311
Tradeswomen United Against Racism 53-54
Transgendered workers 49-50
Transit workers 163-164, 275-278, 280
Translation 247, 302-303, 311, 315. See also Intepreters
Transnationals Information Exchange 340, 343
Transport Workers Union Local 100 275-278, 310, 311
Traylor, Butch 119-120
Trementozzi, Don 132
Tripp, Andrew 224-226
Trusteeship 284
T-shirts, mass wearing of 23, 32, 51, 64, 97-98, 229, 283

Two-tier contract 1, 3, 50-51, 333, 356
Tucker, Jerry 128-129, 145-146, 202
Tyler, Dewey 244-245
Typographical Union Local 18 113
Tyson Foods 15-17, 324, 358

U

Uehlein, Joe 34, 37-38, 147
Undocumented workers 246-259, 261-263, 265-271, 363
Unfair labor practice 118-119, 142, 218, 222, 226, 229, 234, 251, 266
Union-busting consultants 34, 70-71, 237
Union meeting 31, 39, 53, 303, 326
  Speaking at a 115, 206, 274-275
Union Summer 175-176
UNITE 141-143, 173. See also UNITE HERE
United Auto Workers 11, 22-23, 88-89, 333
  Local 235 45-47
  Local 594 195-196
  Local 900 44
  Local 909 76
  Local 1700 76
  Local 2036 195-196
  Local 2244 27-28, 308
  Local 2322 220
  Region 9A 188
United Electrical Workers (UE) 12, 33, 73, 126, 270-271, 305, 315, 328, 348-350
  Local 506 74-77, 349
  Local 896 349
United Farm Workers 48, 140, 322
United Food and Commercial Workers 87-88, 197-198, 221, 251-254, 255, 256, 336
  Local P-9/Hormel strike 113, 203, 362
  Local 789 32, 314-315, 319, 320
  Local 1001 314
  Local 1105 49
United Mine Workers 291
  Local 1189 67
United Nurses and Allied Professionals 224
  Local 5096 64-65
United Steelworkers 37-38, 45, 55, 83, 184-186, 291, 329, 362
  Local 915L 83
  Local 12273 342-343
United Students Against Sweatshops 143, 170, 172, 177, 348
United Transportation Union 35
UNITE HERE 48, 152-155, 210, 256. See also HERE, UNITE
Unity, building 45-50, 53-56, 69-70, 117-118, 202, 245-246, 257, 284-285. See also Multilingual organizing
University of Illinois 171, 217
University of Illinois Medical Center at Chicago 69-72, 77
University Professional and Technical Employees 297
University workers, 13-14, 20, 25-26, 31, 37, 69-72, 171-174, 179-180, 191-193, 215-216, 297-298, 315, 319, 349
Unpaid wages, winning 256-258, 262-263, 268, 270
UPS 63-64, 116-120, 291, 336-337
Uthappa, N. Renuka 43, 271

V

Valerio, Roberto 349
Van Gordon, Michael 219
Velásquez, Baldemar xi, 246-247
Verizon 56-57, 103, 131-134, 230, 317-318, 335
Vermont Workers Center 182, 223-227
Videos (resources) 29, 59, 77, 89, 106, 177, 206, 348, 363
Videotaping picket lines, by union 97, 119

Video, union use of 63, 162, 171, 325, 330, 343
Villa, Frank 197
Vision 299, 303-305, 323, 326, 353-358
"Vote no" (on contract) campaigns, 100-101, 279

W

WAGE (Working At GE) 236-241
Walker, J.D. 312
Walker, Phyllis 355
Wallace, Sharon 347
Walls, Randy 118
Wal-Mart 354
War, opposition to 183, 203, 347, 361
Washington Education Association 110-112
Washington Post 36, 139
WashTech 320-321
Water, clean 185-186
Watson, Mike 309
Watson, Steve 196
Watts, Dave 129
Websites, as organizing tool 99, 100, 165, 306-321, 363
  Design tips 306-308, 312, 313, 314, 321
  For international solidarity 315, 317
  Web stewards 309
Weingarten rights 130, 235, 239
Werlein-Jaén, Lemoin 236
West Coast Waterfront Coalition 198-200
West, Justin 11
White, Chris 283-284
Whitman, Christy 67-68
Wigmore, Dorothy 14, 79
Wildcat strikes 120-122, 358
Wilhelm, John 236
Williams, Barrie 145, 148
Williams, David 218
Williams, Mark 210
Williamson, Steve 351
Wilson, Rand 63, 116, 337
Winston, Jason 164
Winzig, Mary 220-223
Wirshing, Kim 248
Witt, Matt 116
Wohlforth, Nancy 48
Women's Institute for Leadership Development 57-58
Women's Law Project 44, 58
Women workers 2, 4, 13-14, 22-23, 41-42, 43-45, 50-51, 53-56, 57-58, 64-65, 67-69, 69-72, 84-86, 94, 98-101, 110-112, 112-113, 134-135, 141-143, 152-155, 162, 179-180, 188, 223-227, 263, 264, 266-267, 302-303, 311, 317, 325, 344-347, 362, 363
Workers centers 148-152, 251-258, 260-271, 325, 346
  Working with unions 264-266, 270-271
Workers Education Center 128, 200, 206
Workers' Rights Boards, See Jobs with Justice
Workplace Project 263, 265, 266-267
Work to rule 20-22, 29, 67, 74, 111, 127-133, 135-138
World Trade Organization (WTO) 4, 344, 350-351

X-Y-Z

X, Malcolm xi
Yale University 191-193
Yao, David 110, 306
Young Workers United 59
Zanfardino, Dave 132-133
Zielinski, Mike 113-114, 185-186
Zipser, Andy 329, 338
Zorilla-Cruz, Iliana 326